Violence

The International Library of Criminology, Criminal Justice and Penology
Series Editors: Gerald Mars and David Nelken

Titles in the Series:

Violence

Edited by

Elizabeth A. Stanko

Royal Holloway University of London, UK

Published by
Dartmouth Publishing Company
Ashgate Publishing Limited
Gower House
Croft Road
Aldershot
Hants GU11 3HR
England

Ashgate Publishing Company
131 Main Street
Burlington, VT 05401-5600 USA

Ashgate website: http://www.ashgate.com

British Library Cataloguing in Publication Data
Violence. – (The international library of criminology,
   criminal justice and penology)
   1. Violence 2. Violence – Social aspects
   I. Stanko, Elizabeth A. (Elizabeth Anne), 1950–
   303.6

Library of Congress Cataloging-in-Publication Data
Violence / edited by Elizabeth A. Stanko.
       p. cm. — (International library of criminology, criminal justice and penology)
   Includes bibliographical references.
   ISBN 0-7546-2230-4 (alk. paper)
       1. Violent crimes. 2. Violence. I. Stanko, Elizabeth Anne, 1950– II. International
   library of criminology, criminal justice & penology

   HV6493 .V558 2002
   364.15—dc21   2001053585

ISBN 0 7546 2230 4

Printed in Great Britain by The Cromwell Press, Trowbridge, Wiltshire

Contents

PART IV   INTERSECTIONS OF VIOLENT OFFENDING AND VIOLENT VICTIMIZATION

PART V   THEORETICAL EXPLANATIONS OF VIOLENCE

PART VI   EXPLANATIONS OF VIOLENCE AS SOCIALLY CONSTRUCTED

PART VII   POLITICAL VIOLENCE

Acknowledgements

The editor and publishers wish to thank the following for permission to use copyright material.

Academy of Criminal Justice Sciences for the essay: Eric P. Baumer, Steven F. Messner and Richard B. Felson (2000), 'The Role of the Victim Characteristics in the Disposition of Murder Cases', *Justice Quarterly*, **17**, pp. 281–307. Copyright © 2000 Academy of Criminal Justice Sciences. Reprinted with permission of the Academy of Criminal Justice Sciences.

Annual Reviews for the essays: Richard B. Felson (1996), 'Mass Media Effects on Violent Behavior', *Annual Review of Sociology*, **22**, pp. 103–28. Copyright © 1996 Annual Reviews www.AnnualReviews.org; Robert Nash Parker and Kathleen Auerhahn (1998), 'Alcohol, Drugs, and Violence', *Annual Review of Sociology*, **24**, pp. 291–311. Copyright © 1998 Annual Reviews www.AnnualReviews.org; Rogers Brubaker and David D. Laitin (1998), 'Ethnic and Nationalist Violence', *Annual Review of Sociology*, **24**, pp. 423–52. Copyright © 1998 Annual Reviews www.AnnualReviews.org.

Australian Academic Press Pty Ltd for the essay: Ania Wilczynski and Kate Sinclair (1999), 'Moral Tales: Representations of Child Abuse in the Quality and Tabloid Media', *The Australian and New Zealand Journal of Criminology*, **32**, pp. 262–83. www.australianacadmicpress.com.au

Frank Cass Publishers for the essays: Kathleen A. Cavanaugh (1997), 'Interpretations of Political Violence in Ethnically Divided Societies', *Terrorism and Political Violence*, **9**, pp. 33–54; Rachel Monaghan (1997), 'Animal Rights and Violent Protest', *Terrorism and Political Violence*, **9,** pp. 106–16.

Lawrence Erlbaum Associates for the essay: Roy F. Baumeister and W. Keith Campbell (1999), 'The Intrinsic Appeal of Evil: Sadism, Sensational Thrills, and Threatened Egotism', *Personality and Social Psychology Review*, **3**, pp. 210–21.

National Council of Family Relations for the essay: Michael P. Johnson and Kathleen J. Ferraro (2000), 'Research on Domestic Violence in the 1990s: Making Distinctions', *Journal of Marriage and the Family*, **62**, pp. 948–63.

Oxford University Press for the essays: Stephen Tomsen (1997), 'A Top Night: Social Protest, Masculinity and the Culture of Drinking Violence', *British Journal of Criminology*, **37**, pp. 90–102; Shani D'Cruze (1999), 'Sex, Violence and Local Courts: Working-Class Respectability in a Mid-Nineteenth-Century Lancashire Town', *British Journal of Criminology*, **39**, pp. 39–55.

Social Forces for the essay: Matthew R. Lee (2000), 'Community Cohesion and Violent Predatory Victimization: A Theoretical Extension and Cross-National Test of Opportunity

Series Preface

The International Library of Criminology, Criminal Justice and Penology, represents an important publishing initiative to bring together the most significant journal essays in contemporary criminology, criminal justice and penology. The series makes available to researchers, teachers and students an extensive range of essays which are indispensable for obtaining an overview of the latest theories and findings in this fast changing subject.

This series consists of volumes dealing with criminological schools and theories as well as with approaches to particular areas of crime, criminal justice and penology. Each volume is edited by a recognised authority who has selected twenty or so of the best journal articles in the field of their special competence and provided an informative introduction giving a summary of the field and the relevance of the articles chosen. The original pagination is retained for ease of reference.

The difficulties of keeping on top of the steadily growing literature in criminology are complicated by the many disciplines from which its theories and findings are drawn (sociology, law, sociology of law, psychology, psychiatry, philosophy and economics are the most obvious). The development of new specialisms with their own journals (policing, victimology, mediation) as well as the debates between rival schools of thought (feminist criminology, left realism, critical criminology, abolitionism etc.) make necessary overviews that offer syntheses of the state of the art. These problems are addressed by the INTERNATIONAL LIBRARY in making available for research and teaching the key essays from specialist journals.

GERALD MARS
Professor in Applied Anthropology, Universities of North London
and Northumbria Business Schools

DAVID NELKEN
Distinguished Research Professor, Cardiff Law Schoool,
University of Wales, Cardiff

Introduction
Searching for the Meaning of Violence: The Limitations of Theory and Data in our Understanding of Violence

Background

Forms of violence differ. Where and how violence occurs differs. Motivations and meanings differ. Yet politicians continue too often to try to speculate about why 'violence' occurs as if it is one kind of phenomenon. This collection presents an approach to the study of violence that refuses to standardize its meaning by looking solely to criminal statute. Common assault, grievous bodily harm, threatening behaviour, stalking and other forms of criminal violence are defined as 'against the law' by making distinctions about the kind of psychological, physical or sexual harm that an individual experiences. Statutes define criminal violence by specifying the form of injury, threat and harm, placing different violent acts along a continuum that separates seriousness by some 'objective' measure of outcome. In this sense, harm from criminal violence is located within parameters of physical and psychological damage outside of its social context and consequences. Conventional wisdom assumes that criminal law judges forms of violent behaviour to have similar consequences for similar victims if the 'objective' harm is the same. Critics, however, have queried whether such judgements are applied without prejudice. As a consequence, critical commentators on violence wonder whether criminal law acts to protect all citizens equally.

Across the world, crime surveys tell us that people themselves largely eschew law following violence. Crime surveys suggest that people define acts as potential criminal violence in roughly one in three violent encounters. An even smaller proportion of police-recorded violence ends up in any court of law. In contrast to the starting point of criminal law as a determinate in reflecting wider social harm of violence, people themselves consider the 'what happened' in a violent encounter within the context of their interpersonal relations. In effect, people may be traumatized by injury or frightened by the threat, but regularly do not use *legal* definitions in understanding acts of criminal violence. 'What happened was too trivial', 'The matter was private', or 'The police could not do anything anyway' are common categories people choose on crime surveys to account for why they did not involve the police in matters of violence. If asked to explain why they chose not to ring the police about criminal violence, people describe 'what happened' as a way of resolving disputes, as deserved punishment for indiscretions (perceived or actual), or as a form of negotiating social power within complicated social relations.

Research on the administration of justice also suggests that police, prosecutors, juries and judges also differentially define different people's experiences of various forms of violence. Sentences vary for those found guilty for acts of violence that appear to have caused similar levels of injury and impact. Many critical campaigners over the past 20 years in particular have used sentence outcome to demonstrate differential treatment by courts, judges and others (including the way in which police initially laid charges for 'what happened'). Battered women's advocates, rape crisis activists, minority and refugee groups, those supporting the rights of children, those with learning difficulties or gay, lesbian and transgendered groups, for instance, have brought their analysis of differential treatment at the hands of law and law enforcement to the forefront of debates in criminology. Some legislative changes in various jurisdictions have tried to address these concerns. Criminal statutes may specify why aggravating and mitigating circumstances justify differential treatment of 'similar acts of violence' by law. In England and Wales, for example, a recent law specifies that a person convicted of racially motivated violence may be given a longer sentence because of the racial element of the assault. Other examples include criminal statutes that define particular victims as more vulnerable than others, such as a child victim or a victim aged over 75. One question worth asking is: does criminal law account for differential vulnerability of victims of violence? And should criminal law be part of 'righting' the harm of social disadvantage experienced by vulnerable victims in the way in which it determines the seriousness of the damage of violence?

Yet many criminologists and other social scientists evade these questions, focusing instead on the study of *criminal* violence and the application of law to criminal acts rather than study the dynamics of *ordinary* violence in people's lives. I suggest that we cannot understand criminal violence without understanding how 'ordinary' violence works in the lives of people in many different circumstances (see Stanko, 1990). We should then study the application of criminal law within the wider complexities of how violence affects different kinds of people. However, most of our theories attempt to explain violence by addressing the abnormality of the individual, the community or the culture. While there is no doubt that any criminal act is committed by an individual, living within a community which has been influenced throughout his/her life by family, community, culture and society, research evidence suggests that *patterns* of forms of violence have changed over time. For example, in many Western societies there has been a dramatic decline in homicide among the elite (Cooney, 1997). Cooney argues quite convincingly that the modern phenomenon of homicide – that it is confined largely to low-status people (mostly men) – is more a reflection of the development of the modern state. Today, disputes among elites are largely settled through a resort to civil law. Violent conflict, Cooney suggests, is a function of the unavailability of law. Conflict, and the resources for its resolution, is managed though the physical confrontations of those who do not have access to alternative mediation. Those with power are more able to draw upon social and cultural forms of legitimacy, shame and social control than those without. Cooney speculates that many acts of violence are indeed people resolving disputes (literally) by their own hands.

But not all violent acts stem from forms of dispute between parties. People also use violence to assert control, to degrade, to humiliate and to punish. Sexual violence, for instance, may be better understood outside a paradigm of conflict. The medium of violence is sex and sexuality, but the message of the violence is far more complicated. Feminist theorizing about rape and sexual abuse throughout the life course focuses our attention on the way in which sexual intimidation impacts on the lives of (largely) women and children as a form of (largely) men's social control over women (see Stanko, 1985; Kelly, 1988). Research on men's experiences of sexual abuse remains more limited. Nonetheless, as a form of violence, sexual violence must be understood as a phenomenon made distinct because of the way in which sex and violence intersect in a complicated maze of gendered social relations.

By and large, most forms of violence people experience flow from and into their everyday lives. Sites of familiarity feature prominently in its typical forms: home, leisure pursuits, the neighbourhood and the workplace. These contexts mould the way in which violence is understood for individuals, social institutions and social policy. Research also demonstrates that some contexts within which violence occurs are understood better than others. Stranger violence, for instance, continues to overshadow our attention and our fear of crime. Headlines capture the outrage of the public when an unknown predator attacks a child or a deranged and dangerous sex offender rapes a woman. The image of the violent stranger is cast into detective stories and Hollywood movies, as well as our everyday newspapers. We are warned to be on our guard from such strangers, encouraged to use our family and friends as protection against such attackers. This image of danger is compatible with blaming individuals for violence without any attempt to understand that it is our social relationships that set the stage for most violence that takes place.

But little violence is random, most of it is purposeful, and much of it is indeed targeted. All our criminological data tells us so. The significance of this violence is *familiarity*. Crime surveys, for example, consistently demonstrate that young men who go out in the evening and drink alcohol more than once a week assault, and are assaulted by, other young men much like themselves. These young men are the typical victims and perpetrators of personal violence in every modern jurisdiction in the world. Child abusers, too, specialize in familiarity. Empirical evidence shows us that much of the personal violence to children is contained within the home, with parents and close family and friends acting as their violators. Yet school programmes designed to teach children safety commonly attempt to teach children to say 'no' to strangers to avoid personal danger. Women are most at risk to threat and personal assault within intimate, sexual partnerships, and face unsafety at work and while at leisure largely through the harm rendered by known assailants. Neighbours, acquaintances and friends also endanger men most, and men's work-related violence places them at additional risk to the violence of strangers (see Budd, 1999; Chappell and Di Martino, 1998). The adage 'A punch in the mouth is a punch in the mouth no matter where it takes place' simply does not hold. Encouraging the promotion of *criminal* law as a mechanism for managing the impact of violence on the total population, or even special groups in the population, will miss the power of, and the functional uses for, violence. In many settings, systematic threat coerces people and is useful for controlling the behaviour of others despite the fact that no punch need be thrown to achieve compliance of an intimidated party.

Given these empirical realities, current work on violence has important limitations. First, most social science scholarship continues to privilege the problem of random violence (Brownstein, 2000). Although there are now volumes on family and domestic violence, child abuse, racist and other forms of targeted violence, these are largely considered separately from random violence. Second, general texts examining the causes of violence often use a common formula for scholarly scrutiny. In such approaches, research findings are grouped by discipline, with each critiqued by author after author demonstrating the (small) portion of violence in so-called advanced, civilized societies that these theoretical approaches might explain (and by implication that which cannot be explained). Thus:

- Biological research into the causes of violence, for instance, inquires into the genetic make-up, chemical levels of the brain or the hormone levels of *identified* violent males or females.
- Psychological approaches scrutinize the differential impact of anxieties or aggression fuelled by inconsistent, harsh or neglectful parenting, loss of parent or significant adults or childhood experiences of physical or sexual abuse experienced by *identified* violent perpetrators.
- Sociological theories estimate prevalence and incidence and interrogate how the occurrence of violence is affected by the attachment of individuals to a (presumed) peaceful, civil society.

All the above tend to focus on the nature of the *individual* violent offender. If there is a concern about more than one individual, the alarm is raised about the behaviour of 'gangs', rather than groups, of (usually) young people. The assumption is that those who are violent only attack strangers, contrary to our empirical evidence which suggests that, with the exception of robbery, most violence occurs between people who know each other (including groups of youths attacking other groups of youths). The attention to, and panic over, stranger danger continues to eclipse the real problem and consequences of violence (Best, 1999). Any commentary noting how the meaning of violence changes if the actions take place in the name of collective violence (such as that of hunt saboteurs), political violence (such as that involving inter ethnic conflict) and state violence (such as instances of police brutality) is largely absent.

Accounting for Violence: What Information about Violence is Missing from our Debates?

All our available evidence shows that violence is experienced and challenged differently depending on the 'who, where, and why' it occurs. People themselves decide what is 'trivial', what is 'private' and what 'the police can do nothing about'. Which forms of violence are most often treated by its victims as 'trivial'? Our information suggests that the closer the relationship between the perpetrator and the victim, the more likely it is that the act of violence is kept outside the remit of criminal law. For many victims, this is largely an assessment that places the violent act – and its outcome – against the logic of criminal law. The meanings of violence, how and whether it comes to the attention of the criminal justice system, therefore arise in a context wider than the action taken by the perpetrator against the victim. But it is not only familiarity that affects how violence is defined. In a recent study of violence in the night-time economy, for instance, Lister *et al.* (2000) found that few of the many assaults arising from pub fights, and especially attacks by door staff supposedly guarding these pubs and clubs, are recorded as criminal violence by police who intervene. Physical damage to a victim therefore is but one of a host of factors influencing whether people who experience violence, and those who judge it, officially define an act as 'against the law'.

Data collection about violence and its intersection with these places of familiarity limits our understanding of how forms of violence intersect in distinct ways in different settings. We know little about violence in care homes, residential facilities for children, schools, hospitals, pizza shops, public transport and so forth. For example, we have little information about violence in the workplace in England and Wales because of the methods of recording workplace injury.

The Health and Safety Executive requires all employers to report any workplace violence that results in injury leading to an absence of three or more days. The limited information we have about workplace violence in the UK demonstrates that much of the violence experienced at work falls well below that standard (Budd, 1999; Stanko *et al.*, 1998).

Even official evidence about the extent of different forms of violence in society is scant (Stanko *et al.*, 1998). Police collect information about assault, robbery or homicide as categories of criminal law defined by elements such as seriousness of injury, force and/or use of weapons. Yet our knowledge about patterns and trends of violence flows from crime surveys or criminal statistics that group similar criminal elements together. But this official information about violence is confined to these legal and administrative categories. Crime surveys, for instance, ask a representative sample of the population about their experiences of crime and violence. The recent *2000 British Crime Survey* found that only 35 per cent of violent crime was reported to police by victims. Domestic violence was least likely, and so-called 'stranger violence' the most likely to be reported to the police (Kershaw *et al.*, 2000). Criminal Statistics, on the other hand, publish data on reported crimes of violence, but do not specify between the types of violence that the victimization survey is able to distinguish. Official legal categories provide broad-brush data on violent crime. Although we are able to count the number of homicides or woundings, or even common assaults, we have no idea about what happened to the people who experienced these forms of violence and what impact it had on them. Moreover, most people who report violent crime to the police do not see these crimes prosecuted or punished by the state. When figures for violent crime rise or fall, there is a strong presumption that the streets are safer, or that commentary about the rise and fall of violence has anything to do with real danger.

The main problem with official criminal statistics about violence is our inability to make distinctions between the forms of violence that contribute to the overall reported levels of violence. When we say that 'violence is up' or 'violence is down', we may only mean reported domestic violence has risen or alcohol-related violence has dramatically decreased and so forth. Specially commissioned studies of different forms of violence, such as surveys exploring domestic violence, racist violence, sexual violence or homophobic violence, have provided valuable insight into the impact, and perhaps incidence and prevalence, of these forms of violence. These surveys, however, are rarely conducted in a way that allows us to make statements about the changes in these forms of violence *over time*. Cooney's observations about elite violence noted above are an exception.

Data collection about violence, then, feed into the way in which the logic of criminal law dominates our criminological analysis of violence. Theorizing about violence raises current debates in social science about the nature of familiarity, security, risk, postmodernity and the ambiguities about the notions of the certainty of 'the safe place' in modern civil society. But these debates are continually placed in the context of criminal law and social order (Garland, 2001). Moreover, global dialogues about human rights and violence in social conflict intersect criminological thinking, but are generally ignored as related to our thinking about criminal violence.

Debating Ordinary Violence and Criminal Violence

This collection firmly embeds theorizing about forms of violence in diverse, lived cultures. It seeks to encourage a debate that is informed by how different forms of violence affect ordinary people who are situated as actors in multiple social hierarchies. As such the age, gender, class, race, ethnicity, religion, and sexuality and so forth of those who commit and those who experience violence matters. It matters what philosophical and moral dilemmas surface in public debates about violence. It matters that we are left to theorize and debate with very limited empirical evidence that would enable us to sketch the place of criminal violence within its ordinary, socially embedded context.

The collection is divided into seven Parts which deliberately present an interdisciplinary framework that challenges an inevitable connection of explanations of violence with criminal violence alone. Disorder, incivility and a chronic nostalgia for the illusory, peaceable community too often obscure the development of an empirically grounded argument. The work on outlining how we might move beyond social policy approaches that cling to legal statute as a solution to public protection from violence to ones that genuinely take the contexts within which violence thrives seriously comes later. Readers should see the essays in this collection as pieces of a puzzle about the nature of violence and its function in contemporary society. I have drawn many of the essays from criminological work that uses criminal violence to explore explanations for why some forms of violence might occur and why our contemporary theorizing is often incomplete without an interdisciplinary framework. They also show that there are no simple explanations for such a complex issue.

Forms of Violent Behaviour

Part I examines the social contexts of four forms of violence: leisure-related violence; women's 'street' violence (homicide, robbery and assault); rape and black-on-black violence in the USA. As a whole, this first section requires the reader to begin to consider the social context within which offenders choose to use violence. Through an ethnographic study, Stephen Tomsen (Chapter 1) sketches features of pub violence in one city in Australia, exploring how such detailed observation reveals aspects of violence that the perpetrators and their onlookers 'appreciate' as entertaining. He is keen to acknowledge the damage of such violence. Indeed, in England and Wales, this form of violence is responsible for over 1000 facial injuries each week (Magennis *et al.*, 1998). Tomsen concludes that this form of violence is firmly embedded in the homosocial: men, public displays of masculinities, drinking and 'a top night out' routinely include a 'good' fight. Challenging the violence of the night-time economy, then, must acknowledge the way in which public drinking and some forms of masculinity come together to create a cocktail for violence. Following on the theme of gender identity, in Chapter 2 Deborah Baskin and Ira Sommers use criminological data on violent street careers to explore the social factors shaping women's violent offending. This essay challenges any simplistic thinking that women's violence is somehow linked to women's liberation or autonomy – a common myth that emerges in the media with great regularity. However, it also demonstrates that caution against generic and gender-based generalizations is well founded. It is the social context of offenders' lives (both male and female) that exerts a significant influence on the features in women's everyday decisions to use violence. In Chapter 3 Diana Scully's and Joseph Marolla's interviews with rapists reveal that these offenders 'make sense' of their violent offending. In their examination of the function of sexual violence in the lives of convicted rapists, the authors discover that some men use sexual violence as a method of revenge and/or punishment while others use it as a means of gaining access to unwilling or unavailable women. But most men could justify or rationalize their use of violence. The authors found men capable of talking about their sexual assaults as if they had meaning for their own lives. Such meaning says more about the availability of a discourse of sexual conquest as a normal part of men's sexual relations with women. Another form of normativity is explored in the last essay in Part I, that by Marino Bruce, Vincent Roscigno and Patricia McCall exploring black-on-black violence in the USA. High rates of violence in the Afro-American community, the authors argue, stems from the day-to-day experience of disadvantage of subordinated groups. A dynamic approach to the study of violence in its context is necessary, they claim, to show how the interactive patterns of local norms contribute to using violence as a resource and as social–psychological tools for negotiating such norms within relative levels of danger and safety of some geographical areas.

Part I sets the stage for arguments that arise throughout the collection. By and large, no violence occurs without meaning. Such meaning is shaped and legitimated (or condemned) by its given contexts. Perpetrators' actions are explored for what they say about their social worlds as much as what they say about how violent harm might befall others. Questions are raised about economic conditions, masculinities and femininities, social privilege, social change and social exclusion. We must stop thinking about violence as 'natural' and inevitable. Its use has patterns, and these patterns largely (though not exclusively) sketch out patterns of societal privilege and social disadvantage.

Domestic Violence

Part II focuses on a major contribution to rethinking our understanding of violent crime, domestic violence. In Chapter 5 Terrie Moffitt, Robert Krueger, Avshalom Caspi and Jeff Fagan, using traditional criminological approaches, ask whether offenders of partner abuse and general crime share the same criminological features. The authors conclude that partner abuse and general crime represent different constructs that are 'moderately related'. We must study partner abuse as a distinct form of violence. This suggests that perpetrators who abuse intimates are most likely to do so as a 'deliberate', rather than as an impulsive, course of action. The essay by Michael Johnson and Kathleen Ferraro (Chapter 6) extends this idea by demanding that we look more closely at domestic violence in a context of examining the interplay of violence, power and control in relationships. These authors encourage us to look more carefully at partner violence in detail. Making distinctions among types of violence, motives of perpetrators, the social and cultural contexts of the lives of those affected, as well as their wider communities is essential in developing an understanding about partner abuse that challenges its many forms. In Chapter 7 Michael Cruz and Juanita Firestone take this call for distinctions one step further by exploring the dimensions of same sex partner abuse – in this case, the violence between gay male couples. The authors demonstrate how the meanings of (domestic) violence are firmly embedded in how victims and perpetrators understand their complex lives in a complicated, social world.

Part II, in sum, addresses one form of violence and, at the same time, illustrates the importance of making distinctions about violence within this form. In many ways, the work on domestic violence can be credited, I believe, for opening up new ways of thinking about violence in the wider global debate about safety.

Sexual Violence

The debate about the widespread existence of domestic violence links to those around sexual violence. These two forms of violence have been largely exposed despite the overwhelming silence of its victims and it is the foundations of this silence that are the main theme of Part III. Historian Shani D'Cruze's contribution (Chapter 8) explores the contradictions for women who brought charges of sexual assault to public scrutiny via the criminal court during the 1800s. Women's reputations as respectable, then as now, intersect with assessments about their sexuality as proper women. Such reputations take their strength as mechanisms to silence and shame from the power of institutionalized heterosexuality as a mechanism of the social control of women. Christine Helliwell's essay (Chapter 9) challenges our contemporary understanding of this power of sexual reputation by placing its largely Western foundation against the way in which sexual assault was understood by the Dayak community of Gerai in Indonesian Borneo. Her essay is provocative. It illustrates the power of our Western cultural understandings about sexualities, and leads us to question the way in which institutionalized thinking influences our own feelings of personal safety as women. As criminological literature continues to demonstrate, sexual violence is responsible for much of women's feelings of unsafety in public. Helliwell's essay encourages us to move beyond our own taken-for-granted frameworks about ways of challenging the damage and the power of sexual violence as a form of sexualized and gender social control.

Sexual violence thus must be understood within its complexities: gender, sexualities, and the social institutions that support wider notions of social respectability. Heterosexuality – although under challenge within the area of violence research in particular – still influences how we characterize the impact of sexual violence. In Chapter 10 Lana Stermac, Peter Sheridan, Alison Davidson and Sheila Dunn address a less frequently studied aspect of sexual violence – the sexual assault of adult men. It is crucial, they argue, that we place our thinking about the sexual assault of men into a theoretical context that confronts the limitations of casting violence as a problem of stranger danger. The authors find that, as with sexual violence perpetrated on women, men's assailants are largely other men known to them. Finally, Jacquelyn Campbell and Karen Soeken (Chapter 11) explore the damage resulting from sexual violence. Although the consequences for women sexually abused by their partners are significant, far too often we continue to highlight the barbarity of the 'stranger' rapist. Violence, as this collection demonstrates, most often flows from the abuse of familiarity and the violation of personal trust.

Intersections of Violent Offending and Violent Victimization

For criminologists, Part IV examines a link too often overlooked in the study of criminal violence – the overlap between violent offending and violent victimization. Although these studies use 'criminal' violence as a source of their research, they acknowledge that our data are unable to capture this connection in many people's experiences. Much of the work exploring violent victimization, for instance, highlights the damage caused to what many term the innocent, undeserving victim. When we begin to explore the intersection between offending and victimization seriously, I suggest here, we will then be able to approach social policy on violence more creatively. Simon Singer's early study of US inner-city males (Chapter 12) found that a significant proportion of those who committed acts of serious violence had also experienced violent victimization. This study leads us to question the emphasis, in popular discourse, about the random nature of violence. As Singer's essay shows, violent victimization falls more heavily on the shoulders of some groups of the population. In Chapter 13 Kenneth Polk opens this discussion further by methodically wading through the controversial topic of victim-precipitated homicide. He persuasively demonstrates that patterns of victim participation, analysed carefully via the rich texture of homicide case files, require us to examine lethal violence in the context of its social encounter. The more we learn about homicide as a social interaction, the more we understand the contexts of violent acts.

The gender dynamics of these social encounters, as Jody Miller shows in Chapter 14, influence the mix of violent victimization and violent offending in the lives of US girl gang members. The risk of violent victimization for these young women increases substantially. Gang initiation, membership and rivalries all contribute to these girls' more numerous encounters with sexual and physical assault. The girls largely view violence as inevitable. Street drug robbers also understand the inevitability of encountering violence. In Chapter 15 Bruce Jacobs, Volkan Topalli and Richard Wright demonstrate the consequences of often ill-judged use of violence by individual drug robbers for the operations of the illegal, inner-city drug market as a whole. The measures taken by those who violate the unspoken 'rules' of illegal drug sales to protect themselves outline the importance of 'peaceful' trade to this very lucrative market. Violence is not necessarily a consequence of the operations of the illegal market in drugs *per se*. It is a demonstration to all that work within it that some individual drug abusers are unable to manage their drug use without bouts of desperation. Cycles of violence in any one illegal market, the authors suggest, may be an outcome of the unpredictable behaviour of a few 'unmanageable' drug robbers.

Theoretical Explanations of Violence

Part V explores many of the common explanations for violence that dominate today's debates about violence. Ralph Cintron's perceptive approach to explaining violence rests on an assumption that acts of violence have meaning in a highly moral and moralized social order (Chapter 16). Vengeance, he argues, is one concept that captures, for him, an explanation for making sense of how threat and assault are used by some who live under extreme conditions of US poverty. His essay locates violence firmly within its social, psychological and economic contexts. These contexts are often forgotten in debates on the impact of mass media on violent behaviour, the topic of Richard Felson's review (Chapter 17). Is it possible to blame violence on the influence of mass media? Felson's essay analyses the evidence carefully and leads us to question the possibility that we will find any single explanation for violent behaviour.

Blame for violence is also often cast on 'the demon drink' or on the pharmacology induced by the use of illegal drugs. Robert Nash Parker and Kathleen Auerhahn's analysis of this popular excuse for violent behaviour (Chapter 18) analyses the research evidence on the links among alcohol, drugs and violence. The authors emphasize that context is by far the most important factor in locating the influence of substance use and misuse on violent behaviour. Another explanation for violent behaviour can be found in the psychological attributes of perpetrators themselves. In Chapter 19 Roy Baumeister and Keith Campbell ask questions about the psychological appeal of some forms of violence to some perpetrators. Some people who commit violence may do so because they derive some form of psychological satisfaction from doing so. The authors conclude that there is evidence to support this explanation in some situations for some perpetrators.

Matthew Lee's essay (Chapter 20) turns to an exploration of the resilience of communities to violence. Examining the findings of the International Victimization Survey, he argues that the social cohesion of communities may act as a buffer to public violence, particularly robbery and assault outside the home. In the final chapter of this part, Bernard Schissel tackles the problem of building resilience to violence into communities by searching for explanations of young men's violence to young women in order to gain strategic insights for the prevention and minimization of this form of violence. Throughout this essay, and all the other essays making up Part V, the reader is urged to think carefully about the importance of social context in understanding particular forms of violence. As the reader will discover, no one single explanation is sufficient in and of itself to account for 'why' a substantial proportion of violence happens. The reader is encouraged to place many of the insights about violence into a constellation of explanations that enable us to capture the complexities of violence as a social and as an individual problem.

Explanations of Violence as Socially Constructed

Part VI will alert the reader to also keep in mind how we as social commentators, criminal justice actors, historians and others, socially construct the problem of violence. In Chapter 22 the social historian John Archer interrogates our use of official records on violence and wonders how reliable such data are. He demonstrates that we should supplement our reading of official historical information with as many sources about life in the past as possible. Newspapers, he shows, are one such source. Returning to the present, Hazel May's essay (Chapter 23) highlights the way in which English people themselves make sense of acts of violence. Through interviews with relatives of convicted murderers, she reveals the complex way in which people search for explanations about violence, often blurring the distinctions between the victims' and perpetrators' responsibility. The common-sense explanations of violence displayed by those interviewed by May have resonance in how criminal justice actors – prosecutors, judges and juries – treat homicide in the USA. Eric Baumer, Steven Messner and Richard Felson (Chapter 24) find evidence that characterizations of victims' conduct influences the legal outcome of US murder cases. Perpetrators who kill so-called disreputable victims are less likely to be prosecuted, less likely to have their cases decided at trial, and more likely to be found guilty of a lesser charge than murder. Who the victim is and what he or she did at the time of the killing matters in the determination of legal guilt. In the essay in this part Ania Wilczynski and Kate Sinclair return once again to the media, arguing that the media takes an active role in constructing a discourse about *bad* perpetrators of violence – in this case, child abusers. The authors alert the reader to the complex processes involved in the media's construction of violent crime.

As a whole, Part VI seeks to encourage the reader to critique the discourses and the social contexts within which academic disciplines, criminal justice actors and the public make sense of violent behaviour. This sense-making all too often turns solely on trying to explain the individual acts of individual actors. As a consequence, the wider contribution of ideologies, communities, and social and political life is ignored.

Political Violence

This is precisely why I end the collection in Part VII with a discussion of this wider context: state violence, ethnic and nationalist violence and terrorist violence. It is through this piece of the puzzle that we can begin to ask where and how ordinary violence relates to criminal violence. In Chapter 26 Rod Morgan reminds us that some modern states justify the use of violence on their behalf. Torture – the use of violence against individuals by officials of the state – is still practised in some countries. Morgan observes that, today, torture thrives in societies characterized by gross inequities of power or where one ethnic or religious community seeks to repress another. Indeed, forms of violence perpetrated during war are recognized as war crimes, now tried by the International Criminal Tribunal in The Hague, The Netherlands. The acts of violence – be they rape, killing or forms of assault – have managed to become separated from similar acts of violence committed by individuals under 'peacetime' conditions. Yet some countries exist simultaneously under peace and violent-prone conditions. In the following chapter Rogers Brubaker's and David Laitin's discussion on aspects of ethnic and political violence contributes another analysis to the context within which individual violence takes place. These authors plead for multi-featured analyses of violence that give careful attention to its forms and its social and political construction. Kathleen Cavanaugh's essay (Chapter 28) questions the way in which violence in Northern Ireland is characterized. It is, the author argues, the issue of the absence of state legitimacy that is central to understanding the use of violence in Northern Ireland. Rachel Monahan's exploration of violent animal rights protest (Chapter 29) extends this section to consider how small groups of individuals challenge the legitimacy of the state on the matter of animal treatment in biological and medical research. The use of violence by animal rights protectors, or paramilitary groups for that matter, is often analysed as separate and distinct from gang violence or inner-city ethnic conflict in so-called peaceable societies.

Ultimately, the way in which we conceptualize violence is influenced by whether we think the state correctly defines some forms of violence as legitimate, and others as the actions of individuals operating outside state legitimacy. The purpose of Part VII, and of this collection as a whole, is to challenge the way in which criminological analyses have so easily left behind the wider questions of state legitimacy in their debates about violence. Together, the essays in this collection urge the reader to go beyond the individual perpetrator, the individual violent act and the individual victim in considerations of the place of violence in society.

References

Best, J. (1999), *Random Violence*, Berkeley: University of California Press.
Brownstein, H. (2000), *The Social Reality of Violence and Violent Crime*, Boston, MA: Allyn and Bacon.
Budd, T. (1999), *Violence at Work: Findings from the British Crime Survey*, London: Home Office.
Chappell, D. and Di Martino, V. (1998), *Violence at Work*, Geneva: International Labour Office.
Coleman, C. and Moynihan, J. (1996), *Understanding Crime Data*, Buckingham: Open University Press.
Cooney, M. (1997), 'The Decline of Elite Homicide', *Criminology*, **35** (3), pp. 381–407.

Garland, D. (2001), *The Culture of Control*, Oxford: Oxford University Press.

Kelly, L. (1988), *Surviving Sexual Violence*, Oxford: Polity Press.

Kershaw, C. (2000), *The 2000 British Crime Survey*, London: The Stationery Office.

Lister, S., Hobbs, D., Hall, S. and Winlow, S. (2000), 'Violence in the Night-Time Economy. Bouncers: The Reporting, Recording and Prosecution of Assaults', *Policing and Society*, **10** (4), pp. 383–402.

Magennis, P., Shepherd, J., Hutchinson, H. and Brown, A. (1998), 'Trends in Facial Injuries', *British Journal of Medicine*, **316**, pp. 325–6.

Stanko, E. (1985), *Intimate Intrusions*, London: Routledge.

Stanko, E. (1990), *Everyday Violence*, London: Pandora Press.

Stanko, E., Marion, L., Crisp, D., Manning, R., Smith, J. and Cowan, S. (1998), *Taking Stock: What do we know about violence?*, Uxbridge, Middlesex: Brunel University.

Part I
Forms of Violent Behaviour

[1]

BRIT. J. CRIMINOL. VOL. 37   NO. 1   WINTER 1997

A TOP NIGHT

Social Protest, Masculinity and the Culture of Drinking Violence

STEPHEN TOMSEN*

Although a wide research literature suggests a regular connection between drinking, violence and social disorder, much doubt remains as to the actual nature and significance of this link. Some strong insights into this are provided by a dual consideration of the tie between masculine social identity and heavy group drinking, and the importance of issues of male honour in the social interaction that leads to much violent behaviour. But as well as this, information from the author's detailed ethnographic study of assaults in public drinking venues illuminates the subjective experience of participation in acts of disorder and violence. This is filtered through understandings of certain forms and aspects of popular leisure as entailing social protest and resistance to middle class morality. Although masculinist and frequently destructive, this violence is interpreted by many drinkers as providing a liberating and attractive sense of release, group pleasure and carnival.

Drinking, Violence and Popular Culture

There is a vast, diverse and conflicting international literature on the nature of the link between drinking, disorder and violent behaviour. Despite a continuous growth in research which has found a high degree of correlation between assaults, street offences and the presence of alcohol, a direct causal relationship between alcohol use and acts of violence is difficult to prove (Robb 1988; Fagan 1990; Bonney and Kery 1991). However, some criminologists stress that an apparent link to street offences reflects the high level of police action against working class youth and minority groups like Aborigines who regularly engage in public drinking (Cunneen 1988). Feminist researchers have also argued that the alleged link between drinking and violence can serve to excuse attacks on women (McGregor 1990). For reasons such as these, some recent literature has doubted that this link is causal, has criticized exclusively pharmacological approaches, and has noted that aggression, violence and drinking are all closely connected to periods of high levels of social interaction (Greenberg 1982; Collins 1989; Fagan 1990).[1]

One path around this apparent theoretical impasse is to analyse drinking-related violence through an understanding of aspects of the historical and cultural conceptions of various forms of social disorder. Important insights can be obtained from studies of 'people's history', leisure and popular culture, and the group significance of acts of

---

* Department of Sociology and Anthropology, University of Newcastle, Australia. A large number of personal friends helped with this study. The author is especially grateful to Mark Fletcher and John Shewan, uncomplaining companions on many long and late nights of fieldwork. Early versions of this paper were presented and discussed with staff and students at the University of Washington, Seattle in 1993. The author's thanks to Howard Becker, Ken Clatterbaugh, Dian Lye, and Stuart Scheingold for helpful criticism and ideas. More locally, he thanks Terry Leahy and Peter Grabosky for their comments.

[1] Fagan argues that: '... the link between intoxication and aggression is less certain than is implied by the scientific literature and popular opinion. Despite overwhelming evidence that drug and alcohol use and aggression are related ... intoxication does not consistently lead to aggressive behaviour (1990: 243).

A TOP NIGHT

disorder, crowd behaviour and riots (Donajgrodski 1977; Yeo and Yeo 1981; Tilly and Tilly 1981; Rude 1995). This work rejects the conventional left view that popular leisure expresses elements of social control or false consciousness, to argue instead that it frequently embodies collective cultural resistance to efforts to regulate the 'dangerous classes' or the 'lower orders' in different societies. In so doing it becomes a terrain of ongoing and unresolved struggles over social values. These pastimes can, therefore, often be understood as a form of symbolic protest against aspects of bourgeois morality (hard work, saving, self-discipline and useful leisure), and the superior value that is placed on the culture and lifestyles of the middle class.

Middle class complaints about the social habits of the 'lower classes' have been typified by an ongoing struggle over the control and regulation of public drinking. This has been a key popular leisure activity which has offended bourgeois commentators. This was very evident in what have been termed as the symbolic crusades of the early Temperance movements in such nations as the United States and Australia (Gusfield 1963; Sturma 1983).

In more recent times, respectable criticism of excessive drinking has taken the form of warnings about the adverse outcomes of drinking that come from a range of health and medical experts. Alongside this, more obvious moral panics also persist. Politicians, police and media commentators often directly blame drinking for acts of crime and public disorder. Explanations of football hooliganism and youth disorder as resulting from unregulated drinking in Britain are just one frequently cited example of this response (Pearson 1983).

Much of the literature on popular leisure effectively deconstructs elements of official representations of drinking and disorder and the historically contested meanings attached to aspects of working class and youth culture. But the further development of an ethnographic focus in studies of drinking-related disorder that links consciousness to social action, could enhance understanding of apparently irrational or pathological violent behaviour. In this way, studies can be complemented by a fuller consideration of the human view of these acts of violence and disorder as collective social processes that are often experienced and valued by participants as pleasurable and liberating social activities.

The Ethnographic Study

A study of violence and group drinking was conducted by the author throughout 1989 and early 1990.[2] This first-hand study of conflict and assaults in public drinking venues was based on observations conducted over a 12-month period at different locations around Sydney. It was conceived as a covert, long-term, ethnographic study of actual incidents of violence in order to extend insights from previous observational studies of drinking and drinking-related aggression.

Research into public drinking in natural settings has been conducted for many decades since the early observational study of a public house in an English industrial town (Mass Observation: 1943). However, few studies have focused specifically on violence.

[2] This was supervised by Professor Ross Homel at Macquarie University. Funding was provided by the Australian Criminology Research Council and the Directorate of Drug Offensive (New South Wales), and the research results submitted to the National Committee on Violence (1990). The 1993 interviews were arranged and conducted by Mark Swivel with funding from the University of Newcastle.

STEPHEN TOMSEN

These include the research conducted in Vancouver by Graham and her colleagues, and a study of violence among Polynesian drinkers based on security records kept in 12 Auckland hotels (Graham *et al.* 1980; Graves *et al.* 1982). More clearly ethnographic concerns directed a study of 'scrapping' between male drinkers in bars in a western Canadian town, and a detailed account of an evening spent socializing with four increasingly intoxicated working class youths in Boston (Dyck 1980; Burns 1980).

In line with growing interest in the situational causes and prevention of criminal behaviour in a range of settings that include group drinking, the author's research was at first conceived as a study of the many variables in the local drinking environment which could be linked to conflict and violence (Roman 1982).

By following the Vancouver research as a useful model for a systematic study of the many relevant social and physical factors, a situational analysis led to the conclusion that violence in these locations was strongly linked to the interaction of such prominent social variables as the presence of groups of male strangers, patron discomfort, high rates of drunkenness and aggressive and unreasonable bouncers (Tomsen *et al.* 1989). Additionally, it was found that historical aspects of the external regulation of these venues (by management, police and public officials) were critical factors in the occurrence of regular violence. But as the research proceeded, the author's interest also expanded to include the more fully ethnographic goal of exploring patrons' own subjective understandings of their involvements in violence, and how these are reproduced in the shared culture of drinkers and group notions of male identity.

The key venues studied were selected from a range of evidence about regular violence drawn from interviews and discussions conducted with liquor licensing officers and local police, and four private security officers who had all worked as bouncers in a variety of venues throughout the city. In the field, useful information about venues was also obtained from conversations with regular patrons. As the situation allowed, they were asked about their impressions of the venue, their motivations for being there, the usual types and behaviour of patrons and staff, and the regularity and apparent causes of occasions of violence. Most spoke freely or with an evident excitement regarding this topic. To complement this, semi-structured interviews were conducted with a small sample of regular drinkers. These were all young men from Sydney and the city of Newcastle. They comprised a mix of assailants, assault victims and current and former bouncers, who were questioned at length about their own experience of drinking-related violence.

Historically, group drinking in Australia has mostly taken place in local public hotels. These bars have been traditionally frequented by men drinking and socializing away from their families at the end of a day's work (Homel and Clark 1995). In recent decades, this pattern has been complicated in most states by such developments as the lowering of the legal drinking age to 18 years and the extension of trading hours for many venues to midnight, early morning or all night.

These changes have allowed the rise of new and more expansive venues attracting a broader range of people, especially groups of younger men and women seeking a late-night social outlet. These hotel 'complexes' typically offer entertainment in the form of a dance area (with recorded or live music) and adjoining bars to several hundred patrons at once. This shift in the operation of public hotels has been matched by many of the larger licensed (football and returned soldiers') clubs spread throughout Australian cities. These often use auditorium space to run a late-night dance and also succeed in attracting hundreds of young revellers on Friday and Saturday nights.

The field study was focused on five highly violent venues. Three were in hotels and two in licensed clubs and all of these were in this form of large and popular young persons' nightspots with either live music or a discotheque, and late trading till the early morning. Each had a sizeable staff, including groups of bouncers.[3] The most typical patrons in these venues were working class people in their early adulthood and engaged in unskilled or skilled blue-collar employment. This judgement was made from a knowledge of the local area, talking with both male and female patrons, and closely noting such features as their clothing, tattoos, distinctive accents, and the motor vehicles they came and went in. Additionally, at least a dozen patrons met in these venues were known personally to myself or to my different companions who had frequented most of these venues over many years.

All these key venues were visited repeatedly in trips that often lasted more than five hours and until after sunrise. More than 300 hours of observation were conducted in 36 different visits. These were usually conducted with companions, and occasionally solo. This was often tiring and unpleasant. It could also become dangerous due to the witnessing of drug dealing, or because of unavoidable arguments with aggressive patrons or doorstaff. Along with companions I was sometimes abused and challenged, and on a few occasions assaulted without real harm. In all, 37 different assaults, some of them very bloody encounters, were watched and then written up as detailed incidents recorded in fieldnotes.

All records of visits were classified and analysed according to the level of observed violence. Six of these visits were classed as 'violent', being mostly marked by less serious physical assaults such as hard pushing, and attacking with punches and kicks that failed to connect or left no evident injuries. Another five visits were regarded as 'highly violent' because of a predominance of extended fights and brawls that resulted in visible injuries, including bleeding wounds and broken bones, to participants. These also sometimes involved the use of dangerous weapons like knives and metal bars. During the most highly violent of all visits, I witnessed seven serious attacks in only a few hours. The worst of these was an assault on an ejected patron by three bouncers who repeatedly bashed his head against a steel garbage crate.

Drinking Violence and Male Identity

This research attempted to go past common-sense and single cause explanations of violence and disorder associated with public drinking. But despite the simple and deterministic link between violent behaviour and the consumption of alcohol that is implied in some of these, official complaints about the effects of much group drinking are not entirely amiss in their depiction of its relation to disorder and violence. In this study, observed detail rebutted the view that there is a simple direct link between drinking and violent actions. Some occasions had very high rates of drinking and little

[3] This research also confirmed the view expressed in interviews by several liquor licensing police that many local working mens' hotels, although often rough and rowdy locations, have an exaggerated reputation for violence. The violent venues studied here appeared to attract a similar group of patrons, but were physically very distinct from the 'youth pubs' which have been viewed as a growing source of drinking-related disorder in Britain (Tuck 1989).

STEPHEN TOMSEN

aggression or violence. Plenty of patrons who were very drunk did not get involved in arguments and fights.

A growing body of research by social psychologists attempts to explain this great variation in reactions to intoxication in different social contexts. Collective drinking is often marked by behaviour that has been termed as 'power displays' in which an assertion of social power and heightened sensitivity to challenges to it is maintained, and this can make for a very volatile social setting (Boyatzis 1974; Gibbs 1985; Archer 1994). This contextual model of group drinking can be merged with criminologists' accounts of many assaults as interactive incidents characterized by an escalating confrontation over social honour. These may seem trivial in reason, but are often highly meaningful among certain groups of males where the generation and protection of a masculine identity is most valuable (Felson and Steadman 1983; Polk and Ransom 1990).

The importance of this establishment and protection of a tough male identity by surviving slights, challenges and actual assaults in public drinking venues was often raised in interview material. Ben, a 26-year-old welfare worker, was involved in a lot of violence as a teenager in a local country pub where violence was viewed as 'probably the most strident form of expression of masculinity' and a common form of initiation into manhood. But in his experience winning was not always a necessity. In this local context of public male drinking, social standing turned on a willingness to respond quickly to any challenge. Involvement itself was taken as a mark of manhood:

... whether you win or lose or whatever, isn't necessarily the point, it's being involved and having a go. It's often better to be a threat to someone and get done over, than be smacked in the mouth every time you walk in. If a stranger picks on you, if you were a man you would retaliate. It's that 'be a man thing'. You get people saying that to you to get you to hit them. You know, someone who knows they can beat you and they whack you and say 'come on be a man and have a go'.

Ben's description of this whole process as 'emasculating' does not simply refer (as some other interviewees do) to the experience of failing at a fight and being badly bashed, but to the humiliating social consequences of publicly refusing any challenge. He is mindful of the frequent physical dangers of fighting and has himself been injured in pub fights. But Ben comments with some irony that this level headedness can be outweighed by the force of social pressure in the public arena of most disputes, even conflicts with strangers in unfamiliar venues:

People think that there is always that element that if you were a real man you wouldn't get into these sorts of situations. Either you would have some sort of masculine charisma that would make people back off, or else if you did get involved you would be able to solve it quickly, cleanly and violently. Its the old idea of punching somebody once, like in the movies. Only in the real world it never works like that. The mongrels keep getting up, or worse still they don't even fall over, and then you're in trouble. (5 August 1993)

My own observational study also noted many violent incidents which could be understood in terms of this protection of male honour in drinking contexts. These would include matters like fights arising out of allegations of cheating at a game of pool, approaches made to girlfriends, and squabbles over bumping and spilt drinks inflamed by insults, threats and retorts.

A TOP NIGHT

The most common form of encounter of this sort that I observed was around the issues of refusal of entry and ejection from premises by staff. Such actions were often taken by drinkers to be officious, unfair and as comprising a personal slight. This resulted in numerous arguments and some very bloody incidents between doorstaff and already drunken patrons. In one venue, two young men were ejected for having a vocal argument. One protested loudly about the pettiness of this to doorstaff. With their continued refusal to readmit him, he exploded in anger declaring that he 'may as well be thrown out for something real' and began to attack and wrestle his friend at the front of the premises. The bouncers kicked them both and pulled them apart, and by that time the angered youth seemed satisfied that he had made a sufficient response to this insult.

This and similar incidents signalled that this explanatory model of public violence as the outcome of heightened concerns with male honour can also be applied to the actions of doormen and many supervisory staff. The masculinist elements of these occupations appear to create a very great sensitivity to personal slights, and can promote violent responses to them. At least one third of the serious assaults recorded in this study were perpetrated by them. They were responsible for the majority of serious injuries (often involving significant facial and head wounds) that were inflicted on drinkers too intoxicated to defend themselves.

The refusal of entry by doormen at one club to two drunken youths who were told that they 'looked like troublemakers' led to the most violent single encounter witnessed, with extensive injuries to all participants. Despite being obviously outnumbered, these two persisted in a fight with staff for several minutes. They were both severely bashed about the head, and then held on the floor until two bemused police constables arrived and arrested them. One doorman was wounded by a blow delivered with a sharpened steel ring of a type that some drinkers wear for use in these conflicts. He insisted on staying on duty, and his cut and bleeding face provided a macabre sort of welcome to any newly arriving patrons.

Preserving honour was also an obvious concern of floorstaff. One manager was ridiculed by a rowdy crowd of patrons as he failed to control a wild brawl. A few minutes later I watched him in a violent rage, hitting and choking a small youth who he mistakenly thought had begun the trouble. On another occasion, a male patron slipped and badly cut his eye in a dangerously flooded bathroom. I naively suggested to him that the best course of action was to complain to management. This youth quickly acted on my poor advice. Soon afterwards I saw him being abused by a supervisor and punched and roughly ejected by bouncers.

Despite these many examples, a significant level of other observed violence was difficult to understand as obvious encounters built around this concern with the honour of participants, whether patrons or staff. Much violence was more opportunistic than this; it appeared to result from an assailant taking exaggerated offence at some minor act of nuisance behaviour. Furthermore, many victims had no evident role to play in causing a conflict that can hardly be termed as interactive. I witnessed one youth being headbutted, and another small one dowsed with a drink and then punched, for no reason other than their availability as ready victims judged as unable to retaliate effectively. I was myself assaulted and sometimes challenged without having done anything obviously annoying to others. The overriding determination to be involved in violence for reasons other than social pressures towards the preserva-

STEPHEN TOMSEN

tion of honour, and in particular, the positive attractions of involvement, need some further explanation.

Disorderly Drinking as Pleasure

This can be attained by a look at the broader cultural understandings of the social meaning of collective drinking. The anthropological literature suggests a widely varying comportment in drinking styles between cultures (McAndrew and Edgerton 1969). But in contemporary class societies, group drinking is still commonly under-stood as a rejection of the social values of the privileged and respectable. This drinking is viewed as a 'time out' period of social licence and release from conventional con-straints (Cavan 1966). Extensive disorderly behaviour is valued for sharpening the subjective sense of release and rebellion experienced by drinkers.

The cultural link between male identity and regular heavy drinking was often spoken of by interviewees. As Stuart, a 28-year-old clerk, succinctly puts this:

... it's so basic. Even the language people use to you as you're drinking betrays this. If you drink ten schooners you're a great old lad, but if you just have one or two and then want to go home, well you're a girl. (5 August 1993)

Fast and rowdy drinking appears even to have a further meaning than this for working or underclass men. Elements of symbolic protest overlap with conceptions of this activity as constructing a strong or tough male image. This simultaneously involves a rejection of middle-class values and offers an enhanced masculine image and sense of empowerment in what can be best termed as a form of 'protest masculinity' (Connell 1995). It is these wider cultural meanings that often rest behind the social context of local power displays in drinking and the concern with male honour in drinking sce-narios. They also explain part of the strong (but by no means, exclusive) attractiveness of this violence to the groups of men observed and spoken to.

In the field, periods of peak drinking tended to correspond with high levels of vio-lence. The most violent occasions were all characterized by heavy levels of intoxica-tion, as judged by people's drinking rates, speech, gait and mannerisms. This was obvious on occasions of discount drinking when many patrons who have paid a high cover charge in order to see an inferior band or just to enter a disco, seem to decide that they should become quite drunk in order to get their 'money's worth'. The most violent visit of all was a discount night with very high levels of intoxication.

On these occasions, many patrons began the evening with very rapid rates of con-sumption. They would often each scull two or three drinks immediately after buying them, and then return over and over to continuously long lines of people at the hectic bars. In some clubs, including the two studied as key venues, cheaper drink prices often brought on this same pattern. When this form of hastened group drinking is in full swing, barstaff are most hurried and bothered. Empty glasses pile up around bars but cannot be washed in time. Bathrooms are soon crowded with drinkers needing to relieve themselves. Floors are wet in patches, and then littered with a flood tide of small mounds of empty beer cans or plastic cups that glasshops toil to collect and place in large garbage bags.

In this frenzied pattern of drunkenness the social context of collective drinking is of fundamental importance. Rowdy acts of misbehaviour, like pushing, arguing,

96

swearing, loudness and obscenity, are all valued for being part of a continuum of social rule-breaking which heightens the pleasurable experience of drinking as time out. This extended sense of rule-breaking as fun was often evident. A drunken youth returned from a session of group casual sex with other drinkers in a park opposite one venue. He then excitedly told me and some dismayed university friends that having 'got totally pissed', and that having just 'fucked two molls', without any doubt at all, this had been 'a top night'.

Furthermore, arguments, assaults and fights are also widely appreciated as being part of this pattern of shared rule-breaking and the enjoyment of a general sense of disorder. The delight in a sense of pandemonium that violence can play a key role in generating, was evident on many occasions including an evening in one key venue characterized by rough ejections, group brawling, and staff fights with patrons. Drinkers particularly enjoyed the arrival of a police wagon full of confused officers responding to a management call for assistance, a wild argument between a night manager and hotel guests, and the simultaneous appearance of an ambulance treating an overdosed youth. This ongoing melodrama caused a growing crowd of patrons to gather outside for a better view of events.

Drinking Violence, Carnival and Social Power

The common perception that viewing conflicts and violence was an acceptable and enjoyable activity proved to be an unexpected benefit during fieldwork. The field strategy of seeking out and literally following conflicts and fights in and outside of venues, was noticed by many drinkers, doorstaff and bystanders. But rather than betraying the research purpose of my trips, this could often result in a wish to share excited accounts of the detail and outcome of various fights. Fights that moved outside the venue, or resulted from a rough ejection, could be observed on the pretence of buying a hotdog, getting fresh air, or simply waiting around for a taxi. In many locations milling around to wait and see some of this action is a common practice that nobody questions. It is generally understood as comprising one more element of the night's entertainment.

In addition to being subjectively experienced as good fun built on rule-breaking, violence and disorderly behaviour can also take the form of a real power contest with local authorities. A more detailed account of one field visit can illustrate this. On this occasion I arrived with one companion at a very large licensed club. This was one of the key venues studied repeatedly. The refusal of late entry to non-members (who had already paid for tickets to attend an upstairs discotheque) was already resulting in numerous arguments with doormen. By midnight at least a dozen angry people were milling on the front steps.

The level of supervision was among the highest I had seen, with extremely watchful floorstaff who adopted a highly paternal and often petty manner with patrons. One girl was heavily remonstrated for briefly resting herself from dancing by leaning on the front stage area, and two bouncers were put on guard all night to watch for any similar troublemakers. Staff gathered expectantly at one point around a group of people who seemed too loud and jovial. I got a clear view of two girls being led from the disco for having a mild argument over a boyfriend, one with her arm twisted painfully behind her back by a female supervisor. A very drunk male was ejected by staff for reasons I

STEPHEN TOMSEN

could not see. Despite the protests and screams of his girlfriend, they blocked his exit from the club and badly assaulted him.

This repressive atmosphere seemed to be further reinforced by physical aspects of the venue, such as the high levels of lighting and lower than expected music volume. The downwards slope of these premises served to assist with the surveillance of patrons. At closing time, I walked outside. The atmosphere here was obviously more free and excited, with much rowdy behaviour at the club entrance, in the street, and adjoining carpark and mall. One drunk youth threw a drink over a girl in the full view of departing staff, for no apparent reason. There was a great deal of shouting and swearing, and several males were urinating in the street or on the side wall of the club. Many people just stood around with no apparent desire to go home.

A car that pulled up outside was surrounded by a group of youths who began to shout and shake the vehicle. A confusing 15 minutes of abuse and brawling with changing main participants, that involved the driver, the passengers and a variety of onlookers began. A male waiting for a lift intervened to protect the female driver, who was apparently his girlfriend. But she had her own dramatic and quite unsuccessful way of handling matters. She alighted from the vehicle, revealing her full girth to the crowd, and then ordered him loudly to 'shut up and get in the fuckin car' in a commanding manner that caused a lot of laughter and made him want to save face by continuing with the conflict. A few youths who were friends of various participants tried to cool matters without success.

I delivered one of my standard conversation starters to a young man standing next to me by asking, 'What's this all about?' He told me that as he had just left the club he had no idea about this fight or who the people involved were. He stood silently next to me and watched for a few minutes more. Then unexpectedly and without uttering a word, he rushed forward to throw a body punch at one of the passengers who had got out of the car, and became fully involved in the remainder of the conflict. A big crowd of more than one hundred patrons had gathered and watched intensely. One girl snapped 'who cares, piss off' to my questions about the reasons for the conflict, and continued to stare straight at the fight.

Two males, who were not among the original combatants, drifted across the street and punched each other repeatedly. They also wrestled on the ground, where they had greater trouble in landing hits and the wounds from this encounter were not severe. But the embarrassment of this sight outside the club eventually led four doormen to separate the fighters, and the brawl broke up. One drunk standing next to me interpreted my watchfulness as wanting some involvement. He challenged me to a fight by asking me if I thought 'things were funny'. But he was quickly deterred by my companion's loud and gruff 'fuck off' delivered inches from his face.

This occasion is described in detail for its illustration of the pleasurable dimension of collectively watching and engaging in violence and disorderly behaviour that can characterize public drinking contexts. It also illustrates the importance of the experience of these actions as a form of game or symbolic power contest between drinkers and authority figures, in this case club bouncers and staff. Here, ejected or departing patrons appeared to react against an atmosphere of petty supervision within the venue, by delighting in viewing or joining in a lengthy group brawl with rotating participants. The involvement of most participants did not seem to be motivated by threats to male

A TOP NIGHT

honour, but rather, by the subjective attraction of the brawl as a disruptive and self-created form of 'carnival' (Stam 1988).

The rowdy behaviour and regular fights at the front of this club appeared to be a direct reaction against the repressive control of leisure time inside the venue and the exaggerated officiousness of staff. The latter have a local reputation for excessive violence in dealing with patrons. A staff assault on an off-duty police officer a few months previously resulted in problems with local licensing police and temporary closure of the venue. Patrons react against this and the pettiness of their treatment with an evident appreciation of the violence outside. Misbehaviour on a safer terrain where staff have a more ambiguous role can reassert some lost dignity and honour among drinkers. But it is also a form of provocation to staff who are highly embarrassed by this rowdy patron behaviour.

In this and other localized power struggles, patrons' bodies are conceived as sites of resistance to the power and discipline incorporated by bouncers and police. Public urinating, vomiting, spitting and the many bodies which are 'let fly' in fighting are all examples of this. Patrons delight in the evident explosive and unpredictable quality of events that mark their creativity free of supervision. In this and similar venues, the reasons for involvement in a dispute could be weak or non-existent, as they were for the youth who rushed to join the brawl with no knowledge of its cause. These sorts of interventions are readily accepted. The drunk who challenged me to a fight without even the slightest pretext took me by complete surprise. But in his view no really plausible reason for taking offence had to be offered. His challenge was simply an invitation to jointly initiate some further form of performance that would be making a helpful contribution to the sense of disruption and carnival, and would undermine staff efforts to contain the ongoing violence.

Material from recorded interviews with other drinkers also strongly reflected this sense of disorder and violence as entertaining and pleasurable. David, a 30-year old barman, has worked and drunk in a variety of drinking venues, ranging from the genteel to the very rough. But the latter were especially valued by him as 'never boring' and as 'spectators' pubs'. Patrons were always providing a 'real show of some sort' with disruptive actions or fights that were highly appreciated by others, not just as the aggressive displays of drunks, but as the deliberate, generous and often highly inventive provision of entertainment for a grateful audience. David speaks with nostalgia and very excitedly of the theatrical and surreal qualities of much violence in these places:

In each place I saw fantastic wild-west, all-in, total bar room brawls, that I never thought I would see outside of a movie. You know. Engulfing. In cinemascope. Chairs, tables, rolling, fighting, smashing, pool cues, windows, everywhere. They would stay in your memory like a very strong film; you know, for a few days after. I would think, did that really happen? I am going back there to work! (14 July 1993)

As already noted, this disorderly behaviour and violence involves a symbolic rejection of middle-class values, leisure habits and lifestyles. But as this and other references to the 'movie-like' qualities of much violence watched or initiated by drinkers suggests, this also exists in a relationship of parody to the technologized and highly formed fantasies of contemporary cultures. The violent and disruptive events in the lives of these drinkers are not simply further chapters in a linear people's history of transgressive

STEPHEN TOMSEN

leisure. They often reflect a playful, creative and active relation to commodified contemporary popular culture and its own distinctive representations of masculinity, youthful fun, and freedom from social constraint.

Conclusion

This study suggests that although there is no direct and obvious tie between violence and the use of alcohol, there is a complex but powerful link between many incidents of public violence and the social process of collective drinking. This link is built around cultural understandings of the connections between rowdy and violent group drinking, the construction and projection of an empowered masculine identity, and the symbolic rejection of respectable social values.

One well-known contemporary academic work has criticized researchers for overlooking the frequent sensual attractions of criminal actions (Katz 1988). Many incidents of drinking violence could be understood by appreciating this dimension. But this understanding must also be complemented by an appreciation of the elements of social protest with which the pleasurable experience of rule-breaking is so complexly interwoven, as to be practically indistinguishable.

At the local level this behaviour can take the form of a power contest with any authority seeking to order and control the leisure activities of people. Disorder and violence are valued by drinkers as the weapons of this contest, enhancing the enjoyed feelings of time out and the suspension of normal social rules. The explosive quality of much disorder and violence accentuates a general sense of carnival. This unpredictability of drinking violence, as well as the cultural complexity of its significance, will always confound researchers seeking to evolve fully predictive models that isolate the situational factors characterizing violent venues.

Analyses which stress the cultural understandings of masculinity that underlie this violence will also create quandaries for radical and liberal intellectuals. Overall sociological understanding is extended considerably by an analysis of its links to cultural resistance and protest masculinity. But, like accounts which focus too exclusively on the role of male honour in interaction, they also risk trivializing victimization. This violence might be linked to cultural resistance, but it is a social process with real human costs. The great toll of drinking-related serious assaults and killings in different nations attests to this. Much violence that gives a sense of pleasure and enhances a carnivalesque social atmosphere is comprised of unprovoked and unjust assaults.

Furthermore, the constant involvement of local authority figures in provoking, shaping and condoning much violence, suggests that the disruptive and protest qualities of patron disorder and violence in these social spaces are already strictly limited. An appreciation of drinking violence as a symbolic form of protest, ought not to result in a dismissal of concerns about this violence as mere moral panic or cultural snobbery. Where a destructive masculinism dovetails with rebellion in this form of disorder, it is too simple either to romanticize or straightforwardly denounce this behaviour.

GLOSSARY

Bouncer Person (usually a large male) employed to physically supervise and possibly eject patrons in drinking venues

A TOP NIGHT

Discount drink A drink sold at lower than usual prices
Glasshop Person collecting empty glasses
Mongrel Literally a cross-bred dog. A derogatory term for any person
Pissed Intoxicated
Pub Public hotel/bar
Schooner Large glasses of beer that are consumed in heavier drinking sessions
Scull To throw the head back and swallow an entire drink in one action

REFERENCES

ARCHER, J. (1994), 'Violence between Men', in J. Archer, ed., *Male Violence*. London: Routledge.

BONNEY, R., and KERY, L. (1991), *Police Reports of Non Aggravated Assault in New South Wales*. Sydney: New South Wales Bureau of Crime Statistics and Research.

BOYATZIS, R. (1974), 'The Effect of Alcohol Consumption on the Aggressive Behaviour of Men', *Quarterly Journal of Studies in Alcohol*, 35: 959.

BURNS, T. (1980), 'Getting Rowdy with the Boys', *Journal of Drug Issues*, 10: 141.

CAVAN, S. (1966), *Liquor License*. Chicago: Aldine.

COLLINS, J. (1989), 'Alcohol and Interpersonal Violence: Less than Meets the Eye', in N. Weiner and M. Wolfgang, eds., *Pathways to Criminal Violence*. Newbury Park: Sage.

CONNELL, R. W. (1995), *Masculinities*. Sydney: Allen and Unwin.

CUNNEEN, C. (1988), 'The Policing of Public Order', in M. Findlay and R. Hogg, eds., *Understanding Crime and Criminal Justice*. Sydney: Law Book Company.

DONAJGRODSKI, A., ed. (1977), *Social Control in Nineteenth Century Britain*. London: Croom Helm.

DYCK, N. (1980), 'Booze, Barrooms and Scrapping', *Canadian Journal of Anthropology*, 1: 191.

FAGAN, J. (1990), 'Intoxication and Aggression', in M. Tonry and J. Q. Wilson, eds., *Crime and Justice: A Review of Research, Drugs and Crime*, vol. 13. Chicago: Chicago University Press.

FELSON, R., and STEADMAN, H. (1983), 'Situations and Processes Leading to Criminal Violence', *Criminology*, 21: 59.

GIBBS, J. (1985), 'Alcohol Consumption, Cognition and Context: Examining Tavern Violence', in A. Campbell and J. Gibbs, eds., *Violent Transactions: The Limits of Personality*. Oxford: Blackwell.

GRAHAM, K. *et al.* (1980), 'Aggression and Barroom Environments', *Journal of Studies in Alcohol*, 41: 227.

GRAVES, T. *et al.* (1982), 'The Social Context of Drinking and Violence in New Zealand's Multi-Ethnic Pub Settings', in T. Harford and I. Gaines, eds., *Social Drinking Contexts*. Washington, DC: NIAAA.

GREENBERG, S. (1982), 'Alcohol and Crime: A Methodological Critique of the Literature', in J. Collins, ed., *Drinking and Crime*. London: Tavistock.

GUSFIELD, J. (1963), *Symbolic Crusade*. Urbana: University of Illinois Press.

HOMEL, R., and CLARK, J. (1995), 'The Prediction and Prevention of Violence in Pubs and Clubs', *Crime Prevention Studies*, 3.

KATZ, J. (1988), *Seductions of Crime*. New York: Basic Books.

MASS OBSERVATION (1943), *The Pub and the People: A Worktown Study*. London: Gollancz.

McANDREW, C., and EDGERTON, R. (1969), *Drunken Comportment: A Social Explanation*. Chicago: Aldine.

STEPHEN TOMSEN

McGREGOR, H. (1990), 'Domestic Violence: Alcohol and Other Distractions', in J. Vernon, ed., *Alcohol and Crime*. Canberra: Australian Institute of Criminology.

PEARSON, G. (1983), *Hooligan: a History of Respectable Fears*. London: Macmillan.

POLK, K., and RANSOM, D. (1990), 'Patterns of Homicide in Victoria', in D. Chappell *et al.*, eds., *Australian Violence: Contemporary Perspectives*. Canberra: Australian Institute of Criminology.

ROBB, T. (1988), *Police Reports of Serious Assault in New South Wales*. Sydney: New South Wales Bureau of Crime Statistics & Research.

ROMAN, R. (1982), 'Situational Factors in the Relationship between Alcohol and Crime', in J. Collins, ed., *Drinking and Crime*. London: Tavistock.

RUDE, G. (1995), *The Crowd in History*. London: Serif.

STAM, R. (1988), 'Mikhail Bakhtin and Left Cultural Critique', in E. Kaplan, ed., *Postmodernism and its Discontents*. London: Verso.

STURMA, M. (1983), *Vice in a Vicious Society*. St Lucia: University of Queensland Press.

TILLY, C., and TILLY, L., eds. (1981), *Class Conflict and Collective Action*. Beverly Hills: Sage.

TOMSEN, S. *et al.* (1989), 'The Causes of Public Violence: Situational and other Factors in Drinking-Related Assaults', in D. Chappell *et al.*, eds., *Australian Violence: Contemporary Perspectives*. Canberra: Australian Institute of Criminology.

TUCK, M. (1989), *Drinking and Disorder: a Study of Non-Metropolitan Violence*, Home Office Research Study No. 108. London: HMSO.

YEO, E., and YEO, S., eds. (1981), *Popular Culture and Class Conflict, 1590–1914*. Brighton: Harvester.

[2]

FEMALES' INITIATION INTO VIOLENT STREET CRIME*

DEBORAH R. BASKIN
IRA SOMMERS
John Jay College of Criminal Justice

The present study is concerned with understanding when and how women become involved in violent street crime. Specifically, the study explores the correlates or explanatory factors of such offending in a sample
of women arrested and/or incarcerated for violent street crimes in New
York City. The findings suggest that an adequate understanding of female
offending must consider the impact of neighborhood, peer, and addiction
factors which affect both males' and females' participation in criminal violence. In addition, different configurations of these factors appear to contribute to the initiation of violent offending, depending on the age of onset.
Early initiation into violent crime was accompanied by participation in a
wide variety of other offending behaviors and deviant lifestyles. In contrast, those women who began their violent offending later did so in the
context of a criminal career which, until the beginning of substance abuse,
was more specialized and focused on typically nonviolent, gender-congruent activities (e.g., prostitution, shoplifting).

Little research has been directed at uncovering trends and
patterns in women's criminal careers. Unique characteristics of female offender subsamples generally have been masked by the tendency to view women and crime in purely gender-linked, generic
terms. Research typically is limited to women's involvement in
gender-congruent behaviors such as drug abuse, street hustling,
and domestic violence (Browne 1987; Carlen 1988; E. Miller 1986).
Also, women's offending is viewed consistently as an understandable outcome of participation in various "victim" roles such as substance abuser, battered woman, or single, underclass parent
(Arnold 1990; B. Miller, Downs, and Gondoli, 1989). As a result,
the broad range of behaviors and subjectivities that characterize
subsamples of female offenders remains unknown.

Because of the continued reliance on a generic and gender-
based stereotype, very little knowledge has been gained about the

* This paper was supported by a grant from the Harry Frank Guggenheim
Foundation. Points of view or opinions expressed herein are our own and do not
necessarily reflect those of the Guggenheim Foundation.

nature of females' involvement in specific types of crimes—for example, violent street crime (such as, assault or robbery). Underdevelopment of information in this area seems to be due in part to the pervasive belief that an insignificant number of women are involved in crime in general and in violent street crime specifically. UCR data for 1987, for example, show that participation in aggravated assault and robbery is a predominantly male phenomenon: males accounted respectively for 86.7 percent and 91.9 percent of the arrests for these crimes.

Although only a small proportion of women are involved in violent street crime as recorded in UCR statistics, women were arrested, for aggravated assault and robbery in 1987, a total of 50,119 times. This figure represents a significant absolute number and denotes an increase of 17.6 percent from 1978. Also, in New York City arrest data we detect a more dramatic growth in female involvement in violent street crime. Females' offending rates for robbery and aggravated assault increased respectively 75.8 percent and 47.0 percent between 1984 and 1989 (New York City Police Department 1990).

The apparent differences between national (UCR) and New York City data regarding the growth of women's involvement in violent street crime speak to the need for researchers to disaggregate crime data by geographic region, sex, and race. For instance, when New York City arrest data for violent crimes are disaggregated, we find tremendous similarity in violent offending between black females and white males. In fact, the offending rates for robbery and aggravated assault are higher for black females than for white males (Sommers and Baskin 1992). Furthermore, across all violent crime categories, the rates for black and Hispanic females are substantially higher than for white females.

These findings make clear the limitations inherent in generalizing about female offending, especially with regard to street violence. Factors such as geographic location, race, and age may produce important variations both in the relationship between gender and violent crime and in the purported protective role of differential gender role socialization in keeping women out of street violence (Hagan, Simpson, and Gillis, 1987). Nonetheless, scholars have shown little interest in exploring specific correlates or explanatory factors of such offending among women. The present study takes some initial steps towards filling this gap. We are concerned here with exploring when and how women become involved in violent street crime.

PATHWAYS TO VIOLENCE

A significant part of the literature on women and crime contends that women are "forced" into offending by males, drug addiction, histories of victimization, and the responsibilities of single parenthood (Arnold 1990; Huling 1991; E. Miller 1986; Pollack-Byrne 1990; Weisheit and Mahan 1988). Generally, it is argued that domestic arrangements provide two important conduits through which women enter into criminal careers.

When offending begins early in a woman's life, childhood victimization is viewed as the main cause of female offending. Between 50 percent and 80 percent of women surveyed in various correctional institutions in the country report being victims of domestic violence (Bureau of Justice 1991); thus a direct casual relationship is posited between "the experience of being victimized and subsequent offending" (Arnold, 1990). Typically, then, the chain of events leading to criminalization is described as beginning with child physical or sexual abuse; this produces a vicious cycle that includes running away, institutionalization, return to the dysfunctional family unit, running away, and ultimately street deviance (e.g., prostitution, drug use).

When a woman is initiated into offending later in life, single parenthood is regarded as another family-based pathway into offending. In view of data documenting the large proportion of female offenders who are also mothers of young children, it is argued that women are driven into criminal activities by the responsibilities of single parenthood thrust upon them by the desertion of an uncaring and often abusive male partner (Glick and Neto 1977; Moss 1986; Roman 1990).

When pathways stray from home, drug use itself has been said to lead women into criminal careers (Arnold 1990; Huling 1991). In such cases it is argued that heavy involvement as an abuser reduces women's options to engage in other income-producing endeavors. Therefore illegal activities provide women with opportunities to make enough money to buy drugs.

Notable for its absence, however, in the literature on women's initiation into crime is the possibility that women's initiation into *violent* offending, in fact may be linked to the same sets of variables as men's (e.g. peers, opportunity structures, neighborhood effects). This prospect remains unexplored or is openly rejected (Daly and Chesney-Lind 1988). As a result, studies on women's initiation into crime in general, and specifically into violent crime, continue to ignore the advances in criminological theory and research based on the integration of control, strain, learning, and

562   FEMALES' INITIATION INTO VIOLENT CRIME

ecological approaches (Dunford and Elliott 1984; Elliott and Huizinga 1984a; Fagan, Piper, and Moore, 1986).

An integrated model of women's initiation into violent offending would take into account a variety of factors that include but
are not limited to family background variables. Combinations of
individual-level factors as well as peer, school, and other socializing influences, such as neighborhood effects, may be equally
strong correlates of initiation into violent offending for women. In
addition, the salience and the sequence of such factors may vary
with age. That is, different processes may be responsible for initiation into violent offending, depending on age of initiation.

Studies support integrated theory as it applies to serious offending (Dunford and Elliott 1984; Elliott and Huizinga 1984a;
Fagan et al. 1986). As noted above, however, samples have been
almost exclusively male. Also, hardly any qualitative data have
been gathered to describe the behaviors of interest or to interpret
the processes underlying initiation. In the present study we explore factors identified by previous works in integrated theory in
order to understand pathways into violent offending for a specific
sample of serious female offenders.

METHODS

The current study is based primarily on the life histories of 85
women arrested for nondomestic violent felony crimes. We used
arraignment calendars for the period from January to June 1990 in
order to obtain a sample of women arrested for violent felony offenses. Access to complete court records permitted us to weed out
those women whose arrests were related directly to domestic violence. We collected official data on 176 women and sent letters inviting participation in the study to all women for whom a recent
address was available (N=124). Thirty letters were returned as
undeliverable (incorrect addresses, resident moved); 43 women
contacted us and gave us interviews.

In addition to the community-based sample, we consulted New
York State Department of Correctional Services databases to draw
a similar incarceration sample. Females committed to Bedford
Hills and Bayview correctional facilities for a felony offense (mur-
der/manslaughter, assault, robbery, weapons possession, weapons
use, burglary, arson, kidnapping) during 1990 were eligible for participation in the study. Women whose violent acts were domestic
were excluded from the incarceration sample. We collected official records data on 93 incarcerated women who fit criteria for the
study. Forty-two women agreed to be interviewed.

We found no significant differences in comparisons based on criminal histories and sociodemographic characteristics between respondents and those who did not participate in the study. The two groups of women were similar in age, race, education, and marital status; they had similar prior arrest records for violent and nonviolent felony offenses (Table 1). The racial mix of respondents reflected the racial mix of women arrested for violent felonies in New York City. Between 1987 and 1990, blacks accounted for 71 percent of females arrested for homicide, robbery, and assault; Hispanic and white women accounted respectively for 20 percent and 8 percent.

Table 1. Offender Characteristics

	Interviewed	Not Interviewed
Race		
White	12%	10.1%
Black	69	69.7
Hispanic	19	20.2
Age (Mean)	28.94	28.89
Marital Status		
Single	29%	24.6%
Ever married	71	75.4
Education (Years)	10.09	10.86
Official Criminal History		
Prior violent felony arrest	2.08%	1.41%
Prior nonviolent felony arrest	1.62	1.48

Because our sampling frame was constrained by time (only arrests that occurred during 1990) and by geographic location (only arrests made in Manhattan), it is difficult to assess to what extent the women in the study represented the larger population of women in New York City who are involved in violent street crime. Nonetheless, this sample permits some initial analyses of factors associated with pathways into violent offending.

We collected life event histories on 85 women in all. These interviews focused on basic demographics, the women's perceptions of family and neighborhood characteristics, school and employment experiences, official and self-reported involvement in crime, victimization histories (personal victimization, own perpetration of abuse, and witnessing others' abuse), alcohol and drug use as well as treatment for substance abuse, participation in drug selling, and chronologies of peer relationships. The interviews were taped and were open-ended.

564   FEMALES' INITIATION INTO VIOLENT CRIME

We employed the following procedures in this study to secure valid responses: assurances of confidentiality; the exclusive use of experienced interviewers who were familiar with and unfazed by deviant lifestyle, language, and perspectives; interviewers' probes and cross-checks with official police and correctional data; and the use of a semistructured instrument that included checks for internal consistency.

Although the data are retrospective, we employed several procedures to enhance respondents' recall. First, the interviewers were familiar with all official record data available for each respondent. Immediately before the interview itself, the interviewer examined the information contained in the records so that she or he would be able to anchor questions to specific routine as well as to significant events in the respondent's life. Second, the liberal use of cross-checks that emphasized particular periods, places of residence, and relationships with specific individuals further enhanced the women's ability to accurately recall the temporal order of key events. Concern about the use of retrospective data was diminished further by other studies that have examined similarly collected data and have found them to be reliable (Nurco 1985; Nurco et al. 1988).

INITIATION INTO VIOLENT OFFENDING

A considerable body of research argues that for some individual, patterns of violent offending may be an outgrowth of a wide variety of early childhood experiences including involvement in interpersonal conflicts, antisocial behaviors, and academic difficulties (Blumstein et al. 1986; Elliott, Huizinga, and Ageton, 1982; Gottfredson and Hirschi 1987; Loeber and Dishion 1983; McCord 1979; West and Farrington 1976; White et al. 1990). For others, initiation may occur later, among adolescents or young adults with no prior history of antisocial behavior (White et al. 1990).

Given our interest in tracing the study women's initial participation in violent offending, we began our inquiry by interviewing them about their early childhood experiences, specifically those during the lower and middle school years. This focus on early school years seemed appropriate for three reasons. First, research has shown that prehigh school involvement in conduct problems, including fighting, truancy, drug use, and delinquency, predict serious adult criminal careers (Loeber 1987; Loeber and Stouthamer-Loeber 1987; Magnusson, Stattin, and Duner 1983). Second, during this period family influences "make a tremendous difference in a child's ability to be successful in school, to make a favorable entry into the labor market, and to survive the experiments with risk taking that are common in adolescence" (Sullivan 1989:218). Finally, the focus on school-related experiences seemed logical because school is a social domain in which peer associations exert considerable influence on youths' behavior, possibly contributing to the early onset of violent offending patterns (Fagan and Wexler 1987).

Early Experiences with Peer-Related Violence

For the purposes of this study, we determined initial involvement in violent behavior by participants' self-report. We chose this strategy to avoid the problems in behavior definition and timing of first involvement that occur with reliance on official records of juvenile delinquency and criminality (Klein and Maxson 1989). We began the temporal sequence with early school years and continued the line of questioning until the point at which the participant recalled initial involvement or left school permanently.

We asked the study women whether they had engaged in fighting or had carried weapons during their time in school; if so, how frequently (rarely, sometimes, frequently) and at what age. Of the study women, 48 percent stated that they fought frequently while still attending school, 8 percent said they fought sometimes, and another 13 percent said they fought only rarely. These women recalled becoming involved in fighting at a mean age of just under 10 years.

Although the majority of the study women reported that they did not carry weapons during their time at school (60%), another 34 percent regularly left home with a weapon, 4 percent sometimes carried a weapon, and an additional 2 percent carried a weapon on rare occasions. The mean age at which these women began carrying weapons was a little over 11 years.

In regard to initiation into fighting and weapons possession during school years, a closer look at the data revealed that respondents fell into two distinct groups. On the one hand, 60 percent of the women reported early onset. On the basis of measures of moderate to high frequency of involvement in fighting and weapons possession, women in this group became involved in these behavior patterns by the time they were 11 years old. Subsequently we refer to these women as the "early onset group."

On the other hand, a sizable percent (40%) of the women in the study reported no early history of fighting or weapons possession; we refer to these women as the "later onset group." These women were not involved in violent street behavior until after they left school, typically in early adulthood. Because our sample was divided between these two groups, those with early onset and

566   FEMALES' INITIATION INTO VIOLENT CRIME

those who initiated their violent offending in early adulthood, we questioned the extent to which background factors were the same or different for these two groups of women. Also, we wondered whether the timing of initiation was related to the difference in the pathways into such offending.[1]

Family Background Factors

We explored several early childhood factors to identify possible sources of similarity and difference between the two groups. We were concerned about the relationship between family life and initiation into violent offending. In a meta-analysis of available studies exploring juvenile aggressiveness, Loeber and Stouthamer-Loeber (1987:29) found that variables such as parental supervision practices, parental criminality and deviance, marital conflict, and parental absence were among the most powerful predictors of juvenile misconduct and delinquency.

Drawing on this literature review and the work of others (Geller and Ford-Sonoma 1984; Guarino 1985; Laub and Sampson 1988; Van Voorhis et al. 1988; Wells and Rankin 1988), we identified a set of background factors that are relevant to understanding family process and juvenile aggressiveness. We obtained measures on parental absence, parental supervision and punitive practices including intrafamily violence, family reliance on public assistance, and familial criminal, mental health, and substance abuse histories.

Parental absence indicates that the study women grew up in a household in which one or both of the parents were absent because of death, parental estrangement (desertion, separation, divorce), or foster care placement. Parental supervision refers to whether the respondent, while growing up, checked in with guardians after school, told them where she was going, told them when she was coming back, and talked about daily plans, and whether the guardians knew the respondent's friends.

We obtained measures of parental punitive practices through a principal-components analysis of responses to questions about the frequency of childhood experiences with verbal and physical abuse between guardians and with verbal, physical, and sexual abuse between guardian(s) and respondent (see appendix). As a result of this analysis, we identified one factor on the between-guardians abuse scale. That factor is composed of the following six items:

---

[1] We are not defining early onset in terms of criminal violence. Instead we are interested in exploring whether the presence or absence of these early behavioral patterns (i.e., fighting and weapons possession), foreshadows later involvement in violent street behavior that *is* defined as criminal.

yelling, pushing or shoving, having something thrown at the target individual, kicking or punching, beatings, and use of weapon during a domestic encounter. In regard to guardian-respondent abuse, we distinguished two factors. The first included the six items listed above; the second measured frequency of unwanted sexual contact between guardian and respondent. We constructed scales by summing the individual items identified within each factor.

We also obtained dichotomous measures for familial criminality, mental health, and substance abuse. Here we wished to understand whether familial deviance may have influenced the study women's aggressiveness through family functioning. Finally, economic dependence was a dummy variable for which 1 signifies familial support through public assistance. This measure has been linked previously to juvenile misconduct (Laub and Sampson 1988).

Table 2 shows few significant differences between the groups in regard to family background factors. The two groups of women were equally likely to have been raised in single-guardian, usually female-headed, households. Furthermore, we found no significant differences in guardians' level of supervision or punitive methods. Both groups of women consistently received little parental supervision or control of their daily routines or behavior. The two groups were equally likely to be victims of physical and sexual abuse as well as witnesses of these types of abuse between their guardians.

In addition, we found no differences in whether the two groups of women grew up in households that relied on public assistance for their financial resources. Forty-nine percent of the sample was raised in households that were supported by public assistance programs. Also, we found no statistical difference between the groups in familial criminality (65% of the women had at least one family member who had been incarcerated during her childhood) or substance abuse (72% had a family member with a substance abuse problem). The early onset group, however, was significantly more likely to come from families with psychiatric histories, particularly mental health hospitalization. In general, though, we can say that the women in our study, regardless of early or later onset of violent offending, grew up in multiproblem households.

Ecological Dimensions

We continued our investigation by examining some of the ecological dimensions of the neighborhoods in which the study women lived. Studies concerning violent and serious delinquency have

Table 2.   Comparison of Family Characteristics, Early and Later Onset
Groups (Percentages)

Variable	Early Onset (N = 51)	Later Onset (N = 34)
Single-Parent Household	73	68
Primary Type of Discipline		
None	8	15
Talk	8	3
Restrictions	29	32
Physical	55	50
Parent/Child Physical Abuse	10.90 (mean)	8.19 (mean)
Parent/Child Sexual Abuse	24	18
Parent/Parent Physical Abuse	8.24 (mean)	6.00 (mean)
Public Assistance	55	41
Family Member Ever Incarcerated	71	56
Family Member Ever Substance Abuser	78	62
Family Member In Psychiatric Hospital	43	21*

* $p < .05$

suggested consistently that the neighborhood itself, because it offers limited social and economic resources (Fagan et al. 1986; Shannon 1984; Weis and Sederstrom 1981) and poses increased risks of
victimization (Lauritsen, Sampson, and Laub 1991), is related
highly to delinquency. In our study we used levels of poverty, respondent's victimization at the hands of a stranger, and peer involvement in criminal activity as our neighborhood characteristics.

We assigned each respondent a 1990 census tract code based on
her address at the time of arrest.[2] We classified census tracts according to the percentage of families living below the poverty
threshold. Tracts with low concentrations of poverty were those in
which fewer than 20 percent of the families had incomes below the
poverty threshold; *moderate* concentrations of poverty were found
in tracts where 20 to 30 percent of the families had incomes below
the poverty threshold; *high* concentrations of poverty were tracts
in which more than 30 percent of the families had incomes below
the poverty threshold. Fifty-two percent of study respondents
lived in neighborhoods characterized by high concentrations of
poverty, 33 percent in moderately impoverished areas, and 15 percent in neighborhoods not typically characterized as poor.

As for victimization by strangers, a principal-components analysis identified one factor that included frequencies of being yelled

---

[2] We used the most recent address because the study women reported that
this location was quite similar with other neighborhoods named in their residential
history.

at, pushed or shoved, kicked or punched, beaten or threatened with a weapon, raped, or being the target of something thrown. We constructed a scale by summing responses to these individual items (see appendix).

Among the ecological factors we found significant early childhood differences between the groups in regard to the neighborhoods in which they grew up (Table 3). The quality of the neighborhoods in which these women lived as youths was correlated highly with early initiation into violent offending. Those women who were initiated into violence early in their childhoods were more likely to have grown up in neighborhoods characterized by high concentrations of poverty, to have experienced physical and sexual abuse at the hands of a stranger, and to have associated with peers who also were involved in delinquent behavior.

Table 3. Comparison of Neighborhood Characteristics, Early and Later Onset Groups (Percentage)

Variable	Early Onset (N=51)·	Later Onset (N=34)
Concentration of Poverty		
Low	10	24
Moderate	27	41
High	63	35*
Stranger/Child Physical & Sexual Abuse	18.11 (mean)	10.44 (mean)*
Criminal Involvement of School Peers		
Violent Crime	3.15 (mean)	1.74 (mean)*
Nonviolent Crime	2.71 (mean)	2.15 (mean)

* $p < .01$

These findings should come as no surprise. Research has shown consistently that certain neighborhood characteristics, specifically high concentrations of poverty (Kennedy and Forde 1990; Lauritsen et al. 1991; Maxfield 1987; Sampson and Wooldredge 1987), are linked to higher victimization rates among youths who themselves are involved in violent and delinquent lifestyles (Lauritsen et al. 1991; Sampson and Lauritsen 1990).

Although recent research has demonstrated that regardless of race, women from neighborhoods with high concentrations of poverty are involved disproportionately in violent crime (Sommers and Baskin 1992), studies also show that the proportion of the poor who live in ghettos varies dramatically by race (Jargowsky and

Bane 1990; Massey and Eggers 1990). Black women are significantly more likely than Hispanic or white women to live in ghetto neighborhoods. Consequently it is not surprising to find that involvement in nondomestic violent crimes is greater among black women.

Although we found no statistically significant racial difference between the two groups, the early onset group contained a higher percentage of black women than the later onset group (76% vs. 59%). In light of the above discussion, many of the reported differences between the two groups may be attributed to neighborhood effects and to the effect of race on residential location.[3]

School Experiences

To obtain a clearer picture of the participants' experiences as they related to schooling, we compared the two groups' dropout rates (Table 4). Although we found no statistically significant difference between the two groups in terms of percentage of dropouts, the data show that those women who were involved in violent offending earlier in their youth left school a full year earlier than the later onset group.

Table 4.   Comparison of School Experiences, Early and Later Onset Groups (Percentages)

Variable	Early Onset (N=51)	Later Onset (N=34)
School Dropout	84	68
Truant	84	59*
Alcohol Use at School	51	29*
Drug Use at School	71	41*
Involvement with Delinquent Peers at School	78	41*
Juvenile Detention Programs	43	21*
Mean Years of Education	9.68	10.69

* p < .01

In addition, the early onset group was significantly more likely to be truant and to drop out of school in order to commit themselves full-time to hanging out with their friends. Furthermore,

---

[3] Although respective group sample sizes are too small to allow adequate assessment of racial and ethnic differences in initiation into violent offending, our findings support the idea that there is nothing inherent in black (or minority) culture which is conducive to crime. Rather, blacks' persistently high rates of initiation into violence appear to stem from the structural links between race, economic deprivation, and residential location (i.e., high concentration of poor neighborhoods).

their friends were more likely to engage in violent crime than were the peers of the later onset participants. The role of delinquent peers in initiating deviant behavior in others has been well documented elsewhere (Elliott et al. 1982). In light of the above differences (i.e., school problems and involvement with delinquent peer networks), it is not surprising to find that the early onset respondents were significantly more likely than their later onset counterparts to be placed in juvenile detention programs. These findings are consistent with Farrington's work, which showed that troublesome behavior at primary school predicts future criminality (see Farrington, Ohlin, and Wilson 1986).

Notwithstanding the controversy about the effects of dropping out of school on subsequent involvement in criminality (compare Polk et al. 1981 and Thornberry, Moore, and Christenson 1985 with Elliott and Voss 1974), we found that dropping out was preceded by earlier involvement in delinquent behavior and that 62 percent of the women in our study reported having friends who also were involved in delinquent behavior including substance use/abuse and truancy.

Involvement in Substance Use/Abuse

In conducting our analysis of background factors, we explored whether the two groups differed as to other high-risk behaviors. Past research, for instance, has identified a definite link between criminal activity and drug involvement (Anglin and Hser 1987; Hser, Anglin, and Booth 1987; Inciardi and Pottieger 1986). The temporal order and/or causal connection have not been established so clearly, however. Some studies have shown that criminal behavior occurs before drug use (Inciardi, Pottieger, and Faupel 1982). Others have found that the two occur simultaneously as part of a general development toward adolescent antisocial behavior or deviant lifestyles (Adler 1975; Inciardi and Pottieger 1985). Still other studies have produced ambiguous results depending on the user's race, drug(s) used, and/or types of crime(s) committed (Datesman 1984; Hser et al. 1987; James, Gosho, and Wohl 1979; Rosenbaum 1981).

Among the study women as a whole, substance use began later than fighting and weapon possession. Among those women who used alcohol as young girls (45% of the sample), 39 percent reported frequent use and 4 percent moderate use; 2 percent drank only on occasion. Drug use followed a different pattern: 53 percent reported that they frequently got high, 6 percent used drugs more irregularly, and 1 percent used drugs only rarely. These women began both drinking and using drugs at a mean age of just

Table 5.   Comparison of Drug Use, Early and Later Onset Groups

Drug Type	Early Onset (N=51)	Later Onset (N=34)
	X̄ Age of First Use	X̄ Age of First Use
Alcohol	12.95	15.37
Marijuana	13.00	14.84
Amphetamines	18.00	22.75*
Barbiturates	16.83	22.13*
PCP	17.00	19.09
Cocaine	18.00	20.68
Crack	20.00	27.06*
Heroin	18.90	22.33*
Mean Group Age	28.46	29.68
	% Ever Used	% Ever Used
Alcohol	78	76
Marijuana	78	76
Amphetamines	43	50
Barbiturates	39	44
PCP	84	24*
Cocaine	57	56
Crack	67	56
Heroin	31	38
	% Addicted	% Addicted
Cocaine Only	10	15
Crack Only	23	20
Heroin Only	3	10
Combination	65	55
Total Addicted	61	59

* $p < .05$

under 14. Chronologically, then, early involvement in violent behavior preceded substance use.

The data, however, indicate significant differences between the two groups as to age of initiation into drug use and age of becoming addicted (daily drug use). In regard to the gateway drugs of alcohol and marijuana, those reporting earlier involvement in violent behavior were much younger when they tried these substances and when they become addicted to more powerful substances (Table 5). The early onset group had first used alcohol and marijuana by age 13; the later onset group waited two full years longer to begin experimenting with drugs. We found similar patterns for early initiation into and abuse of cocaine, crack, and heroin.

Other notable differences between the groups relate to influences on drug use. The early onset group reported that friends

(31%), family members (27%), and their own curiosity (27%) were the major influences on their drug use. The later onset group cited friends (47%) and boyfriends (24%) as the primary sources of initiation. Also, like Johnson, Marcos, and Bahr (1987), we found that both groups of women were initiated because of "situational pressure to jointly participate" in a primarily social behavior (1987:336).

A great deal of research has explored the relationship between narcotics and crime over the course of an addiction career (Anglin and Speckart 1988; Ball, Shaffer, and Nurco 1983; Hunt et al. 1984; Inciardi 1979; B. Johnson et al. 1985; Nurco et al.) We wished to learn which came first, criminal involvement or drug addiction.

Having computed the age of initiation into drug use and abuse, we developed the same information for criminal involvement (Table 6). We found that the early onset group was significantly more likely to have committed robbery, assault, and burglary at a much younger age. In addition, they were involved in a wide variety of crimes, including violent offenses, before they became addicted (Table 7). In contrast, the preaddiction criminal careers of the later onset group centered mostly on shoplifting, prostitution, and other gender-related crimes such as forgery. One notable exception is this group's preaddiction involvement in assault.

Given the differences between the two groups, we wondered whether they foreshadowed any future patterns of involvement in various types of crime and in drug use. We found that the early onset group was significantly more likely to have been ever involved in drug selling, robbery, and weapons use (Table 8). As for the frequency of such involvement, we found a statistically significant difference for all offenses but robbery. Interpretation of these findings is difficult, however: it is not clear whether the higher lifetime participation rate in the early onset group is a carryover from their preadolescent involvement in these behaviors or whether this rate reflects the exigencies of drug distribution, in which weapons possession and use go hand in hand with the trade.

A notable finding, however, is the change in the women's criminal participation once they become addicted. In each crime category, the criminal involvement of the later onset group increases, especially for violent offenses. Yet their level of participation does not approach that of the early onset group. Thus, the later onset group seems to display a clearer drug-crime connection in regard to initiation into violent offending because this initiation coincides with drug addiction. Patterns of offending in the later

Table 6.   Comparison of Mean Age of First Involvement in Crime,
Early and Later Onset Groups

Crime Type	Early Onset (N=51)	Later Onset (N=34)
Robbery	19.00	23.11*
Assault	17.89	28.29*
Burglary	19.50	22.50
Drug Selling	18.65	24.00*
Weapons Use	15.35	23.00*
Shoplifting	14.35	18.06*
Forgery	19.36	25.14*
Prostitution	19.43	19.65

* p < .05

Table 7.   Comparison of Preaddiction Criminal Histories, Early and
Later Onset Groups (Percent Ever Involved)

Crime Type	Early Onset (N=31)	Later Onset (N=20)
Shoplifting	68	40
Forgery	48	25
Prostitution	55	40
Burglary	39	25
Robbery	58	20*
Assault	52	40
Drug Selling	81	20*
Weapons Use	58	25*
Murder/Manslaughter	10	6

* p < .01

onset group resemble those in a sample of addicts studied by Anglin and Speckart: "while some criminality precedes the addiction
career, the great majority is found during the addiction career
(1988:223). These increases in offending support the findings of
other studies in which such increases consistently occur after the
beginning of addiction (Nurco and Dupont 1977; Voss and Stephens 1973; Weissmann, Katsampes, and Giacinti 1976).

It seems that for the later onset group, the cost of increasing
substance use is a major cause of offending, especially robbery and
drug selling, in which the use of weapons is more common. Thus,
for this group, involvement in violent crime may be a "last resort
precipitated by heavy addiction" (Anglin and Speckart 1988:224).
These findings are consistent with the "compulsion model" that
characterizes the drug-crime relationship (Anglin and Speckart
1988; Chaiken and Chaiken 1982; Goldstein 1985; Nurco et al.

Table 8.   Comparison of Total Criminal Histories, Early and Later
          Onset Groups (Percent Ever Involved)

Crime Type	Early Onset (N=31)	Later Onset (N=20)
Shoplifting	73	65
Forgery	41	50
Prostitution	51	56
Burglary	39	41
Robbery	63	29*
Assault	57	44
Drug Selling	80	47*
Weapons Use	63	26*
Murder/Manslaughter	16	18

* $p < .01$

1988), especially when heroin addiction is involved (Collins, Hubbard, and Rachal 1985; Crawford, Washington, and Senay 1983; Datesman 1984; Hunt et al. 1984).

In the early onset group, drug abuse appears to be less important as a cause of violent behavior in spite of the high correlations between these two behaviors. Instead addiction seems to be part of a more general lifestyle (Collins et al. 1985; Peterson and Braiker 1980) in which involvement in violent criminal careers precedes but may be amplified by addiction.

Yet the fact that violent offending can and does exist without addiction in the early onset group suggests that one is not a necessary precondition of the other and that addiction as a pathway to violent offending may be one factor that differentiates the two groups of women in our study. Thus the persistent commission of violent crime among women in the early onset group may be a function of other factors such as ecological dimensions and involvement with delinquent peers.

DISCRIMINANT FUNCTION ANALYSIS

Findings from the bivariate analyses provide strong evidence for the existence of two distinct groups of women in regard to salient background factors as well as onset of violent criminal careers. For a more complete examination of the relationships among these factors, we turned to discriminant analysis.

We performed a discriminant function analysis using variables related to family background, neighborhood characteristics, peer delinquency, juvenile incarceration, and substance use. The discriminant function calculated from these measures was used to predict membership in the two groups.

576   FEMALES' INITIATION INTO VIOLENT CRIME

Table 9.   Discriminant Function Coefficients, Differences between
Early and Later Onset Groups

Variable	Standardized Coefficient
Family Member Incarcerated	−.214
Family Member Substance Abuser	−.243
Family Member Mental Health	−.192
Parent/Child Physical Abuse	.150
Parent/Child Secual Abuse	.172
Stranger/Child Physical & Sexual Abuse	−.309
School Peers, Violent Cirme	−.328
School Peers, Nonviolent Cirme	−.179
Prior Juvenile Detention	−.212
Alcohol Use (Frequency)	−.176
Marijuana Use (Frequency)	−.376
Cocaine Use (Frequency)	−.177
Crack Use (Frequency)	−.278
Heroin Use (Frequency)	.103
Neighborhood Type	−3.67

Wilks Lambda = .529 p=.022
Canonical Correlation = .810

Classification Success Rates
Group 1 (Later Onset) 82%
Group 2 (Early Onset) 89%
Total   86%

On the basis of the results of the discriminant function analysis, we constructed a classification table that compared true group membership with group membership predicted from the discriminant function. In the entire sample, 86 percent were classified correctly—89 percent of the early onset cases and 82 percent of the later onset cases—with the discriminant function obtained from the 15 predictors (Table 9).

When we compared the classificatory abilities of the individual predictors, we found that neighborhood characteristics (concentration of poverty and stranger victimization), having violent delinquent peers, and frequency of marijuana use during school age years were discriminated most strongly between the two groups.

DISCUSSION

The data reported here came from a larger study of women's involvement in violent street crime. Although the research design is exploratory, it has produced results that challenge contemporary assumptions about offending by females. Our analysis suggests a complex relationship that serves to warn against the generic and gender-based generalizations which have been drawn from time-bound, aggregate-level data sets and from ethnographies of women's involvement in street hustling. Specifically, our findings suggest that an adequate understanding of females' offending must consider the effects of neighborhood, peer, and addiction factors that affect both males' and females' participation in criminal violence. In addition, different configurations of these factors appear to contribute to the initiation of violent offending, depending on age of onset.

These findings, as well as their interpretation, are suggestive and require further validation with a more geographically diverse and larger sample. Nonetheless they support theoretical and substantive explanations that emerge from an integrated perspective. The convergence of social learning, control, and ecological theories helps to explain how weak school attachments and parental supervision, associations with delinquent peers, and other social and economic processes prevalent in severely distressed communities (e.g., relative deprivation, increased opportunities for illegal activities, decrease in conventional role models) combine with individual-level and situational factors to initiate involvement in violent street crime for the 85 women who participated in our study.

Nonetheless, the results suggest variation among the study women. The findings demonstrate that individual-level factors related to onset of violent crime patterns change as youths age through adolescence. Early initiation into violent crime was accompanied by participation in a wide variety of other offending behaviors and deviant lifestyles. In contrast, those women who began their violent offending later in life did so in the context of a criminal career which, until the beginning of substance abuse, was more specialized and focused on typically nonviolent, gender-congruent activities such as prostitution and shoplifting. Therefore, for purposes of prevention and control, criminal justice policies and practices must be geared toward the particularities of these two career paths in regard to timing, content, and breadth of intervention.

In general, however, the overall effect of the present study reaffirms the importance of social factors in accounting for violent career patterns. The data suggest that initiation into violent street crime for the 85 women in the study was influenced strongly by the neighborhood environment. These women came from the most severely distressed communities in New York City, where the stresses of poverty and the increases in illegal opportunities combined with a weakening of the social control capabilities of neighborhood institutions. Therefore these women grew up in

578   FEMALES' INITIATION INTO VIOLENT CRIME

multiproblem households where the absence of conventional role models, social support, and material resources weakened the socialization functions of the family. They were detached from conventional institutions such as school, marriage, and employment; by adulthood, most were entrenched deeply in substance abuse and related deviant lifestyles.

The end result of these processes seems to be pathways to violent street offending for a newer, younger, more heavily addicted group of people—women. Also, with the continuing decline in the quality of life in severely distressed communities, poor women rapidly are becoming one of the fastest-growing (Sommers and Baskin forthcoming) and most resilient segments of the offender population.

REFERENCES

Adler, F. (1975) *Sisters in Crime: The Rise of the New Female Criminal*. New York: McGraw-Hill.

Anglin, D. and Y. Hser (1987) "Addicted Women and Crime." *Criminology* 25:359-97.

Anglin, D. and G. Speckart (1988) "Narcotics Use and Crime: A Multisample, Multimethod Analysis." *Criminology* 26:197-234.

Arnold, R. (1990) "Processes of Victimization and Criminalization of Black Women." *Social Justice* 17:153-66.

Ball, J., J. Shaffer, and D. Nurco (1983) "The Day-to-Day Criminality of Heroin Addicts in Baltimore: A Study in the Continuity of Offense Rates." *Drug and Alcohol Dependence* 12:119-42.

Blumstein, A., J. Cohen, J.A. Roth, and C.A. Visher, eds. (1986) *Criminal Careers and Career Criminals*. Washington, DC: National Academy Press.

Browne, A. (1987) *When Battered Women Kill*. New York: Free Press.

Bureau of Justice (1991) *Women in Prison*. Washington, DC: Bureau of Justice Statistics, U.S. Department of Justice.

Carlen, P. (1988) *Women, Crime and Poverty*. Milton Keynes, mk11134 : Open University Press.

Chaiken, J. and M. Chaiken (1982) *Varieties of Criminal Behavior*. Santa Monica: RAND.

Collins, J., R. Hubbard, and J.V. Rachal (1985) "Expensive Drug Use and Illegal Income: A Test of Explanatory Hypotheses." *Criminology* 23:743-64.

Crawford, G., M.C. Washington, and E. Senay (1983) "Careers with Heroin." *International Journal of the Addictions* 18:701-15.

Daly, K. and M. Chesney-Lind (1988) "Feminism and Criminology." *Justice Quarterly* 5:101-43.

Datesman, S. (1984) "Women, Crime and Drugs." In J. Inciardi (ed.), *The Drugs-Crime Connection*, pp. 85-104. Beverly Hills: Sage.

Dunford, F. and D. Elliot (1984) "Identifying Career Offenders Using Self-Reported Data." *Journal of Research in Crime and Delinquency* 21:57-86.

Elliott, D. and D. Huizinga (1984a) *The Relationship between Delinquent Behavior and ADM Problems*. Boulder: Behavior Research Institute.

——— (1984b) "The Relationship between Delinquent Behavior and ADM problems." Presented at the ADAMHA/OJJDP State-of-the-Art Research Conference on Juvenile Offenders with Serious Drug, Alcohol and Mental Health Problems, Washington, DC.

Elliott, D., D. Huizinga, and S. Ageton (1982) *Explaining Delinquency and Drug Use*. Beverly Hills: Sage.

Elliott, D. and H. Voss (1974) *Delinquency and Dropout*. Lexington, MA: Lexington Books.

Fagan, J., E. Piper, and Y.T. Cheng (1987) "Contributions of Victimization to Delinquency in Inner Cities." *Journal of Criminal Law and Criminology* 78:586-613.

Fagan, J., E. Piper, and M. Moore (1986) "Violent Delinquents and Urban Youth: Correlates of Survival and Avoidance." *Criminology* 24:439-71.

Fagan, J. and S. Wexler (1987) "Crime in the Home and Crime in the Streets: The Relation between Family Violence and Stranger Crime." *Violence and Victims* 2:5-21.

Farrington, D., L. Ohlin, and J.Q. Wilson (1986) *Understanding and Controlling Crime*. New York: Springer-Verlag.

Gandossy, R., J. Williams, J. Cohen, and H. Harwood (1980) *Drugs and Crime: A Survey and Analysis of the Literature*. Washington, DC: U.S. Government Printing Office.

Geller, M. and L. Ford-Sonoma (1984) *Violent Homes, Violent Children: A Study of Violence in the Families of Juvenile Offenders*. Trenton: New Jersey State Department of Corrections.

Glick, R. and V. Neto (1977) *National Study of Women's Correctional Programs*. Washington, DC: U.S. Government Printing Office.

Goldstein, P. (1985) "The Drugs/Violence Nexus: A Tripartite Conceptual Framework." *Journal of Drug Issues* 15:493-506.

Gottfredson, M. and T. Hirschi (1987) "The Methodological Adequacy of Longitudinal Research on Crime." *Criminology* 25:581-614.

Guarino, S. (1985) *Delinquent Youth and Family Violence: A Study of Abuse and Neglect in the Homes of Serious Juvenile Offenders*. Boston: Department of Youth Services.

Hagan, J., J.H. Simpson, and A.R. Gillis (1987) "Class in the Household: A Power-Control Theory of Gender and Delinquency." *American Journal of Sociology* 92:788-816.

Hirschi, T. (1969) *Causes of Delinquency*. Berkeley: University of California Press.

Hser, Y., D. Anglin, and M. Booth (1987) "Sex Differences in Addict Careers: Initiation of Use." *American Journal of Drug and Alcohol Abuse* 13:231-51.

Huba, G. and P. Bentler (1983) "Test of a Drug Use Causal Model Using Asymptotically Distribution Free Methods." *Journal of Drug Education* 13:3-14.

Huling, T. (1991) "New York Groups Call on State lawmakers to Release Women in Prison." Press release, Correctional Association of New York.

Hunt, D., D. Strug, D. Goldsmith, D. Lipton, B. Spunt, L. Truitt, and K. Robertson (1984) "An Instant Shot of 'Aah': Cocaine Use among Metadone Clients." *Journal of Psychoactive Drugs* 16:217-27.

Inciardi, J. (1979) "Heroin Use and Street Crime." *Crime and Delinquency* 25:335-46.

Inciardi, J. and A. Pottieger (1986) "Drug Use and Crime among Two Cohorts of Women Narcotics Users: An Empirical Assessment." *Journal of Drug Issues* 14:91-106.

Inciardi, J., A. Pottieger, and C. Faupel (1982) "Black Women, Heroin and Crime: Some Empirical Notes." *Journal of Drug Issues* 10:241-50.

Jacquith, S. (1981) "Adolescent Marijuana and Alcohol Use: An Empirical Test of Differential Association Theory." *Criminology* 19:271-80.

James, J., C. Gosho, and R.W. Wohl (1979) "The Relationship between Female Criminality and Drug Use." *International Journal of the Addictions* 14:215-29.

Jargowsky, P. and M.J. Bane (1990) "Neighborhood Poverty: Basic Questions." Discussion paper, Malcolm Wiener Center for Social Policy, John F. Kennedy School of Government, Harvard University.

Johnson, B., P. Goldstein, E. Preble, J. Schmeidler, D. Lipton, B. Spunt, and T. Miller (1985) *Taking Care of Business: The Economics of Crime by Heroin Abusers*. Lexington, MA: Lexington Books.

Johnson, R., A. Marcos, and S. Bahr (1987) "The Role of Peers in the Complex Etiology of Adolescent Drug Use." *Criminology* 25:323-39.

Kennedy, L. and D. Forde (1990) "Routine Activities and Crime: An Analysis of Victimization in Canada." *Criminology* 28:137-52.

Klein, M. and C. Maxson (1989) "Street Gang Violence." In N. Weiner and M. Wolfgang (eds.), *Violent Crime, Violent Criminals*, pp. 198-234. Beverly Hills: Sage.

580   FEMALES' INITIATION INTO VIOLENT CRIME

Laub, J. and R. Sampson (1988) "Unraveling Families and Delinquency: A Reanalysis of the Gluecks' Data." *Criminology* 26:355-80.

Lauritsen, J., R. Sampson, and J. Laub (1991) "The Link between Offending and Victimization among Adolescents." *Criminology* 29:265-91.

Loeber, R. (1987) "The Prevalence, Correlates, and Continuity of Serious Conduct Problems in Elementary School Children." *Criminology* 25:615-42.

Loeber, R. and T. Dishion (1983) "Early Predictors of Male Adolescent Delinquency: A Review." *Psychological Bulletin* 94:68-99.

Loeber, R. and M. Stouthamer-Loeber (1987) "Prediction." In H. Quay (ed.), *Handbook of Juvenile Delinquency*, pp. 15-33. New York: Wiley.

Magnusson, D., H. Stattin, and A. Duner (1983) "Aggression and Criminality in a Longitudinal Perspective." In K.T. Van Dusen and S.A. Mednick (eds.), *Antecedents of Aggression and Antisocial Behavior*, pp. 45-61. Boston: Kluwer-Nijhoff.

Massey, D. and M. Eggers (1990) "The Ecology of Inequality: Minorities and the Concentration of Poverty, 1970-1980." *American Journal of Sociology* 95:1153-88.

Maxfield, M. (1987) "Lifestyle and Routine Activity Theories of Crime: Empirical Studies of Victimization, Delinquency and Offender Decision Making." *Journal of Quantitative Criminology* 3:275-82.

McCord, J. (1979) "Some Child-Rearing Antecedents of Criminal Behavior in Adult Men." *Journal of Personality and Social Psychology* 37:1477-86.

Miller, B., W. Downs, and D. Gondoli (1989) "Delinquency, Childhood Violence, and the Development of Alcoholism in Women." *Crime and Delinquency* 35:94-108.

Miller, E. (1986) *Street Woman*. Philadelphia: Temple University Press.

Moss, S. (1986) "Women in Prison: A Case of Pervasive Neglect." *Women and Therapy* 5:5-10.

Nurco, D. (1985) "A Discussion of Validity." In B. Rouse, N. Kozel, and L. Richards (eds.), *Self-Report Methods of Estimating Drug Use Meeting Current Challenges to Validity*, pp. 4-11. Rockville, MD: National Institute on Drug Abuse.

Nurco, D. and R. DuPont (1977) "A Preliminary Report of Crime and Addiction within a Community-Wide Population of Narcotics Addicts." *Drug and Alcohol Dependence* 2:109-21.

Nurco, D., T. Hanlon, T. Kinlock, and K. Duszynski (1988) "Differential Criminal Patterns of Narcotic Addicts over an Addiction Career." *Criminology* 26:407-23.

Peterson, M. and H. Braiker (1980) *Doing Crime: A Survey of California Prison Inmates*. Santa Monica: RAND.

Pettiway, L. (1987) "Participation in Crime Partnerships by Female Drug Users: The Effects of Domestic Arrangements, Drug Use, and Criminal Involvement." *Criminology* 25:741-66.

Polk, K., C. Adler, G. Bazemore, G. Blake, S. Cordray, G. Coventry, J. Galvin, and M. Temple (1981) *Becoming Adult: An Analysis of Maturational Development from Age 16 to 30 of a Cohort of Young Men. Final Report of the Marion County Youth Study*. Eugene: University of Oregon Press.

Pollack-Byrne, J. (1990) *Women, Prison and Crime*. Belmont, CA: Brooks/Cole.

Roman, L. (1990) "Jailed Mothers Risk Losing Their Kids." *New Directions for Women* (March/April):12.

Rosenbaum, M. (1981) *Women on Heroin*. New Brunswick: Rutgers University Press.

Sampson, R. and J. Lauritsen (1990) "Deviant Lifestyles, Proximity to Crime, and the Offender-Victim Link in Personal Violence." *Journal of Research on Crime and Delinquency* 27:110-39.

Sampson, R. and J. Wooldredge (1987) "Linking the Micro- and Macro-Level Dimensions of Lifestyle-Routine Activity and Opportunity Models of Predatory Victimization." *Journal of Quantitative Criminology* 3:371-93.

Shannon, L. (1984) *The Development of Serious Criminal Careers and the Delinquent Neighborhood*. Washington, DC: National Institute for Juvenile Justice and Delinquency Prevention.

Sommers, I. and D. Baskin (1992) "Sex, Race, Age and Violent Offending." *Violence and Victims* 7:191-202.

———— (forthcoming) "The Situational Context of Violent Female Offending." *Journal of Research in Crime and Delinquency*.

Spatz-Widom, C. (1989) "Child Abuse and Adult Criminality." *American Journal of Orthopsychiatry* 59:355-66.

Steffensmeier, D. (1983) "Organization Properties and Sex-Segregation in the Underworld: Building a Sociological Theory of Sex Differences in Crime." *Social Forces* 61:1010-32.

Sullivan, M. (1989) *Getting Paid: Youth, Crime and Work in the Inner City*. Ithaca: Cornell University Press.

Thornberry, T., M. Moore, and R.L. Christenson (1985) "The Effect of Dropping out of High School on Subsequent Criminal Behavior." *Criminology* 23:3-18.

Van Voorhis, P., F. Cullen, R. Mathers, and C. Chenoweth Garner (1988) "The Impact of Family Structure and Quality on Delinquency: A Comparative Assessment of Structural and Functional Factors." *Criminology* 26:235-61.

Voss, H. and R. Stephens (1973) "Criminality History of Narcotic Addicts." *Drug Forum* 2:191-202.

Weis, J. and J. Sederstrom (1981) *The Prevention of Serious Delinquency: What to Do?* Washington, DC: Office of Juvenile Justice and Delinquency Prevention.

Weisheit, R. and S. Mahan (1988) *Women, Crime and Criminal Justice*. Cincinnati: Anderson.

Weismann, J.C., P.L. Katsampes, and T.G. Giacinti (1976) "Opiate Use and Criminality among a Jail Population." *Addictive Diseases* 1:269-81.

Wells, L.E. and J.H. Rankin (1985) "The Broken Homes Model of Delinquency: Analytic Issues." *Journal of Research in Crime and Delinquency* 23:68-93.

West, D. and D. Farrington (1976) *Who Becomes Delinquent?* London: Heinemann.

White, J., T. Moffitt, F. Earls, L. Robins, and P. Silva (1990) "How Early Can We Tell? Predictors of Childhood Conduct Disorder and Adolescent Delinquency." *Criminology* 28:50734.

582   FEMALES' INITIATION INTO VIOLENT CRIME

Appendix.   Factor Loadings for Variables Used to Compute Scales

Factors and Individual Variables	Factor Loading
Parent/Respondent Physical Abuse	
Verbal	.678
Push/Shove	.764
Throw Something	.661
Kick/Hit	.608
Beat	.744
Use Weapons	.658
Mean = 9.80 (0 = never ... 3 = frequently)	
SD = 10.03	
Parent/Respondent Sexual Abuse	
Unwanted Sexual Contact	.698
Mean = .212 (0 = never ... 3 = frequently)	
SD = .315	
Parent/Parent Physical Abuse	
Verbal	.823
Push/Shove	.938
Throw Something	.932
Kick/Hit	.953
Beat	.892
Use Weapons	.786
Mean = 7.33 (0 = never ... 3 = frequently)	
SD = 7.59	
Stranger/Respondent Physical & Sexual Violence	
Verbal	.762
Push/Shove	.871
Slap	.876
Throw Something	.838
Kick/Hit	.910
Beat	.844
Use Weapons	.846
Unwanted Sexual Contact	.616
Mean = 15.02 (0 = never ... 3 = frequently)	
SD = 9.77	
School Peers: Violent Crime	
Assault	.649
Robbery	.759
Burglary	.611
Weapons Possession	.756
Weapons Use	.786
Murder/Manslaughter	.671
Mean = 2.53 (0 = no, 1 = yes)	
SD = 2.03	

School Peers: Nonviolent Crime

Auto Theft	.598
Shoplifting	.758
Forgery	.718
Prostitution	.734
Drug Possession	.772
Drug Selling	.777

Mean= 2.46   (0=no, 1=yes)
SD=   1.75

[3]

SOCIAL PROBLEMS, Vol. 32, No. 3, February 1985

"RIDING THE BULL AT GILLEY'S":
CONVICTED RAPISTS DESCRIBE THE REWARDS OF RAPE*

DIANA SCULLY
JOSEPH MAROLLA
Virginia Commonwealth University

In this paper we argue that the popular image of rape, a nonutilitarian act committed by a few "sick" men, is too limited a view of sexual violence because it excludes culture and social structure as pre-disposing factors. Our data come from interviews with 114 convicted, incarcerated rapists. Looking at rape from the perspective of rapists, we attempt to discover the function of sexual violence in their lives; what their behavior gained for them in a society seeming prone to rape. Our analysis reveals that a number of rapists used sexual violence as a method of revenge and/or punishment while others used it as a means of gaining access to unwilling or unavailable women. In some cases, rape was just a bonus added to burglary or robbery. Rape was also a recreational activity and described as an "adventure" and an "exciting" form of impersonal sex which gained the offender power over his victim(s).

Over the past several decades, rape has become a "medicalized" social problem. That is to say, the theories used to explain rape are predicated on psychopathological models. They have been generated from clinical experiences with small samples of rapists, often the therapists' own clients. Although these psychiatric explanations are most appropriately applied to the atypical rapist, they have been generalized to all men who rape and have come to inform the public's view on the topic.

Two assumptions are at the core of the psychopathological model; that rape is the result of idiosyncratic mental disease and that it often includes an uncontrollable sexual impulse (Scully and Marolla, 1985). For example, the presumption of psychopathology is evident in the often cited work of Nicholas Groth (1979). While Groth emphasizes the nonsexual nature of rape (power, anger, sadism), he also concludes, "Rape is always a symptom of some psychological dysfunction, either temporary and transient or chronic and repetitive" (Groth, 1979:5). Thus, in the psychopathological view, rapists lack the ability to control their behavior; they are "sick" individuals from the "lunatic fringe" of society.

In contradiction to this model, empirical research has repeatedly failed to find a consistent pattern of personality type or character disorder that reliably discriminates rapists from other groups of men (Fisher and Rivlin, 1971; Hammer and Jacks, 1955; Rada, 1978). Indeed, other research has found that fewer than 5 percent of men were psychotic when they raped (Abel et al., 1980).

Evidence indicates that rape is not a behavior confined to a few "sick" men but many men have the attitudes and beliefs necessary to commit a sexually aggressive act. In research conducted at a midwestern university, Koss and her coworkers reported that 85 percent of men defined as highly sexually aggressive had victimized women with whom they were romantically involved (Koss and Leonard, 1984). A recent survey quoted in *The Chronicle of Higher Education* estimates that more than 20 percent of college women are the victims of rape and attempted rape (Meyer, 1984). These findings mirror research published several decades earlier which also concluded that sexual aggression was commonplace in dating relationships (Kanin, 1957, 1965, 1967, 1969; Kirkpatrick and

* This research was supported by a grant (R01 MH33013) from the National Center for the Prevention and Control of Rape, National Institute of Mental Health. We are indebted to the Virginia Department of Corrections for their cooperation and assistance in this research. Correspondence to: Scully, Department of Sociology/Anthropology, Virginia Commonwealth University, 312 Shafer Street, Richmond, Virginia 23284.

Kanin, 1957).[1] In their study of 53 college males, Malamuth, Haber and Feshback (1980) found that 51 percent indicated a likelihood that they, themselves, would rape if assured of not being punished.

In addition, the frequency of rape in the United States makes it unlikely that responsibility rests solely with a small lunatic fringe of psychopathic men. Johnson (1980), calculating the lifetime risk of rape to girls and women aged twelve and over, makes a similar observation. Using Law Enforcement Assistance Association and Bureau of Census Crime Victimization Studies, he calculated that, excluding sexual abuse in marriage and assuming equal risk to all women, 20 to 30 percent of girls now 12 years old will suffer a violent sexual attack during the remainder of their lives. Interestingly, the lack of empirical support for the psychopathological model has not resulted in the de-medicalization of rape, nor does it appear to have diminished the belief that rapists are "sick" aberrations in their own culture. This is significant because of the implications and consequences of the model.

A central assumption in the psychopathological model is that male sexual aggression is unusual or strange. This assumption removes rape from the realm of the everyday or "normal" world and places it in the category of "special" or "sick" behavior. As a consequence, men who rape are cast in the role of outsider and a connection with normative male behavior is avoided. Since, in this view, the source of the behavior is thought to be within the psychology of the individual, attention is diverted away from culture or social structure as contributing factors. Thus, the psychopathological model ignores evidence which links sexual aggression to environmental variables and which suggests that rape, like all behavior, is learned.

CULTURAL FACTORS IN RAPE

Culture is a factor in rape, but the precise nature of the relationship between culture and sexual violence remains a topic of discussion. Ethnographic data from pre-industrial societies show the existence of rape-free cultures (Broude and Green, 1976; Sanday, 1979), though explanations for the phenomena differ.[2] Sanday (1979) relates sexual violence to contempt for female qualities and suggests that rape is part of a culture of violence and an expression of male dominance. In contrast, Blumberg (1979) argues than in pre-industrial societies women are more likely to lack important life options and to be physically and politically oppressed where they lack economic power relative to men. That is, in pre-industrial societies relative economic power enables women to win some immunity from men's use of force against them.

Among modern societies, the frequency of rape varies dramatically, and the United States is among the most rape-prone of all. In 1980, for example, the rate of reported rape and attempted rape for the United States was eighteen times higher than the corresponding rate for England and Wales (West, 1983). Spurred by the Women's Movement, feminists have generated an impressive body of theory regarding the cultural etiology of rape in the United States. Representative of the feminist view, Griffin (1971) called rape "The All American Crime."

The feminist perspective views rape as an act of violence and social control which functions to "keep women in their place" (Brownmiller, 1975; Kasinsky, 1975; Russell, 1975). Feminists see rape

---

1. Despite the fact that these data have been in circulation for some time, prevention strategies continue to reflect the "lunatic fringe" image of rape. For example, security on college campuses, such as bright lighting and escort service, is designed to protect women against stranger rape while little or no attention is paid to the more frequent crime—acquaintance or date rape.
2. Broude and Green (1976) list a number of factors which limit the quantity and quality of cross-cultural data on rape. They point out that it was not customary in traditional ethnography to collect data on sexual attitudes and behavior. Further, where data do exist, they are often sketchy and vague. Despite this, the existence of rape-free societies has been established.

as an extension of normative male behavior, the result of conformity or overconformity to the values and prerogatives which define the traditional male sex role. That is, traditional socialization encourages males to associate power, dominance, strength, virility and superiority with mascu-linity, and submissiveness, passivity, weakness, and inferiority with femininity. Furthermore, males are taught to have expectations about their level of sexual needs and expectations for corresponding female accessibility which function to justify forcing sexual access. The justification for forced sexual access is buttressed by legal, social, and religious definitions of women as male property and sex as an exchange of goods (Bart, 1979). Socialization prepares women to be "legitimate" victims and men to be potential offenders (Weis and Borges, 1973). Herman (1984) concludes that the United States is a rape culture because both genders are socialized to regard male aggression as a natural and normal part of sexual intercourse.

Feminists view pornography as an important element in a larger system of sexual violence; they see pornography as an expression of a rape-prone culture where women are seen as objects avail-able for use by men (Morgan, 1980; Wheeler, 1985). Based on his content analysis of 428 "adults only" books, Smith (1976) makes a similar observation. He notes that, not only is rape presented as part of normal male/female sexual relations, but the woman, despite her terror, is always depicted as sexually aroused to the point of cooperation. In the end, she is ashamed but physically gratified. The message — women desire and enjoy rape — has more potential for damage than the image of the violence *per se*.[3]

The fusion of these themes — sex as an impersonal act, the victim's uncontrollable orgasm, and the violent infliction of pain — is commonplace in the actual accounts of rapists. Scully and Marolla (1984) demonstrated that many convicted rapists denied their crime and attempted to justify their rapes by arguing that their victim had enjoyed herself despite the use of a weapon and the infliction of serious injuries, or even death. In fact, many argued, they had been instrumental in making *her* fantasy come true.

The images projected in pornography contribute to a vocabulary of motive which trivializes and neutralizes rape and which might lessen the internal controls that otherwise would prevent sexually aggressive behavior. Men who rape use this culturally acquired vocabulary to justify their sexual violence.

Another consequence of the application of psychopathology to rape is it leads one to view sexual violence as a special type of crime in which the motivations are subconscious and uncontrollable rather than overt and deliberate as with other criminal behavior. Black (1983) offers an approach to the analysis of criminal and/or violent behavior which, when applied to rape, avoids this bias.

Black (1983) suggests that it is theoretically useful to ignore that crime is criminal in order to discover what such behavior has in common with other kinds of conduct. From his perspective, much of the crime in modern societies, as in pre-industrial societies, can be interpreted as a form of "self help" in which the actor is expressing a grievance through aggression and violence. From the actor's perspective, the victim is deviant and his own behavior is a form of social control in which the objective may be conflict management, punishment, or revenge. For example, in socie-ties where women are considered the property of men, rape is sometimes used as a means of avenging the victim's husband or father (Black, 1983). In some cultures rape is used as a form of punish-ment. Such was the tradition among the puritanical, patriarchal Cheyenne where men were valued for their ability as warriors. It was Cheyenne custom that a wife suspected of being unfaithful could be "put on the prairie" by her husband. Military confreres then were invited to "feast" on the prairie

---

3. This factor distinguishes rape from other fictional depictions of violence. That is, in fictional murder, bombings, robberys, etc., victims are never portrayed as enjoying themselves. Such exhibits are reserved for pornographic displays of rape.

(Hoebel, 1954; Llewellyn and Hoebel, 1941). The ensuing mass rape was a husband's method of punishing his wife.

Black's (1983) approach is helpful in understanding rape because it forces one to examine the goals that some men have learned to achieve through sexually violent means. Thus, one approach to understanding why some men rape is to shift attention from individual psychopathology to the important question of what rapists gain from sexual aggression and violence in a culture seemingly prone to rape.

In this paper, we address this question using data from interviews conducted with 114 convicted, incarcerated rapists. Elsewhere, we discussed the vocabulary of motive, consisting of excuses and justifications, that these convicted rapists used to explain themselves and their crime (Scully and Marolla, 1984).[4] The use of these culturally derived excuses and justifications allowed them to view their behavior as either idiosyncratic or situationally appropriate and thus it reduced their sense of moral responsibility for their actions. Having disavowed deviance, these men revealed how they had used rape to achieve a number of objectives. We find that some men used rape for revenge or punishment while, for others, it was an "added bonus" — a last minute decision made while committing another crime. In still other cases, rape was used to gain sexual access to women who were unwilling or unavailable, and for some it was a source of power and sex without any personal feelings. Rape was also a form of recreation, a diversion or an adventure and, finally, it was something that made these men "feel good."

METHODS[5]

Sample

During 1980 and 1981 we interviewed 114 convicted rapists. All of the men had been convicted of the rape or attempted rape (n = 8) of an adult woman and subsequently incarcerated in a Virginia prison. Men convicted of other types of sexual offense were omitted from the sample.

In addition to their convictions for rape, 39 percent of the men also had convictions for burglary or robbery, 29 percent for abduction, 25 percent for sodomy, 11 percent for first or second degree murder and 12 percent had been convicted of more than one rape. The majority of the men had previous criminal histories but only 23 percent had a record of past sex offenses and only 26 percent had a history of emotional problems. Their sentences for rape and accompanying crimes ranged from ten years to seven life sentences plus 380 years for one man. Twenty-two percent of the rapists were serving at least one life sentence. Forty-six percent of the rapists were white, 54 percent black. In age, they ranged from 18 to 60 years but the majority were between 18 and 35 years. Based on a statistical profile of felons in all Virginia prisons prepared by the Virginia Department of Corrections, it appears that this sample of rapists was disproportionately white and, at the time of the research, somewhat better educated and younger than the average inmate.

All participants in this research were volunteers. In constructing the sample, age, education, race, severity of current offense and past criminal record were balanced within the limitations imposed by the characteristics of the volunteer pool. Obviously the sample was not random and thus may not be typical of all rapists, imprisoned or otherwise.

All interviews were hand recorded using an 89-page instrument which included a general background, psychological, criminal, and sexual history, attitude scales and 30 pages of open-ended

---

4. We also introduced a typology consisting of "admitters" (men who defined their behavior as rape) and "deniers" (men who admitted to sexual contact with the victim but did not define it as rape). In this paper we drop the distinction between admitters and deniers because it is not relevant to most of the discussion.

5. For a full discussion of the research methodology, sample, and validity, see Scully and Marolla (1984).

questions intended to explore rapists' own perceptions of their crime and themselves. Each author interviewed half of the sample in sessions that ranged from three to seven hours depending on the desire or willingness of the participant to talk.

Validity

In all prison research, validity is a special methodological concern because of the reputation inmates have for "conning." Although one goal of this research was to understand rape from the perspective of men who have raped, it was also necessary to establish the extent to which rapists' perceptions deviated from other descriptions of their crime. The technique we used was the same others have used in prison research; comparing factual information obtained in the interviews, including details of the crime, with reports on file at the prison (Athens, 1977; Luckenbill, 1977; Queen's Bench Foundation, 1976). In general, we found that rapists' accounts of their crime had changed very little since their trials. However, there was a tendency to understate the amount of violence they had used and, especially among certain rapists, to place blame on their victims.

HOW OFFENDERS VIEW THE REWARDS OF RAPE

Revenge and Punishment

As noted earlier, Black's (1983) perspective suggests that a rapist might see his act as a legitimized form of revenge or punishment. Additionally, he asserts that the idea of "collective liability" accounts for much seemingly random violence. "Collective liability" suggests that all people in a particular category are held accountable for the conduct of each of their counterparts. Thus, the victim of a violent act may merely represent the category of individual being punished.

These factors — revenge, punishment, and the collective liability of women — can be used to explain a number of rapes in our research. Several cases will illustrate the ways in which these factors combined in various types of rape. Revenge-rapes were among the most brutal and often included beatings, serious injuries and, even murder.

Typically, revenge-rapes included the element of collective liability. This is, from the rapist's perspective, the victim was a substitute for the woman they wanted to avenge. As explained elsewhere, (Scully and Marolla, 1984), an upsetting event, involving a woman, preceded a significant number of rapes. When they raped, these men were angry because of a perceived indiscretion, typically related to a rigid, moralistic standard of sexual conduct, which they required from "their woman" but, in most cases, did not abide by themselves. Over and over these rapists talked about using rape "to get even" with their wives or other significant woman.[6] Typical is a young man who, prior to the rape, had a violent argument with his wife over what eventually proved to be her misdiagnosed case of venereal disease. She assumed the disease had been contracted through him, an accusation that infuriated him. After fighting with his wife, he explained that he drove around "thinking about hurting someone." He encountered his victim, a stranger, on the road where her car had broken down. It appears she accepted his offered ride because her car was out of commission. When she realized that rape was pending, she called him "a son of a bitch," and attempted to resist. He reported flying into a rage and beating her, and he confided,

> I have never felt that much anger before. If she had resisted, I would have killed her . . . The rape was for revenge I didn't have an orgasm. She was there to get my hostile feelings off on.

---

6. It should be noted that significant women, like rape victims, were also sometimes the targets of abuse and violence and possibly rape as well, although spousal rape is not recognized in Virginia law. In fact, these men were abusers. Fifty-five percent of rapists acknowledged that they hit their significant woman "at least once," and 20 percent admitted to inflicting physical injury. Given the tendency of these men to under-report the amount of violence in their crime, it is probably accurate to say, they under-reported their abuse of their significant women as well.

Although not the most common form of revenge rape, sexual assault continues to be used in retaliation against the victim's male partner. In one such case, the offender, angry because the victim's husband owed him money, went to the victim's home to collect. He confided, "I was going to get it one way or another." Finding the victim alone, he explained, they started to argue about the money and,

> I grabbed her and started beating the hell out of her. Then I committed the act,' I knew what I was doing. I was mad. I could have stopped but I didn't. I did it to get even with her and her husband.

Griffin (1971:33) points out that when women are viewed as commodities, "In raping another man's woman, a man may aggrandize his own manhood and concurrently reduce that of another man."

Revenge-rapes often contained an element of punishment. In some cases, while the victim was not the initial object of the revenge, the intent was to punish her because of something that transpired after the decision to rape had been made or during the course of the rape itself. This was the case with a young man whose wife had recently left him. Although they were in the process of reconciliation, he remained angry and upset over the separation. The night of the rape, he met the victim and her friend in a bar where he had gone to watch a fight on TV. The two women apparently accepted a ride from him but, after taking her friend home, he drove the victim to his apartment. At his apartment, he found a note from his wife indicating she had stopped by to watch the fight with him. This increased his anger because he preferred his wife's company. Inside his apartment, the victim allegedly remarked that she was sexually interested in his dog, which he reported, put him in a rage. In the ensuing attack, he raped and pistol-whipped the victim. Then he forced a vacuum cleaner hose, switched on suction, into her vagina and bit her breast, severing the nipple. He stated:

> I hated at the time, but I don't know if it was her (the victim). (Who could it have been?) My wife? Even though we were getting back together, I still didn't trust her.

During his interview, it became clear that this offender, like many of the men, believed men have the right to discipline and punish women. In fact, he argued that most of the men he knew would also have beaten the victim because "that kind of thing (referring to the dog) is not acceptable among my friends."

Finally, in some rapes, both revenge and punishment were directed at victims because they represented women whom these offenders perceived as collectively responsible and liable for their problems. Rape was used "to put women in their place" and as a method of proving their "manhood" by displaying dominance over a female. For example, one multiple rapist believed his actions were related to the feeling that women thought they were better than he was.

> Rape was a feeling of total dominance. Before the rapes, I would always get a feeling of power and anger. I would degrade women so I could feel there was a person of less worth than me.

Another, especially brutal, case involved a young man from an upper middle class background, who spilled out his story in a seven-hour interview conducted in his solitary confinement cell. He described himself as tremendously angry, at the time, with his girl friend whom he believed was involved with him in a "storybook romance," and from whom he expected complete fidelity. When she went away to college and became involved with another man, his revenge lasted eighteen months and involved the rape and murder of five women, all strangers who lived in his community. Explaining his rape-murders, he stated:

---

7. This man, as well as a number of others, either would not or could not, bring himself to say the word "rape." Similarly, we also attempted to avoid using the word, a technique which seemed to facilitate communication.

I wanted to take my anger and frustration out on a stranger, to be in control, to do what I wanted to do. I wanted to use and abuse someone as I felt used and abused. I was killing my girl friend. During the rapes and murders, I would think about my girl friend. I hated the victims because they probably messed men over. I hated women because they were deceitful and I was getting revenge for what happened to me.

An Added Bonus

Burglary and robbery commonly accompany rape. Among our sample, 39 percent of rapists had also been convicted of one or the other of these crimes commited in connection with rape. In some cases, the original intent was rape and robbery was an after-thought. However, a number of the men indicated that the reverse was true in their situation. That is, the decision to rape was made subsequent to their original intent which was burglary or robbery.

This was the case with a young offender who stated that he originally intended only to rob the store in which the victim happened to be working. He explained that when he found the victim alone,

I decided to rape her to prove I had guts. She was just there. It could have been anybody.

Similarly, another offender indicated that he initially broke into his victim's home to burglarize it. When he discovered the victim asleep, he decided to seize the opportunity "to satisfy an urge to go to bed with a white woman, to see if it was different." Indeed, a number of men indicated that the decision to rape had been made after they realized they were in control of the situation. This was also true of an unemployed offender who confided that his practice was to steal whenever he needed money. On the day of the rape, he drove to a local supermarket and paced the parking lot, "staking out the situation." His pregnant victim was the first person to come along alone and "she was an easy target." Threatening her with a knife, he reported the victim as saying she would do anything if he didn't harm her. At that point, he decided to force her to drive to a deserted area where he raped her. He explained:

I wasn't thinking about sex. But when she said she would do anything not to get hurt, probably because she was pregnant, I thought, 'why not.'

The attitude of these men toward rape was similar to their attitude toward burglary and robbery. Quite simply, if the situation is right, "why not." From the perspective of these rapists, rape was just another part of the crime—an added bonus.

Sexual Access

In an effort to change public attitudes that are damaging to the victims of rape and to reform laws seemingly premised on the assumption that women both ask for and enjoy rape, many writers emphasize the violent and aggressive character of rape. Often such arguments appear to discount the part that sex plays in the crime. The data clearly indicate that from the rapists' point of view rape is in part sexually motivated. Indeed, it is the sexual aspect of rape that distinguishes it from other forms of assault.

Groth (1979) emphasizes the psychodynamic function of sex in rape arguing that rapists' aggressive needs are expressed through sexuality. In other words, rape is a means to an end. We argue, however, that rapists view the act as an end in itself and that sexual access most obviously demonstrates the link between sex and rape. Rape as a means of sexual access also shows the deliberate nature of this crime. When a woman is unwilling or seems unavailable for sex, the rapist can seize what isn't volunteered. In discussing his decision to rape, one man made this clear.

All the guys wanted to fuck her . . . a real fox, beautiful shape. She was a beautiful woman and I wanted to see what she had.

The attitude that sex is a male entitlement suggests that when a woman says "no," rape is a suitable method of conquering the "offending" object. If, for example, a woman is picked up at a party

258   SCULLY AND MAROLLA

or in a bar or while hitchhiking (behavior which a number of the rapists saw as a signal of sexual availability), and the woman later resists sexual advances, rape is presumed to be justified. The same justification operates in what is popularly called "date rape." The belief that sex was their just compensation compelled a number of rapists to insist they had not raped. Such was the case of an offender who raped and seriously beat his victim when, on their second date, she refused his sexual advances.

> I think I was really pissed off at her because it didn't go as planned. I could have been with someone else. She led me on but wouldn't deliver . . . I have a male ego that must be fed.

The purpose of such rapes was conquest, to seize what was not offered.

Despite the cultural belief that young women are the most sexually desirable, several rapes involved the deliberate choice of a victim relatively older than the assailant.[8] Since the rapists were themselves rather young (26 to 30 years of age on the average), they were expressing a preference for sexually experienced, rather than elderly, women. Men who chose victims older than themselves often said they did so because they believed that sexually experienced women were more desirable partners. They raped because they also believed that these women would not be sexually attracted to them.

Finally, sexual access emerged as a factor in the accounts of black men who consciously chose to rape white women.[9] The majority of rapes in the United States today are intraracial. However, for the past 20 years, according to national data based on reported rapes as well as victimization studies, which include unreported rapes, the rate of black on white (B/W) rape has significantly exceeded the rate of white on black (W/B) rape (La Free, 1982).[10] Indeed, we may be experiencing a historical anomaly, since, as Brownmiller (1975) has documented, white men have freely raped women of color in the past. The current structure of interracial rape, however, reflects contemporary racism and race relations in several ways.

First, the status of black women in the United States today is relatively lower than the status of white women. Further, prejudice, segregation and other factors continue to militate against interracial coupling. Thus, the desire for sexual access to higher status, unavailable women, an important function in B/W rape, does not motivate white men to rape black women. Equally important, demographic and geographic barriers interact to lower the incidence of W/B rape. Segregation as well as the poverty expected in black neighborhoods undoubtedly discourages many whites from choosing such areas as a target for house-breaking or robbery. Thus, the number of rapes that would occur in conjunction with these crimes is reduced.

---

8. When asked towards whom their sexual interests were primarily directed, 43 percent of rapists indicated a preference for women "significantly older than themselves." When those who responded, "women of any age" are added, 65 percent of rapists expressed sexual interest in women older than themselves.

9. Feminists as well as sociologists have tended to avoid the topic of interracial rape. Contributing to the avoidance is an awareness of historical and contemporary social injustice. For example, Davis (1981) points out that fictional rape of white women was used in the South as a post-slavery justification to lynch black men. And LaFree (1980) has demonstrated that black men who assault white women continue to receive more serious sanctions within the criminal justice system when compared to other racial combinations of victim and assailant. While the silence has been defensible in light of historical racism, continued avoidance of the topic discriminates against victims by eliminating the opportunity to investigate the impact of social factors on rape.

10. In our sample, 66 percent of black rapists reported their victim(s) were white, compared to two white rapists who reported raping black women. It is important to emphasize that because of the biases inherent in rape reporting and processing, and because of the limitations of our sample, these figures do not accurately reflect the actual racial composition of rapes committed in Virginia or elsewhere. Furthermore, since black men who assault white women receive more serious sanctions within the criminal justice system when compared to other racial combinations of victim and assailant (LaFree, 1980), B/W rapists will be overrepresented within prison populations as well as over-represented in any sample drawn from the population.

Reflecting in part the standards of sexual desirability set by the dominant white society, a number of black rapists indicated they had been curious about white women. Blocked by racial barriers from legitimate sexual relations with white women, they raped to gain access to them. They described raping white women as "the ultimate experience" and "high status among my friends. It gave me a feeling of status, power, macho." For another man, raping a white woman had a special appeal because it violated a "known taboo," making it more dangerous and, thus more exciting, to him than raping a black woman.

Impersonal Sex and Power

The idea that rape is an impersonal rather than an intimate or mutual experience appealed to a number of rapists, some of whom suggested it was their preferred form of sex. The fact that rape allowed them to control rather than care encouraged some to act on this preference. For example, one man explained,

> Rape gave me the power to do what I wanted to do without feeling I had to please a partner or respond to a partner. I felt in control, dominant. Rape was the ability to have sex without caring about the woman's response. I was totally dominant.

Another rapist commented:

> Seeing them laying there helpless gave me the confidence that I could do it . . . With rape, I felt totally in charge. I'm bashful, timid. When a woman wanted to give in normal sex, I was intimidated. In the rapes, I was totally in command, she totally submissive.

During his interview, another rapist confided that he had been fantasizing about rape for several weeks before committing his offense. His belief was that it would be "an exciting experience—a new high." Most appealing to him was the idea that he could make his victim "do it all for him" and that he would be in control. He fantasized that she "would submit totally and that I could have anything I wanted." Eventually, he decided to act because his older brother told him, "forced sex is great, I wouldn't get caught and, besides, women love it." Though now he admits to his crime, he continues to believe his victim "enjoyed it." Perhaps we should note here that the appeal of impersonal sex is not limited to convicted rapists. The amount of male sexual activity that occurs in homosexual meeting places as well as the widespread use of prostitutes suggests that avoidance of intimacy appeals to a large segment of the male population. Through rape men can experience power and avoid the emotions related to intimacy and tenderness. Further, the popularity of violent pornography suggests that a wide variety of men in this culture have learned to be aroused by sex fused with violence (Smith, 1976). Consistent with this observation, recent experimental research conducted by Malamuth et al., (1980) demonstrates that men are aroused by images that depict women as orgasmic under conditions of violence and pain. They found that for female students, arousal was high when the victim experienced an orgasm and *no* pain, whereas male students were highly aroused when the victim experienced an orgasm and pain. On the basis of their results, Malamuth et al., (1980) suggest that forcing a woman to climax despite her pain and abhorrence of the assailant makes the rapist feel powerful, he has gained control over the only source of power historically associated with women, their bodies. In the final analysis, dominance was the objective of most rapists.

Recreation and Adventure

Among gang rapists, most of whom were in their late teens or early twenties when convicted, rape represented recreation and adventure, another form of delinquent activity. Part of rape's appeal was the sense of male camaraderie engendered by participating collectively in a dangerous activity. To prove one's self capable of "performing" under these circumstances was a substantial challenge and also a source of reward. One gang rapist articulated this feeling very clearly,

260 SCULLY AND MAROLLA

We felt powerful, we were in control. I wanted sex and there was peer pressure. She wasn't like a person, no personality, just domination on my part. Just to show I could do it—you know, macho.

Our research revealed several forms of gang rape. A common pattern was hitchhike-abduction rape. In these cases, the gang, cruising an area, "looking for girls," picked up a female hitchhiker for the purpose of having sex. Though the intent was rape, a number of men did not view it as such because they were convinced that women hitchhiked primarily to signal sexual availability and only secondarily as a form of transportation. In these cases, the unsuspecting victim was driven to a deserted area, raped, and in the majority of cases physically injured. Sometimes, the victim was not hitchhiking; she was abducted at knife or gun point from the street usually at night. Some of these men did not view this type of attack as rape either because they believed a woman walking alone at night to be a prostitute. In addition, they were often convinced "she enjoyed it."

"Gang date" rape was another popular variation. In this pattern, one member of the gang would make a date with the victim. Then, without her knowledge or consent, she would be driven to a predetermined location and forcibly raped by each member of the group. One young man revealed this practice was so much a part of his group's recreational routine, they had rented a house for the purpose. From his perspective, the rape was justified because "usually the girl had a bad reputation, or we knew it was what she liked."

During his interview, another offender confessed to participating in twenty or thirty such "gang date" rapes because his driver's license had been revoked making it difficult for him to "get girls." Sixty percent of the time, he claimed, "they were girls known to do this kind of thing," but "frequently, the girls didn't want to have sex with all of us." In such cases, he said, "It might start out as rape but, then, they (the women) would quiet down and none ever reported it to the police." He was convicted for a gang rape, which he described as "the ultimate thing I ever did," because unlike his other rapes, the victim, in this case, was a stranger whom the group abducted as she walked home from the library. He felt the group's past experience with "gang date" rape had prepared them for this crime in which the victim was blindfolded and driven to the mountains where, though it was winter, she was forced to remove her clothing. Lying on the snow, she was raped by each of the four men several times before being abandoned near a farm house. This young man continued to believe that if he had spent the night with her, rather than abandoning her, she would not have reported to the police.[11]

Solitary rapists also used terms like "exciting," "a challenge," "an adventure," to describe their feelings about rape. Like the gang rapists, these men found the element of danger made rape all the more exciting. Typifying this attitude was one man who described his rape as intentional. He reported:

It was exciting to get away with it (rape), just being able to beat the system, not women. It was like doing something illegal and getting away with it.

Another rapist confided that for him "rape was just more exciting and compelling" than a normal sexual encounter because it involved forcing a stranger. A multiple rapist asserted, "it was the excitement and fear and the drama that made rape a big kick."

Feeling Good

At the time of their interviews, many of the rapists expressed regret for their crime and had empirically low self-esteem ratings. The experience of being convicted, sentenced, and incarcerated for

---

11. It is important to note that the gang rapes in this study were especially violent, resulting in physical injury, even death. One can only guess at the amount of hitchhike-abduction and "gang-date" rapes that are never reported or, if reported, are not processed because of the tendency to disbelieve the victims of such rapes unless extensive physical injury accompanies the crime.

rape undoubtedly produced many, if not most, of these feelings. What is clear is that, in contrast to the well-documented severity of the immediate impact, and in some cases, the long-term trauma experienced by the victims of sexual violence, the immediate emotional impact on the rapists is slight.

When the men were asked to recall their feelings immediately following the rape, only eight percent indicated that guilt or feeling bad was part of their emotional response. The majority said they felt good, relieved or simply nothing at all. Some indicated they had been afraid of being caught or felt sorry for themselves. Only two men out of 114 expressed any concern or feeling for the victim. Feeling good or nothing at all about raping women is not an aberration limited to men in prison. Smithyman (1978), in his study of "undetected rapists" — rapists outside of prison — found that raping women had no impact on their lives nor did it have a negative effect on their self-image.

Significantly a number of men volunteered the information that raping had a positive impact on their feelings. For some the satisfaction was in revenge. For example, the man who had raped and murdered five women:

> It seems like so much bitterness and tension had built up and this released it. I felt like I had just climbed a mountain and now I could look back.

Another offender characterized rape as habit forming: "Rape is like smoking. You can't stop once you start." Finally one man expressed the sentiments of many rapists when he stated,

> After rape, I always felt like I had just conquered something, like I had just ridden the bull at Gilley's.

CONCLUSIONS

This paper has explored rape from the perspective of a group of convicted, incarcerated rapists. The purpose was to discover how these men viewed sexual violence and what they gained from their behavior.

We found that rape was frequently a means of revenge and punishment. Implicit in revenge-rapes was the notion that women were collectively liable for the rapists' problems. In some cases, victims were substitutes for significant women on whom the men desired to take revenge. In other cases, victims were thought to represent all women, and rape was used to punish, humiliate, and "put them in their place." In both cases women were seen as a class, a category, not as individuals. For some men, rape was almost an after-thought, a bonus added to burglary or robbery. Other men gained access to sexually unavailable or unwilling women through rape. For this group of men, rape was a fantasy come true, a particularly exciting form of impersonal sex which enabled them to dominate and control women, by exercising a singularly male form of power. These rapists talked of the pleasures of raping — how for them it was a challenge, an adventure, a dangerous and "ultimate" experience. Rape made them feel good and, in some cases, even elevated their self image.

The pleasure these men derived from raping reveals the extreme to which they objectified women. Women were seen as sexual commodities to be used or conquered rather than as human beings with rights and feelings. One young man expressed the extreme of the contemptful view of women when he confided to the female researcher.

> Rape is a man's right. If a women doesn't want to give it, the man should take it. Women have no right to say no. Women are made to have sex. It's all they are good for. Some women would rather take a beating, but they always give in; it's what they are for.

This man murdered his victim because she wouldn't "give in."

Undoubtedly, some rapes, like some of all crimes, are idiopathic. However, it is not necessary to resort to pathological motives to account for all rape or other acts of sexual violence. Indeed, we find that men who rape have something to teach us about the cultural roots of sexual aggres-

262   SCULLY AND MAROLLA

sion. They force us to acknowledge that rape is more than an idiosyncratic act committed by a few "sick" men. Rather, rape can be viewed as the end point in a continuum of sexually aggressive behaviors that reward men and victimize women.[12] In the way that the motives for committing any criminal act can be rationally determined, reasons for rape can also be determined. Our data demonstrate that some men rape because they have learned that in this culture sexual violence is rewarding. Significantly, the overwhelming majority of these rapists indicated they never thought they would go to prison for what they did. Some did not fear imprisonment because they did not define their behavior as rape. Others knew that women frequently do not report rape and of those cases that are reported, conviction rates are low, and therefore they felt secure. These men perceived rape as a rewarding, low risk act. Understanding that otherwise normal men can and do rape is critical to the development of strategies for prevention.

We are left with the fact that all men do not rape. In view of the apparent rewards and cultural supports for rape, it is important to ask why some men do not rape. Hirschi (1969) makes a similar observation about delinquency. He argues that the key question is not "Why do they do it?" but rather "Why don't we do it?" (Hirschi, 1969:34). Likewise, we may be seeking an answer to the wrong question about sexual assault of women. Instead of asking men who rape "Why?", perhaps we should be asking men who don't "Why not?"

---

12. It is interesting that men who verbally harass women on the street say they do so to alleviate boredom, to gain a sense of youthful camaraderie, and because it's fun (Benard and Schlaffer, 1984) — the same reason men who rape give for their behavior.

REFERENCES

Abel, Gene, Judith Becker, and Linda Skinner
   1980   "Aggressive behavior and sex." Psychiatric Clinics of North America 3:133–51.
Athens, Lonnie
   1977   "Violent crime: a symbolic interactionist study." Symbolic Interaction 1:56–71.
Bart, Pauline
   1979   "Rape as a paradigm of sexism in society — victimization and its discontents." Women's Studies International Quarterly 2:347–57.
Benard, Cheryl and Edit Schlaffer
   1984   "The man in the street: why he harasses." Pp. 70–73 in Alson M. Jaggar and Paula S. Rothenberg (eds.), Feminist Frameworks. New York: McGraw-Hill.
Black, Donald
   1983   "Crime as social control." American Sociological Review 48:34–45.
Blumberg, Rae Lesser
   1979   "A paradigm for predicting the position of women: policy implications and problems." Pp. 113–42 in Jean Lipman-Blumen and Jessie Bernard (eds.), Sex Roles and Social Policy. London: Sage Studies in International Sociology.
Broude, Gwen and Sarah Greene
   1976   "Cross-cultural codes on twenty sexual attitudes and practices." Ethnology 15:409–28.
Brownmiller, Susan
   1975   Against Our Will. New York: Simon and Schuster.
Davis, Angela
   1981   Women, Race and Class. New York: Random House.
Fisher, Gary and E. Rivlin
   1971   "Psychological needs of rapists." British Journal of Criminology 11:182–85.
Griffin, Susan
   1971   "Rape: the all American crime." Ramparts, September 10:26–35.
Groth, Nicholas
   1971   Men Who Rape. New York: Plenum Press.
Hammer, Emanuel and Irving Jacks
   1955   "A study of Rorschack flexnor and extensor human movements." Journal of Clinical Psychology 11:63–67.
Herman, Dianne
   1984   "The rape culture." Pp. 20–39 in Jo Freeman (ed.), Women: A Feminist Perspective. Palo Alto: Mayfield.

Hirschi, Travis
1969   Causes of Delinquency. Berkeley: University of California Press.
Hoebel, E. Adamson
1954   The Law of Primitive Man. Boston: Harvard University Press.
Johnson, Allan Griswold
1980   "On the prevalence of rape in the United States." Signs 6:136–46.
Kanin, Eugene
1957   "Male aggression in dating-courtship relations." American Journal of Sociology 63:197–204.
1965   "Male sex aggression and three psychiatric hypotheses." Journal of Sex Research 1:227–29.
1967   "Reference groups and sex conduct norm violation." Sociological Quarterly 8:495–504.
1969   "Selected dyadic aspects of male sex aggression." Journal of Sex Research 5:12–28.
Kasinsky, Renee
1975   "Rape: a normal act?" Canadian Forum, September:18–22.
Kirkpatrick, Clifford and Eugene Kanin
1957   "Male sex aggression on a university campus." American Sociological Review 22:52–58.
Koss, Mary P. and Kenneth E. Leonard
1984   "Sexually aggressive men: empirical findings and theoretical implications." Pp. 213–32 in Neil M. Malamuth and Edward Donnerstein (eds.), Pornography and Sexual Aggression. New York: Academic Press.
LaFree, Gary
1980   "The effect of sexual stratification by race on official reactions to rape." American Sociological Review 45:824–54.
1982   "Male power and female victimization: towards a theory of interracial rape." American Journal of Sociology 88:311–28.
Llewellyn, Karl N., and E. Adamson Hoebel
1941   The Cheyenne Way: Conflict and Case Law in Primitive Jurisprudence. Norman: University of Oklahoma Press.
Luckenbill, David
1977   "Criminal homicide as a situated transaction." Social Problems 25:176–87.
Malamuth, Neil, Scott Haber and Seymour Feshback
1980   "Testing hypotheses regarding rape: exposure to sexual violence, sex difference, and the 'normality' of rapists." Journal of Research in Personality 14:121–37.
Malamuth, Neil, Maggie Heim, and Seymour Feshback
1980   "Sexual responsiveness of college students to rape depictions: inhibitory and disinhibitory effects." Social Psychology 38:399–408.
Meyer, Thomas J.
1984   " 'Date rape': a serious problem that few talk about." Chronicle of Higher Education, December 5.
Morgan, Robin
1980   "Theory and practice: pornography and rape." Pp. 134–40 in Laura Lederer (ed.), Take Back the Night: Women on Pornography. New York: William Morrow.
Queen's Bench Foundation
1976   Rape: Prevention and Resistence. San Francisco: Queen's Bench Foundation.
Rada, Richard
1978   Clinical Aspects of Rape. New York: Grune and Stratton.
Russell, Diana
1975   The Politics of Rape. New York: Stein and Day.
Sanday, Peggy Reeves
1979   The Socio-Cultural Context of Rape. Washington, DC: United States Department of Commerce, National Technical Information Service.
Scully, Diana and Joseph Marolla
1984   "Convicted rapists' vocabulary of motive: excuses and justifications." Social Problems 31:530–44.
1985   "Rape and psychiatric vocabulary of motive: alternative perspectives." Pp. 294–312 in Ann Wolbert Burgess (ed.), Rape and Sexual Assault: A Research Handbook. New York: Garland Publishing.
Smith, Don
1976   "The social context of pornography." Journal of Communications 26:16–24.
Smithyman, Samuel
1978   The Undetected Rapist. Unpublished Dissertation: Claremont Graduate School.
West, Donald J.
1983   "Sex offenses and offending." Pp. 1–30 in Michael Tonry and Norval Morris (eds.), Crime and Justice: An Annual Review of Research. Chicago: University of Chicago Press.
Weis, Kurt and Sandra Borges
1973   "Victimology and rape: the case of the legitimate victim." Issues in Criminology 8:71–115.
Wheeler, Hollis
1985   "Pornography and rape: a feminist perspective." Pp. 374–91 in Ann Wolbert Burgess (ed.), Rape and Sexual Assault: A Research Handbook. New York: Garland Publishing.

[4]

Theoretical Criminology
© 1998 SAGE Publications
London, Thousand Oaks
and New Delhi.
1362–4806(199802)2:1
Vol. 2(1): 29–55; 002281.

Structure, context, and agency in the reproduction of black-on-black violence

MARINO A. BRUCE, VINCENT J. ROSCIGNO
AND PATRICIA L. McCALL
*University of Wisconsin-Madison, Ohio State
University* and *North Carolina State University,
USA*

Abstract _____

Violence has a substantial impact on morbidity and mortality within the African-American community. While certainly providing insight into macro- and micro-level forces, existing conceptualizations of the race and violence linkage are limited. We discuss these limitations and then offer a more comprehensive and integrated theoretical framework for understanding disparate patterns. Rather than reducing race-specific violence outcomes to social-psychological or deterministic structural factors, the theoretical model we construct suggests that violence among African Americans (and other subordinated racial/ethnic groups for that matter) is best conceived of as a dynamic and emergent phenomenon, patterned by the intersection of social structure, local context, and agency.

Key Words _____

context • race • violence

African-American communities across the nation are being torn apart by high levels of violence. Official reports cite that African-American males have a 1 in 30 chance of being murdered (Bureau of Justice Statistics, 1990). Such estimates have led public health officials to conclude that homicide is the leading cause of death in this group (Gibbs, 1988; Jaynes and Williams, 1989; Palley and Robinson, 1990). Perhaps the most sobering aspect of this crisis is that the individuals most susceptible to victimization are also the ones most likely to fill the role of perpetrator (Jeff, 1981; Staples, 1986).

Criminological research focusing on disparate race-specific patterns of violence tends to fall into one of two general categories (see Hawkins, 1985, 1986). Subcultural perspectives concentrate on cultural and/or normative attributes allegedly specific to African Americans and other disproportionately poor, non-white groups. That is, these theoretical accounts hold that high rates of violence result from a culture where criminality in general, and violence in particular, are more acceptable forms of behavior (e.g. Curtis, 1975; Elkins, 1959; Wolfgang and Ferracuti, 1967). Structural perspectives, in contrast, argue that intraracial violence among African Americans, and higher rates of criminality more generally, stem from the disadvantaged material conditions that they disproportionately face, such as high levels of poverty and unemployment (e.g. Blau and Blau, 1982; Hagan and Peterson, 1995; Hawkins, 1983, 1986; Sampson, 1987).

Though some research supports the subcultural account (Messner, 1982, 1983; McCall, Land, and Cohen, 1992), similar amounts of research indicate that structural factors are better predictors of violence and crime outcomes within a given community (Loftin and Hill, 1974; Blau and Blau, 1982; Hagan, 1985; Sampson, 1985, 1987; Parker, 1989; Roscigno and Bruce, 1995). We believe that inconsistent empirical findings are attributable, at least in part, to an inadequate conceptualization of race and its relation to violence. Specifically, taking an exclusive structural or subcultural approach limits the ability of researchers to consider the complex, and often interacting, economic and social contexts from which violence emerges.

In this paper, we address theoretical limitations of traditional frameworks. First, we discuss subcultural and structural approaches, highlighting factors that appear to be central to our understanding of disparate levels of violence among African Americans. It is our position that a more plausible conceptualization of intraracial violence in general, and African-American intraracial violence in particular, would incorporate both macro- and micro-level factors into a single framework (see Hagan, 1993; Sampson and Wilson, 1995).[1] Relative to subcultural accounts, this would involve the specification of structural conditions and processes that create and/or shape normative patterns and boundaries. Structural work, too, must be developed in such a way that it acknowledges the emergence of cultural and/or normative patterns under certain conditions and, perhaps more importantly, specifies processes that underlie and reproduce group disadvantage in the first place. To each of these ends, we construct a theoretical model of intraracial violence grounded in structuration theory.

Our conceptualization extends contemporary frameworks by accounting for stratification processes that make context meaningful, by relating structural context to normative and micro-interactional outcomes, and by avoiding the theoretically problematic assumptions of existing perspectives.

The framework we present, particularly our emphases on local context, stratification process, and agency, represents a general theoretical approach to understanding social phenomena—in this case disparate violence outcomes. Thus, our theoretical approach and the general ideas we offer will be of use for those attempting to understand disparate violence outcomes among other social groups (e.g. Rodriguez, 1990; Martinez, 1996) or among those within certain geographic locales (e.g. Nelson, Corzine, and Huff-Corzine, 1994; McCall et al., 1992). At the same time, we believe that general theorizing regarding group or locally specific patterns must be supplemented with auxiliary information about the historical and political nuances of race and/or class stratification that may vary somewhat across group or place (for an elaboration of this approach, see Tomaskovic-Devey and Roscigno, 1996). Thus, following our overview of existing criminological frameworks, we pose an alternative and general conceptual frame and then supplement it with knowledge of historical and political forces that influence levels of violence within a certain group in the US racial/ethnic hierarchy, African Americans.

The subculture of violence

Of theories examining the relationship between race and violence, the most widely cited is the 'subculture of violence' thesis. Its major premise is that value systems of particular groups, including African Americans, differ qualitatively from those of Caucasians. One result is that African Americans have not embraced conventional norms, including those condemning illegitimate forms of violence (Auletta, 1982; Moynihan, 1965; Wolfgang and Ferracuti, 1967). Rather, a subculture of violence has developed and exists as part of an alternative normative structure for minority racial group members.[2]

Wolfgang and Ferracuti (1967), in their formulation of these ideas, suggest that African-American social institutions themselves contribute to the development and persistence of a subculture conducive to criminality and violence. The disintegration of particular institutions (i.e. churches, families and schools), it is argued, denies African Americans the opportunity to learn conventional norms and values (see also Auletta, 1982; Moynihan, 1965). What evolves is a normative system that does not necessarily operate in accordance with that of conventional society.

The result of these processes, it is argued, is that African Americans are more likely to use violence in their day-to-day encounters. They are thought to resolve disputes through violence rather than through more 'legitimate' means, such as verbal negotiation (Gibbs, 1988). Thus, whether historically based in their social practices or in their institutional setup, the argument is that intraracial violence is rooted in counter-normative attributes of the African-American community itself.

Despite its appeal, the subcultural framework has been criticized on the grounds that it assumes a unique subculture based in and adhered to by members of the African-American community. A number of researchers have disputed this claim, arguing that what is often thought of as a unique subcultural tendency is, in fact, an emergent phenomenon—a manifestation of local structural conditions and general levels of opportunity (Taylor, 1979; Wilson, 1987; Anderson, 1990). More structurally-oriented researchers have clearly noted the lack of community structural context in subcultural interpretations of race, criminal activity, and violence (Hawkins, 1985, 1987; Staples, 1986; Sampson, 1987).

The tendency to assume unique cultural attributes, Sampson and Wilson (1995) suggest, has had the effect of directing attention to alleged problems within African-American communities while, at the same time, ignoring more macro-societal processes at work. We know, for instance, that more fundamental structural attributes of a given locality, such as poverty and unemployment, have consequences for the disproportionate breakdown of African-American families, churches, and schools (Hawkins, 1985; Staples, 1986). Yet, *subcultural approaches tend to overlook the interrelation of normative process and institutional deterioration with more structural features of a given community.* The result, of course, is an understanding that erroneously places the blame for disproportionately high rates of intraracial violence on African Americans themselves, on the African-American family, or on African-American culture.

Structural criminological approaches

Rather than concentrating on pathological or cultural deficiencies associated with disadvantaged groups, structural criminological theories examine relationships between economic conditions within a given locality and levels of violence. These perspectives suggest that harsh material conditions facing a substantial proportion of the African-American population, coupled with very high levels of residential segregation, account for the disparate rates of within-group violence. While quite similar, there are at least two strands within the structural camp, each of which varies theoretically on the question of why structure is crucial to the patterning of crime.

Strain perspectives posit that crime results from a disjuncture between aspirations espoused by the dominant culture and the 'legitimate' resources to obtain them. It is argued that the absence of legitimate avenues of opportunity, such as education and employment, can motivate disadvantaged individuals to pursue alternative and illegitimate structures of opportunity, including those that tend to be more violent, in order to obtain societally desired ends (Agnew, 1992; Merton, 1938). The other structuralist strand, social disorganization theory, argues that crime can be linked to the disintegration of social bonds between residents and the larger community. Specifically, limited structures of opportunity within a given locality hinder the formation of, or tear down, institutional social control structures, thus reducing a given community's ability to guard against crime (Bursik, 1988; Bursik and Grasmick, 1993; Shaw and McKay, 1942). Independently, strain and social disorganization perspectives propose different mediating pathways between local structures of opportunity and crime. Regardless of these differences, however, both have influenced the direction of research by introducing the idea that it is the material conditions of a given locality, rather than cultural or normative systems, that precipitate crime.

Researchers have constructed empirical models in an attempt to identify the most crucial structural factors associated with violence (see Braithwaite, 1979; Blau and Blau, 1982; Messner, 1982, 1989; Sampson, 1985; Golden and Messner, 1987; Balkwell, 1990; Harer and Steffensmeier, 1992; Lafree, Drass, and O'Day, 1992; Messner and Golden, 1992). However, findings tend to offer little support for the prioritization of any one influential structural factor over others. This is true even for empirical work now considered to be classic by those working in the area. For instance, in an analysis of spatial variation in crime outcomes across metropolitan statistical areas, Braithwaite (1979) suggests that poverty plays the central role in violent behavior, particularly among non-white racial groups. Blau and Blau (1982), in contrast, find that the level of racial inequality in a given locality has a greater influence on violence than does poverty.[3] A recent study of methodological problems associated with violence research concludes that inconsistencies in findings result from misspecified empirical models (Land, McCall, and Cohen 1990).[4] We, too, argue that inconsistent findings may result from misspecified models, though model misspecification may itself be as much produced by theoretical limitations as by methodological shortcomings.

A clear theoretical limitation of much contemporary structural research is that *it neglects processes involved in the disadvantaged status and the day-to-day experiences of African Americans and other subordinated groups in a race-stratified society*. Aggregate data sets with large units of analysis often fail to include measures that account for inequality processes, based largely on ascribed status, that members of the African-American community must deal with on a continual basis (Feagin and Sikes, 1994). An unfortunate consequence is that macro-level analyses, while certainly uncovering crucial linkages between structure and crime, often prevent researchers from considering the processes that generate group disadvantage in the first place. Such perspectives also tend to overlook the

importance of normative and social-psychological processes that undeniably mediate the relation between community context and violence.

Theoretical reconceptualization

Efforts to explain disparate levels of violence from an exclusively subcultural or structural framework have led criminological research to overlook crucial and often interrelated dynamics involved in the process.
Gaining a better understanding, we believe, requires theorists to work
within a framework that accurately represents the environment in which
the group exists. Indeed, because human action (including violence) evolves
as a response to individual- and structural-level stimuli, one must consider
the relationships among structure, context specific processes, and action.

In what follows, we draw from Giddens' (1984) theory of structuration
and pose an alternative theoretical account of disparate levels of violence
among African Americans. The resulting framework places action in a
given structural, processual, and interactional context while also taking
into account potential recursive effects on structure. Combining these
elements into a unitary framework does not occur by simply merging
theories operating at different levels of analysis. Rather, new conceptual
tools must be introduced.

Structuration as a starting point

According to structuration theory, human action results from the interaction between individual- and structural-level factors. Thus, a theory of
violence constructed within this framework can avoid some of the problematic assumptions and stifling determinism associated with previous
research. Individuals are assumed to be cognizant and rational human
beings whose actions are often influenced but by no means completely
determined by the interplay of social-psychological factors and structural
context. For our purposes, this means that African Americans and other
subordinate racial/ethnic groups are not merely 'dupes', driven to disparate
violent behavior by overwhelming structural conditions, indoctrinated
norms and values, or uncontrollable innate tendencies. Rather, a theory of
criminality or violence grounded in the structuration paradigm would
suggest that criminality in general, and violence in particular, are shaped by
shifting normative boundaries and social-psychological processes that are,
at least in part, a function of the structure in which they are embedded.

Social structure gives shape and form to social life (Giddens, 1984;
Messerschmidt, 1993). However, unlike traditional depictions, structure
here is seen as having a recursive, interdependent relationship with action
(Messerschmidt, 1993). Thus, social structures are malleable entities which
are defined by recurrent social practices. *By viewing structure as malleable,
our concern moves to processes that shape and reproduce it.*

This conceptualization of structure and human action holds exciting possibilities for advancing theoretical discussion about disparate rates of criminality and violence. In order to tap into this potential, we first draw from racial stratification research to identify key actors and processes that create and reproduce a structural context conducive to violence. However, we do not stop there. Individual and group action are influenced, mediated, and reinforced by normative structures and rules that are emergent in nature, and that are shaped by structures of opportunity. Following our discussion of race and class-based processes influencing opportunity, we focus on the manifestation of normative patterns and the shifting boundaries within a context of limited opportunity. Finally, we suggest that structural and normative considerations ultimately interact and shape social-psychological processes and perceptions of danger in a given locality, resulting in local and race-specific variations in violence that are so apparent in many urban areas of the USA.

Inequality processes, key actors, and the shaping of local context

We begin by taking into consideration the embeddedness of a disadvant-aged group in a given social context, and how this context is affected by important actors and social processes relating to race and class inequality. That is, we ground our general framework in the historical, political, and local specifics and experiences of African Americans. Giddens (1984) suggests that structuration is a process that generally begins at the indi-vidual level. However, the recursive nature of the interaction between structure and action allows the theoretical freedom to begin conceptualiz-ing at the structural level.

A fundamental attribute of a given locality that has been implicated in deprivation and inequality among particular racial/ethnic groups is the presence of group members or, more specifically, the size of a minority group relative to the dominant racial group. Stratification research has been clear in pointing out that a large or growing minority group population represents a threat to the economic and political welfare of majority group members (Blalock, 1967). As a result of this threat, dominant racial/ethnic group members respond with discriminatory acts in order to maintain their advantaged position (Lieberson, 1980; Olzak, 1992; Wilson, 1978). In what follows, we briefly consider 'competition' and 'exploitation' accounts of these processes, each of which deals with the development of racial antagonism and the consequences of that antagonism for group disadvant-age. Unlike structural criminological work, *these perspectives acknowledge the role that important and powerful societal actors play in the generation of group disadvantage. Perhaps even more important, they specify the processes through which group disadvantage is reproduced and local opportunity context is created.*[5]

Competition theorists (e.g. Blalock, 1967; Olzak, 1992) focus largely on manifestation of racial antagonism and its consequences for discriminatory

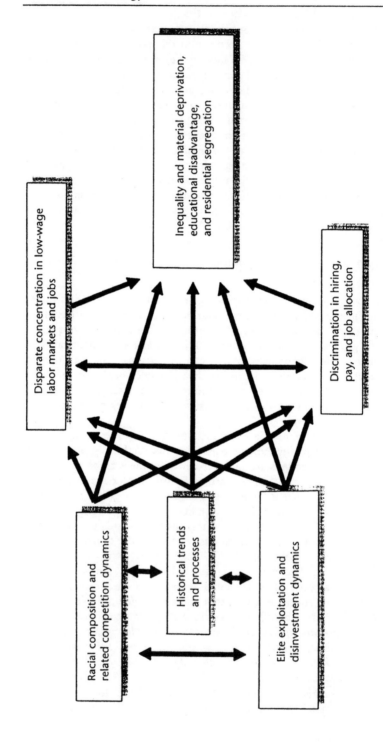

Figure 1 General conceptualization of race and class-based processes in relation to the context of structural opportunity

action by working-class whites. Race relations, it is suggested, remain relatively stable until a significant amount of African-American (or other racial/ethnic minority group) labor becomes available for use by capital. Under these circumstances, Caucasian workers perceive increasing numbers of African-American workers as a threat to their economic status, since employers can easily replace them at a lower cost. When this has occurred historically, white workers set up exclusionary rules and practices, such as the denial of access to unions or guilds, thus fortifying their advantaged status (Bonacich, 1976; Lieberson, 1980). The outcome is a wage differential, or split-labor market, between majority and minority group workers even when efficiency and productivity are held constant (Bonacich, 1972; Brown and Boswell, 1995; Tomaskovic-Devey, 1993). Both in the past and today, these tendencies have also been observed to lead to higher levels of racial residential segregation, poverty and unemployment (Massey and Denton, 1987; Massey and Gross, 1991; Falk and Rankin, 1992; Olzak, 1992).

In contrast to the racial competition argument, exploitation theorists argue that racial antagonism is instigated by more powerful class factions in an effort to drive down the wages of all workers (Reich, 1981; Szymanski, 1976). Basically, owners threaten working-class white material interests by proposing to bring in low-wage, non-white workers (Szymanski, 1976). Rather than perceived threat, exploitation theory suggests that economic threat to working-class white workers is real. Thus, more politically and economically powerful individuals and groups take an active role in spurring racial antagonism by pitting groups of workers against each other for material gain.

Both competition and exploitation theories assert that racial antagonism exists because minority racial group members represent a threat, perceived or real, to the material well-being of working-class whites (Tomaskovic-Devey and Roscigno, 1996). White workers are prompted to take steps to secure their economic and political stability (Wilson, 1978; Lieberson, 1980). The discriminatory methods employed secure the material interest of dominant racial group members or a certain class faction while intensifying economic, political, and social disadvantages for African Americans and other racial/ethnic minority groups.

Figure 1 displays processes through which racial inequality, deprivation, and limited structural opportunity have been and continue to be reproduced. General and race-specific opportunity is manifested, in part, through job and labor market discrimination, exclusion, and/or concentration. At the level of the job, racial disadvantage results from discriminatory pay and hiring as well as from the relegation of African Americans to less prestigious and, therefore, lower-paying jobs (Tomaskovic-Devey, 1993). Kirshenman and Neckerman (1990), in their research on corporate hiring practices in urban areas of the US, show how employers continue to discriminate against non-whites despite federal guidelines making discrimination on the basis of race illegal. As a result of limited access to gainful employment, African Americans continue to face substantial social and economic hardships in the US.[6]

Coupled with disadvantages at the job level are those having to do with the disproportionate concentration of African Americans in poorer labor market areas (Wilson, 1987; Lichter, 1989; Wacquant and Wilson, 1989; Tomaskovic-Devey and Roscigno, 1996). Some explain this concentration in terms of general historical and ecological trends. Wilson (1978, 1987), for instance, suggests that the changing economic structure of major urban areas of the US, coupled with the rising cost of maintaining industry, has forced business either to shut down or to relocate outside of central cities, especially in localities that are disproportionately black and Latino/a. Because many of the former employees of these transplanted industries lack the human capital or monetary resources to relocate in areas with better employment opportunity, many are compelled to seek employment in the local, low-paying service sector or abandon the labor market completely (Wilson, 1987; Kasarda, 1989). This scenario presents a situation where limited opportunities for African Americans stem from a changing economy as opposed to intentional exclusionary or discriminatory practices.[7]

There are other, more recent lines of theoretical and empirical work that, rather than relying on ecological interpretations, focus on the influence of elite and corporate investment/disinvestment dynamics and local class- and race-based struggles. New urban theorizing in particular is more explicit with regard to the influence of elite activity and human agency more generally on the crises facing many urban areas (Gottdiener and Feagin, 1988). Recent evidence, for instance, suggests that elite investment/disinvestment patterns and local growth machine politics systematically bypass localities with large minority populations, thereby shaping economic development and creating racial inequality through spatial patterns of investment (Logan and Molotch, 1987; Molotch, 1988; Wilson, 1992). Redlining of disproportionately black and Latino/a areas by banks and insurance companies most assuredly plays a role in reproducing patterns of depressed economic development and racial concentration both by limiting the formation of new businesses and also by contributing to the speed at which an area physically declines and is deemed undesirable by potential investors (Squires, Valez, and Taeuber, 1991). Finally, the concentration of blacks in poorer labor market areas may be a function of the distorting consequences of racial antagonism, exclusion, and discrimination for long-term economic development or of the dependence of local elites on the persistence of a low-wage, labor-intensive labor market (Tomaskovic-Devey and Roscigno, 1996).

The patterns described above have both resulted in and reinforced levels of residential segregation, which itself has further consequences for structures of opportunity available to African Americans. Even though federal law prohibits the intentional separation of the races, residential 'steering' by realtors, federally sponsored public housing, as well as whites' prejudices have had the effect of keeping urban areas segregated (Massey and Denton, 1987; Massey and Gross, 1991; Farley and Frey, 1994).

Coupled with manufacturing disinvestment and suburbanization, residentially segregated non-white communities have smaller tax bases relative to suburban locales and, as a result, tend to receive a smaller share of state and local funding allocations. One consequence is that inner city schools with large minority youth populations have low levels of funding, poor facilities, and an environment which is anything but conducive to learning (Jaynes and Williams, 1989; Roscigno, 1995). Two ramifications of these processes are clear. First, students in these areas become discouraged and, as a result, drop out of school at much higher rates. Second, those who do make it through school in these localities and graduate are less likely to have the educational or vocational training necessary for college or for a skilled labor market (Wilson, 1987). As with economic disinvestment, the life chances of African Americans diminish because educational disadvantages cause the window of economic and political opportunity to shrink even further.

Overall, then, racial inequality processes continue to have serious implications for the social structural contexts in which African Americans are disproportionately embedded. Disadvantages at the level of job and labor market, individual and institutional discriminatory practices, and patterns of economic investment/disinvestment—all a function of historical trends, racial dynamics, and class politics—continue to limit opportunity. Structuration theory postulates that individuals take action to cope with their circumstances. Thus, we should not expect any group, including African Americans, to be complacent actors in a context where opportunity is constricted or perhaps increasingly limited. Rather, we should expect formation and shifts in normative/cultural patterns. *Unlike traditional depictions employed by cultural deprivation theorists, cultural formation and normative boundary shifts would not be viewed here as necessarily characteristic of a particular racial/ethnic group. Rather, they are emergent in nature and characteristic of individuals and groups within a particular social structural context.*

Normative boundary shifts and cultural formation

Thus far, we have noted several stratification-related processes and key actors implicated in limiting structures of opportunity for African Americans and, more generally, the context in which they are disproportionately embedded. It is unlikely, however, that macro and more material forces directly influence social behavior and, in our case, levels of violence within a given community. Rather, *structures of opportunity serve as an impetus for the formation of normative structures which, in turn, will have more of a direct influence on behavior.* Individuals engage in purposive behavior in accordance with social structure (Giddens, 1984; Messer-schmidt, 1993). Thus, social structure organizes how individuals interpret their circumstances and generate methods for dealing with them.

Consider Bourdieu's (1977) stress that 'culture' or normative structures and the behavior it dictates may have more to do with access to material resources than it does to group attributes, personal characteristics, or taste. If this is so, the children of the affluent may have a working knowledge of the fine arts and literature because their parents can afford to pay for trips to concert halls, museums, and theaters. The development of this type of culture, shaped by structural location and status, may have benefits in a variety of institutional arenas, such as the education system, because elite cultural resources are revered in western industrialized societies. DiMaggio (1982) demonstrates this dynamic in his examination of student achievement. He finds that students possessing elite cultural resources are often perceived as gifted and tend to receive more attention and special assistance in the classroom.

In the above-mentioned example, what is viewed as culture is a manifestation of structural position and class status. The life experiences and cultural attributes that emerge serve to reproduce an individual's or a group's advantaged status. This is not to suggest, however, that cultural/normative manifestation due to structural location is merely reflective of the experiences of those at the top of status hierarchies. It is not. The manifestation of cultural/normative attributes in relation to structural disadvantage is apparent as well. This is evidenced in a small body of literature dealing with class and race-based educational disadvantages, ethnicity and racial separation, and seemingly antagonistic normative attributes of adolescent peer groups located in limited opportunity structure areas.

With regard to peer group antagonism that is aversive toward education, evidence suggests that such normative attributes are more likely to emerge in regions where class- and race-based opportunities and the socio-economic return to education are more severely limited (Hargreaves, 1967; Ogbu, 1978; Willis, 1981; Fordham and Ogbu, 1986). It is no coincidence that such areas in the US tend to be disproportionately non-white and highly residentially segregated. This suggests a reflexive process whereby peer group attitudes and normative structures are shaped by what adolescents see as their own opportunities in life. Given that perfect information regarding future opportunities is virtually impossible to acquire, it is likely that this type of information is supplied to a particular adolescent by his or her perceptions and observations regarding the current economic and occupational status of adults in close proximity (Roscigno, 1995).

Similar arguments pertaining to the emergent character of culture and normative attributes can be found in research examining the ethnic character of particular groups within the USA (see especially Yancey, Ericksen, and Juliani, 1976; Taylor, 1979; Tomaskovic-Devey and Tomaskovic-Devey, 1983; Burr and Mutchler, 1993). Taylor (1979), for instance, in his analysis of African-American identity, finds that group identity and related normative attributes, often perceived as ethnicity, are profoundly shaped by the character of the locality in which the group is embedded and, most importantly, the extent to which the group is structurally segregated.[8]

Ethnographic research has likewise revealed that the permanency associated with the plight of many African Americans in poorer urban areas has led to the development of normative structures with behavioral outcomes, including violence, that further limit life chances (Liebow, 1967; Anderson, 1978, 1990; Keiser, 1979). In an analysis of inner city youth and sex codes, Anderson notes that norms for conduct among poorer inner city youth, while arguably destructive, are 'nothing less than the cultural manifestation of persistent urban poverty' (1990: 112). Figure 2 highlights the basic argument and relationships we are suggesting.

The lesson here is that what is often perceived of as the unique and pre-existent cultural characteristics of a given subordinate group may actually be more a function of a group's structural location. This point is highlighted in a recent piece of research by Alex-Assensoh (1995), who finds that 'underclass behaviors' typically thought of as a reflection of African-American culture are, in fact, a reflection of the poverty-stricken neighborhoods in which the group exists. She compares the behavior of whites and blacks who are embedded in a similar structural situation and finds that the level of 'underclass behavior' is virtually indistinguishable across groups, both statistically and substantively.[9] Thus, *normative structures and practices often thought of as culture may be as much the outcome of the material conditions in which a given group is embedded.*

Linking structure, normative patterns, and action

In the previous discussion, we outlined how inequality processes influence the social structural context within which African Americans are disproportionately embedded and how this continues to have consequences for the current life experiences and well-being of the African-American community. We also suggested that cultural patterns and normative boundary shifts often manifest themselves in relation to racial inequality and general opportunity. The real challenge, however, is to identify mechanisms linking structural disadvantage to the perpetration of violence within the African-American community. Drawing from the ideas presented earlier, we argue that *social structure influences levels of violence within a given community through the interaction of normative pressures and social psychological processes, often generated by economic deprivation and dangerous living conditions.* Figure 3 represents our modeling of these processes.

Incorporating a social psychological dimension within our theoretical framework provides insight into the life experiences of African Americans. As African Americans grow up in disadvantaged communities, they become cognizant of the constraints on their existence. The recognition of the sur-

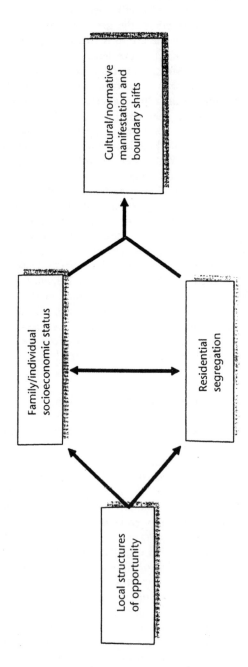

Figure 2 General conceptualization of linkage between structural opportunity and normative manifestation

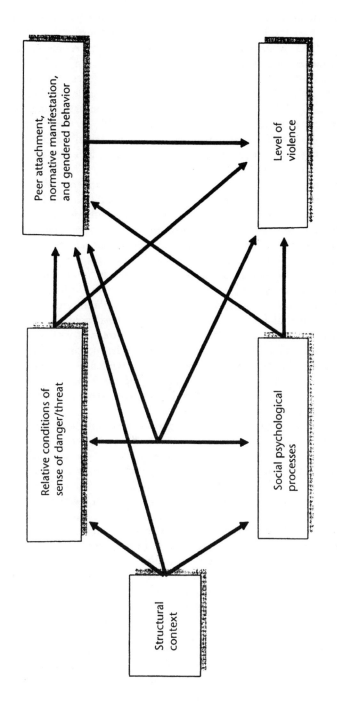

Figure 3   General conceptual linkages between structural context, normative manifestation, and disparate racial outcomes pertaining to violence

rounding restrictions can come through first-hand experience of material
constraint, such as the lack of educational and job opportunities (Duster,
1987; Gibbs, 1988; Majors and Billson, 1992). They also become aware of
their powerlessness through direct observation (Anderson, 1978, 1990;
Majors and Billson, 1992). Many African-American children, for instance,
observe how poor educational and employment opportunities limit the
degree to which adults in the community can perform traditional roles
such as protector and provider (Majors and Billson, 1992). The barrage of
indicators which signify their powerlessness shape social psychological
well-being and certainly may lead to anger, frustration, and despair (Grier
and Cobbs, 1968; Gibbs, 1988).

A second dimension to consider when attempting to understand violence
involves the emergence and existence of dangerous conditions, and perhaps
'illegitimate' avenues of opportunity, within materially-deprived areas.
Because relatively few legitimate opportunities exist for poorer inner city
residents, a relatively large number of individuals participate in underground economic activities such as drugs and weapons trafficking
(Hawkins, 1986). Within these enterprises, order is often maintained
through brute force as well as by intimidation. The disproportionate
involvement in illegal activities, coupled with the availability of weapons,
increases the potential for guns to be used in the settlement of disputes.
This phenomenon triggers a process whereby the threat of violence spurs
those who spend time on the streets to arm themselves (Scott, 1993). One
result is that the object used for protection from violence may, in effect,
contribute to its perpetuation. The outcome of these processes is the
transformation of peaceful neighborhoods into tense areas gripped by the
ever-present threat of violent confrontation.

Social psychological processes and dangerous conditions may *independently* factor into the perpetration of violence. However, we also contend
that violence may result given the *interaction* between social psychological
processes and the threat of danger. The reality of living in an area where
individuals have to depend on illegitimate activities for survival can have
negative consequences for social psychological processes which, in turn,
may increase the potential for violence. Ethnographic accounts of inner city
gang members exemplify this interactional tendency, revealing a general
devaluation of human life in such a context (Scott, 1993). Because gang
members hold such grim prospects for life, minor incidents such as
accidentally bumping into someone or wearing a particular color create the
possibility that an individual will be attacked.

The threat of violence, often apparent from the availability of guns,
likewise has the potential to affect social psychological processes in a way
which can lead to higher levels of violence. Indeed, the lives of inner city
African-American children are often touched by violence at an early age. By
the time these children reach adolescence, it is quite likely that they or their
friends have faced life-threatening confrontations. Growing up in environments filled with violence can lead to psychological states such as nihilism.

Nihilistic world views are evident in qualitative studies, where adolescents speak about their slim chances of seeing adulthood (see Majors and Billson, 1992). The interplay among danger, social psychological processes, and shifts in normative boundaries discussed earlier, holds serious consequences for many African-American communities.

As a means to cope with their bleak surroundings, inner city African-American youth, especially males, participate in and are strongly bonded with their peer groups (Fordham and Ogbu, 1986; Majors and Billson, 1992; Scott, 1993). Peer groups offer these young people a rare opportunity to gain and maintain status and self-respect (Messerschmidt, 1993). Unfortunately, given constraints on legitimate opportunities, status structures and processes in these peer groups often involve placing individual group members or outsiders at risk of serious injury or death (Gibbs, 1988; Jaynes and Williams, 1989). Specifically, it has been suggested that within a limited-opportunity context young people often gain status among their peers by engaging in dangerous and destructive behaviors because bravery and toughness are held in high regard (Gibbs, 1988; Messerschmidt, 1993; Scott, 1993; McCall, 1994). 'Reps' (status among peers) depend not only on surviving dangerous conflict but also on the amount of damage done. For instance, killing another human being during a confrontation gives one tremendous prestige (Brown, 1965; McCall, 1994; Scott, 1993). This 'code of honor' resembles that which exists during times of war.

Messerschmidt (1993) extends the theoretical discussion of normative pressure and violence outcomes to the issue of gender. He argues that young males seek the respect given to 'men' through public displays of 'manhood'. This means that being recognized as a man, in most cases, depends upon access to power and resources. Middle-class youth can demonstrate their manhood more easily through the pursuit of legitimate prestige structures. Since such avenues to publicly display manhood are not readily available to poorer inner city youth, they seek recognition within the confines of their circumstances. Displaying physical superiority over another has traditionally been the means by which many lower-class men gain respect in their neighborhoods (Keiser, 1979; Liebow, 1967). As a result, any confrontation, regardless of triviality, grants a valued opportunity for young males to get respect (or 'juice'). In a recent ethnographic piece, Anderson (1994) suggests that peer group participation allows African-American males the opportunity to obtain and maintain gender-specific respect within the confines of their structural location. He illustrates how young African-American males within a given limited-opportunity context would rather risk death than be disrespected ('dissed') by others:

> . . . there are always people around looking for a fight to increase their share of respect—or 'juice,' as it is sometimes called on the street. Moreover, if a person is assaulted, it is important, not only in the eyes of his opponent but also in the eyes of his 'running buddies,' for him to avenge himself.

Otherwise he risks being 'tried' (challenged) or 'moved on' by any number
of others. To maintain his honor he must show that he is not someone to be
'messed with' or 'dissed'.

(Anderson, 1994: 88)

Traditionally, physical superiority to the point of violence has served as a
consistent and easily accessible resource to gain recognition within peer
groups in areas of limited opportunity. It is, in essence, a form of accom-
modation to the powerlessness associated with impoverished material
conditions (Messerschmidt, 1986, 1993).

Our understanding is one in which disproportionate violence among
African Americans is viewed as an emergent phenomenon, taking place
within a detailed economic, historical, and social context. Structure and
action are linked here via the manifestation of material conditions, normative structures, and social psychological outcomes. Our emphasis on process rather than structure on both ends—in the creation and reproduction
of structure on the one hand, and on the committing of a violent act on the
other—is an important theoretical step relative to existing approaches
because it moves us beyond structurally overdetermined models of disparate criminality and violence while also addressing questionable assumptions of race-specific cultural approaches.

Conclusion

Culture of violence approaches that pervaded much sociological and
criminological thought on racial inequality during and after the 1960s are
limited in their acknowledgment of social structures and the often constraining situation facing many non-white groups. Such approaches likewise overlook the possibility that what is viewed as a unique subcultural
tendency is, in actuality, a normative manifestation of structural conditions
and group status. More structural approaches, in contrast, have tended to
overlook both normative structures and social psychological influences that
have relevance for understanding violent behavior. Rather than simply
drawing from each, we have integrated and combined these focuses into a
structuration approach to sociological theorizing, that is, one that makes
clear the emergent character of behavior within a given historical and social
context, that focuses on processes relevant to the creation of structure and
outcomes, and that leaves open the possibility of human agency.

Consistent with what a structuration approach to sociological theorizing
would suggest, we believe that a more complete theoretical understanding
of high levels of intraracial violence will systematically incorporate a
discussion of processes and key actors relevant to the historical and
contemporary creation of structure. By doing so, we avoid mistaken
assumptions about the stagnant or somehow natural state of structure and
opportunity. As a result, our models are not theoretically overdetermined.
In fact, they are more open to the possibility of change.

But social action does not arise simply from local structural context. Rather, as we have argued, local structures of opportunity tend to shape social action through the patterning of normative boundaries, social-psychological attributes, and relative levels and perceptions of danger across locales. It is here that structural research is lacking and can be informed by ethnographic and historical accounts of inequality and criminological processes. Drawing from such accounts as well as more general sociological theorizing of 'emergent culture', we argue that it is through the dynamic and reciprocal interplay of context, emergent normative phenomena, and social psychological processes that disparate levels of violence are manifested.

As noted earlier, human action and social structure can influence one another in a reciprocal fashion. We have suggested most clearly the ways in which structure can ultimately impact the level of violence within a given community. We also pointed out the possibility that human action can impact structure (e.g. elites through investment/disinvestment, dominant racial groups through exclusionary policies and discrimination). Another way in which structure may be shaped is through levels of crime and violence themselves. Criminogenic activity and violence may certainly shape economic investment/disinvestment patterns. Geographic areas where violence occurs (or where it is believed to occur) can pose problems for corporations on at least two levels. Firstly, firms may have trouble attracting employees with skills or expertise not available in the surrounding environment, due to the threat or the fear of violence. Second, choosing to invest in an impoverished environment may hinder profitability. Locating a work site in or near what is seen as a violent community carries the financial burden of additional insurance and security (Squires, DeWolfe, and DeWolfe, 1979). Similarly, companies that desire to locate in central cities may have difficulty securing capital for projects such as machine procurement or facility renovation. As a result of these obstacles, firms that could conceivably employ entire communities often bypass central cities in favor of safer and often less expensive suburban environments (Fusfield and Bates, 1984; Jaynes and Williams, 1989).

Violence can also intensify the degree to which disadvantaged minority communities are isolated. Crime, in combination with other adverse behavioral outcomes, tends to cause higher income sections of the community (including those belonging to non-white racial/ethnic groups) to seek less dangerous residential, educational, and work environments (Alba, Logan, and Bellair, 1994). One result is the further erosion of inner city tax bases. This limits the leverage of the remaining residents to get State and local funding for community improvement projects such as school renovations. In each of these scenarios, action—violence and criminality—that partially results from the inability to acquire economic and political resources contributes to their increasing scarcity.

Our discussion and theoretical framework imply the need for a multi-method approach to the analysis of crime. Ethnographic, community, and/

or qualitative research endeavors, for example, have been quite successful in pointing out both more proximate causal mechanisms in the (re)production of social action and also the importance of experiential knowledge. That is, the experiences of subjects are crucial in making sense of social processes, including those having to do with violence (Wardell and Zajicek, 1995). Historical treatments, moreover, have uncovered macro-level societal changes that have clear ramifications for the phenomena we investigate and whether we should expect the problems we research to be perpetuated or even intensified. Coupled with social structural and aggregate analyses, this multi-method approach lends itself to generalizability and to a clearer understanding of the spatial character of these processes. We believe all of the above are crucial to sound sociological analysis. Whether at the level of literature review and theory or at the level of an actual research project, a multi-method undertaking will lead to the acknowledgment of multiple contexts at varying levels, will reveal more clearly the dynamic character of social action, and will clarify conceptualization and modeling of criminological outcomes. Indeed, these issues are relevant to most sociological theorizing and research.

Notes

An earlier version of this paper was presented at the 1995 Meeting of the American Sociological Association, Washington DC, August. The authors wish to thank Maureen Bruce, Jeffrey Davis, L. Richard Della Fave, Gary Hill, Jacqueline Johnson, Alan Lizotte, Donald Tomaskovic-Devey and the editor and anonymous reviewers of *Theoretical Criminology* for helpful comments on earlier drafts. Direct correspondence to Marino A. Bruce, Department of Sociology, University of Wisconsin-Madison, 8128 Social Science Building, 1180 Observatory Drive, Madison, WI 53706 or via internet: mbruce@ssc.wisc.edu.

1. Despite the fact that violence has been a major topic of research for decades, little if any research has considered, much less addressed, the ambiguity surrounding its use as a concept. Although dealing with such conceptual distinctions is beyond the scope of this paper, we acknowledge that conceptualizing violence to include such forms as rape, robbery, assault, and homicide may be too broad. We suspect that the ideas we offer are most applicable to street and gang-related manifestations of violence, and perhaps weaker (but still somewhat significant) when applied to issues of domestic and personal (i.e. drug use, suicide, etc.) violence.
2. These ideas regarding subcultural tendencies and violence encompass explanations of differential rates of poverty, family dissolution, and substance abuse across racial/ethnic groups as well. In this regard, see especially Moynihan (1965) and Auletta (1982).
3. In this now landmark article, Blau and Blau (1982) attempted to establish the role of racial inequality (as opposed to just general deprivation) in the

creation of urban violent crime across 125 Standard Metropolitan Statistical Areas (SMSAs). The distinction made in this article between absolute deprivation and relative deprivation was important, as it was an issue overlooked in most analyses of crime prior to that time. In recent years, a growing body of research has attempted to determine which type of deprivation offers the more plausible explanation of African-American violence. For examples of research findings in this regard, see especially Messner (1982, 1983, 1989), Messner and Golden (1992), and Golden and Messner (1987).

4. The major methodological critique here was that research exploring violence outcomes often makes use of measures that are highly correlated. The result, it is argued, are collinearity problems that skew both the findings and subsequent conclusions. For elaboration of this point, see Land, McCall, and Cohen (1990).

5. For elaboration of these two frameworks, see Beck (1980) and Tomaskovic-Devey and Roscigno (1996).

6. Residential segregation practices, which are sometimes more intentional, have been implicated in the inability of non-whites to follow industry to other, often more suburban, locations (see Farley and Frey, 1994). We deal with the issue of residential segregation and its relation to economic and educational opportunity momentarily.

7. For a discussion of contemporary discrimination in pay, see Thomas, Herring, and Horton (1994) and Tomaskovic-Devey (1993).

8. Yancey, Ericksen, and Juliani (1976) demonstrate that many first generation immigrants formed enclaves with compatriots in order to have access to goods and services without the problems affiliated with language barriers.

9. Although the focus of this research is not on violence per se, Alex-Assensoh (1995) does focus on a variety of social behavioral outcomes that are typically thought of as representative of the underclass. These include welfare dependency, low educational attainment, perceptions of criminal activity, unemployment, lack of neighborhood role models, and diminished social and political participation.

References

Agnew, Robert (1992) 'Foundation for A General Strain Theory of Crime and Delinquency', *Criminology* 30: 47–66.

Alba, Richard D., John R. Logan and Paul E. Bellair (1994) 'Living with Crime: The Implications of Racial/Ethnic Differences in Suburban Location', *Social Forces* 73: 395–434.

Alex-Assensoh, Yvette (1995) 'Myths About Race and the Underclass: Concentrated Poverty and "Underclass Behaviors"', *Urban Affairs Review* 31: 3–19.

Anderson, Elijah (1978) *A Place on the Corner*. Chicago: University of Chicago Press.

Anderson, Elijah (1990) *Streetwise: Race Class and Change in an Urban Community.* Chicago: University of Chicago Press.

Anderson, Elijah (1994) 'The Code of the Streets', *Atlantic Monthly* 273: 80–91.

Auletta, Kenneth (1982) *The Underclass.* New York: Random House.

Balkwell, James W. (1990) 'Ethnic Inequality and the Rate of Homicide', *Social Forces* 69: 53–70.

Beck, E.M. (1980) 'Discrimination and White Economic Loss: A Time Series Examination', *Social Forces* 59: 148–68.

Blalock, Hubert M. (1967) *Toward a Theory of Minority Group Relations.* New York: John Wiley.

Blau, Judith R. and Peter M. Blau (1982) 'The Cost of Inequality: Metropolitan Structure and Violent Crime', *American Sociological Review* 47: 114–29.

Bonacich, Edna (1972) 'The Theory of Elite Antagonism: The Split Labor Market', *American Sociological Review* 37: 547–59.

Bonacich, Edna (1976) 'Advanced Capitalism and Black/White Race Relations in the United States: A Split Labor Market Interpretation', *American Sociological Review* 41: 35–51.

Bourdieu, Pierre (1977) *Reproduction in Education.* Beverly Hills, CA: Sage.

Braithwaite, John (1979) *Inequality, Crime and Public Policy.* London: Cambridge University Press.

Brown, Claude (1965) *Manchild in the Promised Land.* New York: MacMillan.

Brown, Cliff and Terry Boswell (1995) 'Strikebreaking or Solidarity in the Great Steel Strike of 1919: A Split Labor Market, Game-Theoretic, and QCA Analysis', *American Journal of Sociology* 100: 1479–519.

Bureau of Justice Statistics (1990) *BJS Data Report, 1989.* Washington, DC: US Government Printing Office.

Burr, Jeffrey A. and Jan E. Mutchler (1993) 'Ethnic Living Arrangements: Cultural Convergence or Cultural Manifestation', *Social Forces* 72: 169–79.

Bursik, Robert J. (1988) 'Social Disorganization and Theories of Crime and Delinquency', *Criminology* 26: 519–51.

Bursik, Robert J. and Harold G. Grasmick (1993) *Neighborhoods and Crime.* New York: Lexington Books.

Curtis, Lyn (1975) *Violence, Race and Culture.* Lexington, MA: Heath.

DiMaggio, Paul (1982) 'Cultural Capital and School Success: The Impact of Status Culture Participation on the Grades of U. S. High School Students', *American Sociological Review* 47: 189–201.

Duster, Troy (1987) 'Crime, Youth Unemployment, and the Black Urban Underclass', *Crime and Delinquency* 33: 300–16.

Elkins, Stanley (1959) *Slavery.* New York: Grossett and Dunlap.

Falk, William and Bruce Rankin (1992) 'The Cost of Being Black in the Black Belt', *Social Problems* 39: 299–313.

Farley, Reynolds and William H. Frey (1994) 'Changes in the Segregation of Whites from Blacks during the 1980s: Small Steps toward a More Integrated Society', *American Sociological Review* 59: 23–45.

Feagin, Joe R. and Melvin Sikes (1994) *Living with Racism*. Boston: Beacon Press.

Fordham, Signithia and John U. Ogbu (1986) 'Black Students' School Success: Coping with the Burden of Acting White', *Urban Review* 18: 176–206.

Fusfield, Daniel R. and Timothy Bates (1984) *The Political Economy of the Urban Ghetto*. Carbondale: Southern Illinois University Press.

Gibbs, Jewel T. (1988) *Young, Black, and Male in America: An Endangered Species*. New York: Auburn House.

Giddens, Anthony (1984) *The Constitution of Society*. Cambridge: Cambridge University Press.

Golden, Reid M. and Steven F. Messner (1987) 'Dimensions of Racial Inequality and Rates of Violent Crime', *Criminology* 25: 525–41.

Gottdiener, Mark and Joe Feagin (1988) 'The Paradigm Shift in Urban Sociology', *Urban Affairs Quarterly* 24: 163–87.

Grier, William H. and Price M. Cobbs (1968) *Black Rage*. New York: Basic Books, Inc.

Hagan, John (1985) 'Toward a Structural Theory of Crime, Race, and Gender: The Canadian Case', *Crime and Delinquency* 31: 129–46.

Hagan, John (1993) 'The Social Embeddedness of Crime and Unemployment', *Criminology* 31: 465–91.

Hagan, John and Ruth D. Peterson (1995) 'Criminal Inequality in America: Patterns and Consequences', in John Hagan and Ruth D. Peterson (eds) *Crime and Inequality*, pp. 14–36. Stanford, CA: Stanford University Press.

Harer, M.D. and Darnell Steffensmeier (1992) 'The Differing Effects of Economic Inequality on Black and White Rates of Violence', *Social Forces* 70: 1035–54.

Hargreaves, D.H. (1967) *Social Relations in Secondary School*. London: Tinling.

Hawkins, Darnell F. (1983) 'Black and White Homicide Differentials: Alternatives to an Inadequate Theory', *Criminal Justice and Behavior* 10: 407–40.

Hawkins, Darnell F. (1985) 'Black Homicide: The Adequacy of Existing Research for Devising Prevention Strategies', *Crime and Delinquency* 31: 83–103.

Hawkins, Darnell F. (1986) *Homicide Among Black Americans*. New York: University Press of America.

Hawkins, Darnell F. (1987) 'Beyond Anomalies: Rethinking the Conflict Perspective on Race and Criminal Punishment', *Social Forces* 65: 719–66.

Jaynes, Gerald D. and Robin M. Williams (1989) *A Common Destiny: Blacks and American Society*. Washington, DC: National Academy Press.

Jeff, Morris F. (1981) 'Why Black-On-Black Crime?', *The Urban League Review* 6: 25–34.

Kasarda, John D. (1989) 'Urban Industrial Transition and the Underclass', *AAPSS* 501: 26–47.

Keiser, R.L. (1979) *The Vice Lords: Warriors of the Streets*. New York: Holt, Rinehart and Winston.

Kirshenman, Joleen and Katherine M. Neckerman (1990) 'We'd Love To Hire Them But . . .: The Meaning of Race for Employers', in Christopher Jencks and Paul Petersen (eds) *The Urban Underclass*, pp. 203–32. Washington, DC: The Brookings Institution.

Lafree, Gary, K.A. Drass and Patrick O'Day (1992) 'Race and Crime in Postwar America: Determinants of African-American and White Rates, 1957–1988', *Criminology* 30: 157–88.

Land, Kenneth, Patricia L. McCall and Lawrence E. Cohen (1990) 'Structural Covariates of Homicide Rates: Are There Any Invariates Across Time and Social Space?', *American Journal of Sociology* 95: 922–63.

Lichter, Daniel T. (1989) 'Race, Employment Hardship and Inequality in the American Nonmetropolitan South', *American Sociological Review* 54: 436–46.

Lieberson, Stanley (1980) *A Piece of the Pie: Black and White Immigrants Since 1880*. Berkeley, CA: University of California Press.

Liebow, Elliot (1967) *Tally's Corner*. Boston: Little Brown and Company.

Loftin, C. and R.H. Hill (1974) 'Regional Subculture and Homicide: An Examination of the Gastil-Hackney Thesis', *American Sociological Review* 39: 714–24.

Logan, J. and Harvey Molotch (1987) *Urban Fortunes: The Political Economy of Place*. Berkeley, CA: University of California Press.

Majors, Richard and Janet M. Billson (1992) *Cool Pose: The Dilemmas of Black Manhood in America*. New York: Touchstone.

Martinez, Ramiro (1996) 'Latinos and Lethal Violence: The Impact of Poverty and Inequality', *Social Problems* 43: 131–46.

Massey, Douglas S. and Nancy A. Denton (1987) 'Trends in the Residential Segregation of Blacks, Hispanics, and Asians: 1970–1980', *American Sociological Review* 52: 802–25.

Massey, Douglas S. and Andrew B. Gross (1991) 'Explaining Trends in Residential Segregation, 1970–1980', *Urban Affairs Quarterly* 27: 13–35.

McCall, Nathan (1994) *Makes Me Wanna Holler*. New York: Vintage Books.

McCall, Patricia L., Kenneth Land and Lawrence Cohen (1992) 'Violent Criminal Behavior: Is There a General and Continuing Influence of the South?', *Social Science Research* 21: 286–310.

Merton, Robert K. (1938) 'Social Structure and Anomie', *American Sociological Review* 3: 672–82.

Messerschmidt, James W. (1986) *Capitalism, Patriarchy and Crime: Toward a Socialist Feminist Criminology*. Totowa, NJ: Rowman and Littlefield.

Messerschmidt, James W. (1993) *Masculinities and Crime: Critique and Reconceptualization of Theory*. Lanham, MD: Rowman and Littlefield.

Messner, Steven F. (1982) 'Poverty, Inequality, and the Urban Homicide Rate: Some Unexpected Findings', *Criminology* 20: 103–14.

Messner, Steven F. (1983) 'Regional and Racial Effects on the Urban Homicide Rate: The Subculture of Violence Revisited', *American Journal of Sociology* 88: 997–1007.

Rates: Further Evidence on the Cost of Inequality', *American Sociological Review* 54: 597–6

Messner, Steven F. and Reid M. Golden (1992) 'Racial Inequality and Racially Disaggregated Homicide Rates: An Assessment of Alternative Theoretical Explanations', *Criminology* 30: 421–45.

Molotch, Harvey (1988) 'Strategies and Constraints of Growth Elites', in Scott Cummings (ed.) *Business Elites and Urban Development*, pp. 25–47. Albany, NY: SUNY Press.

Moynihan, Daniel P. (1965) *The Negro Family*. Washington, DC: United States Department of Labor.

Nelson, Candace, Jay Corzine and Lin Huff-Corzine (1994) 'The Violent West Reexamined: A Research Note on Regional Homicide Rates', *Criminology* 32: 135–48.

Ogbu, John (1978) *Minority Education and Caste: The American System in Cross-Cultural Perspective*. New York: Academic Press

Olzak, Susan (1992) *The Dynamics of Ethnic Competition & Conflict*. Stanford: Stanford University Press.

Palley, H.A. and D.A. Robinson (1990) 'Black-On-Black Crime: Poverty, Marginality, and the Underclass Debate from a Global Perspective', *Social Development Issues* 12: 52–61.

Parker, Robert N. (1989) 'Poverty, Subculture of Violence and Type of Homicide', *Social Forces* 67: 983–1007.

Reich, Michael (1981) *Racial Inequality: A Political Economic Analysis*. Princeton: Princeton University Press.

Rodriguez, Orlando (1990) 'Hispanics and Homicide in New York City', in Jess Kraus, Susan Sorenson, and Paul Juarez (eds) *Research Conference on Violence and Homicide in Hispanic Communities*, pp. 67–84. Washington, DC: Office of Minority Health, Dept. of Health and Human Services.

Roscigno, Vincent J. (1995) 'The Social Embeddedness of Racial Educational Inequality: The Black–White Gap and the Impact of Racial and Local Political–Economic Contexts', *Research in Social Stratification and Mobility* 14: 137–68.

Roscigno, Vincent J. and Marino A. Bruce (1995) 'Racial Inequality and Social Control: Historical and Contemporary Patterns in the U.S. South', *Sociological Spectrum* 15: 323–49.

Sampson, Robert J. (1985) 'Race and Criminal Violence: A Demographically Disaggregated Analysis of Urban Homicide', *Crime and Delinquency* 31: 47–82.

Sampson, Robert J. (1987) 'Urban Black Violence: The Effect of Male Joblessness and Family Disruption', *American Journal of Sociology* 93: 348–82.

Sampson, Robert J. and William J. Wilson (1995) 'Toward a Theory of Race, Crime and Urban Inequality', in John Hagan and Ruth D. Peterson (eds) *Crime and Inequality*, pp. 37–54. Stanford,CA: Stanford University Press.

Scott, Kody (1993) *Monster: The Autobiography of an L.A. Gang Member*. New York: Peguin.

Shaw, Clifford R. and Henry D. McKay (1942) *Juvenile Delinquency and Urban Areas*. Chicago: University of Chicago Press.

Squires, Gregory D., Ruthanne DeWolfe, and Alan S. DeWolfe (1979) 'Urban Decline or Disinvestment: Uneven Development, Redlining, and the Role of the Insurance Industry', *Social Problems* 27: 79–95.

Squires, Gregory D., William Valez, and Karl E. Taeuber (1991) 'Insurance Redlining, Agency Location, and the Process of Urban Disinvestment', *Urban Affairs Quarterly* 26: 567–88.

Staples, Robert (1986) 'The Masculine Way of Violence', in Darnell Hawkins (ed.) *Homicide Among Black Americans*, pp. 137–53. New York: University Press of America.

Szymanski, Albert (1976) 'Racial Discrimination and White Gain', *American Sociological Review* 41: 403–14.

Taylor, Ronald L. (1979) 'Black Ethnicity and the Persistence of Ethnogenesis', *American Journal of Sociology* 84: 1401–23.

Thomas, Melvin E., Cedric Herring and Haywood Derrick Horton (1994) 'Discrimination Over the Life Course: A Synthetic Cohort Analysis of Earnings Differences Between Black and White Males, 1940–1990', *Social Problems* 41: 608–28.

Tomaskovic-Devey, Barbara and Donald Tomaskovic-Devey (1983) 'The Social Structural Determinants of Ethnic Group Behavior: Single Ancestry Rates Among Four White American Ethnic Groups', *American Sociological Review* 53: 650–9.

Tomaskovic-Devey, Donald (1993) *Gender & Racial Inequality at Work: The Sources and Consequences of Job Segregation*. Ithaca, NY: ILR Press.

Tomaskovic-Devey, Donald and Vincent J. Roscigno (1996) 'Racial Economic Subordination and White Gain in the U.S. South', *American Sociological Review* 61: 565–89.

Wacquant, Loic J.D. and William J. Wilson (1989) 'The Cost of Racial and Class Exclusion in the Inner City', *AAPSS* 501: 8–25.

Wardell, Mark and Anna M. Zajicek (1995) 'Social Problems: Pathways for Transcending Exclusive Sociology', *Social Problems* 42: 301–17.

Willis, Paul (1981) *Learning to Labor: How Working Class Kids Get Working Class Jobs*. New York: Columbia University Press.

Wilson, C.A. (1992) 'Restructuring and the Growth of Concentrated Poverty in Detroit', *Urban Affairs Quarterly* 28: 187–205.

Wilson, William J. (1978) *The Declining Significance of Race*. Chicago: University of Chicago Press.

Wilson, William J. (1987) *The Truly Disadvantaged: The Inner City, the Underclass and Public Policy*. Chicago: University of Chicago Press.

Wolfgang, Marvin E. and Franco Ferracuti (1967) *The Subculture of Violence: Towards an Integrated Theory in Criminology*. London: Tavistock Publications.

Yancey, William L., Eugene P. Ericksen, and Richard N. Juliani (1976) 'Emergent Ethnicity: A Review and Reformulation', *American Sociological Review* 41: 391–403.

MARINO A. BRUCE is currently an Anna Julia Cooper Fellow and Assistant Professor of Sociology at the University of Wisconsin-Madison. His research deals with stratification, context and their consequences for inequality reproduction and criminological outcomes. Currently he is exploring structures of race and class-based opportunity in the contemporary US and its implications for the unfolding of masculinity, including various forms of violence. [email: mbruce@ssc.wisc.edu]

VINCENT J. ROSCIGNO is an Assistant Professor in the Department of Sociology at the Ohio State University. His research focuses on political and group mobilization processes as they pertain to race, gender, and class inequality, as well as education and educational opportunity. Some of this work has recently been published in *Sociological Spectrum* (1995), *Research in Social Stratification and Mobility* (1995), and *American Sociological Review* (1996). [email: Roscigno.1@osu.edu]

PATRICIA L. MCCALL is Associate Professor of Sociology at North Carolina State University. Her recent research interests include the study of the effects of structural covariates on suicide and race-specific homicide, micromodeling of criminal careers, and the evaluation of delinquency prevention programs. [email: Patty@server.sasw.ncsu.edu]

Part II
Domestic Violence

[5]

PARTNER ABUSE AND GENERAL CRIME: HOW ARE THEY THE SAME? HOW ARE THEY DIFFERENT?*

TERRIE E. MOFFITT
UNIVERSITY OF LONDON
UNIVERSITY OF WISCONSIN-MADISON

ROBERT F. KRUEGER
UNIVERSITY OF MINNESOTA-TWIN CITIES

AVSHALOM CASPI
UNIVERSITY OF LONDON
UNIVERSITY OF WISCONSIN-MADISON

JEFF FAGAN
COLUMBIA UNIVERSITY

Both partner abuse and general crime violate the rights and safety of victims. But are these phenomena the same or are they distinct, demanding their own research and intervention specialties? Are persons who abuse their partners the same people who commit other criminal behavior? Do partner abuse and general crime share the same correlates? We investigated these questions in a birth cohort of over 800 young adults, by testing whether a personality model known to predict general crime would also predict partner abuse. Personality data were gathered at age 18, and self-reported partner abuse and general criminal offending were measured at age 21. Results from modeling latent constructs showed that partner abuse and general crime represent different constructs that are moderately related; they are not merely two expressions of the same underlying antisocial propensity. Group comparisons showed many, but not all, partner abusers also engaged in violence against nonintimates. Personality analyses showed that partner abuse and general crime shared a strong propensity from a trait called Negative Emotionality. However, crime was related to weak Constraint (low self-control), but partner abuse was not. All findings applied to women as well as to men, suggesting that women's partner abuse may

* This study was supported by grants from the National Institute of Mental Health (MH45070, MH49414, MH56344), by fellowships from the University of Wisconsin, and by the U.K. Medical Research Council. The Dunedin Multidisciplinary Health and Development Research Unit is supported by the New Zealand Health Research Council. We are grateful to the Dunedin Unit director, Phil Silva, the investigators and staff, and the Study members.

200   MOFFITT ET AL.

be motivated by the same intra-personal features that motivate men's abuse. The results are consistent with theoretical and applied arguments about the "uniqueness" of partner violence relative to other crime and violence.

A longstanding conviction that intimate violence is unique has fostered the growth of specialist research and intervention fields for partner abuse. As a result, most theory and research into partner abuse has remained separate from theory and research into crime, and this separation has diverted attention from questions about associations between partner abuse and crime. Such questions are worth looking into, because if partner abuse were found to be empirically indistinct from general crime, the premise that partner abuse needs its own specialist research effort fueled by its own funding initiatives may be unfounded. Existing and emerging theories of criminal, antisocial, and violent behavior might well explain partner abuse with parsimony. Moreover, if partner abuse is not distinct from general crime, justice policies of tailoring special preventions, reha- bilitations, therapies, and controls for perpetrators of partner violence may be misguided and uneconomical. Thus, the important goals of parsi- monious theory and frugal resource management make research into the relation between partner abuse and other crime a priority for science and for policy. These questions have received some attention in the research literature (Avakame, 1998; Fagan and Wexler, 1987; Hotaling et al., 1990; Marvell and Moody, 1999; Shields et al., 1988), but more attention seems warranted, given what is at stake.

In the research reported here, we investigated the relation between partner abuse and general criminal offending among the young men and women of the Dunedin birth cohort (Silva and Stanton, 1996). We also applied to partner abuse a personality model that has already been shown in this journal and elsewhere to predict crime and violent offending (Caspi et al., 1994) to test how well the personality profile derived for general crime would fit partner abuse.

PRIOR STUDIES OF RELATIONS BETWEEN PARTNER ABUSE AND CRIME

The relation between partner abuse and general crime has been approached via two methods of analysis. Most analyses have asked whether individuals who commit partner abuse are the *same people* who commit violence toward nonintimates. A few complementary analyses have asked whether measured partner abuse and nonintimate violence share the *same correlates*. Both approaches are needed, because even 100% overlap between partner abusers and general criminals would not

PARTNER ABUSE AND GENERAL CRIME 201

rule out the possibility that the two forms of behavior represent distinct theoretical constructs with different causal origins. Likewise, zero overlap between partner abusers and general criminals would not rule out the possibility that partner abuse and general crime have the same causes. In the next sections, we review findings from studies using these two approaches.

ARE PARTNER ABUSERS AND OTHER OFFENDERS THE SAME PEOPLE?

Partner violence theorizing originally emerged from the unexamined premise that batterers are specialists in violence who specialize further, victimizing women intimates exclusively as victims. This specialization premise remained largely unexamined for some time because of the bifurcation between the fields of domestic violence research and criminology. Until recently, neither group measured each other's dependent variable, and domestic violence researchers seemed unaware of the ongoing debate within criminology about whether offense specialization exists. Uncovering whether anyone at all specializes in violence has been a significant challenge for criminology (Brennan et al., 1989; Britt, 1996; Lattimore et al., 1994), and thus it is reasonable to remain skeptical about whether anyone specializes further in violence against intimates. The existence of a significant proportion of partner-abuse perpetrators who are not selective with regard to their choice of offense and victim would challenge theories of partner abuse.

Consistent with this healthy skepticism, evidence is accumulating to suggest that many, if not most, partner abusers do not specialize, but engage in violence against nonintimates as well as a variety of nonviolent crimes (Fagan and Wexler, 1987). Reviews of this literature conclude that the overlap between partner violence and other crime exceeds the amount of co-occurrence expected by chance and is substantial, although the overlap is far from 100% (Fagan and Browne, 1994; Holtzworth-Munroe and Stuart, 1994; Hotaling et al., 1990; Marvell and Moody, 1999). There is some evidence of overlap among female as well as male perpetrators (Felson and Messner, 1998; Greenfield et al., 1998; Hotaling et al., 1990; McNeely and Mann, 1990). The true extent of overlap varies widely across studies depending on the source of research subjects and the methods of measurement, and therefore, it remains uncertain. One reason that knowledge about overlap remains uncertain is that past studies have usually compared pairs of partner violence measures and crime measures that had different sources of measurement error and bias and have covered different reporting periods or different crime-recording jurisdictions. For example, some studies compare official conviction records of one type of violence (which undercount illegal behavior a lot) with self-reports or victim reports of the other type (which undercount much less).

202   MOFFITT ET AL.

In the present study, we analyzed the relation between partner abuse and general crime using confirmatory factor analysis to model the latent structure underlying observed indicators of partner abuse and general crime. We analyzed measures of *general partner abuse* that included acts of both psychological and physical abuse and measures of *general crime* that included acts of theft, fraud, vice, and physical force. The observed indicators were matched as closely as possible on measurement method, reporting period, and reliability. This modeling strategy tested whether partner abuse and general crime are manifestations of a single underlying construct versus two separate constructs. We also separately analyzed measures restricted to physical acts of violence; we calculated percentages of overlapping cases between groups who committed *violent partner abuse* and *violent crime*, and we quantified the *odds* that a person who hits partners also hits nonintimates. However, as noted earlier, even if 100% of partner abusers also engaged in general crime, this would not preclude the possibility that the two behaviors have different causes. Thus, an important complementary test is whether antisocial behavior toward an intimate versus nonintimate victim is predicted by the same correlates.

DO PARTNER ABUSE AND OTHER CRIME SHARE THE SAME CORRELATES?

Prospective longitudinal studies reveal that the childhood and adolescent antecedents of adult partner violence are remarkably reminiscent of the risk factors for general crime (Farrington, 1994; Magdol et al., 1998a). In addition, longitudinal studies show strong continuity from childhood and adolescent antisocial behaviors to later partner abuse across the individual life course and across generations (Capaldi and Clark, 1998; Farrington, 1994; Giordano et al., 1999; Huesmann et al., 1984; Magdol et al., 1998a; Simons et al., 1998; Simons et al., 1995). These studies provide conceptual evidence that the causes of partner abuse may be the same as the causes of general crime, but direct empirical comparisons of the relative strength of correlates of partner abuse and general crime measured in the same sample are needed. There are two direct comparisons of the predictors and correlates in the backgrounds of partner-violence versus other-violence perpetrators (Farrington, 1994; Shields et al., 1988), and a direct comparison of intimate versus stranger victimizations among 22,000 1980 to 1982 homicides (Avakame, 1998). These studies show that partner abuse and general crime share many of the demographic, developmental, and macrolevel correlates that have strong effects. However, they also provide evidence that partner abuse may have some unique correlates, albeit with weaker effects. To add to the growing evidence base on this question, we analyzed the relation between partner abuse and general

PARTNER ABUSE AND GENERAL CRIME 203

crime by comparing whether the personality profiles that predict the two forms of perpetrators' behavior are the same or different.

THE PERSONALITY MODEL OF GENERAL CRIME

In the past, criminologists were skeptical about personality (Stitt and Giacopassi, 1992), but recent studies have demonstrated that personality psychology can make a contribution to crime research by using personality instruments that overcome methodological concerns and by integrating personality with other criminological theory (Farrington, 1994; Wright et al., 1999). One personality profile has proven to play a particularly useful role in understanding crime. This profile has replicated robustly across males and females, whites and African Americans, adults and young adolescents, and samples from different nations, using either official or self-report measures of crime, and using several different instruments for assessing personality (Caspi et al., 1994; Elkins et al., 1997; Krueger et al., 1994). The personality profile has been found to relate to a developmental trajectory of life-course-persistent antisocial behavior (Moffitt et al., 1996) and to predict conviction for violent crime (Caspi et al., 1997). Personality is most often assessed via self-reports, but the same criminal personality profile is obtained when another informant provides the data (Moffitt et al., 1995). Moreover, a naive observer's impressions of a child's personality recorded at age 3 can predict recidivistic criminal conviction 18 years later, albeit with modest accuracy (Caspi et al., 1996).

The method for assessing crime-prone personality characteristics used in our research is the Multidimensional Personality Questionnaire (MPQ; Tellegen, 1982). With respect to research into crime—and partner abuse—the MPQ assessment is a systematic method of gathering psychological clues as to why behaviors occur by considering the attitudes, values, and beliefs that perpetrators have about themselves and others, the emotions perpetrators tend to experience readily, and the kinds of activities and settings that perpetrators prefer. The MPQ is simply a systematic way of quantifying these characteristics and organizing them into a proven theoretical model of the structure of human personality. The MPQ model emphasizes three primary personality factors that are derived from a large number of descriptors. Some of these descriptors are theoretically relevant to antisocial behavior (although they share no content with measures of criminal behavior). The MPQ asks about one's beliefs about close relationships ("I could pull up my roots, leave my home, my parents, and my friends without regretting it"), about one's expectations about the behavior of others ("Most people stay friendly only as long as it is to their advantage"), about one's attitudes towards aggression ("When someone hurts me, I try to get even"), about how one usually reacts to stress ("I often get irritated at little annoyances"), about one's values ("As young people grow up, they ought to try to carry out some of their rebellious ideas instead of just settling down"), and about one's preferred style of approaching the environment ("It would be fun to explore an old abandoned house at night"). In the MPQ (and other instruments), the personality profile that robustly predicts general crime features two primary personality characteristics, called Constraint and Negative Emotionality, which are described next.

As anticipated by many criminologists, criminal behavior is predicted by a lack of Constraint. This personality characteristic is already well-known to criminologists as "low self-control," which plays the starring role in one of the most important contemporary theories of general crime (Gottfredson and Hirshi, 1990). In the MPQ system, this personality factor is labeled "Constraint" and operationalized when research participants describe themselves as reflective, cautious, careful, rational, and planful; when they say they endorse high moral standards and feel most comfortable in a conservative social environment; and when they say they avoid excitement and danger, preferring safe activities even if they are tedious. A large body of psychometric research has demonstrated that these qualities empirically factor together, forming one broad feature of human personality (Church and Burke, 1994; Tellegen and Waller, 2000).

A finding that was less anticipated by criminology theory was that self-control is not the lone star that predicts crime. A characteristic labeled "Negative Emotionality" is just as essential. Although less well-known to criminological theorists, Negative Emotionality has a rich empirical and theoretical nomological net in other behavioral sciences (Watson et al., 1994). In the MPQ, it is operationalized when research participants describe themselves as nervous, vulnerable, prone to worry, and unable to cope with stress; when they say they have a low threshold for feeling tense, fearful, and angry; when they feel suspicious, expect mistreatment, and see the world as being peopled with potential enemies; and when they say they seek revenge for slights, take advantage of other people, and find it fun to frighten others. These qualities, too, empirically factor together (Church and Burke, 1994; Tellegen and Waller, 2000).

PERSONALITY AND PARTNER VIOLENCE

Some partner abuse researchers, like criminologists in the past, are likely to greet a personality model of partner abuse with ambivalence. One author wrote that, "The search for psychological causal factors or distinct personality configurations associated with wife abuse has not proven very useful" (Bograd, 1988:17), and a National Academy of Sciences review concurred (Fagan and Browne, 1994). This pessimism is justified

PARTNER ABUSE AND GENERAL CRIME 205

because partner abuse research has not availed itself of modern systems of personality measurement nor been guided by proven theories of personality structure. Nonetheless, some batterer intervention programs assess personality disturbances for treatment planning (Healey et al., 1998) and a few theorists embrace personality concepts (Browne, 1987; Dutton, 1998). However, when we read the literature, it is clear that the field relies heavily, albeit implicitly, on personality constructs. Clinical descriptions of male abusers use adjectives such as anxious, angry, hostile, alienated, remorseless, compulsive, suspicious, emotionally volatile, overcontrolling, dominant, aggressive, impulsive, or undercontrolled. Summarizing the results of 14 studies, Hotaling et al. (1990:439) describe male partner-abusers as "over-controlled loners, cowards, approval seeking, extremely jealous, dependent and passive, fearing abandonment, lacking in assertiveness, having low self-esteem, having no impulse control, neurotic, frustration-displacing, moody, immature and hysterical, angry, and having feelings of incompetence, inadequacy, and worthlessness." Many of these adjectives are reminiscent of the known personality characteristics of generally criminal persons: high Negative Emotionality and weak Constraint (impulsivity or low self-control).

Clinical descriptions of the psychological makeup of abusers are echoed in the motivations attributed to abusers by specialized theories of domestic violence. We highlight two features of these theories. First, these theories tacitly assume that partner abuse is unique and specialized, and they imply that partner abuse should not be subsumed by general theories of criminal behavior (Hotaling et al., 1990). In essence, each of the theories of partner abuse is a theory of victim choice. Each theory attempts to explain the behavior of individuals who are prone to antisocial behavior uniquely directed at their intimate partners, for reasons unique to an intimate relationship. Thus, the victim's female gender and her intimate relationship to the perpetrator are the mainsprings that drive most theories of partner violence (Marvell and Moody, 1999). Second, a closer look at these theories reveals that they make implicit use of personality characteristics of the individual. They tacitly imply that men who abuse their partners tend to experience certain emotions, prefer certain behavioral styles, and hold certain beliefs, attitudes, and values about the self and others; i.e., individual differences in personality.

Feminist theory suggests that partner abuse is special because, unlike general crime, it can be uniquely attributed to the influence of patriarchal cultural values on the behavior of individual male perpetrators (Dobash and Dobash, 1992; Yllö, 1993). That is, violence is a tool for ensuring men's domination over women (Dobash and Dobash, 1992). "Batterers. . . choose to use or threaten violence because of its effectiveness in controlling their partners" (Healey et al., 1998:24). The motives that drive the

206   MOFFITT ET AL.

abuser's strategic use of violence are articulated by feminist theorists in personality terms suggestive of Negative Emotionality: Men's emotional arousal, such as fear or anger, is channeled by patriarchal ideology into aggression against women. Feminist writers speak of abusers' needs for power, control and domination, hypersensitivity to perceived threats to control, and overreaction to self-vulnerability (Fagan and Browne, 1994), all of which are aspects of Negative Emotionality. In contrast, feminist writers would seem to take a dim view of a role for Constraint in explaining abuse. "According to the feminist model, although they may claim to feel out of control, batterers are *not* out of control: battering is a decision, a choice" (Healey et al., 1998:24). In this view, abuse of a partner is deliberately and strategically employed by an abuser to manipulate the partner's behavior so as to meet the abuser's needs. Translation of this theoretical tenet to personality terms yields the hypothesis that partner abusers are not impulsive, and therefore, partner abuse may be unrelated to individual differences in Constraint. Interestingly, this feminist hypothesis contradicts the aforementioned clinical description of batterers as "having no impulse control" and "immature and hysterical" (Hotaling et al., 1990).

Sociobiological accounts of partner abuse also emphasize its uniqueness from general crime based on the victim's gender and her relationship to the perpetrator. For example, Daly and Wilson's (1988) evolutionary theory of wife beating and murder emphasizes sexual proprietariness as a motivation for men's coercing women through violence. From an evolutionary perspective, if men are to invest in offspring, they will be motivated to ensure their paternity. For this reason, they will take whatever steps are necessary—including violence against their wives—to prevent or punish real or suspected extramarital sex. Translating this perspective to personality terms, risk for partner abuse should be enhanced by a tendency to experience jealousy, expect rejection, and suspect betrayal (Downey and Feldman, 1996), which are aspects of Negative Emotionality.

Other theorists have also suggested that intimate abuse may necessitate unique theories. These writers, including family sociologists, marital therapists, and criminologists (Gelles and Straus, 1979; Giles-Sims, 1983; Megargee, 1982), argue that partner abuse is unlike general crime because it is part of a continuing pattern of intrafamilial interaction. In this view, partner abuse will be difficult to understand if separated from its intimate context. In particular relation to personality, in the context of an intimate relationship, an individual's tendency to perceive all arousal as anger (Healey et al., 1998) and to experience negative emotions, such as anger, fear, and rage, very rapidly and with extreme intensity are thought to contribute to the escalation of conflict from verbal to physical violence

(Jacobson et al., 1994). Such tendencies are central to Negative Emotionality.

Our reading of the abuse literature suggests the hypothesis that, like crime, partner abuse will be related to Negative Emotionality. The literature does not point to a clear hypothesis about Constraint; the writings of some clinicians suggest that partner abuse will relate to it, but the writings of some feminist theorists suggest that partner abuse will not. Although empirical research on the personality characteristics of partner-abusive individuals has implicated some of the same personality characteristics known to predict crime (see O'Leary, 1993), we report here the first systematic comparison to address the question of whether partner abuse has the same personality profile as general crime.

STUDYING BOTH MEN AND WOMEN

Our sample contains both sexes, and we examined both men and women as perpetrators of general crime and partner abuse. Because this may surprise some readers, we explain why. Our prior reports showed that, although females produce less crime than males, the personality profiles associated with male and female offending do not differ (Krueger et al., 1994). The gender story for partner abuse may not be so straightforward. There is much controversy about whether women commit partner abuse and if the abuse they commit is worthy of research attention (Straus, 1998). Contributing to the controversy is the fact that epidemiological studies have generated discrepant estimates of female perpetration. These discrepant findings appear to depend on whether the data collection method emphasizes the context of crime versus the context of the partner relationship (Mihalic and Elliott, 1997). When victims are asked about the identity of their assailant in the context of an interview about their assault victimization experiences, female and male victims report very low overall rates of partner abuse and male victims report relatively low rates of perpetration by women (e.g., Bachman and Saltzman, 1995; Langley et al., 1997; Tjaden and Thoennes, 1998). In contrast, when respondents are asked about abusive acts in the context of an interview about their relationships with partners, they report much higher overall rates of partner-abuse, and the rates and types of reported partner-abuse perpetration by women are similar to (or even slightly greater than) those of men. Moreover, in these studies, the finding that women commit abuse has been corroborated by reports from both male victims and women perpetrators (Magdol et al., 1997; Morse, 1995; Straus, 1998), in some cases, within the same couple (Moffitt et al., 1997). The sample for the present research contains women who reported partner abuse and general crime. Given our prior finding that men and women who commit general crime have the same personality profile, it is important to ask whether this gender similarity extends to partner abuse. There is some reason to expect that men and women who report partner abuse will not share personality features, and we turn to this next.

The finding that women participate in partner abuse is generally met with the observation that any acts attributed to women must have been motivated by self-defense. Personality research can address this hypothesis, because the hypothesis implies that women's perpetration does not originate from the same structure of deviant attitudes, beliefs, values, emotions, and preferred behavioral styles that promotes men's perpetration. If women's perpetration represents mainly self-defense, we would not expect personality characteristics that predict male perpetration to replicate for female perpetration. Self-defensive acts should not be predicted by Negative Emotionality characteristics, such as the tendency to anger when dominance is threatened, finding enjoyment in frightening others, or irrational suspiciousness, nor by Constraint characteristics, such as disregard for social norms or a preference for excitement over safety. Some personality variables linked to abuse perpetration among men (e.g., aggressivity) have also been linked to abuse perpetration by women (O'Leary et al., 1994), but the matter has not been studied in depth. In this study, we explicitly tested the hypothesis that there would be sex differences in the relation between personality and abuse perpetration.

METHODS

RESEARCH PARTICIPANTS

Our research participants were part of an unselected birth cohort that has been studied extensively for over 20 years as part of the Dunedin Multidisciplinary Health and Development Study (Silva and Stanton, 1996). It is a longitudinal investigation of the health, development, and behavior of a cohort of 1,037 births (52% boys) between April 1, 1972 and March 31, 1973, in Dunedin, New Zealand, a city of 120,000. The children's families were representative of the social class and ethnic distribution in the general population of New Zealand's South Island. Fewer than 7% identify themselves as nonwhite.

The Dunedin birth cohort includes persons who had experienced all levels of partner abuse, from no abuse to injurious abuse (Langley et al., 1997), thereby improving the generalizability of findings over studies of the personalities and criminal histories of batterers recruited from treatment programs, in which unrepresentativeness may bias and distort true effect sizes (Karney et al., 1995). Assessing a birth cohort also obviated difficulties with finding appropriate comparisons for abusers; prior studies' "control" groups have been found to show rates of intimate violence approaching 33% (Holtzworth-Munroe et al., 1992). Because partner violence is concentrated among young adults, unmarried cohabitors, and those with low income and education (Bachman and Saltzman, 1995; Magdol et al., 1998b), we studied this cohort of young adults who were involved in dating and cohabiting relationships, as well as marriage, and who represented a wide range of socioeconomic circumstances.

Published cross-national comparisons of rates of social problems lend confidence about generalizing findings from the Dunedin study to other industrialized nations. With specific reference to this report, New Zealand and the United States show very comparable prevalence rates of assault, rape, robbery, burglary, and auto theft in national victimization surveys (Van Dijk and Mayhew, 1992), and the Dunedin sample closely matches the prevalence among young adults of similar age from international and American surveys of self-reports of delinquent offenses (Junger-Tas et al., 1994) and partner abuse (for comparisons, see Magdol et al., 1997).

The Dunedin sample has been reassessed every two or three years, most recently at age 21. The basic research procedure involves bringing each study member into the research unit, where various research topics are presented in different private interview rooms as standardized modules, each given by a different examiner, in counterbalanced order across study members (e.g., partner abuse interview, physical exam, self-report delinquency interview, dental exam; or the opposite order). At age 18, 938 (92%) of the 1,020 still-living study members participated in the personality assessment. At age 21, 956 (94%) were interviewed about crime participation and 941 (92%) were interviewed about their intimate relationships, although 80 unable to report about partner abuse because they had not dated anyone in the past 12 months were dropped from the analyses reported here. The final sample size for analyses requiring data about personality, crime, and partner abuse was $N = 815$; for analyses requiring data only about crime and partner abuse, $N = 849$.

PERSONALITY ASSESSMENT AT AGE 18

Sample members completed the MPQ to assess individual differences in three primary factors of personality: Behavioral Constraint, Negative Emotionality, and Positive Emotionality (Tellegen and Waller, 2000). Individuals high on Constraint tend to avoid thrills, endorse social norms, and act in a cautious and restrained manner. Individuals high on Negative Emotionality have a low general threshold for the experience of negative emotions, such as anxiety and anger, tend to break down under stress, and perceive the world as threatening. Individuals high on Positive Emotionality value close relationships with others, are confident, have a low threshold for the experience of positive emotions, such as contentment or

210   MOFFITT ET AL.

happiness, and tend to view life as being essentially a pleasurable experience.

We measured personality prospectively, at age 18, three years before assessing partner abuse or crime for the current research. In studies of adjudicated or clinical samples, in which personality is assessed after abuse has been identified, it is difficult to determine whether the personality profile antedated partner abuse or whether, to the contrary, the dynamics of a relationship influenced the personality profile. In addition, self-reports of personality may be distorted if research participants in legal or clinical settings do not trust confidentiality guarantees, or if they surmise the study's aims. Prospective personality assessment avoided some of these pitfalls.

MEASUREMENT OF GENERAL CRIME AND PARTNER ABUSE AT AGE 21

The measures of general crime and of partner abuse tapped different content, but were matched as closely as possible on method. First, for clarity of interpretation, our two measures contained no overlapping item content. Second, both measures indexed the *variety* of antisocial actions taken by perpetrators. Third, both of these "variety" measures covered a *range* of antisocial behaviors, from nonviolent to severe, physically violent acts. Fourth, to control for source variance, both our measures were derived from perpetrators' self-reports. Fifth, we used a one-year reporting period for both measures.

CRIMINAL BEHAVIOR AT AGE 21

We used the Self-Report Delinquency Interview (Elliott and Huizinga, 1989), a method that has good reliability and validity under circumstances such as those in our study: The reporting period is one year, and the respondents have a long history of unbroken trust in our guarantee of confidentiality. In this research, we used 49 items, encompassing four major classes of criminal behaviors: theft (12 criminal behaviors), fraud (9 criminal behaviors), vice (23 criminal behaviors), and force (5 criminal behaviors). The five interview questions used to assess crimes of physical force had been reworded to instruct respondents to exclude force against a partner. Two other items that inquire about attacking and hitting intimates were omitted from this scale in the present analyses to avoid content overlap with our measure of partner abuse. Items were dummy-recoded for this study into a "yes" or "no" format for a reporting period of the past 12 months.

PARTNER ABUSE AND GENERAL CRIME 211

PARTNER ABUSE AT AGE 21

To allow privacy while overcoming any problems with literacy, the interviewer read each partner abuse item aloud and the respondent circled "yes" or "no" on an answer sheet to show whether the behavior happened in the past year. The study members interviewed about partner abuse comprised 91% who reported about partner abuse with their current or most recent intimate partner over the past year, and a further 9% who reported that they had dated *at least once or twice each month* over the past year and were therefore asked questions about partner abuse in their dating experiences. The average length of the relationships about which the study members reported was 17 months (S.D. = 17 mos.). The correlation between length of the relationship and variety of abusive behaviors was .29. Only 14% of the relationships had begun before the age-18 personality assessment.

In this research we used 33 items encompassing two major classes of abusive behaviors. The item list has been published elsewhere (Moffitt et al., 1997). It includes physical violence (13 items) and psychological abuse that captures controlling, demeaning, and other psychologically abusive behavior (20 items). The set of items was thus conceptually similar to the counterpart set of items measuring self-reported crime, which comprised both physically violent and nonviolent offenses. In our previous study of inter-partner agreement on this instrument with 360 couples, latent correlations between perpetrator and victim reports of perpetrators' abuse ranged from .71 to .83 and did not differ according to the perpetrator's sex (Moffitt et al., 1997). Because both partners' reports measured the same construct (i.e., perpetrator's abuse), these correlations are "coefficients of determination," which are directly interpreted as the variance explained without being squared (Ozer, 1985), suggesting that the men's and women's reports of their own perpetration obtained for this study are reliable and valid.

RESULTS

Our analyses addressed the following three questions: (1) How much overlap is there between partner abuse and general crime in a representative sample of young adults? That is, are partner abuse and general crime the same or different phenomena? (2) Would the personality characteristics that predict partner abuse and general crime be the same or different? (3) Narrowing the focus from abuse and crime to physical acts, would the same or different personality characteristics predict *physical partner violence* and *violent criminal offending*?

212   MOFFITT ET AL.

PARTNER ABUSE AND CRIMINAL BEHAVIOR: ONE FACTOR OR TWO?

Are partner abuse and criminal behavior the same or different things? To answer this question, we conducted a confirmatory factor analysis (CFA) using LISREL 8.03 and PRELIS 2.03. Regarding fit indices, we report the commonly reported model chi-square and goodness-of-fit index (GFI) as well as the root mean square error of approximation (RMSEA; Browne and Cudeck, 1993). As a first step in our analysis, we divided the partner abuse and self-report delinquency items into conceptually coherent groups (or "item parcels"), to be used as indicators for the CFA. The partner abuse items were divided into four different groups: humiliating items, isolating items, intimidating items, and physically abusive items. The self-reported crime items were also divided into four groups: vice items, fraud items, theft items, and physical force items.[1] By modeling indicators of vice, fraud, and theft as well as indicators of physical force, we were able to address the issue of whether a general antisocial propensity explains partner abuse. We used the weighted least squares fitting function in LISREL 8.03 to fit a model to the polychoric correlations among these eight indicators and their asymptotic variances and covariances. Initially, we computed these matrices separately for men and women to determine if we could reject the null hypothesis that the polychoric correlation matrices were the same for men and women. Because the results showed that the correlation matrices for men and women were indistinguishable, $\chi^2(36, N = 421$ women, $N = 428$ men) = 44.91, $p = .15$, GFI = 1.00, RMSEA = .02, it was correct to fit a CFA model for the whole sample, collapsed across gender.

The path diagram describing this CFA model, and standardized fitted values for the freely estimated paths (all significant at $p < .01$), can be seen in Figure 1. In this model, the four crime parcels and the four partner abuse parcels indicated, respectively, crime and partner abuse factors, which were allowed to correlate freely. This model provided an excellent fit to these data: $\chi^2(19, N = 849) = 48.69, p = .00$, GFI = .99, RMSEA = .04. Moreover, as shown in the path diagram of Figure 1, the crime and partner abuse factors consisted of both unique and overlapping variance, as

---

1. We modeled "parcels" of items because they are more reliable than individual items, and when many items may be reduced to fewer parcels, the resulting smaller number of model parameters can be estimated with more precision (cf. West et al., 1995). Weighted least squares was chosen rather than maximum likelihood because the indicators were ordinal and positively skewed, and, unlike maximum likelihood, weighted least squares does not assume multivariate normalcy of the joint distribution of the measured variables in the model. Because the asymptotic variance-covariance matrix necessary for analysis of the polychoric correlation matrix is quite large, it is not printed here, but is available upon request.

PARTNER ABUSE AND GENERAL CRIME 213

revealed by the correlation of .39 between the two factors. We tested this two-factor proposition statistically by estimating a model in which all eight crime and partner abuse parcels were constrained to load on a single "crime and partner abuse" factor. This one-factor model did not fit as well as the two-factor model in Figure 1, $\chi^2(20, N = 849) = 290.39$, $p = .00$, GFI $= .96$, RMSEA $= .13$; difference between the models is $\chi^2(1) = 241.70$, $p < .001$. In sum, partner abuse and crime, as measured in this study, appear to be distinct, albeit moderately correlated phenomena.

Figure 1.   Crime and Partner Abuse: Same or Different Phenomena?

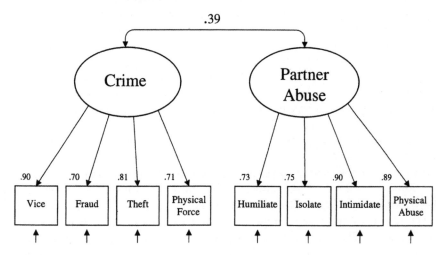

CONSTRUCTING SCALES TO MEASURE GENERAL CRIME AND PARTNER ABUSE

Note that in Figure 1 the physical abuse (violent) items loaded as well as the psychological abuse (nonviolent) items did on the partner abuse factor. This was consistent with the strong bivariate Pearson correlation between physical and psychological abuse scales ($r = .74$) and with the high internal consistency of a single scale comprising all 33 physical and psychological abuse items (Cronbach's alpha = .88). Similarly, Figure 1 shows that the physical force (violent) items loaded as well on the general crime factor as the other (nonviolent) items. This was in keeping with the strong correlation between violent and nonviolent crime scales ($r = .50$) and with the high internal consistency of a single scale comprising all 49 violent and nonviolent items (alpha = .85). These patterns suggested that it was advisable to present the analyses in this article using scales measuring

214   MOFFITT ET AL.

general crime and general abuse. (However, in a later section of the article, analyses separate out physical violence for special focus.) In constructing a scale to measure each of the constructs of general crime and partner abuse, we took the sum of how many different acts of each type were committed at least once during the past 12 months.[2]

PERSONALITY PREDICTING PARTNER ABUSE AND GENERAL CRIME

We began our analysis of the personality predictors of partner abuse and general crime at the bivariate level by examining the zero-order correlations linking each personality factor with both outcomes. Because both outcomes were positively skewed, the variety scales were log-transformed prior to estimation of these correlations, which are presented in Table 1, separately for men and women. Table 1 reveals two notable features. First, Z-tests of sex differences in these correlations presented in the last two columns of Table 1 show that there were no statistically significant sex differences in the personality correlates of general crime or partner abuse. Second, general crime and partner abuse have both common and distinctive personality correlates. Positive Emotionality was not consistently related to either general crime or partner abuse. Negative Emotionality was equally predictive of general crime and of partner abuse. Constraint was more strongly related to general crime than to partner abuse; the correlation between Constraint and partner abuse was only half the size of the correlation between Constraint and general crime.

The results of multivariate regression analyses amplify these conclusions (see Table 2). The goal of these analyses was to examine the correlations between each of the personality factors with partner abuse (after controlling for its association with general crime), and with general crime (after controlling for its association with partner abuse). That is, what personality features are uniquely associated with partner abuse and what personality features are uniquely associated with crime more generally? The results showed that, for both men and women, high Negative Emotionality and

---

2.   Variety scales are useful for several reasons (Elliott and Huizinga, 1989). First, variety scores are less skewed than frequency scores. Second, they give equal weight to all antisocial acts, unlike frequency scores, which give more weight to nonserious acts committed frequently (e.g., public drunkeness, slapping a partner) and give less weight to serious, but infrequent acts (e.g., strong-arm robbery, using a knife on a partner). Third, variety scales are more reliable than frequency reports because "Has X happened?" is a more accurate response than the "How many times has X happened?" format, especially among respondents whose offenses have lost their salience because they offend at a high frequency. Finally, variety measures of antisocial behaviors have been shown to be highly correlated in this sample with scores weighted for act seriousness ($r = .95$ at age 15) and frequency scores ($r = .65$ at age 21), and they are recommended as the strongest predictors of future violence (Robins, 1978).

PARTNER ABUSE AND GENERAL CRIME 215

Table 1. Correlations Between Personality Factors and
Measures of Partner Abuse and General Crime
Among Women and Men

	Women		Men		Z-Test for Sex Differences	
	Crime N = 446	Partner Abuse N = 405	Crime N = 458	Partner Abuse N = 410	Crime	Partner Abuse
Personality Factors						
Positive Emotionality	−.07	−.15**	−.01	−.10	−.90	−.72
Negative Emotionality	.25***	.27***	.35***	.36***	−1.65	−1.42
Constraint	−.37***	−.17***	−.41***	−.21***	.72	.58

NOTE: Z-tests = pairwise comparison of the correlation for men versus correlation for women.
** $p < .01$.
*** $p < .001$.

Table 2. Multiple Regression Analyses Predicting Partner
Abuse and General Crime Among Women and
Men Using Personality Factors

	Women		Men	
	Crime	Partner Abuse	Crime	Partner Abuse
	N = 405		N = 410	
Personality Factors				
Positive Emotionality	−.04	−.12*	−.02	−.06
Negative Emotionality	.17***	.21***	.24***	.24***
Constraint	−.32***	−.06	−.32***	−.05

NOTE: Values in the table are beta weights from multiple regression analyses in which each MPQ factor was used to predict partner abuse (after controlling for general crime) and general crime (after controlling for partner abuse).
* $p < .05$.
*** $p < .001$.

216   MOFFITT ET AL.

low Constraint were associated with general crime. In contrast, the results showed that, for both men and women, high Negative Emotionality was significantly associated with partner abuse, but Constraint was not when general crime was controlled. Apparently, the correlation between Constraint and partner abuse (Table 1) originated because some partner abusers had also engaged in crime.

We next sought to summarize the complete, multivariate pattern of relations between the personality factors and the outcome variables. To accomplish this, we fit a maximum-likelihood, just identified ($df = 0$) path model to the matrix of covariances among the three personality factors and the two outcomes.[3] The fitted path model, the values for the freely estimated paths, and the significance levels of the freely estimated path coefficients, may be seen in Figure 2. Because the model is just identified, there are no indices of fit (i.e., the model is saturated). The path coefficients in the model show that, when personality traits were conceptualized as predictors in a multivariate system, controlling for all other personality traits, Positive Emotionality was predictive of neither crime nor partner abuse; Negative Emotionality was predictive of both crime and of partner abuse; and Constraint was predictive of crime, but not of partner abuse.

To test whether Negative Emotionality was an equally good predictor of both general crime and of partner abuse, we refit the path model in Figure 2, forcing both paths emanating from Negative Emotionality to be equal. By forcing the two Negative Emotionality paths to be equal, we had one less parameter to estimate and gained a degree of freedom that we used to test the fit of this "modified" model. This modification produced $\chi^2(1, N = 815) = 1.97$, $p = .16$, GFI = 1.00, RMSEA = .04. Thus, statistically, Negative Emotionality predicted both general crime and partner abuse with equal magnitude. We performed the same test for Constraint, which produced $\chi^2(1, N = 815) = 48.36$, $p = .00$, GFI = .98, RMSEA = .24. Statistically, the two Constraint paths were clearly different; Constraint was a significantly better predictor of general crime than of partner abuse.

Examination of the structural equations in Figure 2 revealed that both multiple correlations were less than 1.0 (personality predicting crime R = .49 and predicting partner abuse R = .26), attesting that variables beyond the personality traits of perpetrators are needed to fully account for each outcome. However, the .20 correlation shown on Figure 2 between the

---

3. Before conducting this analysis, we computed the covariance matrices separately for men and women to determine if we could safely retain the null hypothesis that the matrices were the same for men and women, thereby allowing us to collapse across gender. Because the results showed that the covariance matrices for men and women were indistinguishable, χ^2 (15, $N = 405$ women, $N = 410$ men) = 13.87, $p = .54$, GFI = .99, RMSEA = .00, we proceeded to fit a model for the whole sample, collapsed across gender.

Figure 2. Personality Factors as Predictors of General Crime and Partner Abuse

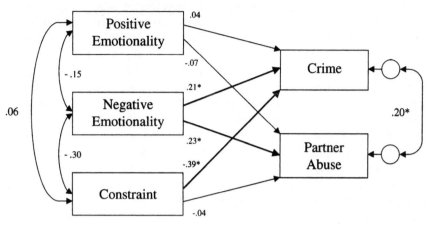

Note: * = *p* < .01.

components of unexplained variance (disturbances) in both outcome variables indicated that some of the unexplained variance in general crime was the same as the unexplained variance in partner abuse. That is, the two outcomes must share explanatory variables other than personality traits.

PERSONALITY PREDICTS PHYSICAL PARTNER VIOLENCE AND VIOLENT CRIME

To ensure that our results held when considering only physically violent behaviors, we formed two dichotomous outcome variables. First, we formed a variable that was "true" only for persons in the sample who said they had perpetrated one or more acts of physical violence against an intimate partner (32% of the total sample; 39.6% of women; 24.5% of men) and a separate variable that was "true" only for persons in the sample who said they had committed one or more violent crimes against someone other than an intimate partner (21.1% of the total sample; 9.6% of women; 32.1% of men). We next formed 2 x 2 tables by cross-tabulating these two outcomes for the total sample, and we examined the resulting odds ratios (OR). In the total sample, there was a clear conjunction between the two types of violence, OR = 1.61, and the 95% confidence interval (CI) did not include zero, as it ranged from 1.15 to 2.25, indicating statistical significance. This conjunction was also apparent when we examined women (OR = 4.44, 95% CI 2.14 – 9.19) and men (OR = 1.81, 95% CI 1.15 – 2.84) separately. As shown by the overlapping confidence intervals for women and men, the conjunction between physical partner violence and violent criminal offending did not differ significantly between

218   MOFFITT ET AL.

the sexes. Men and women who violently abused their partners often had
also committed violence against other people.

Next, we classified the study members into one of four groups formed
by our cross-tabulation of the dichotomous partner violence and criminal
violence variables. Over half of the study members (55% of the total sample; 57% of women and 53% of men) were involved in neither violent
crime nor in partner violence, 12% of the study members (3% of the
women; 22% of men) were involved in violent crime, but not in partner
violence, 23% (33% of women; 14% of men) were involved in partner
violence, but not in violent crime, and 9% (7% of women and 11% of
men) were involved in both partner violence and in violent crime.

We compared these four groups on the three MPQ personality factors
by conducting univariate ANOVAs. To control for the effects of the une-
qual distribution of females and males in the four groups on the results,
and to test for possible sex-interaction effects, we included a sex main
effect as well as an interaction term between sex and group membership in
the analyses. The main effects for group differences, controlling for sex,
were significant for Negative Emotionality [F (3,809) = 16.47, p = .001]
and for Constraint [F (3,809) = 5.00, p = .002], but not for Positive Emotionality [F (3,809) = 1.77, p = .152]. The interaction between sex and
group membership was not statistically significant for any of the three
MPQ personality factors [Negative Emotionality: F (3,806) = 1.22, p =
.301; Constraint: F (3,806) = 1.16, p = .323; Positive Emotionality: F (3,806)
= 1.64, p = .178]. This indicated that the means of the four groups on the
three MPQ factors did not vary as a function of the perpetrator's sex, and
thus, men and women should be collapsed into the groups compared in
Figure 3.

Figure 3 shows the means (T-scores, where M = 50 and S.D. = 10) of the
four groups on the three MPQ personality factors. Post-hoc LSD tests
were made for differences between pairs of groups. No groups differed
significantly on Positive Emotionality, but all four groups were significantly different from each other (p < .05) on both Negative Emotionality
and Constraint, with three exceptions. The "Only Violent Crime" group
and the "Partner and Criminal Violence" group were not different on
Negative Emotionality or Constraint. Of particular interest, the "Only
Partner Violence" group was significantly different from the "Non-Violent" group on Negative Emotionality, but not on Constraint. These
results mesh well with the results from the prior analyses: With regard to
Negative Emotionality, persons who committed either violent crime (M =
54) or partner violence (M = 51) had significantly higher scores than persons who committed neither type of violence (M = 48), and persons who
committed both types of violence had especially high Negative Emotionality scores (M = 55). In contrast, with regard to Constraint, persons who

PARTNER ABUSE AND GENERAL CRIME 219

Figure 3. Personality Profiles of Persons Involved in
Violent Crime and Partner Violence

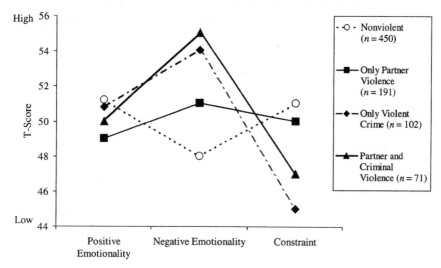

committed violent crime (either alone [$M = 45$] or in addition to partner
violence [$M = 47$]) were characterized by significantly weak Constraint,
whereas persons who committed only partner violence ($M = 50$) were similar to those who engaged in neither type of violence ($M = 51$).[4]

DISCUSSION

The goal of this research was to investigate the extent of overlap
between partner abuse and general criminal offending using matched measurement methods and to test whether these two forms of antisocial
behavior share the same or different correlates. Our analysis of antisocial
behaviors as observable indicators of latent constructs suggests that partner abuse and general crime represent different constructs that are moderately related; they are not merely two expressions of the same underlying
antisocial propensity. This impression was buttressed by further construct-

---

4. The "Only Partner Violence" group and the "Partner and Criminal Violence"
group reported a similar variety of abusive acts ($M = 2.29$, S.D. = 1.64 and $M = 2.68$,
S.D. = 1.94, respectively, a less than .2 S.D. difference, which was not significant).
Because these two groups did not differ on their level of abuse, it is not the case that the
"Partner and Criminal Violence" group scored worse on Constraint because it contains
more seriously violent abusers than the "Only Partner Violence" group. Incidentally,
the "Only Violent Crime" group and the "Partner and Criminal Violence" group
reported a similar variety of violent crime ($M = 1.19$, S.D. = .46 and $M = 1.28$, S.D. =
.61, respectively).

validation analyses. We found that partner abuse and general crime share a propensity from strong Negative Emotionality, but do not share a propensity from weak Constraint. Although perpetrators who engage in both partner abuse and general crime have weak Constraint, multivariate analysis revealed that the trait is unrelated to abuse of their partner. The balance of findings suggests that partner abuse and general crime are not conceptually equivalent, even when performed by the same individual.

ARE PERSONS WHO ABUSE THEIR PARTNERS THE SAME PEOPLE WHO COMMIT OTHER CRIMINAL BEHAVIORS?

First, the results revealed statistically significant associations between abuse and general crime whether the data were analyzed using latent dimensional variables or when persons in categories were compared. Second, the results revealed significant associations between partner abuse and general crime when we compared global measures of partner abuse that included acts of both psychological and physical abuse with global measures of general crime that included acts of theft, fraud, vice, and force, as well as when we narrowed our comparison to acts of physical violence against partners with acts against nonintimates. Third, the results revealed that the association between partner abuse and general crime was the same for both men and women, regardless of how these behaviors were modeled or measured.

Some inferential limitations need to be kept in mind. First, the one-year reporting period used in this research provides information only about the concurrent overlap between partner abuse and general crime. The presence in our study of persons engaged in partner violence alone or in violence against nonintimates alone should not be interpreted as evidence for specialization at other ages or across the life course, because some persons involved in violence against partners alone could have engaged in violence against others at some earlier point, and vice versa.[5] Second, although the measures were well matched on data collection method (private and confidential self-report interviews), reliability (> .85), and reporting period (past 12 months), partner violence was measured with 13 items, whereas

---

5. We are able to provide some, albeit inconclusive, evidence that perpetration patterns in this sample at age 21 appeared to reflect long-standing victim preferences. We checked the Study members' histories of violent delinquency using data gathered when they were 15 years old, before most of them began dating partners. Study members classified at age 21 in the "Non-Violent" or in the "Only Partner Violence" groups had similar and minimal histories of violence (*M* variety of violent acts at age 15 = .20 versus .29). Both of those groups had significantly less adolescent violence (*p* < .05) than Study members classified at age 21 in the "Only Violent Crime" group (*M* = .69) or in the "Partner and Criminal Violence" group (*M* = 1.16). Thus, the adults who were exclusively partner abusers did not have a notable prior history of general violence.

PARTNER ABUSE AND GENERAL CRIME 221

violence against someone other than an intimate was measured with 5 items. The higher prevalence for partner violence may in part reflect the larger number of items, or it is possible that there are more private than public violent offenders. This study cannot tell. Therefore, we caution that it is unwise to draw conclusions from the categorical comparisons in this study about the relative point-prevalence rates of the two forms of violence, or their precise amount of co-occurrence in the population. It is possible to deduce from the various analyses we conducted that there is a moderate, though nonperfect, association between partner abuse and general crime, which is in keeping with previous studies (for reviews, see Fagan and Browne, 1994; Hotaling et al., 1990; Marvell and Moody, 1999).

SIMILARITIES BETWEEN THE CORRELATES OF PARTNER ABUSE AND CRIME

We applied to the prediction of partner abuse a personality model that was known to predict general crime. Some prospective personality factors predicted partner abuse and general crime equally well, whereas other personality factors predicted partner abuse and general crime differently. This partly-the-same/partly-different conclusion was robust across latent continuous variables or observed categorical variables, across general offending or physical violence, and across men or women. Although in this study we only tested the relevance of a personality model to understanding sources of similarities and differences between partner abuse and general crime, the results confirmed that these two forms of antisocial behavior have shared and unique correlates other than personality. A growing literature is beginning to identify some of the many shared correlates of partner abuse and general crime as well as some of the unique factors implicated in each (Avakame, 1998; Farrington, 1994; Shields et al., 1988).

Partner abuse and general crime are the same in that (1) Positive Emotionality predicts neither of these two outcomes and (2) Negative Emotionality predicts both of these two outcomes. It should not be surprising that Positive Emotionality is not related to antisocial behavior in general nor to partner abuse in particular. Positive Emotionality (the capacity to experience well-being and enjoy interpersonal relationships) is not implicated in any theory of crime or partner violence. In fact, research shows that individuals who engage in antisocial behavior are capable of experiencing well-being (Baumeister et al., 1996), and they appear to enjoy relationships, as a great deal of offending takes place in peer groups (Warr, 1993) and partner abuse, by definition, takes place in the context of an intimate relationship. On the whole, Positive Emotionality tends to be less related to antisocial problems than it is related to other social problems, such as depression (Clark et al., 1994).

222   MOFFITT ET AL.

Negative Emotionality is a shared risk factor for both partner abuse and
general crime. Negative Emotionality is a generalized propensity for
experiencing aversive affective states, including anger, anxiety, suspiciousness, and irritability. People with chronically high levels of Negative Emotionality are emotionally brittle; they live in a world darkened by a rapid,
excessive response to minor stressors, a sense that others are malicious,
and a propensity to react to even slight provocation with rage. For example, to a person with an excess of Negative Emotionality, events that
would be perceived by others as mildly irritating or simply annoying cause
serious upset and distress. Thus, it is not surprising that persons with a
stable, lowered threshold for the experience of negative emotions are at
higher risk for a variety of aggressive, antisocial outcomes—for both abuse
in intimate relationships and violence in the world at large. In one typology, Holtzworth-Munroe and Stuart (1994) suggested that traits comprised
by Negative Emotionality (e.g., dysphoria, excessive jealousy, emotional
volatility, anger) might distinguish one subtype within abusers. However,
the findings here extend the predictive power of Negative Emotionality
very broadly to all of the forms of antisocial behavior we studied regardless of victim choice.

The important contribution of Negative Emotionality to criminal behavior in general has been documented in our own previous studies as well as
in the research of others (Elkins et al., 1997; Krueger et al., 1994; Moffitt
et al., 1995). We suggested that individuals with chronically high levels of
Negative Emotionality are predisposed to construe events in a biased way,
perceiving threat in the acts of others and menace in the vicissitudes of
everyday life. The current study extends this finding to suggest that individual differences in Negative Emotionality can foretell involvement in
partner abuse. Although criminological theories have overlooked the role
of Negative Emotionality in the prediction of crime (cf. Gottfredson and
Hirschi, 1990), reference to specific facets of Negative Emotionality
appears in virtually all theories of partner abuse. For example, feminist
theories emphasize that men perpetrate partner violence because they are
incapable of tolerating threats to their status and patriarchial ideology
channels emotional arousal into aggression toward women; evolutionary
theories emphasize that men perpetrate partner violence when they
become excessively suspicious of their partner's fidelity; and social-inter-
actional theories suggest that conflicts during dyadic interactions become
abusive as a result of intense and rapid escalation of anger. It should be
noted that none of these partner-abuse theories is a theory of individual
differences. Rather, each of these theories invokes a causal mechanism
that is general in the sense that it is supposed to apply to all men, and that
is at the same time quite specific in that it is supposed to apply to men, but

PARTNER ABUSE AND GENERAL CRIME   223

not to women. A personality model contrasts in two ways. First, it suggests that the mechanisms do not apply to all persons; the fact that some people abuse their partners and others do not may be accounted for, in part, by individual variation in Negative Emotionality. Second, it allows that Negative Emotionality is a personality characteristic that varies among both males and females, affecting the behavior of both sexes. Thus, personality psychology can account for two facts that are ignored by mainstream abuse theories: that not all men abuse their women, and that some women abuse their men.

DIFFERENCES BETWEEN THE CORRELATES OF PARTNER ABUSE AND CRIME

Partner abuse and general crime are different in that Constraint predicts crime, but does not predict partner abuse. Constraint indexes individual differences in the ability to modulate and control impulsive expression. The ability to modulate impulses is the most ubiquitous demand that society places on the developing child and, fundamentally, Constraint is about the successful outcome of the socialization process—it is about heeding societal prohibitions against the expression of impulses. The importance of weak Constraint (described as "low self-control") to antisocial behavior has been recognized by psychologists for some time and is a central construct in contemporary theory and research on crime (Gottfredson and Hirschi, 1990).

But how should Constraint relate to partner violence? According to Gottfredson and Hirschi's (1990) "general theory of crime," Constraint should relate to partner abuse just as strongly as it relates to other criminal behaviors and analogous acts. This prediction is likewise derived from clinical studies, in which poor self-control is invoked as an important feature of the psychological makeup of the batterer (Hotaling et al., 1990). Holtzworth-Munroe and Stuart (1994) offered a different view. Based on a large literature review, they suggested that partner abusers who also victimize nonintimates should be impulsive (weak Constraint), but abusers who victimize only intimates should not be impulsive. Our comparison on "Partner and Criminal Violence" versus "Only Partner Violence" groups fits this suggestion because only the former group had weak Constraint. However, our multivariate analysis of the personality correlates of partner abuse controlling for participation in other crime revealed that, to the extent that some partner abusers show weak Constraint, the personality trait is only related to their other criminal behavior, not to their abuse of their partner. In other words, the same individual who attacks someone impulsively in a bar, at a sports event, or during a robbery may use violence strategically to control his or her partner in the privacy of home. This finding was consistent with our reading of feminist and evolutionary theories, which have suggested that partner violence is strategic, planful, and willful. This view that perpetrators abuse intimates as a deliberate, rather than an impulsive, course of action anticipated our finding that Constraint is unrelated to partner violence.

GENDER SIMILARITY IN THE PERSONALITY CORRELATES OF PARTNER ABUSE

In this research, we examined both young men and young women as perpetrators of general crime and of abusive behaviors toward a partner. Our earlier reports demonstrated that, although females produce less crime than males, male and female offenders share the personality profile of high Negative Emotionality and low Constraint (Caspi et al., 1994). Our current findings demonstrate that male and female partner abusers share high Negative Emotionality and low Constraint (the latter only if they also victimize nonpartners).

Many studies have found that a substantial number of women self-report abusive behaviors toward male partners (for a meta-analysis, see Archer, 2000; for a bibliography, see Fiebert, 1997). These reports are often countered with the argument that women's perpetration represents only self-defense. The personality research reported here may be pertinent to the debate because personality was measured prospectively, in most cases at least one or two years before the women entered their abusive relationship.

If all women are uniformly vulnerable to male abuse and women's apparent perpetration represents solely a reasonable defensive reaction to male attack, we would not expect individual differences in personality to predict perpetration among Dunedin women as well they do in Dunedin men. Yet, the findings revealed that preexisting characteristics, such as approval of the use of aggression, suspiciousness about others' motives, a tendency to experience intense and rapid negative emotions, and, in some cases, poor self-control, predicted which Dunedin women were to engage in abusive behavior toward their partners (and toward nonintimates too). In this regard, it is important to note that, although self-defense may account for women's behavior toward their intimate partners, self-defense is less intuitive as an account of their general crime toward nonintimates; yet, the pattern of overlap between partner abuse and general crime was approximately the same for Dunedin women as for Dunedin men. Together, with earlier findings that women's perpetration is related to their aggressivity (O'Leary et al., 1994), and their childhood and adolescent history of delinquency (Giordano et al., 1999; Magdol et al., 1998a), our findings weigh in on the side of women's perpetration being more than self-defense alone, at least in a substantial proportion of young couples.

PARTNER ABUSE AND GENERAL CRIME   225

The significance, or lack thereof, of women's self-reports of perpetration is unlikely to be resolved in the near future, because it is inherently difficult to conduct a definitive empirical test of the self-defense hypothesis. Our findings reported here, though not definitive, are consistent with the possibility that a self-defense account of women's perpetration is incomplete. Undeniably, many women's perpetration is self-defense, but the data suggest that some women's perpetration is motivated by the same intrapersonal factors that motivate men's perpetration. If true, this poses a challenge to theories that ascribe the mainsprings of partner abuse to male-specific concerns about patriarchy and paternity.

IMPLICATIONS FOR INTERVENTION AND RESEARCH POLICY

Individual differences in Negative Emotionality measured via the MPQ are known to be partly heritable (Tellegen et al., 1988), predictable from early childhood (Caspi and Silva, 1995), and stable over adulthood (McGue et al., 1993). Stability implies that, in the absence of radical environmental change, people with behavior driven by strong negative emotions are likely to continue responding this way throughout adulthood. However, this information need not imply pessimism about treating or preventing partner abuse. Neither knowledge of partial heritability nor the high-stability coefficients obtained in longitudinal studies of natural development address the question of whether personality can be changed. Existing longitudinal data tell us only that, in the normal course of an uninterrupted life, individual differences in personality usually do not change dramatically. We actually do not know how much people's personalities can be changed by deliberate intervention, as fewer than 10% of people ever encounter psychological intervention of any kind, and only a tiny fraction of those get treatment of the quality required to promote change in basic personality structures (Caspi and Moffitt, 1993).

Many of the predominant treatment models of partner abuse employ cognitive restructuring as their main therapeutic approach (Healey et al., 1998). Such programs directly attempt to extinguish violence-promoting attitudes, values, and beliefs that perpetrators have about themselves and their social world. The programs also attempt to restructure how perpetrators interpret their own emotional arousal during interpersonal conflict. The goal of treatment is to replace violence-promoting social cognitions with violence-inhibiting social cognitions and to instill abusers with preferences for healthier patterns of interpersonal behavior. In essence, the dominant intervention models attempt to alter how the personality characteristic Negative Emotionality works in the specific domain of intimate relationships. Some psychologists have speculated pessimistically that therapeutic change is unlikely for partner abusers with a history of crime, negative emotions, and extreme personality traits (Jacobson et al., 1995).

226   MOFFITT ET AL.

However, the efficacy of interventions for partner abuse has not been extensively evaluated (Chalk and King, 1998), and we think it is important to remind readers that personality profiles are not inherently permanent. Meanwhile, research on the link between partner abuse and general crime is beginning to support interventions and theories that acknowledge the link and to address the particularly unique aspects of partner violence.

REFERENCES

Archer, John
   2000   Sex differences in aggression between heterosexual partners: A meta-analytic review. Psychological Bulletin. In Press.

Avakame, Edem F.
   1998   How different is violence in the home? An examination of some correlates of stranger and intimate homicide. Criminology 36:601–632.

Bachman, Ronet and Linda E. Saltzman
   1995   Violence Against Women: Estimates from the Redesigned Survey. Washington, D.C.: U.S. Department of Justice.

Baumeister, Roy F., Laura Smart, and Joseph M. Boden
   1996   Relation of threatened egotism to violence and aggression: The dark side of high self esteem. Psychological Review 103:5–33.

Bograd, Michele
   1988   How battered women and abusive men account for domestic violence: Excuses, justifications, or explanations? In Gerald T. Hotaling, David Finkelhor, John T. Kirkpatrick, and Murray A. Straus (eds.), Coping with Family Violence: Research and Policy Perspectives. Newbury Park, Calif.: Sage.

Brennan, Patty, Sarnoff Mednick, and Richard John
   1989   Specialization in violence: Evidence of a criminal subgroup. Criminology 27:437–453.

Britt, Chester L.
   1996   The measurement of specialization and escalation in the criminal career: An alternative modelling strategy. Journal of Quantitative Criminology 12:193–222.

Browne, Angela
   1987   When Battered Women Kill. New York: Free Press.

Browne, Michael W. and Robert Cudeck
   1993   Alternative ways of assessing model fit. In Ken A. Bollen and J. Scott Long (eds.), Testing Structural Equation Models. Newbury Park, Calif.: Sage.

Capaldi, Deborah M. and Sara Clark
   1998   Prospective family predictors of aggression toward female partners for young at-risk males. Developmental Psychology. 34:1175–1188.

Caspi, Avshalom and Terrie E. Moffitt
   1993   When do individual differences matter? A paradoxical theory of personality coherence. Psychological Inquiry 4:247–271.

Caspi, Avshalom and Phil A. Silva
　　1995　Temperamental qualities at age 3 predict personality traits in young adulthood: Longitudinal evidence from a birth cohort. Child Development 66:486–498.

Caspi, Avshalom, Dot Begg, Nigel Dickson, Honalee Harrington, John Langley, Terrie E. Moffitt, and Phil A. Silva
　　1997　Personality differences predict health-risk behaviors in young adulthood: Evidence from a longitudinal study. Journal of Personality and Social Psychology 73:1052–1063.

Caspi, Avshalom, Terrie E. Moffitt, Denise L. Newman, and Phil A. Silva
　　1996　Behavioral observations at age 3 predict adult psychiatric disorders: Longitudinal evidence from a birth cohort. Archives of General Psychiatry 53:1033–1039.

Caspi, Avshalom, Terrie E. Moffitt, Phil A. Silva, Magda Stouthamer-Loeber, Pamela S. Schmutte, and Robert Krueger
　　1994　Are some people crime prone? Replications of the personality-crime relation across nation, gender, race and method. Criminology 32:301–333.

Chalk, Rosemary and Patricia A. King
　　1998　Violence in Families: Assessing Prevention and Treatment Programs. Washington, D.C.: National Academy Press.

Church, A. Timothy and Peter J. Burke
　　1994　Exploratory and confirmatory tests of the Big Five and Tellegen's three- and four-dimensional models. Journal of Personality and Social Psychology 66:93–114.

Clark, Lee A., David Watson, and Susan Mineka
　　1994　Temperament, personality, and the mood and anxiety disorders. Journal of Abnormal Psychology 103:103–116.

Daly, Martin and Margo Wilson
　　1988　Evolutionary social psychology and family homicide. Science 242:519–523.

Dobash, Russell E. and Rebecca P. Dobash
　　1992　Women, Violence and Social Change. London: Routledge.

Downey, Geraldine and Scott I. Feldman
　　1996　Implications of rejection sensitivity for intimate relationships. Journal of Personality and Social Psychology 70:1327–1343.

Dutton, Donald G.
　　1998　The Abusive Personality: Violence and Control in Intimate Relationships. New York: Guilford.

Elkins, Irene J., William G. Iacono, A. E. Doyle, and Matt McGue
　　1997　Characteristics associated with the persistence of antisocial behavior: Results from recent longitudinal research. Aggression and Violent Behavior 2:101–124.

Elliott, Delbert S. and David Huizinga
　　1989　Improving self-reported measures of delinquency. In Malcolm W. Klein (ed.), Cross-National Research in Self-Reported Crime and Delinquency. Dordrecht: Kluwer Academic.

228   MOFFITT ET AL.

Fagan, Jeffrey and Angela Browne
    1994   Violence between spouses and intimates: Physical aggression between
            women and men in intimate relationships. In Albert J. Reiss, Jr. and
            Jeffrey A. Roth (eds.), Understanding and Preventing Violence. Vol. 3.
            Social Influences. Washington, D.C.: National Academy Press.

Fagan, Jeffrey and Sandra Wexler
    1987   Crime at home and in the streets: The relationship between family and
            stranger violence. Violence and Victims 2:5–23.

Farrington, David P.
    1994   Childhood, adolescent, and adult features of violent males. In L. Rowell
            Huesmann (ed.), Aggressive Behavior: Current Perspectives. New York:
            Plenum Press.

Felson, Richard B. and Steven F. Messner
    1998   Disentangling the effects of gender and intimacy on victim precipitation in
            homicide. Criminology 36:405–423.

Fiebert, Martin S.
    1997   References examining assaults by women on their spouses/partners.
            Sexuality and Culture 1:273–286.

Gelles, Richard J. and Murray A. Straus
    1979   Determinants of violence in the family: Towards a theoretical integration.
            In Wesley R. Burr, R. Hill, F. Ivan Nye, and Ira L. Reiss (eds.),
            Contemporary Theories About the Family. Vol. 1. New York: Free Press.

Giles-Sims, Jean
    1983   Wife Battering: A Systems Theory Approach. New York: Guilford.

Giordano, Peggy, Toni J. Millhollin, Stephen A. Cernkovich, M.D. Pugh, and
Jennifer L. Rudolph
    1999   Delinquency, identity, and women's involvement in relationship violence.
            Criminology 37:17–40.

Gottfredson, Michael and Travis Hirschi
    1990   A General Theory of Crime. Stanford, Calif.: Stanford University Press.

Greenfield, Lawrence A., Michael R. Rand, Diane Craven, Patsy A. Klaus, Craig A.
Perkins, Cheryl Ringel, Greg Warchol, Cathy Maston, and James A. Fox
    1998   Violence by Intimates: Analysis of Data on Crimes by Current or Former
            Spouses, Boyfriends, and Girlfriends. Washington, D.C.: Bureau of
            Justice Statistics.

Healey, Kerry, Christine Smith, and Chris O'Sullivan
    1998   Batterer Intervention: Program Approaches and Criminal Justice Strate-
            gies. Washington, D.C.: U.S. Department of Justice.

Holtzworth-Munroe, Amy and Gregory L. Stuart
    1994   Typologies of male batterers: Three subtypes and the differences among
            them. Psychological Bulletin 116:476–497.

Holtzworth-Munroe, Amy, Jennifer Waltz, Neil S. Jacobson, Valerie Monaco, Peter
A. Fehrenbach, and John M. Gottman
    1992   Recruiting nonviolent men as control subjects for research on marital
            violence: How easily can it be done? Violence and Victims 7:79–88.

PARTNER ABUSE AND GENERAL CRIME 229

Hotaling, Gerald T., Murray A. Straus, and Alan J. Lincoln
1990   Intrafamily violence and crime and violence outside the family. In Murray A. Straus and Richard J. Gelles (eds.), Physical Violence in American Families: Risk Factors and Adaptions to Violence in 8,145 Families. New Brunswick, N.J.: Transaction.

Huesmann, L. Rowell, Leonard D. Eron, Monroe M. Lefkowitz, and Leopold O. Walder
1984   Stability of aggression over time and generations. Developmental Psychology 20:1120–1134.

Jacobson, Neil S., John M. Gottman, and Joann W. Shortt
1995   The distinction between Type 1 and Type 2 batterers—Further Considerations: Reply to Ornduff et al. (1995), Margolin et al. (1995) and Walker (1995). Journal of Family Psychology 9:272–279.

Jacobson, Neil S., John M. Gottman, Jennifer Waltz, Regina Rushe, Julia C. Babcock, and Amy Holtzworth-Munroe
1994   Affect, verbal content, and psychophysiology in the arguments of couples with a violent husband. Journal of Consulting and Clinical Psychology 62:982–988.

Junger-Tas, Josine, Gert-Jan Terlouw, and Malcolm Klein
1994   Delinquent Behavior Among Young People in the Western World. Amsterdam: Kugler.

Karney, Benjamin R., Joanne Davila, Catherine L. Cohan, Kieran T. Sullivan, Matthew D. Johnson, and Thomas N. Bradbury
1995   An empirical investigation of sampling strategies in marital research. Journal of Marriage and the Family 57:909–920.

Krueger, Robert, Pamela S. Schmutte, Avshalom Caspi, Terrie E. Moffitt, Kathleen Campbell, and Phil A. Silva
1994   Personality traits are linked to crime among males and females: Evidence from a birth cohort. Journal of Abnormal Psychology 103:328–338.

Langley, John, Judy Martin, and Shyamala Nada Raja
1997   Physical assault among 21-year-olds by partners. Journal of Interpersonal Violence 12:675–684.

Lattimore, Pamela K., Christy Visher, and Richard L. Linster
1994   Specialization in juvenile careers: Markov results for a California cohort. Journal of Quantitative Criminology 10:291–316.

Magdol, Lynn, Terrie E. Moffitt, Avshalom Caspi, and Phil A. Silva
1998a   Developmental antecedents of partner abuse: A prospective-longitudinal study. Journal of Abnormal Psychology 107:375–389.
1998b   Hitting without a license: Testing explanations of differences in partner abuse between young adult daters and cohabitors. Journal of Marriage and the Family 60:41–55.

Magdol, Lynn, Terrie E. Moffitt, Avshalom Caspi, Denise L. Newman, Jeffrey Fagan, and Phil A. Silva
1997   Gender differences in partner violence in a birth-cohort of 21-year-olds: Bridging the gap between clinical and epidemiological approaches. Journal of Consulting and Clinical Psychology 65:68–78.

230   MOFFITT ET AL.

Marvell, Thomas B. and Carlisle E. Moody
    1999   Female and male homicide victimization rates: Comparing trends and
            regressors. Criminology. 37:879–900.

McGue, Matt, Steven Bacon, and David T. Lykken
    1993   Personality stability and change in early adulthood: A behavioral genetic
            analysis. Developmental Psychology 29:96–109.

McNeely, R.L. and Coramae Richey Mann
    1990   Domestic violence is a human issue. Journal of Interpersonal Violence
            5:129–132.

Megargee, Edwin I.
    1982   Psychological determinants and correlates of criminal violence. In Marvin
            E. Wolfgang and Neil A. Weiner (eds.), Criminal Violence. Newbury
            Park, Calif.: Sage.

Mihalic, Sharon W. and Delbert S. Elliot
    1997   If violence is domestic, does it really count? Journal of Family Violence
            12:293–311.

Moffitt, Terrie E., Avshalom Caspi, Phil A. Silva, and Magda Stouthamer-Loeber
    1995   Individual differences in personality and intelligence are linked to crime:
            Cross-context evidence from nations, neighborhoods, genders, races and
            age-cohorts. In John Hagan (ed.), Current Perspectives on Aging and the
            Life Cycle. Vol. 4. Delinquency and Disrepute in the Life Course:
            Contextual and Dynamic Analyses. Greenwich, Conn.: JAI Press.

Moffitt, Terrie E., Avshalom Caspi, Nigel Dickson, Phil A. Silva, and Warren Stanton
    1996   Childhood-onset versus adolescent-onset antisocial conduct in males:
            Natural history from age 3 to 18. Development and Psychopathology
            8:399–424.

Moffitt, Terrie E., Avshalom Caspi, Robert F. Krueger, Lynn Magdol, Gayla
    Margolin, Phil A. Silva, and Ros Sydney
    1997   Do partners agree about abuse in their relationship? A psychometric
            evaluation of interpartner agreement. Psychological Assessment 9:47–56.

Morse, Barbara
    1995   Beyond the Conflict Tactics Scale: Assessing gender differences in partner
            violence. Violence and Victims 10:251–261.

O'Leary, K. Daniel
    1993   Through a psychological lens: Personality traits, personality disorders, and
            levels of violence. In Richard J. Gelles and D. Loeske (eds.), Current
            Controversies Regarding Psychological Explanations of Family Violence.
            Newbury Park, Calif.: Sage.

O'Leary, K. Daniel, Jean Malone, and Andrea Tyree
    1994   Physical aggression in early marriage: Prerelationship and relationship
            effects. Journal of Consulting and Clinical Psychology 62:594–602.

Ozer, Dan
    1985   Correlation and the coefficient of determination. Psychological Bulletin
            97:307–315.

Robins, Lee N.
    1978   Sturdy childhood predictors of antisocial behaviour: Replications from
            longitudinal studies. Psychological Medicine 8:611–622.

PARTNER ABUSE AND GENERAL CRIME 231

Shields, Nancy M., George J. McCall, and Christine R. Hanneke
1988   Patterns of family and nonfamily violence: Violent husbands and violent men. Violence and Victims 3:83–97.

Silva, Phil A. and Warren Stanton (eds.)
1996   From child to adult: The Dunedin Multidisciplinary Health and Development Study. Auckland, U.K.: Oxford University Press.

Simons, Ronald L., Kuei-Hsiu Lin, and Leslie C. Gordon
1998   Socialization in the family of origin and male dating violence: A prospective study. Journal of Marriage and the Family 60:467–478.

Simons, Ronald L., Chyi-In Wu, Christine Johnson, and Rand D. Conger
1995   A test of various perspectives on the intergenerational transmission of domestic violence. Criminology 33:141–171.

Stitt, B. Grant and David J. Giacopassi
1992   Trends in the connectivity of theory and research in criminology. The Criminologist 17:1–6.

Straus, Murray A.
1998   The controversy over domestic violence by women: A methodological, theoretical, and sociology of science analysis. In Ximena B. Arriaga and Stuart Oskamp (eds.), Violence in Intimate Relationships. Thousand Oaks, Calif.: Sage.

Tellegen, Auke
1982   Brief Manual for the Multidimensional Personality Questionnaire. Minneapolis: University of Minnesota.

Tellegen, Auke and Neils G. Waller
2000   Exploring personality through test construction: Development of the Multidimensional Personality Questionnaire. In Steve R. Briggs and Jonathan M. Cheek (eds.), Personality Measures: Development and Evaluation. Greenwich, Conn.: JAI Press. In Press.

Tellegen, Auke, David T. Lykken, Tom J. Bouchard, Kimberly J. Wilcox, Nancy L. Segal, and S. Rich
1988   Personality similarity in twins reared apart and together. Journal of Personality and Social Psychology 6:1031–1039.

Tjaden, Patricia G. and Nancy Thoennes
1998   Prevalence, Incidence, and Consequences of Violence Against Women: Findings from the National Violence Against Women Survey. Washington, D.C.: U.S. Department of Justice.

Van Dijk, Jan and Pat Mayhew
1992   Criminal Victimization in the Industrialized World. The Hague: Ministry of Justice.

Warr, Mark
1993   Age, peers, and delinquency. Criminology 31:17–40.

Watson, David, Lee Anna Clark, and Alan R. Harkness
1994   Structures of personality and their relevance to psychopathology. Journal of Abnormal Psychology 103:18–31.

232   MOFFITT ET AL.

West, Stephen G., John F. Finch, and Patrick J. Curran
    1995   Structural equation models with nonnormal variables. In Rick H. Hoyle
            (ed.), Structural Equation Modeling: Concepts, Issues, and Applications.
            Newbury Park, Calif.: Sage.

Wright, Bradley Entner, Avshalom Caspi, Terrie E. Moffitt, and Phil A. Silva
    1999   Low self-control, social bonds, and crime: Social causation, social
            selection, or both? Criminology. 37:479–514.

Yllö, Kirsty A.
    1993   Through a feminist lens: Gender, power, and violence. In Richard J.
            Gelles and Donileen R. Loseke (eds.), Current Controversies on Family
            Violence. Newbury Park, Calif.: Sage.

Terrie Moffitt is Professor in the Department of Psychology at the University of Wisconsin, Madison; Professor of Social Behaviour and Development at the Social, Genetic, and Developmental Psychiatry Research Centre, Institute of Psychiatry, University of London; and Associate Director of the Dunedin Multidisciplinary Health and Development Study at the Medical School of Otago, New Zealand. Her research interests include the developmental origins of antisocial behavior and theoretical explanations for antisocial behavior across the life course.

Robert Krueger is Assistant Professor in the Department of Psychology at the University of Minnesota-Twin Cities. His research interests include the relations between personality and psychopathology and measuring the structure of symptoms of psychopathology.

Avshalom Caspi is Professor in the Department of Psychology at the University of Wisconsin, Madison, and in the Social, Genetic, and Developmental Psychiatry Research Centre, Institute of Psychiatry, University of London. His work focuses on personality development and psychopathology across the life course.

Jeffrey Fagan is Professor in the Schools of Public Health and Law at Columbia University. His research interests include the causes, consequences, and control of interpersonal violence.

[6]

MICHAEL P. JOHNSON   *Pennsylvania State University*

KATHLEEN J. FERRARO   *Arizona State University**

Research on Domestic Violence in the 1990s:

Making Distinctions

This review of the family literature on domestic violence suggests that two broad themes of the 1990s provide the most promising directions for the future. The first is the importance of distinctions among types or contexts of violence. Some distinctions are central to the theoretical and practical understanding of the nature of partner violence, others provide important contexts for developing more sensitive and comprehensive theories, and others may simply force us to question our tendency to generalize carelessly from one context to another. Second, issues of control, although most visible in the feminist literature that focuses on men using violence to control "their" women, also arise in other contexts, calling for more general analyses of the interplay of violence, power, and control in relationships. In addition to these two general themes, our review covers literature on coping with violence, the effects on victims and their children, and the social effects of partner violence.

She wandered the streets, looking in shop windows. Nobody knew her here. Nobody knew what he did when the door was closed. Nobody knew.

(Brant, 1996, pp. 281)

Department of Sociology, 211 Oswald Tower, University Park, PA 16802 (mpj@psu.edu).

*Women's Studies, Box 873404, Arizona State University, Tempe, AZ 85287-3404.

Key Words: battering, domestic violence, partner violence.

In everyday speech and even in most social science discourse, "domestic violence" is about men beating women. It is estimated that somewhere in the neighborhood of two million women in the United States are terrorized by husbands or other male partners who use violence as one of the tactics by which they control "their woman." Most of the literature on domestic violence is about men controlling women in intimate relationships through the use of violence. This is not, however, the only form of violence between adult or adolescent partners in close relationships, and our review will therefore cover "partner violence" in a broad range of couple relationships, including the marital, cohabiting, and dating relationships of same-gender and opposite-gender couples.

Our reading of the literature on partner violence has led us to the conclusion that two broad themes of the 1990s provide the most promising directions for the future. The first theme is about the importance of making distinctions. Partner violence cannot be understood without acknowledging important distinctions among types of violence, motives of perpetrators, the social locations of both partners, and the cultural contexts in which violence occurs. We will argue that it is difficult to find a question about partner violence for which these distinctions are not relevant and that our ability to draw firm conclusions and to develop effective policies is broadly handicapped by a failure to make distinctions among types of partner violence.

Control, the second promising theme, is most visible in the feminist literature, which has argued that partner violence is primarily a problem of men using violence to maintain control over "their women," a control to which they feel they are entitled and that is supported by a patriarchal culture. We would agree that "domestic violence" or "battering" as it is generally understood by professionals and by the public is primarily a problem of heterosexual male control of women partners. Nonetheless, battering does happen in gay male couples and in lesbian couples, and some heterosexual women do physically assault their male partners and there are forms of partner violence that are quite different from the systematic violence that we call battering.

THE CENTRALITY OF DISTINCTIONS

Types of Violence Against Partners

One of the clearest illustrations of the importance of making distinctions among types of violence arose in the context of the long-standing debate about "battered husbands," and the alleged gender symmetry of partner violence. Johnson (Johnson, 1995, 2000a) argued that at the relationship level, one can distinguish four major patterns of partner violence, which he called "common couple violence" (CCV), "intimate terrorism" (IT), "violent resistance" (VR), and "mutual violent control" (MVC). The distinctions are based not on behavior in a single incident, but on more general patterns of control exercised across the many encounters that comprise a relationship, patterns that are rooted in the motivations of the perpetrator and his or her partner.

Common couple violence. The first type of partner violence identified by Johnson is that which is not connected to a general pattern of control. It arises in the context of a specific argument in which one or both of the partners lash out physically at the other. In a series of empirical papers, Johnson has demonstrated that CCV (compared to IT) has a lower per-couple frequency, is not as likely to escalate over time, is not as likely to involve severe violence, and is more likely to be mutual (Johnson, 1998, 2000a, 2000b). He also has shown that virtually all of the violence in a general sample is CCV, suggesting that research using such samples may be relevant only to this type of partner violence.

Intimate terrorism. The basic pattern in IT is one of violence as merely one tactic in a general pattern of control. The violence is motivated by a wish to exert general control over one's partner. IT involves more per-couple incidents of violence than does CCV, is more likely to escalate over time, is less likely to be mutual, and is more likely to involve serious injury. Nonetheless, IT is not merely "severe violence," as defined in much of the literature. There is considerable variability of severity in both CCV and IT, with some CCV involving homicides and some IT involving a rather low level of violence (Johnson, 2000a). The distinguishing feature of IT is a pattern of violent and nonviolent behaviors that indicates a general motive to control.

The controlling behaviors of IT often involve emotional abuse (Follingstad, Rutledge, Berg, Hause, & Polek, 1990). Kirkwood (1993) provided detailed insights into the processes of emotional abuse that can gradually alter women's views of themselves, their relationships, and their place in the world. Chang's (1996) detailed accounts of psychological abuse also illustrate the processes through which women become demoralized and trapped in abusive relationships. Renzetti's work (1992) on battering in lesbian relationships demonstrates that emotional abuse is not the sole prerogative of men.

Violent resistance. We prefer the term "violent resistance" over "self-defense," because "self-defense" has meanings that are defined (and changing) in the law. Given that the issue of VR has been central to the debate about the gender asymmetry of partner violence and that there is considerable discussion of the "battered woman" self-defense plea in the law, research on the general dynamics of VR is surprisingly meager. One might almost think from the literature that the only women who fight back are the ones who kill their partners (Browne, Williams, & Dutton, 1999; Roberts, 1996). Johnson (2000a) reported that VR is perpetrated almost entirely by women, but he presented no detailed analysis of its characteristics. There is some evidence elsewhere regarding the immediate dangers of VR (Bachman & Carmody, 1994), and Jacobson & Gottman (1998, see pages 160–162) viewed VR as one important indicator that a woman will soon leave her abusive partner. It is time that we give more research attention to the incidence and nature of VR in partner violence.

Mutual violent control. Johnson (1999, 2000a) identified a couple pattern in which both husband and wife are controlling and violent, in a situation that could be viewed as two intimate terrorists battling for control. The pattern seems to be rare and we know little about it, but it raises questions again about the importance of distinctions. Until recently the literature on mutual violence was either framed in terms of "self-defense" or "mutual combat," (Saunders, 1988), but the little we do know about VR, MVC, and mutual violence in CCV suggests a need for much more focused research on what it means when both partners in a relationship are violent.

General implications. We have given these distinctions considerable attention because in our review we found our understanding of the literature to be improved by making distinctions among types of violence. For example, the marital violence literature is rife with studies that claim to show that partner violence is gender symmetric, if not perpetrated more often by women than by men, continuing to leave readers of this literature with the impression that men and women are equally abusive. Almost all of these studies, however, use the sort of general heterosexual sample in which aggregated violence only appears to be gender symmetric because it lumps together IT, which is essentially perpetrated by men; CCV, which is perpetrated slightly more often by men than by women; and VR, which is clearly perpetrated more often by women than by men (Johnson, 2000b). Similarly, Macmillan and Gartner (1999) demonstrated the centrality of such distinctions in causal research. They found three qualitatively distinct forms of spousal violence against women, two of which they identified with CCV and IT. When they used these classes as dependent variables in multivariate analyses, the models for CCV and IT were clearly different.

Types of Perpetrators

We see a major convergence in the many attempts to develop typologies of male batterers, suggesting three types: one involved in CCV and two types of perpetrators of IT.

Holtzworth-Munroe and Stuart (1994) referred to these types as "family-only," "generally-violent-antisocial," and "dysphoric-borderline." It appears to us that the family-only type may involve primarily CCV because they were described by the authors as involved in "the least severe

marital violence and . . . the least likely to engage in psychological and sexual abuse" (p. 481). The other types (whom we see as involved in IT) come to their terrorism through two quite different developmental histories and psychological profiles, one type broadly sociopathic and violent, the other deeply emotionally dependent on their relationship with their partner (see also Dutton, 1995).

The types identified by Jacobson and Gottman (1998) in a sample of men that seems to include only intimate terrorists bear a striking similarity to generally-violent-antisocials and dysphoric-borderlines. The sample of couples they studied had identified themselves as involved in violent relationships, and Jacobson and Gottman reported that practically all of the men were emotionally abusive (p. 155) in addition to being violent. The Jacobson and Gottman research is unique in that in addition to being interviewed, observed, and given psychological tests, the couples were monitored physiologically during arguments in the laboratory. One group of men (labeled memorably as "cobras") exhibited a "cold" physiology even in the heat of vicious verbal attacks on their partners, with heart rate and other physiological indicators that suggest a chilling internal calmness. The characteristics of this group and their personal histories resembles those of generally-violent-antisocial batterers. The second group identified by Jacobson and Gottman ("pit bulls") was more physiologically in tune with the emotional displays involved in their verbal attacks on their partner, and in other respects they resembled the dysphoric-borderline type in that they are dependent and needy. Holtzworth-Munroe and Stuart's hypotheses about the development of different types of batterers have received general empirical support in a number of empirical tests (e.g., Hamberger, Lohr, Bonge, & Tolin, 1996; Holtzworth-Munroe, Meehan, Herron, Rehman, & Stuart, in press).

Types of perpetrators within types of violence. We believe that major advances in our understanding of the origins of partner violence will come from bringing together and extending the work on types of violence and types of perpetrators. These distinctions have already demonstrated their usefulness in understanding the causes of battery and in developing treatment programs for batterers (Saunders, 1996), and the Jacobson and Gottman (1998) book is an accessible and compelling demonstration of the importance of such distinctions in matters as far ranging as the childhood precursors of partner violence, the developmental course of violent relationships, the process of escaping such relationships, and matters of public policy and intervention strategies. Most of this perpetrator work is focused on male IT, but we believe it might also be useful to attempt to develop typologies of male and female CCV perpetrators as well (Holtzworth-Munroe & Stuart, 1994; Holtzworth-Munroe et al., in press).

Types of Relationships

The 1990s have also seen an explosion in information about violence in different types of partner relationships. There is now a massive literature on dating and courtship violence and a growing literature on violence in cohabiting relationships. Some of this work has focused on same-gender relationships.

Same-sex relationships. Although a recent issue of the *Journal of Gay and Lesbian Social Services* was devoted to violence within both male and female same-gender relationships (Renzetti & Miley, 1996), we still seem to know more about lesbian battering than we do about violence in gay men's relationships, in part because of the important role of the women's movement in generating research on domestic violence (Dobash & Dobash, 1992) and in part because of Claire Renzetti's (1992) groundbreaking research on lesbian relationships. Her conclusion that psychological abuse was present in all of the violent relationships that she studied, that these abusive partners were extremely threatened by their partner's efforts to establish independent friendships and activities, that jealousy was a major problem, and that power and control were major sources of conflict all suggest to us that her sample tapped into IT. Furthermore, the fact that the majority of women in Renzetti's sample (68%) indicated that their partner's dependency was a source of conflict suggests a similarity to Jacobson and Gottman's "pit bulls" and Holtzworth-Munroe and Stuart's dysphoric-borderline type. Thus, it may be possible that some variation or elaboration of the models developed with heterosexual couples can provide insight into violence in lesbian couples.

Some of the most striking differences between lesbian battery and heterosexual battery have to do with links to the external environment of the relationship. Threats of "outing" women to family members or employers are common forms of psychological abuse and are of course unique to

same-gender couples; battered lesbians are evidently less likely to be supported by friends, who often refuse to believe that a lesbian can be an abuser; and social service workers are often unsupportive as well, assuming that only men batter their partners (Renzetti, 1992).

Although the women's movement has made efforts to educate service providers and the public about lesbian battering (Elliot, 1990), specialized services are rare and research is still quite limited. We still know little about the varieties of partner violence in same-gender relationships (for example, the extent of CCV or IT). The inability to collect information from random samples means that we know almost nothing about incidence. These gaps in our knowledge are troubling not only because they leave policy makers and service providers somewhat on their own, but also because research on partner violence in diverse types of relationships could be an important source of insights into the inadequacies of our "general" theories. Both Merrill and Renzetti (Merrill, 1996; Renzetti, 1992) have pointed out aspects of partner violence in same-gender relationships that seem to fly in the face of theories developed in a heterosexual context. This may be an arena in which much can be gained in terms of the testing and revision of general theory.

Dating and courtship. Research on partner violence in heterosexual dating and courtship relationships began early in the 1980s and has continued throughout the 1990s (Lloyd & Emery, 2000). Although we appear to know a good deal about what was initially a most surprising incidence of partner violence in dating relationships, this literature is as plagued by lack of distinctions as is the marital violence literature. Frequent statements in the literature that there is as much violence in these relationships as there is in marriage imply that there is as much IT, but because the data are drawn from general social surveys, they probably include only CCV.

Rather than review this extensive literature here, we would simply like to point out that it has been a rich source of theoretical insight regarding partner violence. A great many of the multivariate analyses of the correlates of violence have been done in this context (Bookwala, Frieze, Smith, & Ryan, 1992; Foo & Margolin, 1995; Riggs & O'Leary, 1996; Riggs, O'Leary, & Breslin, 1990; Tontodonato & Crew, 1992; Wyatt, 1994). Stets's theoretical work on the centrality of control issues grew from her work on dating violence (Stets &

Pirog-Good, 1990), and Lloyd & Emery's (Lloyd & Emery, 2000) recent book develops a general theoretical framework for understanding physical violence in dating relationships that could be used to address partner violence in all types of relationships.

Cohabitation. Serious discussion of the extent of partner violence in cohabiting relationships can be traced to Stets and Straus's (1990) puzzling finding that cohabiting couples reported more violence than did either married or dating couples, even with controls for age, education, and occupation. Recent studies in New Zealand and Canada also report a higher rate of violence in cohabiting relationships, compared with dating (Magdol, Moffitt, Caspi, & Silva, 1998), and marriage (Johnson, 1996). Although in the United States, the National Violence Against Women Survey appears to present data on cohabitation (Tjaden & Thoennes, 1999, pp. 27–29), the data actually refer to lifetime victimization of respondents who have a history of cohabitation and do not allow for easy interpretation. One possible complication in this cohabitation literature is the confounding of age, length of relationship, and marital status. In Canada, Johnson (1996, pp. 166–168) found that the difference between married and cohabiting unions held only for couples who had been together for 3 years or less.

Stets and Straus (1990) introduced three possible explanations of marital status differences: social isolation, autonomy–control, and investment. Although Stets (1991) claimed to demonstrate that social isolation "explains" the effect, the only measure of social isolation that works in her analysis is "ties to spouse," as measured by the respondents' report of the chances that they will separate. We think it makes more sense to see this as a measure of commitment to the relationship, suggesting only that low commitment is either a consequence or a cause of partner violence in cohabiting relationships. Gaertner and Foshee's (1999) data support this interpretation, showing a negative relationship between commitment and violence in dating relationships. They also reported data relevant to the investment explanation, finding that both duration of relationship and reported investment are *positively* related to violence, the opposite of what Stets and Straus predicted.

Stets and Straus's data actually show that the pattern of more violence occurring in cohabitation than in marriage does not hold for couples in which only the man was violent (p. 240). Perhaps

the pattern is relevant only to CCV. Macmillan and Gartner (1999) reported that marriage is negatively related to CCV, but positively to IT. Perhaps marriage, although not a license to hit, is for some people a license to terrorize. Once again, we see an area in which distinctions among types of violence would help to clarify matters.

Demographics, Social Location, and Identity

Gender. The most longstanding and acrimonious debate in the family literature involves the issue of gender symmetry of partner violence (Archer, 2000; Dobash & Dobash, 1992; Dobash, Dobash, Wilson, & Daly, 1992; Johnson, 1995; Kurz, 1989, 1993; Straus, 1990a, 1993). Although papers continue to appear regularly that claim to demonstrate that women are as violent as men in intimate relationships of one kind or another, or in one country or another, a careful assessment of the literature and a look at the few studies that do distinguish among types of violence both indicate that IT is almost entirely a male pattern (97% male in Johnson, 2000a). The evidence seems to indicate that VR is primarily perpetrated by women (Browne, Williams, et al., 1999; Cascardi & Vivian, 1995; Dobash & Dobash, 1992; Johnson, 2000a; Ogle, Maier-Katkin, & Bernard, 1995; Saunders, 1988). CCV appears to be roughly gender symmetric (56% male perpetrators in Johnson, 2000a; see also Milardo, 1998).

Most studies define gender symmetry in terms of the percent of men and women who have perpetrated at least one act of violence in their relationship. To call this gender symmetry, however, is to ignore different male and female frequencies of violence and the different physical consequences of male-to-female and female-to-male violence. As for the former, Johnson (1999) showed that in 31% of the relationships involving "mutual" CCV, the husbands were clearly more frequently violent than were their wives, compared with 8% in which the wives were more frequently violent. With regard to injury, the more serious physical consequences of male-to-female violence are well-established (Brush, 1990; Sorenson, Upchurch, & Shen, 1996; Straus, 1990a, 1999; Tjaden & Thoennes, 1999).

A number of studies have focused on the possibility that the causes of violence are not the same for men and women. Foo and Margolin (1995) reported in a dating context that a set of standard predictor variables explains 41% of the variance in male-to-female violence, but only 16%

for female-to-male violence (see also Anderson, 1997).

Although work on the gender symmetry issue is of interest in itself, it has also provided an important site for both methodological developments and theoretical insights into the nature of partner violence. Methodologically, the debate has prompted a number of developments, including a new version of the CTS (Straus, Hamby, Boney-McCoy, & Sugarman, 1996), a major reconsideration of the interview context of assessments of violence (Straus, 1999; Tjaden & Thoennes, 1999), and discussions of couple-data issues (Szinovacz & Egley, 1995). The debate has also generated attention to the sampling issues involved in various research designs (Johnson, 2000b; Straus, 1990a).

With regard to theory, the debate has prompted Straus to consider some of the social roots of women's violence toward their male partners (Straus, 1999). He discussed factors such as women's assumption that their violence is harmless (Fiebert & Gonzalez, 1997) and that under some conditions slapping a man is an appropriately "feminine" behavior. Johnson (1995) also provided a rudimentary list of gendered causal factors in partner violence, and he argued that some combinations of them might produce CCV, whereas others produce IT. Other theoretical work of the decade that has arisen from a focus on gender includes theory focused on the broader social context (Dobash & Dobash, 1992, 1998; Straus, 1999), social construction of gender models (Anderson, 1997; Dobash & Dobash, 1998), and evolutionary models (Buss & Shackelford, 1997; Wilson & Daly, 1996, 1998). Of course, gender also is centrally implicated in the literature on gay and lesbian relationships in ways that may prompt further theoretical development as we are forced to ask ourselves which aspects of the gendering of partner violence are a function of male-female differences and which are more related to the specifically gendered nature of heterosexual relationships (Renzetti & Miley, 1996; West, 1998).

Race and ethnicity in North America. Most of the earliest race and ethnicity scholarship did not give serious attention to ethnic differences in experiences of abuse or responses to it, focusing instead primarily on Black-White differences in incidence (Crenshaw, 1994). That literature has continued into the 1990s with survey research regularly indicating higher levels of partner violence among Blacks than among Whites (Anderson, 1997; Ca-

zenave & Straus, 1990; Greenfield & Rand, 1998; Sorenson, 1996; Tjaden & Thoennes, 1999). Recent work has broadened ethnic comparisons to cover other groups, however. For example, only 13% of Asian and Pacific Islander women in the 1995–1996 National Violence Against Women Survey (Tjaden & Thoennes, pp. 22–26) reported having been physically assaulted by an intimate partner. For White women, the figure is 21%, for African Americans 26%, for American Indian and Alaska Natives 31%, and for Mixed Race 27%.

There are two important questions we have to ask about these differences. First, what kind of violence are we talking about? These surveys do not make distinctions among the various types of violence discussed above. We do not know if higher incidence of violence reported in these surveys necessarily means more IT. It is more likely to be CCV. We cannot develop good theories about race differences until we make such distinctions. Second, we have to ask about the extent to which "race" differences have less to do with race and ethnicity than they do with socioeconomic status, as has been shown in National Family Violence Survey data (Cazenave & Straus, 1990). Lockheart's (1991) more recent survey of 307 African American and European American women, drawn equally from high-, middle-, and low-income brackets, found no significant racial differences in rates of violence.

Beyond questions of incidence, there is now a growing literature that focuses on more institutional and cultural matters. Are the dominant social institutions addressing domestic violence effectively in various cultural and ethnic contexts? Are the services women need available in their communities? Are kin, friends, and community willing to face issues of domestic violence and to work to eliminate it? Are the psychological and social consequences the same in different groups? For example, Eng (1995) noted that acknowledgment of battering is highly shameful for many immigrant Asian women who are socialized to believe that marital failure is always the fault of a wife (see also Song, 1996). Gondolf, Fisher, & McFerron (1991) examined 5,708 Texas shelter residents and found no significant differences in the amounts of violence experienced by White, African American, and Hispanic women but did find that Hispanic women were relatively disadvantaged economically and tended to endure battering for a longer time than White and African American women. Crenshaw (1994) was one of the first scholars to identify gaps in domestic violence services for women of color and insensitivity to issues of race and ethnicity in developing policy agendas such as mandatory arrest. Such issues are beginning to be addressed for a number of major ethnic and racial groups in North America, including American Indian people (Bachman, 1992; Fairchild, Fairchild, & Stoner, 1998; McEachern, Winkle, & Steiner, 1998; Norton & Manson, 1995; Tom-Orme, 1995; Waller, Risley-Curtis, Murphy, Medill, & Moore, 1998), Asian and Pacific Island people (Abraham, 1995; Ho, 1990; Song, 1996; Yick & Agbayani-Siewert, 1997), Latino groups (Perilla, Bakerman, & Norris, 1994), and African Americans (Dennis, Key, Kirk, & Smith, 1995; Marsh, 1993; Richie, 1996).

As this literature grows, it will be important to attend to two general questions. First, can we identify social forces that shape experiences similarly across subsets of "minority" groups, such as similarities produced by common experiences of exclusion and domination, or the experience of recent immigration (Cervantes & Cervantes, 1993; Root, 1996; Sorenson, 1996)? Second, what are the unique ways in which each particular racial and ethnic context shapes domestic violence, its consequences, and community responses to it? Even within "standard" racial and ethnic categories, there are important distinctions that cannot be ignored. In one illustration of the importance of making such distinctions, Sorenson and Telles (1991, pp. 3) reported no difference between non-Hispanic Whites and Mexican Americans in their sample until immigration status was taken into account: "Mexican Americans born in the US reported rates 2.4 times higher than those born in Mexico." This finding can serve to remind us not only of the importance of differences among specific groups in North America, but also of matters of cultural roots and immigrant status that have global implications (Kane, 1999).

Global complexities. We can only begin to address the global complexity of partner violence in this review, involving as it does issues of cultural differences, economic and social structure, effects of conflict and warfare, and the position of immigrant and refugee populations. To begin, we can simply draw attention to a number of overviews of the international scope of partner violence (Heise, 1996; Heise, Raikes, Watts, & Zwi, 1994; Human Rights Watch, 1995; Klein, 1998; Levinson, 1989; Sewall, Vasan, & Schuler, 1996; United Nations, 1989). In addition, scholarly work in English on domestic violence in specific other coun-

tries is beginning to become available (Alexander, 1993; Dawud-Noursi, Lamb, & Sternberg, 1998; Fawcett, Heise, Isita-Espejel, & Pick, 1999; Glantz, Halperin, & Hunt, 1998; Gondolf & Shestakou, 1997; Grandin & Lupri, 1997; Haj-Yahia, 1998; Handwerker, 1998; Kalu, 1993; Ofei-Aboagye, 1994; Schuler, Hashemi, Riley, & Akhter, 1996; Stewart, 1996; Tang, 1994). Finally, we would like to address briefly a few specific international issues.

First, in a global context domestic violence has now been defined as a human rights issue (Richters, 1994). Second, there appears to be considerable variability in the incidence of partner violence in various countries (Heise, 1994). Of course, we do not know what type of violence these statistics reference. Furthermore, as we consider these clues to the social and cultural roots of partner violence, it will be important to monitor our interpretations for ethnocentrism. For example, Bhattacharjee (1997) questions the assumption of Western White feminism that Southeast Asian women are more subservient to husbands.

Third, a literature is developing that explores the effects of war, internal conflict, and terrorism on matters related to partner violence. McWilliams (1998) framed the issue as one of "societies under stress," using the case of Northern Ireland as her major example. Community resources are diverted to the conflict, a higher priority is placed on keeping families together, public agencies may be controlled by the "enemy," calls for ingroup solidarity militate against making internal conflicts such as domestic violence public, and "warrior" images reinforce patriarchal ideology. As we read McWilliams' chapter, we were intrigued by the possibility that many of these same processes might be relevant to racial and ethnic minorities in the United States who are under siege, albeit a "siege" that generally falls short of the open intergroup violence that applies in the cases McWilliams discusses.

In countries recovering from war, pronatalist policies may limit access to contraceptive devices or reduce women's ability to procure employment that might allow them to escape an abusive situation. Additionally, people suffering from the continuing effects of occupation, such as the majority of indigenous groups worldwide, have high rates of interpersonal and domestic violence related to the destruction of culture and oppressive economic and social conditions (McWilliams, 1998, p. 123–124). Scholarship on the effects of colonization, decolonization, war, and development on rates and forms of partner violence is in its infancy. Filling this gap is an important task for the next decade of research.

Finally, immigrant and refugee status (sometimes a result of flight from the kind of societal stress discussed above) creates special difficulties for women trying to escape abusive relationships. Immigrant women experiencing violence in their homes often are restricted by language barriers, fear of deportation, lack of transportation, fear of loss of child custody, and cultural taboos (Hogeland & Rosen, 1990).

Summary

Some distinctions are central to the theoretical and practical understanding of the nature of partner violence (e.g., types of violence and perpetrators), others provide important contexts for developing more sensitive and comprehensive theories (e.g., types of relationships or gender differences), and others may simply force us to question our tendency to generalize carelessly from one context to another. Such distinctions were a major theme of the domestic violence literature of the 1990s, and they must continue to be so into the next decade.

CONTROL

A second major theme of the 1990s has been control. Whatever the immediate precipitator of violence may be, it generally gives the perpetrator some measure of control, but once again we see distinctions among types of violence as central. The control may be specific, focused narrowly on winning a particular argument or having one's way in some narrowly defined matter (CCV). In other cases the control may be broad, involving the establishment or maintenance of general control over one's partner (IT, MVC). Sometimes the control issue is one of wresting some modicum of control from a generally abusive partner (VR). We believe that the most progress will be made in our understanding of domestic violence by assuming that the origins and dynamics of the different kinds of control motives are not the same.

In our review of this literature, we want to make a somewhat arbitrary distinction. Some writers have come to their focus on control issues through an analysis of the patriarchal roots of wife beating (Dobash & Dobash, 1992; Johnson, 1995; Pence & Paymar, 1993). Although this is our own primary orientation, we believe that a full understanding of partner violence must go beyond this

feminist analysis to ask questions about the role of control in the generation of violence that may have little to do either with patriarchal traditions and structures or with individual patriarchal motives.

The Gender Context

Johnson's (1995) discussion of IT as violence embedded in a general pattern of control tactics draws heavily on the work of the Duluth shelter activists Pence and Paymar (1993). The "power and control wheel" that is the heart of the Duluth educational model for intervention with batterers is drawn directly from the accounts of women who have come to shelters for help. Kirkwood's (1993) study of women who left abusive relationships also relied heavily on an analysis of the dynamics of control. Dobash and Dobash's (1992); analysis of the dynamics of wife beating was likewise formed by the perspectives of battered women, in this case women whom they interviewed in their early research in Scotland, but they also drew heavily on a more sociological and historical analysis of the patriarchal form of the family and other institutions. They now are beginning to explore control issues from the perspective of the violent men themselves (Dobash & Dobash, 1998). Their arguments regarding the importance of context refer not only to the relationship context in which a particular man may feel he has the right to control "his woman," but also the more general context in which relations between men and women are formed and in which other institutions react to men's violence against their female partners.

Whereas Dobash and Dobash, as well as other feminists, tend to move the analysis up from the relationship to the broader societal context of wife beating, Jacobson and Gottman (1998) moved down to the individual level, asking questions about the childhood roots of the personalities of the two types of perpetrators whom they identified among their sample of men who batter their partners. Similarly, other psychologists who focus on wife beating but do not rely heavily on a feminist analysis search for the developmental roots of men's violent behavior toward their female partners (Dutton, 1995; Dutton & Starzomski, 1993; Holtzworth-Munroe et al., in press; Holtzworth-Munroe, Stuart, & Hutchinson, 1997).

Prospects for a More General Analysis of Control

The problem with the analyses of control discussed above is that they are so focused on male

IT that they probably provide little insight into CCV or VR, and they seem to have little relevance for any type of partner violence in same-gender relationships. We need a more general approach to issues of violence and control that can encompass IT in heterosexual relationships but also go beyond it.

Beginning with a study that focused on the connection between relationship control and violence, Jan Stets and her colleagues have developed two lines of analysis of the role of control in intimate relationships (Stets & Pirog-Good, 1990). One line of work focuses on a "compensatory model" in which it is assumed that individuals act to maintain a reasonable level of control in their lives, becoming more controlling of their partner when their level of control is threatened either within the relationship itself (Stets, 1993, 1995b) or in other areas of their life (Stets, 1995a). In a slightly different approach, paying more attention to individual differences, the concepts of "control identity" and "mastery identity" were explored in terms of their relationships to gender, gender identity, and controlling behavior in intimate relationships (Stets, 1995c; Stets & Burke, 1994, 1996).

If this literature could be brought back to its initial connection with violence, and perhaps informed more by feminist analyses of the gendering of control issues in relationships, it might provide a context for major theory development. We expect that the most fruitful approaches will bring together a variety of levels of analysis from the societal through the interpersonal to the individual (for example, see Lloyd & Emery, 2000).

SOME OTHER CONTINUING THEMES

Coping With Partner Violence

Most of the literature on coping with violence is focused on IT. In the 1990s, the dominant view shifted from seeing women in abusive relationships as victims to defining them as "survivors," focusing on the decisions women make to escape, to end the violence, or to cope with it in some other manner (Ferraro, 1997). Campbell and her colleagues (Campbell, Miller, Cardwell, & Belknap, 1994; Campbell, Rose, Kub, & Nedd, 1998) argued that the women they studied over a 2½-year period showed great resourcefulness in their resistance to the pattern of violent control in which they were enmeshed. Strategies included (a) active problem solving, (b) responding to iden-

tifiable pivotal events, and (c) negotiating first with oneself and then directly or indirectly with the male partner. By the end of the 2½ years, three fourths of the battered women were no longer in a violent relationship, 43% having left and 32% having successfully negotiated an end to the violence. This is yet another area in which distinctions among types of violence and types of relationship are likely to be useful. Strategies of negotiation and barriers to leaving are likely to differ rather dramatically for IT and CCV and across dating, cohabiting, same-gender and cross-gender relationships.

Leaving. The coping strategy that has received the most attention is "leaving," all-too-often addressed from a misguided sense of puzzlement that women do not leave abusive relationships. We still see papers and sections of literature reviews and textbooks headed "Why do they stay?" Well, the truth is, they don't stay (Campbell et al., 1994; Holtzworth-Munroe, Smutzler, & Sandin, 1997, pp. 194–95). We need to watch our language; there is no good reason why a study in which two thirds of the women have left the violent relationship is subtitled, "How and why women stay" instead of "How and why women leave" (Herbert, Silver, & Ellard, 1991).

One theoretical approach that seems promising draws upon commitment theory. Rusbult and Martz (1995) make use of Rusbult's investment model to investigate the effects of commitment, rewards, costs, alternatives, and investments on whether women in abusive relationships stay or leave within the time frame of the study. We believe, however, that the best work on staying and leaving will have to treat leaving as a process. Choice & Lamke (1997) did that to some extent, identifying two stages of leaving in which women ask themselves first "Will I be better off?" and second "Can I do it?" But there is other work that focuses in more detail on the process of leaving.

Kirkwood's (1993) marvelous book takes us into both the process by which abusive men entrap their partners and the process by which those women engineer their escape. Her two metaphors of a "web" of entrapment and of a "spiral" of escape capture the details of the process simply and vividly. These men use a wide range of tactics of control not only to control the intact relationship, but also to ensure as best they can that their partner will never be able to leave them. Johnson's (1998) analysis of the shelter movement addressed this process in terms of the abuser's manipulation of personal, moral, and structural commitments to the relationship in order to entrap his partner. He argued that the major strategies of the battered women's movement (temporary safe housing, support groups, empowerment counseling, networking with social support services, legal advocacy, coordinated community response) empower women to neutralize those commitments. Kirkwood also acknowledged the role of shelter advocates in helping the women she studied as they went through a process of leaving and returning, each time gaining more psychological and social resources, each time coming closer to escaping for good, metaphorically spiraling outward until they escaped from the web.

Psychological and Behavioral Consequences of Partner Violence

As we approach the end of this article, we come upon a huge research literature dealing with the psychological consequences of partner violence for the adults involved and for their children. Once again, however, we have to note the difficulties created by not taking care to distinguish among types of violence. Although some of the studies in this literature make use of samples in which the violence is clearly IT, others analyze survey data in which the measurement of violence does not attend to differences that may have critical implications in terms of consequences. A slap in the face sometime in the last 12 months is likely to have little impact on self-esteem and may not even be witnessed by the children. A systematic pattern of assault and psychological abuse is another story.

The victims. Nevertheless, the literature confirms that IT and perhaps other forms of partner violence *against women* have negative effects in terms of injuries and longer-term physical and psychological health (Giles-Sims, 1998; Holtz-worth-Munroe et al., 1997, pp. 184–189; Johnson & Leone, 2000). The psychological effects include posttraumatic stress disorder, depression, and lowered self-esteem.

There is another interesting line of research that focuses not on psychological health, but on women's attributions regarding the causes of the violence they are experiencing. Holtzworth-Munroe and her colleagues (Holtzworth-Munroe, Jacobson, Fehrenbach, & Fruzzetti, 1992) argue, on the basis of a literature review, that the evidence

shows women do not generally blame themselves for their partner's violence (see also Cantos, Neidig, & O'Leary, 1993). Nonetheless, the fact that issues of victim self-blame are raised often in the more qualitative literature suggests that research on attributions as moderating variables, affecting the consequences of violence, might be useful (Andrews & Brewin, 1990; Fincham, Bradbury, Arias, Byrne, & Karney, 1997).

Studies that have compared physical and psychological consequences for men and women find more serious consequences for women (Browne, Williams, et al., 1999; Brush, 1990; Dobash et al., 1992; Grandin, Lupri, & Brinkerhoff, 1998; Sorenson et al., 1996; Straus, 1999; Vivian & Langhinrichson-Rohling, 1994). Of course, the danger in these comparisons is that they may be comparing apples and oranges because most of them deal with survey data in which no distinctions among types of violence are made. It is unlikely that many of the men in such surveys are experiencing IT, whereas a significant number of the female victims of violence are (Johnson, 2000a). Qualitative and anecdotal evidence suggest that the consequences of terroristic violence may be as severe for men as they are for women (Cook, 1997; Island & Letellier, 1991; Letellier, 1996).

The children. There is also a substantial literature regarding the effects of partner violence on children who witness it (Kolbo, Blakely, & Engleman, 1996; Wolak & Finkelhor, 1998). Behavioral effects include aggression and delinquency, among others. Psychological effects include anxiety, depression, and low self-esteem. There is even evidence of long-term effects, with college-age women who remember violence between their parents having lower self-esteem, greater depression, and lower levels of social competence (Henning, Leitenberg, Coffey, Bennett, & Jankowski, 1997; Silvern, Karyl, Waelde, Hodges, & Starek, 1995). Again, however, we have to point out that although some of these studies deal with populations in which the nature of the parental violence is relatively clear, in most cases the measures do not allow the necessary distinctions. The reported effects are generally small, but we do not know if exposure to IT might in fact have powerful effects that are muted by their aggregation with the effects of CCV.

Intergenerational nontransmission of violence. One particular type of long-term effect on children has been studied enough to merit its own section.

Although it is not unusual for scholars to take the position that "violence in the family of origin is probably the mostly widely accepted risk marker for the occurrence of partner violence (Kantor & Jasinski, 1998, p.16), we are struck by the weakness of the relationship in the studies we reviewed. In this as in other areas of socialization research, the widespread use of the metaphor of "transmission" introduces a gross distortion of the reality of family-of-origin effects on the adult lives of children. Nevertheless, scholars have moved on to assessment of the mechanisms by which "transmission" takes place, in many cases with data that effectively show no "transmission" to begin with. For example, Simons, Lin, & Gordon (1998) presented structural equation models of the process by which parental behavior affects dating violence of their children, failing to draw our attention to the fact that the largest zero-order correlation they find is .12, representing roughly 1% of the variance in dating violence. Then there is a study of marriage and marriagelike relationships (Lackey & Williams, 1995) that takes intergenerational transmission for granted and restricts its major analyses to investigating the conditions under which men whose parents were violent do not become violent themselves. Buried in their appendix is the correlation that represents the intergenerational effect in their data ($r = .10$), once again an explained variance of 1%. Foshee, Bauman, and Linder (1999) similarly tested models of intervening variables for effects the largest of which represent 2% of the variance in dating violence.

The important point here is not just that the effects are small. Social scientists indeed often do make much of such small effects in other areas as well. Our concern is that the metaphor of transmission, and the use of terms such as "cycle of violence," imply that partner violence is inexorably passed on from generation to generation. We want to drive home our concern here with widely cited data that may represent the strongest intergenerational effect ever reported in this literature. Analyzing data from the first National Family Violence Survey, Straus, Gelles, and Steinmetz (1988, p.101) reported that "the sons of the most violent parents have a rate of wife-beating 1,000 percent greater than that of the sons of nonviolent parents . . . ." What we deleted with our ellipses is the actual rate of 20%, meaning that even among this group of men whose parents were two standard deviations above average in level of partner violence, 80% of the adult sons had not even

once in the last 12 months committed any acts of severe violence toward their partners as defined by the CTS. What about the 20% who *were* violent? We must return to our old refrain that we have no way of knowing which type of violence these men (or their parents) perpetrated.

Social Consequences of Partner Violence

During the 1990s, scholarship began to focus on the interconnections of partner violence, poverty, welfare, and homelessness. This work became particularly relevant with the passage of so-called welfare reform in 1996, which included the possibility for states to exempt battered women from some of its most restrictive mandates (Kurz, 1998). Research focusing specifically on low-income women has uncovered an extraordinarily high level of interpersonal violence, which interferes with social and economic success. Zorza (1991) found that at least half of homeless women were forced from residences because of violence from their intimate partners. Browne and Bassuk (1997) interviewed 220 homeless and 216 housed low-income women in Massachusetts about childhood abuse and adult intimate violence. Nearly one third of respondents reported that their current or most recent partner had perpetrated severe physical violence against them. Browne and her colleagues (Browne, Salomon, & Bassuk, 1999) also reported that "Controlling for a variety of factors, women who experienced physical aggression/violence by male partners during a 12-month period had only one third the odds of maintaining employment for at least 30 hrs per week for 6 months or more during the subsequent year as did women without these experiences." Other examinations of the effects of battering on women's employment (Brandwein, 1998; Lloyd, 1999) have reported that abusive men deliberately undermine women's employment by depriving them of transportation, harassing them at work, turning off alarm clocks, beating them before job interviews, and disappearing when they promised to provide child care. Some abusers simply prohibit their partners from working. Battering also indirectly undermines employment by (a) causing repeated absences; (b) impairing women's physical health, mental agility and concentration; and (3) lowering self-esteem and aspirations. Thus, although surveys and crime statistics indicate higher levels of partner violence among low-income couples and in lower income neighborhoods (Anderson, 1997; Lupri, Grandin, & Brinkerhoff, 1994;

Miles-Doan, 1998; Straus, 1990b), for many women violence may be the *precipitating* factor for poverty, and it is surely a barrier to raising income and employment status.

CONCLUSION

The 1990s were a time of tremendous growth in the literature on partner violence, including considerable growth in attention to the need to make distinctions among various types of violence. Unfortunately, our major conclusion from this review of the decade is that in spite of increasing evidence of the importance of distinctions, almost all of our general theoretical and empirical work is severely handicapped by the failure to attend to these distinctions. The modeling of the causes and consequences of partner violence will never be powerful as long as we aggregate behaviors as disparate as a "feminine" slap in the face, a terrorizing pattern of beatings accompanied by humiliating psychological abuse, an argument that escalates into a mutual shoving match, or a homicide committed by a person who feels there is no other way to save her own life.

Even more troubling, however, is the possibility that the aggregation of such disparate phenomena can produce serious errors, as it did in the gender symmetry debate. Everything from lists of risk factors, to inferences about causal processes from multivariate analyses, to statements about differences in incidence across groups or across time—all of it—is called into question. Going back through this review, one can hardly find a section in which we did not feel the need to question generalization across types of violence. We need to return to our research, make distinctions among types of violence, and find out which of our pronouncements apply to which forms of violence.

We hope that the beginning of this century will see work on partner violence that is more careful to make important distinctions among types of violence and to develop theories that take into account the different causes, dynamics, and consequences of the different forms of violence. Equally important is the presentation of our knowledge to each other and to the general public in terms that clearly reflect those differences, so that public opinion and policy development can make *appropriate* use of what we learn.

REFERENCES

Abraham, M. (1995). Ethnicity, gender, and marital violence: South Asian women's organizations in the United States. *Gender and Society, 9,* 450–468.

Alexander, R. (1993). Wife battering—An Australian perspective. *Journal of Family Violence, 8,* 229–251.

Anderson, K. L. (1997). Gender, status and domestic violence: An integration of feminist and family violence approaches. *Journal of Marriage and the Family, 59,* 655–669.

Andrews, B., & Brewin, C. R. (1990). Attributions of blame for marital violence: A study of antecedents and consequences. *Journal of Marriage and the Family, 52,* 757–767.

Archer, J. (in press). Sex differences in aggression between heterosexual partners: A meta-analytic review. *Psychological Bulletin.*

Bachman, R. (1992). *Death and violence on the reservation: Homicide, family violence, and suicide in American Indian populations.* Westport, CT: Autumn House.

Bachman, R., & Carmody, D. (1994). Fighting fire with fire: The effects of victim resistance in intimate versus stranger perpetrated assaults against females. *Journal of Family Violence, 9,* 317–331.

Bhattacharjee, A. (1997). The public/private mirage: Mapping homes and undomesticating violence work in the South Asian immigrant community. In M. J. Alexander & C. T. Mohanty (Eds.), *Feminist genealogies, colonial legacies, democratic futures* (pp. 308–329). New York: Routledge.

Bookwala, J., Frieze, I. H., Smith, C., & Ryan, K. (1992). Predictors of dating violence: A multivariate analysis. *Violence and Victims, 7,* 297–311.

Brandwein, R. A. (1998). *Battered women, children, and welfare reform: The ties that bind.* Thousand Oaks, CA: Sage.

Brant, B. (1996). Wild Turkeys. In S. Koppelman (Ed.), *Women in the trees: U.S. women's short stories about battering & resistance, 1839-1994* (pp. 199–230). Thousand Oaks, CA: Sage.

Browne, A., & Bassuk, S. S. (1997). Intimate violence in the lives of homeless and poor housed women: Prevalence and patterns in an ethnically diverse sample. *American Journal of Orthopsychiatry, 67,* 261–278.

Browne, A., Salomon, A., & Bassuk, S. S. (1999). The impact of recent partner violence on poor women's capacity to maintain work. *Violence Against Women, 5,* 393–426.

Browne, A., Williams, K. R., & Dutton, D. G. (1999). Homicide between intimate partners: A 20-year review. In M. D. Smith & M. A. Zahn (Eds.), *Homicide: A sourcebook of social research* (pp. 149–164). Thousand Oaks, CA: Sage.

Brush, L. D. (1990). Violent acts and injurious outcomes in married couples: Methodological issues in the National Survey of Families and Households. *Gender & Society, 4,* 56–67.

Buss, D. M., & Shackelford, T. K. (1997). From vigilance to violence: Mate retention tactics in married couples. *Journal of Personality and Social Psychology, 72,* 346–361.

Campbell, J. C., Miller, P., Cardwell, M. M., & Belknap,

R. A. (1994). Relationship status of battered women over time. *Journal of Family Violence, 9,* 99–111.

Campbell, J. C., Rose, L., Kub, J., & Nedd, D. (1998). Voices of strength and resistance: A contextual and longitudinal analysis of women's responses to battering. *Journal of Interpersonal Violence, 13,* 743–762.

Cantos, A. L., Neidig, P. H., & O'Leary, K. D. (1993). Men and women's attributions of blame for domestic violence. *Journal of Family Violence, 8,* 289–302.

Cascardi, M., & Vivian, D. (1995). Context for specific episodes of marital violence: Gender and severity of violence differences. *Journal of Family Violence, 10,* 265–293.

Cazenave, N. A., & Straus, M. A. (1990). Race, class, network embeddedness, and family violence: A search for potent support systems. In M. A. Straus & R. J. Gelles (Eds.), *Physical violence in American families* (pp. 321–339). Brunswick, NJ: Transaction.

Cervantes, N. N., & Cervantes, J. M. (1993). A multi-cultural perspective in the treatment of domestic violence. In M. Harway & M. Hansen (Eds.), *Battering and family therapy: A feminist perspective* (pp. 156–174). Newbury Park, CA: Sage.

Chang, V. N. (1996). *I Just lost myself: Psychological abuse of women in marriage.* Westport, CT: Praeger.

Choice, P., & Lamke, L. K. (1997). A conceptual approach to understanding abused women's stay/leave decisions. *Journal of Family Issues, 18,* 290–314.

Cook, P. W. (1997). *Abused men: the hidden side of domestic violence.* Westport, CT: Praeger/Greenwood.

Crenshaw, K. (1994). Mapping the margins: Intersectionality, identity politics, and violence against women of color. In M. A. Fineman & R. Mykitiuk (Eds.), *The public nature of private violence: The discovery of domestic abuse* (pp. 93–118). New York: Routledge.

Dawud-Noursi, S., Lamb, M. E., & Sternberg, K. J. (1998). The relations among domestic violence, peer relationships, and academic performance. In C. Feiring (Ed.), *Families, risk, and competence* (pp. 207–226). Mahwah, NJ: Erlbaum.

Dennis, R. E., Key, L. J., Kirk, A. L., & Smith, A. (1995). Addressing domestic violence in the African American community. *Journal of Health Care for the Poor and Underserved, 6,* 284–293.

Dobash, R. E., & Dobash, R. P. (1992). *Women, violence and social change.* New York: Routledge.

Dobash, R. E., & Dobash, R. P. (1998). Violent men and violent contexts. In R. E. Dobash & R. P. Dobash (Eds.), *Rethinking violence against women* (pp. 141–168). Thousand Oaks, CA: Sage.

Dobash, R. P., Dobash, R. E., Wilson, M., & Daly, M. (1992). The myth of sexual symmetry in marital violence. *Social Problems, 39,* 71–91.

Dutton, D. G. (1995). *The batterer: A psychological profile* (with Susan K. Golant). New York: Basic Books.

Dutton, D. G., & Starzomski, A. J. (1993). Borderline personality in perpetrators of psychological and physical abuse. *Violence and Victims, 8,* 327–338.

Elliot, P. (Ed.). (1990). *Confronting lesbian battering: A manual for the battered women's movement.* St. Paul, MN: Minnesota Coalition for Battered Women.

Eng, P. (1995). Domestic violence in Asian/Pacific Island communities. In D. L. Adams (Ed.), *Health is-sues for women of color* (pp. 78–88). Thousand Oaks, CA: Sage.

Fairchild, D. G., Fairchild, M. W., & Stoner, S. (1998). Prevalence of adult domestic violence among women seeking routine care in a Native American health care facility. *American Journal of Public Health, 88,* 1515–1517.

Fawcett, G., Heise, L. L., Isita-Espejel, L., & Pick, S. (1999). Changing community responses to wife abuse: A research and demonstration project in Iztacalco, Mexico. *American Psychologist, 54,* 41–49.

Ferraro, K. J. (1997). Battered women: Strategies for survival. In A. Carderelli (Ed.), *Violence among intimate partners: Patterns, causes and effects* (pp. 124–140). New York: Macmillan.

Fiebert, M. S., & Gonzalez, D. M. (1997). College women who initiate assaults on their male partners and the reasons offered for such behavior. *Psychological Reports, 80,* 583–590.

Fincham, F. D., Bradbury, T. N., Arias, I., Byrne, C. A., & Karney, B. R. (1997). Marital violence, marital distress, and attributions. *Journal of Family Psychology, 11,* 367–372.

Follingstad, D. R., Rutledge, L. L., Berg, B. J., Hause, E. S., & Polek, D. S. (1990). The role of emotional abuse in physically abusive relationships. *Journal of Family Violence, 5,* 107–120.

Foo, L., & Margolin, G. (1995). A multivariate investigation of dating aggression. *Journal of Family Violence, 10,* 351–377.

Foshee, V. A., Bauman, K. E., & Linder, G. F. (1999). Family violence and the perpetration of adolescent dating violence: Examining social learning and social control processes. *Journal of Marriage and the Family, 61,* 331–342.

Gaertner, L., & Foshee, V. (1999). Commitment and the perpetration of domestic violence. *Personal Relationships, 6,* 227–239.

Giles-Sims, J. (1998). The aftermath of partner violence. In J. L. Jasinski & L. M. Williams (Eds.), *Partner violence: A comprehensive review of 20 years of research* (pp. 44–72). Thousand Oaks, CA: Sage.

Glantz, N. M., Halperin, D. C., & Hunt, L. M. (1998). Studying domestic violence in Chiapas, Mexico. *Qualitative Health Research, 8,* 377–392.

Gondolf, E. W., Fisher, E., & McFerron, J. R. (1991). Racial differences among shelter residents: A comparison of Anglo, Black and Hispanic battered women. In R. L. Hampton (Ed.), *Black family violence.* Lexington, MA: Lexington Books.

Gondolf, E. W., & Shestakou, D. (1997). Spousal homicide in Russia versus United States: Preliminary findings and implications. *Journal of Family Violence, 12,* 63–74.

Grandin, E., & Lupri, E. (1997). Intimate violence in Canada and United States: A cross-national comparison. *Journal of Family Violence, 12,* 417–443.

Grandin, E., Lupri, E., & Brinkerhoff, M. B. (1998). Couple violence and psychological distress. *Canadian Journal of Public Health, 89,* 43–47.

Greenfield, L. A., & Rand, M. R. (1998). *Violence by Intimates* (NCJ-167237). Washington, DC: U.S. Department of Justice.

Haj-Yahia, M. M. (1998). A patriarchal perspective of beliefs about wife beating among Palestinian men from the West Bank and the Gaza Strip. *Journal of Family Issues, 19,* 595–621.

Hamberger, L. K., Lohr, J. M., Bonge, D., & Tolin, D. F. (1996). A large sample empirical typology of male spouse abusers and its relationship to dimensions of abuse. *Violence & Victims, 11,* 277–292.

Handwerker, W. P. (1998). Why violence? A test of hypotheses representing three discourses on the roots of domestic violence. *Human Organization, 57,* 200–208.

Heise, L. L. (1994). *Violence against women: The hidden health burden.* Washington, DC: World Bank.

Heise, L. L. (1996). Violence against women: Global organizing for change. In J. L. Edleson & Z. C. Eisikovits (Eds.), *Future interventions with battered women and their families* (pp. 7–33). Thousand Oaks, CA: Sage.

Heise, L. L., Raikes, A., Watts, C. H., & Zwi, A. B. (1994). Violence against women: A neglected public health issue in less developed countries. *Social Science and Medicine, 39,* 1165–1179.

Henning, K., Leitenberg, H., Coffey, P., Bennett, T., & Jankowski, M. K. (1997). Long-term psychological adjustment to witnessing interparental physical conflict during childhood. *Child Abuse and Neglect, 21,* 501–515.

Herbert, T. B., Silver, R. C., & Ellard, J. H. (1991). Coping with an abusive relationship: I. How and why do women stay? *Journal of Marriage and the Family, 53,* 311–325.

Ho, C. K. (1990). An analysis of domestic violence in Asian American communities: A multicultural approach to counseling. *Women and Therapy, 9,* 129–150.

Hogeland, C., & Rosen, K. (1990). *Dreams lost, dreams found: Undocumented women in the land of opportunity.* San Francisco: Coalition for Immigrant and Refugee Rights and Services.

Holtzworth-Munroe, A., Jacobson, N. S., Fehrenbach, P. A., & Fruzzetti, A. (1992). Violent married couples' attributions for violent and nonviolent self and partner behaviors. *Behavioral Assessment, 14,* 53–64.

Holtzworth-Munroe, A., Meehan, J. C., Herron, K., Rehman, U., & Stuart, G. L. (in press). Testing the Holtzworth-Munroe and Stuart batterer typology. *Journal of Consulting and Clinical Psychology.*

Holtzworth-Munroe, A., Smutzler, N., & Sandin, E. (1997). A brief review of the research on husband violence: Part II: The psychological effects of husband violence on battered women and their children. *Aggression and Violent Behavior, 2,* 179–213.

Holtzworth-Munroe, A., & Stuart, G. L. (1994). Typologies of male batterers: Three subtypes and the differences among them. *Psychological Bulletin, 116,* 476–497.

Holtzworth-Munroe, A., Stuart, G. L., & Hutchinson, G. (1997). Violent versus nonviolent husbands: Differences in attachment patterns, dependency, and jealousy. *Journal of Family Psychology, 11,* 314–331.

Human Rights Watch (Ed.). (1995). Domestic violence. In *The Human Rights Watch Global Report on Women's Human Rights* (pp. 341–409). New York: Author.

Island, D., & Letellier, P. (1991). *Men who beat the men who love them: Battered gay men and domestic violence.* New York: Haworth Press.

Jacobson, N., & Gottman, J. (1998). *When men batter women: New insights into ending abusive relationships.* New York: Simon & Schuster.

Johnson, H. (1996). *Dangerous domains: Violence against women in Canada.* Toronto: Nelson Canada.

Johnson, M. P. (1995). Patriarchal terrorism and common couple violence: Two forms of violence against women. *Journal of Marriage and the Family, 57,* 283–294.

Johnson, M. P. (1998, June). *Commitment and entrapment.* Paper presented at the Ninth International Conference on Personal Relationships, Saratoga Springs, NY.

Johnson, M. P. (1999, November). *Two types of violence against women in the American family: Identifying patriarchal terrorism and common couple violence.* Paper presented at the National Council on Family Relations annual meetings, Irvine, CA.

Johnson, M. P. (2000a). Conflict and control: Images of symmetry and asymmetry in domestic violence. In A. Booth, A. C. Crouter, & M. Clements (Eds.), *Couples in conflict.* Hillsdale, NJ: Erlbaum.

Johnson, M. P. (2000b). Domestic violence is not a unitary phenomenon: A major flaw in the domestic violence literature. Unpublished manuscript.

Johnson, M. P., & Leone, J. (2000, July). *The differential effects of patriarchal terrorism and common couple violence: Findings from the National Violence Against Women Survey.* Paper presented at the International Conference on Personal Relationships, Brisbane, Australia.

Kalu, W. J. (1993). Battered spouse as a social concern in work with families in two semi-rural communities of Nigeria. *Journal of Family Violence, 8,* 361–373.

Kane, E. W. (1999, August). *Race, ethnicity, and beliefs about gender inequality.* Paper presented at the Society for the Study of Social Problems, Chicago.

Kantor, G. K., & Jasinski, J. L. (1998). Dynamics and risk factors in partner violence. In J. L. Jasinksi & L. M. Williams (Eds.), *Partner violence: A comprehensive review of 20 years of research* (pp. 1–43). Thousand Oaks, CA: Sage.

Kirkwood, C. (1993). *Leaving abusive partners: From the scars of survival to the wisdom for change.* Newbury Park, CA: Sage.

Klein, R. C. A. (Ed.). (1998). *Multidisciplinary perspectives on family violence.* New York: Routledge.

Kolbo, J. R., Blakely, E. H., & Engleman, D. (1996). Children who witness domestic violence: A review of empirical literature. *Journal of Interpersonal Violence, 11,* 281–293.

Kurz, D. (1989). Social science perspectives on wife abuse: Current debates and future directions. *Gender and Society, 3,* 489–505.

Kurz, D. (1993). Physical assaults by husbands: A major social problem. In R. J. Gelles & D. R. Loseke (Eds.), *Current controversies on family violence* (pp. 88–103). Newbury Park, CA: Sage.

Kurz, D. (1998). Women, welfare, and domestic violence. *Social Justice, 25,* 105–122.

Lackey, C., & Williams, K. R. (1995). Social bonding and the cessation of partner violence across generations. *Journal of Marriage and the Family, 57,* 295–305.

Letellier, P. (1996). Twin epidemics: Domestic violence

and HIV infection among gay and bisexual men. In C. M. Renzetti & C. H. Miley (Eds.), *Violence in gay and lesbian domestic partnerships* (pp. 69–81). New York: Harrington Park Press.

Levinson, D. (Ed.). (1989). *Family violence in a cross-cultural perspective.* Newbury Park, CA: Sage.

Lloyd, S. (1999). The effects of male violence on female employment. *Violence Against Women, 5,* 370–392.

Lloyd, S. A., & Emery, B. C. (2000). *The dark side of courtship: Physical and sexual aggression.* Thousand Oaks, CA: Sage.

Lockheart, L. L. (1991). Spousal violence: A cross-racial perspective. In R. L. Hampton (Ed.), *Black family violence* (pp. 85–101). Lexington, MA: Lexington Books.

Lupri, E., Grandin, E., & Brinkerhoff, M. B. (1994). Socioeconomic status and male violence in the Canadian home: A reexamination. *Canadian Journal of Sociology, 19,* 47–73.

Macmillan, R., & Gartner, R. (1999). When she brings home the bacon: Labour-force participation and the risk of spousal violence against women. *Journal of Marriage and the Family, 61,* 947–958.

Magdol, L., Moffitt, T. E., Caspi, A., & Silva, P. A. (1998). Hitting without a license: Testing explanations for differences in partner abuse between young adult daters and cohabitors. *Journal of Marriage and the Family, 60,* 41–55.

Marsh, C. E. (1993). Sexual assault and domestic violence in the African American community. *Western Journal of Black Studies, 17,* 149–155.

McEachern, D., Winkle, M. V., & Steiner, S. (1998). Domestic violence among the Navajo: A legacy of colonization. In E. A. Segal & K. M. Kilty (Eds.), *Pressing issues of inequality and American Indian communities* (pp. 31–46). New York: Haworth Press.

McWilliams, M. (1998). Violence against women in societies under stress. In R. E. Dobash & R. P. Dobash (Eds.), *Rethinking violence against women* (pp. 11–140). Thousand Oaks, CA: Sage.

Merrill, G. S. (1996). Ruling the exceptions: Same-sex battering and domestic violence theory. In C. M. Renzetti & C. H. Miley (Eds.), *Violence in gay and lesbian domestic partnerships* (pp. 9–21). New York: Haworth Press.

Milardo, R. M. (1998). Gender asymmetry in common couple violence. *Personal Relationships, 5,* 423–438.

Miles-Doan, R. (1998). Violence between spouses and intimates: Does neighborhood context matter? *Social Forces, 77,* 623–645.

Norton, I. M., & Manson, S. M. (1995). A silent minority: Battered American Indian women. *Journal of Family Violence, 10,* 307–318.

Ofei-Aboagye, R. O. (1994). Altering the strands of fabric: A preliminary look at domestic violence in Ghana. *Signs, 19,* 924–938.

Ogle, R. S., Maier-Katkin, D., & Bernard, T. J. (1995). A theory of homicidal behavior among women. *Criminology, 33,* 173–193.

Pence, E., & Paymar, M. (1993). *Education groups for men who batter: The Duluth model.* New York: Springer.

Perilla, J. L., Bakerman, R., & Norris, F. H. (1994). Culture and domestic violence: The ecology of abused Latinas. *Violence & Victims, 9,* 325–339.

Renzetti, C. M. (1992). *Violent betrayal: Partner abuse in lesbian relationships.* Thousand Oaks, CA: Sage.

Renzetti, C. M., & Miley, C. H. (1996). *Violence in gay and lesbian domestic partnerships.* New York: Haworth Press.

Richie, B. (1996). *Compelled to Crime: The gender entrapment of battered Black women.* New York: Routledge.

Richters, A. (1994). *Women, culture and violence: a development, health and human rights issue.* Leiden, The Netherlands: Women and Autonomy Centre.

Riggs, D. S., & O'Leary, K. D. (1996). Aggression between heterosexual dating partners: An examination of a causal model of courtship aggression. *Journal of Interpersonal Violence, 11,* 519–540.

Riggs, D. S., O'Leary, K. D., & Breslin, F. C. (1990). Multiple correlates of physical aggression in dating couples. *Journal of Interpersonal Violence, 5,* 61–73.

Roberts, A. R. (1996). Battered women who kill: A comparative study of incarcerated participants with a community sample of battered women. *Journal of Family Violence, 11,* 291–304.

Root, M. P. (1996). Women of color and traumatic stress in "domestic captivity": Gender and race as disempowering statuses. In A. J. Marsella & M. J. Friedman (Eds.), *Ethnocultural aspects of posttraumatic stress disorder: Issues, Research, and Clinical Applications* (pp. 363–387). Washington, DC: American Psychological Association.

Rusbult, C. E., & Martz, J. M. (1995). Remaining in an abusive relationship: An investment model analysis of nonvoluntary dependence. *Personality and Social Psychology Bulletin, 21,* 558–571.

Saunders, D. G. (1988). Wife abuse, husband abuse, or mutual combat? A feminist perspective on the empirical findings. In K. Yllo & M. Bograd (Eds.), *Feminist perspectives on wife abuse* (pp. 90–113). Newbury Park, CA: Sage.

Saunders, D. G. (1996). Feminist-cognitive-behavioral and process-psychodynamic treatments for men who batter: Interactions of abuser traits and treatment model. *Violence and Victims, 4,* 393–414.

Schuler, S. R., Hashemi, S. M., Riley, A. P., & Akhter, S. (1996). Credit programs, patriarchy and men's violence against women in rural Bangladesh. *Social Science and Medicine, 43,* 1729–1742.

Sewall, R. P., Vasan, A., & Schuler, M. A. (Eds.). (1996). *State responses to domestic violence: current status and needed improvements.* Washington, DC: Institute for Women, Law & Development.

Silvern, L., Karyl, J., Waelde, L., Hodges, W., & Starek, J. (1995). Retrospective reports of parental partner abuse: Relationships to depression, trauma symptoms and self-esteem among college students. *Journal of Family Violence, 10,* 177–202.

Simons, R. L., Lin, K.-H., & Gordon, L. C. (1998). Socialization in the family of origin and male dating violence: A prospective study. *Journal of Marriage and the Family, 60,* 467–478.

Song, Y. (1996). *Battered women in Korean immigrant families: The silent scream.* New York: Garland.

Sorenson, S. B. (1996). Violence against women: Examining ethnic differences and commonalities. *Evaluation Review, 20,* 123–145.

Sorenson, S. B., & Telles, C. A. (1991). Self-reports of spousal violence in a Mexican American and a non-

Hispanic White population. *Violence and Victims, 6,* 3–16.

Sorenson, S. B., Upchurch, D. M., & Shen, H. (1996). Violence and injury in marital arguments: Risk patterns and gender differences. *American Journal of Public Health, 86,* 35–40.

Stets, J. E. (1991). Cohabiting and marital aggression: The role of social isolation. *Journal of Marriage and the Family, 53,* 669–680.

Stets, J. E. (1993). Control in dating relationships. *Journal of Marriage and the Family, 55,* 673–685.

Stets, J. E. (1995a). Job autonomy and control over one's spouse: A compensatory process. *Journal of Health and Social Behavior, 36,* 244–258.

Stets, J. E. (1995b). Modeling control in relationships. *Journal of Marriage and the Family, 57,* 489–501.

Stets, J. E. (1995c). Role identities and person identities: Gender identity, mastery identity, and controlling one's partner. *Sociological Perspectives, 38,* 129–150.

Stets, J. E., & Burke, P. J. (1994). Inconsistent self-views in the control identity model. *Social Science Research, 23,* 236–262.

Stets, J. E., & Burke, P. J. (1996). Gender, control, and interaction. *Social Psychology Quarterly, 59,* 193–220.

Stets, J. E., & Pirog-Good, M. A. (1990). Interpersonal control and courtship aggression. *Journal of Social and Personal Relationships, 7,* 371–394.

Stets, J. E., & Straus, M. A. (1990). The marriage license as hitting license: A comparison of assaults in dating, cohabiting, and married couples. In M. A. Straus & R. J. Gelles (Eds.), *Physical violence in American families: risk factors and adaptations to violence in 8,145 families* (pp. 227–244). New Brunswick, NJ: Transaction.

Stewart, S. (1996). Changing attitudes toward violence against women: The Musasa Project. In S. Zeidenstein & K. Moore (Eds.), *Learning about sexuality: A practical beginning* (pp. 343–362). New York: International Women's Health Coalition, Population Council.

Straus, M. A. (1990a). Injury and frequency of assault and the 'representative sample fallacy' in measuring wife beating and child abuse. In R. J. Gelles & M. A. Straus (Eds.), *Physical violence in American families: Risk factors and adaptations to violence in 8,145 families* (pp. 75–91). New Brunswick, NJ: Transaction.

Straus, M. A. (1990b). Social stress and marital violence in a national sample of American families. In M. A. Straus & R. J. Gelles (Eds.), *Physical violence in American families: Risk factors and adaptations to violence in 8,145 families* (pp. 181–201). New Brunswick, NJ: Transaction.

Straus, M. A. (1993). Physical assaults by wives: A major social problem. In R. J. Gelles & D. R. Loseke (Eds.), *Current controversies on family violence.* Newbury Park, CA: Sage.

Straus, M. A. (1999). The controversy over domestic violence by women: A methodological, theoretical, and sociology of science analysis. In X. B. Arriaga & S. Oskamp (Eds.), *Violence in intimate relationships* (pp. 17–44). Thousand Oaks, CA: Sage.

Straus, M. A., Gelles, R. J., & Steinmetz, S. K. (1988).

Behind closed doors: Violence in the American family. Newbury Park, CA: Sage. (Original work published 1980)

Straus, M. A., Hamby, S. L., Boney-McCoy, S., & Sugarman, D. B. (1996). The revised Conflict Tactics Scales (CTS2): Development and preliminary psychometric data. *Journal of Family Issues, 17,* 283–316.

Szinovacz, M. E., & Egley, L. C. (1995). Comparing one-partner and couple data on sensitive marital behaviors: The case of marital violence. *Journal of Marriage and the Family, 57,* 995–1010.

Tang, C. S.-K. (1994). Prevalence of spouse aggression in Hong Kong. *Journal of Family Violence, 9,* 347–356.

Tjaden, P., & Thoennes, N. (1999). *Extent, nature, and consequences of intimate partner violence: Findings from the national violence against women survey.* Washington, DC: National Institute of Justice/Centers for Disease Control and Prevention.

Tom-Orme, L. (1995). Native American women's health concerns. In D. L. Adams (Ed.), *Health issues for women of color* (pp. 27–41). Thousand Oaks, CA: Sage.

Tontodonato, P., & Crew, B. K. (1992). Dating violence, social learning theory, and gender: A multivariate analysis. *Violence and Victims, 7,* 3–14.

United Nations. (1989). *Violence against women in the family.* New York: United Nations.

Vivian, D., & Langhinrichson-Rohling, J. (1994). Are bi-directionally violent couples mutually victimized? A gender-sensitive comparison. *Violence and Victims, 9,* 107–124.

Waller, M. A., Risley-Curtis, C., Murphy, S., Medill, A., & Moore, G. (1998). Harnessing the positive power of language: American Indian women, a case example. In E. A. Segal & K. M. Kilty (Eds.), *Pressing issues of inequality and American Indian communities* (pp. 63–81). New York: Haworth.

West, C. M. (1998). Leaving a second closet: Outing partner violence in same-sex couples. In J. L. Jasinksi & L. M. Williams (Eds.), *Partner violence: A comprehensive review of 20 years of research* (pp. 163–183). Thousand Oaks, CA: Sage.

Wilson, M. I., & Daly, M. (1996). Male sexual proprietariness and violence against wives. *Current Directions in Psychological Science, 5,* 2–7.

Wilson, M., & Daly, M. (1998). Lethal and nonlethal violence against wives and the evolutionary psychology of male sexual proprietariness. In R. E. Dobash & R. P. Dobash (Eds.), *Rethinking violence against women* (pp. 199–230). Thousand Oaks, CA: Sage.

Wolak, J., & Finkelhor, D. (1998). Children exposed to partner violence. In J. L. Jasinski & L. M. Williams (Eds.), *Partner violence: A comprehensive review of 20 years of research* (pp. 73–112). Thousand Oaks, CA: Sage.

Wyatt, G. E. (1994). Sociocultural and epidemiological issues in the assessment of domestic violence. *Journal of Social Distress and the Homeless, 3,* 1,7–21.

Yick, A. G., & Agbayani-Siewert, P. (1997). Perceptions of domestic violence in a Chinese-American community. *Journal of Interpersonal Violence, 12,* 832–846.

Zorza, J. (1991). Woman battering: A major cause of homelessness. *Clearinghouse Review, 25,* 421.

[7]

Exploring Violence and Abuse
in Gay Male Relationships

J. Michael Cruz
Texas Woman's University, Denton
Juanita M. Firestone
The University of Texas at San Antonio

The purpose of this study was to examine gay male relationships where domestic violence was present. Qualitative data for this endeavor were collected by conducting in-depth interviews over an 8-month period with 25 men who self-identified both as homosexual and as victims or perpetrators of domestic violence. Implications are made throughout this piece for further research and analysis regarding gay male domestic violence. Findings include the prominent similarities between heterosexual domestic violence and the perceptions of abuse experienced by the respondents in this study with respect to definitions of the situation, actual experiences and reasons for remaining in abusive relationships. Additionally, the need for both family-based and community-based support services are documented.

Domestic violence as it occurs in same-sex male relationships[1] lacks sufficient research and analysis. Intimate violence has been identified as a problem in the gay community (Ammerman & Hersen, 1991; Bartolomeo, 1990; Gelles, 1997; Island & Letellier, 1991a; Island & Letellier, 1991b; Kirby, 1994; Renzetti & Miley, 1996; Szymanski, 1991; Tuller, 1994; Zuniga, 1995), however, "Domestic violence with gay male relationships is not a well-documented phenomenon..." and "is considerably more widespread than the gay community would dare to admit" (Kirby, 1994, p. 46; see Tessina, 1989, for an exception). While no national database exists for actual numbers of victims or perpetrators of gay-male domestic violence, it has been estimated that between 350,000 and 650,000 gay men in the United States are victims of domestic violence perpetrated by their partners (Island & Letellier, 1991a). However, as pointed out by Renzetti (1997), to date, none of the studies of partner abuse in gay male and lesbian relationships has been able to measure an accurate prevalence. Research does show that abuse in same-sex relationships is well known, does not appear to occur only infrequently or in isolated cases, and seems to follow the same cycle of violence found in heterosexual abuse (see Renzetti, 1997, for a review of this research).

Importantly, the issue of domestic violence has been named the third largest health problem facing gay men today, next to AIDS and substance abuse (Singer & Deschamps, 1994). The purpose of this study was to examine gay male relationships where domestic violence was present. Qualitative data for this endeavor were collected by conducting in-depth interviews over an 8-month period with 25 men who self-identified both as homosexual and as victims and/or perpetrators of domestic violence.

LITERATURE REVIEW

A small body of literature does exist with respect to domestic violence in homosexual male relationships. Typically, these appear in community newspapers and books written for the gay and lesbian community (Silverstein & Picano, 1992). Island and Letellier (1991a) outline an organizational framework for theory development of gay male domestic violence. Harris and Cook (1994) conducted a study examining the reactions of college students to stories of family violence. Three types of scenarios were presented, one in which a woman beat her heterosexual husband; another in which a man beat his heterosexual wife and a third in which a gay man beat his same-sex partner. The findings are that "...suggestions of negative attitudes toward homosexuals [were present], most notably the fact that the battered gay partner was the least liked of the three victims. . . On the rating of whether the victim should leave the batterer, subjects most strongly said that the gay partner should, perhaps because the relationship was seen to be less permanent than the marriage bond in the other two cases" (Harris & Cook, 1994, p. 54).

In examining the issue of domestic violence in gay relationships, we use the perspective of symbolic interaction, specifically, negative symbolic interaction (see, for example, Denzin, 1984).

Denzin (1984) links intimate violence directly to negative interactions. Thus, the violent man (or individual) is never free of negative emotion, nor are his victims, because they are bound together in a structure of negative experience (see also Hepburn, 1973, p. 427). This negative interaction structure includes the use of emotional and physical force to regain the sense of intimacy, closeness, and "we-ness" that characterizes all primary groups and which was lost as violence escalated. Denzin (1984) cites several stages through which family violence moves:

> ... denial of the violence; pleasure derived from violence; the building of mutual hostility between spouses and other family members; the development of misunderstandings; jealousy, especially sexual; increased violence and either eventual collapse of the relationship or the resolution of violence into an unsteady, yet somewhat stable state of recurring violence (pp. 490-491).

Several family characteristics have been associated with family violence, and these characteristics seem equally applicable to homosexual as well as heterosexual families (see Gelles & Strauss, 1988). For example, time spent together is such a trait. Because we spend so much time around the person we live with, we tend to develop a deep intimate involvement and a knowledge base, which may lead to more sensitivity when it comes to insults, failures, etc. Additionally, such factors as inequality with regard to income and household duties can result in tensions, as do similar stresses from the outside world. These may be particularly problematic if they are associated with status inconsistencies (Gelles & Strauss, 1988, pp. 78-88). Thus, if internal or external stresses make the perpetrator feel inadequate compared to his own self-image, he may choose a violent means of reestablishing dominance.

Goode (1971) argues that the particular structure of each family is fairly rigid with regard to the roles contained within it. Family relations often become strained if the members of the family begin to feel as though they are contributing in excess, e.g., contributing love, money and respect of the others present. Thus, "one or more members begins to feel a sense of anger and frustration, of being cheated by the exchanges in which they engage" (Goode, 1971, p. 632). Furthermore, because the people involved within this unit are usually already emotionally close, they know each other's weaknesses and have learned how to successfully hurt one another (Goode, 1971, pp. 624-632).

Hepburn (1973) like Goode (1971) addresses factors that facilitate the initiation of family violence. These factors include the acceptance of violence as legitimate to use against another person, the successful use of violence in the past, overuse of intoxicants, whether or not an audience is present, and the cost of failure.

Gelles (1993) also highlights the wide variety of activities and interactions which occur with family members as well as the intensity of involvement when family members interact. The zero-sum aspect of these activities can lead to a perception of a winner and a loser. For example, selecting a television show: One person will get his or her way and watch the show of choice, while the other will not. (If the issue is as simplistic as this, neither negotiation nor compromise is present.) Thus, a winner and a loser are present in certain situations and decisions. Age and sex differences, as well as stress resulting from ascribed roles, may provide the basis for influencing the winner. Perceptions of winning (or losing) can then, in turn, impact one's self-concept and feelings of self-esteem.

GAY MALE RELATIONSHIPS

While some have suggested that same-sex couples may be less prone to domestic violence because partners are more likely on an equal footing with respect to gender, Bohan (1996) notes that "...in fact some gay and lesbian individuals have the same dysfunctional coping styles and the same relational deficits as do some heterosexual individuals" (p. 183).

When the problem of gay male domestic violence is alluded to in the social science literature, the fact that socialization is the same for most gay men as for most heterosexual men is emphasized. The male sex role as dictated by our society has several dimensions. The display of certain emotions like "fear, tenderness, trust, love, and weakness is discouraged" (Franklin, 1988, p. 63; Rofes, 1996). These are attributes associated with being feminine, and men are socialized to not exhibit these types of characteristics. Most men typically go through a similar socialization process, therefore homosexual men are no different than heterosexual men, in this regard.

Another aspect of the male sex role focuses on respect. A male is socialized to desire to be respected, and to earn respect through economic success. Men are also taught to display an air of confidence, to be self-reliant, and to be strong. The last aspect of the male sex role is one which involves being violent and daring. An important part of the male socialization process is the casual use of violence. "Some...men with a problem of being abusive have been taught, perhaps through sports or the military, to react to problems violently" (Tessina, 1989, p. 104). Franklin (1988) concurs with this and states, "aggression and violence in male sports beginning with Little League and extending through high school and into professional leagues is unabashedly supported, encouraged, and often demanded by parents, coaches, and spectators" (p. 65). Island and Letellier (1991a) conclude that it is almost impossible to grow up as a nonviolent male in this society because of the influences of the TV, movies, sports, advertising and the military on male socialization (p. 50).

Studies on violence in intimate relationships suggest that some forms of power, particularly those related to one's relative status in the relationship, are related to frequency and severity of abuse (Byrne, 1996; Coleman, 1994; Smith, 1990). In heterosexual relationships, the male is typically the partner with higher status, and abuse is more likely when the male partner considers himself less powerful than his female partner or perceives his power as declining (Gondolf, 1988). While there are no similar studies with respect to gay relationships, Renzetti (1992) found that among lesbian couples, the greater the batterer's dependency and the greater the target's inclination for independence, the greater the frequency and the number of types of abuse. Batterers, whether gay or heterosexual, have been profiled as having negative self-concepts and low self-esteem, which lead to high dependency needs (see Byrne, 1996; Coleman, 1994; Walker, 1989). This process is likely to be exacerbated by the combination of male sex role socialization and homophobia, which are inherent in society. As pointed out by Renzetti (1997), homophobia can be internalized to produce negative self-esteem, and may also be used as a weapon of abuse when the abuser threatens to "out" or expose the target's sexual preference.

HOMOPHOBIA AND VIOLENCE

The literature on gay men discusses the problem of internalized homophobia as an unhealthy mental state affecting many in the gay community. To clarify, "Internalized homophobia refers to the direction of societal negative attitudes toward the self" (Meyer, 1995, p. 40). Franklin (1988) believes there are specific dynamics to the roles men play in our society that include the establishment of sufficient distance from femininity; the need to be looked up to and respected; the requirements of being tough, confident and self-reliant; and the aura of aggression and violence, all of which contribute to internalized homophobia (pp. 63-65).

McWhirter and Mattison (1982) state that while antigay attitudes permeate American society, they seem to have an extreme affect on the homosexual community. The issues of ignorance, prejudice, oppression and homophobia are dealt with in every same-sex relationship (see also Robes, 1996). Furthermore, the authors believe that most gay men are either unaware of these issues, or are unaware of how profoundly they are affected by them, specifically their own homophobia or self-oppression (McWhirter & Mattison, 1982, p. 87). Silverstein and Picano (1992) extend internalized homophobia and self-oppression to include hostility toward the partner (p. 57). As emphasized by Moore and Bundy (1983) internalized, self-deprecating messages are likely to result in depression, despair, and/or other forms of self-destructive behavior. Bohan (1996) states that problems in openly portraying a gay identity might exacerbate violence through internalized homophobia (p. 183).

Stress to fulfill some preconceived notion of a masculine role in the relationship might be another manifestation of internalized homophobia. Prince and Arias (1994) cite findings of personality traits of batterers who are characterized as, "having low self-esteem and feelings of inadequacy and inferiority" (p. 126). Furthermore, they state these men often have a strong need for power and control; ascribe to traditional sex-roles; are extremely rigid and oversocialized; and maintain a dogma of strength and dominance that is central to their self-concepts as men.

As noted previously, homophobia can also be used as a tool of violence. In a homophobic society the threat to publicly "out" a partner can be a powerful means of control. While the negative consequences can include the loss of a job or the support of family or friends, there is no legal recourse for the target (Renzetti, 1992). This aspect of the problem can be intensified with the presence of HIV or AIDS. Letellier (1996) argues that AIDS may increase the difficulty victims of abuse have in trying to leave their batterers because they may be completely dependent on their partner for support and care. On the other hand, if the abuser has AIDS, the target may feel such intense guilt for either leaving, or for not having AIDS, that he has difficulty exiting the relationship.

CYCLE OF VIOLENCE

Intergenerational transmission, or the cycle of violence, is used to help understand why such behavior occurs in intimate relationships (see, for example, Pagelow, 1984, and Utech, 1994). Pagelow (1984) begins by defining it as the notion that interpersonal violence is "bequeathed" from one generation to the next (p. 223). Thus the fact that children learn those behaviors and associated attitudes from their parents or models becomes the key to understanding the problem (Utech, 1994, p. 126).

Pagelow (1984) states that some evidence has been offered in support of the theory stating that abused children will most likely become spousally abusive adults, but the information is not conclusive, especially with regard to whether the abused child will become the perpetrator or the victim. In particular, Coleman (1994) and Renzetti (1992) found that intergenerational transmission was not a significant predictor of abuse in gay relationships. In either case, this concept may also prove helpful in understanding intimate violence in gay relationships.

While much of the information relating to the terms family and family violence has clearly focused on the relationships where those involved are of the opposite sex, it seems likely that homosexual relationships would endure as many of the same problems associated with domestic violence as do their heterosexual counterparts. In addition to those problems that are the same, internalized homophobia may exacerbate the context in which family violence occurs for gay couples. The objective of this research is to analyze the problems that homosexual men encounter at home and in the community when they are involved in a relationship where intimate violence is present.

METHODS

This study was conducted in a large metropolitan area in the southwestern United States. In-depth interviews were conducted with 25 respondents. This method of data collection is pertinent for gaining sociological insight in the social phenomenon of domestic violence in same-sex male relationships, and for a better understanding of the issues surrounding men in same-sex unions who are faced with the dilemma of interpersonal violence within their relationships. This study was exploratory and designed to discover heretofore undiscovered knowledge rather than to test any specific hypotheses.

THE SAMPLING PROCESS

At the onset of the research project, two social contact persons introduced one of the authors to potential respondents. One was a counselor for a local AIDS Resource Center, and the other was a member of the Gay/Lesbian Alliance and was associated with the Domestic Violence Project. Different contacts were established by becoming an active member of the Gay/Lesbian Alliance and by contacting different social service agencies in the gay community. Participation as a panelist as part of the Domestic Violence Project during a monthly meeting of the Gay/Lesbian Alliance also provided contacts. In many instances, after initial contacts were made with respondents, they introduced other potential respondents in the community who had experienced domestic violence with same-sex relationships. Thus, the respondents themselves became contact persons. This kind of strategy provides a nonprobability-based snowball sample (Berg, 1995).

A description of this study was provided to agencies such as a legal hospice, various AIDS organizations, a therapist, the local gay church, and other such organizations asking for help in making the study known to potential respondents. Additionally, some contacts were made at a health club and through a personal friendship network.

The criteria used in the selection of the sample were twofold: (1) respondents were chosen for their past experiences with interpersonal violence in a same-sex relationship, (2) the respondents were at least 23 years of age. Age 23 was selected because personal experience and consultations with counseling faculty in a university social work program suggested that that age was old enough for respondents to both have come to terms with their homosexuality and to have formed experience in relationship(s). The upper-age limit of 45 was an artifact of the snowball-sampling process.

SAMPLE CHARACTERISTICS

All respondents self-identified as gay when asked if they were gay or bisexual. Four stated they had been in a heterosexual marriage previously, but had since come to terms with their homosexuality. Respondents' lifestyles varied with respect to the degree of self-identification as gay. Thus, an analysis of various interview sites revealed that some of the respondents' homes were replete with gay "touches" (i.e., homoerotic art, symbols of the gay community such as the rainbow flag, the pink triangle, etc.) while others were void of any visible gay-identifying objects or symbols.[2]

Age of respondents ranged from 23 to 45. Racial and ethnic identity of respondents was not obtained. On average respondents had 4.24 siblings and about half of them had one or both parents living in the same state where this research was conducted.

Because the Human Immunodeficiency Virus (HIV) and Acquired Immune Deficiency Syndrome (AIDS) have had such a dramatic impact on the gay community, the HIV status of the respondents was obtained. All of the respondents stated they had been tested for the HIV virus. Fourteen of the respondents indicated they were HIV negative, while 11 indicated their HIV status as positive.

The educational attainment of respondents ranged from an 11th grade education to postgraduate credit hours. Employment status ranged from unemployed/disabled to full employment. The former were typically men who were HIV-positive and were diagnosed with AIDS. Specific occupations ranged from clerical jobs to business professionals. One man owned his own business.

Twelve respondents grew up in self-identified violent families, and two persons reported having personally experienced violence. Information related to previous experience with counseling or a therapeutic relationship with an individual was not obtained from the respondents.

All of the respondents, except for two, reported their violent or abusive relationships had been terminated. The length of time from the termination varied from 9 months to 10 years. The length of time spent in the abusive relationship varied from 10 months to 10 years.

Victimization status of the respondents proved to be interesting. While only one person initially identified himself as a perpetrator, he also identified himself as a victim during the interview process. While all other respondents (24) initially identified themselves as victims, many of them suggested culpability in provoking violence, thus becoming perpetrators as well as victims. Because we had no clear distinction between victims and perpetrators, perhaps due to the small sample size, we were unable to classify responses based on victimization status. No information about prior treatment history was collected, as the focus of the interviews was on the stories the respondents wanted to tell.

INTERVIEW PROCESS

The research questions that guided this study were:

1. How do you define domestic violence? How do you define abuse?
2. Describe the kind of domestic violence or abuse you have encountered in a same-sex relationship.
3. Why do you think these forms of domestic violence or abuse occur in same-sex relationships?

Frequent probes through the use of follow-up questions and comments were used to illicit more in-depth responses about the problems faced and issues encountered as a gay male confronted with interpersonal domestic violence.

The actual formal interview (which occurred both before and after the informal visits) was recorded on tape and ranged from 1-hour to a 4-hour visit. These followed a specific interview guide. Interviews were conducted in the home of the respondent, in the home of one of the researchers, and in various public places, such as coffeehouses and delicatessens. These sites were suitable and conducive to the interview process, as well as having been mutually agreed upon by one of the authors and the respondents. The atmosphere at these sites was typically relaxed and conversations flowed freely. The interviews that were conducted at the homes of the respondents were invaluable because they allowed observations of the respondent in an informal, comfortable setting.

Informal discussions with respondents ranged from 3 to 4 hours. The topics of the conversations ranged from issues relating to homosexuality, issues of domestic violence, the respondents' theories of male socialization and the effects it had on same-sex relationships, to the impact of AIDS on the gay/lesbian community. Conversations were not recorded if the respondents indicated statements were off the record.

At the time of the interviews all respondents were guaranteed confidentiality. To accomplish this, precautions were taken in the presentation of the data. In order for the voices of the respondents to be heard without being identified, quotes are the result of using composite cases (see Sjoberg & Nett, 1968). This method involves combining like quotes from two or more respondents.

The data were collected over an 8-month period—September 1995 through May 1996. All of the respondents were guaranteed confidentiality and were assured that one of the researchers would be the only person collecting the data for this project, transcribing the interview tapes, analyzing the data, and writing the findings and conclusions. Consent was obtained from all respondents to tape-record as well as to take notes during the interviews through the use of formal consent forms. The form informed the respondents that the interviews were confidential and voluntary.

FINDINGS

Lillian Rubin's(1976) *World's of Pain: Life in the Working Class Family* provided the guide for organizing our findings. Her techniques included an examination of the information based on specific issues or themes. She then quotes from interviews so as to provide the reader with a comprehension of how the respondents have defined their life situations. These data describe the personal perceptions of the gay men who have experienced family violence in their romantic relationships with other men, and represent their definitions of the situation. Therefore, we organized our findings around the themes relevant to the literature on domestic violence, and present them in the words of our respondents.

DEFINITION OF DOMESTIC VIOLENCE OR ABUSE

The first major finding that emerged from the data was the extent to which respondents focused on power and control when defining violence and abuse. By way of illustration, examples of how respondents defined violence included:

> ... an imbalance in the delegation of power in the relationship. One partner seems, in a domestic violence situation, to have a...an...extreme need to control the other person.

> ... abusive, emotional and physical attacks. These might be even nonviolent sick manipulations, or control. Control games that go on. Hitting and bruising and overall fighting. Fist fighting.

> exactly as you would in a heterosexual relationship...physical, mental and verbal abuse. It's far deeper than just physical abuse. Just abusive, verbally. It can be physical at times, or just not...

Most did not define violence and abuse as separate concepts. One respondent reported:

> Violence and abuse, to me, it's pretty close to the same thing. I've seen it in one of my relationships and between my parents. Whenever I've seen violence it's been abuse too. So it's the same thing, to me.

Another participant said:

> Abuse encompasses domestic violence. Violence would be more physical and more exaggerated [emotionally]. Abuse certainly includes more understated or manipulative or controlling experience. Abuse would be mental and physical...and violence, I would pretty much say, is physical.

A couple of responses clearly reflected the use of insider family knowledge as expressed in the literature:

Verbal abuse, that's when you know somebody for a long time, for a lot of years, then you know them like a clock and you take the things that would hurt them the worst and crank it out, just really pump the hell out of it. Argumentative.

There was a lot of verbal abuse and emotional abuse. I mean he was...in his violent moods he would degrade me, tell me I was stupid or I was nothing but a...faggot and he was always belittling me [and] my family. Family is very important to me. See, he knew what buttons to push and he'd push them.

DOMESTIC VIOLENCE OR ABUSE EXPERIENCED

Questions regarding details of a specific violent or abusive episode were posed, and responses indicated a variety of experiences. Once again the focus was on control over the partner who is the target of the abuse. Respondents reported experiencing physical abuse, verbal abuse, emotional abuse, and mental abuse. This coincides with the literature on gay men's domestic violence found in the media targeting this population (Bartolomeo, 1990; Island & Letellier, 1991a; Island & Letellier, 1991b; Kirby, 1994; Letellier, 1994a; Letellier, 1994b; McCoy, 1995; Moore & Bundy, 1983), and also reflects the types of violence described by Gelles (1987) and Gelles and Strauss (1988) in the social science literature written about heterosexual relationships.

When asked about the type of violence or abuse encountered in the relationship, one respondent told about having been at a party where he kissed someone else on the cheek, sending his partner into a jealous rage:

And my lover was extremely jealous, dragged me into the bedroom by my leg and proceeded to beat the [crap] out of me.

Another respondent said:

Mostly it was emotional and kind of controlling, manipulative things. There were three specific instances when it became physical violence and that was enough.

Others described abusive experiences in this way:

Very controlling. I can't have friends. If I have a friend, even if it's male or female, it induces a fight because if I spend more than an hour away from the house, other than work, I'm abandoning him...can't have friends. I can't go out and do things with friends that would be completely platonic, [because] he automatically assumes and accuses me of having an affair... Physical violence, hitting, pulling hair, scratching. Then of course the verbal abuse, shrieking at the top of the lungs, profanity, and damage of property, broken mirrors, broken pictures, scratched paint, flattened tires, broken windshields...a lot of physical [violence]....the last relationship, gosh we've locked each other out of the house. My lover would get upset and beat his head into the wall.

Verbal abuse patterns often reflected the insider knowledge associated with family membership.

Well, there was a lot of verbal [abuse] you know. A lot of belittling, a lot of damage to one's self-esteem, one's ego. There was some physical...There were fights, but mostly verbal or emotional types...the belittling, to the point where you start to wonder or question yourself.

Additionally, one respondent stated:

...And if there wasn't enough money around the house and he couldn't see that his drinking and doing drugs was the reason, then there was another fight and that was verbally as well as physically. And this got to where it was a couple of times a month...I mean a lot of trips to the emergency room.

One respondent stated that he often brought work consisting of personnel files home. His partner would peruse the information in the files and use that as a type of insider knowledge:

...he would see that if two people who had similar positions, one might make more than the other. Well, if we were ever in a situation where they're both there, he'd bring that up [to the individuals].

REASONS FOR SAME-SEX VIOLENCE OR ABUSE

The third major finding deals with reported reasons that men would abuse their same-sex partners. Responses to the question, "Why do you think these forms of domestic violence or abuse occur in same-sex relationships?" relate issues of internalized homophobia (Meyer, 1995), control (Prince & Arias, 1994; Hendricks-Matthews, 1992) jealousy and insecurity, money (Berger, 1990), drugs or alcohol (Levine & Rosich, 1996), and inter-generational transmission of physical violence as learned behavior (Gelles & Cornell, 1990; Tolman & Bennett, 1990). For example, one respondent alluded to internalized homophobia as addressed by Meyer (1995) and stated:

Well, the main reason is because in a gay, in a same-sex relationship there's so many other pressures that the straight community does not realize. The ridicule, the discrimination, the bias that we face just identifying ourselves as gay men in gay relationships... Also, not only that, but when you're in a relationship with another gay man, ...you're also having to deal with the emotional baggage that they bring to the relationship. The problems that they've had growing up and coming out, coming to grips with their homosexuality and sometimes you've got so many emotions...

With respect to jealousy and insecurity, one person replied:

Yeah, he's insecure about everything. He's insecure about me. I think insecurity has a lot to do with it and...Insecurities got him a lot. Well, I guess, not just insecurity, but.. jealousy.

One respondent concluded, as did Hamberger, Feurbach, and Borman (1990) that, at times, men do not know how to relate to one another:

Because men don't know how to deal with each other, they don't know how to talk to each other on a respectful, understanding level. I think one or both parties are unable to communicate. I think, and this is strange, that the only reason two men are really together is sex. Or it starts out to be the sex and then it falls into a comfortable pattern and they don't want to break the pattern. I can't truly notice or see love between two men. I can't see that. I think that men just use men for whatever they want and that's where the violence starts, because they don't really care about each other.

Another described a similar experience based on use of control:

Men are conditioned to be the ones who are in charge of a relationship and the ones who make all the calls. And so when you get two men in a relationship together, they both expect that power and I think a lot of men don't know any other way to get that power except to hit whomever they're with. Too much testosterone! He's a control freak about me. It's just an unhealthy need to want to control another human being for whatever, you know, the perpetrator's reasons are.

Money and/or drug and alcohol abuse can exacerbate relationship problems. Our respondents also described these problems:

I'd say alcohol. Alcohol plays a big factor and then maybe there's underlying reasons of personal problems. I think anything, be it alcohol, drugs, anything that alters your way of thinking at all, is a contributing factor to domestic violence.

Strains from finances were also mentioned:

He is constantly aggravated and bitching about money. Financial strains put a lot of stress on our relationship.

Finally, the theme of intergenerational transmission of violence as a learned behavior recurred during the interviews. Quotes from two individuals are illustrative:

I think that if we're talking about men, I think that there's a societal approval of men being violent with each other. I think there's violence in same-sex relationships for the same reasons that there are in heterosexual relationships, you know? The perpetrator learns violence in his household...when he's growing up that carries over with him into his own relationships...you were brought up in that environment so you think that's the way it's done.

And:

I think it has to do something with...it's your upbringing. I think to a point, you're taught by your parents. And in my opinion, they teach you these skills and you're around this environment and you're learning this. And I think you tend to do the same things in your relationship. And you see how your father treated your mother and I think in a sense it works out that way.

Lastly, all respondents reported the perceived need for formal assistance and support for the gay community. Suggestions ranged from money and a safe house, to counseling, and then to more education and a dissemination of information to the persons involved about domestic violence and the options available to those in need. Respondents said some sort of public assistance is needed and their thoughts are illustrated by the following two quotes documenting the exact types of social support:

Awareness. I believe that as a community people need to educate themselves as to what same-sex violence is...and I think armed with that kind of education people should try to reach out to the victim and let [him] know that they do not need to stay in the relationship...I think counseling is a very good idea. Therapy of some sort...I think they need a shelter of some kind. They need some kind of financial aid set-up...when you don't have any place to go and you don't have any place to stay it's hard to leave somebody.

Another said:

Some place where people would be comfortable enough to go and discuss their personal lives and to see what's going on. Having a comfort zone. Some place they can go and work these things out. Like a center.

CONCLUSION

One of the most important goals in this study was to learn the respondents' definitions of abuse and domestic violence rather than beginning with definitions imposed by researchers.

Our findings indicate similarities between social science literature documenting heterosexual domestic violence and the abuse experienced by the respondents participating in this study. While similarities were far more prevalent than comments focusing on internalized homophobia, male sex role behaviors seem to interact with homophobia to produce contextual differences within the cycles of violence experienced by our sample.

The types of domestic violence and abuse experienced by the respondents in this study mirror the experiences endured by women in the heterosexual community who are living in abusive relationships. We found strong similarities in their definitions and those reported by heterosexuals involved in these types of relationships (see Gelles & Strauss, 1988). Respondents' beliefs about why domestic violence or abuse occurs in same-sex relationships are also similar to earlier studies focusing on heterosexual relationships. In addition, issues of control and power (Prince & Arias, 1994; Hendricks-Matthews, 1992); alcohol and drug abuse (Levine & Rosich,1996); and intergenerational transmission of violence (Gelles & Cornell, 1990; Tolman & Bennett, 1990) were all reported by respondents in this sample.

Based upon the recommendations of the respondents and the literature existing on gay male domestic violence, a call for further research and analysis is in order. Because few research studies in the area of gay male domestic violence exist, and those that exist are typically based on anecdotal accounts of violence and abuse experienced rather than on empirical research, this study fills an important breach in the available literature.

Respondents believed that agencies should be more sensitive to issues relating to gay male abuse. Specifically, respondents and social scientists (see Short, 1996) call for social service providers to be made sensitive to the needs of all groups within the population being served. Thus, services designed only to address the needs of heterosexual families may not fully address the needs of gay couples. Respondents taking part in this project stated a desire for support services such as a safe house for gay men, counseling services with trained professionals who can deal effectively with the special dynamics of same-sex male relationships, and funding from the federal government to aid in maintaining these social support services.

Additionally, Gelles (1987) calls for clinical practices to be based on scientific research to insure as broad an application as possible. Those taking part in this study believed it was important for researchers, as well as those who had previous experience with violence in gay male relationships to share information and to educate those who might need to be enlightened.

Finally, as is the case in abusive heterosexual relationships, stronger family ties between persons in the gay community and their families of origin could provide much needed support. Many men involved in this study believed they had no place to seek refuge and no one to talk to regarding their life situations. Because a jealous, controlling, and abusive significant other typically isolated his victim from friends, immediate family is the most prominent source of hope for a victim of domestic violence. Unfortunately, family ties may already be strained or severed due to prevailing homophobia and/or isolation created by the abuser. Thus, dealing with homophobia may be the necessary first step in providing support for targets of abuse in gay male relationships.

Clearly our findings both fill a gap in the existing literature and highlight the need for more such studies. Gaining real understanding of abusive relationships depends on developing an awareness of the similarities and differences in experiences based on the structural context in which the abuse takes place. Gay males may describe their abuse similarly to heterosexual targets, but are also aware of their positions as gay men in a homophobic society. Using their own words to gain an understanding of their experiences helps provide the contextual basis for making meaningful comparisons to the experiences of other groups. Such comparisons may eventually provide the basis for creating meaningful programs and policies which benefit members of all groups, not just members of the majority.

NOTES

[1]The terms same-sex male relationships, gay male relationships, and homosexual male relationships will be used interchangeably.

[2]While these descriptions highlight the natural settings in which interviews took place, analysis of respondents' statements revealed no discernable connection between the decor of the homes and victimization status.

REFERENCES

Ammerman, R. T., & Hersen, M. (Eds.) (1991). *Case studies in family violence.* New York: Plenum Press.

Bartolomeo, N. (1990). Domestic violence: A serious problem lacking in resources. *Washington Blade,* July 27 (7).

Berg, B. L. (1995). *Qualitative research methods for the social sciences.* (Second ed.) Boston, MA: Allyn and Bacon.

Berger, R. M. (1990). Men together: Understanding the gay couple. *Journal of Homosexuality, 19,* 31-49.

Bohan, J. S. (1996). *Psychology and sexual orientation: Coming to terms.* New York: Routledge.

Byrne, D. (1996). Clinical models for the treatment of gay male perpetrator of domestic violence. In C. Renzetti and C. H. Miley (Eds.), *Violence in gay and lesbian domestic partnerships* (pp. 107-116). New York: Harrington Park.

Coleman, V. E. (1994). Lesbian battering: The relationship between personality and the perpetration of violence. *Violence and Victims, 9,* 139-152.

Denzin, N. K. (1984). Toward a phenomenology of domestic, family violence. *American Journal of Sociology, 90,* 483-512.

Franklin II, C. W. (1988). *Men and society.* Chicago: Nelson-Hall.

Gelles, R. J. (1997). *Intimate violence in families.* (Third ed.) Thousand Oaks: Sage Publications.

Gelles, R. J. (1987). *Family violence.* Newbury Park: Sage Publications.

Gelles, R. J. (1993). Through a sociological lens: Social structure and family violence. In R. J. Gelles and D. R. Loseke (Eds.), *Current controversies on family violence* (pp.31-46). Newbury Park: Sage Publications

Gelles, R. J., & Cornell, C. P. (1990). *Intimate violence in families.* Newbury Park: Sage Publications.

Gelles, R. J., & Strauss, M. A. (1988). *Intimate violence.* New York: Simon and Schuster.

Gondolf, E. W. (1988). *Research on men who batter: An overview, bibliography and resource guide.* Bradenton, FL: Human Services Institute.

Goode, W. J. (1971). Force and violence in the family. *Journal of Marriage and the Family, 33,* 624-636.

Hamberger, L. K., Feurbach, S. P., & Borman, R. J. (1990). Detecting the wife batterer. *Medical Aspects of Human Sexuality*, September, 32-39.

Harris, R. J., & Cook, C. A. (1994). Attributions about spouse abuse: It matters who the batterers and victims are. *Sex Roles, 30,* 553-565.

Hendricks-Matthews, M. (1992). Family physicians and violence: Looking back, looking ahead. *American Family Physician, 45,* 2033-2035.

Hepburn, J. R. (1973). Violent behavior in interpersonal relationships. *The Sociological Quarterly, 14,* 419-429.

Island, D., & Letellier, P. (1991a). *Men who beat the men who love them.* Binghampton, NY: The Hawthorne Press.

Island, D., & Letellier, P. (1991b). *The scourge of domestic violence.* Gaybook, 11. San Francisco, CA: Rainbow Ventures.

Kirby, N. (1994). Love hurts. *Attitude, 1,* 46-50.

Letellier, P. (1996). Twin epidemics: domestic violence and HIV infection among gay and bisexual men. In C. M. Renzetti and C. H. Miley (Eds.), *Violence in gay and lesbian domestic partnerships* (pp. 69-81). New York: Harrington Park.

Letellier, P. (1994a). Gay and bisexual male domestic violence victimization: Challenges to feminist theory and responses to violence. *Violence and Victims, 9,* 95-106.

Letellier, P. (1994b). Identifying and treating battered gay men. *San Francisco Medicine,* April, 16-19.

Levine, F. J., & Rosich, K. J. (1996). *Social causes of violence: Crafting a science agenda.* Washington, DC: American Sociological Association.

McCoy, J. (1995). Domestic violence among gay and lesbian families an unexplored issue. *Dallas Voice,* August 4, 7-8.

McWhirter, D. P., & Mattison, A. M. (1982). Psychotherapy for gay male couples. *Journal of Homosexuality, 7,* 79-91.

Meyer, I. H. (1995). Minority stress and mental health in gay men. *Journal of Health and Social Behavior, 36,* 38-56.

Moore, E., & Bundy, A. (1983). Battery between gay men: An exploratory study of domestic violence in the San Francisco gay men's community. Social Work Masters Research Project, San Francisco State University, Department of Social Work.

Pagelow, M. D. (1984). *Family violence.* New York: Praeger Publishers.

Prince, J. E., & Arias, I. (1994). The role of perceived control and the desirability of control among abusive and nonabusive husbands. *The American Journal of Family Therapy, 22,* 126-134.

Renzetti, C. M. (1997). Violence in lesbian and gay relationships. In L. L. O'Toole & J. R. Schiffman (Eds.), *Gender Violence: Interdisciplinary perspectives* (pp. 285-293). New York: New York University Press.

Renzetti, C. M. (1992). *Violent betrayal: Partner abuse in lesbian relationships.* Newbury Park, CA: Sage.

Renzetti, C. M., & Miley, C. H. (Eds.) (1996). *Violence in gay and lesbian domestic partnerships.* New York: Harrington Park.

Rofes, E. (1996). *Reviving the tribe: Sexuality and culture in the ongoing epidemic.* Binghampton, NY: Harrington Park Press.

Rubin, L. B. (1976). *Worlds of pain: Life in the working class family.* New York: Basic Books.

Short, B. J. (1996). *Provision of services to gay male victims of domestic violence.* Master's thesis, University of Minnesota, School of Public Health, Division of Epidemiology.

Silverstein, C., & Picano, F. (1992). *The new joy of gay sex.* New York: HarperCollins Publishers.

Singer, B. L., & Deschamps, D. (Eds.) (1994). *Gay and lesbian stats.* New York: The New York Press.

Sjoberg, G., & Net, R. (1968). *A methodology for social research.* New York: Harper and Row.

Smith, M. (1990). Sociodemographic risk factors in wife abuse: Results from a survey of Toronto women. *Canadian Journal of Sociology 15*(1), 39-58.

Szymanski, M. (1991). Battered husbands: Domestic violence in gay relationships. *Genre,* 32-73.

Tessina, T. (1989). *Gay relationships.* Los Angeles: Jeremy P. Tarcher.

Tolman, R. M., & Bennett, L. W. (1990). A review of quantitative research on men who batter. *Journal of Interpersonal Violence, 5,* 87-118.

Tuller, D. (1994). When gays batter their partners. *San Francisco Chronicle,* January 3, A1-A8.

Utech, M. R. (1994). *Violence, abuse and neglect: The American home.* Dix Hills, NY: General Hall.

Walker, L.W. (1989). *Terrifying love.* New York: Harper Perennial.

Zuniga, J. (1995). Gay couples not immune from domestic violence, figures show. *Dallas Voice,* November 24, 10-11.

Part III
Sexual Violence

Part III

Special Questions

[8]

BRIT. J. CRIMINOL. VOL. 39 NO.1 SPECIAL ISSUE 1999

SEX, VIOLENCE AND LOCAL COURTS

Working-Class Respectability in a Mid-Nineteenth-Century Lancashire Town

SHANI D'CRUZE*

Complex issues of class and gender were highlighted when sexual and physical violence against women came up in mid-nineteenth-century local courts. In Middleton, Lancashire, despite its large female industrial workforce, these cases mostly associated working women's social identities with home and neighbourhood. They presented masculinities that contradicted the increasing respectability of working men's organization and politics. Proceedings were published to a courtroom audience and in local newspapers. Men's sexual and physical violence, often associated with leisure and drunkenness, affiliation cases and women's neighbourhood quarrels, produced a composite picture of disorder which middle-class magistrates aimed to discipline. Respectable working-class opinion must also have disapproved. Local courts gave working women a public forum to air grievances, but one that entailed a real risk to their own reputation.

The historical persistence of the double standard that has disadvantaged women trying to obtain justice in cases involving sexual assault is by now an established truism of academic research from the medieval to the modern period, despite other far-reaching changes in law and legal practice (Clark 1987). Legal judgments frequently served the interests of patriarchy and depended (as research for the nineteenth century has demonstrated) on assessments of character, rather than on the strict circumstances of an assault. A woman jeopardized her respectability (and thus her reliability as a witness) in even bringing a case of this kind, first because she was sexually compromised and secondly because she dared (and was forced by the legal system) to speak immodestly in open court. Had she brought it upon herself, either through carelessness or wanton behaviour? By contrast, working-class masculine respectability, derived from workplace and family as well as public identity, was in the end easier to maintain.[1] With the extension of magistrates' powers of summary jurisdiction by mid-century legislation and before motoring offences brought the middle classes to the attention of the police courts, petty sessions dealt almost exclusively with the working class (Skyrme 1991). I have argued in a wider study that the kinds of sexual assaults that these courts dealt with were far from comprising the totality of sexual violence in that society, even amongst the working class. As an aspect of (some) working-class masculinities, however, sexual aggression was one part of the uses of violence within working-class culture more generally, intersecting with (for example) domestic violence, men's street fighting, neighbourhood quarrels and routine violence by adults against children (D'Cruze 1998; Hammerton 1992).

* Manchester Metropolitan University.
[1] Bashar (1983); Clark (1983); Clark (1987); Carter (1985); Conley (1986).

SHANI D'CRUZE

Women's reputations in all social classes had a crucial sexual component. Dominant discourse had a tendency to reduce all components of working women's reputations (good housekeeping, neighbourliness, workplace skills) to that of sexuality. Working women themselves could reproduce such discourses. They sometimes fought over each other's sexual reputations. Most obviously, promiscuity, sexual assertiveness, drink, prostitution, avoiding marriage whilst bringing up children and/or having sexual relationships could all call a woman's reputation into question. In Middleton, in the early 1860s, Hannah Collinge blacked Sarah Ogden's eye after she had 'caught her husband with Ogden'. Part of the cause of a row between Ann Kent and Elizabeth Ramsden was that Elizabeth had spread the rumour that Ann was 'neither married or single'.[2] Nevertheless, 'bourgeois' paradigms of pre and extra-marital sexual abstinence did not dominate. Numerous bastardy cases show sexual intercourse to be part of 'serious courtship' and some examples of maternity outside marriage are redolent of those in handloom weaving areas earlier in the century where women's earning potential enabled a range of household and family forms (Gandy 1978). Cohabitation and illegitimate pregnancies did not necessarily mean outright social ostracism in mid-century Middleton, particularly when economic hardship destabilized the process of family formation.

Neighbours and Kin

At this period, Middleton working people lived in small, nucleated clusters of streets, which spatially defined the parameters of the neighbourhood. Within local, face-to-face networks, reciprocal support between women resulted in tangible material and social benefit, but tensions could also arise (Ross 1983, 1993; Tebbutt 1995). The neighbourhood featured strongly in court cases as the context for women's violence against women. Any interpretation of men's violence against women needs also to take into consideration other ways in which interpersonal violence featured in working women's lives. Numerous quarrels between neighbours, reaching the court if they turned violent, demonstrated the strain under which neighbourly relations could find themselves, and often turned on the good reputation of a woman and her household. A frequent cause of quarrel was the conduct of children. Margaret Mather and Agnes Hannah came to blows because Margaret's children constantly made mock of Agnes since her own children were in prison for theft and '. . . the children were sent by their mother to shout at her'. Thus provoked, Agnes beat one of the children and when Margaret arrived at her house to complain, threw water over her.[3] Reputation was ascribed through the mechanisms of gossip, and sometimes of wider community action. A woman, thought to have mistreated her stepdaughter so badly that the child attempted suicide, was burned in effigy by a large crowd. On two evenings, '. . . some hundreds of persons congregated together . . .' outside the house and 'commenced hooting, shouting and groaning' to 'show its dissatisfaction of the conduct of the stepmother. . .'[4]

---

[2] *Middleton Albion (Midd Alb)* 9.6.1860; Lancashire Record Office (LRO), PsMi/1/3, Middleton PS, 11.4.1861.
[3] *Midd Alb*, 21.4.1866.
[4] *Midd Alb*, 7.7.1866, 14.7.1866; *Midd Alb*, 21.4.1866.

SEX, VIOLENCE AND LOCAL COURTS

Charles Butterworth had been sent to gaol for raping Mary Taylor's daughter in Royton, a village just outside Middleton. There had been some doubt over the identity of the attacker, but Salford Quarter Sessions had found against him. Butterworth was obviously popular in Royton. Mary brought an unsuccessful case at Royton Petty Sessions against a group of boys who repeatedly stoned her and shouted abuse, singing, 'When Charley comes marching home again.'[5] In important if problematic ways, the petty sessions could act to extend and formalize the local public forum at the same time as it sought to police the conduct of the working class.

Personal, sexual and material factors in combination comprised women's reputations. A fracas arose when Henry Simpson's wife and adult daughter went to secure some contribution from him towards doctor's bills for his sick children. He had decamped to live with a 'tally' wife. He beat his wife and in retribution the daughter broke his windows. The disturbance must have made the dispute a matter of neighbourhood knowledge. It had certainly become so by the time it reached the court. The sympathy of the magistrates and the public gallery was with the 'real' wife, but it was Henry Simpson, not the 'other' woman, who was hissed when he tried to pass her off as his 'wash woman, she had just brought in my clothes'. In another case, Margaret Cranshaw was assaulted by James Webster (a cooper). This assault was a continuation of a quarrel that had begun between Margaret and 'the woman who cohabited' with Webster, that is, his tally wife. The tally wife did not appear in court and was not named, but seems to have initiated the row by trying to recover some household goods that Margaret claimed to have purchased from her.[6] Therefore one discourse about reputation and sexuality was masked by another around the 'material appurtenances' of respectability (Perkin 1989: 122).

If Sessions Minutes show ample evidence of women perpetrating violence, they also demonstrate women supporting each other. Alice Greaves ran to a neighbour, Mrs Coop, for sanctuary when her house had been invaded by (unusually) a police constable who 'addressed her in . . . indecent language . . . [and] . . . asked her to have a kiss'. Ann Smith, a miner's wife, was periodically harassed by her estranged husband, who '. . . had come home many a time and disturbed herself and the neighbourhood'. She took him to court for assault after a particularly severe beating and a neighbour, Eliza Simpson, 'gave corroborative evidence, she happening to be with Smith's better half at the time'. Eliza had received a '"gentle" tap in the fray'. The husband protested that Eliza 'had been telling tales about him . . . [and] . . . if she got touched, it was through meddling.'[7] Women also helped obtain redress for daughters, relatives and neighbours subjected to violence, sexual assault or seeking financial support from the father of an illegitimate child. Sarah Ann Ashworth, a dyer's wife, found a new job as a live-in servant for Alice Wild. Sarah Ann had testified in court when Alice brought an unsuccessful case of indecent assault against the son of the family where Alice had previously lived and worked.[8] It fell to Mary Hardman, rather than her husband, to turn out the lodger who had raped her nine-year-old daughter, to seek medical help first from a local 'wise woman', then from the doctor, and to appear in court as witness.[9]

---

[5] *Midd Alb*, 20.10.1866.
[6] *Midd Alb*, 9.6.1860, 26.1.1867.
[7] *Midd Alb*, 13.10.1866; 7.6.1865.
[8] LRO, PsMi/1/1 21.12.1859, *Midd Alb*, 21.12.1859.
[9] LRO, PsMi/1/1 27.4.1861; *Midd Alb*, 27.4.1861.

SHANI D'CRUZE

Middleton in the Mid-Nineteenth Century

This discussion is based on records of local court proceedings in and around Middleton, Lancashire in the 1850s and 1860s. Middleton was an industrial town some six miles north of Manchester with a population of 19,635 in 1861.[10] This discussion uses 88 Middleton cases of violence against women drawn from local petty sessions between 1858 and 1867, and 42 other bastardies (see Table 1).[11] These 88 cases represent a significant proportion of the 311 violence and disorder cases the petty sessions in Middleton dealt

TABLE 1   *Cases of physical and sexual assault against women, Middleton, 1858–67*

	1858	1859	1860	1861	1862	1863	1864	1865	1866	1867	All years
Physical and sexual violence against women											
Affiliation (coerced sex)		1		1	1			1			4
Indecent exposure						1					1
Indecent assault	3	3	2	3			1	5			17
Common assault (sexual element)		1						2	1		4
Common assault	3	5	1	5	4	3	2	2	5	5	35
Assault by women		4	7	1	3	3	2	1	2	4	27
Total	6	12	12	9	8	8	4	4	15	10	88
Affiliation (Coercion not argued)	1	4	10	7	7	7	5	1			42
Men's violence against men											
Common assault		9	6	8	7	4	6	2			42
Drunk, disorderly		8	30	28	29	27	6	11			139
All disorder	7	33	58	52	51	46	21	18	15	10	311
Other cases											
Debt	5	4	6	16	22	11	6				70
Theft	3	6	9	7	10	5	1				41
Traffic	11	7	6		11	5	7				47
Trading (weights and measures etc.)	6	10	11	8	2	1	1				39
Beerhouse (trading without licence etc.)	2	13	16	17	8	3	5				64
Gaming		5		15	1		8				29
Damage	3	4	7	2	2	1	2				21
Nuisance (dunghill, obstruction etc.)	1	3			1						5
Other			1	1	1		1				4
Total other cases	31	52	56	66	58	26	31				320

Sources: Middleton and Tonge Petty Sessions Minutes 1859–1865 (PsMi/1/1, 1859–61; PsMi/1/2, 1861–65; PsMi/1/3, 1859–1865) and reports of petty sessions from the *Middleton Albion* between 1858 and 1867 for Middleton, Tonge and Royton sessions. Neither the minutes nor the newspapers provide a complete listing of cases and even with the overlap of sources these figures cannot be assumed to represent the entirety of cases heard.

---

[10] Slater's *Lancashire Directory* (1869: 505).

[11] These examples are selected from a far broader collection of 909 cases from Lancashire, Cheshire and Suffolk. Middleton Petty Sessions revived in 1851 but records are only available in the County Record Office from 1859. This article uses the first three volumes of Sessions Minutes available in Lancashire Record Office, PsMi/1/1, 1.9.1859-2.11.1861; PsMi/1/2, 4.12.1861-31.5.1865; PsMi/1/3, which includes Middleton Sessions from 17.8.1859-6.121.1864 and Tonge Sessions, 30.12.1863-14.6.1865. The *Middleton Albion (Midd Alb)* was printed from 1857, and has been searched from 1859 (when reporting of the sessions becomes regular) until 1867, collecting relevant cases from Middleton, Tonge and nearby Royton sessions.

SEX, VIOLENCE AND LOCAL COURTS

with in those years. That 311 made up almost half the total business of the court, indicating, I would argue, that the disorder of working people in all its manifestations was a central preoccupation of the petty sessions at this period. Of these 88, 25 were sexual assaults, although only 17 were tried as such. A good deal of sexual violence in petty sessions was hidden in cases of common assault, domestic violence, even theft and minor misdemeanours as well as affiliation cases. This finding resonates with modern, sociological studies of the ways that sexual assaults are filtered out of the legal system (Kelly 1988; Stanko 1985). It emphasizes the fragility of this evidence as a basis for determining any overall incidence of sexual assault and questions research based on courts' own definitions of offences, which produce comparatively low figures for sexual assaults (e.g. Philips 1977).

Since 1780 Middleton had changed from a gentry-dominated semi-rural pastoral-agricultural community with some handloom weaving in cotton and silk, to an urban, industrial town where the manufacturing and trading middle classes held positions of authority amidst a well-defined public culture of middle and working-class respectability. Cotton mills employed women and young people as well as men. The hand weaving of silk was put out to women and men who worked at home or in small workshops. Women's paid work was a fundamental constituent of working-class domestic economies. Men and boys also worked at the dyeworks which had around 900 hands by 1868, and in nearby collieries. The growing commercial and shopkeeping sector employed young men and women.[12] The 1801 population of 3,976 had grown to 12,548 in 1851 and continued to expand. However, by the 1860s Middleton people experienced economic downturn and unemployment. After prosperity in the 1850s, the Cotton Famine from 1860 exacerbated a severe slump in the silk trade from 1858.

Middleton working people had engaged in radical and sometimes violent causes throughout the first half of the nineteenth century, a period established by social historians as crucial to the political and labour activism that forged working-class consciousness. Women and men had besieged a mill and burned down the house of its owner in 1812. In 1819 they had marched to Peterloo (Bamford 1903). They participated in riots and 'plug drawing' (industrial sabotage) in August 1843 (Baines 1868: 476) and were active Chartists in the 'Hungry 40s'.[13] Historians have argued that from the mid-century there were changes in the character of working-class activism and of class relations more generally in the direction of 'reformism' and respectability, and Middleton people participated in this trend (Kirk 1985). Although organization and action continued, they were of a restrained and sober character. The Cotton Famine did not produce riot or demonstration. Silk weavers' traditions of 'artisan independence' were expressed chiefly through their own ratepayers' association in the 1860s, whose main concern was to check the expenditure of the highway surveyor.[14]

Mid-century Middleton local government was led by a group of affluent manufacturers, clergy and merchants who involved themselves institutionally in everything from the Agricultural Society, the Public Baths and the National School to the Gas Company and the Improvement Commissioners. The Commissioners dealt with

[12] For detailed references, see D'Cruze (1998).

[13] Wright (1988: 66); Mather (1980); Hovell (1925); Read (1959).

[14] For hardship amongst the Middleton silk weavers, see *Midd Alb,* 19.12.1857, 24.12.1858, 14.5.1859, 21.5.1858, 9.7.1859, 20.8.1859.

SHANI D'CRUZE

amenities and public health issues. Two of the most active magistrates, Thomas Ashton and Thomas Dickens were also Improvement Commissioners. Ashton was a native of Middleton, a Manchester merchant who resided at Parkfield House. He was a close associate of the Rector Richard Durnford. Durnford sat on the Board of Guardians, chaired the Board of Surveyors, established a National School and Sunday Schools and chaired the Improvement Commissioners. Thomas Dickens owned Spring Vale Works, Tonge, was a director of the Middleton and Tonge Cotton Mill Company and chairman of the Baths Company. The magistrates were therefore well known to the local populace, as some less than deferential responses from witnesses testify. When James Cheetham was asked from the Bench by Thomas Ashton to account for why he had punched Lucy Gregory he replied, 'Well, Tommy, I'll tell you about it . . .' Local knowledge and energetic elite paternalism were nevertheless underpinned by recent memories of aggressive popular political radicalism and anxieties about diverse forms of working-class disorder. Fortnightly petty sessions were held at the Old Boars Head Inn. A new town clerk, Henry Wheeler, set up better record keeping, which can in part account for the escalation in recorded drunk and disorderly cases, affiliation hearings and instances of violence and sexual assault in the economically difficult early 1860s (Table 1). Nevertheless, these statistics indicate the sharpened institutional gaze on working-class disorder at this period.[15]

The work of the magistrates on the Petty Sessions bench was thus complementary to their work as Improvement Commissioners. The Victorian Health of Towns movement involved more than a disinterested concern with public welfare. Its morally inflected rhetoric elided poor health and sanitation in working-class neighbourhoods with sexual licence and all round depravity (Midwinter 1969; Wohl 1983; Hamlin 1988). We can perhaps associate a vociferous campaign over Middleton street lighting at least in part with such social control intentions as well as cost-conscious preoccupations about the profits of the private Gas Company.[16] Such meta-narratives can begin to make connections between the differing activities of Middleton's governing elite. In dealing with cases of violence, drunkenness and aggressive sexuality as JPs, they were in fact engaged in projects of 'bringing to light' and 'cleaning up' some of the nastier aspects of working-class disorder (Yeo 1993; Douglas 1966; Levy 1991). Newspaper reports communicated to the town their moral as well as their legal pronouncements. When William Jagger, 'a debauched character' who worked at the dyeworks, was tried for attempting to sexually assault his adolescent daughter in a drunken fit, the case collapsed as her evidence became contradictory. Unable to find a guilty verdict, the magistrate, Thomas Ashton, nevertheless took the opportunity to moralize at length. Jagger was 'morally guilty;—a more base, more brutal transaction was not within his [Ashton's] knowledge. He [the prisoner] deserved horsewhipping.'[17]

On one occasion the bench 'complimented . . . [Alice Morvel] . . . for bringing the case [against two drunks who had torn her shawl] . . . and said they would afford every protection to females'.[18] Respectable 'females' apparently required chivalric, paternalistic protection so that they could preserve their sexual chastity for marriage, an

---

[15] Garrard (1983); *Midd Alb*, 5.11.1864. For detailed local history references see D'Cruze (1998).
[16] *Midd Alb*, 5.2.1859.
[17] *Midd Alb*, 7.7.1866, 14.7.1866.
[18] *Midd Alb*, 9.7.1859.

institution which the magistrates also felt called upon to defend. George Halliwell beat up his wife and threatened her with a knife. However, because her screams did not reach the ears of a police sergeant outside, the bench was inclined to lenience and 'admonished [the couple] to live more comfortably together'.[19] Petty sessions and police were at this period essentially local, overstretched institutions which tended to see their social control functions (except at particular crises and moral panics) in terms of ringfencing and surveillance, rather than repression. To the extent that the Middleton working class was infused with clean-living respectability, it could share the magistrate's disapproval of the sexual attacks, child abuse and wife beating that came before the sessions.

At that period, local courts and police were the chief institutional means of regulating certain kinds of sexual and physical violence alongside lingering customs such as the 'riding' or 'charivari'.[20] It cannot necessarily be supposed that the possibilities open to women in the past to complain about such abuse were necessarily less useful to them than those in contemporary society (Bacchi and Jose 1994). Within the limitations of the source material, it is possible to detect vociferous protests by women against sexual and physical violence. Sometimes these accounts ran counter to both the legal definitions and the practices of the court and were able to capture some of the discursive space created by the operation of the patriarchal legal institution.

Mary Gradgrind and Lillie Garrett

Where men were the aggressors, situations from physical injuries associated with sexual assault, to domestic violence or even sexual insult used in a neighbour's quarrel, each problematized any neat separation between physical and sexual violence. Recent studies have begun to explore the specific discursive and institutional strategies that disadvantaged women in court. Historical specificity is important in understanding the social and cultural meanings of sexual violence beneath the overarching continuities of the double standard. It is also a valuable tactic in challenging the construction of women as always-already-entirely victim, particularly if the 'humble modalities' of disciplinary power are understood invariably to involve resistance (Foucault 1979*b*).

Two examples indicate contrasting ways for sexual assault to become the business of Middleton Petty Sessions. Mary Gradgrind appeared in 1863 at the behest of the Poor Law Guardians who wanted to recoup their costs from James Bamford (also known as 'Joe Twin') for the maintenance of Mary's illegitimate daughter. James Bamford and Mary Gradgrind had known each other only a month when the child was conceived. On the day of James's uncle's wedding, they were part of a drinking party of four women and two men. James decided to have sex with Mary. He pulled her on to his lap and kissed her, then (according to William Heywood) 'shoved' her into the back room. After some 20 minutes, Ann Berry went into the kitchen. James had Mary backed up against the wall with 'her thigh as bare as her face'. He swore at Ann and sent her out. Hannah Tetlow and Ann Ogden went into the kitchen on the excuse of fetching some coals and, to his

---

[19] *Midd Alb*, 30.7.1859.
[20] An attorney in the small village of Cowan Bridge, Lancashire, was the subject of a 'riding' or charivari after his quarrel with his wife had become known through the village. *Lancaster Guardian*, 8.1.1850.

SHANI D'CRUZE

annoyance, stopped James in the middle of intercourse. The women then took Mary to another friend's house, but he followed. Even so, the situation seems to have returned to normal sociability until it was time to go home. As she left the protection of her friend's house, James again appropriated Mary, took her up Coalpit Lane and this time succeeded in having sex with her, even though she 'cried and asked [Ann Ogden] not to leave her'. He apparently saw Mary's body as the site of a leisure activity which like his beer, he could pay for. According to Ann Ogden he said, 'if anything came he wd either pay for it or have her'. The court ordered James Bamford to pay 2s per week.[21]

The court's interest in proving the paternity of Mary's child and avoiding a charge on the poor rates has inscribed the story of its conception in the sources. People also tried to solve such problems informally—through visits by male or female kin, offers of monetary compensation or occasionally the use of traditional shaming rituals (D'Cruze 1998). The court hearing that generated the written record seems to have been resorted to only when informal methods failed or, as in this case, where the poor law authorities or police had a direct interest. Amongst this circle of acquaintances, James Bamford's conduct was seen as out of line, but not so outrageous as to call for complete ostracism. Both men and women saw a bit of dalliance in a back kitchen as an acceptable component of the party. The women attempted to rescue Mary, but because the boundaries of light-hearted flirtation were ambiguous, the assault on Mary was the outcome. A courtship relationship would have legitimated sexual access in Mary's eyes and explained it satisfactorily for the court. Mary, however, said in evidence, 'I never courted with the def[endan]t.' Ann Berry said, 'we left Jos and *we women* went up to [Elizabeth] Kay's house—Bamford followed us' (my emphasis). He had constructed as sexual a relationship which Mary and her women friends saw as primarily social.

A case conforming to the more accepted paradigm of rape occurred in 1861. Lillie Garrett (aged 11) was raped by a plainly dressed, working-class man, Charles Brown.[22] She was returning home one evening and accepted a lift in his cart. Lillie was thrown down on her back, silenced by a hand over her mouth and raped. A man arriving, apparently summoned by the girl's screams, interrupted Brown. She returned directly home to her mother, who called the police. Two constables went off in hot pursuit. Brown was found guilty of an indecent assault and fined 1s; a sum which represented something like 10 per cent of the weekly earnings of local handloom weavers at that period (Baines 1868: 475). The evidence in court made a guilty verdict likely. This was an attack apparently by a stranger on a child of 11. The police had intervened at once. But presumably because Lillie had been out alone, had accepted the ride in the cart and apparently had not sustained extensive external physical injuries, Brown was found guilty only of a minor misdemeanour. Taken together, these two cases indicate just something of the ways that sexual assault (then as now) was but one option embedded in complex webs of power relations by gender. Both describe situations which men exploited by forcing themselves sexually on to a girl or a woman who had agreed to social interaction. Stevi Jackson's notion of 'sexual scripts' is useful here (Jackson 1978). Such 'scripts' facilitate differential readings of an encounter by the social actors involved. Scripts that license sexual intercourse provide a prior neutralization of sexual aggression for men

---

[21] *Midd Alb*, 9.5.1863, LRO, PsMi/1/2, Middleton PS, 20.5.1863.
[22] *Midd Alb*, 2.2.1861, LRO PsMi/1/1, Middleton PS, 30.1.1861.

SEX, VIOLENCE AND LOCAL COURTS

who interpret women's social behaviour and conversation as an invitation to sexual activity. For this nineteenth-century material, scripts involving either courtship and/or familial rights of sexual access by dominant males (husbands, fathers or even employers) seem to have been most commonly invoked.

Although the court held that Brown should not have taken advantage of Lillie Garrett, they did not treat the assault as a particularly serious matter. She had agreed to have a 'ride' with him. Another contemporary Middleton case discussed below uses 'ride' as a euphemism for sexual intercourse. Two years afterwards, the same court accepted that James Bamford was the father of Mary Gradgrind's child, but ignored the sexual assault involved. Had Mary attempted to bring a charge of indecent assault, she would have been less likely to succeed. Courts tended to accept that if a woman's behaviour could be explained as 'courtship', men who took sexual advantage could not be too strongly condemned. Emma Bamford in 1860 stated that 'A man pulled me about—got hold of me—tried to get me into the [petty]—the def[endan]t tried to master me—he sd he wd keep me out all night if I wd not'. Back yards and privies (or petties) were not infrequent resorts of courting couples. It was very hard for Emma to argue that she did not consent to courtship sex after being found there with a man; he was found not guilty. A case that invoked both courtship and the rights of sexual access of older men in domestic space was brought by Elizabeth Cranmer. She lost her case for indecent assault against William Lancaster. He was a neighbour, an older man, who had called to her from his doorstep as she passed. She had accepted his invitation into his bedroom, apparently to deal with some household chore, and been subjected to his indecent proposals.[23] Jurisprudence accepted that a woman's consent to sexual intercourse could be legitimately 'obtained' through physical coercion (Clark 1983: 17). However, broad strands of respectable opinion also included assumptions of women's diminished responsibility for their own sexual chastity in the face of male sexual potency and called upon men to accept responsibility for women they had 'seduced' (Frost 1995; Israel 1997).

Working-Class Masculinity: Sex, Courtship and Popular Leisure

The social history of popular leisure provides a context for much male disorderly behaviour.[24] Although popular leisure (and its traditional association with carnival) was transformed in the nineteenth century to become more appropriate to people's industrial work patterns and earning power, even the most respectable sections of the late Victorian working class still retained some association with it. As well as the self-improving cultures of leisure associated with artisan autodidacticism, the Mechanics Institutes, the Co-operative and temperance movements, Middleton also had flourishing leisure traditions, including the annual wakes (Walton and Poole 1982: 106). Wakes carts elaborately decorated with rushes were the centres of processions and ceremony. These carts, symbolizing fertility and sexuality as well as handicraft traditions and 'local pride and prosperity', were drawn through the streets by young men, described by one hostile observer as 'men-horses' (Poole 1983: 75–6). As well as dressing up, grotesque and

[23] Middleton PS, PsMi/1/1, 4.7.1860, *Midd Alb*, 22.9.1858.
[24] For example, Malcolmson (1973); Golby and Purdue (1984); Yeo and Yeo (1981); Burke (1978); Storch (1982).

SHANI D'CRUZE

blackened faces, morris dancing (doubtless in its less polite manifestations) and the raucous 'rough music' of fife and drum bands, processions were accompanied by heavy drinking, blood sports and fighting. Ribald carnival laughter, the tropes of inversion and indulgence, could be horribly uncomfortable for the dignity of elites—particularly aspiring groups like the nineteenth-century middle class—and had the potential to symbolize resistance and subversion (Bakhtin 1984; Le Roy Ladurie 1980). The *Middleton Albion* of 1864 announced with some relief that 'the wakes had passed off with very few instances of rioting and disorderly conduct'.[25]

A key figure in the Middleton wakes, who built and decorated the rush carts and organized the morris dancing, was Thomas Thorp—a robust and long-lived local character, whose carts were blazoned with his catch phrase, 'NO GRUMBLING'. Thorp was nicknamed 'Old Stiff', a name he acquired because he was in the habit of exposing himself to little girls. This predilection brought him into court in 1863, largely through the complaints of local women who argued that their children were 'actually frightened of him'. 'Old Stiff' put up a spirited show in court, to the amusement of the local newspaper, which represented him as a comic character—in fact, a grotesque. He was 'notorious for displaying his stentorian powers'. When asked by the bench to provide character witnesses, he turned to a crowded court, saying, 'You o nown me; some o you step up'. Though two of his (male) neighbours had not 'known anything wrong of him', one did remark he was known 'for his eccentricities'; eccentricities which included both a very active role in local popular culture and subjecting young girls to frightening and abusive treatment.[26]

Although blood sports declined, heavy drinking and punch-ups continued. Only broader social and economic change, the increasing cost of cart building and the growing availability of cheap railway transport, enabling whole communities to transfer the carnival licence of the wakes to the seaside, eventually made these festivals less relevant in the late nineteenth century (Poole 1983, 1985). Other popular festivals and celebrations, including friendly society processions, fairs, works outings, however superficially rational, even paternalistic, could still provide the opportunity to indulge in elements of the carnivalistic, even if this was limited to heavy eating and a spot too much to drink (Neave 1988; D'Cruze and Turnbull 1995; Joyce 1980). Carnival is of course a cultural arena with a rich symbolic language. Walton and Poole see the Lancashire wakes as 'affirmative' celebrations of 'communal sociability' and emphasize the dimensions of hospitality, of spring-cleaning and reinforced domesticity (Walton and Poole 1982:105). Whilst relations of power and control over material resources construct one or some meanings as dominant—the harmonious industrial community, the solidarities of a respectable working-class—other meanings are not lost, but muted and thus available for recuperation (Moore 1986: 74–80).

Carnivalistic practices also informed a wider tradition of drunken masculine excess in Middleton. In April 1861, John Oldham, *alias* Hollin Lane Monk and John Buckley *alias* Jack 'ut Paul's were arrested as being drunk and disorderly. They had blacked up and were being wheeled round the town in handcarts by two rival factions, in the character of two carnival Lord Mayors, begging drinking money from passers-by.[27] This was no

---

[25] *Midd Alb*, 27.8.1864.
[26] *Midd Alb*, 10.10.1863.
[27] *Midd Alb*, 13.4.1861.

SEX, VIOLENCE AND LOCAL COURTS

spontaneous bit of larking about, but a well-established practice. Buckley pointed out in court that he felt entitled to the role of Lord Mayor since he had served his apprenticeship. The Lord Mayor was elected on Easter Tuesdays and chaired around the town daubed with soot and grease. Drink and fighting were an integral aspect of the event (Partington 1900: 131–2). Wakes and fairs were also a good opportunity for sexual licence, courtship or, indeed, marriage. Jane Ramsden fell pregnant through having sex at Middleton Wakes with James Jackson. He asked her to marry him that night. They had pub-crawled with a group of friends through the Trowell 'then to the Britannia—up and down Middleton and then came home'—alone via a dark lane.[28] Bakhtin's interpretation of carnival pays no heed to gender and the potential dangers for women that its potent mixture of physical and sexual excess could pose (Bakhtin 1984). Not all aspects of working-class male sexual aggression were associated with traditional leisure. Nevertheless, the broader cultural metaphor of leisure and licence, combined with the unbuttoning effects of drink, could neutralize violent lapses in respectability within working-class culture more generally.

Peter Bailey has argued that some individuals and families could sequentially adopt both 'rough' *and* 'respectable' leisure practices (Bailey 1979). Hammerton has pointed out the ambiguities in attitudes to domestic violence evident in Lancashire dialect poetry of this period, indicating an affective investment in family and domesticity whilst acknowledging lapses into violence (Hammerton 1992). The division between 'rough' and 'respectable' could not simply be drawn according to occupation, wage level or region. One individual could be disorderly in some social situations, whilst in others appearing the epitome of sober and self-helping respectability. Working men were called upon to negotiate physically tough, hard-drinking and sexually predatory tropes of working-class masculinity which co-existed with models shared in part with the lower middle class, that emphasized sobriety, domesticity, sexual restraint and promise-keeping (Frost 1995). This contradiction was reinforced by traditions of plebian culture, which were differentiated by gender and sometimes directly misogynist (Clark 1995).

In the affiliation case in which Elizabeth Jacques named Amos Hilton as the father of her illegitimate child, a dense network of friends, kin and neighbours gave evidence. Amos Hilton had once courted Elizabeth, but had since married someone else. He was therefore very keen to deny that her child was his, particularly as Elizabeth was also claiming that she became pregnant as the result of a rape. Elizabeth gave evidence of Amos Hilton's repeated attempts to force her into intercourse. She said '. . . he came many a time but c[oul]d not o'erset me'. Mary Ann Jacques and neighbour Lucy Page testified to finding Amos and Elizabeth alone in the house. Alice Sutcliffe and Elizabeth's brother Thomas both said that Amos had approached them, offering money to 'settle' the matter, demonstrating the kinds of informal strategies which had they worked would have prevented the court case. Amos Hilton's brother, Charles told the court about a conspiracy between themselves, Elizabeth's brother-in-law, Jacob Sutcliffe, and one Richard Kenyon, a man on whom they were trying to pin the paternity of her child. Kenyon was a bricklayer, a neighbour and the friend of Elizabeth's father. This is what Charles Hilton said in court:

[28] LRO, PsMi/1/3, Middleton PS, 18.7.1860.

49

SHANI D'CRUZE

I have been [in] comp[any] of Richd Kenyon—He told me to get [Elizabeth's brothers] . . . out of the house and he wd go in and ride her—we got them out and went down Mid[dleton] with them and walked about until 10 o'clock—Richard Kenyon about that Period said he sent one other [woman] up for Jacob Sutcliffe and that he wd have Eliza for payment.[29]

I interpret the clerk's abbreviated and ungrammatical transcript as describing an alleged agreement between Kenyon and the Hilton brothers that the Hiltons would invite Elizabeth's brothers to go out 'on the town' one evening so that Kenyon could have sex with Elizabeth. Kenyon had paid her brother-in-law for this service and had previously procured a prostitute for him. These events probably never happened; the court decided that Amos Hilton was the father of Elizabeth's child. Nevertheless, the testimony carried into the court the payload of numerous discourses of the sexual availability of women, of men's lack of compunction over consent, the notion that Elizabeth's body was the property of her male kin. Furthermore, that sex-with-violence was (for the parties, the bench *and* the public gallery) a not unimaginable component of young male adult leisure pursuits. There is evidence that male leisure association involved talking about and hence imagining sex as an athletic, competitive practice (McLelland 1991: 81–2). Alfred Dixon's friend recalled him 'plaguing me about being married myself—we were chaffing one another'. Dixon was apparently bragging that he had had sex with one woman 'many a time' without the inconveniences of having a wife.[30] In Rawenstall, another Lancashire textile town, Aaron Elton recalled a conversation with James Hayle about Hayle's relationship with Alice Ratcliffe. Hayle 'sd he did it twice without pulling out. I sd thou art in capital blow'.[31]

Returning to the Hilton brothers in Middleton, their courtroom story was a serious attempt to influence the magistrates' decision. It acquired plausibility because it described exactly the kind of leisure and sexual practices that the bench officially disapproved of. Indeed, it might have deliberately played up to what the Hiltons assumed the bench would believe about how working-class young men behaved. At the same time, of course, it paid court to broader discourses of masculine sexual fantasy which respectable middle-class males might (if covertly or transiently) enjoy. In court it did a good deal of imaginative work, particularly as the woman who was its focal point was standing in the public court as it was told. The local knowledges of witnesses, magistrates, police, court officials and women and men in the public gallery could all give the story credence from different points of view.

Thus these public court hearings undertook surveillance of disorderly working-class masculinity, principally by adjudicating what were the acceptable boundaries of conduct. These stories of the impact of sexual and physical violence on the reputations of working women and men provided regular and staple fare for both the courtroom audience and a local, popular newspaper readership. Considered separately they were titillating anecdotes about neighbours, friends or friends of friends. Together, they formed an ongoing, if unstable and heteroglossial, meta-narrative about the classed and gendered nature of respectability. Such stories repeatedly examined the areas of leisure, courtship, drink, patriarchal rights to control women. Women could express anger and outrage at

[29] PsMi/1/2 10.9.1862, *Midd Alb* 13.9.1862, 20.9.1862, 16.8.1862.
[30] LRO, PsMi/1/5, Middleton PS, 4.10.1894.
[31] LRO, PsRd/1/34, Rawenstall PS, 3.3.1873.

SEX, VIOLENCE AND LOCAL COURTS

such abuse, nevertheless, that opportunity remained contingent. Elizabeth Jacques did not *need* to assert that Amos Hilton '. . . overcame me with violence' since in an affiliation case, the court was only interested in whether they had had intercourse, not in whether force was used. Mary Ann Jacques did not *need* to underline that Elizabeth had 'looked very rough' when Mary Ann had walked in and found Amos standing over Elizabeth with the blinds drawn. Both these testimonies represent Amos's conduct as unacceptable. However, women's and girls' reputations could become fragile once they were subject to this degree of public scrutiny. Simply by revealing their conduct in this degree of detail women's evidence invited questions about their collusion. Who had let down the blinds? Why did Elizabeth continue to entertain an ex-sweetheart, now married, when she was alone? And however neat and respectable she appeared in court, her own and other witnesses' descriptions of her disordered dress, her hair unfastened, brought contradictory representations of her into imaginative view. This public negotiation of the boundaries of rough and respectable revealed not only the class interests of the court to whom working-class disorder was very recently connected with political radicalism and insurrection (Clark 1995), but also the contradictory tropes of working-class masculinity. Lastly the sessions enabled working-class women to voice a somewhat different perception of acceptable masculine conduct, in resistance to assumptions of patriarchal access to women's bodies shared in some measure by both working and middle-class men.

Conclusion

Interestingly, in a Lancashire textile town, cases involving violence in the workplace are comparatively scarce. The industrial workplace had its own procedures for dealing with disorder, though the extent to which physical and sexual violence was directly used as a disciplinary strategy (particularly against the large female textile workforce) remains a speaking silence in these sources (Lambertz 1985). Consequently, the operation and reporting of the Middleton sessions had the effect of predominantly locating working women's social identities firmly within the context of household, neighbourhood and social networks. However, the courts also provided an institutional and discursive framework for the positive assertion of those identities, and a means of airing certain kinds of grievances and achieving justice following certain kinds of injury. As well as widespread involvement in paid work, women's control of household management and consumption gave them a considerable tenacity in defence of the reputations of their households. In these records women represented their agency as contingent and collaborative (Smith and Valenze 1980: 377). This was particularly true where women spoke as advocates for each other.

Women's ability to use the petty sessions in this way would seem to be related to the fact that these were *local* courts. To the extent that Middleton women used the courts to obtain redress for the physical or sexual violence of working men, they colluded with the court's agendas of disciplining the disorderly aspects of working-class masculinity. However, women avoided total subordination within the mid-century petty sessions, if for no other reason than that they spoke not only to the magistrates on the bench but also to their friends and neighbours in the public gallery. From the 1850s the petty sessions

SHANI D'CRUZE

were local, regular and frequent. They were open to the public and judging by newspaper reports could be well attended, particularly one imagines in periods of slack work. A working-class accustomed to attend public meetings on pay, on parliamentary reform, as well as that section given to public entertainments and in search of cheap leisure, could well be attracted to the Wednesday afternoon petty sessions, particularly when the cases involved intimate and sexual revelations of neighbours or acquaintances.

In conclusion, I have reviewed evidence which reflects a specific (though far from unique) local situation at a particular historical conjuncture. Middleton in the mid-nineteenth century experienced acute economic stress, though was still a fast-developing industrial town. Only later, in the 1880s, did it acquire large mills and factories and infilling between what in 1860 were small, localized working-class neighbourhoods separated by field and moor. A middle-class elite was developing overlapping administrative institutions and spheres of influence. A diverse and heterogeneous working class was rethinking its earlier aggressive radicalism and transmuting artisan independence into ratepayer activism. Unruly, disorderly and alcoholic patterns of working-class masculinity, preserved in part by a 'traditional' leisure culture of wakes and carnival, co-existed with the sober respectability of the Mechanics Institute and the Co-operative tea party. In terms of sexual mores and family formation the breadwinner nuclear family was not the only practice, particularly since local organization of production, especially in textiles, made women's and children's earnings vital to working people's domestic economies.

The Petty Sessions thus became a point of intersection of several competing discourses about sexuality and sexual violence, deeply implicated in projects of social control and working-class resistance. Because disciplinary power has positive as well as negative effects, the courtroom opened an albeit unstable and risky public space for women to air their grievances. Official condemnation of disorderly working-class masculinity facilitated women's complaints. However, disapproval of working-class masculinity went hand in hand with dominant views that subsumed broader criteria of working women's respectability (household management, good neighbourliness etc.) into a definition of reputation predicated on sexual chastity. Women's sexual reputation could prove fragile and unstable when the material realities of working-class life (exacerbated by social and economic upheaval) meant that courtship, marriage, even walking from place to place in the dark involved potential sexual dangers. In court, the act of speaking was a risk in itself. A further layer of uncertainty lay in the possibilities of assumptions of women's sexual availability shared, if ever so covertly, between middle-class and working-class patriarchy.

REFERENCES

BACCHI, C. and JOSE, J. (1994), 'Historicising sexual harassment', *Women's History Review*, 3: 263–70.

BAILEY, P. (1979), 'Will the real Bill Banks please stand up? Towards a role analysis of mid-Victorian working-class respectability', *Journal of Social History*, 12: 336–53.

BAINES, E. (1868), *The History of the County Palatine and Duchy of Lancaster, Vol 1*. London and Manchester.

BAKHTIN, M. (1984), *Rabelais and His World*, trans. H. Iswolsky. Bloomington, IN: Indiana University Press.

SEX, VIOLENCE AND LOCAL COURTS

BAMFORD, S.(1903), *Passages in the Life of a Radical*. T. Fisher and Unwin, London.

BASHAR, N. (1983), 'Rape in England between 1550 and 1700', in London Feminist History Group, *The Sexual Dynamics of History*. London: Pluto.

BURKE, P.(1978), *Popular Culture in Early Modern Europe*. London: Maurice Temple Smith.

BUTTERWORTH, E. (1840), *Historical Notices of the Town and Parish of Middleton*. Middleton.

CARTER, J. M. (1985), *Rape in Medieval England: An Historical and Sociological Study*. Lantham, NY: University Press of America.

CHINN, C. (1988), *They Worked All Their Lives: Women Of The Urban Poor In England, 1880–1939*. Manchester: Manchester University Press.

CLARK K. and HOLQUIST, M. (1984), *Mikhail Bakhtin*. Cambridge, MA: Harvard University Press.

CLARK, A. (1983), 'Rape or seduction? A controversy over sexual violence in the nineteenth century', in London Feminist History Group, *The Sexual Dynamics of History*. London: Pluto.

——(1987), *Women's silence, men's violence: sexual assault in England, 1770–1845*. London: Pandora.

——(1992), 'Humanity or Justice? Wifebeating and the law in the eighteenth and nineteenth centuries', in C. Smart, ed., *Regulating Womanhood*, 187–206. London: Routledge.

——(1995), *The struggle for the breeches: gender and the making of the British working class*. Berkeley: University of California Press.

CONLEY, C. (1986), 'Rape and Justice in Victorian England', *Victorian Studies*, 29/4: 519–36.

——(1991), *The Unwritten Law: Criminal Justice in Victorian Kent*. Oxford: Oxford University Press.

D'CRUZE, S. (1998), *Crimes of outrage: sex, violence and Victorian working women*. London: UCL Press.

D'CRUZE, S. and TURNBULL, J. (1995), 'Fellowship and Family: Oddfellows' Lodges in Preston and Lancaster, c. 1830-c. 1890', *Urban History*, 22: 25–47.

DAVIS, J. (1984), 'A poor man's system of justice; the London police courts in the second half of the nineteenth century', *Historical Journal*, 27: 309–35.

DOUGLAS, M. (1966), *Purity and danger; an analysis of concepts of pollution and taboo*. London: Routledge and Kegan Paul.

FOUCAULT M. (1979a), *The History of Sexuality*, vol. 1, trans. Robert Hurley. Harmondsworth: Allen Lane.

——(1979b), *Discipline and Punish*, trans. Alan Sheridan. Harmondsworth: Penguin.

FROST, G. (1995), *Promises Broken: Courtship, Class, and Gender in Victorian England*. Charlottesville and London: University Press of Virginia.

GANDY, G. N. (1978), Illegitimacy in a handloom weaving community: fertility patterns in Culcheth, Lancashire, 1781–1860. PhD, Oxford University.

GARRARD, J. (1983), *Leadership and Power in Victorian Industrial Towns 1830–80*. Manchester: Manchester University Press.

GARRATT, M. (1987), 'The Development of Local Government In Middleton; The Early Years of the Middleton And Tonge Improvement Commissioners, 1861-c1875', MA Dissertation, Manchester Polytechnic.

GILLIS, J. (1985), *For Better for Worse: British Marriages 1600 to the present*. Oxford: Oxford University Press.

GOLBY, J M and PURDUE, A. W., (1984), *The Civilization of the Crowd; Popular Culture in England, 1750–1900*. London: Batsford.

HAMLIN, C. (1988), 'Muddling in Bumbledom; on the enormity of large sanitary improvements in four British towns, 1855–1885', *Victorian Studies*, 32: 55–84.

HAMMERTON, A. J. (1992), *Cruelty and Companionship: Conflict in Nineteenth-Century Married Life*. London: Routledge.

HARRISON, J. F. C. (1971), *The Early Victorians 1832–1851*. London: Weidenfeld and Nicolson.

SHANI D'CRUZE

HOLQUIST, M. (1990), *Dialogism: Bakhtin and his World*. London: Routledge.

HOVELL, M. (1925), *The Chartist Movement*. Manchester: Manchester University Press.

HUNT, M. (1992), 'Wife-beating, domesticity and independence in eighteenth-century London', *Gender and History*, 4/1: 10–33.

ISRAEL, K. (1997), 'French vice and British liberties: gender, class and narrative competition in a late Victorian sex scandal', *Social History*, 22: 1–26.

JACKSON, S. (1978), 'The social context of rape; sexual scripts and motivation', *Women's Studies International Quarterly*, 1: 27–39.

JOYCE, P. (1980), *Work, Society and Politics; the Culture of the Factory Town in Late Victorian England*. Brighton: Harvester.

——(1991), *Visions of the People*. Cambridge: Cambridge University Press.

KELLY, L. (1988), *Surviving Sexual Violence*. Cambridge: Polity.

KIRK, N. (1985), *The growth of working-class reformism in mid-Victorian England*. London: Croom Helm.

LE ROY LADURIE, E. (1980), *Le Carnaval de Romans*. London: Scolar.

LAMBERTZ, J. (1985), 'Sexual harassment in the nineteenth-century English cotton industry', *History Workshop Journal*, 19: 29–61.

LEVY, A. (1991), *Other Women; The writing of class, race and gender, 1842–1898*. Princeton, New Jersey: Princeton University Press.

MALCOLMSON, R. W. (1973), *Popular Recreations in English Society*. Cambridge: Cambridge University Press.

MATHER, F. C. (1980), *Chartism and Society: An Anthology of Documents*. London: Bell and Hayman.

McLELLAND, K. (1991), 'Masculinity and the 'representative artisan' in Britain, 1850–80', in M. Roper and J. Tosh, eds., *Manful assertions: masculinities in Britain since 1800*, 74–91. London: Routledge.

MIDWINTER, E. C. (1969), *Social administration in Lancashire, 1830–1860: Poor law, public health and police*. Manchester: Manchester University Press.

MOORE, H. (1986), *Space, Text and Gender*. Cambridge: Cambridge University Press.

MORSON, G. S. and EMERSON, C., eds. (1989), *Rethinking Bakhtin: Extensions and challenge*. Evanston, IL: Northwestern University Press.

NEAVE, D. R. J. (1988), *East Riding Friendly Societies*. East Yorks. Local History Society.

PARTINGTON, S. (1900), *A Record of Events in the Past History of the Borough*. Middleton.

PEMBER REEVES, M. (1980), *Round About a Pound a Week*. London: Garland.

PERKIN, J. (1989), *Women and Marriage in Nineteenth Century England*. London: Routledge.

PHILIPS, D. (1977), *Crime and Authority in Victorian England*. London: Croom Helm.

POOLE, R. (1983), 'The Oldham Wakes', in J. K. Walton and J. Walvin, eds., *Leisure in England, 1780–1939*, 75–93. Manchester: Manchester University Press.

——(1985), 'Wakes holidays and pleasure fairs in the Lancashire cotton district, c.1790–1890', PhD thesis, History Department, Lancaster University.

READ, D. (1959), 'Chartism in Manchester', in A. Briggs, ed., *Chartist Studies*, 29–64. London: Macmillan.

ROBERTS, E. (1984), *A Woman's Place*. Oxford: Basil Blackwell.

ROSS E. (1982), 'Fierce questions and taunts; married life in working-class London, 1870–1914', *Feminist Studies*, 8/3: 575–602.

——(1983), 'Survival networks: women's neighbourhood sharing in London before World War 1', *History Workshop Journal*, 15: 4–27.

54

SEX, VIOLENCE AND LOCAL COURTS

——(1993), *Labour and Love; Motherhood in Outcast London, 1870–1891.* Oxford: Oxford University Press.

ROTHWELL, N. (1971), The Growth and Development of Middleton. Manchester College of Education, dissertation.

SKYRME, T. (1991), *A History of the Justices of the Peace,* vol 2. Chichester: Barry Rose.

SMITH R. and VALENZE, D.(1980), 'Mutuality and Marginality: Liberal moral theory and working-class women in nineteenth-century England', *Signs,* 1980: 377.

STAM, R. (1981), 'Mikhail Bakhtin and left cultural critique', in E. Ann Kaplan, ed., *Postmodernism and its Discontents, Theories and Practices,* 116–143. London: Verso.

STANKO, E. A. (1985), *Intimate intrusions: Women's experience of male violence.* London: Routledge and Kegan Paul.

STORCH, R. D., ed. (1982), *Popular Culture and Custom in England.* London: Croom Helm.

TEBBUTT, M. (1992), 'Women's Talk? Gossip and Women's Words in Working-Class Communities, 1880–1939', in A. Davies and S. Fielding, eds., *Worker's Worlds: Cultures and Communities in Manchester and Salford, 1880–1939,* 49–73. Manchester: Manchester University Press.

——(1995), *Women's Talk: A social history of gossip in working-class neighbourhoods, 1880–1960.* Aldershot: Scolar Press.

TURNER, V. W. (1969), *The Ritual Process: Structure and anti structure.* London: Routledge and Kegan Paul.

WALTON, J. K. (1987), *Lancashire: A Social History.* Manchester: Manchester University Press.

WALTON, J. K. and POOLE, R. (1982), 'The Lancashire wakes', in R. D. Storch, ed., *Popular Culture And Custom,* 100–24. London: Croom Helm.

WALTON J. K. and WALVIN J., eds. (1983), *Leisure in England, 1780–1939.* Manchester: Manchester University Press.

WEEKS, J. (1981), *Sex, Politics and Society: The regulation of sexuality since 1800.* London: Longman.

WOHL, A. S. (1983), *Endangered Lives: Public health in Victorian Britain.* Cambridge, MA: Harvard University Press.

WRIGHT, D. G. (1988), *Popular Radicalism: The Working Class Experience, 1780–1880.* London and New York: Longman

YEO, E. (1993) 'The Body Metaphor in British Social Science', unpublished paper presented at Lancaster University, 10 September 1993.

YEO E. and YEO, S., eds. (1981), *Popular Culture and Class Conflict, 1590–1914: Explorations in the history of labour and leisure.* Brighton: Harvester.

[9]

Christine Helliwell

"It's Only a Penis": Rape, Feminism, and Difference

In 1985 and 1986 I carried out anthropological fieldwork in the Dayak community of Gerai in Indonesian Borneo. One night in September 1985, a man of the village climbed through a window into the freestanding house where a widow lived with her elderly mother, younger (unmarried) sister, and young children. The widow awoke, in darkness, to feel the man inside her mosquito net, gripping her shoulder while he climbed under the blanket that covered her and her youngest child as they slept (her older children slept on mattresses nearby). He was whispering, "be quiet, be quiet!" She responded by sitting up in bed and pushing him violently, so that he stumbled backward, became entangled with her mosquito net, and then, finally free, moved across the floor toward the window. In the meantime, the woman climbed from her bed and pursued him, shouting his name several times as she did so. His hurried exit through the window, with his clothes now in considerable disarray, was accompanied by a stream of abuse from the woman and by excited interrogations from wakened neighbors in adjoining houses.

I awoke the following morning to raucous laughter on the longhouse verandah outside my apartment where a group of elderly women gathered regularly to thresh, winnow, and pound rice. They were recounting this tale loudly, and with enormous enjoyment, to all in the immediate vicinity. As I came out of my door, one was engaged in mimicking the man climbing out the window, sarong falling down, genitals askew. Those others working or lounging near her on the verandah — both men and women — shrieked with laughter.

When told the story, I was shocked and appalled. An unknown man had tried to climb into the bed of a woman in the dead, dark of night? I knew what this was called: attempted rape. The woman had seen the man and recognized him (so had others in the village, wakened by her shouting). I knew what he deserved: the full weight of the law. My own fears

I am grateful to Francis Elliott for a crucial reference, to the editors and referees of *Signs* for their thoughtful comments and suggestions, to Barbara Sullivan for many helpful discussions, and to Barry Hindess for his customary blend of perceptive criticism and encouragement.

[*Signs: Journal of Women in Culture and Society* 2000, vol. 25, no. 3]

about being a single woman alone in a strange place, sleeping in a dwelling that could not be secured at night, bubbled to the surface. My feminist sentiments poured out. "How can you laugh?" I asked my women friends; "this is a very bad thing that he has tried to do." But my outrage simply served to fuel the hilarity. "No, not bad," said one of the old women (a particular friend of mine), "simply stupid."

I felt vindicated in my response when, two hours later, the woman herself came onto the verandah to share betel nut and tobacco and to broadcast the story. Her anger was palpable, and she shouted for all to hear her determination to exact a compensation payment from the man. Thinking to obtain information about local women's responses to rape, I began to question her. Had she been frightened? I asked. Of course she had— Wouldn't I feel frightened if I awoke in the dark to find an unknown person inside my mosquito net? Wouldn't I be angry? Why then, I asked, hadn't she taken the opportunity, while he was entangled in her mosquito net, to kick him hard or to hit him with one of the many wooden implements near at hand? She looked shocked. Why would she do that? she asked—after all, he hadn't hurt her. No, but he had wanted to, I replied. She looked at me with puzzlement. Not able to find a local word for *rape* in my vocabulary, I scrabbled to explain myself: "He was trying to have sex with you," I said, "although you didn't want to. He was trying to hurt you." She looked at me, more with pity than with puzzlement now, although both were mixed in her expression. "Tin [Christine], it's only a penis," she said. "How can a penis hurt anyone?"

Rape, feminism, and difference

A central feature of many feminist writings about rape in the past twenty years is their concern to eschew the view of rape as a natural function of male biology and to stress instead its bases in society and culture. It is curious, then, that so much of this work talks of rape in terms that suggest—either implicitly or explicitly—that it is a universal practice. To take only several examples: Pauline Bart and Patricia O'Brien tell us that "every female from nine months to ninety years is at risk" (1985, 1); Anna Clark argues that "all women know the paralyzing fear of walking down a dark street at night. . . . It seems to be a fact of life that the fear of rape imposes a curfew on our movements" (1987, 1); Catharine MacKinnon claims that "sexuality is central to women's definition and forced sex is central to sexuality," so "rape is indigenous, not exceptional, to women's social condition" (1989b, 172) and "all women live all the time under the shadow of the

S I G N S Spring 2000 I 791

threat of sexual abuse" (1989a, 340); Lee Madigan and Nancy Gamble write of "the global terrorism of rape" (1991, 21–22); and Susan Brison asserts that "the fact that all women's lives are restricted by sexual violence is indisputable" (1993, 17). The potted "world histories" of rape—which attempt to trace the practice in a range of different societies against a single historical/evolutionary timeline—found in a number of feminist writings on the topic, further illustrate this universalizing tendency.[1] Just as I, an anthropologist trained to be particularly sensitive to the impact of cultural difference, nevertheless took for granted the occurrence of rape in a social and cultural context that I knew to be profoundly different from my own, so most other feminists also unwittingly assume that the practice occurs in all human societies.[2] This is particularly puzzling given that Peggy Reeves Sanday, for one, long ago demonstrated that while rape occurs widely throughout the world, it is by no means a human universal: some societies can indeed be classified as rape free (1981).

There are two general reasons for this universalization of rape among Western feminists. The first of these has to do with the understanding of the practice as horrific by most women in Western societies. In these settings, rape is seen as "a fate worse than, or tantamount to, death" (S. Marcus 1992, 387): a shattering of identity that, for instance, left one North American survivor feeling "not quite sure whether I had died and the world went on without me, or whether I was alive in a totally alien world" (Brison 1993, 10). While any form of violent attack may have severe emotional consequences for its victims, the *sexualization* of violence in rape greatly intensifies those consequences for women in Western societies: "To show power and anger through rape—as opposed to mugging or assault—men are calling on lessons women learn from society, from history and religion, to defile, degrade and shame in addition to inflicting physical pain. Rapists have learned, *as have their victims,* that to rape is to do something worse than to assault" (Gordon and Riger 1989, 45; see also Koss and Harvey 1991). Clearly, the intermeshing of sexuality and personal identity in contemporary Western societies—such that Michel Foucault refers to sex as "that secret which seems to underlie all that we are" (1978, 155)—imbues

---

[1] For recent examples of such histories, see Madigan and Gamble 1991, 11ff.; McColgan 1996, 12–27.

[2] There are some exceptions to this. For example, Peggy Sanday's work on rape among the Minangkabau (1986) and within U.S. college fraternities (1990b) emphasizes very much its contextualized character. In fact, Sanday is one of the few feminists who has attempted to formulate a more general theory concerning the conditions under which rape occurs and under which it does not occur (1981; 1986; 1990b, 8).

the practice of rape with particular horror for most victims from those societies, since there it involves a violation of personhood itself.[3]

Significantly, almost one-third of the respondents in Bart and O'Brien's sample of U.S. women subject to rape attempts were more afraid of being raped by their attackers than they were of being murdered and/or mutilated by them (1985, 52–53) — an extraordinarily large number given that American women are reported to fear murder more than any other crime (Gordon and Riger 1989, 2).[4] Rape is the second most feared crime among women in America, a situation that is no doubt exacerbated by the frequency with which it occurs there.[5] Margaret Gordon and Stephanie Riger (1989) have documented at length the way fear of rape — "the female fear" or "this special fear," as they call it — pervades the lives and shapes the actions of American women. So deep is this fear for many Western women

[3] It is clear from the ethnographic record that while for women in many non-Western societies the experience of rape is similar to that of most Western women, this is not the case in all societies. Material from, e.g., Mehinaku (Gregor 1990) and some Papua New Guinea societies suggests that rape takes on rather different meanings and significances in these settings and, in particular, that rape is not everywhere experienced by women victims in the deeply traumatic terms taken for granted by most Western feminist writers on the topic. Indeed, there is evidence to suggest that, even within specific Western contexts, rape can mean rather different things to different people: Bourque 1989, for instance, has shown that within a single community in southern California, definitions of rape vary enormously, both between men and women and between different women. It is important to point out in this context that to acknowledge the social and cultural variability of the meaning of rape is not to deny its horror or invalidate its trauma for most women victims in the West. The work of such disparate thinkers as Maurice Merleau-Ponty, Foucault, and Pierre Bourdieu has demonstrated that bodily (including emotional) responses are largely socially constituted; the fact that they are therefore not universally shared renders them no less real for those who experience them. Iris Marion Young's classic account (1990) of how Western women's oppression is lived in their bodily experience, for instance, makes very clear the connection between social institutions and practices and the bodily/emotional responses of individuals.

[4] Twenty-nine women out of ninety-two were more afraid of being raped by their attackers than of being murdered and/or mutilated by them. Forty-seven women were more afraid of being murdered and/or mutilated, and sixteen were unclear on this point (Bart and O'Brien 1985, 53). Bart and O'Brien suggest that women who are more afraid of being raped than of being murdered and/or mutilated are more likely to avoid rape when attacked by a potential rapist.

[5] Madigan and Gamble state that an estimated 15 to 40 percent of women (presumably of American women) are "victims of attempted or completed rapes during their lifetimes" (1991, 4; see also Russell 1984; Bart and O'Brien 1985, 129–30; Kilpatrick et al. 1987; Koss and Harvey 1991, 22–29). Koss and Harvey cite a study showing that one in 3.6 American college women has been subject to rape or attempted rape in her lifetime (1991, 24). While the frequency rates are lower in most other Western countries, they are nonetheless high; McColgan, e.g., refers to a 1982 study in London that found that one woman in every six had been raped and a further one in five had been subject to attempted rape (1996, 94).

S I G N S Spring 2000 I 793

that they anticipate the possibility of rape everywhere: rape comes to be understood simply as part of the "natural" human condition. Susan Griffin puts it eloquently: "I have never been free of the fear of rape. From a very early age I, like most women, have thought of rape as part of my natural environment — something to be feared and prayed against like fire and lightning. I never asked why men raped; I simply thought it one of the many mysteries of human nature" (1986, 3). Since feminists are, undoubtedly, as subject to this fear as any other Western women, our tendency to universalize rape is almost overwhelming.

In addition, because within Western feminist discourse rape is depicted as a shockingly barbaric practice — "illuminat[ing] gendered relations of power in their rawest, most brutal forms" (Dubinsky 1993, 8) — there is a tendency to view it as atavistic. Because the practice is widespread in "civilized" Western countries, it is assumed to pervade all other societies as well, since these latter are understood as located closer to the savagery end of the evolutionary ladder. This relates very closely to what Chandra Mohanty has described as "the third world difference": "that stable ahistorical something" that, in many feminist accounts, oppresses the women of Third World countries in addition to their oppression by men (1991, 53). Under this logic, practices deemed oppressive to women that are not commonly found in the West, such as clitoridectomy and *sati,* are explained as resulting from the barbarism of Third World peoples, while oppressive practices that are common in the West, such as rape, are explained in universalistic terms.[6] The related tendency within Western iconography to sexualize black female bodies (see Gilman 1985) means that rape is readily assumed to be a characteristic of "other" — especially black — societies. In fact, the link between this racist iconography and the frequency with which white men rape black women in countries like the United States should lead us to be extremely wary of this kind of assumption. Feminists cannot sidestep this problem by claiming that apparently universalizing statements about rape are meant to refer to Western societies only, since the assumption that

---

[6] Kathleen Barry's recent book on prostitution provides a good example of this kind of approach. Without providing any historical or ethnographic evidence whatsoever, she claims that in "pre-industrial and feudal societies" (the first of four progressive historical "stages of sexual exploitation"), "women's reduction to sex is a fact of their status as the property of their husbands. Under such conditions women are governed by marital relations of power through the exploitation of their unpaid labor in the home, their reproduction, and their sexuality. . . . Men may sexually exploit their wives, take concubines, and buy prostitutes with impunity as the privilege of male domination that services their promiscuity. By contrast, as women are sexual property of men, any sexual act outside of their marriage, including rape and forced prostitution, is usually considered infidelity and the victims are severely punished" (Barry 1995. 51)

unmarked statements should automatically be read in this way is itself suggestive of a form of racism. This is a point to which Western feminists, of
all people, should be particularly sensitive, having ourselves been engaged
in a protracted battle to fracture universalizing masculinist discourses.

A second, equally deep-seated reason for the feminist tendency to universalize rape stems from Western feminism's emphasis on difference between men and women and from its consequent linking of rape and
difference. Two types of difference are involved here. The first of these is
difference in social status and power; thus rape is linked quite explicitly, in
contemporary feminist accounts, to patriarchal social forms. Indeed, this
focus on rape as stemming from difference in social position is what distinguishes feminist from other kinds of accounts of rape (see Ellis 1989, 10).
In this view, inequality between men and women is linked to men's desire
to possess, subjugate, and control women, with rape constituting a central
means by which the freedom of women is limited and their continued
submission to men ensured. For this reason, rape has assumed a significant
role within many feminist narratives, with Carole Pateman's account of the
social contract as based on an originary rape of a woman by a man providing perhaps the best-known example (1988). Since many feminists continue to believe that patriarchy is universal — or, at the very least, to feel
deeply ambivalent on this point — there is a tendency among us to believe
that rape, too, is universal.[7]

However, the view of women as everywhere oppressed by men has been
extensively critiqued within the anthropological literature. A number of
anthropologists have argued that in some societies, while men and women
may perform different roles and occupy different spaces, they are nevertheless equal in value, status, and power.[8] In addition, Marilyn Strathern, for
one, has pointed out that notions such as "inequality" and "domination"
cannot necessarily be applied in societies with very different conceptions
of agency and personhood: "To argue that what happens to women qua
women is a function of what happens to men qua men is not to postulate
that women's concerns are relative to or subsumed by those of men but
that neither can be understood without comprehending the relationship
between them" (1988, 34; see also Strathern 1987). As Strathern sees it,
the Western tendency to distinguish between subject and object makes it
impossible for Westerners to recognize that in some societies (in this case,

[7] Among "radical" feminists such as Andrea Dworkin and Catharine MacKinnon this belief reaches its most extreme version, in which all sexual intercourse between a man and a
woman is viewed as akin to rape (Dworkin 1987; MacKinnon 1989a, 1989b).

[8] Leacock 1978 and Bell 1983 are well-known examples. Sanday 1990a and Marcus 1992
are more recent examples, on Minangkabau and Turkish society, respectively.

S I G N S Spring 2000 I 795

Melanesian ones) a person (whether male or female) is, at the same time, both subject and object. Feminist distinctions between male subjects and female objects—and corresponding notions of asymmetry—thus do not make sense in these contexts (Strathern 1988). Viewed in this light, feminist claims concerning the universality of rape begin to look even more problematic.[9]

But there is a second type of difference between men and women that also, albeit largely implicitly, underlies the assumption that rape is universal, and it is the linkage between this type of difference and the treatment of rape in feminist accounts with which I am largely concerned in this article. I refer to the assumption by most Western feminists writing on rape that men and women have different bodies and, more specifically, different genitalia: that they are, in other words, differently sexed. Furthermore, it is taken for granted in most feminist accounts that these differences render the former biologically, or "naturally," capable of penetrating and therefore brutalizing the latter and render the latter "naturally" able to be brutalized. While this assumption was quite explicit in earlier feminist accounts of rape—in particular, in Susan Brownmiller's (1975) argument that men rape primarily because they are biologically equipped with the "tools" (penises) to do so—it is largely implicit in more recent feminist work, where the concern is to eschew biological explanations and to stress instead the social bases of rape.[10] Rape of women by men is thus assumed to be universal because the same "biological" bodily differences between men and women are believed to exist everywhere.

Unfortunately, the assumption that preexisting bodily difference between men and women underlies rape has blinded feminists writing on the subject to the ways the practice of rape itself creates and inscribes such difference. This seems particularly true in contemporary Western societies

[9] MacKinnon suggests, for instance, that Khalka Mongol men's assertion (as quoted by Sanday) that "our women never resist" evokes a society in which sex can be equated with rape (1989a, 322). This suggestion clearly assumes that the individuated "subject" of Western experience is found also among the Khalka Mongol, such that the observer can separate out the "autonomous" interests of husband and wife and thus describe sexual relations between them in the familiar Western terms of "consent" and "resistance." While any categorization of Khalka Mongol society as "rape free" cannot be based simply on male claims of this type, categorization of it as "rape prone" purely on this basis is equally absurd, since it assumes that these kinds of male claims serve the same function here as they often do in the United States: namely, to legitimate male objectification of women. Work such as Strathern's throws into question precisely this kind of assumption.

[10] Some contemporary feminist accounts, however, are more explicit in their adoption of this kind of position. Aileen McColgan, e.g., states that most rapists "are not armed with . . . anything other than their fists, their penises and their superior strength" (1996, 9).

where the relationship between rape and bodily/genital dimorphism appears to be an extremely intimate one. Judith Butler (1990, 1993) has argued (following Foucault 1978) that the Western emphasis on sexual difference is a product of the heterosexualization of desire within Western societies over the past few centuries, which "requires and institutes the production of discrete and asymmetrical oppositions between 'feminine' and 'masculine,' where these are understood as expressive attributes of 'male' and 'female'" (1990, 17).[11] The practice of rape in Western contexts can only properly be understood with reference to this heterosexual matrix, to the division of humankind into two distinct—and in many respects opposed—types of body (and hence types of person).[12] While it is certainly the case that rape is linked in contemporary Western societies to disparities of power and status between men and women, it is the particular discursive form that those disparities take—their elaboration in terms of the discourse of sex—that gives rape its particular meaning and power in these contexts.

Sharon Marcus has already argued convincingly that the act of rape "feminizes" women in Western settings, so that "the entire female body comes to be symbolized by the vagina, itself conceived of as a delicate, perhaps inevitably damaged and pained inner space" (1992, 398). I would argue further that the *practice* of rape in these settings—both its possibility and its actualization—not only feminizes women but masculinizes men as well.[13] This masculinizing character of rape is very clear in, for instance, Sanday's ethnography of fraternity gang rape in North American universities (1990b) and, in particular, in material on rape among male prison inmates. In the eyes of these rapists the act of rape marks them as "real men" and marks their victims as not men, that is, as feminine.[14] In this iconography, the "masculine" body (along with the "masculine" psyche), is

---

[11] See Laqueur 1990 for a historical account of this process.

[12] On the equation of body and person within Western (especially feminist) thought, see Moore 1994.

[13] See Plaza 1980: "[Rape] is very sexual in the sense that [it] is frequently a sexual activity, but especially in the sense that it opposes men and women: it is *social sexing* which is latent in rape. . . . Rape is sexual essentially because it rests on the very social difference between the sexes" (31).

[14] The material on male prison inmates is particularly revealing in this respect. As an article by Stephen Donaldson, a former prisoner and the president of the U.S. advocacy group Stop Prisoner Rape, makes clear, "hooking up" with another prisoner is the best way for a prisoner to avoid sexual assaults, particularly gang rapes. Hooking up involves entering a sexual liaison with a senior partner ("jocker," "man," "pitcher," "daddy") in exchange for protection. In this arrangement, the rules are clear: the junior partner gives up his autonomy and comes under the authority of the senior partner; he is often expected by the senior partner "to be as feminine in appearance and behaviour as possible," including shaving his legs, growing long hair,

S I G N S   Spring 2000   I   **797**

viewed as hard, penetrative, and aggressive, in contrast to the soft, vulnerable, and violable "feminine" sexuality and psyche. Rape both reproduces and marks the pronounced sexual polarity found in these societies.

Western understandings of gender difference have almost invariably started from the presumption of a presocial bodily difference between men and women ("male" and "female") that is then somehow acted on by society to produce gender. In particular, the possession of either male genitals or female genitals is understood by most Westerners to be not only the primary marker of gender identity but, indeed, the underlying cause of that identity. Most feminist models of gender, while wishing to draw attention to the socially constructed character of difference, have nevertheless assumed—however reluctantly—that gender ultimately relates "back" to sex, that is, to the differences between "male" and "female" bodies. Yet this assumption is problematic in light of both feminist challenges to the notion that "sex" is given (and therefore universal) (Butler 1990, 1993) and historical research suggesting that dimorphic "sexing" of bodies is a relatively recent phenomenon in West European history (Trumbach 1989, 1993; Laqueur 1990; van der Meer 1993). This kind of model is especially problematic for using with cross-cultural material, such as that described below.[15]

I seek to do two things in this article. First, in providing an account of a community in which rape does not occur, I aim to give the lie to the widespread assumption that rape is universal and thus to invite Western feminists to interrogate the basis of our own tendency to take its universality for granted.[16] The fundamental question is this: Why does a woman of Gerai see a penis as lacking the power to harm her, while I, a white Australian/New Zealand woman, am so ready to see it as having the capacity to defile, to humiliate, to subjugate and, ultimately, to destroy me?

Second, by exploring understandings of sex and gender in a community

---

using a feminine nickname, and performing work perceived as feminine (laundry, cell cleaning, giving backrubs, etc.) (Donaldson 1996, 17, 20). See also the extract from Jack Abbott's prison letters in Halperin 1993 (424–25).

[15] Henrietta Moore has pointed out some of the problems with the conventional sex/gender model. These include its assumption that difference lies between bodies (whereas in many societies gender differences are understood to reside within individual bodies) and its stress on the body as the ultimate repository of identity, which relates to the Western belief in the unified, continuous person located in an individual body (a belief that is by no means universal) (Moore 1994, chaps. 1 and 2).

[16] While I am primarily concerned here with the feminist literature (believing that it contains by far the most useful and insightful work on rape), it needs to be noted that many other (nonfeminist) writers also believe rape to be universal. See, e.g., Ellis 1989; Palmer 1989.

that stresses identity, rather than difference, between men and women (including men's and women's bodies), I aim to demonstrate that Western beliefs in the "sexed" character of bodies are not "natural" in basis but, rather, are a component of specifically Western gendering and sexual regimes. And since the practice of rape in Western societies is profoundly linked to these beliefs, I will suggest that it is an inseparable part of such regimes. This is not to say that the practice of rape is always linked to the kind of heterosexual regime found in the West; even the most cursory glance at any list of societies in which the practice occurs indicates that this is not so.[17] But it is to point out that we will be able to understand rape only ever in a purely localized sense, in the context of the local discourses and practices that are both constitutive of and constituted by it. In drawing out the implications of the Gerai stress on identity between men and women for Gerai gender and sexual relations, I hope to point out some of the possible implications of the Western emphasis on gender difference for Western gender and sexual relations — including the practice of rape.

Gender, sex, and procreation in Gerai

Gerai is a Dayak community of some seven hundred people in the Indonesian province of Kalimantan Barat (West Borneo).[18] In the twenty months I spent in the community, I heard of no cases of either sexual assault or attempted sexual assault (and since this is a community in which privacy as we understand it in the West is almost nonexistent — in which surveillance by neighbors is at a very high level [see Helliwell 1996] — I would certainly have heard of any such cases had they occurred). In addition, when I questioned men and women about sexual assault, responses ranged from puzzlement to outright incredulity to horror.

While relations between men and women in Gerai can be classified as

---

[17] For listings of "rape-prone" societies, see Minturn, Grosse, and Haider 1969; Sanday 1981.

[18] I carried out anthropological fieldwork in Gerai from March 1985 to February 1986 and from June 1986 to January 1987. The fieldwork was funded by an Australian National University Ph.D. scholarship and carried out under the sponsorship of Lembaga Ilmu Pengetahuan Indonesia. At the time that I was conducting my research a number of phenomena were beginning to have an impact on the community — these had the potential to effect massive changes in the areas of life discussed in this article. These phenomena included the arrival of a Malaysian timber company in the Gerai region and the increasing frequency of visits by Malay, Bugis, Chinese, and Batak timber workers to the community; the arrival of two American fundamentalist Protestant missionary families to live and proselytize in the community; and the establishment of a Catholic primary school in Gerai, resulting in a growing tendency among parents to send their children (both male and female) to attend Catholic secondary school in a large coastal town several days' journey away.

relatively egalitarian in many respects, both men and women nevertheless say that men are "higher" than women (Helliwell 1995, 364). This is especially the case in the context of formal community-wide functions such as village meetings and moots to settle legal disputes. While women are not required to remain silent on such occasions, their voices carry less authority than those of men, and, indeed, legal experts in the community (all men) told me that a woman's evidence in a moot is worth seven-tenths of a man's (see also Tsing 1990). In addition, a husband is granted a degree of formal authority over his wife that she does not have over him; thus a wife's disobedience of her husband is theoretically a punishable offense under *adat*, or local law. I have noted elsewhere that Gerai people stress the ideal of *diri*, literally meaning "standing" or "to stand," according to which each rice group should take primary responsibility for itself in all spheres of life and make its own decisions on matters concerning its members (Helliwell 1995). It is on the basis of their capacity to stand that rice groups within the community are ranked against one another. The capacity to stand is predicated primarily on the ability to produce rice surpluses: yet, significantly, although men and women work equally at rice-field work, it is only men who occasionally are individually described as standing. As in some other societies in the same region (Ilongot, Wana), Gerai people link men's higher status to their greater bravery.[19] This greater bravery is demonstrated, they say, by the fact that it is men who *mampat* (cut down the large trees to make a rice field), who burn off the rice field to prepare for planting, and who enter deep primary jungle in search of game and jungle products such as aloe wood—all notoriously dangerous forms of work.

This greater status and authority does not, however, find expression in the practice of rape, as many feminist writings on the subject seem to suggest that it should. This is because the Gerai view of men as "higher" than women, although equated with certain kinds of increased potency vis-à-vis the world at large, does not translate into a conception of that potency as attached to and manifest through the penis—of men's genitals as able to brutalize women's genitals.

Shelly Errington has pointed out that a feature of many of the societies of insular Southeast Asia is a stress on sameness, even identity, between men and women (1990, 35, 39), in contrast to the Western stress on difference between the passive "feminine" object and the active, aggressive "masculine" subject.[20] Gerai understandings of gender fit Errington's

[19] On the Ilongot, see Rosaldo 1980a; on the Wana, see Atkinson 1990.

[20] The Wana, as described by Jane Atkinson (1990), provide an excellent example of a society that emphasizes sameness. Emily Martin points out that the explicit Western opposition between the "natures" of men and women is assumed to occur even at the level of the cell, with biologists commonly speaking of the egg as passive and immobile and the sperm as

model very well. In Gerai, men and women are not understood as fundamentally different types of persons: there is no sense of a dichotomized
masculinity and femininity. Rather, men and women are seen to have the
same kinds of capacities and proclivities, but with respect to some, men
are seen as "more so" and with respect to others, women are seen as "more
so." Men are said to be braver and more knowledgeable about local law
(*adat*), while women are said to be more persistent and more enduring.
All of these qualities are valued. Crucially, in terms of the central quality
of nurturance (perhaps the most valued quality in Gerai), which is very
strongly marked as feminine among Westerners, Gerai people see no
difference between men and women. As one (female) member of the community put it to me: "We all must nurture because we all need."[21] The
capacity both to nurture and to need, particularly as expressed through the
cultivation of rice as a member of a rice group, is central to Gerai conceptions of personhood: rice is the source of life, and its (shared) production
humanizes and socializes individuals (Helliwell, forthcoming). Women
and men have identical claims to personhood based on their equal contributions to rice production (there is no notion that women are somehow
diminished as persons even though they may be seen as less "high"). As in
Strathern's account of Hagen (1988), the perceived mutuality of rice-field
work in Gerai renders inoperable any notion of either men or women as
autonomous individual subjects.

It is also important to note that while men's bravery is linked to a notion
of their greater physical strength, it is not equated with aggression—aggression is not valued in most Gerai contexts.[22] As a Gerai man put it to
me, the wise man is the one "who fights when he has to, and runs away
when he can"; such avoidance of violence does not mark a man as lacking
in bravery. This does not mean that in certain contexts male warriorship—
the ability to fight and even to take heads—is not valorized; on the con-

---

active and aggressive even though recent research indicates that these descriptions are erroneous and that they have led biologists to misunderstand the fertilization process (1991). See
also Lloyd 1984 for an excellent account of how (often latent) conceptions of men and
women as having opposed characteristics are entrenched in the history of Western philosophical thought.

[21] The nurture-need dynamic (that I elsewhere refer to as the "need-share dynamic") is
central to Gerai sociality. Need for others is expressed through nurturing them; such expression is the primary mark of a "good" as opposed to a "bad" person. See Helliwell (forthcoming) for a detailed discussion.

[22] In this respect, Gerai is very different from, e.g., Australia or the United States, where,
as Michelle Rosaldo has pointed out, aggression is linked to success, and women's constitution as lacking aggression is thus an important element of their subordination (1980b, 416;
see also Myers 1988, 600).

trary, the most popular myths in Gerai are those that tell of the legendary warrior hero (and headhunter without peer) Koling. However, Gerai people make a clear distinction between the fantastic world of the heroes of the past and the mundane world in which the present man of Gerai must make his way.[23] While it is recognized that a man will sometimes need to fight — and skill and courage in fighting are valued — aggression and hotheadedness are ridiculed as the hallmarks of a lazy and incompetent man. In fact, physical violence between adults is uncommon in Gerai, and all of the cases that I did witness or hear about were extremely mild.[24] Doubtless the absence of rape in the community is linked to this devaluing of aggression in general. However, unlike a range of other forms of violence (slapping, beating with a fist, beating with an implement, knifing, premeditated killing, etc.), rape is not named as an offense and accorded a set punishment under traditional Gerai law. In addition, unlike these other forms of violence, rape is something that people in the community find almost impossible to comprehend ("How would he be able to do such a thing?" one woman asked when I struggled to explain the concept of a man attempting to put his penis into her against her will). Clearly, then, more is involved in the absence of rape in Gerai than a simple absence of violence in general.

Central to all of the narratives that Gerai people tell about themselves and their community is the notion of a "comfortable life": the achievement of this kind of life marks the person and the household as being of value and constitutes the norm to which all Gerai people aspire. Significantly, the content of such a life is seen as identical for both men and women: it

---

[23] The practice of headhunting — seeking out enemies in order to sever their heads, which were then brought back to one's own village and treated with ritual reverence — was, in the past, widely found among Borneo Dayak groups. Gerai people claim that their not-too-distant ancestors practiced headhunting, but my own sense is that they are more likely to have been the hunted than the hunters. While in many respects Gerai resembles some of the "nonviolent" societies found throughout the region — including the Semai (Dentan 1968, 1978) and Chewong (Howell 1989) of Peninsular Malaysia and the Buid (Gibson 1986) of Mindoro in the Philippines — its celebration of violence in certain specified contexts marks it as rather different from many of them. Howell, for instance, claims that none of the indigenous peoples of Peninsular Malaysia "has any history of warfare, either recorded by the outside world or represented in myths and legends" (1989, 35), while Gibson notes that the Buid language "lacks words expressing a positive evaluation of courage or the reciprocation of violence" (1986, 107–8). Gerai people are, in fact, very similar in this respect to another Borneo Dayak people, the Bidayuh, who also valorize male violence in myth but tend to devalue and avoid it in everyday life and who also have a tradition of headhunting but are likely to have been hunted rather than hunters (Geddes 1957).

[24] See Helliwell 1996, 142–43, for an example of a "violent" altercation between husband and wife.

is marked by the production of bountiful rice harvests each year and the successful raising of a number of healthy children to maturity. The core values and aspirations of men and women are thus identical; of the many life histories that I collected while in the community—all of which are organized around this central image—it is virtually impossible to tell those of men from those of women. Two points are significant in this respect. First, a "comfortable life" is predicated on the notion of a partnership between a man and a woman (a conjugal pair). This is because while men and women are seen to have the same basic skills and capacities, men are seen to be "better" at certain kinds of work and women to be "better" at other kinds. Second, and closely related to this, the Gerai notion of men's and women's work does not constitute a rigid division of labor: both men and women say that theoretically women can perform all of the work routinely carried out by men, and men can perform all of the work routinely carried out by women. However, men are much better at men's work, and women are much better at women's work. Again, what we have here is a stress on *identity* between men and women at the expense of radical difference.

This stress on identity extends into Gerai bodily and sexual discourses. A number of people (both men and women) assured me that men sometimes menstruate; in addition, menstrual blood is not understood to be polluting, in contrast to how it is seen in many societies that stress more strongly the difference between men and women. While pregnancy and childbirth are spoken of as "women's work," many Gerai people claim that under certain circumstances men are also able to carry out this work—but, they say, women are "better" at it and so normally undertake it. In line with this claim, I collected a Gerai myth concerning a lazy woman who was reluctant to take on the work of pregnancy and childbirth. Her husband instead made for himself a lidded container out of bark, wood, and rattan ("like a betel nut container"), which he attached around his waist beneath his loincloth and in which he carried the growing fetus until it was ready to be born. On one occasion when I was watching a group of Gerai men cut up a boar, one, remembering an earlier conversation about the capacity of men to give birth, pointed to a growth in the boar's body cavity and said with much disapproving shaking of the head: "Look at this. He wants to carry his child. He's stupid." In addition, several times I saw fathers push their nipples into the mouths of young children to quieten them; while none of these fathers claimed to be able to produce milk, people nevertheless claimed that some men in the community were able to lactate, a phenomenon also attested to in myth. Men and women are thought to produce the same genital fluid, and this is linked in complex

S I G N S Spring 2000 I 803

ways to the capacity of both to menstruate. All of these examples demonstrate the community's stress on bodily identity between men and women.

Furthermore, in Gerai, men's and women's sexual organs are explicitly conceptualized as the same. This sexual identity became particularly clear when I asked several people who had been to school (and hence were used to putting pencil to paper) to draw men's and women's respective organs for me: in all cases, the basic structure and form of each were the same. One informant, endeavoring to convince me of this sameness, likened both to wooden and bark containers for holding valuables (these vary in size but have the same basic conical shape, narrower at the base and wider at the top). In all of these discussions, it was reiterated that the major difference between men's and women's organs is their location: inside the body (women) and outside the body (men).[25] In fact, when I pressed people on this point, they invariably explained that it makes no sense to distinguish between men's and women's genitalia themselves; rather, it is location that distinguishes between penis and vulva.[26]

Heterosexuality constitutes the normative sexual activity in the community and, indeed, I was unable to obtain any information about homosexual practices during my time there. In line with the stress on sameness, sexual intercourse between a man and a woman in Gerai is understood as an equal coming together of fluids, pleasures, and life forces. The same stress also underlies beliefs about conception. Gerai people believe that repeated acts of intercourse between the same two people are necessary for conception, since this "prepares" the womb for pregnancy. The fetus is deemed to be created through the mingling of equal quantities of fluids and forces from both partners. Again, what is seen as important here is not the fusion of two different types of bodies (male and female) as in Western understandings; rather, Gerai people say, it is the similarity of the two bodies that allows procreation to occur. As someone put it to me bluntly: "If they were not the same, how could the fluids blend? It's like coconut oil and water: they can't mix!"

---

[25] I have noted elsewhere that the inside-outside distinction is a central one within this culture (Helliwell 1996).

[26] While the Gerai stress on the sameness of men's and women's sexual organs seems, on the face of it, to be very similar to the situation in Renaissance Europe as described by Laqueur 1990, it is profoundly different in at least one respect: in Gerai, women's organs are not seen as emasculated versions of men's—"female penises"—as they were in Renaissance Europe. This is clearly linked to the fact that, in Gerai, as we have already seen, *people* is not synonymous with *men*, and women are not relegated to positions of emasculation or abjection, as was the case in Renaissance Europe.

What needs to be stressed here is that both sexual intercourse and conception are viewed as involving a mingling of similar bodily fluids, forces,
and so on, rather than as the penetration of one body by another with a
parallel propulsion of substances from one (male) body only into the other,
very different (female) one. Nor is there anything in Gerai understandings
that equates with the Western notion of conception as involving an aggressive active male cell (the sperm) seeking out and penetrating a passive,
immobile female cell (the egg) (Martin 1991). What Gerai accounts of
both sexual intercourse and conception stress are tropes of identity, mingling, balance, and reciprocity. In this context it is worth noting that many
Gerai people were puzzled by the idea of gender-specific "medicine" to
prevent contraception—such as the injectable or oral contraceptives promoted by state-run health clinics in the area. Many believed that, because
both partners play the same role in conception, it should not matter
whether husband or wife received such medicine (and indeed, I knew of
cases where husbands had taken oral contraceptives meant for their wives).
This suggests that such contraceptive regimes also serve (like the practice
of rape) to reinscribe sex difference between men and women (see also
Tsing 1993, 104–20).

When I asked why, if conception is predicated on the mingling of two
similar bodies, two men or two women could not also come together to
create a child, the response was that a man and a woman "fit" with one
another *(sedang)*. But while there is some sense of physical compatibility
being suggested here, Gerai people were adamant that what is more important in constituting "fit" is the role of each individual's "life force" *(semongan')* and its intimate connection to particular forms of work. The *semongan'* is the spiritual essence or force that animates the person, that gives the
person his or her individual life. Without his or her *semongan'*, a human
being cannot live (this is true of all other elements in the universe as well),
and thus when a person dies, the *semongan'* is understood to have left the
body and journeyed away. In turn, an individual's *semongan'* is centrally
linked to the kind of work he or she routinely performs—particularly during the rice-cultivation cycle, which is understood as the source of life itself
in Gerai.

While Gerai people stress sameness over difference between men and
women, they do, nevertheless, see them as being different in one important
respect: their life forces are, they say, oriented differently ("they face
different ways," it was explained to me). This different orientation means
that women are "better" at certain kinds of work and men are "better" at
other kinds of work—particularly with respect to rice-field work. Gerai
people conceive of the work of clearing large trees for a new rice field as

the definitive man's work and regard the work of selecting and storing the rice seed for the following year's planting—which is correlated in fundamental ways with the process of giving birth—as the definitive woman's work. Because women are perceived to lack appropriate skills with respect to the first, and men are perceived to lack appropriate skills with respect to the second, Gerai people say that to be viable a household must contain both adult males and adult females. And since a "comfortable life" is marked by success in production not only of rice but also of children, the truly viable household must contain at least one conjugal pair. The work of both husband and wife is seen as necessary for the adequate nurturance of the child and successful rearing to adulthood (both of which depend on the successful cultivation of rice). Two women or two men would not be able to provide adequately for a child since they would not be able to produce consistently successful rice harvests; while such a household might be able to select seed, clear a rice field, and so grow rice in some rudimentary fashion, its lack of expertise at one of these tasks would render it perennially poor and its children perennially unhealthy, Gerai people say. For this reason, households with adults of only one gender are greatly pitied by Gerai people, and single parents seek to marry or remarry as quickly as they can. It is the mingling of the respective life forces of a man and a woman, then—linked, as they are, to the work skills of each—that primarily enables conception. It is this, Gerai people say, that allows the child's *semongan'* to come into being. Mingling of the parental bodily fluids, in turn, creates the child's bodily substance, but this substance must be animated in some prior sense by a life force, or the child will die.

Gender difference in Gerai, then, is not predicated on the character of one's body, and especially of one's genitalia, as in many Western contexts. Rather, it is understood as constituted in the differential capacity to perform certain kinds of work, a capacity assigned long before one's bodily being takes shape.[27] In this respect it is important to note that Gerai ontology rests on a belief in predestination, in things being as they should (see Helliwell 1995). In this understanding, any individual's *semongan'* is linked in multifarious and unknowable ways to the cosmic order, to the "life" of the universe as a whole. Thus the new fetus is predestined to become someone "fitted" to carry out either men's work or women's work as part of the maintenance of a universal balance. Bodies with the appropriate characteristics—internal or external genitalia, presence or absence of breasts, and so

---

[27] In this respect Gerai is similar to a number of other peoples in this region (e.g., Wana, Ilongot), for whom difference between men and women is also seen as primarily a matter of the different kinds of work that each performs.

on — then develop in line with this prior destiny. At first sight this may not seem enormously different from Western conceptions of gender, but the difference is in fact profound. While, for Westerners, genitalia, as signifi-cant of one's role in the procreative process, are absolutely fundamental in determining one's identity, in Gerai the work that one performs is seen as fundamental, and genitalia, along with other bodily characteristics, are relegated to a kind of secondary, derivative function.

Gerai understandings of gender were made quite clear through circum-stances surrounding my own gender classification while in the community. Gerai people remained very uncertain about my gender for some time after I arrived in the community because (as they later told me) "I did not . . . walk like a woman, with arms held out from the body and hips slightly swaying; I was "brave," trekking from village to village through the jungle on my own; I had bony kneecaps; I did not know how to tie a sarong in the appropriate way for women; I could not distinguish different varieties of rice from one another; I did not wear earrings; I had short hair; I was tall" (Helliwell 1993, 260). This was despite the fact that people in the community knew from my first few days with them both that I had breasts (this was obvious when the sarong that I wore clung to my body while I bathed in the river) and that I had a vulva rather than a penis and testicles (this was obvious from my trips to defecate or urinate in the small stream used for that purpose, when literally dozens of people would line the banks to observe whether I performed these functions differently from them). As someone said to me at a later point, "Yes, I saw that you had a vulva, but I thought that Western men might be different."

My eventual, more definitive classification as a woman occurred largely fortuitously. My initial research proposal focused on the creation of subjec-tivity and sociality through work and, accordingly, as soon as I arrived in the community, I began accompanying people to work in the rice fields. Once I had negotiated a longhouse apartment of my own in which to live (several weeks after arrival), I also found myself, in concert with all other households in the community, preparing and cooking rice at least twice daily. These activities rapidly led to a quest for information concerning rice itself, particularly concerning the different strains, how they are cultivated, and what they are used for. As I learned to distinguish types of rice and their uses, I became more and more of a woman (as I realized later), since this knowledge — including the magic that goes with it — is understood by Gerai people as foundational to femininity. However, while people eventu-ally took to referring to me as a woman, for many in the community my gender identity remained deeply ambiguous, partly because so many of my characteristics and behaviors were more like those of a man than a woman,

S I G N S Spring 2000 I 807

but also, and more importantly, because I never achieved anything approaching the level of knowledge concerning rice-seed selection held by even a girl child in Gerai.

In fact, Gerai people talk of two kinds of work as defining a woman: the selection and storage of rice seed and the bearing of children.[28] But the first of these is viewed as prior, logically as well as chronologically. People are quite clear that in the womb either "someone who can cut down the large trees for a ricefield is made, or someone who can select and store rice." When I asked if it was not more important whether or not someone could bear a child, it was pointed out to me that many women do not bear children (there is a high rate of infertility in the community), but all women have the knowledge to select and store rice seed. In fact, at the level of the rice group the two activities of "growing" rice and "growing" children are inseparable: a rice group produces rice in order to raise healthy children, and it produces children so that they can in turn produce the rice that will sustain the group once their parents are old and frail (Helliwell, forthcoming). For this reason, any Gerai couple unable to give birth to a child of their own will adopt one, usually from a group related by kinship. The two activities of growing rice and growing children are constantly talked about together, and the same imagery is used to describe the development of a woman's pregnancy and the development of rice grains on the plant. Indeed, the process of pregnancy and birth is seen as intimately connected to the process of rice selection and storage. As one woman explained to me, "It is because we know how to hold the seed in the storage baskets that we are able to hold it in our wombs." But just as the cultivation of rice is seen as in some sense prior to the cultivation of children, so it is said that "knowledge about childbirth comes from knowledge about rice seed."

Gerai, then, lacks the stress on bodily — and especially genital — dimorphism that most feminist accounts of rape assume. Indeed, the reproductive organs themselves are not seen as "sexed." In a sense it is problematic even to use the English categories *woman* and *man* when writing of this community, since these terms are saturated with assumptions concerning the priority of biological (read, bodily) difference. In the Gerai context, it would be more accurate to deal with the categories of, on the one hand, "those responsible for rice selection and storage" and, on the other, "those responsible for cutting down the large trees to make a ricefield." There is no discursive space in Gerai for the distinction between an active, aggressive,

---

[28] In Gerai, pregnancy and birth are seen not as semimystical "natural" processes, as they are for many Westerners, but simply as forms of work, linked very closely to the work of rice production.

penetrating male sexual organ (and sexuality) and a passive, vulnerable, female one. Indeed, sexual intercourse in Gerai is understood by both men and women to stem from mutual "need" on the part of the two partners; without such need, people say, sexual intercourse cannot occur, because the requisite balance is lacking. Since, as I have described at length elsewhere (Helliwell, forthcoming), a relationship of "needing" is always reciprocal (it is almost inconceivable, in Gerai terms, to need someone who does not need you in return, and the consequences of unreciprocated needing are dire for both individual and rice group), the sexual act is understood as preeminently mutual in its character, including in its initiation. The idea of having sex with someone who does not need you to have sex with them—and so the idea of coercing someone into sex—is thus almost unthinkable to Gerai people. In addition, informants asserted that any such action would destroy the individual's spiritual balance and that of his or her rice group and bring calamity to the group as a whole.[29]

   In this context, a Gerai man's astonished and horrified question "How can a penis be taken into a vagina if a woman doesn't want it?" has a meaning very different from that of the same statement uttered by a man in the West. In the West, notions of radical difference between men and women—incorporating representations of normative male sexuality as active and aggressive, normative female sexuality as passive and vulnerable, and human relationships (including acts of sexual intercourse) as occurring between independent, potentially hostile, agents—would render such a statement at best naive, at worst misogynist. In Gerai, however, the stress on identity between men and women and on the sexual act as predicated on mutuality validates such a statement as one of straightforward incomprehension (and it should be noted that I heard similar statements from women). In the Gerai context, the penis, or male genitalia in general, is not admired, feared, or envied, nor is the phallus a central signifier in the way postulated by Lacanians. In fact, Gerai people see men's sexual organs as more vulnerable than women's for the simple reason that they are outside the body, while women's are inside. This reflects Gerai understandings of "inside" as representing safety and belonging, while "outside" is a place of strangers and danger, and it is linked to the notion of men as braver than women.[30] In addition, Gerai people say, because the penis is "taken

---

[29] Sanday 1986 makes a similar point about the absence of rape among the Minangkabau. See Helliwell (forthcoming) for a discussion of the different kinds of bad fate that can afflict a group through the actions of its individual members.

[30] In Gerai, as in nearby Minangkabau (Sanday 1986), vulnerability is respected and valued rather than despised.

into" another body, it is theoretically at greater risk during the sexual act than the vagina. This contrasts, again, quite markedly with Western understandings, where women's sexual organs are constantly depicted as more vulnerable during the sexual act—as liable to be hurt, despoiled, and so on (some men's anxieties about *vagina dentata* not withstanding). In Gerai a penis is "only a penis": neither a marker of dimorphism between men and women in general nor, in its essence, any different from a vagina.

Conclusions

The Gerai case suggests that, in some contexts at least, the practice of rape is linked to sexual dimorphism and, indeed, that in these contexts discourses of rape (including the act of rape itself) reinscribe such dimorphism. While the normative sexual practice in Gerai is heterosexual (between men and women), it is not accompanied by a heterosexual regulatory regime in the sense meant by Foucault (1978) in his discussion of the creation of sex as part of the heterosexualization of desire in the West, nor is it part of what Butler terms "the heterosexual matrix" (Butler 1990, 1993). The notion of "heterosexualization" as used by these thinkers refers to far more than the simple establishment of sexual relations between men and women as the normative ideal; it denotes the entire governmental regime that accompanies this normative ideal in Western contexts. Gerai stresses sameness between men and women more than difference, and such difference as occurs is based on the kinds of work people perform. Although this process certainly naturalizes a division between certain kinds of tasks—and the capacity to perform those tasks effectively—clearly, it does not involve sex or sexed bodies in the way Westerners normally understand those terms—as a naturalized difference between bodies (located primarily in the genitals) that translates into two profoundly different types of person. In this context, sexual assault by a man on a woman is almost unthinkable (both by women and by men).

With this background, I return now to the case with which I began this article—and, particularly, to the great differences between my response to this case and that of the Gerai woman concerned. On the basis of my own cultural assumptions concerning the differences—and particularly the different sexual characters—of men and women, I am inclined (as this case showed me) to read any attempt by a man to climb into a woman's bed in the night without her explicit consent as necessarily carrying the threat of sexual coercion and brutalization. This constant threat has been inscribed onto my body as part of the Western cultural process whereby I was "girled" (to use Butler's felicitous term [1993, 7]), or created as a gendered being in a context where male and female sexualities are perceived as penetrative and aggressive and as vulnerable and self-protective, respectively. The Gerai woman, in contrast, has no fear of coerced sexual intercourse when awakened in the dark by a man. She has no such fear because in the Gerai context "girling" involves the inscription of sexual sameness, of a belief that women's sexuality and bodies are no less aggressive and no more vulnerable than men's.

In fact, in the case in question, the intruding man did expect to have intercourse with the woman.[31] He claimed that the woman had already agreed to this through her acceptance of his initiatory gifts of soap.[32] The woman, however, while privately agreeing that she had accepted such gifts, claimed that no formal agreement had yet been reached. Her anger, then, did not stem from any belief that the man had attempted to sexually coerce her ("How would he be able to do such a thing?"). Because the term "to be quiet" is often used as a euphemism for sexual intercourse in Gerai, she saw the man's exhortation that she "be quiet" as simply an invitation to engage in sex with him, rather than the implicit threat that I read it to be.[33] Instead, her anger stemmed from her conviction that the correct protocols had not been followed, that the man ought to have spoken with

[31] The man left the community on the night that this event occurred and went to stay for several months at a nearby timber camp. Community consensus—including the view of the woman concerned—was that he left because he was ashamed and distressed, not only as a result of having been sexually rejected by someone with whom he thought he had established a relationship but also because his adulterous behavior had become public, and he wished to avoid an airing of the details in a community moot. Consequently, I was unable to speak to him about the case. However, I did speak to several of his close male kin (including his married son), who put his point of view to me.

[32] The woman in this particular case was considerably younger than the man (in fact, a member of the next generation). In such cases of considerable age disparity between sexual partners, the older partner (whether male or female) is expected to pay a fine in the form of small gifts to the younger partner, both to initiate the liaison and to enable its continuance. Such a fine rectifies any spiritual imbalance that may result from the age imbalance and hence makes it safe for the relationship to proceed. Contrary to standard Western assumptions, older women appear to pay such fines to younger men as often as older men pay them to younger women (although it was very difficult to obtain reliable data on this question, since most such liaisons are adulterous and therefore highly secretive). While not significant in terms of value (women usually receive such things as soap and shampoo, while men receive tobacco or cigarettes), these gifts are crucial in their role of "rebalancing" the relationship. It would be entirely erroneous to subsume this practice under the rubric of "prostitution."

[33] Because Gerai adults usually sleep surrounded by their children, and with other adults less than a meter or two away (although the latter are usually inside different mosquito nets), sexual intercourse is almost always carried out very quietly.

her rather than taking her acceptance of the soap as an unequivocal expression of assent. She was, as she put it, letting him know that "you have sexual relations together when you talk together. Sexual relations cannot be quiet."[34]

Yet, this should not be taken to mean that the practice of rape is simply a product of discourse: that brutality toward women is restricted to societies containing particular, dimorphic representations of male and female sexuality and that we simply need to change the discourse in order to eradicate such practices.[35] Nor is it to suggest that a society in which rape is unthinkable is for that reason to be preferred to Western societies. To adopt such a position would be still to view the entire world through a sexualized Western lens. There are, in fact, horrific things that may be done to women in places such as Gerai—things that are no less appalling in their implications for the fact that they do not involve the sexualized brutality of rape. In Gerai, for instance, while a woman does not fear rape, she does fear an enemy's bewitchment of her rice seed (the core of her gendered identity in this context) and the subsequent failure of the seed to sprout, resulting in hunger and illness for herself and her rice group. In extreme cases, bewitchment of rice seed can lead to malignancy of the growing fetus inside the woman; her subsequent death in childbirth, killed by her own "seed"; and her resultant transformation into a particularly vile kind of demon. Gerai women live constantly with the fear of this bewitchment (much as Western women live with the fear of rape), and even talking of it (always in whispers) reduces them to a state of terror.[36] The fact that this kind of attack can be carried out on a woman by either a woman or a man, and that it strikes not at her alone but at her rice group as a whole, marks it as belonging to a very different gendering regime from that which operates in the West. But it is no less horrific in its implications for that.

In order to understand the practice of rape in countries like Australia

[34] In claiming that "sexual relations cannot be quiet," the woman was playing on the expression "be quiet" (meaning to have sexual intercourse) to make the point that while adulterous sex may need to be even "quieter" than legitimate sex, it should not be so "quiet" as to preclude dialogue between the two partners. Implicit here is the notion that in the absence of such dialogue, sex will lack the requisite mutuality.

[35] Foucualt, e.g., once suggested (in a debate in French reprinted in *La Folle Encerclee* [see Plaza 1980]) that an effective way to deal with rape would be to decriminalize it in order to "desexualize" it. For feminist critiques of his suggestion, see Plaza 1980; de Lauretis 1987; Woodhull 1988.

[36] Men fear a parallel form of bewitchment that causes death while engaged in the definitive "men's work" of cutting down large trees to make a rice field. Like women's death in childbirth, this is referred to as an "evil death" *(mati jat)* and is believed to involve the transformation of the man into an evil spirit.

and the United States, then — and so to work effectively for its eradication there — feminists in these countries must begin to relinquish some of our most ingrained presumptions concerning difference between men and women and, particularly, concerning men's genitalia and sexuality as inherently brutalizing and penetrative and women's genitalia and sexuality as inherently vulnerable and subject to brutalization. Instead, we must begin to explore the ways rape itself *produces* such experiences of masculinity and femininity and so inscribes sexual difference onto our bodies. In a recent article, Moira Gatens asks of other feminists, "Why concede to the penis the power to push us around, destroy our integrity, 'scribble on us,' invade our borders and boundaries, and . . . occupy us in our (always already) conquered 'privacy'?" (1996, 43). This article echoes her lament. The tendency among many Western feminists writing on rape to accept as a seeming fact of nature the normative Western iconography of sexual difference leads them to reproduce (albeit unwittingly) the very discursive framework of Western rapists themselves, with their talk of "tools" and "holes," the very discursive framework in which rape is possible and which it reinscribes. For rape imposes difference as much as it is produced by difference. In fact, the highly racialized character of rape in many Western contexts suggests that the practice serves to police not simply sexual boundaries but racial ones as well. This is hardly surprising, given the history of the present "heterosexual matrix" in the West: as Stoler (1989, 1995) has demonstrated, the process of heterosexualization went hand-in-hand with that of colonialism. As a result, in contemporary Western settings sexual othering is inextricably entangled with racial othering. Unfortunately, in universalizing rape, many Western feminists risk naturalizing these othering processes and so contributing to a perpetuation of the very practices they seek to eradicate.

Department of Archaeology and Anthropology
Australian National University

References

Atkinson, Jane Monnig. 1990. "How Gender Makes a Difference in Wana Society." In *Power and Difference: Gender in Island Southeast Asia,* ed. Jane Monnig Atkinson and Shelly Errington, 59–93. Stanford, Calif.: Stanford University Press.

Barry, Kathleen. 1995. *The Prostitution of Sexuality.* New York and London: New York University Press.

Bart, Pauline B., and Patricia H. O'Brien. 1985. *Stopping Rape: Successful Survival Strategies.* New York: Pergamon.

Bell, Diane. 1983. *Daughters of the Dreaming.* Melbourne: McPhee Gribble.

Bourque, Linda B. 1989. *Defining Rape.* Durham, N.C., and London: Duke University Press.

Brison, Susan J. 1993. "Surviving Sexual Violence: A Philosophical Perspective." *Journal of Social Philosophy* 24(1):5–22.

Brownmiller, Susan. 1975. *Against Our Will: Men, Women, and Rape.* New York: Simon & Schuster.

Butler, Judith. 1990. *Gender Trouble: Feminism and the Subversion of Identity.* New York and London: Routledge.

———. 1993. *Bodies That Matter: On the Discursive Limits of "Sex."* New York and London: Routledge.

Clark, Anna. 1987. *Women's Silence, Men's Violence: Sexual Assault in England, 1770–1845.* London and New York: Pandora.

de Lauretis, Teresa. 1987. "The Violence of Rhetoric: Considerations on Representation and Gender." In her *Technologies of Gender: Essays on Theory, Film and Fiction,* 31–50. Bloomington and Indianapolis: Indiana University Press.

Dentan, Robert Knox. 1968. *The Semai: A Nonviolent People of Malaya.* New York: Holt, Rinehart & Winston.

———. 1978. "Notes on Childhood in a Nonviolent Context: The Semai Case (Malaysia)." In *Learning Non-Aggression: The Experience of Non-Literate Societies,* ed. Ashley Montagu, 94–143. New York: Oxford University Press.

Donaldson, Stephen. 1996. "The Deal behind Bars." *Harper's* (August): 17–20.

Dubinsky, Karen. 1993. *Improper Advances: Rape and Heterosexual Conflict in Ontario, 1880–1929.* Chicago and London: University of Chicago Press.

Dworkin, Andrea. 1987. *Intercourse.* London: Secker & Warburg.

Ellis, Lee. 1989. *Theories of Rape: Inquiries into the Causes of Sexual Aggression.* New York: Hemisphere.

Errington, Shelly. 1990. "Recasting Sex, Gender, and Power: A Theoretical and Regional Overview." In *Power and Difference: Gender in Island Southeast Asia,* ed. Jane Monnig Atkinson and Shelly Errington, 1–58. Stanford, Calif.: Stanford University Press.

Foucault, Michel. 1978. *The History of Sexuality.* Vol. 1, *An Introduction.* Harmondsworth: Penguin.

Gatens, Moira. 1996. "Sex, Contract, and Genealogy." *Journal of Political Philosophy* 4(1):29–44.

Geddes, W. R. 1957. *Nine Dayak Nights.* Melbourne and New York: Oxford University Press.

Gibson, Thomas. 1986. *Sacrifice and Sharing in the Philippine Highlands: Religion and Society among the Buid of Mindoro.* London and Dover: Athlone.

Gilman, Sander L. 1985. "Black Bodies, White Bodies: Toward an Iconography of Female Sexuality in Late Nineteenth-Century Art, Medicine, and Literature." In *"Race," Writing, and Difference,* ed. Henry Louis Gates, Jr., 223–40. Chicago and London: University of Chicago Press.

Gordon, Margaret T., and Stephanie Riger. 1989. *The Female Fear.* New York: Free Press.

Gregor, Thomas. 1990. "Male Dominance and Sexual Coercion." In *Cultural Psychology: Essays on Comparative Human Development,* ed. James W. Stigler, Richard A. Shweder, and Gilbert Herdt, 477–95. Cambridge: Cambridge University Press.

Griffin, Susan. 1986. *Rape: The Politics of Consciousness.* San Francisco: Harper & Row.

Halperin, David M. 1993. "Is There a History of Sexuality?" In *The Lesbian and Gay Studies Reader,* ed. Henry Abelove, Michele Barale, and David M. Halperin, 416–31. New York and London: Routledge.

Helliwell, Christine 1993. "Women in Asia: Anthropology and the Study of Women." In *Asia's Culture Mosaic,* ed. Grant Evans, 260–86. Singapore: Prentice Hall.

———. 1995. "Autonomy as Natural Equality: Inequality in 'Egalitarian' Societies." *Journal of the Royal Anthropological Institute* 1(2):359–75.

———. 1996. "Space and Sociality in a Dayak Longhouse." In *Things as They Are: New Directions in Phenomenological Anthropology,* ed. Michael Jackson, 128–48. Bloomington and Indianapolis: Indiana University Press.

———. Forthcoming. *"Never Stand Alone": A Study of Borneo Sociality.* Williamsburg: Borneo Research Council.

Howell, Signe. 1989. *Society and Cosmos: Chewong of Peninsular Malaysia.* Chicago and London: University of Chicago Press.

Kilpatrick, Dean G., Benjamin E. Saunders, Lois J. Veronen, Connie L. Best, and Judith M. Von. 1987. "Criminal Victimization: Lifetime Prevalence, Reporting to Police, and Psychological Impact." *Crime and Delinquency* 33(4):479–89.

Koss, Mary P., and Mary R. Harvey. 1991. *The Rape Victim: Clinical and Community Interventions.* 2d ed. Newbury Park, Calif.: Sage.

Laqueur, Thomas. 1990. *Making Sex: Body and Gender from the Greeks to Freud.* Cambridge, Mass., and London: Harvard University Press.

Leacock, Eleanor. 1978. "Women's Status in Egalitarian Society: Implications for Social Evolution." *Current Anthropology* 19(2):247–75.

Lloyd, Genevieve. 1984. *The Man of Reason: "Male" and "Female" in Western Philosophy.* London: Methuen.

MacKinnon, Catharine A. 1989a. "Sexuality, Pornography, and Method: 'Pleasure under Patriarchy.'" *Ethics* 99: 314–46.

———. 1989b. *Toward a Feminist Theory of the State.* Cambridge, Mass., and London: Harvard University Press.

Madigan, Lee, and Nancy C. Gamble. 1991. *The Second Rape: Society's Continued Betrayal of the Victim.* New York: Lexington.

Marcus, Julie. 1992. *A World of Difference: Islam and Gender Hierarchy in Turkey.* Sydney: Allen & Unwin.

Marcus, Sharon. 1992. "Fighting Bodies, Fighting Words: A Theory and Politics of Rape Prevention." In *Feminists Theorize the Political,* ed. Judith Butler and Joan W. Scott, 385–403. New York and London: Routledge.

Martin, Emily 1991. "The Egg and the Sperm: How Science Has Constructed a

S I G N S   Spring 2000   I   815

Romance Based on Stereotypical Male-Female Roles." *Signs: Journal of Women in Culture and Society* 16(3):485–501.

McColgan, Aileen. 1996. *The Case for Taking the Date Out of Rape.* London: Pandora.

Minturn, Leigh, Martin Grosse, and Santoah Haider. 1969. "Cultural Patterning of Sexual Beliefs and Behaviour." *Ethnology* 8(3):301–18.

Mohanty, Chandra Talpade. 1991. "Under Western Eyes: Feminist Scholarship and Colonial Discourses." In *Third World Women and the Politics of Feminism,* ed. Chandra Talpade Mohanty, Ann Russo, and Lourdes Torres, 51–80. Bloomington and Indianapolis: Indiana University Press.

Moore, Henrietta L. 1994. *A Passion for Difference: Essays in Anthropology and Gender.* Cambridge and Oxford: Polity.

Myers, Fred R. 1988. "The Logic and Meaning of Anger among Pintupi Aborigines." *Man* 23(4):589–610.

Palmer, Craig. 1989. "Is Rape a Cultural Universal? A Re-Examination of the Ethnographic Data." *Ethnology* 28(1):1–16.

Pateman, Carole. 1988. *The Sexual Contract.* Cambridge: Polity.

Plaza, Monique. 1980. "Our Costs and Their Benefits." *m/f* 4:28–39.

Rosaldo, Michelle Z. 1980a. *Knowledge and Passion: Ilongot Notions of Self and Social Life.* Cambridge: Cambridge University Press.

———. 1980b. "The Use and Abuse of Anthropology: Reflections on Feminism and Cross-cultural Understanding." *Signs* 5(3):389–417.

Russell, Diana E. H. 1984. *Sexual Exploitation: Rape, Child Abuse, and Workplace Harassment.* Beverly Hills, Calif.: Sage.

Sanday, Peggy Reeves. 1981. "The Socio-Cultural Context of Rape: A Cross-Cultural Study." *Journal of Social Issues* 37(4):5–27.

———. 1986. "Rape and the Silencing of the Feminine." In *Rape,* ed. Sylvana Tomaselli and Roy Porter, 84–101. Oxford: Blackwell.

———. 1990a. "Androcentric and Matrifocal Gender Representations in Minangkabau Ideology." In *Beyond the Second Sex: New Directions in the Anthropology of Gender,* ed. Peggy Reeves Sanday and Ruth Gallagher Goodenough, 141–68. Philadelphia: University of Pennsylvania Press.

———. 1990b. *Fraternity Gang Rape: Sex, Brotherhood, and Privilege on Campus.* New York and London: New York University Press.

Stoler, Ann Laura. 1989. "Carnal Knowledge and Imperial Power: Gender, Race, and Morality in Colonial Asia." In *Gender at the Crossroads of Knowledge: Feminist Anthropology in the Postmodern Era,* ed. Micaela di Leonardo, 51–101. Berkeley and Los Angeles: University of California Press

———. 1995. *Race and the Education of Desire: Foucault's* History of Sexuality *and the Colonial Order of Things.* Durham, N.C., and London: Duke University Press.

Strathern, Marilyn 1987. "Conclusion." In *Dealing with Inequality: Analysing Gender Relations in Melanesia and Beyond,* ed. Marilyn Strathern, 278–302. Cambridge: Cambridge University Press.

816 I Helliwell

————. 1988. *The Gender of the Gift: Problems with Women and Problems with Society in Melanesia.* Berkeley and Los Angeles: University of California Press.

Trumbach, Randolph. 1989. "Gender and the Homosexual Role in Modern Western Culture: The Eighteenth and Nineteenth Centuries Compared." In *Homosexuality, Which Homosexuality?* ed. Dennis Altman, 149–69. Amsterdam: An Dekker/Schorer; London: GMP.

————. 1993. "London's Sapphists: From Three Sexes to Four Genders in the Making of Modern Culture." In *Third Sex, Third Gender: Beyond Sexual Dimorphism in Culture and History,* ed. Gilbert Herdt, 111–36. New York: Zone.

Tsing, Anna Lowenhaupt. 1990. "Gender and Performance in Meratus Dispute Settlement." In *Power and Difference: Gender in Island Southeast Asia,* ed. Jane Monnig Atkinson and Shelly Errington, 95–125. Stanford, Calif.: Stanford University Press.

————. 1993. *In the Realm of the Diamond Queen: Marginality in an Out-of-the-Way Place.* Princeton, N.J.: Princeton University Press.

van der Meer, Theo. 1993. "Sodomy and the Pursuit of a Third Sex in the Early Modern Period." In *Third Sex, Third Gender: Beyond Sexual Dimorphism in Culture and History,* ed. Gilbert Herdt, 137–212. New York: Zone.

Woodhull, Winifred. 1988. "Sexuality, Power, and the Question of Rape." In *Feminism and Foucault: Reflections on Resistance,* ed. Irene Diamond and Lee Quinby, 167–76. Boston: Northeastern University Press.

Young, Iris Marion. 1990. "Throwing like a Girl: A Phenomenology of Feminine Body Comportment, Motility, and Spatiality." In her *Throwing like a Girl and Other Essays in Feminist Philosophy and Social Theory,* 141–59. Bloomington and Indianapolis: Indiana University Press.

[10]

The circumstances and characteristics of sexual assaults against adult males presenting to a crisis unit in a large metropolitan area were examined. Twenty-nine men, ranging in age from 18 to 65, who were victims of sexual assaults or attempted sexual assaults, were seen over a 16-month period. Information extracted from the unit database included client demographics and personal history, assault characteristics, and presentation information. Twenty-five (86%) of the reported assaults involved male perpetrators, one involved a single female perpetrator, and two involved both male and female perpetrators. Half the male-male assaults and all the female-male assaults were acquaintance sexual assaults. Only a minority of the stranger assaults were suggestive of antigay violence. Most victims were young gay men, many of whom had physical or cognitive disabilities making them particularly vulnerable. The results suggest a need for increased awareness of acquaintance sexual assault in adult males.

Sexual Assault of Adult Males

LANA STERMAC
*The Ontario Institute for Studies
in Education and Women's College Hospital*

PETER M. SHERIDAN
York University

ALISON DAVIDSON
*The Ontario Institute for Studies
in Education and Women's College Hospital*

SHEILA DUNN
Women's College Hospital

The sexual assault of adult males has been largely ignored in the clinical and research literature until relatively recently. Despite estimates of occurrence ranging from 5% to 10% of all sexual assault victims (Forman, 1982; Kaufman, Divasto, Jackson, Voorhees, & Christy, 1980), little attention has been paid to males who experience sexual violence as adults. Ignorance and disbelief about the phenomenon of male sexual assault has perpetuated numerous myths that find expression in the popular media, in films and literature, even in medicine, psychology, and law (Sheridan & Hucker, 1994). These include the belief that males cannot be, or are rarely, sexual assault

Authors' Note: The first and second authors contributed equally to this study. Correspondence concerning this article should be addressed to Lana Stermac, Department of Applied Psychology, The Ontario Institute for Studies in Education, 252 Bloor Street West, Toronto, Ontario, M5S 1V6.

JOURNAL OF INTERPERSONAL VIOLENCE, Vol. 11 No.1, March 1996 52-64
© 1996 Sage Publications, Inc.

victims (Mezey & King, 1987; Sheridan & Hucker, 1994), that sexual assaults against males are committed only within sex-segregated institutions (Cotton & Groth, 1982; Nacci & Kane, 1983; Sagarin, 1976; Weiss & Friar, 1974; Wooden & Parker, 1982), that sexual assault of males is committed by homosexual rapists overpowering heterosexual men and boys (Groth & Burgess, 1980; Mezey & King, 1987), and that women are seldom, if ever, perpetrators against males (Sarrel & Masters, 1982; Smith, Pine, & Hawley, 1988).

The few published empirical studies of male sexual assault provide some information on circumstances of the offenses and characteristics of both victims and assailants. An early study of the psychological motives in cases of male sexual assault by Groth and Burgess (1980) revealed that assaults were committed predominantly by young White males who were strangers to the victims. In this study, about 13% of the perpetrators were described as homosexual; an additional 38% were described as bisexual, a number of whom were in heterosexual marriages. Fifty percent of the victims were described as homosexual. Reported assault behaviors typically consisted of receptive oral and anal penetration or attempted penetration of the victim. The majority of victims reported significant distress and disruption of their lives following the assault. Although this report provides interesting details and insights into male sexual assault, the sample consisted of convicted sexual offenders undergoing evaluation at a center for sexually dangerous persons, which seriously limits generalizability.

Kaufman and his colleagues (1980) compared 14 male victims with 100 female victims of sexual assault. Unlike Groth and Burgess (1980), these authors found male victims to be ethnically diverse. Compared to female victims, males tended to be younger, to be attacked more frequently by multiple assailants, to be assaulted multiple times, and to have been held captive for longer durations. Male victims as a group were also more likely to have been beaten, and they suffered greater physical trauma than the female group. In contrast to the females, the males appeared more reluctant to reveal the sexual component of their assaults, preferred to seek treatment for nongenital trauma, and used denial to minimize the impact of the assault and to control their affective reactions. Kaufman et al. (1980) note that a high percentage of the male victims experienced economic and social instability and suggest that such lifestyle characteristics may place them at higher risk for victimization of many kinds. In this study, neither the sexual orientation nor the degree of relationship between perpetrator and victim was examined.

Mezey and King (1989) describe the circumstances of sexual assaults against 22 males. In this study, the majority of assaulted men and their assailants were White homosexual or bisexual men. About 82% knew their assailants. In half of these cases, the assailant was a close acquaintance, lover, or former lover; the remaining cases consisted primarily of brief acquaintances or sexual "pickups." Alcohol was involved in the majority of assaults, but it was determined to play a role in incapacitating the victim in only one case.

Mezey and King's (1989) findings—that the majority of victims are gay or bisexual and are at least acquainted with their assailants—have been supported by other recent investigations of sexual assault of males and studies of sexual coercion in the dating relationships of adult males. Hillman, O'Mara, Taylor-Robinson, and Harris (1990) reported that 62% of the 100 male victims of sexual assault in their study were homosexual or bisexual, and 75% knew their assailants. A minority of the cases involved multiple assailants or use of a weapon. As in other studies, many victims did not immediately report the assault to the authorities and tended to minimize the emotional trauma. Myers (1989) reports clinical data from 14 men seen in private practice, most of whom were sexually assaulted as adults. The majority of men (64%) identified themselves as homosexual or bisexual. In only one case was the assailant a stranger. According to Myers, these men nearly uniformly used repression, denial, and minimizing of trauma as psychological defenses in dealing with the sequelae of the assaults. Kaszniak, Nussbaum, Berren, and Santiago (1988) likewise report a case study of a male presenting with functional amnesia resulting from the psychological trauma of a sexual assault. These authors hypothesize that the immediate consequences of assault for some male victims may be massive denial and repression of the experience.

Although there is a dearth of research examining sexual aggression in gay male relationships, three studies suggest this is a significant phenomenon. Duncan (1990) found that gay and bisexual males reported a significantly higher lifetime prevalence of sexual victimization than did heterosexual subjects (11.8% vs. 3.6%). McConaghy and Zamir (cited in McConaghy, 1993) found that male students who admitted to homosexual feelings were more likely to report being sexually coerced than were heterosexual students. Finally, Waterman, Dawson, and Bologna (1990) reported a prevalence rate of 12% for sexual coercion in gay male couples.

As seen in these studies examining the characteristics of male sexual assault, there are a number of inconsistencies that deserve examination. Several researchers have raised questions about the degree of similarity between male and female sexual assault. For example, both Groth and Burgess (1980) and Mezey and King (1987) suggest that reactions of male victims of sexual assault are similar to those of female victims. Other researchers note that male victims usually experience greater physical trauma than female victims and are more prone to use psychological defenses such as denial and minimization following their assaults. Some researchers (e.g., Kaufman et al., 1980) have also suggested that certain characteristics, such as degree of violence and number of assailants, may differentiate assaults against males from those perpetrated against females. Furthermore, the sexual orientation of male perpetrators and victims of sexual assault and the relationship between perpetrator and victim appear inconsistent across studies. As a result, early studies suggest a pattern of stranger rape in which perpetrators are ostensibly heterosexual, whereas more recent investigations report what appears to be acquaintance rape in gay men.

In none of these studies to date has the issue of antigay violence been examined. Antigay/lesbian violence is defined as words or actions intended to intimidate or harm individuals because they are lesbian or gay. Such violence is referred to as hate or bias crime because it specifically targets members of a minority group because of their membership in that group. In early formulations of male sexual assault, Groth (1979; Groth & Burgess, 1980) considers the sexual assault of males to be the sexualized expression of aggression and hostility, with sexual gratification of secondary, or nonexistent, importance. Groth understands male rape to serve a variety of motives, including the expression of mastery and control through conquest, a desire for revenge and retaliation provoked by anger toward the victim, the punishment of another as a means of warding off anxiety resulting from unresolved conflict over one's sexual orientation, or the need for status and affiliation, as in gang rape (Sheridan & Hucker, 1994). This early formulation, in which ostensibly heterosexual males, and males known to be conflicted about their sexuality, were seen to commit sexual assault against adult males as a means of symbolically defeating some unresolved aspect of themselves, is thought to be a motive operative in antigay violence, or "gay bashing."

Recent studies of antigay/lesbian violence document the characteristics of this form of violence. Herek (1989) indicates that as many as 92% of lesbians and gay men report that they have been the target of verbal abuse and 24% the target of physical abuse because of their sexual orientation. In one study, for example, 36% of gay men reported being chased or followed; 27% had objects thrown at them; 24% were punched, kicked, hit, or beaten; 8% were spat upon; and 11% were assaulted with a weapon (Comstock, 1989). In addition, approximately 5% to 10% of male victims of gay bashing report experiencing sexual assault by heterosexual male perpetrators (Berrill, 1990; Comstock, 1989). Such assaults are understood as a form of degradation and humiliation of the victim (Cotton, 1992).

A number of variables appear to characterize incidents of antigay violence (Berk, 1990; Comstock, 1989; Harry, 1990). These include temporal patterns (greater frequency of nighttime and weekend assaults); occurrence near

56   JOURNAL OF INTERPERSONAL VIOLENCE / March 1996

gay-identified locations (e.g., outside gay bars or businesses, in known gay "cruising" areas); perpetration by multiple assailants, usually youth gangs, who are unknown to the victim; specific use of antigay (e.g., "faggot," "queer") or AIDS-related (e.g., "plague-carrying faggot") epithets; and malicious, gratuitous physical violence with weapons (baseball bats, use of objects for anal penetration).

Antigay violence is currently receiving increased attention in lay and professional communities, especially in large urban centers where such violence is known to be escalating ("Antigay Crimes," 1992; Cotton, 1992; Gerard, 1991). Increased knowledge of and sensitization to this issue suggests that some male victims of stranger sexual assault may be unidentified victims of gay bashing (see also Mezey & King, 1989).

The purpose of the present study was to examine the circumstances and characteristics of sexual assaults against adult males. As there is a dearth of clinical or research literature on this topic, this article presents a description of male sexual assault cases seen at a sexual assault crisis unit in Toronto, Canada. The nature and type of assault, the degree of relationship between assailant(s) and victim, the amount of coercion and violence perpetrated, and the use of weapons, drugs, and alcohol are discussed. This study also examined incidents of sexual assault of adult males to determine whether any fit the pattern of antigay violence as identified in the literature. Summary data and clinical case descriptions are presented.

METHOD

Subjects

Subjects consisted of 29 males who presented to the sexual assault crisis unit of a university teaching hospital in Toronto, Canada, between January 1992 and April 1993. This center provides multidisciplinary assessment and treatment services to all adult sexual assault victims within the metropolitan area. Male victims in this sample constitute 7% of the total number of victims presenting to the unit over the period of the study. These 29 males were all victims of sexual assault or attempted sexual assault.

Procedure

Variables describing the subjects, as well as the characteristics of the sexual assault, were obtained from the sexual assault crisis unit database. This database contains both client information and detailed characteristics of the sexual assaults as recorded by intake and treatment personnel at the hospital. Information extracted from the database included client demographics and personal history, assault characteristics, presentation information, medical and/or psychological intervention, and disposition of the case.

RESULTS

Demographic Information

About 31% (9) of the males presented at the sexual assault care center were accompanied by friends or relatives; 45% (13) were accompanied by police. The mean age of the men was 26.86 (*SD* = 10.36, range 18 to 65), with 55% (16) between the ages of 18 and 25, 28% (8) between ages 26 and 30, and 10% (3) between ages 31 and 35. The remaining two men were 55 and 65 years old. About 93% (27) of the victims were age 35 or under. The distribution of ages is thus highly skewed toward males in young and middle adulthood.

About 93% (27) of the males were single. Of those for whom information was available, 28% (8) reported living alone, 28% (8) lived with family, 7% (4) lived with nonrelatives, and 14% (4) reported living on the streets or in shelters/hostels. Over half (59%, *N* = 17) of the men reported being currently without employment; of these, however, 17% (5) were students and 7% (2) collected disability.

Victim vulnerability. In addition to the economic and social disadvantages of some men in the sample (4 were indigent and 10 unemployed), a surprisingly high number of the men had disabilities; 14% (4) had physical disabilities and 21% (6) were cognitively impaired. About 34% (10) of the sample voluntarily reported childhood sexual abuse, and 14% (4) reported previous adult sexual assault. Qualitative data, as presented below, revealed that a common pattern of assault involved the exploitation of vulnerable individuals.

> A 30-year-old physically disabled male, who was confined to a wheelchair and living on a pension, arrived at the crisis unit shortly after midnight, reporting a sexual assault by two unknown assailants. The assailants approached the client several hours earlier in a park and attacked him with a knife while shouting antigay epithets. The client was assaulted anally by both assailants and sustained numerous lacerations from the violent attack. He did not call the police and arrived at the unit unaccompanied.

58   JOURNAL OF INTERPERSONAL VIOLENCE / March 1996

Characteristics of the Sexual Assaults

Gender, sexual orientation, and relationship of assailants. About 86% (25) of the reported assaults involved male perpetrators; 7% involved both male and female perpetrators; and one involved a single female assailant. One victim said he had been sexually assaulted while intoxicated and could not recall details of the assault.

In the three cases involving women, all assailants were known to the victims. In the two cases involving both female and male perpetrators, both victims met only the male perpetrator initially. The following is a brief description of one of these cases.

> A 24-year-old male arrived at the crisis unit reporting confinement and sexual assault by a male and a female. The client stated that he had willingly gone to the home of a man he met at a bar and had engaged in consensual sex. During this, a female known to the perpetrator arrived, and the victim was tied up by both perpetrators and assaulted. Numerous sexual acts, including forced vaginal intercourse, were committed. The victims's genital area was shaved. He suffered various physical injuries in addition to psychological trauma and came accompanied to the unit by the police.

Half (50%, $N = 14$) of the male assailants were complete strangers to the victims, and half were known to some degree by the victim. About 21% (6) were known for less than, and 29% (8) for more than, 24 hours. Known assailants were typically acquaintances or friends; in one case, the assailant was a relative of the victim. Many of these victims reported that they were in relationships with the men who assaulted them. Assailants known less than 24 hours were typically individuals met casually, for example, in bars. In cases where information was volunteered by clients, it was revealed that all were gay and appeared to be victims of acquaintance sexual assault.

In keeping with the finding that assailants were frequently known to victims, 43% (12) of assaults occurred in either the victim's or the assailant's home. About 14% (4) occurred in private vehicles and 21% (6) in public parks. This pattern, as described below, likewise suggests a phenomenon akin to acquaintance sexual assault, or "date rape," in heterosexual dyads.

> A 25-year-old male arrived at the crisis unit in the early morning hours reporting a sexual assault by an acquaintance. He revealed that he met another man that evening and had consented to accompany him home to have drinks. After the two men began to drink, the client believes that he fell asleep. He was awakened some time later by the assailant who was attempting to anally assault him. The client left and consulted a physician before coming to the crisis unit with a friend. He did not suffer physical injuries but was very traumatized psychologically.

Another victim reported that he met a man in a gay bar and was assaulted by him and several of his friends in their vehicle. Several of the men reported that they were sexually assaulted in parks that were known to be gay cruising areas. These were not homophobic assaults, however. Both victim and perpetrator were gay and initially consented to a casual pickup.

Stranger assaults in this sample were not suggestive of antigay violence. Few clear markers of antigay assaults were reported by victims. No evidence of a seasonal or temporal pattern of assaults was found, conforming to known patterns of gay bashing. Despite the prevalence of multiple assailants (see below) in a number of cases, and the fact that a number of assaults did occur in or near gay-identified locations (bars, parks known for cruising), the relationship between victims and perpetrators and the sexual orientation of both men mitigates identifying these assaults as antigay violence. A minority of attendees did report the use of antigay or AIDS-related epithets, and their assaults are suggestive of antigay violence.

Details of assaults. Assaults involving multiple assailants occurred with alarming frequency: 21% (6) of victims reported two assailants, 11% (3) reported three, and another 11% (3) reported four perpetrators. Where information was available on the total number of assaults that occurred, 48% (11) of victims indicated that they had been assaulted more than once and as many as six times.

Assault behaviors included touching and fondling (7%, $N = 2$), fellatio performed on the assailant (43%, $N = 12$), and receptive anal intercourse (54%, $N = 15$) or attempted intercourse (11%, $N = 3$). Two men reported that they were forced to perform vaginal intercourse with female perpetrators. About 17% of men (5) reported that they were unsure of what assaults had occurred because they were assaulted when intoxicated, drugged, or sleeping. In only four cases did the perpetrator ejaculate, and this was, in each case, as a result of oral sex.

Alcohol and Drug Use

Victims reported using alcohol in 46% (13) of cases and drugs in 18% (5). Assailants were reported to have used alcohol in 39% (11) of cases and drugs in 14% (4). Five men were actually unconscious when the sexual assault occurred due to alcohol or drug intoxication. In the vast majority of cases, however, alcohol and drugs did not appear to be deliberately used to incapacitate the victim. In those cases where victims were assaulted when unconscious, this appeared to be an opportunistic rather than a premeditated assault.

Use of Violence

Coercion was reported in nearly all cases of assault; five men reported that they were unsure of what degree of force had been used as they were either using substances or were asleep. Verbal threats were reported in 21% (6) of cases, and physical violence such as kicking, punching, and slapping in 11% (3). About 39% (11) of victims reported being confined or restrained. A high percentage of cases (21%, $N = 6$) involved the use of weapons; these included knives, household objects, and, in one case, a gun.

Victim Impact

Emotional trauma was evident in the initial presentation of the clients at the crisis unit in the majority of cases (59%, $N = 17$). In two cases, clients had to be admitted to hospital due to their emotional state following the attack. Tranquilizers were also dispensed to a number of men. Although these assaults were emotionally traumatic for all victims, few suffered physical injury. About 19% (5) reported soft-tissue damage, such as bruises, and an equal number reported lacerations and abrasions. None had to be admitted to hospital due to physical trauma.

DISCUSSION

The results of this study revealed that sexual assaults against adult males in a large urban area are reported at rates similar to those described in other studies (Forman, 1982; Kaufman et al., 1980). This study also revealed that most clients presenting to the crisis unit following sexual assault were young gay men. This also is consistent with other studies (e.g., Mezey & King, 1987), which have indicated a high prevalence of gay male victims of sexual assault. Although it remains unclear whether gay men are more likely than heterosexual men to be victims of sexual assault, whether they are more aware of and more likely to use victim services, or whether they simply feel less stigmatized by sexual assault than heterosexual men, several studies using diverse methodologies in sample recruitment have now documented this finding.

Several unexpected results emerged from this study. It was revealed that 35% of the victims had physical or cognitive disabilities, and 21% were assaulted when unconscious. A number of the victims reported histories of child- and early adulthood abuse. A large number were also indigent or unemployed. This may reflect the exploitation of vulnerable individuals who have a decreased capacity to prevent their victimization. Kaufman et al. (1980) similarly reported a high rate of family disruption, unemployment, and social dysfunction in their group of male sexual assault victims. These authors hypothesized that a lifestyle characterized by frequent mobility and economic and social instability may place such men at higher risk for diverse forms of victimization.

The results of this study also revealed that physical violence in the sexual assaults reported to this unit was not as prevalent as other researchers have reported. Although a high rate of weapon use was found, no serious physical damage was inflicted. This finding may reflect the fact that more violent assaults were directed to other units or to emergency departments where victims either were not asked about sexual aspects of their assaults or did not volunteer this information. This notion is supported by the finding that male sexual assault victims are reluctant to report sexual trauma, focusing attention instead on physical, nongenital trauma and minimizing emotional distress (Hillman et al., 1990; Kaufman et al., 1980; Kaszniak et al., 1988; Mezey & King, 1989; Myers, 1989). Another explanation for the low rate of physical trauma to victims in the present study is that most assaults in this study were coercive acquaintance sexual assaults, in which psychological and emotional coercion are more prevalent.

Consistent with other reports in the literature (Hillman et al., 1990; Mezey & King, 1989; Myers, 1989), it appears that a significant number of the men presenting to this unit are young gay males who are victims of acquaintance sexual assaults by other males. The majority of the victims had known their assailants at least briefly and had engaged in a social encounter with them or were in longer-term relationships with them. Some of these latter cases may parallel the phenomenon of marital rape in heterosexual couples. Waterman et al. (1990) reported that 12% of gay men in their sample reported being a victim of forced sex with their current or most recent long-term partner.

Only a minority of cases in the present study were suggestive of antigay assaults. Mezey and King (1989) suggested that in certain cases in their study, the sexual assault represented an extension of "queer bashing." Although rape of gay males by heterosexuals is considered to be rare, about 5% to 10% of victims of antigay violence do report sexual assault in the context of violence directed at them because of their sexual orientation (Sheridan & Hucker, 1994). Our clinical impression is that such offenses may represent symbolically the perpetrator's wish to control, punish, or destroy an unwanted aspect of himself, namely, his conflict or ambivalence regarding his own sexual orientation. Although we have seen perpetrators in our clinical practice, our failure to find a significant number of victims in this sample suggests that victims of such crimes are unlikely to attend this hospital following their assaults.

Our reading of the scant literature on male sexual assault revealed two general trends in identifying perpetrators and victims. Groth's early studies (Groth, 1979; Groth & Burgess, 1980) suggest a preponderance of ostensibly heterosexual perpetrators and a mixed group of heterosexual, bisexual, and homosexual victims. In the vast majority of cases, the offender was completely unknown to the victim. It is important to note that Groth's data on perpetrators came directly from the convicted offenders themselves. Later studies (Hillman et al., 1990; Mezey & King, 1989; Myers, 1989) suggest a preponderance of homosexual perpetrators and victims, usually known to one another. In these studies, data is obtained from victims. In the former case, the sexual assaults parallel stranger sexual assaults; in the latter, the assaults are consistent with a date-rape paradigm.

These patterns of male sexual assault likely represent two distinct groups of perpetrators: heterosexual males who rape other males as a means of punishing and degrading them, possibly in an extension of other forms of violence targeted specifically toward subordinate males (e.g., gay men, prison inmates), and gay males who coerce partners or acquaintances into sexual activity by use of threats or intimidation, as in date rape (Sheridan & Hucker, 1994). In our opinion, the first of these groups is rare. The relatively recent emergence in the research literature of the date-rape pattern may reflect the growing awareness among clinicians and researchers of this form of sexual violence, as well as the increased willingness of victims to acknowledge their sexual orientation. Research with offenders, as opposed to victims, would appear to be particularly biased in terms of reporting sexual orientation; sex offenders are known to misrepresent their sexual preferences, and those who assault males may be loath to admit that they are gay (see, for example, Groth & Burgess, 1980).

The longer-term effects of sexual assault on males cannot be determined in the present study. Two men were admitted to hospital as a result of emotional distress, but the vast majority were discharged without further follow-up. These men did not wish to avail themselves of further support services offered at this center. Previous research has demonstrated that the psychological effects of sexual assaults on men appear similar to those women experience (Groth & Burgess, 1980; Kaufman et al., 1980; Mezey & King, 1989), although special needs have been identified. The heterosexual victim may have fundamental beliefs about his sexuality and masculinity challenged as a result of sexual assault. The gay male victim may experience fearful or aversive feelings associated with normal sexual behavior and may blame himself—as female victims of date rape do—for not resisting vehemently enough, or being somehow complicitous in the rape (Garnets, Herek, & Levy, 1990). Victims of antigay violence, in which sexual assault is a part, have special treatment needs that must be addressed, including internalized homophobia, stigmatization, and marginalization (Stermac & Sheridan, 1993).

The results of this study suggest that sexual assaults against adult males in a large urban center are targeted toward young gay males. Although physical violence was used less frequently than other studies have reported, coercive patterns of assault such as those seen in acquaintance sexual assaults of females were evident. These results suggest that a growing awareness of the phenomenon of acquaintance sexual assault in adult male victims is needed.

REFERENCES

Antigay crimes are reported on rise in 5 cities. (1992, March 20). *The New York Times.*

Berk, R. A. (1990). Thinking about hate-motivated crimes. *Journal of Interpersonal Violence, 5,* 334-349.

Berrill, K. T. (1990). Antigay violence and victimization in the United States: An overview. *Journal of Interpersonal Violence, 5,* 274-294.

Comstock, G. D. (1989). Victims of anti-gay/lesbian violence. *Journal of Interpersonal Violence, 4,* 101-106.

Cotton, D. J., & Groth, A. N. (1982). Inmate rape: Prevention and intervention. *Journal of Prison and Jail Health, 2,* 47-57.

Cotton, P. (1992). Attacks on homosexual persons may be increasing, but many "bashings" still aren't reported to police. *Journal of the American Medical Association, 267,* 2999-3000.

Duncan, D. F. (1990). Prevalence of sexual assault victimization among heterosexual and gay/lesbian university students. *Psychological Reports, 66,* 65-66.

Forman, B. D. (1982). Reported male rape. *Victimology, 7,* 235-236.

Garnets, L., Herek, G. M., & Levy, B. (1990). Violence and victimization of lesbians and gay men. *Journal of Interpersonal Violence, 5,* 366-383.

Gerard, W. (1991, June 29). Is gay bashing out of control? *The Toronto Star.*

Groth, A. N. (1979). *Men who rape: The psychology of the offender.* New York: Plenum.

Groth, A. N., & Burgess, A. W. (1980). Male rape: Offenders and victims. *American Journal of Psychiatry, 137,* 806-810.

Harry, J. (1990). Conceptualizing antigay violence. *Journal of Interpersonal Violence, 5,* 350-358.

Herek, G. M. (1989). Hate crimes against lesbians and gay men: Issues for research and policy. *American Psychologist, 44,* 948-955.

Hillman, R. J., O'Mara, N., Taylor-Robinson, D., & Harris, J. R. W. (1990). Medical and social aspects of sexual assault of males: A survey of 100 victims. *British Journal of General Practice, 40,* 502-504.

Kaszniak, A. W., Nussbaum, P. D., Berren, M. R., & Santiago, J. (1988). Amnesia as a consequence of male rape: A case report. *Journal of Abnormal Psychology, 97,* 100-104.

Kaufman, A., Divasto, P., Jackson, R., Voorhees, D., & Christy, J. (1980). Male rape victims: Noninstitutionalized assault. *American Journal of Psychiatry, 137,* 221-223.

McConaghy, N. (1993). *Sexual behavior: Problems and management.* New York: Plenum.

Mezey, G., & King, M. (1987). Male victims of sexual assault. *Medicine, Science, and the Law, 27*, 122-124.

Mezey, G., & King, M. (1989). The effects of sexual assault on men: A survey of 22 victims. *Psychological Medicine, 19*, 205-209.

Myers, M. F. (1989). Men sexually assaulted as adults and sexually abused as boys. *Archives of Sexual Behavior, 18*, 203-215.

Nacci, P. L., & Kane, T. R. (1983). The incidence of sex and sexual aggression in federal prisons. *Federal Probation, 47*, 31-36.

Sagarin, E. (1976). Prison homosexuality and its effect on post-prison sexual behaviour. *Psychiatry, 39*, 245-257.

Sarrel, P., & Masters, W. (1982). Sexual molestation of men by women. *Archives of Sexual Behavior, 11*, 117-133.

Sheridan, P. M., & Hucker, S. J. (1994). Rape and sadomasochistic paraphilias. In J. Krivacska & J. Money (Eds.), *The handbook of forensic sexology* (pp. 104-125). New York: Prometheus.

Smith, R. E., Pine, C. J., & Hawley, M. E. (1988). Social cognitions about male victims of female sexual assault. *Journal of Sex Research, 24*, 101-112.

Sternac, L., & Sheridan, P. M. (1993). Anti-gay/lesbian violence: Treatment issues. *Canadian Journal of Human Sexuality, 2*, 33-38.

Waterman, C. K., Dawson, L. J., & Bologna, M. J. (1989). Sexual coercion in gay male and lesbian relationships: Predictors and implications for support services. *Journal of Sex Research, 26*, 118-124.

Weiss, C., & Friar, D. (1974). *Terror in the prisons.* New York: Bobbs-Merrill.

Wooden, W. S., & Parker, J. (1982). *Men behind bars: Sexual exploitation in prison.* New York: Plenum.

Lana Sternac is an Associate Professor in the Department of Applied Psychology, Ontario Institute for Studies in Education, University of Toronto, and a Research Consultant at Womens College Hospital in Toronto, Canada. Her research interests focus mainly on the examination of social and cultural factors in sexual violence against both adults and children.

Peter Sheridan is a Doctoral Candidate in Clinical Psychology at York University. He is a counselor in the Lesbian, Gay and Bisexual Youth Program at Central Toronto Youth Services. His area of specialization is forensic psychology, and his doctoral dissertation research is on cognitions about adult male victims of seuxal assault.

Alison Davidson is a Doctoral Candidate in Community Psychology at the Ontario Institute for Studies in Education. Her doctoral research is in the area of barriers to womens activism in the Canadian labor movement.

Sheila Dunn is a Family Physician at Womens College Hospital and Medical Director of the Bay Centre for Birth Control at the Regional Womens Health Centre, Womens College Hospital. Her research interests include the examination of doctor-patient relationships and the medical effects of violence.

[11]

Forced Sex and Intimate Partner Violence:

Effects on Women's Risk and Women's Health

JACQUELYN C. CAMPBELL
Johns Hopkins University
KAREN L. SOEKEN
University of Maryland

A volunteer community sample of 159 primarily (77%) African American battered women were interviewed about forced sex by their partner (or ex-partner). Almost half (45.9%) of the sample had been sexually assaulted as well as physically abused. Except for ethnicity, there were no demographic differences between those who were forced into sex and those who were not, and there was no difference in history of child sexual abuse. However, those who were sexually assaulted had higher scores on negative health symptoms, gynecological symptoms, and risk factors for homicide even when controlling for physical abuse and demographic variables. The number of sexual assaults (childhood, rape, and intimate partner) was significantly correlated with depression and body image.

There is now significant research demonstrating that women's health is seriously affected by domestic violence (e.g., McCauley et al., 1995; Plichta, 1996). The Commonwealth Fund national random survey estimates that 4.4 million adult women are physically assaulted by a spouse or cohabitant in this country every year (Plichta, 1996). Although the survey only included women currently living with or married to someone, it found an 8% prior year prevalence of physical abuse and a 3.2% rate of severe abuse. The women abused by spouses in that sample were significantly more likely to rate their health as fair or poor than women not battered, a finding supported in at least one other population-based study (Gelles & Straus, 1990). Neither survey specifically asked about forced sex in these battering relationships.

Battering is defined here as repeated physical and/or sexual assault by an intimate partner within a context of coercive control

AUTHORS' NOTE: Research reported in this study was supported by the National Institutes of Health, National Institute of Nursing Research R29#NR01678.

VIOLENCE AGAINST WOMEN, Vol. 5 No. 9, September 1999   1017-1035

1018   VIOLENCE AGAINST WOMEN / September 1999

(J. C. Campbell & Humphreys, 1993). Emotional abuse is almost always part of the coercive control and has serious psychological consequences according to women themselves (Marshall, 1996). However, the actual effects of emotional abuse on women's health have seldom been measured separately. The sexual assault aspect of battering has also seldom been considered as a separate phenomenon with particular effects on women's health and separate implications for women's safety. Diana Russell's (1982, 1997) groundbreaking research alerted the domestic violence and women's health communities that forced relationship sex was a separate and important type of violence against women. More recently, Tjaden and Thoennes (1998), in the population-based National Violence Against Women Survey, determined that 7.7% of U.S. women (7.75 million) reported that they had been raped by an intimate partner (current and former spouses, opposite and same-sex cohabitating partners, dates, and boyfriends) in their lifetime and 0.2% (201,000) were during the past year.

From two different empirical investigations, it has been estimated that 40% to 45% of all battered women are forced to have sex by their male partners (J. C. Campbell, 1989; Finkelhor & Yllo, 1985). Forced sex can range from clearly communicated unwanted rough, painful, or particular sexual acts to threatened violence if sexual demands are not met, actual beatings prior, during, or after sex, and/or sex with objects (J. C. Campbell & Alford, 1989). In an earlier analysis with a different sample, Campbell (1989) found forced sex to be associated with increased severity and frequency of violent tactics and a greater number of risk factors for homicide. As part of a second study of women's physical, mental, and behavioral responses to battering (J. C. Campbell, Kub, Belknap, & Templin, 1997), this analysis specifically focused on the prevalence and consequences of forced sex in battering relationships.

It was hypothesized that forced sex would have a negative effect on women's self-esteem and health status, especially gynecological symptoms, over and above the physical and emotional abuse incurred. From a trauma framework, self-esteem is related to the shame associated with sexual assault as well as prolonged coercive control (Herman, 1992). The physical health problems would be part of a physiological stress response as well as those specifically related to gynecological health (Koss, 1993; Koss &

Harvey, 1991). It was also hypothesized that forced sex would be positively related to lethality risk factors controlling for frequency and severity of physical and emotional abuse.

LITERATURE REVIEW

Forced sex in intimate partner relationships is often termed *wife rape* or *marital rape*, but this terminology is problematic because of the frequency of women forced into sex by partners in nonmarital (and often noncohabiting) but nonetheless ongoing relationships. The term *rape* also often implies strangers or acquaintances as perpetrators rather than well-known partners. The forced sex acts can be occasional, occurring among many other consensual and often desired and satisfying sexual acts, further confusing the issue. Other acts that are sexual and coercive but not violent and not actual sexual acts with the battered woman per se, such as refusing to wear condoms, being emotionally abusive or threatening when discussing safe sex, refusing to use birth control, having unprotected sex with other women, refusing to have sex, or being otherwise demeaning or emotionally abusive in terms of sex, further complicate definitions and descriptions (J. C. Campbell, Pugh, Campbell, & Visscher, 1995; Wingood & DiClemente, 1997). For purposes of clarification, an act of forced sex that includes sexual acts with actual violence or threats of violence (and thereby meeting criminal sexual assault criteria) as described above will be referred to in this article as sexual assault. Repeated sexual assault or sexual assault within a context of coercive control is within the definition of battering given above.[1] Other sexually related acts that are controlling, degrading, demeaning, and/or detrimental to women's health (physical and/or mental) will be defined as sexual abuse.

HEALTH EFFECTS OF FORCED SEX

Increased rates of pelvic inflammatory disease, heightened risk of sexually transmitted diseases (STDs) including HIV/AIDS, unexplained vaginal bleeding, and other genital-urinary related health problems have been documented for battered women in several population-based and health care setting controlled studies (Bergman & Brismar, 1991; Chapman, 1989; Coving-ton, Maxwell, Clancy, Churchill, & Ahrens, 1995; Plichta, 1996; Plichta & Abraham, 1996; Saunders, Hamberger, & Hovey, 1993). However, in those studies, forced sex was not specifically queried, so that it is only possible to surmise that these health outcomes were linked to forced sex rather than other forms of physical vio-lence. Two shelter sample studies particularly linked the sexually violent aspects of battering relationships with physical health problems. In a descriptive study, sexually assaulted battered women described vaginal and anal tearing, bladder infections, dysmenorrhea, sexual dysfunction, pelvic pain, urinary tract infections, and increased STDs as a result of that form of battering (J. C. Campbell & Alford, 1989). In the second shelter-based study, Eby and Campbell (1995) documented that the increased risk for STDs, including HIV/AIDS, in this sample of battered women was related to the lack of using protection during intercourse (67%)—primarily at the male partner's insistence or when sex was forced—rather than other risky behavior on the woman's part (e.g., multiple casual sexual partners or IV drug use). A third study showed that for sexually active young African American women, those in abusive relationships were less likely to use con-doms, more afraid to ask their partner to use condoms, and more likely to be emotionally abused or threatened with physical abuse when discussing safe sex than young women in nonviolent rela-tionships (Wingood & DiClemente, 1997).

Battered women in focus groups also linked forced sex in bat-tering relationships, as well as male partner control of contracep-tive use, with unintended pregnancy, a connection also shown in two other large sample studies (J. C. Campbell et al., 1995; Gazma-rarian et al., 1995). When asked directly about sexual abuse by health care professionals, women respond without objection, and the health care system may be the only place where women are likely to receive appropriate care for this aspect of their battering experience (Weingourt, 1985, 1990).

WOMEN'S MENTAL HEALTH CONSEQUENCES

The primary mental health response of women to being bat-tered in an ongoing intimate relationship and the primary reason for battered women going to a primary health care setting is depression (McCauley et al., 1995; Saunders et al., 1993). Prevalence of depression in abused women has ranged from 10.2% (Weissman & Klerman, 1992) to 21.3% (Kessler et al., 1994) to 31.9% when also including anxiety diagnoses (Plichta, 1996) in general population studies.

Using psychiatric diagnostic procedures, Gleason (1993) found a significantly higher prevalence of major depression in 62 battered women than in the National Institute of Mental Health Epidemiological Catchment Area study. In that same study, there was a higher prevalence of major depression (63%) than of diagnosed post-traumatic stress disorder (PTSD) (40%). In comparison, depression in women in general is estimated at 9.3% point prevalence and 20% to 25% lifetime risk.

In a study exploring the dynamics of depression in battered women in the same sample as used for this analysis, significant predictors of depression included the frequency and severity of current physical abuse and stress, more strongly than prior history of mental illness or demographic, cultural, or childhood characteristics (J. C. Campbell et al., 1997). Forced relationship sex was not a significant predictor of depression in that analysis.

Although PTSD has been linked with both rape and battering in many independent analyses (e.g., Resnick, Kilpatrick, Dansky, Saunders, & Best, 1993; Saunders, 1992; Saunders et al., 1993), the specific relationships between relationship sexual assault and PTSD have only been examined by Riggs, Kilpatrick, and Resnick (1992). Those investigators found women raped in the context of a marital relationship were no more likely to have PTSD or other measures of psychological distress than women physically assaulted by a husband or a stranger or raped by a stranger; however, all victim groups were more distressed than those not victimized. One of the problems with that study was the wide variation in time since the assault in question and the omission of women in nonmarital intimate partner relationships. Yet, it is the first such study in an area that needs more investigation.

Lowered self-esteem is another frequently reported mental health outcome of battering. In an earlier sample, J. C. Campbell (1989) found sexual assault to be significantly related to self-esteem (and especially the body image component of self esteem), even controlling for physical abuse.

METHOD

Women were recruited for the study from a large midwestern city using newspaper advertisements and bulletin board postings. Women with "serious problems in an intimate relationship with a man" were offered $15 compensation for participation. The words *abuse* or *battering* were avoided in the advertisement, recognizing that many women physically assaulted by an intimate partner do not consider themselves to be abused or battered (J. C. Campbell, Miller, Cardwell, & Belknap, 1994). When women called, they were screened for battering using the Conflict Tactics Scale (Straus & Gelles, 1990). Women who reported having had more than one of the less severe violent tactics (pushing, shoving, slapping, kicking, biting) used against them during the prior year by an intimate partner or one of the severely violent tactics (punching, beating up, weapon threat or use) were eligible for the study. Because of the fear of being too intrusive at first contact, forced sex was not included in the questions, although battering was considered to include sexual as well as physical assault (J. C. Campbell & Humphreys, 1993).

Battered women were invited to come to a university setting for a research appointment that would last approximately 2 hours. They were also asked about safe times and places to call to remind them about the appointment. Informed consent was obtained at the time of interview, including the warning that current child abuse, although not specifically asked about, would be reported if the woman talked about this happening to any children in the home. The consent and interview protocol was approved by the affiliated university Institutional Review Board.

SAMPLE DESCRIPTION

Sample size was determined by power analysis for multivariate analysis (Cohen & Cohen, 1983) for 80% power, alpha at .05, and a medium effect size. The sample for the study consisted of 159 women, with the demographic characteristics as follows: The women had a mean age of 31.6 years, were relatively well educated (70% with a high school education or more), and had an average of 2.2 children, with 21% having no children. The sample was relatively poor (average income of $14,478 with 65% having a total family income of less than $10,000 per year). Almost half (49%) of the women were unemployed, but the other half covered the full range of occupational categories, with 11% holding jobs in professional occupations. In terms of ethnicity, 123 (76.6%) described themselves as African American, 10 (6.1%) as Anglo American (White, without strong ethnic identification), 14 (8.5%) as European American (White, strongly identifying with a European ethnicity, primarily Polish), 1 (0.6%) Mexican American, 1 (0.6%) Asian American, 1 (0.6%) Arab American, and 9 (5.5%) other or mixed. This ethnic distribution and the general demographic profile are close to the overall demographic characteristics of women in that city.

MEASUREMENT

Sample items and psychometric information from the measures in the study are listed in Table 1. The two subscales of the Index of Spouse Abuse (ISA) were used to measure physical and sexual (ISA-P) and emotional abuse (ISA-NP) (Hudson & McIntosh, 1981). The ISA (Hudson & McIntosh, 1981) is a 30-item scale designed to measure the severity or magnitude of physical and nonphysical abuse inflicted on a woman by her spouse or partner. The ISA items represent varying degrees of abuse, taken into account in the weighted scoring and interpretation of the responses. Two scores (ranging from 0 to 100) are computed for each respondent: an ISA-P score that represents the severity of physical abuse and an ISA-NP score that represents the severity of nonphysical abuse.

The ISA has been partially validated in five studies (Hudson & McIntosh, 1981). The first two were student studies using the original ISA in Hawaii, finding support for reliability and factorial validity. The third sample established support for the ability of the ISA to successfully discriminate between abused and nonabused women in a large sample from four different sites and to establish cut-off scores (Hudson & McIntosh, 1981). D. W. Campbell, Campbell, Parker, King, and Ryan (1994) found independent reliability and factor analysis support in samples of African American women. Subsequently, Attala, Hudson, and McSweeney

TABLE 1
Measurement

Construct	Instrument	Sample Items	Reliability Support	Validity Support	Alpha
Self-esteem	Tennessee Self-Concept Scale (TSCS)	I have a healthy body. I am a decent sort of person. (false-true, 1-5)	Test-retest (.61-92); alpha = .80-.90 (Fitts, 1972)	Construct (convergent and divergent), predictive (Fitts, 1972)	.921
Physical and nonphysical abuse	Index of Spouse Abuse—Physical (ISA-P, ISA-NP)	My partner belittles me. My partner threatens me with a weapon. (Frequency 1-5)	Alpha = .90-93 (D. W. Campbell, Campbell, & et al., 1994; Hudson & McIntosh, 1981)	Construct (convergent, factorial, discriminate group) (D. W. Campbell, Campbell, et al., 1994; Hudson & McIntosh, 1981)	.937
Risk of homicide	Danger Assessment (DA)	Has he ever forced you to have sex when you did not wish to? Have you ever been beaten by him while you were pregnant? (yes/no)	Five studies: alpha = .60 (n = 30) –.86 (n = 156); test-retest = .89-.94 (J. C. Campbell, 1995)	Construct (convergent and discriminate group) (J. C. Campbell, 1995)	.678
Depression	Beck Depression Inventory (BDI)	I do not feel sad. I do not feel particularly guilty. (0-3 scale)	Alpha = .90+ (Beck, 1972)	Construct (discriminate group, predictive (Beck, 1972)	.885
Health (negative symptoms and positive health)	Health Responses Scale (HRS)	Lower abdominal cramping or pain. Decreased sexual desire. (yes/no, frequency 1-4; severity 1-4)	Alpha = .89 (Brown, 1986)	Construct (Brown, 1986)	.887

(1994) found additional support for reliability and construct validity of the modified version of the ISA (PAS). In this sample, the internal consistency of the ISA was .94.

The Danger Assessment (DA) measured serious abuse in terms of risk factors for homicide (either partner as victim) in intimate partner relationships (J. C. Campbell, 1995). It is a 15-item yes/no instrument without a cut-off score, with a higher score indicating more risk. The DA has support for internal consistency, test-retest reliability, and construct validity over six studies using ethnically heterogeneous samples from a variety of community and clinical settings (J. C. Campbell, 1989; McFarlane, Parker, Soeken, & Bullock, 1992). The DA had an internal consistency coefficient of .68 in this sample.

Self-esteem was measured by the normed instrument of the Tennessee Self-Concept Scale (TSCS) (Fitts, 1972). Short- and long-term test-retest reliability (.61 to .92) and internal consistency (.80 to .90) of both the total and the subscales have been supported in many studies (Fitts, 1972). Content validity was addressed in instrument development and has been supported by other self-concept experts (Wells & Marwell, 1976). The instrument has shown both discriminate (Fitts, 1972) and construct validity (Thompson, 1972). One of the subscales is physical health or body image. In this sample, the TSCS alpha was .92.

The Beck Depression Inventory (BDI) was chosen to measure depression because of its ability to indicate enduring behavioral manifestations of depression rather than a more transitory mood state, with a higher score indicating more depression. Internal consistency of the instrument was determined by split-half reliability and internal consistency measurement (Beck, Ward, Mendelson, Mock, & Erbaugh, 1961). Validity has been supported by discriminant ability and agreement with clinical psychiatric evaluations of depression. In addition, the instrument has been used in numerous research studies that have shown associations in predicted directions with other constructs (Beck, 1972). Internal consistency of the BDI in this sample was .89.

Functional health was measured by the Health Responses Scale (HRS) (Brown, 1986). In prior research, the HRS internal consistency was supported by an alpha coefficient of .89. Construct validity was supported by significant correlations in expected directions with other constructs (Brown, 1986). The instrument was chosen because it measures positive health as well as problematic symptoms. The subscale of positive health is subtracted from the score of problematic health symptoms (higher score, more symptoms) for an overall health score, with a higher score representing poorer health or health problems (the HRS difference score, or HRSDIF). In this sample, internal consistency of the HRS was .89.

The Daily Hassles Scale (DHS) is a widely used instrument to measure stress as it is experienced in ongoing situations rather than major life events. It is hypothesized as a more salient construct for women, especially as related to domestic violence. Reliability has been addressed in terms of strong support for stability on a monthly basis (Lazarus & Folkman, 1989). Validity, especially in terms of health outcomes, has been supported by the instrument, explaining more of the variance in psychological and physical health symptoms than major life events. In this study, the internal consistency of the DHS was .86.

RESULTS

Almost half (45.9%) of the battered women reported that they were also being forced into sex by their intimate partners. Using *t*-test analysis of the demographic variables, the sexually assaulted and nonsexually assaulted women did not differ in terms of age, education, or total family income. They also did not differ in terms of employment or in terms of a history of child sexual abuse, with the sexually assaulted women no more likely to be unemployed or sexually abused as a child than those not forced into sex by their intimate partner. However, there was a significant ($p = .035$) difference (by chi-square) in terms of ethnicity, with 50.4% of the African American women sexually assaulted by their partner as compared to 30.6% of the non–African American women.

Hotelling's multivariate T^2 test was performed to compare the sexually assaulted women with those not sexually assaulted by their partner on seven dependent variables: the BDI, the TSCS, the DA, the HRSDIF, the DHS, and the ISA, both physical and nonphysical aspects (see Table 2). The average correlation among these variables was .356, and the assumption of equal covariance

TABLE 2
Scale Score Mean (standard deviation) by Whether Sexually Assaulted

| | Sexually Assaulted | |
Scale	Yes	No
Beck Depression Inventory	19.1 (10.56)	15.8 (9.43)
Danger Assessment*	6.7 (2.71)	4.5 (2.58)
Daily Hassles Scale	114.1 (56.07)	101.7 (59.71)
HRS —Positive health	7.5 (4.44)	8.1 (4.19)
HRS —Negative symptoms*	17.9 (7.48)	15.0 (8.36)
HRS —Difference	10.3 (8.90)	6.9 (9.21)
ISA—Physical*	44.5 (20.75)	31.2 (19.30)
ISA—Nonphysical*	61.4 (24.85)	50.6 (23.59)
Tennessee Self-Concept Scale	290.9 (37.36)	303.2 (43.51)
Physical Self	57.8 (7.39)	60.5 (9.52)

NOTE: HRS = Health Responses Scale; ISA = Index of Spouse Abuse.
*Significantly different by directional univariate t test at adjusted .015.

matrices was met according to Box's M test ($p = .489$), supporting the use of multivariate procedure. Results indicated that the combined dependent variable differed significantly based on whether the woman was sexually assaulted by her partner, $T^2 = .205$, $p < .001$, reflecting a modest association ($O^2 = .17$). To investigate the differences for each of the dependent variables, univariate t tests were used with an adjusted I-level of .015 for each test.

Although the univariate t tests indicated that the overall HRS score was not related to sexual assault by the partner, the positive and negative symptoms subscores were examined separately. These component scores each correlate with the overall HRS score, but they measure different aspects of health and are not correlated with each other ($p = .862$). Results indicate that women sexually assaulted by their partners had a significantly higher mean health symptoms score than those not assaulted (17.9 vs. 15.0; $t = 2.24$, $p = .013$). There were no differences on the positive health subscale (7.5 vs. 8.1; $t = .89$. $p = .38$).

Four items on the HRS refer to gynecological problems: abdominal cramping or pain, experienced by 48% of the sexually abused women; urinary problems, experienced by 26%; decreased sexual desire, reported by 54%; and genital irritation, indicated by 26%. Overall, the mean number of gynecological problems reported by the women was 1.5 ($SD = 1.19$). The only single gynecological symptom related to intimate partner sexual abuse was abdominal cramping or pain (experienced by 56% of

TABLE 3
Health Responses Scale Gynecological Problems Results

Sexual Abuse	Abdominal Cramping/ Pain (%)	Urinary Problems (%)	Decreased Sexual Desire (%)	Genital Irritation (%)	Mean Number of Problems
No	41.7	22.6	49.4	21.2	1.31
Yes	55.6	29.6	60.0	30.6	1.71
Overall	48.1	25.8	54.2	25.5	1.50
Test Statistic	$x^2 = 3.0$ $(p = .08)$	$x^2 = 0.97$ $(p = .32)$	$x^2 = 1.72$ $(p = .19)$	$x^2 = 1.81$ $(p = .18)$	$t = 2.24$ $(p = .026)$

$x^2 df = 1$

the sexually abused and 42% of the nonsexually abused women). However, when the number of problems were examined, there was a difference between the two groups, with the sexually abused women reporting significantly more gynecological problems ($t = 2.24$, $p = .013$) (see Table 3). Only 14% of those abused reported no problems as compared to 27% of the nonabused women. Using a multiple regression approach and controlling for age, race, tangible resources, and stress, sexual assault by the partner remained a significant predictor ($p = .03$) of the number of problems. The adjusted odds ratio for whether the woman would experience gynecological problems based on sexual assault by her partner was 2.65 (95% CI: 1.11 to 6.32).

Women who were sexually assaulted by their partner had significantly higher scores on the DA (risk factors for homicide) and both the physical and nonphysical subscales of the ISA. Controlling for physical abuse (ISA-P), the correlation between forced sex and the rest of the DA was .259 ($p < .05$). Controlling for both physical and nonphysical abuse (ISA-NP), the correlation was the same, indicating that nonphysical abuse did not contribute to explained variance of homicide risk when physical abuse was already controlled. The mean DA score adjusting for ISA-P was 4.95 for those not forced into sex and 6.2 for those who were. Also adjusting for nonphysical abuse made no discernible difference in DA scores.

All women were queried about childhood sexual abuse, but only after the study began were women asked about rape by someone other than the current intimate partner. Therefore, we have complete data on all forms of prior sexual assault on 91 women. Although childhood sexual abuse (43% of the sample) did not differ between those sexually assaulted by the intimate partner and those who were not, having been raped did, $\chi^2(1) = 5.71, p = .017$. Overall, 44% of the women reported that they had been raped—56.5% of the women who experienced forced sex with an intimate partner and 31.9% of the women who were not sexually assaulted within a relationship. These three variables—intimate partner forced sex, rape, and childhood sexual abuse—were then examined in combination for their relationship to depression and self-esteem. The number of forced sex experiences was found to correlate significantly with depression ($r = .189, p = .018$); women having experienced more of the sexual assaults also tended to report increased levels of depression. A different pattern was found with respect to self-esteem, however. Although the overall level of self-esteem as measured by the TSCS did not correlate with the number of different forms of sexual assaults or differ by the type of assault, the physical self-dimension did. Based on one-way ANOVA ($F = 3.20, df = 2 \& 75, p = .046$), there was a difference among those experiencing no sexual assault (mean = 64.6), those experiencing 1 or 2 types (mean = 58.9), and those experiencing all 3 types (mean = 60.1). Women with no sexual assault had a more positive image of physical self than women experiencing sexual assault.

DISCUSSION

The results of this analysis are similar to those in an earlier sample that was recruited in a similar manner. Although there was a greater proportion of Anglo and European American women (White) in that sample (55% vs. 15% in the current study), the demographic profile was otherwise similar (J. C. Campbell, 1989). Thus, three comparable studies now indicate that 40% to 45% of physically abused women are also being forced into sex by their intimate partner or ex-intimate partner (J. C. Campbell, 1989; Finkelhor & Yllo, 1985). The difference in proportions between the African American and non–African American battered women forced into sex found in this sample needs to be interpreted with caution. The non–African American subsample was extremely small and of mixed ethnicity, and this result was not found in the prior study that had a more balanced ethnic representation (J. C.

Campbell, 1989). Therefore, the finding needs to be viewed as tentative and warranting further investigation only. Even so, there were no significant differences between the two ethnic groupings in severity and frequency of either physical or nonphysical abuse as measured by the ISA or in the total DA score, so the observed difference cannot be attributed to overall abuse differentials. There is other documentation that sexual assault is a horrifically common experience for young African American women across their lifetime (Riggs et al., 1992), although we did not find any association of number of lifetime types of sexually assaultive experiences with ethnicity.

Associations between ethnicity and frequency or prevalence of sexual assault may be more associated with poverty than ethnicity, a confounding relationship across violence research that needs more careful disaggregation (Hawkins, 1993). When we included ethnic group and income in our multivariate analyses, neither was a significant predictor of health outcomes, but we were hampered by the small size of our non–African American group in controlling for income with the prevalence association.

There is an extreme paucity of research on intimate partner forced sex experiences for African American women in terms of both specific risk factors and sequelae. Plichta and Abraham (1996) did control for race and other demographic factors in their analysis (13.1% of their sample was African American) and found that past-year spouse abuse was still significantly predictive of gynecological problems. However, that study did not measure forced sex specifically. African American women also are more at risk for STDs and other gynecological problems that may have associations with forced sex that have not been determined. Our results suggest important directions for further inquiry in this area but no definitive conclusions.

There are clearly detrimental physical and mental health effects to women sexually abused that are apparently somewhat different from those incurred by women only physically (and emotionally) abused. Unfortunately, most health measurement instruments do not include all of the particular health problems most frequently mentioned by sexually assaulted battered women. The Health Responses Scale used in this study only had 4 (of 50 total) such items: lower abdominal (pelvic) pain, urinary problems, decreased sexual desire, and genital itching or irritation. Even so, there was a significantly higher score on the total physical health symptoms scale of the HRS, and the relationship held even when controlling for demographics and physical violence. Thus, it is important for health care professionals to assess battered women separately and specifically for forced sex and to further investigate the specific health care problems that may be a result of this kind of abuse. Clearly, it is particularly important that those who provide gynecological, obstetric, and primary care to women routinely screen for physical violence (Bohn, 1993; Chez & Jones, 1995; McCauley et al., 1995) and then further inquire about forced sex when physical abuse is present. If there is sexual assault, there also are often the sexually abusive tactics that present particular risk of unintended pregnancy and STDs. Programs that target reducing unintended pregnancy, repeat STDs, and preventing HIV/AIDS need to include routine assessment for forced sex and other forms of intimate partner violence and information about these issues in teaching materials (Wingood & DiClemente, 1997).

It is also important for other professionals working with battered women to inquire specifically about sexual assault, so that these women can be referred to the appropriate health care professionals. Often-battered women do not connect health care problems (such as chronic pelvic pain) with their relationship violence and need to be helped to see possible connections and to have their health care providers realize these linkages. They are also often extremely ashamed of the sexually abusive and assaultive acts and unlikely to volunteer the presence and especially the extent of these tactics. Support group sessions devoted to forced sex can be helpful to women in helping to dispel the stigma, but leaders need to bring the topic up and be sure to indicate that if women are not comfortable in disclosing sexual assault in a group setting, it can be discussed individually with counselors.

In terms of mental health consequences related to forced sex, it is a serious limitation of this study that PTSD was not measured. The analytic approach used here that demonstrated a significant impact of repeated different kinds of sexual assault over a lifetime on depression and self esteem supports other studies showing that repeated sexual trauma is related to chronic and serious mental health problems (Plichta & Abraham, 1996; Riggs et al., 1992). The relationship with the body image (Physical Self) subscale of the TSCS with sexual assault suggests that body image is the aspect of self-esteem damage that is affected particularly from forced relationship sex. These insights are important for therapeutic interventions specific to forced relationship sex as have been outlined by Weingourt (1985, 1990).

Finally, the indication from this study that men who sexually assault their partners as well as physically abuse them are particularly dangerous men was also supported in the earlier investigation (J. C. Campbell, 1989). This means that women who are being sexually assaulted need to be warned of this reality as part of a lethality risk safety planning intervention (J. C. Campbell, in press).

Other limitations of this study include the nonrepresentative volunteer nature of the sample, the relatively small sample size, the incomplete mental health measurement (e.g., not including panic disorders, not differentiating between acute and chronic depression), the lack of data on previous experiences of rape on more than a third of the participants, and the relatively few specific gynecological questions. Even so, it is valuable for its attention to this neglected area of investigation related to violence against women.

CONCLUSIONS

It is still extremely difficult for women to prove forced relationship sex in court, whether it is called "date rape" or "marital rape" (Family Violence Prevention Fund, 1997), and this form of domestic violence has been neglected in our research and practice across disciplines. More knowledge about the deleterious health effects and particular dangers specific to this form of violence against women would be helpful in health, mental health, and criminal justice sectors in order to decrease its impact. This study has demonstrated that there are physical health effects and increased danger for women beyond what is associated with the physical and emotional abuse that they are also experiencing from a battering intimate partner. It is not enough for service providers to assess for other forms of violence; they need to ask specifically about forced sex. Health care professionals especially are in a unique position to address this kind of abuse and need to be alert for its occurrence in primary care and gynecological settings as well as in emergency departments.

NOTE

1. Although it is useful to differentiate sexual from physical assault when considering domestic violence, it is also useful to use terminology that allows for repeated sexual assault (without physical violence in other contexts) to be considered as part of the battering terminology. Some women (albeit few) do report sexual assault as the only form of violence from an intimate partner with all the other same dynamics as a battering relationship.

REFERENCES

Attala, J. M., Hudson, W. W., & McSweeney, M. (1994). A partial validation of two short-form partner abuse scales. *Women & Health, 21,* 125-139.

Beck, A. T. (1972). *Depression: Causes and treatment.* Philadelphia: University of Pennsylvania Press.

Beck, A. T., Ward, C. H., Mendelson, M., Mock, J., & Erbaugh, J. (1961). An inventory for measuring depression. *Archives of General Psychiatry, 4,* 53-63.

Bergman, B., & Brismar, B. (1991). A 5-year follow-up study of 117 battered women. *American Journal of Public Health, 81,* 1486-1488.

Bohn, D. K. (1993). Nursing care of native American battered women. *AWHONN's Clinical Issues in Perinatal and Women's Health Nursing* (Special Issue), 4, 424-436.

Brown, M. A. (1986). Social support, stress, and health: A comparison of expectant mothers and fathers. *Nursing Research, 35,* 72-76.

Campbell, D. W., Campbell, J. C., Parker, B., King, C., & Ryan, J. (1994). The reliability and factor structure of the Index of Spouse Abuse with African American women. *Violence and Victims, 9,* 259-274.

Campbell, J. C. (1989). Women's responses to sexual abuse in intimate relationships. *Women's Health Care International, 8,* 335-347.

Campbell, J. C. (1995). Prediction of homicide of and by battered women. In J. C. Campbell (Ed.), *Assessing the risk of dangerousness: Potential for further violence of sexual offenders, batterers, and child abusers* (pp. 96-113). Thousand Oaks, CA: Sage.

Campbell, J. C. (in press). Safety planning based on lethality assessment for partners of batterers in treatment. In R. Geffner (Ed.), *Family violence and sexual assault.* Binghamton, NY: The Hayworth Maltreatment and Trauma Press.

Campbell, J. C., & Alford, P. (1989). The dark consequences of marital rape. *American Journal of Nursing, 89,* 946-949.

Campbell, J. C., & Humphreys, J. (1993). *Nursing care of survivors of family violence.* St. Louis, MO: Mosby.

Campbell, J. C., Kub, J., Belknap, R. A., & Templin, T. (1997). Predictors of depression in battered women. *Violence Against Women, 3,* 276-293.

Campbell, J. C., Miller, P., Cardwell, M. M., & Belknap, R. A. (1994). Relationship status of battered women over time. *Journal of Family Violence, 9,* 99-111.

Campbell, J. C., Pugh, L. C., Campbell, D., & Visscher, M. (1995). The influence of abuse on pregnancy intention. *Women's Health Issues, 5,* 214-223.

Chapman, J. D. (1989). A longitudinal study of sexuality and gynecologic health in abused women. *Journal of the American Osteopathic Association, 89,* 946-949.

Chez, R. A., & Jones, R. F. (1995). The battered woman. *American Journal of Obstetrics and Gynecology, 173,* 677-679.

Cohen, J., & Cohen, P. (1983). *Applied multiple regression/correlation analysis for the behavioral sciences.* New York: John Wiley.

Covington, D. L., Maxwell, J. G., Clancy, T. V., Churchill, M. P., & Ahrens, W. L. (1995). Poor hospital documentation of violence against women. *Journal of Trauma: Injury, Infection and Critical Care, 38*, 412-416.

Eby, K. K., & Campbell, J. C. (1995). Health effects of experiences of sexual violence for women with abusive partners. *Women's Health Care International, 14*, 563-576.

Family Violence Prevention Fund. (1997). Family Violence Prevention Fund's news and tips for the domestic violence community. In *Speaking up*, (p. 3). Washington, DC: Author.

Finkelhor, D., & Yllo, K. (1985). *License to rape: Sexual abuse of wives*. New York: Holt, Rinehart & Winston.

Fitts, W. H. (1972). *The self-concept and behavior: Overview and supplement*. Los Angeles: Western Psychological Services.

Gazmararian, J. A., Adams, M. M., Saltzman, L. E., Johnson, C. H., Bruce, F. C., Marks, J. S., & Zahniser, S. C. (1995). The relationship between intendedness and physical violence in mothers of newborns. *Obstetrics and Gynecology, 85*, 131-138.

Gelles, R. J., & Straus, M. A. (1990). The medical and psychological costs of family violence. In M. A. Straus & R. J. Gelles (Eds.), *Physical violence in American families: Risk factors and adaptations to violence*. New Brunswick, NJ: Transaction.

Gleason, W. J. (1993). Mental disorders in battered women: An empirical study. *Violence and Victims, 8*, 53-68.

Hawkins, D. F. (1993). Inequality, culture, and interpersonal violence. *Health Affairs, 12*, 80-95.

Herman, J. (1992). *Trauma and recovery*. New York: Basic Books.

Hudson, W. W., & McIntosh, S. R. (1981). The assessment of spouse abuse: Two quantifiable dimensions. *Journal of Marriage and the Family, 43*, 873-885.

Kessler, R., McGonagle, K., Nelson, C., Hughes, M., Swartz, M., & Blazer, D. (1994). Sex and depression in the National Comorbidity Survey. II. Cohort effects. *Journal of Infectious Disease, 30*, 15-26.

Koss, M. P. (1993). Rape: Scope, impact, intervention, and public policy response. *American Psychologist, 4*, 1062-1069.

Koss, M. P., & Harvey, M. R. (1991). *The rape victim: Clinical and community intervention*. Newbury Park, CA: Sage.

Lazarus, R. S., & Folkman, S. (1989). *Manual for the hassles and uplifts scales: Research edition*. Palo Alto, CA: Consulting Psychologists Press.

Marshall, L. (1996). Psychological abuse of women: Six distinct clusters. *Journal of Family Violence, 11*, 379-410.

McCauley, J., Kern, D. E., Kolodner, K., Dill, L., Schroeder, A. F., DeChant, H., Ryden, J., Bass, E., & Derogatis, L. (1995). The "Battering Syndrome": Prevalence and clinical characteristics of domestic violence in primary care internal medicine practices. *Annals of Internal Medicine, 123*, 737-746.

McFarlane, J., Parker, B., Soeken, K., & Bullock, L. (1992). Assessing for abuse during pregnancy: Severity and frequency of injuries and associated entry into prenatal care. *Journal of the American Medical Association, 267*, 2370-2372.

Plichta, S. B. (1996). Violence and abuse: Implications for women's health. In M. M. Falik & K. S. Collins (Eds.), *Women's health: The Commonwealth Survey* (pp. 237-272). Baltimore: Johns Hopkins University Press.

Plichta, S. B., & Abraham, C. (1996). Violence and gynecologic health in women < 50 years old. *American Journal of Obstetrics and Gynecology, 174*, 903-907.

Resnick, H., Kilpatrick, D., Dansky, B., Saunders, B., & Best, C. (1993). Prevalence of civilian trauma and posttraumatic stress disorder in a representative national sample of women. *Journal of Consulting & Clinical Psychology, 61*, 984-991.

Riggs, C., Kilpatrick, D., & Resnick, H. (1992). Longterm psychological distress associated with marital rape and aggravated assault: A comparison to other crime victims. *Journal of Family Violence, 7*, 283-296.

Russell, D. (1982). *Rape in marriage.* New York: Macmillan.

Russell, D. (1997). Wife rape. In A. Parrot & L. Bechhofer (Eds.), *Acquaintance rape: The hidden crime* (pp. 129-139). New York: John Wiley.

Saunders, D. G. (1992). Posttraumatic stress symptom profiles of battered women: A comparison of survivors in two settings. *Violence & Victims, 9,* 31-44.

Saunders, D. G., Hamberger, K., & Hovey, M. (1993). Indicators of woman abuse based on a chart review at a family practice center. *Archives of Family Medicine, 2,* 537-543.

Straus, M. A., & Gelles, R. J. (1990). *Physical violence in American families: Risk factors and adaptations to family violence in 8,145 families.* New Brunswick, NJ: Transaction.

Thompson, W. (1972). *Correlates of the self concept.* Los Angeles: Western Psychological Services.

Tjaden, P., & Thoennes, N. (1998). *Prevalence, incidence and consequences of violence against women: Findings from the National Violence Against Women Survey* (NCJ Publication No. 172837). Washington, DC: U.S. Department of Justice, National Institute of Justice.

Weingourt, R. (1985). Wife rape: Barriers to identification and treatment. *Journal of Psychotherapy, 39,* 187-192.

Weingourt, R. (1990). Wife rape in a sample of psychiatric patients. *Image: Journal of Nursing Scholarship, 22,* 144-147.

Weissman, M., & Klerman, G. (1992). Depression: Current understanding and changing trends. *Annual Review of Public Health, 13,* 319-339.

Wells, L. E., & Marwell, G. (1976). *Self-esteem: Its conceptualization and measurement.* Beverly Hills, CA: Sage.

Wingood, G. M., & DiClemente, R. J. (1997). The effects of an abusive primary partner on the condom use and sexual negotiation practices of African-American women. *American Journal of Public Health, 87,* 1016-1018.

Jacquelyn C. Campbell received a BSN from Duke University, an MSN from Wright State University, and a Ph.D. in nursing from the University of Rochester. She is the Anna D. Wolf Endowed Professor and associate dean for doctoral education programs and research at Johns Hopkins University School of Nursing with a joint appointment in the School of Hygiene and Public Health. As principal investigator (PI) of five major nationally funded research studies on battering, she is author or coauthor of more than 80 articles and five books on the subject. Campbell has worked with wife-abuse shelters and policy-related committees on domestic violence for more than 18 years.

Karen L. Soeken received her B.S. in psychology and mathematics from Valparaiso University in 1965, an M.S. in mathematics from the University of Maryland in 1969, a Ph.D. in educational measurement and statistics from the University of Maryland in 1979, and a masters of theological studies from Wesley Seminary in 1996. She is currently associate professor at the University of Maryland School of Nursing where she teaches research methods and statistics. She has coauthored more than 50 databased publications in content areas that include spirituality and nursing care, measurement of patient intensity for nursing care, and domestic abuse.

Part IV
Intersections of Violent Offending and Violent Victimization

[12]

Violence and Victims, Vol. 1, No. 1, 1986
© 1986 Springer Publishing Company

Victims of Serious Violence and Their Criminal Behavior: Subcultural Theory and Beyond

Simon I. Singer*

This paper looks at the relationship between the experiences of the victim of a serious crime and that of the offender. It shows that, in some cases, the victim experience is an important predictor of criminal behavior. An analysis of self-reported and officially recorded offense and victimization data supports the hypothesized relationship between victim and offender experiences. The results have implications for subcultural theory and a dynamic analysis of how patterns of assaultive violence are created and maintained.

A perplexing issue in sociological theories of crime is the relationship between violent victimization and criminal conduct. There is reason to believe that, under some conditions, victimization experience precedes and facilitates criminal behavior. For example, in reaction to their victimization, juveniles may seek the support of a gang or possession of a weapon. Similarly, violent victimization experienced in the home or school may contribute to the lack of attachment and involvement juveniles feel toward their parents or formal education.[1]

Some theorists of criminal behavior argue explicitly that victimization increases the likelihood of offenses or alters the nature of offenses committed by the victim. The perception of being the victim rather than the perpetrator of crime is a prominent neutralization technique among delinquents (Matza, 1964). It may also explain why black offenders select white victims (Silberman, 1978) and why racial violence exists in maximum security institutions (Carroll, 1974). Black (1983) has argued that what are often viewed as random acts of violence are, in reality, responses to a perceived wrong.

In theories of criminal violence, the symmetry between the roles of victim and offender is taken into account in perspectives that emphasize the internecine qualities of subcultural values and attitudes. That is, that violent behavior tends to be a reciprocal exchange in which violence is followed by retaliation. The social

---

*Department of Sociology, State University of New York at Buffalo.

61

patterning of victim-precipitated incidents, or violence involving homicide (Wolfgang, 1958) and assault (Pittman & Handy, 1964) implies a mutual support for the use of violence to resolve intergroup conflicts. Wolfgang and Ferracuti (1967) contend that there is a subculture of violence in which a violent response is encouraged and even demanded at the risk of further victimization. The offenders in such a subculture are also frequently the victims, because of subcultural norms that justify retaliation.

The premise that the internecine qualities of violence lead to the development of violent values and attitudes is a key deduction of the subculture of violence thesis. It is also suggested in other subcultural studies that stress the social learning of violence. Cloward and Ohlin (1960, p. 175) argue that juveniles become embroiled in a conflict subculture not only because of their desire for status and prestige among peers, but also because of their initial exposure to violence. Short and Strodtbeck's (1965) "group process perspective" of subcultural violence is more explicit about the mechanisms in which violence is learned. They argue that victimization, like mental illness and unemployment, is one of the hazards of lower-class life that leads to criminal conduct. The threat of victimization is seen as a motivating force of violent gang activity, whether in the name of protection or self-defense (Short & Strodtbeck, 1965, pp. 257–258).

Studies that attempt to test subcultural perspectives of violence have generally confined their analysis to correlating demographic characteristics with attitudes toward the use of violence (Ball-Rokeach, 1973; Erlanger, 1975) or with aggregate rates of criminal violence (Gastil, 1971; Hackney 1969). There are serious method-ological problems with both approaches (Fine & Kleinman, 1979; Hindelang, 1978; Magura, 1975; Loftin & Hill, 1974). The measures of violent attitudes are of questionable validity, and there is a tendency to infer the presence of violent cultural patterns from the presence of violent behavior. Consequently, there is a need for data on individuals and for behavioral indicators that reflect a commitment to serious assaultive violence.

THE PRESENT HYPOTHESIS

The present study uses data collected from a sample of intercity males to examine the subcultural theory proposition that victims of serious violence are frequently offenders. It is shown that, for this sample, experience as a victim of serious criminal behavior is highly correlated with committing serious criminal violence, even when a variety of demographic and offense-related characteristics are controlled. There is strong evidence that these males have alternated their position as victims and offenders with regularity. This is exactly the type of experience that generates and maintains the values, attitudes, and conduct norms that Wolfgang and others have characterized as the subculture of violence.

Other theoretical perspectives are compatible with the hypothesis. For example, victimization among delinquents might account for their social alienation (Covin & Pauly, 1983) and lack of legitimate social bonds (Hirschi, 1969). Similarly, learning theory can be reconceptualized to reflect the possible social reinforcement of behavior (Burgess & Akers, 1966) that victims receive in displacing their victimization experiences onto others. To some extent this is a reflection of the integrative capacity of the subculture of violence thesis (Wolfgang & Ferracuti, 1967), but it is not critical at this stage to distinguish among competing general theories. The primary objective here is to document the victim/offender pattern.

MEASURING VICTIM AND OFFENDER EXPERIENCES

In the follow-up to the *Delinquency in a Birth Cohort* study (Wolfgang, Figlio, & Sellin, 1972), a survey of self-reported delinquency and victimization was conducted on a 10% sample of the 1945 Philadelphia birth cohort. These follow-up data are used in the present study.

The original cohort population consisted of males born in 1945 who resided in Philadelphia from age 10 to age 18 or longer (Wolfgang et al., 1972). Of the 975 sample subjects in the follow-up sample, 567 cohort members were interviewed, at age 26, about their social background, victimization, and delinquent activity. In addition to interview information, arrest data were collected from the Philadelphia Police Department (Wolfgang et al., 1972). A comparison of the interview sample with the entire population indicates that the interviewed population is under-represented by nonwhite offenders. When measures of sample bias are computed controlling for race, the impact of sampling variation due to nonresponse error on the magnitude of correlational analysis is insignificant (Singer, 1977).[2]

Surveyed victimizations were measured by asking cohort members to respond to whether an incident occurred during three distinct chronological periods in the respondent's life: before age 12, from ages 12 to 18, and from ages 19 to 26, when all cohort members were interviewed. The cohort follow-up survey included incidents of victimization ranging from simple to aggravated forms of assault as well as property offenses. No follow-up questions were asked concerning a reported incident of victimization so that the characteristics of the victim's offender can not be determined, nor can the sequence of offenses and victimizations.

To test the aspect of subcultural theory that predicts serious assaultive violence, only victimizations involving serious assault with a weapon are measured. The analysis, thus, is confined to those incidents in which respondents said they were either shot or stabbed.[3]

Self-reported serious offender status was measured with incidents of serious assault or theft with injury. This includes rape and homicide, as well as any aggravated forms of assault in which the victim was seriously injured. In addition to the self-reported offenses, criminal offense records from police records were used. These officially recorded arrests (actually "contacts" with the police for juveniles) controlled in part for response bias in the self-report data (Sudman & Bradburn, 1974).

The purpose of the analysis was not to determine whether victimization precedes criminal behavior. Consistent with the subculture of violence theory, it was expected that offenders would alternate in their roles as victims and offenders. The purpose of the analysis was simply to empirically demonstrate the reciprocal pattern of victimization and criminal behavior.

Self-Reported Serious Assaults

Bivariate results. Nineteen percent of the surveyed cohort members said they were either shot or stabbed before age 26. The percentage declines from 12% in the juvenile years to 8% in the adult years. The proportion of cohort members who were victims is lower than those indicating they were offenders, 19% compared to 35%. This difference can be attributed to the fact that the victimization incidents used involved more serious injury than the self-reported offenses.

Victimization is highly related to self-reported, violent offenses. Among cohort members who said they were victims of serious violence, more than two-thirds indicated having committed an act of serious violence. In contrast, less than a third of the nonvictims reported committing a serious violent offense (Table 1). That is, violent offenses are three times as likely among victims as nonvictims.

Gang membership was also strongly related to offender status: nearly twice as many gang members as nonmembers indicated they had committed an act of assaultive violence. Weapon use produced similar results.[4]

Race is an important social background variable predicting offender status; 46% of blacks compared to 32% of whites were offenders. Other social background variables, such as socioeconomic status, area income, educational level, and marital and employment status are insignificant when race is controlled. This difference between whites and blacks in self-reported serious violence is comparable to the results of the original cohort study (Wolfgang et al., 1972).[5]

Multivariate results. To test the hypothesized relationship between serious assaultive offenses, gang membership, weapon use, and victimization experience, logit models were computed using Goodman's (1972) modified multiple regression technique. The procedure is appropriate for a model with a binary dependent variable such as whether or not a respondent reports having committed a serious assault.

In Table 2, summary statistics for six models based on race, assaultive offense, victimization, weapon use, and gang membership are presented. The probability of a cohort member having committed a serious assault can be accurately prediced with race, victimization, weapon use, and gang membership.

Model 2, which includes all of the independent variables, fits the model well as indicated by the small chi-square value (10.65 with 11 degrees of freedom). However, Model 3, which excludes race, is more parsimonious and fits the data just

TABLE 1. Proportion Who Report Serious Assaultive Violence by Race and Offense- Related Characteristics (*N* = 567)

Characteristic	Number[a]	Proportion
Whites	453	.32
Blacks	114	.46
Victims	106	.68
Nonvictims	461	.27
Gang Members	94	.52
Nonmembers	473	.23
Weapon	70	.67
Nonweapon	497	.30

[a]Number of respondents with the specified characteristic.

as well (chi-square of 10.65 with 12 degrees of freedom). The relationship between race and offender status can be explained by the difference between whites' and blacks' membership in gangs, use of weapons, and having been either shot or stabbed.

When gang membership is eliminated (Model 4), the chi-square value is significant, indicating its importance in accounting for offender status. Without victimization status (Model 5), the fit is poor. Finally, when weapon use is eliminated (Model 6), the model is insignificant at the .05 level, although it is not nearly as good a fit as Model 3, which excludes the impact of race.

As shown in Table 3, when the best fitting model (Model 3) is partitioned to determine the relative contribution of victimization, gang membership, and weapon use, victim status appears to make the strongest contribution to the overall fit of the data. Goodman's coefficient of multiple determination (1972, p. 43) is .77 for victimization, .63 for gang membership, and .48 for weapon use.[6]

Official Arrests

For the officially recorded arrest data, victim experiences were significantly related to a criminal record for a cohort member's adult years. Victims were substantially more likely to have an official adult arrest than nonvictims: 64% compared to 21%. By race, blacks were much more likely than whites to experience an adult arrest: 48% compared to 18%. Similarly, cohort members who said they were gang members were more than twice as likely to have had an official arrest: 46% compared to 20%.

Despite the significance of the relationship between self-reported victim experiences and the probability of an official arrest, it falls short of the intended objective to measure serious criminality. Even in the adult years, arrests may involve relatively minor offenses. Therefore, to control for the seriousness of an official offense history, arrests during adulthood were totaled and transformed to measures of career seriousness based on an index of severity developed by Sellin and Wolfgang (1964). The Sellin-Wolfgang index has two important advantages as a measure of career seriousness. First, as mentioned above, it allows for an event to be weighted for the severity of injury or theft. Second, the index provides a measure of the cumulative seriousness of offenses over time.

TABLE 2. Possible Models for the Association of Assaultive Violence [A], Victimization [V], Weapon Use [W], Gang Membership [G], and Race [R]

Model	Fitted marginals	Degrees of freedom	Likelihood ratio chi-square	Probability
1	[VWGR] [A]	15	105.61	<.01
2	[VWGR] [AV] [AW] [AG] [AR]	11	10.65	.47
3	[VWGR] [AV] [AW] [AG]	12	10.65	.56
4	[VWGR] [AV] [AW]	13	29.00	<.01
5	[VWGR] [AG] [AW]	13	45.95	<.01
6	[VWGR] [AV] [AG]	13	20.39	.09

TABLE 3. Coefficient of Partial Determination and Net Contribution of Variables in Model 3

Comparison	Source	D.F.	L^{2a}	R^{2b}	p
Model 4–Model 3	G	1	18.35	.63	<.01
Model 5–Model 3	V	1	35.30	.77	<.01
Model 6–Model 3	W	1	9.74	.48	<.01

[a]Likelihood-ratio chi-square.
[b]Goodman's coefficient of multiple determination for a logit model (1972, p. 43).

To predict total adult seriousness scores, the results of various models estimated with ordinary least squares procedures are presented in Table 4.[7] As in the original cohort study, race is the most important predictor of the seriousness of total arrests. Of a cohort member's offense-related characteristics, the total seriousness of prior juvenile arrests, gang membership, and victimization were significantly correlated with adult arrests. In total, these variables accounted for 32% of the variance in seriousness scores. When weapon use is included, it contributes only slightly to the explained variance.

The impact of offense-related characteristics is examined further by estimating separate models for whites and blacks. For blacks, the proportion of variance explained by juvenile arrests, gang membership, and victimization increases to 36%. If gang membership and juvenile arrests were not included in the model, victimization alone would account for 11% of the variance in the seriousness of black adult arrests. Gang membership and victimization contribute equally to predicting adult seriousness scores. Without the victim experience included in the model, only 29% of the variance could be explained by juvenile arrests and gang membership.

For whites, the relationships are weaker and not statistically significant at the conventional .05 level, but the general pattern of relationships is the same as for blacks. Juvenile arrests, gang membership, and victimization are positively associated with adult seriousness scores. Thus, the official data is consistent with a model in which victim experience as well as other offense-related characteristics increase the likelihood of serious adult offenses. The effects are stronger for blacks than whites, but are positive in both groups.[8]

SUMMARY

For the whole sample, having been shot or stabbed is strongly correlated with both self-reported offenses and recorded official arrests. When other offender-related characteristics are controlled, such as gang membership and the use of a weapon, victimization is still a significant predictor of criminal behavior. For self-reported offenses, the best predictor of committing an act of violence is being the victim of serious violence. In particular, the victim experience accounted for the relationship between race and serious offender status. Thus, the overrepresentation of blacks in violent crime was explained by the greater likelihood of blacks experiencing violent victimization.

TABLE 4. Factors Affecting the Seriousness of Total Adult Arrests

	Unstandardized coefficients	Standard error	t	Standardized coefficients
	All Adult Offenders			
Race	12.835	3.406	3.77	.294
Juvenile arrests	.414	.141	2.94	.223
Gang membership	9.003	3.708	2.43	.198
Victimization	8.439	4.153	2.03	.160
$(R^2 = .295)$				
	Black Offenders			
Juvenile arrests	.630	.190	3.32	.395
Gang membership	12.303	5.59	2.20	.269
Victimization	13.367	6.00	2.23	.268
$(R^2 = .357)$				
	White Offenders			
Juvenile arrests	.0478	.226	.21	.025
Gang membership	4.566	4.870	.94	.113
Victimization	6.500	5.95	1.09	.136
$(R^2 = .044)$				

With the official arrest data, self-reported victimization is still a significant predictor of the seriousness of an adult criminal career, especially for blacks. Although race and the seriousness of prior juvenile arrests are more strongly correlated with adult seriousness scores than victimization, the estimated effects of the victim experience is equal to gang membership, which has traditionally been considered a major correlate of subcultural involvement. However, the victimization experiences of cohort members may have been a result of their criminal activity. Unfortunately, incidents in which cohort members perceived themselves as victims but were actually the offenders cannot be determined with the available data.

CONCLUSION

Subcultural perspectives that emphasize the internecine qualities of violent conduct are supported with both the self-reported and officially recorded cohort data. The results of the analysis suggest that subcultural violence is not likely to arise in social environments where the likelihood of violent victimization and rationalization is low.

The mutual support violent offenders may feel in association with others is more loosely structured than previous analysis would suggest. Group criminal or gang behavior may be a consequence of the social hazards of lower-class life that is reflected in the greater risks of experiencing a violent victimization. Efforts to reduce the risk of victimization may include carrying a weapon as well as membership in a gang. The role offenders play in alternating their position as victims would appear to support the maintenance of violent values.

An incident of serious violent victimization is a life experience that may also help to predict initial involvement in crime, although this could not be tested with available data. Specific segments of the general population can be expected to legitimate more readily the use of violence because of their victimization experiences.[9] If there is an absence of legitimate forms of social control (and thus, moral development) to sanction the perpetrator of a violent offense, then the victim experience may be seen as justification for criminal conduct. Victimization, in the absence of other forms of social control, would seem to provide the situational conditions for further acts of violence. Thus, the development of subcultural attitudes and values may reflect general norms of reciprocity (Gouldner, 1960) based on initial experiences with violence.

It is important to remember that these analyses were conducted using data from an inner-city sample of males and thus the findings are specific to that group. For most people, being shot or stabbed does not lead to the commission of a criminal act in response. There are cultural values which intercede, causing victims to repress the expression of aggressive impulses. Dominant cultural values dictate calling the police or seeking the help of other representatives of legal authority. Victims may further counterbalance their victimization experiences by invoking certain moral dicta, such as "two wrongs don't make a right" or "turn the other cheek." An incident of victimization, rather than producing aggression, often leads to greater caution and even desistance from involvement in criminal behavior. Recognition of the risk of further victimization may also be one of the motivating factors causing violent offenders to grow out of their delinquent behavior.

In conclusion, violent victimization is a unique kind of social experience that, until now, has been mainly examined simply in terms of its patterns of occurrence. Its impact on criminal behavior needs to be examined in more detail in other research settings, if theories of victims and offenders are to provide a more complete understanding of crime. Further analysis is needed on the situational factors that produced the victim experience. Although perceived incidents of having been shot or stabbed are assumed to reflect actual events, they may represent acts of crime in which self-reported victims were the main perpetrators of the offense. In any case, the victim experience should be considered in all sociological analyses that attempt to account for the emergence and maintenance of violent criminal behavior.

REFERENCES

Ball-Rokeach, S. (1973). Values and violence: A test of the subculture of violence thesis. *American Sociological Review, 38*, 736–750.

Black, D. (1983). Crime as social control. *American Sociological Review, 48*, 34–45.

Burgess, R., & Akers, R. (1966). A differential association reinforcement theory of criminal behavior. *Social Problems, 14*, 128–147.

Carroll, L. (1974). *Hacks, blacks, and cons: Race relations in a maximum security prison.* Lexington, MA: Lexington Books.

Cloward, R. A., & Ohlin, L. E. (1960). *Delinquency and opportunity: A theory of delinquent gangs.* New York: The Free Press.

Colvin, M., and Pauly, J. (1983). A critique of criminology: toward an integrated structural-Marxist theory of delinquency production. *American Journal of Sociology, 89*, 513-551.

Dostoyevsky, F. (1950). *Brothers Karamozov*. New York: Modern Library.

Erlanger, H. S. (1975). Is there a 'subculture of violence' in the South? *Journal of Criminal Law and Criminology, 66*, 483-490.

Fine, G. A., & Kleinman, S. (1979). Rethinking subculture: An interactionist analysis. *American Journal of Sociology, 85*, 1-20.

Gastil, R. D. (1971). Homicide and a regional culture of violence. *American Sociological Review, 36*, 412-427.

Gouldner, A. W. (1960). The norm of reciprocity: A preliminary statement. *American Sociological Review, 25*, 161-178.

Goodman, L. (1972). A modified multiple regression approach to the analysis of dichotomous variables. *American Sociological Review, 37*, 28-46.

Hackney, S. (1969). Southern violence. *American Historical Review, 74*, 906-925.

Hindelang, M. (1978). Race and involvement in personal crimes. *American Sociological Review, 43*, 93-109.

Hirschi, T. (1969). *Causes of delinquency*. Berkeley: University of California Press.

Kornhauser, R. R. (1978). *Social sources of delinquency*. Chicago: University of Chicago Press.

Loftin, C., & Hill R. (1974). Regional subculture and homicide: An examination of the Gastil-Hackney thesis. *American Sociological Review, 39*, 714-724.

Magura, S. (1975). Is there a subculture of violence? *American Sociological Review, 40*, 831-836.

Matza, D. (1964). *Delinquency and drift*. New York: John Wiley.

Messner, S. G. (1983). Regional and racial effects on the urban homicide rate: The subculture of violence revisited. *American Journal of Sociology, 88*, 997-1007.

Piaget, J. (1965). *The moral judgment of the child*. New York: The Free Press.

Pittman, D., & Handy, W. (1964). Patterns in criminal aggravated assault. *Journal of Criminal Law and Criminology, 55*, 462-470.

Sellin, T., & Wolfgang, M. E. (1964). *The measurement of delinquency*. New York: John Wiley.

Short, J. F., & F. C. Strodtbeck (1965). *Group process and gang delinquency*. Chicago: University of Chicago Press.

Singer, S. I. (1977). "The effect of non-response in the birth-cohort follow-up." Unpublished manuscript, University of Pennsylvania, Center for Studies in Criminology and Criminal Law, Philadelphia.

Silberman, C. E. (1978). *Criminal violence, criminal justice*. New York: Random House.

Sudman, S., & Bradburn, N. M. (1974). *Response effects in surveys*. Chicago: Aldine.

Wolfgang, M. E. (1958). Patterns in criminal homicide. Philadelphia: University of Pennsylvania Press.

Wolfgang, M. E. & Ferracuti, F. (1967). *The subculture of violence*. London: Tavistock.

Wolfgang, M. E., Figlio, R. M., & Sellin, T. (1972). *Delinquency in a birth cohort*. Chicago: University of Chicago Press.

NOTES

[1]There are many literary examples of the significance of the victim experience on criminal behavior. One is De Sica's classic film, *The Bicycle Thief*, in which the victim of a bicycle theft steals someone else's bicycle after a fruitless search. The significance of the victimization experience is clear in that it involves imitating a perceived wrong, but only after the normal avenues of justice fail to provide any form of relief or compensation.

In Dostoyevsky's novels, a perceived victimization is also an important explanation of what may appear at times as random acts of violence. In attempting to understand why he was assaulted, the main character in *The Brothers Karamazov*, Aloysha, tries to explain his victimization by asking his offender in what way he has been harmed.

> Though I don't know you and it's the first time I've seen you . . . I must have done something to you—you wouldn't have hurt me like this for nothing. So what have I done? How have I wronged you, tell me? (1950, p. 213)

[2]For the entire population, there is a .35 chance of a juvenile arrest compared to .30 for those interviewed. However, the difference appears specific to race, with less than a 2% difference between interviewed whites and their population values, while for blacks the difference is about 9%. Although blacks are underrepresented in their probability of arrest in the interviewed sample, once measures of the standard error are computed the added variance due to nonresponse does not appear to alter the chance of observed differences at the .95 level of confidence.

[3]Recall error is a special concern, since the recall period covers 26 years. However, the length of the period is compensated for, to some degree, by the fact that we are only dealing with incidents in which respondents were shot or stabbed. Since the victimization is very serious, recall error should be minimal.

[4]Weapon use was measured by asking cohort members if they had "used a weapon to threaten another person." Gang membership was measured by asking: "Were you ever a member of a gang?"

[5]In the original cohort study, race was a significant predictor of the probability of an arrest and the seriousness of a delinquent career. Blacks had a higher probability of having two or more arrests and accounted for more than four times the total amount of harm committed based on total offender rates weighted for seriousness.

[6]This is not the same coefficient of determination that one finds in the context of ordinary least squares regression analysis.

[7]Seriousness scores were transformed to their square root values. The plotted residuals indicate that the variances are stable at each level of the independent variables.

[8]One reason the effects are not statistically significant for whites is that the range of seriousness scores is more restricted for whites than for blacks. It seems more reasonable to conclude, at least tentatively, that the effects are positive than to conclude that they are zero just because they do not meet the arbitrary .05 level of significance. Future research should investigate the reasons of the apparent differences between black and white offenders.

[9]The victim experience would appear to have its greatest impact on children. According to Piaget (1965, p. 217), cooperation and mutual respect are essential ingredients in the moral development of the child. Before complex relationships and a balanced sense of justice can develop, the child needs some basis for establishing the legitimacy of various forms of social conduct.

Acknowledgments. I would like to thank Marvin Wolfgang and Lionel Lewis for comments on earlier versions of the paper. My thanks also to Colin Loftin and Kirk Williams for assistance in revisions of the final paper.

Reprints: Requests for reprints should be directed to Simon I. Singer, Department of Sociology, SUNY-Buffalo, Ellicott Complex, Buffalo, NY 14261.

Received: July 1985
Accepted: September 1985

[13]

A Reexamination of the Concept of Victim-Precipitated Homicide

KENNETH POLK

University of Melbourne

This article draws on a qualitative analysis of homicide in Victoria, Australia, to examine the concept of "victim precipitated homicide." Despite the enduring popularity of the term, there are many problems in its use for the present-day study of homicide, including the lack of adequate detail in files for the determination of the role of the victim for a large number of cases, as well as the fact that inevitably, the various actors in a homicide scene have different views of what happened, so it may be difficult to establish the facts of the case (especially given that the voice of the victim will not be present). Understanding the nature of the interactions that link victims, offenders, and bystanders in unfolding homicide scenarios may prove theoretically richer than focusing on what may be the unanswerable question of "who started it?"

For more than 30 years, the study of homicide has been influenced by the pioneering work of Marvin Wolfgang. His 1958 study of murder in Philadelphia still provides a base of useful data on homicide. Wolfgang's influence can be seen in the prominence of the relationship between victim and offender in most research since his initial study. Investigations continue to make use of concepts he suggested. Among the terms that can still be found in both research and textbooks is "victim-precipitated homicide." The purpose of the present analysis is to examine in some detail the empirical and theoretical adequacy of this term, and to suggest ways of extending and expanding the ideas that underlie the concept.

A starting point is the definition provided by Wolfgang (1958):

> The term *victim-precipitated* homicide is applied to those criminal homicides in which the victim is a direct, positive precipitator in the crime. The role of the victim is characterized by his having been

HOMICIDE STUDIES, Vol. 1 No. 2, May 1997 141-168
© 1997 Sage Publications, Inc.

the first in the homicide drama to use physical violence directed against his subsequent slayer. The victim-precipitated cases are those in which the victim was the first to show and use a deadly weapon, to strike a blow in an altercation—in short, the first to commence the interplay of resort to physical violence. (p. 252)

Explicit in this account is the image of the active victim, one whose own willingness to resort to violence has brought the lethal consequences back onto the initial perpetrator of violence. Wolfgang then goes on to provide several illustrative case examples, which typically took the form of an individual starting a fight; for example, a man striking his wife, with the husband then becoming the victim of reactive violence (i.e., homicide) by the wife.

Of the 558 homicides within the Philadelphia data, Wolfgang (1958) asserted that there was "sufficient background information to establish much about the nature of the victim-offender relationship" (p. 254), including the finding that 120, or 26%, were examples of victim-precipitated homicides. No further information was provided regarding the nature of the process of determining whether cases fell into the victim-precipitated or non-victim-precipitated categories. Later studies provided differing levels of victim precipitation in homicide. These range from 13% in a recent study in Buffalo (Sobol, 1995), 22% in 17 American cities in 1967 (Curtis, 1974a), 33% in the case studies examined by Allen (1980), and 38% in a Chicago study (Voss & Hepburn, 1968). Reviewing a number of overseas studies, Curtis (1974a, pp. 84-85) reported that levels of victim-precipitated homicide tended to be low, ranging from 0 to 20% in a number of African jurisdictions, although Polish and Slovenian data indicated that as much as half of all homicide could be viewed as victim-precipitated. Among more recent studies, an Australian finding falls in the low end of this range, with Wallace (1986, p. 68) reporting that only 10.4% of homicides in New South Wales, Australia, were precipitated by victims; a figure close to the 11.0% observed by Wikstrom (1991) in Stockholm.

One place where the term "victim precipitation" has had an indelible imprint is in discussions of homicide in criminology textbooks. A textbook writer is attempting to give a broad overview of crime and to find concepts that will capture the imagination of a student in their first exposure to the field. Victim precipitation is one of those ideas that can be counted on to jar the imagination because, to many protected undergraduates, it will pose what at first may be a counterintuitive idea (e.g., why would a person engage in behavior that would bring about his/her own death?). A selection of such text discussions of victim precipitation includes

> Wolfgang found that some of the victims of homicide were not totally innocent parties. Wolfgang used the term *victim precipitation* to describe a type of homicide in which the victim took some active role in his or her own victimization. In his Philadelphia data, Wolfgang reported that 25% of the murders were victim-precipitated in that the victim struck the first blow or was the first to use a weapon. (Meier, 1989, p. 178)

> There is growing evidence that many homicide victims precipitate their own deaths. . . . This is most likely to occur when those involved know each other and are attuned to each other's personality. Tensions and mutual aggravations may reach the point where both personalities see reconciliation only through violence. . . . In any event, the violence is to be understood as an outcome of action and responses by both parties and not merely those of the subsequent slayer. . . . Estimates of the number of victim-precipitated homicides are difficult to make, because doing so requires intimate knowledge of the interaction before the killing took place. Since one party is dead, recreation of the incident must rely on personal accounts by the killer and by any witnesses who might be available. Estimates have nevertheless been made, and these range from around 25% of homicides to upwards of 50%. (Barlow, 1984, pp. 142-143)

> One of the most important innovations in the study of homicide was Wolfgang's notion of "victim-precipitated homicide"—a term for acts of violence in which the victim initiated the fatal outburst by making the first menacing gesture or striking the first blow. Homicides often take place between persons who have been in social interaction with each other, but victim-precipitation killings involve more than prior interaction. In the victim-precipitated case, the victim induced his or her death through his or her own menacing actions. (Gibbons, 1992, pp. 257-258)

From these observations it will be seen that there is little in the way of qualification of Wolfgang's (1958) original concept. One place where the general idea of victim precipitation has taken firm root is in that branch of criminology known as victimology. Fattah (1991), as one example, has provided a vigorous defence of the general idea of victim precipitation and provides what he regards as a sharpened and more focused definition of the term, defining victim precipitation as

> A form of overt, aggressive, and provocative behavior by the victim that *triggers* the action of the criminal. It is an actualizing factor, the stimulus that elicits the violent response. . . . To establish victim-precipitation, then, is to demonstrate that had it not been for the precipitating actions of the victim, the victimization would not have occurred against that particular victim in that particular situation. (p. 295)

Fattah (1991) here is trying to narrow the term to those situations where the victim's actions were a necessary part of the event. He goes on in his analysis to talk about a wider range of ways that victims may actively engage in an interaction that becomes part of a crime:

> Certain behaviors by the victim may not attain extreme levels of precipitation but may still play a major or a minor causal role. And whereas victim-precipitation is usually (and justly) confined to conscious, deliberate, and active behavior, the functional role of the victim may be in the form of inadvertent behavior, or the failure to act (i.e., nonfeasance). In other words, acts of negligence, carelessness, recklessness, and imprudence, which create a temptation or opportunity situation or make it easier for the potential offender to commit a certain crime, are contributing factors, even though they may not fit a narrow operational definition of victim precipitation. (Fattah, 1991, p. 297)

In short, if one reads the literature of criminology, and in particular the literature on victimology, one of the enduring concepts that weaves through general writings on homicide is the idea that victims often contribute to (i.e., precipitate) their own deaths by playing an antagonistic role in the events preceding the fatal encounter. Indeed, Rasche (1993) has concluded recently that despite problems regarding the development of appropriate operational definitions, "victim precipitation has remained a vital theoretical concept in the field of homicide research" (p. 199). This idea continues to provide a focal point for homicide research, as can be seen in the work by Mann (1996) on homicide by women, the attempt to examine the relevance of victim precipitation in "homicide contests" by Savitz, Kumar and Turner (1993), or the attempt to examine the interweaving of participation and precipitation in the study of homicide in Buffalo by Sobol (1995).

Wolfgang (1993) himself has recently observed that "the term 'victim precipitation' is now deeply ingrained in the scientific literature, so I am content to retain it" (p. 170).

At the same time, it is noteworthy that the concept plays little or no role in the theoretical analysis of homicide, such as those of Daly and Wilson (1988), and that at least some writers have questioned the empirical adequacy of the data available to assess precipitation (Block, 1993a, 1993b). The extended discussion that follows suggests that it is time to reassess the concept of victim-precipitated homicide. It will be argued that many of the problems with the term hinge on difficulties in extracting the information needed, and that these problems extend even to relatively rich homicide data that are based on extensive case information. Given these problems, the view to be taken here is that it is probably not possible in most available homicide data sets to extract with any precision an indication of the level of victim precipitation. Equally important are a number of questions that can be raised about the theoretical or conceptual relevance of the term. It will be suggested that although there is value in continuing to focus on how victims and offenders actively participate in mutually reinforcing behavior that leads to lethal violence, there may be conceptual approaches that produce richer returns than are possible with victim precipitation.

DATA INFORMING THE DISCUSSION

The data for the present investigation, which is part of an ongoing investigation of homicide (Polk, 1994; Polk & Ranson, 1991), are drawn from the files of the Office of the Coroner of Victoria, Australia. These files contain a number of reports that are collected for the purpose of carrying out the coronial inquest. They include an initial police report of the incident; an autopsy report regarding the cause of death; a toxicology report, if such is relevant; a police prosecutor's brief; and the report of the inquest itself. The most helpful of these documents is the prosecutor's brief, which typically contains lengthy witness statements as well as transcripts of interviews with defendants where these have been taken.

There were a total of 384 homicides reported during the years 1985 through 1989. For each homicide, a lengthy case history was prepared, drawing on the material in the coronial files. These case studies were then subjected to a qualitative analysis of the themes that characterized the relationship between the victim and the offender. The resulting narratives can be examined to ascertain the specific role of the contribution of the victim to the events that are part of the unfolding homicide drama.

METHODOLOGICAL ISSUES IN DETERMINING VICTIM PRECIPITATION

Lack of Information

The first methodological issue that arises in reviewing homicide data is the large number of cases where the available information does not permit any analysis of the question of precipitation on the part of the victim. This is true even in the present data, despite its being considerably richer in narrative material than that available to most researchers. Lack of information is obviously an issue in those cases where what is known is simply too scanty. For example

> A woman's body was found lying in the sand. She obviously had been sun-bathing, and her death had been caused by a blow to the head. A piece of wood found nearby was identified as the weapon. No further information has come to light about the circumstances of the death. No perpetrator was identified. (Case No. 0099-86)

Any set of homicide data is likely to contain cases such as this one where beyond the fact that a death has occurred, and that it was a homicide, little else can be established. There are even instances where it is not clear that the case is a homicide, as in the Victorian files where the body of a known chronic alcoholic was found early in the morning in a large park, with the death caused by head injuries consistent with either an accident or a beating. Such cases might be homicides, perhaps ones where the individual participated actively in the circumstances that brought about his or, much less often, her death. Deaths of this nature often result from the common drunken brawl. In this instance, however, no other relevant facts could be established other than the deceased having died from head injuries. In contemporary Western cities, it virtually is assured that there will be narratives like this where little can be determined other than cause of death and the coroner is not even able to say categorically that the death was a homicide.

There are other cases where the uncertainty is caused more by the confusion inherent to many of the scenes that give rise to homicides. The following case illustrates this difficulty:

> Giles collected his pay packet one Friday night and set off on a night of drinking. At the Railway Hotel, he met up with Carl, and the two had several drinks together, being the last to leave at closing time. At some point after leaving the pub, the two apparently began an argument which led to a fight. Giles was badly beaten and kicked about the head. Carl took the remaining money from Giles's wallet and wandered off to continue drinking, leaving Giles on the sidewalk (he was found by a passer-by, and taken to a hospital where he died the next morning). When questioned later, Carl admitted that there had been a fight, but apparently as a consequence of the heavy alcohol consumption, was unable to provide any details of what provoked their confrontation. (Case No. 1121-86)

In this instance, we know that there was a fight between two males, that the fight fits the classic pattern of the pub brawl honor contest, and that these are precisely the kinds of situations where the victim may have precipitated the fight. From the available facts, however, such precipitation cannot be established, nor can it be rejected. The death of one and the drunkenness of the other, coupled with the absence of other witnesses, make it impossible to determine who began either the argument or the fatal fight. Even where data are relatively extensive concerning victim, offender, and the circumstances that brought them together (there were a number of witnesses in this case to what happened prior to the two leaving the pub), the very lack of clarity of some of the critical events will mean that the central elements of precipitation can not be determined.

This difficulty has manifested itself in a number of studies. Although Wolfgang (1958) apparently was able to state with some confidence that 26% of his cases were victim premeditated and 74% were not, most other researchers have not been so fortunate. Voss and Hepburn (1968), for example, found that they were unable to determine the degree of victim precipitation in 21% of cases. Curtis (1974b), similarly, was not able to determine the presence of victim precipitation in 44% of the cases of criminal homicide in the U.S. cities examined, whereas for various African populations reviewed in that analysis, the unknown category ranged from 3 to 77%. When the necessary information is not available in up to half or more of the files, the assertion that a given percentage of cases is victim-precipitated becomes problematic indeed.

Competing or Conflicting Accounts

A second issue has to do with the adversarial nature of the interpretation of the role of victim and offender in the homicide. This might be termed the "Rashomon" problem. In the film of that title, the story of a rape-murder is told from the viewpoint of the offender, the homicide victim (speaking through a soothsayer), the woman victim of the rape (and wife of the homicide victim), and an onlooker. Each of their stories is dramatically different (a major point of the film), because as the tale unfolds, it becomes clear that all the characters had something to hide; therefore, each had a self-interested stake in determining what the official story would be. Similarly, real homicides may involve situations where, for many different reasons, the main actors (e.g., victims, offenders, onlookers, relatives, friends) have different narratives about the event. Consider the following account:

> In the crowded disco, mixed among others attending, were representatives of two distinctive youth styles that are known as "Bogans" (basically a working class style, identifiable at the time by such clothing as tight jeans and black tee shirts) and "Head Bangers." A group of Bogan males, including Colin, became involved in an argument with a group of girls who were hanging out that night with Head Bangers. An exchange of taunts and insults occurred, which then led to one of the girls punching Colin, who punched back in return. One of the Head Bangers, Charles, then came over, tried to separate the group, and pull the girls away. Colin then called Charles a coward and a wimp, and began to throw punches at Charles. At this point, a general brawl involving members of both groups broke out. In the midst of this, Charles pulled out a knife and stabbed Colin several times in the chest, causing Colin's death. (Case No. 1931-87)

This appears to be a straightforward account and a clear example of victim precipitation; Colin threw the punches at Charles that preceded the brawl, and then was fatally wounded by Charles. As plausible as this text appears, however, it is a compilation from a number of accounts by both participants and onlookers. No sooth-sayer is available to extract Colin's account, and narratives provided by his friends would not agree on all points in the above synopsis of the events of that night. It has to be acknowledged that Charles's description of events is advantaged because Colin's version of the tale cannot be told; thus Colin is more easily labeled as the precipitator of the fatal event. What can be stated with more plausibility is that both Colin and Charles were active participants in these events, thereby supporting the underlying idea of Wolfgang's original argument that the victim and offender were engaged in mutually reinforcing behavior that resulted in the initial violence and ultimately, the death of Colin.

There are a number of accounts such as this one, especially those involving groups of males where, because of the issues of both criminal culpability and personal pride, the question of "who started the fight?" is highly contentious. Although it is often possible to describe the general outline of the case, and even to have reasonable confidence in the way in which witness and participant accounts converge, it must be underscored that these are conditional narratives. In all but a few cases, the voice of a central actor, the victim, has been removed (occasionally victims linger and can be questioned before death, but this is rare). As the Rashomon story makes clear, even onlookers may have a stake in the particular way the story comes to be told.

At issue here is what is routinely knowable. It may be possible in many of these situations to determine if the main actors in the events were engaged in some mutually defined interaction, such as the steps leading to a fight. The scene in the immediately preceding narrative had many features central to "contest of honor" (Daly & Wilson, 1988) or "confrontational homicides" (Polk, 1994). It took place in a public scene, the central actors were male, there was a social audience that provided an important and active presence in the violence, and alcohol had been consumed in the scene. In the above, it is safer to assert that Colin and Charles both were active participants in a brawl than to draw the more problematic conclusion that Colin precipitated his own death. We shall return to this point in more detail later.

150   HOMICIDE STUDIES / May 1997

Issues of Time

The third problem is one having to do with time and events that link victim and offender that extend backward beyond the time of the final exchange. Some accounts are clear in that the victim and offender have not known each other before, and the lethal violence evolves out of a single interaction that proceeds relatively quickly, for example, from argument, to fight, and then to use of a lethal weapon. It is not uncommon, however, for interactions in the final event to have their roots in earlier exchanges. As illustrated in the following case, many homicide narratives refer back to past arguments or grudges held between offender and victim.

> A feud began to develop in an outer-metropolitan suburb after a group of mainly "old Australian" young males, led by Reginald, crashed a party at the local Italian Social Club, which led to verbal exchanges, arguments and finally a fight. In the local culture, this was viewed as a clash involving "the Skips" vs. "the Wogs." After the fight, trouble simmered between the two groups until Reginald left town to spend several months in Queensland. When Reginald returned, however, he was eager to restore the row. Over the next few days, there were several verbal clashes between the groups until one night the Wog group decided to take more drastic action. A large number of them converged on a small school hall where the Skips were gathered. Outnumbered, the Skips attempted to lock the doors, but once entry was gained through an unlocked window, a general brawl developed in the hall as the Wogs poured in. In the middle of the melee, Reginald suddenly appeared with a rifle, and began firing into the attacking group, wounding several and killing Brian instantly when a bullet penetrated his heart. (Case No. 3641-86)

The problem posed by this case in determining victim precipitation is to establish when the clock starts ticking on precipitation. In the immediate sense, Brian and the rest of the Wogs precipitated the violence by converging in a mass on the school hall. But what of the earlier provocations? How does one figure in the fight at the social club that was the beginning point of this narrative, an incident that took place many weeks before, and where it was the Skips who "started it"?

Equally important, from many accounts similar to this one, it is clear only that a number of other interactions had happened previously. Allegations sometimes are made in homicide narratives about fights in the past, for which there will be little reliable information. The nature of those events, and whether they involved violence in which the victim can be said to have precipitated the events leading to the homicide, simply cannot be determined even when fairly rich data are routinely available.

THEORETICAL AND CONCEPTUAL ISSUES REGARDING VICTIM PRECIPITATION

Of at least equal importance are a number of theoretical problems that arise in the use of the concept of victim precipitation. Central to these for present purposes is the question of whether the term precipitation, and the behavior to which it refers, provides the most useful guide to the study of interaction between victims, offenders, and (an often important feature) a social audience in situations of homicides. Assuming the importance of a close examination of victim-offender interaction for the study of homicide, are there better ways of addressing this interaction that may provide more theoretically complex and satisfying information than does a focus on precipitation?

Polk (1994) has carried out a qualitative analysis of a large number of homicides and has advanced the proposition that much of contemporary homicide can be described as falling within four masculine themes (alternatively, scenarios) of violence. One possible way of assessing the contribution of the term precipitation is to examine how the term fits within the four scenarios of masculine violence.

Sexual Intimacy

The first of the scenarios identified by Polk (1994) was that concerning the use of exceptional violence by males as a means of control in situations of sexual intimacy. Much of the homicide that is described in this scenario is emphatically not victim-precipitated homicide. In the Victorian data, there were no cases where, when males killed their female sexual partner, the woman had precipitated the homicide by her being the first to use violence (a few such cases, however, are reported in Philadelphia by Wolfgang, 1958). The situation is dramatically different, however, when the focus shifts to women who kill their sexual partners. Such cases are much less common in the Australian data, there being at least four cases where men kill their female sexual partners for every one case where a woman kills a male partner. This is somewhat different than in the United States, where in some cities the proportions can be about equal (see Daly & Wilson, 1988).

The Victorian data show that when women kill their sexual partners, in roughly 8 out of 10 cases, they are doing so in direct response to prior masculine violence. In some of these cases, the male can be seen as directly precipitating his death, as in one case where a recently separated husband forced his way into his wife's house, threatened her with a knife, and used the knife to force her to engage in sexual acts with him. The events ended when the woman was able to gain control of the knife and stabbed the male, causing fatal injuries. In this case, there is no question that the homicide was directly and immediately triggered by the initial use of violence by the victim of the homicide.

Also found in these homicide files, however, are those cases where the woman has been routinely terrified by the male, but in taking counter measures she calculates that because of the overwhelming physical strength of the male, she must somehow wait or organize propitious circumstances to engage in counter-violence. In one such case, a prostitute became progressively frightened and angry by the increasing and dangerous use of violence against her by her pimp. She sought help from another prostitute and two male companions, who together accosted the violent male when he was sleeping and beat him to death. Although in both of these cases, it is the violence of the male that provokes the woman to kill her partner, the legal and theoretical status of these two are different. Because in cases like the second one, where the woman has planned the homicide, she will be vulnerable to a criminal charge of murder because the act was clearly intentional. Also, whereas in the first case the woman was found to have engaged in legitimate self-defence (i.e., the homicide was justified in a legal sense), the woman in the second case was convicted of murder and sentenced to a term in prison.[1]

Turning now to an examination of the concept of victim precipitation, it is clear that there are important differences within this scenario that have to do with whether prior violence triggers the homicide. One of the first observations is that the killing by men of their women partners (or, incidentally, the killing of men's sexual rivals) occurs without prior violence on the part of the victim. That is, an understanding of such events means that we must look elsewhere than victim precipitation for an explanation of the violence. When women kill their male partners, on the other hand, in a large proportion of the cases it is precisely the prior violence of the male that sets the stage for the lethal violence that follows. At the same time, there is a continuum of such circumstances, ranging from highly spontaneous, defensive acts (which are likely to be treated as legitimate self-defence by the criminal justice authorities) to calculated, premeditated acts at the other extreme (which may attract the harshest penalties available in law). Although a common thread to these diverse events is something that is contained in the concept of victim precipitation, is the one term itself theoretically adequate?

In a recent discussion, even Wolfgang (1993) recognizes that it may be useful to separate out from victimization the legal concept of provocation, which concerns specific legal grounds whereby the circumstances surrounding a criminal homicide may lessen the degree of culpability for the killing. Although the males in the present narratives precipitated the violence that led to their deaths, there are important internal variations within this scenario that may remain hidden if the analysis fails to penetrate deeper than examining simply the question "who started it?"

Masculine Honor Contests

Rather different results are obtained when we examine the other three masculine scenarios of violence suggested by Polk (1994). A feature of these three is that, unlike the first scenario, they are predominately male-on-male events. The most common of these is what might be termed the masculine honor contest (Polk also used the term "confrontational homicide"), where males come together in a public scene. Typically, these are settings where groups of young males, mostly single and working class, are engaged in leisure activities. These activities often involve drinking at pubs, discos, parties, BBQs, or perhaps in streets or transport locations used in going to, or coming from, another leisure setting. Typically, some form of social friction occurs between individuals within this setting, that friction resulting from an insult, a push, comments toward a woman companion, or perhaps even provocative looks. The presence of a social audience that provides a backdrop for the drama to be acted out by a victim and offender is central, because it is the audience that raises the stakes in the honor game. Words are exchanged, a challenge to combat is laid down, and a fight results that, in turn, leads to a lethal outcome. In these honor contests, the initial intent is not to kill, and the murder commonly emerges spontaneously; in contrast, many cases where men kill their female sexual partners involve a homicide that is planned and the offender has an overt intent of physically destroying his victim.

In the honor contest scenario, there is active participation by individuals who play out the roles of offender, victim, and social audience. Still, the issue of precipitation is complicated. Take the following case example:

> Fred (born in Turkey) was drinking in a well known "blood house" (a pub with a reputation for violence) when Dennis and a group of his friends came in. It was not long before one of the friends of Dennis caught Fred's eye, and the two began "eyeing each other off." The friend turned to Dennis and made a comment to the effect that Fred was an "arsehole Turk" and "sleazy." Fred then came over to the friend and said, "What are you staring at?" Another of the group attempted to break off the argument, whereupon Fred told him to "fuckin' keep out of it." In reply, the friend said, "well, then fuckin' cop this" and punched Fred in the head. In a short time, a major brawl had broken out. As this escalated, Fred pulled out a knife, first slashing his opponent in the staring contest across the stomach. Surrounded by a group of angry males, Fred sought shelter behind the bar. Dennis reached over the bar to try to pull Fred out and was stabbed in the chest. One of Dennis's friends, known as "Dogsbody," then beat Fred over the head several times with a pool cue, but Fred twisted away, stabbing his attacker as he did so. This further enraged the group and one was heard to shout "Let's kill him, he's stabbed Dogsbody, let's kill him." Fred sought shelter in a small room of the bar where the publican (innkeeper) was standing counting his money, locking the door behind him, pleading "don't let them get me, they're going to kill me." In a couple of minutes, the group managed to kick the door in, whereupon Fred held his knife to the throat of the publican, threatening to kill him if they advanced any closer. The group then started throwing bottles at Fred, enabling the publican to break loose. Fortunately for Fred, at this moment the police arrived and broke up the fight. When the confusion cleared, Dennis was found on the floor dead as a result of his stab wounds. (Case No 3631-87)

In any body of homicide data, there are likely to be many stories such as these. The initial provocations consisted of what would appear to be trivial forms of eye contact. It is the aggressive character of that eye contact, however, and probably other non-verbal cues that have to do with posture and bearing, that were the triggering events. The action quickly shifted from the individual making the eye contact to another person altogether who punched Fred (the first apparent violent act in this encounter). The brawl then widened; others, initially part of the social audience, became involved in violence directed toward Fred, Dogsbody received a knife wound, then Dennis was fatally stabbed.

In this account, how important, or even relevant, is it to ask who precipitated this violence? One can sort through the various accounts and come to some agreement among the witnesses that it was after an onlooker attempted to intercede, but was rebuffed in a challenging way, that the first blow was struck by the onlooker whose role in the violence does not appear centrally after that act. Thus, in a technical sense, this would be considered as a non-victim-precipitated homicide.

But, is not this scenario best understood as being composed of the complex and mutually reinforcing behaviors that make up masculine honor contests? Reciprocally challenging eye contact was the immediate precursor to the verbal exchange that, in turn, led to the physical exchange. This exchange would seem to be as important to the telling of the story as would be the specific fact of who hit whom first.

Consider, for example, the role of Dennis. In one sense, he was neither the original offender nor the original victim, because both the eyeing off contest and the first blows involved others in the role of initiator and responder to the escalating interaction. Yet Dennis was an important part of the scene, at a certain point becoming a participant in the violence, and ultimately a victim of that violence. Using technical operational rules, Dennis's death would be classified with reasonable reliability as a non-victim-precipitated homicide. However, is this information useful in a theoretical sense? To what extent does that attempt at classification in any way capture the nature of the complex dynamics that were played out in the pub? For example, how would the interpretative meaning be affected if, rather than Dennis, it had been the friend who struck the first blow who was killed? Unquestionably, it would then be a victim-precipitated homicide, but that classification would hardly change the sense of what happened.

What distinguishes this homicide case for theoretical purposes is that it represents a classic example of the masculine honor contest. The events fit the form of conflict that Daly and Wilson (1988) refer to as an "escalated showing-off contest" involving unrelated males who are "trying to best one another before an audience of mutual acquaintances" (p. 176), or what Polk (1994) refers to as a "confrontational homicide." The central issue is the threat to the honor of a male and the public defense of that honor with violence. The violence is likely to involve complex interactions between offender, victim, and a social audience; and certainly the person who becomes the victim in most circumstances has been an active participant in the evolving events.

It is an inevitable quality of many such masculine honor contests that the roles of victim and offender become confused, especially where many individuals are involved as the violence unfolds. It may be, in fact, that the original protagonists, those who started it, may not appear as either victim or offender in the final steps of the homicide drama. It is common that individuals who are originally part of the audience of mutual acquaintances become swept up in the violence; often, it is they who become the ultimate victim and offender of the homicide as described in typical police files.

There are some events involving masculine honor contests in which the victim is a totally innocent bystander to the precipitating events. In one case, for example, an argument broke out in a parking lot between two teenagers and two young adult males. Both groups climbed into their cars and continued the dispute by engaging in a combination race and chase. The car being driven by the teenagers swerved at one point, went out of control, and killed a total stranger who just happened to be walking along the road. In another case, a single male had been drinking heavily in a pub, and as he became progressively more drunk, he became more of a nuisance to the female patrons. Finally, a bouncer intervened, an argument erupted between the male and the bouncer, and the male was ejected from the pub. Enraged, the male went to his van, and to get even began to drive at great speed in circles in the parking lot of the pub, swerving in a threatening manner toward patrons as they left the pub. On one of his passes, as he swerved, a piece of metal tubing flew off and struck a male patron who was coming out of the door of the pub, killing him. In this case, the victim was an innocent bystander to the central events of this narrative, which involved the prior conflicts in the pub between the offender, patrons, and the bouncer. The events emerged out of the escalated rancor between the male and the bouncer, and the victim neither precipitated nor participated (as far as can be determined) in any of the interaction until he had the misfortune to step out of the door of the pub at the wrong moment.

What this case demonstrates is that whereas victims may in some fashion participate in many of the masculine honor contest homicides, the events can be behaviorally complex, so much so that the victim may enter late, even accidentally, into the scenario. The defining events concern the focal challenges and responses to threats to masculine honor, and it is these that are of theoretical interest. To be sure, one may wish to explore in more precise detail how it is that both offenders and victims become caught up in these potentially life threatening contests. There is evidence from studies of pub violence, for example, that aggressive males may choose opponents to fight who are smaller, more drunk, and weaker (Tomsen, Homel, & Thommeny, 1991).

The previous pub narrative, where Dennis was the victim, also shows in theoretical terms how artificial the question of "who started it?" may be. The actual precipitating events involved nonverbal behavior in the form of challenging eye contact. This led to verbal exchanges between two males. The violence started, however, when one of these men was hit by a third male, after the verbal and unknowable other nonverbal challenges had shifted to take in that third party. If an attempt is made to begin the account by identifying the point at which actual violence began, then important information would be lost about the nature of this complex story and many like it. Certainly, little of this would be knowable from the simple classification of this as a non-victim-precipitated homicide, however correct such a classification might be.

Of course, it must be acknowledged that in some of the honor contest homicides, there exists the precise conditions that define the concept of victim precipitation. The following narrative exemplifies such a case.

> Gregor and his friend Ned had been doing the rounds of pubs one night. When Gregor was walking back to the bar from the toilet, there was an exchange with a woman (who was also feeling the effects of drink) that led to an argument, which widened when the woman's young friend Arthur came over to intervene on her behalf. The heated argument attracted the attention of the bouncer, who ejected Gregor. Ned came out a few minutes later to find Gregor fuming because he had been called a "wog." Gregor then went home and fetched a shot gun, which he brought back to the scene despite the pleas of both his wife and his friend (it was, he said, something he simply had to do). Gregor confronted Arthur when he came out of the pub, insisting that he apologize. In a moment when his attention was diverted, Arthur grabbed the shotgun and fired it at Gregor, killing him instantly. (Case No. 2069-86)

Using standard coding rules, this case, and others like it, would be considered a good example of victim-precipitated homicide. Such a classification would be accurate and reliable. However, bearing in mind that the intent of the exercise is to understand the nature of what happens between victims and offenders, is it meaningful to have a classification system where the previous honor contests are put in one category and this one in another? We are not questioning here the importance of knowing how victims and offenders act and react to each other as the violence unfolds. However, the active participation of offender, victim, and social audience are essential features of this violence and it is an understanding of their patterns of participation, rather than precipitation, that best captures the collaborative acts resulting in honor contest homicides.

Homicides Committed During the Course of Another Crime

The third and fourth of the masculine scenarios suggested by Polk (1994) are quite different in character. One involves situations where the homicide can be viewed as originating in the course of other crimes. These events involve mostly males who are highly marginal and most often are enmeshed in a long history of criminal behavior. They have reached the point where they are willing to consider the taking of exceptional risks with their lives and the lives of others as they engage in such acts as armed robbery, armed burglary, or sexual assault where a weapon is used. As was the case with homicides where men kill their sexual partners, in most cases where homicide results during the course of another crime, victim precipitation is not an issue, because the ultimate victim of the homicide was the initial victim of the original predatory crime, and thus such victims can be called "double victims." In some cases, however, the risks are turned back on the perpetrator and the original offender becomes a "reverse victim." Such reverse victimization, of course, represents another variety of victim precipitation, although certainly very different in character to that observed in the cases cited above.

Homicide as Dispute Resolution

The final of the four scenarios suggested by Polk (1994) consists of those situations where violence is chosen by males as an intentional method for resolving what is, in most instances, a long-simmering dispute. This theme, like the previous one, tends to be limited to individuals caught in a world of criminality that by its very nature seals off its participants from conventional procedures for settling personal disputes (e.g., the courts, arbitration, use of attorneys as go-betweens). Further, the individuals tend to know each other well because the nature of this scenario hinges on some conflict between the parties extending through time. Here, as is the case with armed robbery, plans and reality may not correspond, and any planned action may be turned back on the one who first engaged in the violence. This happened in a case where a group of individuals decided to punish one of their group whom they suspected of stealing from its members. He was taken for a ride in the country where the others planned to give him beating. During the course of the journey, they started to punch the alleged thief, but when they arrived at their destination in the bush, the would-be victim pulled a knife, stabbed to death the leader of his attackers, then escaped by running into the scrub. In this case, the facts are densely enough packed in time so that the elements of precipitation are clear. In many other cases, however, the simmering disputes involve earlier use of violence, so that it becomes difficult to establish with any certainty who started it. The dispute can fester over considerable time, and the central protagonists may have engaged in a number of mutually provocative and violent acts over a long period. Thus, whereas they are both active participants in the dispute, it is difficult to establish with any certainty when the violence started and/or who was the first to use violence.

Looking across all four of these scenarios, it is clear that contexts can be defined where violent actions on the part of the victim are often an important part of the interactions that result in homicide. Thus there is verification of Wolfgang's (1958) original notion that the active role of the victim is an important aspect of some lethal encounters. Furthermore, these homicides stand in contrast to others where the role of the victim is qualitatively different, as in the cases where depressed and often elderly husbands decide to end not only their own lives, but their wives' as well, where a child is killed in the first hours of life, or where a mass murderer shoots at random to claim his victims (examples of all of these are found in the Victorian data). In some homicides, the victim's role is passive; in others, the actions of the victim are an important part of the homicide drama, including being the person who initiates the violence. At issue, then, is how this dimension of activity-passivity is best captured empirically and theoretically.

RECONCEPTUALIZING VICTIM PRECIPITATION

In the foregoing discussion, two distinct sets of issues have dominated concerns regarding the concept of victim precipitation. The first set relates to the concept's reliability and concerns attempts to operationalize the term victim precipitation. These issues have been raised in previous research. In a methodological note in one of the reports of the long-running study of homicide in Chicago, it was commented that

> In the Chicago Homicide Study, we made an intensive effort for a number of years (1965 to 1978) to collect data on victim precipitation of homicides, but our coder reliability was such that we ultimately dropped the variable (still retaining, however, variables capturing victim participation, revenge motives, etc.). Given that one of the key sources of information about "who started it" is dead, and given the difficulty of differentiating between precipitation of the specific event versus retaliation or revenge from an earlier incident, we question whether the concept of victim precipitation is measurable or even definable. (Block, 1993a, p. 329)

In another discussion, Block (1993b) has pointed out similar empirical problems that plague researchers attempting to obtain valid data on victim precipitation. These include the absence of the victim's interpretative account, that in rapidly evolving events precise determination of time sequences may be impossible to obtain, and that the time order of a given event may be confounded when there are a succession of events central to a particular scene. Similar observations about victim precipitation in violent confrontations have been made by Felson and Steadman (1983), who, in their research, found that they were unable to identify with any regularity the specific person who precipitated the violent event. In sum, the research evidence suggests that given the host of problems that arise in attempts to operationalize the term victim precipitation, its reliability is unacceptably low. Thus the ability to state with confidence that there is any given percentage of victim precipitated homicides within a set of homicide data has to be questioned.

A second issue is theoretical in nature and concerns the crucial necessity of retaining the essence of precipitation—that in some circumstances, the victim may in one way or another play an active role in the violence. Indeed, in some cases, the victim is the individual who overtly pushes the interaction in a direction that results in the violent outcome.

One way of preserving that kernel of information is to attempt to redefine and refocus the term. In an early review of victim precipitation, Silverman (1973) found a number of problems with the concept. These included difficulties of reliability in the operational definitions employed in different studies; situational problems whereby the victims' words or behavior intend no offence, but are misinterpreted as antagonistic by offenders; the fact that what is deemed to be a provocation in one setting may not be in another setting (e.g., small towns vs. metropolitan communities); and the use by immigrants of what are to them routine, nonthreatening gestures or words, but that in their new culture, precipitate a violent act by some offender.

Despite these problems, Silverman's (1973) review led him to advocate that the term be refocused rather than discarded. Thus he proposed a new definition of victim precipitation, one that included crimes such as rape and burglary as well as homicide. According to Silverman,

> Victim precipitation occurs when the offender's action in commit-
> ting or beginning to commit a crime is initiated after and directly
> related to, an action (be it physical or verbal, conscious or uncon-
> scious) on the part of the victim. The offender perceives the victims
> [sic] behavior as a facilitating action (including temptation, invita-
> tion) to the commission of the crime. The action of the victim might
> be said to have triggered the offender's behavior. (1973, p. 107)

Unfortunately, at least in terms of the present discussion, the
suggested redefinition has, if anything, more difficulties than
Wolfgang's (1958) original conceptualization. It still presumes that
such a distinction can be made from data where detailed information simply is not available in many cases, it makes assumptions
about narratives and the timing of events that are highly questionable, and it focuses on a feature of the event (i.e., the assumed
precipitating acts of a victim) that may be at best only marginally
relevant to a theoretical understanding of the ongoing homicide
scenario.

In fact, Silverman's (1973) definition could lead to what would
appear to be unhelpful conclusions. For example, does the process
of being born involve action on the part of the newborn that
precipitates the resulting neonaticide? If a robbery victim stutters
and stammers in response to questioning, has he precipitated his
being shot by an overly aggressive, anxious robber? When a
young child repeatedly sticks its tongue out at the drunken step-
father, does he precipitate the beating that takes his life? When,
after years of a brutal and violent marriage, the wife leaves, does
she precipitate the offender to kill her because "if he can't have
her, no one else will"? In each of these cases, given the broad
definition, the offender would perceive the behavior of the victim
"as a facilitating action . . . to the commission of the crime." It is
unlikely, though, that such interpretations will contribute to a
theoretical understanding of violence.

THE PERSPECTIVE OF VICTIM PARTICIPATION

The essence of what has been argued in this article is that there
are both empirical and theoretical grounds for a refocusing of the
concept of victim precipitation to victim participation. At a prac-

tical level, there are simply too many cases where the data are not available, where the inherently competing accounts make it difficult to assess accurately the specific question of "who started it," or where the data suggest that the events between victim and offender are deeply imbedded in a time sequence too complex to be unraveled with typical homicide files, even those relatively rich with information.

More important, from a theoretical perspective, the precipitation question is likely to be secondary to understanding the dynamics of a scenario within which the violence occurs. Although there are some scenes in which the victim plays an important participatory role in the violence, the nature of that participation is better comprehended by a careful description of the central elements of the ongoing scenario that links victim, offender, and social audience.

Such an analysis in no way diminishes the theoretical significance of the active, participatory role of the victim in some scenarios of violence. Consequently, the present comments are supportive of the overall intent of Wolfgang (1958) (and before him, von Hentig, 1948) in their emphasis on the mutually reinforcing actions that can exist between victims and offenders. In the concluding section of *Patterns in Criminal Homicide* (1958), Wolfgang observed that

> In many cases, the victim has most of the major characteristics of an offender; in some cases, two offenders come together in a homicide situation and it is probably only chance that results in one becoming a victim and the other an offender. At any rate, connotations of a victim as a weak and passive individual, seeking to withdraw from an assaultive situation, and of an offender as a brutal, strong, and overly aggressive person seeking out his victim, are not always correct. (p. 265)

Acknowledged here is the obvious fact that in some cases, a homicide involves much more than simply overt aggression on the part of an offender. Similarly, in a recent statement regarding victim precipitation, Silverman and Kennedy (1993) noted

> The conceptualizations of violent episodes as victim-precipitated or situational transactions all suggest that it is useful to view such episodes as more than a product of the will or motivation of the violent offender. They imply the need to understand violent crime,

in general, and homicide, in particular, as an outcome of a dynamic interplay between offenders and victims. The archetype of this kind of homicide is the barroom brawl. (p. 92)

In the intervening years since Wolfgang's (1958) original investigation, much has been learned from the analysis of victim/ offender interactions. For example, as more recent empirical analysis suggests, it may be useful in homicide studies to note the degree to which the victim participated in the events leading to the homicide (Block, 1993a, 1993b; Block & Block, 1991; Sobol, 1995; Wilbanks, 1984). There are many situations where it may not be possible to determine with an acceptable level of reliability who actually initiated the violence in an exchange. However, establishing that a group of individuals were active participants in the violence is much more likely to be discerned with some accuracy.

BEYOND VICTIM PARTICIPATION

Even this shifting of the focus to participation is not by itself completely satisfactory. In the Chicago study, for example, the code book distinguishes between participation as a result of committing a crime, of revenge for an earlier predatory crime, or in retaliation for an earlier confrontation (Block, 1993b, p. 186). In another context, Block and Block (1991) use the Chicago data to distinguish between expressive violence, which typically begins as an interpersonal confrontation, and instrumental violence, which begins as a predatory attack. From that distinction, they develop a cluster of homicide syndromes that provide one possible avenue for exploring patterns of victim/offender relationships. For some purposes, especially when focusing on patterns of instrumental homicide such as killings in the course of such crimes as robbery or burglary, researchers may find the multiple categories and close attention to reliability suggested by the Blocks a more satisfying way of approaching the issue of victim participation than the approach suggested in the foregoing discussion. On the other hand, the lack of gendered content, as well as the lumping together of diverse lethal encounters (e.g., husband/ wife, honor contest killings) in a common category of expressive homicide represents an approach that may prove problematic for other researchers.

Ultimately, the call here is for a theoretical focus on the dimension of participation. There is a common element of active involvement across all four of the masculine scenarios discussed earlier that represents the dynamic identified by Wolfgang (1958) as "victim precipitation." Within these four situations, however, there would appear to be rather important differences in the quality of that active involvement. The pattern of sustained violence by males toward their female partners, which at times produces lethal counterviolence by the women, contains elements that are in some ways quite different than the interactional dynamics found in the typical honor contest. Similarly, the exceptional risk taking involved in committing an armed robbery or attempting to resolve a dispute with violence, originates in different interpersonal dynamics and involves quite different characters than does either spousal violence or honor contest homicides. Although one could say that a common feature of all of these is victim precipitation, the present argument is that much would be lost if only that term is employed.

Within the scenarios examined here, the victim and actor are to some degree mutually participating in a set of activities that ultimately lead to the death of the victim. Put bluntly, the victim is clearly more than just an innocent bystander; instead, there has been action involving violence on the part of the victim that is a feature of the interactional dynamics that contributed to the lethal violence. What is of primary theoretical interest, though, is not the question of the identity of the precipitator, but the nature of the mutually reinforcing actions taken by the parties involved that result in the violence. In conceptual terms, it is the content of the scenario that needs to be addressed, especially the active roles played by all participants—the offender, the social audience, and, of course, the victim. Thus the intent of this discussion has been to advocate that it is the wider social pattern within which victim precipitation and participation occurs that is of major theoretical interest in understanding the evolution of most incidents of lethal violence.

CROSS-NATIONAL CAVEATS

In some respects, the fact that these data derive from a cultural setting different than that described by Wolfgang (1958) reinforces more strongly the importance of his assertion that a primary focus of homicide research should be on the interaction between victims and offenders. To be sure, some differences should be expected when one compares these Australian data with those of other countries. For example, important variations should be expected when these patterns are contrasted with those in the United States. In the United States, there will be a role for gang homicide that is rarely apparent in Australia, although there are killings in both countries that involve loose collectives of young males who become involved in honor contests. The role of drugs in the United States would probably alter the scenario patterns of both conflict resolution homicides and homicides committed in the course of other crimes (although a few drug-related homicides are found in both of these homicide patterns in Australia).

In general, however, the content of the four masculine scenarios discussed here are quite compatible with descriptions of general homicide patterns found in most other countries and in other qualitative studies of homicide (e.g., Lundsgaarde, 1977), although some variation in other cultural contexts is to be expected in terms of the relative frequencies of these scenarios.

CONCLUDING OBSERVATIONS

The intent of the present discussion ultimately is to support the essential proposition of Wolfgang (1958) that a central element in the study of homicide should be the interactions that occur between victims and offenders. However, it is now possible to expand on that initial insight by moving on to identify distinctive scenarios of violence, most of which evolve around the playing out of themes of aggressive masculinity. Within these scenarios, theoretical attention is appropriately focused on the issue of the participation of victim, offender, and the social audience in the steps that lead to the homicide.

An especially fruitful line of further inquiry might be focused on the masculine character of these patterns of violence. Works by Daly and Wilson (1988), Dobash and Dobash (1992), or Newburn and Stanko (1994) are beginning to probe into the theoretical terrain that will help expand our understandings about the themes that describe such violence. The weight of current theoretical work would suggest that more will be gained by understanding the specific contexts within which forms of masculine violence are played out rather than focusing on the specific issue of precipitation by the victim.

NOTE

1. Most women in the Victorian sample, if they were convicted, were convicted of manslaughter, and only a handful of women were sentenced to prison.

REFERENCES

Allen, N. H. (1980). *Homicide: Perspectives on prevention.* New York: Human Sciences Press.

Barlow, H. D. (1984). *Introduction to criminology.* Boston: Little, Brown.

Block, C. R. (1993a). Lethal violence in the Chicago Latino community. In A. V. Wilson (Ed.), *Homicide: The victim/offender connection* (pp. 267-342). Cincinnati, OH: Anderson.

Block, C. R. (1993b). The meaning and measurement of victim precipitation. In C. R. Block & R. L. Block (Eds.), *Questions and answers in lethal and nonlethal violence* (pp. 185-194). Washington, DC: National Institute of Justice.

Block, C. R., & Block, R. (1991). Beginning with Wolfgang: An agenda for homicide research. *Journal of Crime and Justice, 14,* 31-70.

Curtis, L. A. (1974a). *Criminal violence: National patterns and behavior.* Lexington, MA: D. C. Heath.

Curtis, L. A. (1974b). Victim precipitation and violent crime. *Social Problems, 21,* 594-605.

Daly, M., & Wilson, M. (1988). *Homicide.* New York: de Gruyter.

Dobash, R. E., & Dobash, R. P. (1992). *Women, violence, and social change.* New York: Routledge.

Fattah, E. A. (1991). *Understanding criminal victimization: An introduction to theoretical victimology.* Englewood Cliffs, NJ: Prentice Hall.

Felson, R., & Steadman, H. (1983). Situational factors in disputes leading to criminal violence. *Criminology, 21,* 59-74.

Gibbons, D. (1992). *Society, crime, and criminal behavior.* Englewood Cliffs, NJ: Prentice Hall.

Lundsgaarde, H. P. (1977). *Murder in space city.* New York: Oxford University Press.

Mann, C. R. (1996). *When women kill.* Albany: State University of New York Press.

Meier, R. F. (1989). *Crime and society.* Boston: Allyn & Bacon.

Newburn, T., & Stanko, E. A. (1994). *Just boys doing business: Men, masculinities, and crime.* London: Routledge.

Polk, K. (1994). *When men kill: Scenarios of masculine violence.* Melbourne: Cambridge University Press.

Polk, K., & Ranson, D. (1991). Patterns of homicide in Victoria. In D. Chappell, P. Grabosky, & H. Strang (Eds.), *Australian violence: Contemporary perspectives* (pp. 53-118). Canberra: Australian Institute of Criminology.

Rasche, C. E. (1993). Victim precipitation and social policy: Clemency for battered women who kill. In C. R. Block & R. L. Block (Eds.), *Questions and answers in lethal and nonlethal violence* (pp. 199-204). Washington, DC: National Institute of Justice.

Savitz, L. D., Kumar, K. S., & Turner, S. H. (1993). Victim-precipitated killings and "homicide contests." In C. R. Block & R. L. Block (Eds.), *Questions and answers in lethal and nonlethal violence* (pp. 195-198). Washington, DC: National Institute of Justice.

Silverman, R. A. (1973). Victim precipitation: An examination of the concept. In I. Drapkin & E. Viano (Eds.), *Victimology: A new focus* (pp. 99-109). Lexington, MA: D. C. Heath.

Silverman, R. A., & Kennedy, L. (1993). *Deadly deeds: Murder in Canada.* Scarborough, Ontario: Nelson Canada.

Sobol, J. J. (1995, November). *Victim characteristics and behavioral attributes in criminal homicide: A case study in Buffalo, 1992-1993.* Paper presented at the annual meeting of the American Society of Criminology, Boston.

Tomsen, S., Homel, R., & Thommeny, J. (1991). The causes of public violence: Situational and other factors. In D. Chappell, P. Grabosky, & H. Strang (Eds.), *Australian violence: Contemporary perspectives* (pp. 177-194). Canberra: Australian Institute of Criminology.

von Hentig, H. (1948). *The criminal and his victim.* New Haven, CT: Yale University Press.

Voss, H., & Hepburn, J. (1968). Patterns in criminal homicide in Chicago. *Journal of Criminal Law, Criminology, and Police Science, 59,* 499-508.

Wallace, A. (1986). *Homicide: The social reality.* Sydney: Bureau of Research and Criminal Statistics of New South Wales.

Wikstrom, P. H. (1991). Cross-national comparisons and context specific trends in criminal homicide. *Journal of Crime & Justice, 14,* 71-96.

Wilbanks, W. (1984). *Murder in Miami: An analysis of homicide patterns and trends in Dade County (Miami) Florida, 1917-1983.* Lanham, MD: University Press of America.

Wolfgang, M. (1958). *Patterns in criminal homicide.* Philadelphia: University of Pennsylvania Press.

Wolfgang, M. (1993). Victim precipitation in victimology and in law. In C. R. Block & R. L. Block (Eds), *Questions and answers in lethal and nonlethal violence* (pp. 167-184). Washington, DC: National Institute of Justice.

Kenneth Polk *is a reader in criminology in the criminology department at the University of Melbourne. He received his M.A. at Northwestern University and his Ph.D. at the University of California, Los Angeles. He went to Australia in 1985 after serving for many years as a professor of sociology at the University of Oregon. Dr. Polk's books include* When Men Kill: Scenarios of Masculine Violence *(Cambridge University Press, 1994),* Schools and Delinquency *(with W. Schafer; Prentice Hall, 1972), and* Scouting the War on Poverty *(D. C. Heath, 1972). With funding from the Criminology Research Council of Australia, he is currently completing a large study of children as victims of homicide.*

[14]

GENDER AND VICTIMIZATION RISK AMONG YOUNG WOMEN IN GANGS

JODY MILLER

Research has documented the enhancement effects of gang involvement for criminal offending, but little attention has been given to victimization. This article examines how gang involvement shapes young women's risks of victimization. Based on interviews with active gang members, the author suggests that (1) gang participation exposes youths to victimization risk and (2) it does so in gendered ways. Young women can use gender to decrease their risk of being harmed by rival gangs or other street participants by not participating in "masculine" activities such as fighting and committing crime. However, the consequence is that they are viewed as lesser members of their gangs and may be exposed to greater risk of victimization within their gangs. The author suggests that more research is needed to examine whether and how gang involvement enhances youths' exposure to victimization risk, and that researchers should maintain a recognition of the role of gender in shaping these processes.

An underdeveloped area in the gang literature is the relationship between gang participation and victimization risk. There are notable reasons to consider the issue significant. We now have strong evidence that delinquent lifestyles are associated with increased risk of victimization (Lauritsen, Sampson, and Laub 1991). Gangs are social groups that are organized around delinquency (see Klein 1995), and participation in gangs has been shown to escalate youths' involvement in crime, including violent crime (Esbensen and Huizinga 1993; Esbensen, Huizinga, and Weiher 1993; Fagan 1989, 1990; Thornberry et al. 1993). Moreover, research on gang violence indicates that the primary targets of this violence are other gang members (Block and Block 1993; Decker 1996; Klein and Maxson 1989; Sanders 1993). As such, gang

An earlier version of this article was presented as a paper at the 1997 National Research and Evaluation Conference, Washington, DC. Thanks to David Curry, Kathy Daly, Scott Decker, Janet Lauritsen, Cheryl Maxson, Richard Wright, and anonymous *Journal of Research in Crime and Delinquency* reviewers for constructive remarks on earlier versions of this article. This work was supported by a grant from the National Institute of Justice (grant 951642394). Opinions expressed are those of the author and do not necessarily reflect those of the funding agency.

JOURNAL OF RESEARCH IN CRIME AND DELINQUENCY, Vol. 35 No. 4, November 1998 429-453
© 1998 Sage Publications, Inc.

430 JOURNAL OF RESEARCH IN CRIME AND DELINQUENCY

participation can be recognized as a delinquent lifestyle that is likely to involve high risks of victimization (see Huff 1996:97). Although research on female gang involvement has expanded in recent years and includes the examination of issues such as violence and victimization, the oversight regarding the relationship between gang participation and violent victimization extends to this work as well.

The coalescence of attention to the proliferation of gangs and gang violence (Block and Block 1993; Curry, Ball, and Decker 1996; Decker 1996; Klein 1995; Klein and Maxson 1989; Sanders 1993), and a possible disproportionate rise in female participation in violent crimes more generally (Baskin, Sommers, and Fagan 1993; but see Chesney-Lind, Shelden, and Joe 1996), has led to a specific concern with examining female gang members' violent activities. As a result, some recent research on girls in gangs has examined these young women's participation in violence and other crimes as offenders (Bjerregaard and Smith 1993; Brotherton 1996; Fagan 1990; Lauderback, Hansen, and Waldorf 1992; Taylor, 1993). However, an additional question worth investigation is what relationships exist between young women's gang involvement and their experiences and risk of victimization. Based on in-depth interviews with female gang members, this article examines the ways in which gender shapes victimization risk within street gangs.

GENDER, VIOLENCE, AND VICTIMIZATION

Feminist scholars have played a significant role in bringing attention to the overlapping nature of women's criminal offending and patterns of victimization, emphasizing the relationships of gender inequality and sexual exploitation to women's participation in crime (Arnold 1990; Campbell 1984; Chesney-Lind and Rodriguez 1983; Daly 1992; Gilfus 1992). In regard to female gang involvement, recent research suggests that young women in gangs have disproportionate histories of victimization before gang involvement as compared with nongang females (Miller 1996) and gang males (Joe and Chesney-Lind 1995; Moore 1991). Moreover, there is evidence that young women turn to gangs, in part, as a means of protecting themselves from violence and other problems in their families and from mistreatment at the hands of men in their lives (Joe and Chesney-Lind 1995; Lauderback et al. 1992).

This is not surprising, given the social contexts these young women face. Many young women in gangs are living in impoverished urban "underclass" communities where violence is both extensive and a "sanctioned response to

[the] oppressive material conditions" associated with inequality, segregation, and isolation (Simpson 1991:129; see also Sampson and Wilson 1995; Wilson 1996). Moreover, violence against *women* is heightened by the nature of the urban street world, where gendered power relations are played out (Connell 1987), crack markets have intensified the degradation of women (Bourgois and Dunlap 1993; Maher and Curtis 1992), and structural changes may have increased cultural support for violence against women (Wilson 1996).

The social world of adolescence is highly gendered as well (Eder 1995; Lees 1993; Thorne 1993). It is a period in which peer relationships increase in significance for youths, and this is magnified, especially for girls, with increased self-consciousness and sensitivity to others' perceptions of them (Pesce and Harding 1986). In addition, it is characterized by a "shift from the relatively asexual gender system of childhood to the overtly sexualized gender systems of adolescence and adulthood" (Thorne 1993:135). Young women find themselves in a contradictory position. Increasingly, they receive status from their peers via their association with, and attractiveness to, young men, but they are denigrated for their sexual activity and threatened with the labels *slut* and *ho* (Eder 1995; Lees 1993). The contexts of adolescence and the urban street world, then, have unique features likely to make young women particularly vulnerable to victimization. Thus, for some young women, gang involvement may appear to be a useful means of negotiating within these environments.

However, as Bourgois (1995) notes, actions taken to resist oppression can ultimately result in increased harm. Among young women in gangs, an important question to examine is how participation in gangs itself shapes young women's risk of victimization, including the question of whether gang involvement places girls at higher risks of victimization because of a potential increased involvement in crime. Lauritsen et al. (1991) found that "adolescent involvement in delinquent lifestyles strongly increases the risk of both personal and property victimization" (p. 265). Moreover, gender as a predictor of victimization risk among adolescents decreases when participation in delinquent lifestyles is controlled for (Lauritsen et al. 1991). That is, much of young men's greater victimization risk can be accounted for by their greater participation in offending behaviors. Among gang members, then, involvement in crime is likely associated with increased risk for victimization. Gang girls' participation in crime is thus an important consideration if we hope to understand the relationship between their gang membership and victimization risk.

GIRLS, GANGS, AND CRIME

Research comparing gang and nongang youths has consistently found that serious criminal involvement is a feature that distinguishes gangs from other groups of youths (Bjerregaard and Smith 1993; Esbensen and Huizinga 1993; Esbensen et al. 1993; Fagan 1989, 1990; Klein 1995; Thornberry et al. 1993; Winfree et al. 1992). Until recently, however, little attention was paid to young women's participation in serious and violent gang-related crime. Most traditional gang research emphasized the auxiliary and peripheral nature of girls' gang involvement and often resulted in an almost exclusive emphasis on girls' sexuality and sexual activities with male gang members, downplaying their participation in delinquency (for critiques of gender bias in gang research, see Campbell 1984, 1990; Taylor 1993).

However, recent estimates of female gang involvement have caused researchers to pay greater attention to gang girls' activities. This evidence suggests that young women approximate anywhere from 10 to 38 percent of gang members (Campbell 1984; Chesney-Lind 1993; Esbensen 1996; Fagan 1990; Moore 1991), that female gang participation may be increasing (Fagan 1990; Spergel and Curry 1993; Taylor 1993), and that in some urban areas, upward of one-fifth of girls report gang affiliations (Bjerregaard and Smith 1993; Winfree et al. 1992). As female gang members have become recognized as a group worthy of criminologists' attention, we have garnered new information regarding their involvement in delinquency in general, and violence in particular.

Recent research on female gang involvement indicates that the pattern of higher rates of criminal involvement for gang members holds for girls as well as their male counterparts (Bjerregaard and Smith 1993; Esbensen and Winfree forthcoming; Thornberry et al. 1993). The enhancement effect of gang membership is most noticeable for serious delinquency and marijuana use (Thornberry et al. 1993). Bjerregaard and Smith (1993) summarize:

> The traditional gang literature has generally suggested that gang membership enhances delinquent activity, and particularly serious delinquent activity for males, but not for females. In contrast, our study suggests that for females also, gangs are consistently associated with a greater prevalence and with higher rates of delinquency and substance use. Furthermore, the results suggest that for both sexes, gangs membership has an approximately equal impact on a variety of measures of delinquent behavior. (P. 346)

An interesting counterpart is provided by Bowker, Gross, and Klein (1980), who suggest there is evidence of "the structural exclusion of young women from male delinquent activities" within gangs (p. 516). Their (male) respondents suggested that not only were girls excluded from the planning of delinquent acts, but when girls inadvertently showed up at the location of a planned incident, it was frequently postponed or terminated. Likewise, Fagan (1990) reports greater gender differences in delinquency between gang members than between nongang youths (pp. 196-97). Male gang members were significantly more involved in the most serious forms of delinquency, whereas for alcohol use, drug sales, extortion, and property damage, gender differences were not significant.

However, Fagan also reports that "prevalence rates for female gang members exceeded the rates for non-gang males" for all the categories of delinquency he measured (see also Esbensen and Winfree 1998). Fagan (1990) summarizes his findings in relation to girls as follows:

> More than 40% of the female gang members were classified in the least serious category, a substantial difference from their male counterparts [15.5 percent]. Among female gang members, there was a bimodal distribution, with nearly as many multiple index offenders as petty delinquents. Evidently, female gang members avoid more serious delinquent involvement than their male counterparts. *Yet their extensive involvement in serious delinquent behaviors well exceeds that of non-gang males or females.* (P. 201, my emphasis)

Few would dispute that when it comes to serious delinquency, male gang members are involved more frequently than their female counterparts. However, this evidence does suggest that young women in gangs are more involved in serious criminal activities than was previously believed and also tend to be more involved than nongang youths—male or female. As such, they likely are exposed to greater victimization risk than nongang youths as well.

In addition, given the social contexts described above, it is reasonable to assume that young women's victimization risk within gangs is also shaped by gender. Gang activities (such as fighting for status and retaliation) create a particular set of factors that increase gang members' victimization risk and repeat victimization risk—constructions of gender identity may shape these risks in particular ways for girls. For instance, young women's adoption of masculine attributes may provide a means of participating and gaining status within gangs but may also lead to increased risk of victimization as a result of deeper immersion in delinquent activities. On the other hand, experiences of victimization may contribute to girls' denigration and thus increase their risk for repeat victimization through gendered responses and labeling—for example, when sexual victimization leads to perceptions of sexual availabil-

434   JOURNAL OF RESEARCH IN CRIME AND DELINQUENCY

ity or when victimization leads an individual to be viewed as weak. In addition, femaleness is an individual attribute that has the capacity to mark young women as "safe" crime victims (e.g., easy targets) or, conversely, to deem them "off limits." My goal here is to examine the gendered nature of violence within gangs, with a specific focus on how gender shapes young women's victimization risk.

METHODOLOGY

Data presented in this article come from survey and semistructured in-depth interviews with 20 female members of mixed-gender gangs in Columbus, Ohio. The interviewees ranged in age from 12 to 17; just over three-quarters were African American or multiracial (16 of 20), and the rest (4 of 20) were White. The sample was drawn primarily from several local agencies in Columbus working with at-risk youths, including the county juvenile detention center, a shelter care facility for adolescent girls, a day school within the same institution, and a local community agency.[1] The project was structured as a gang/nongang comparison, and I interviewed a total of 46 girls. Gang membership was determined during the survey interview by self-definition: About one-quarter of the way through the 50+ page interview, young women were asked a series of questions about the friends they spent time with. They then were asked whether these friends were gang involved and whether they themselves were gang members. Of the 46 girls interviewed, 21 reported that they were gang members,[2] and an additional 3 reported being gang involved (hanging out primarily with gangs or gang members) but not gang members. The rest reported no gang involvement.

A great deal of recent research suggests that self-report data provide comparatively reliable and valid measures of youths' gang membership (see Bjerregaard and Smith 1993; Fagan 1990; Thornberry et al. 1993; Winfree et al. 1992). This research suggests that using more restrictive measures (such as initiation rituals, a gang name, symbolic systems such as colors or signs) does not change substantive conclusions concerning gang members' behaviors when comparing self-defined gang members to those members who meet these more restrictive definitions. Although most researchers agree that the group should be involved in illegal activities in order for the youth to be classified as a gang member (see Esbensen et al. 1993; Esbensen and Huizinga 1993; Fagan 1989), other research that has used self-nomination without specifying crime as a defining feature has nonetheless consistently found serious criminal involvement as a feature that distinguishes gangs from other groups of youths (Fagan 1990; Thornberry et al. 1993; Winfree et al.

1992). All the gang members in my sample were members of groups they described as delinquent.

Cooperation from agency personnel generally proves successful for accessing gang members (see Bowker et al. 1980; Fagan 1989; Short and Strodtbeck 1965). However, these referrals pose the problem of targeting only officially labeled gang youth. I took several steps to temper this problem. First, I did not choose agencies that dealt specifically with gang members, and I did not rely on agency rosters of "known" gang members for my sample. As a result of the gang/nongang comparative research design, I was able to avoid oversampling girls who were labeled as gang members by asking agency personnel to refer me not just to girls believed to be gang involved but also any other girls living in areas in Columbus where they might have contact with gangs. Second, although I was only moderately successful, throughout the project I attempted to expand my sample on the basis of snowball techniques (see Fagan 1989; Hagedorn 1988). I only generated one successful referral outside of the agency contexts. However, I was successful at snowballing *within* agencies. Several girls I interviewed were gang involved but without staff knowledge, and they were referred to me by other girls I interviewed within the facilities. Thus, in a limited capacity, I was able to interview gang members who had not been detected by officials. Nonetheless, my sample is still limited to youths who have experienced intervention in some capacity, whether formal or informal, and thus it may not be representative of gang-involved girls in the community at large.

The survey interview was a variation of several instruments currently being used in research in a number of cities across the United States and included a broad range of questions and scales measuring factors that may be related to gang membership.[3] On issues related to violence, it included questions about peer activities and delinquency, individual delinquent involvement, family violence and abuse, and victimization. When young women responded affirmatively to being gang members, I followed with a series of questions about the nature of their gang, including its size, leadership, activities, symbols, and so on. Girls who admitted gang involvement during the survey participated in a follow-up interview to talk in more depth about their gangs and gang activities. The goal of the in-depth interview was to gain a greater understanding of the nature and meanings of gang life from the point of view of its female members. A strength of qualitative interviewing is its ability to shed light on this aspect of the social world, highlighting the meanings individuals attribute to their experiences (Adler and Adler 1987; Glassner and Loughlin 1987; Miller and Glassner 1997). In addition, using multiple methods, including follow-up interviews, provided me with a means of detecting inconsistencies in young women's accounts of their experiences.

Fortunately, no serious contradictions arose. However, a limitation of the data is that only young women were interviewed. Thus, I make inferences about gender dynamics, and young men's behavior, based only on young women's perspectives.

The in-depth interviews were open-ended and all but one were audiotaped. They were structured around several groupings of questions. We began by discussing girls' entry into their gangs—when and how they became involved, and what other things were going on in their lives at the time. Then, we discussed the structure of the gang—its history, size, leadership, and organization, and their place in the group. The next series of questions concerned gender within the gang; for example, how girls get involved, what activities they engage in and whether these are the same as the young men's activities, and what kind of males and females have the most influence in the gang and why. The next series of questions explored gang involvement more generally—what being in the gang means, what kinds of things they do together, and so on. Then, I asked how safe or dangerous they feel gang membership is and how they deal with risk. I concluded by asking them to speculate about why people their age join gangs, what things they like, what they dislike and have learned by being in the gang, and what they like best about themselves. This basic guideline was followed for each interview subject, although when additional topics arose in the context of the interview, we often deviated from the interview guide to pursue them. Throughout the interviews, issues related to violence emerged; these issues form the core of the discussion that follows.

SETTING

Columbus is a particular type of gang city. Gangs are a relatively new phenomenon there, with their emergence dated around 1985 (Maxson, Woods, and Klein 1995). In addition, it is thriving economically, experiencing both population and economic growth over the last decade (Rusk 1995). As such, it is representative of a recent pattern of gang proliferation into numerous cities, suburbs, and towns that do not have many of the long-standing problems associated with traditional gang cities, such as deindustrialization, population loss, and the deterioration of social support networks (see Curry et al. 1996; Hagedorn 1988; Klein 1995; Maxson et al. 1995; Spergel and Curry 1993). Even as Columbus has prospered, however, its racial disparities have grown (Columbus Metropolitan Human Services Commission 1995:17). In fact, in relative terms (comparing the gap between African Americans and Whites), racial disparities in measures such as income and percentage poverty in Columbus are equal to or even greater than in many cities experiencing economic and population declines.[4]

According to recent police estimates, Columbus has about 30 active gangs, with 400 to 1,000 members (LaLonde 1995). Most of these groups are small in size (20 or fewer members) and are either African American or racially mixed with a majority of African American members (Mayhood and LaLonde 1995). Gangs in Columbus have adopted "big-city" gang names such as Crips, Bloods, and Folks, along with the dress styles, signs, and graffiti of these groups, although gangs are and have been primarily a "homegrown" problem in Columbus rather than a result of organized gang migration (Huff 1989). Local police view these groups as criminally oriented, but not especially sophisticated. On the whole, gangs in Columbus seem to match those described in other cities with emergent gang problems—best characterized as "relatively autonomous, smaller, independent groups, poorly organized and less territorial" than in older gang cities (Klein 1995:36).

The young women I interviewed described their gangs in ways that are very much in keeping with these findings. All 20 are members of Folks, Crips, or Bloods sets.[5] All but 3 described gangs with fewer than 30 members, and most reported relatively narrow age ranges between members. Half were in gangs with members who were 21 or over, but almost without exception, their gangs were made up primarily of teenagers, with either one adult who was considered the OG ("Original Gangster," leader) or just a handful of young adults. The majority (14 of 20) reported that their gangs did not include members under the age of 13.

Although the gangs these young women were members of were composed of both female and male members, they varied in their gender composition, with the vast majority being predominantly male. Six girls reported that girls were one-fifth or fewer of the members of their gang; 8 were in gangs in which girls were between a quarter and a third of the overall membership; 4 said girls were between 44 and 50 percent of the members; and 1 girl reported that her gang was two-thirds female and one-third male. Overall, girls were typically a minority within these groups numerically, with 11 girls reporting that there were 5 or fewer girls in their set.

This structure—male-dominated, integrated mixed-gender gangs—likely shapes gender dynamics in particular ways. Much past gang research has assumed that female members of gangs are in auxiliary subgroups of male gangs, but there is increasing evidence—including from the young women I spoke with—that many gangs can be characterized as integrated, mixed-gender groups. For example, from interviews with 110 female gang members in three sites (Boston, Seattle, and Pueblo, Colorado), Curry (1997) found integrated mixed-gender gangs to be the predominant gang structure of female gang members, with 57.3 percent of girls describing their gangs as mixed-gender.[6] It is likely that gang structure shapes both status orientations and criminal involvement among gang members (Brotherton 1996), and that these differences may also be mediated by ethnicity (Brotherton 1996; Joe and Chesney-Lind 1995; Moore and Hagedorn, 1996). Generalizability beyond mixed-gender, predominantly African American gangs in emergent gang cities, then, is questionable.

GENDER, GANGS, AND VIOLENCE

Gangs as Protection and Risk

An irony of gang involvement is that although many members suggest one thing they get out of the gang is a sense of protection (see also Decker 1996; Joe and Chesney-Lind 1995; Lauderback et al. 1992), gang membership itself means exposure to victimization risk and even a willingness to be victimized. These contradictions are apparent when girls talk about what they get out of the gang, and what being in the gang means in terms of other members' expectations of their behavior. In general, a number of girls suggested that being a gang member is a source of protection around the neighborhood. Erica,[7] a 17-year-old African American, explained, "It's like people look at us and that's exactly what they think, there's a gang, and they respect us for that. They won't bother us. . . . It's like you put that intimidation in somebody." Likewise, Lisa, a 14-year-old White girl, described being in the gang as empowering: "You just feel like, oh my God, you know, they got my back. I don't need to worry about it." Given the violence endemic in many inner-city communities, these beliefs are understandable, and to a certain extent, accurate.

In addition, some young women articulated a specifically gendered sense of protection that they felt as a result of being a member of a group that was predominantly male. Gangs operate within larger social milieus that are characterized by gender inequality and sexual exploitation. Being in a gang with young men means at least the semblance of protection from, and retaliation against, predatory men in the social environment. Heather, a 15-year-old White girl, noted, "You feel more secure when, you know, a guy's around protectin' you, you know, than you would a girl." She explained that as a gang member, because "you get protected by guys . . . not as many people mess with you." Other young women concurred and also described that male gang members could retaliate against specific acts of violence against girls in the gang. Nikkie, a 13-year-old African American girl, had a friend who was raped by a rival gang member, and she said, "It was a Crab [Crip] that raped my girl in Miller Ales, and um, they was ready to kill him." Keisha, an African American 14-year-old, explained, "If I got beat up by a guy, all I gotta do is go tell one of the niggers, you know what I'm sayin'? Or one of the guys, they'd take care of it."

At the same time, members recognized that they may be targets of rival gang members and were expected to "be down" for their gang at those times even when it meant being physically hurt. In addition, initiation rites and internal rules were structured in ways that required individuals to submit to, and be exposed to, violence. For example, young women's descriptions of the qualities they valued in members revealed the extent to which exposure to violence was an expected element of gang involvement. Potential members, they explained, should be tough, able to fight and to engage in criminal activities, and also should be loyal to the group and willing to put themselves at risk for it. Erica explained that they didn't want "punks" in her gang: "When you join something like that, you might as well expect that there's gonna be fights. . . . And, if you're a punk, or if you're scared of stuff like that, then don't join." Likewise, the following dialogue with Cathy, a White 16-year-old, reveals similar themes. I asked her what her gang expected out of members and she responded, "to be true to our gang and to have our backs." When I asked her to elaborate, she explained,

> *Cathy:* Like, uh, if you say you're a Blood, you be a Blood. You wear your rag even when you're by yourself. You know, don't let anybody intimidate you and be like, "Take that rag off." You know, "you better get with our set." Or something like that.
> *JM:* Ok. Anything else that being true to the set means?
> *Cathy:* Um. Yeah, I mean, just, just, you know, I mean it's, you got a whole bunch of people comin' up in your face and if you're by yourself they ask you what's your claimin', you tell 'em. Don't say "nothin'."
> *JM:* Even if it means getting beat up or something?
> *Cathy:* Mmhmm.

One measure of these qualities came through the initiation process, which involved the individual submitting to victimization at the hands of the gang's members. Typically this entailed either taking a fixed number of "blows" to the head and/or chest or being "beaten in" by members for a given duration (e.g., 60 seconds). Heather described the initiation as an important event for determining whether someone would make a good member:

> When you get beat in if you don't fight back and if you just like stop and you start cryin' or somethin' or beggin' 'em to stop and stuff like that, then, they

440   JOURNAL OF RESEARCH IN CRIME AND DELINQUENCY

ain't gonna, they'll just stop and they'll say that you're not gang material
because you gotta be hard, gotta be able to fight, take punches.

In addition to the initiation, and threats from rival gangs, members were
expected to adhere to the gang's internal rules (which included such things
as not fighting with one another, being "true" to the gang, respecting the
leader, not spreading gang business outside the gang, and not dating members
of rival gangs). Breaking the rules was grounds for physical punishment,
either in the form of a spontaneous assault or a formal "violation," which
involved taking a specified number of blows to the head. For example, Keisha
reported that she talked back to the leader of her set and "got slapped pretty
hard" for doing so. Likewise, Veronica, an African American 15-year-old,
described her leader as "crazy, but we gotta listen to 'im. He's just the type
that if you don't listen to 'im, he gonna blow your head off. He's just crazy."

It is clear that regardless of members' perceptions of the gang as a form
of "protection," being a gang member also involves a willingness to open
oneself up to the possibility of victimization. Gang victimization is governed
by rules and expectations, however, and thus does not involve the random
vulnerability that being out on the streets without a gang might entail in
high-crime neighborhoods. Because of its structured nature, this victimization risk may be perceived as more palatable by gang members. For young
women in particular, the gendered nature of the streets may make the
empowerment available through gang involvement an appealing alternative
to the individualized vulnerability they otherwise would face. However, as
the next sections highlight, girls' victimization risks continue to be shaped
by gender, even within their gangs, because these groups are structured
around gender hierarchies as well.

Gender and Status, Crime and Victimization

Status hierarchies within Columbus gangs, like elsewhere, were male
dominated (Bowker et al. 1980; Campbell 1990). Again, it is important to
highlight that the structure of the gangs these young women belonged
to—that is, male-dominated, integrated mixed-gender gangs—likely shaped
the particular ways in which gender dynamics played themselves out.
Autonomous female gangs, as well as gangs in which girls are in auxiliary
subgroups, may be shaped by different gender relations, as well as differences
in orientations toward status, and criminal involvement.

All the young women reported having established leaders in their gang,
and this leadership was almost exclusively male. While LaShawna, a 17-year-

old African American, reported being the leader of her set (which had a membership that is two-thirds girls, many of whom resided in the same residential facility as her), all the other girls in mixed-gender gangs reported that their OG was male. In fact, a number of young women stated explicitly that only male gang members could be leaders. Leadership qualities, and qualities attributed to high-status members of the gang—being tough, able to fight, and willing to "do dirt" (e.g., commit crime, engage in violence) for the gang—were perceived as characteristically masculine. Keisha noted, "The guys, they just harder." She explained, "Guys is more rougher. We have our G's back but, it ain't gonna be like the guys, they just don't give a fuck. They gonna shoot you in a minute." For the most part, status in the gang was related to traits such as the willingness to use serious violence and commit dangerous crimes and, though not exclusively, these traits were viewed primarily as qualities more likely and more intensely located among male gang members.

Because these respected traits were characterized specifically as masculine, young women actually may have had greater flexibility in their gang involvement than young men. Young women had fewer expectations placed on them—by both their male and female peers—in regard to involvement in criminal activities such as fighting, using weapons, and committing other crimes. This tended to decrease girls' exposure to victimization risk comparable to male members, because they were able to avoid activities likely to place them in danger. Girls *could* gain status in the gang by being particularly hard and true to the set. Heather, for example, described the most influential girl in her set as "the hardest girl, the one that don't take no crap, will stand up to anybody." Likewise, Diane, a White 15-year-old, described a highly respected female member in her set as follows:

> People look up to Janeen just 'cause she's so crazy. People just look up to her 'cause she don't care about nothin'. She don't even care about makin' money. Her, her thing is, "Oh, you're a Slob [Blood]? You're a Slob? You talkin' to me? You talkin' shit to me?" Pow, pow! And that's it. That's it.

However, young women also had a second route to status that was less available to young men. This came via their connections—as sisters, girlfriends, cousins—to influential, high-status young men.[8] In Veronica's set, for example, the girl with the most power was the OG's "sister or his cousin, one of 'em." His girlfriend also had status, although Veronica noted that "most of us just look up to our OG." Monica, a 16-year-old African American, and Tamika, a 15-year-old African American, both had older brothers in their

442   JOURNAL OF RESEARCH IN CRIME AND DELINQUENCY

gangs, and both reported getting respect, recognition, and protection because of this connection. This route to status and the masculinization of high-status traits functioned to maintain gender inequality within gangs, but they also could put young women at less risk of victimization than young men. This was both because young women were perceived as less threatening and thus were less likely to be targeted by rivals, and because they were not expected to prove themselves in the ways that young men were, thus decreasing their participation in those delinquent activities likely to increase exposure to violence. Thus, gender inequality could have a protective edge for young women.

Young men's perceptions of girls as lesser members typically functioned to keep girls from being targets of serious violence at the hands of rival young men, who instead left routine confrontations with rival female gang members to the girls in their own gang. Diane said that young men in her gang "don't wanna waste their time hittin' on some little girls. They're gonna go get their little cats [females] to go get 'em." Lisa remarked,

> Girls don't face much violence as [guys]. They see a girl, they say, "we'll just smack her and send her on." They see a guy—'cause guys are like a lot more into it than girls are, I've noticed that—and they like, well, "we'll shoot him."

In addition, the girls I interviewed suggested that, in comparison with young men, young women were less likely to resort to serious violence, such as that involving a weapon, when confronting rivals. Thus, when girls' routine confrontations were more likely to be female on female than male on female, girls' risk of serious victimization was lessened further.

Also, because participation in serious and violent crime was defined primarily as a masculine endeavor, young women could use gender as a means of avoiding participation in those aspects of gang life they found risky, threatening, or morally troubling. Of the young women I interviewed, about one-fifth were involved in serious gang violence: A few had been involved in aggravated assaults on rival gang members, and one admitted to having killed a rival gang member, but they were by far the exception. Most girls tended not to be involved in serious gang crime, and some reported that they chose to exclude themselves because they felt ambivalent about this aspect of gang life. Angie, an African American 15-year-old, explained,

> I don't get involved like that, be out there goin' and just beat up people like that or go stealin', things like that. That's not me. The boys, mostly the boys do all that, the girls we just sit back and chill, you know.

Likewise, Diane noted,

> For maybe a drive-by they might wanna have a bunch of dudes. They might
> not put the females in that. Maybe the females might be weak inside, not strong
> enough to do something like that, just on the insides. . . . If a female wants to
> go forward and doin' that, and she wants to risk her whole life for doin' that,
> then she can. But the majority of the time, that job is given to a man.

Diane was not just alluding to the idea that young men were stronger than
young women. She also inferred that young women were able to get out of
committing serious crime, more so than young men, because a girl shouldn't
have to "risk her whole life" for the gang. In accepting that young men were
more central members of the gang, young women could more easily participate in gangs without putting themselves in jeopardy—they could engage in
the more routine, everyday activities of the gang, like hanging out, listening
to music, and smoking bud (marijuana). These male-dominated mixed-gender gangs thus appeared to provide young women with flexibility in their
involvement in gang activities. As a result, it is likely that their risk of
victimization at the hands of rivals was less than that of young men in gangs
who were engaged in greater amounts of crime.

Girls' Devaluation and Victimization

In addition to girls choosing not to participate in serious gang crimes, they
also faced exclusion at the hands of young men or the gang as a whole (see
also Bowker et al. 1980). In particular, the two types of crime mentioned most
frequently as "off-limits" for girls were drug sales and drive-by shootings.
LaShawna explained, "We don't really let our females [sell drugs] unless they
really wanna and they know how to do it and not to get caught and everything." Veronica described a drive-by that her gang participated in and said,
"They wouldn't let us [females] go. But we wanted to go, but they wouldn't
let us." Often, the exclusion was couched in terms of protection. When I asked
Veronica why the girls couldn't go, she said, "so we won't go to jail if they
was to get caught. Or if one of 'em was to get shot, they wouldn't want it to
happen to us." Likewise, Sonita, a 13-year-old African American, noted, "If
they gonna do somethin' bad and they think one of the females gonna get hurt
they don't let 'em do it with them. . . . Like if they involved with shooting or
whatever, [girls] can't go."

Although girls' exclusion from some gang crime may be framed as
protective (and may reduce their victimization risk vis-à-vis rival gangs), it

also served to perpetuate the devaluation of female members as less significant to the gang—not as tough, true, or "down" for the gang as male members.
When LaShawna said her gang blocked girls' involvement in serious crime,
I pointed out that she was actively involved herself. She explained, "Yeah, I
do a lot of stuff 'cause I'm tough. I likes, I likes messin' with boys. I fight
boys. Girls ain't nothin' to me." Similarly, Tamika said, "girls, they little
peons."

   Some young women found the perception of them as weak a frustrating
one. Brandi, an African American 13-year-old, explained, "Sometimes I
dislike that the boys, sometimes, always gotta take charge and they think,
sometimes, that the girls don't know how to take charge 'cause we're like
girls, we're females, and like that." And Chantell, an African American
14-year-old, noted that rival gang members "think that you're more of a
punk." Beliefs that girls were weaker than boys meant that young women had
a harder time proving that they were serious about their commitment to the
gang. Diane explained,

> A female has to show that she's tough. A guy can just, you can just look at him.
> But a female, she's gotta show. She's gotta go out and do some dirt. She's gotta
> go whip some girl's ass, shoot somebody, rob somebody or something. To show
> that she is tough.

   In terms of gender-specific victimization risk, the devaluation of young
women suggests several things. It could lead to the mistreatment and victimization of girls by members of their own gang when they didn't have specific
male protection (i.e., a brother, boyfriend) in the gang or when they weren't
able to stand up for themselves to male members. This was exacerbated by
activities that led young women to be viewed as sexually available. In
addition, because young women typically were not seen as a threat by young
men, when they did pose one, they could be punished even more harshly than
young men, not only for having challenged a rival gang or gang member but
also for having overstepped "appropriate" gender boundaries.

   Monica had status and respect in her gang, both because she had proven
herself through fights and criminal activities, and because her older brothers
were members of her set. She contrasted her own treatment with that of other
young women in the gang:

> They just be puttin' the other girls off. Like Andrea, man. Oh my God, they
> dog Andrea so bad. They like, "Bitch, go to the store." She like, "All right, I
> be right back." She will go to the store and go and get them whatever they want
> and come back with it. If she don't get it right, they be like, "Why you do that

bitch?" I mean, and one dude even smacked her. And, I mean, and, I don't, I told my brother once. I was like, "Man, it ain't even like that. If you ever see someone tryin' to disrespect me like that or hit me, if you do not hit them or at least say somethin' to them. . . . " So my brothers, they kinda watch out for me.

However, Monica put the responsibility for Andrea's treatment squarely on the young woman: "I put that on her. They ain't gotta do her like that, but she don't gotta let them do her like that either." Andrea was seen as "weak" because she did not stand up to the male members in the gang; thus, her mistreatment was framed as partially deserved because she did not exhibit the valued traits of toughness and willingness to fight that would allow her to defend herself.

An additional but related problem was when the devaluation of young women within gangs was sexual in nature. Girls, but not boys, could be initiated into the gang by being "sexed in"—having sexual relations with multiple male members of the gang. Other members viewed the young women initiated in this way as sexually available and promiscuous, thus increasing their subsequent mistreatment. In addition, the stigma could extend to female members in general, creating a sexual devaluation that all girls had to contend with.

The dynamics of "sexing in" as a form of gang initiation placed young women in a position that increased their risk of ongoing mistreatment at the hands of their gang peers. According to Keisha, "If you get sexed in, you have no respect. That means you gotta go ho'in' for 'em; when they say you give 'em the pussy, you gotta give it to 'em. If you don't, you gonna get your ass beat. I ain't down for that." One girl in her set was sexed in and Keisha said the girl "just do everything they tell her to do, like a dummy." Nikkie reported that two girls who were sexed into her set eventually quit hanging around with the gang because they were harassed so much. In fact, Veronica said the young men in her set purposely tricked girls into believing they were being sexed into the gang and targeted girls they did not like:

> If some girls wanted to get in, if they don't like the girl they have sex with 'em. They run trains on 'em or either have the girl suck their thang. And then they used to, the girls used to think they was in. So, then the girls used to just come try to hang around us and all this little bull, just 'cause, 'cause they thinkin' they in.

Young women who were sexed into the gang were viewed as sexually promiscuous, weak, and not "true" members. They were subject to revictimization and mistreatment, and were viewed as deserving of abuse by other members, both male and female. Veronica continued, "They [girls who are sexed in] gotta do whatever, whatever the boys tell 'em to do when they want 'em to do it, right then and there, in front of whoever. And, I think, that's just sick. That's nasty, that's dumb." Keisha concurred, "She brought that on herself, by bein' the fact, bein' sexed in." There was evidence, however, that girls could overcome the stigma of having been sexed in through their subsequent behavior, by challenging members that disrespect them and being willing to fight. Tamika described a girl in her set who was sexed in, and stigmatized as a result, but successfully fought to rebuild her reputation:

> Some people, at first, they call her "little ho" and all that. But then, now she startin' to get bold. . . . Like, like, they be like, "Ooh, look at the little ho. She fucked me and my boy." She be like, "Man, forget y'all. Man, what? What?" She be ready to squat [fight] with 'em. I be like, "Ah, look at her!" Uh huh. . . . At first we looked at her like, "Ooh, man, she a ho, man." But now we look at her like she just our kickin' it partner. You know, however she got in that's her business.

The fact that there was such an option as "sexing in" served to keep girls disempowered, because they always faced the question of how they got in and of whether they were "true" members. In addition, it contributed to a milieu in which young women's sexuality was seen as exploitable. This may help explain why young women were so harshly judgmental of those girls who were sexed in. Young women who were privy to male gang members' conversations reported that male members routinely disrespect girls in the gang by disparaging them sexually. Monica explained,

> I mean the guys, they have their little comments about 'em [girls in the gang] because, I hear more because my brothers are all up there with the guys and everything and I hear more just sittin' around, just listenin'. And they'll have their little jokes about "Well, ha I had her," and then and everybody else will jump in and say, "Well, I had her, too." And then they'll laugh about it.

In general, because gender constructions defined young women as weaker than young men, young women were often seen as lesser members of the gang. In addition to the mistreatment these perceptions entailed, young women also faced particularly harsh sanctions for crossing gender boundaries— causing harm to rival male members when they had been viewed as nonthreatening. One young woman[9] participated in the assault of a rival female gang member, who had set up a member of the girl's gang. She explained, "The female was supposingly goin' out with one of ours, went back and told a bunch of [rivals] what was goin' on and got the [rivals] to jump my boy. And he ended up in the hospital." The story she told was unique but nonetheless significant for what it indicates about the gendered nature of gang violence and victimization. Several young men in her set saw the girl walking down the street, kidnapped her, then brought her to a member's house. The young woman I interviewed, along with several other girls in her set, viciously beat the girl, then to their surprise the young men took over the beating, ripped off the girl's clothes, brutally gang-raped her, then dumped her in a park. The interviewee noted, "I don't know what happened to her. Maybe she died. Maybe, maybe someone came and helped her. I mean, I don't know." The experience scared the young woman who told me about it. She explained,

> I don't never want anythin' like that to happen to me. And I pray to God that it doesn't. 'Cause God said that whatever you sow you're gonna reap. And like, you know, beatin' a girl up and then sittin' there watchin' somethin' like that happen, well, Jesus that could come back on me. I mean, I felt, I really did feel sorry for her even though my boy was in the hospital and was really hurt. I mean, we coulda just shot her. You know, and it coulda been just over. We coulda just taken her life. But they went farther than that.

This young woman described the gang rape she witnessed as "the most brutal thing I've ever seen in my life." While the gang rape itself was an unusual event, it remained a specifically gendered act that could take place precisely because young women were not perceived as equals. Had the victim been an "equal," the attack would have remained a physical one. As the interviewee herself noted, "we coulda just shot her." Instead, the young men who gang-raped the girl were not just enacting revenge on a rival but on a *young woman* who had dared to treat a young man in this way. The issue is not the question of which is worse—to be shot and killed, or gang-raped and left for dead. Rather, this particular act sheds light on how gender may function to structure victimization risk within gangs.

DISCUSSION

Gender dynamics in mixed-gender gangs are complex and thus may have multiple and contradictory effects on young women's risk of victimization and repeat victimization. My findings suggest that participation in the delinquent lifestyles associated with gangs clearly places young women at risk for victimization. The act of joining a gang involves the initiate's submission to victimization at the hands of her gang peers. In addition, the rules governing gang members' activities place them in situations in which they are vulnerable to assaults that are specifically gang related. Many acts of violence that girls described would not have occurred had they not been in gangs.

It seems, though, that young women in gangs believed they have traded unknown risks for known ones—that victimization at the hands of friends, or at least under specified conditions, was an alternative preferable to the potential of random, unknown victimization by strangers. Moreover, the gang offered both a semblance of protection from others on the streets, especially young men, and a means of achieving retaliation when victimization did occur.

Lauritsen and Quinet (1995) suggest that both individual-specific heterogeneity (unchanging attributes of individuals that contribute to a propensity for victimization, such as physical size or temperament) and state-dependent factors (factors that can alter individuals' victimization risks over time, such as labeling or behavior changes that are a consequence of victimization) are related to youths' victimization and repeat victimization risk. My findings here suggest that, within gangs, gender can function in both capacities to shape girls' risks of victimization.

Girls' gender, as an individual attribute, can function to lessen their exposure to victimization risk by defining them as inappropriate targets of rival male gang members' assaults. The young women I interviewed repeatedly commented that young men were typically not as violent in their routine confrontations with rival young women as with rival young men. On the other hand, when young women are targets of serious assault, they may face brutality that is particularly harsh and sexual in nature because they are female—thus, particular types of assault, such as rape, are deemed more appropriate when young women are the victims.

Gender can also function as a state-dependent factor, because constructions of gender and the enactment of gender identities are fluid. On the one hand, young women can call upon gender as a means of avoiding exposure to activities they find risky, threatening, or morally troubling. Doing so does not expose them to the sanctions likely faced by male gang members who attempt to avoid participation in violence. Although these choices may insulate young women from the risk of assault at the hands of rival gang members, perceptions of female gang members—and of women in general—as weak may contribute to more routinized victimization at the hands of the male members of their gangs. Moreover, sexual exploitation in the form of "sexing in" as an initiation ritual may define young women as sexually available, contributing to a likelihood of repeat victimization unless the young woman can stand up for herself and fight to gain other members' respect.

Finally, given constructions of gender that define young women as nonthreatening, when young women do pose a threat to male gang members, the sanctions they face may be particularly harsh because they not only have caused harm to rival gang members but also have crossed appropriate gender boundaries in doing so. In sum, my findings suggest that gender may function to insulate young women from some types of physical assault and lessen their exposure to risks from rival gang members, but also to make them vulnerable to particular types of violence, including routine victimization by their male peers, sexual exploitation, and sexual assault.

This article has offered preliminary evidence of how gender may shape victimization risk for female gang members. A great deal more work needs to be done in this area. Specifically, gang scholars need to address more systematically the relationships between gang involvement and victimization risk rather than focusing exclusively on gang members' participation in violence as offenders. My research suggests two questions to be examined further, for both female and male gang members. First, are gang members more likely to be victimized than nongang members living in the same areas? Second, how does victimization risk fluctuate for gang members before, during, and after their gang involvement? Information about these questions will allow us to address whether and how gang involvement has an enhancement effect on youths' *victimization*, as well as their delinquency.

With the growing interest in masculinities and crime (see Messerschmidt 1993; Newburn and Stanko 1994), an important corollary question to be examined is how masculinities shape victimization risk among male gang members. The young women I interviewed clearly associated serious gang violence with the enactment of masculinity and used gender constructions to avoid involvement in those activities they perceived as threatening. Young men thus may be at greater risk of serious physical assaults, because of their greater involvement in serious gang crime and violence, and because gender constructions within the gang make these activities more imperative for young men than for young women.

NOTES

1. I contacted numerous additional agency personnel in an effort to draw the sample from a larger population base, but many efforts remained unsuccessful despite repeated attempts and promises of assistance. These included persons at the probation department, a shelter and outreach agency for runaways, police personnel, a private residential facility for juveniles, and three additional community agencies. None of the agencies I contacted openly denied me permission to interview young women; they simply chose not to follow up. I do not believe that

450   JOURNAL OF RESEARCH IN CRIME AND DELINQUENCY

much bias resulted from the nonparticipation of these agencies. Each has a client base of "at-risk" youths, and the young women I interviewed report overlap with some of these same agencies. For example, a number had been or were on probation, and several reported staying at the shelter for runaways.

2. One young woman was a member of an all-female gang. Because the focus of this article is gender dynamics in mixed-gender gangs, her interview is not included in the analysis.

3. These include the Gang Membership Resistance Surveys in Long Beach and San Diego, the Denver Youth Survey, and the Rochester Youth Development Study.

4. For example, Cleveland, Ohio provides a striking contrast with Columbus on social and economic indicators, including a poverty rate double that found in Columbus. But the poverty rate for African Americans in Cleveland is just over twice that for Whites, and it is more than three times higher in Columbus.

5. The term *set* was used by the gang members I interviewed to refer to their gangs. Because they adopted nationally recognized gang names (e.g., Crips, Bloods, Folks), they saw themselves as loosely aligned with other groups of the same name. This term was used to distinguish their particular gang (which has its own distinct name, e.g., Rolling 60s Crips) from other gangs that adopted the broader gang name. I will use the terms *set* and *gang* interchangeably.

6. This was compared to 36.4 percent who described their gangs as female auxiliaries of male gangs, and only 6.4 percent who described being in independent female gangs (Curry 1997; see also Decker and Van Winkle 1996).

7. All names are fictitious.

8. This is not to suggest that male members cannot gain status via their connections to high-status men, but that to maintain status, they will have to successfully exhibit masculine traits such as toughness. Young women appear to be held to more flexible standards.

9. Because this excerpt provides a detailed description of a specific serious crime, and because demographic information on respondents is available, I have chosen to conceal both the pseudonym and gang affiliation of the young woman who told me the story.

REFERENCES

Adler, Patricia A. and Peter Adler. 1987. *Membership Roles in Field Research*. Newbury Park, CA: Sage.

Arnold, Regina. 1990. "Processes of Victimization and Criminalization of Black Women." *Social Justice* 17 (3): 153-66.

Baskin, Deborah, Ira Sommers, and Jeffrey Fagan. 1993. "The Political Economy of Violent Female Street Crime." *Fordham Urban Law Journal* 20:401-17.

Bjerregaard, Beth and Carolyn Smith. 1993. "Gender Differences in Gang Participation, Delinquency, and Substance Use." *Journal of Quantitative Criminology* 4:329-55.

Block, Carolyn Rebecca and Richard Block. 1993. "Street Gang Crime in Chicago." Research in Brief. Washington, DC: National Institute of Justice.

Bourgois, Philippe. 1995. *In Search of Respect: Selling Crack in El Barrio*. Cambridge, UK: Cambridge University Press.

Bourgois, Philippe and Eloise Dunlap. 1993. "Exorcising Sex-for-Crack: An Ethnographic Perspective from Harlem." Pp. 97-132 in *Crack Pipe as Pimp: An Ethnographic Investigation of Sex-for-Crack Exchanges*, edited by Mitchell S. Ratner. New York: Lexington Books.

Bowker, Lee H., Helen Shimota Gross, and Malcolm W. Klein. 1980. "Female Participation in Delinquent Gang Activities." *Adolescence* 15 (59): 509-19.

Brotherton, David C. 1996. " 'Smartness,' 'Toughness,' and 'Autonomy': Drug Use in the Context of Gang Female Delinquency." *Journal of Drug Issues* 26 (1): 261-77.

Campbell, Anne. 1984. *The Girls in the Gang*. New York: Basil Blackwell.

————. 1990. "Female Participation in Gangs." Pp. 163-82 in *Gangs in America*, edited by C. Ronald Huff. Beverly Hills, CA: Sage.

Chesney-Lind, Meda. 1993. "Girls, Gangs and Violence: Anatomy of a Backlash." *Humanity & Society* 17 (3): 321-44.

Chesney-Lind, Meda and Noelie Rodriguez. 1983. "Women under Lock and Key: A View from the Inside." *The Prison Journal* 63 (2): 47-65.

Chesney-Lind, Meda, Randall G. Shelden, and Karen A. Joe. 1996. "Girls, Delinquency, and Gang Membership." Pp. 185-204 in *Gangs in America*, 2d ed., edited by C. Ronald Huff. Thousand Oaks, CA: Sage.

Columbus Metropolitan Human Services Commission. 1995. *State of Human Services Report— 1995*. Columbus, OH: Columbus Metropolitan Human Services Commission. March, Orlando, FL.

Connell, R. W. 1987. *Gender and Power*. Stanford, CA: Stanford University Press.

Curry, G. David. 1997. "Selected Statistics on Female Gang Involvement." Paper presented at the Fifth Joint National Conference on Gangs, Schools, and Community, March, Orlando, FL.

Curry, G. David, Richard A. Ball, and Scott H. Decker. 1996. Estimating the National Scope of Gang Crime from Law Enforcement Data. Research in Brief. Washington, DC: National Institute of Justice.

Daly, Kathleen. 1992. "Women's Pathways to Felony Court: Feminist Theories of Lawbreaking and Problems of Representation." *Review of Law and Women's Studies* 2 (1): 11-52.

Decker, Scott H. 1996. "Collective and Normative Features of Gang Violence." *Justice Quarterly* 13 (2): 243-64.

Decker, Scott H. and Barrik Van Winkle. 1996. *Life in the Gang*. Cambridge, UK: Cambridge University Press.

Eder, Donna. 1995. *School Talk: Gender and Adolescent Culture*. New Brunswick, NJ: Rutgers University Press.

Esbensen, Finn-Aage. 1996. Comments presented at the National Institute of Justice/Office of Juvenile Justice and Delinquency Prevention Cluster Meetings, June, Dallas, TX.

Esbensen, Finn-Aage and David Huizinga. 1993. "Gangs, Drugs, and Delinquency in a Survey of Urban Youth." *Criminology* 31 (4) 565-89.

Esbensen, Finn-Aage, David Huizinga, and Anne W. Weiher. 1993. "Gang and Non-Gang Youth: Differences in Explanatory Factors." *Journal of Contemporary Criminal Justice* 9 (2): 94-116.

Esbensen, Finn-Aage and L. Thomas Winfree. 1998. "Race and Gender Differences between Gang and Non-Gang Youth: Results from a Multi-Site Survey." *Justice Quarterly* 15(3):505-25.

Fagan, Jeffrey. 1989. "The Social Organization of Drug Use and Drug Dealing among Urban Gangs." *Criminology* 27(4): 633-67.

————. 1990. "Social Processes of Delinquency and Drug Use among Urban Gangs." Pp. 183-219 in *Gangs in America*, edited by C. Ronald Huff. Newbury Park, CA: Sage.

Gilfus, Mary E. 1992. "From Victims to Survivors to Offenders: Women's Routes of Entry and Immersion into Street Crime." *Women and Criminal Justice* 4 (1): 63-89.

Glassner, Barry and Julia Loughlin. 1987. *Drugs in Adolescent Worlds: Burnouts to Straights*. New York: St. Martin's.

Hagedorn, John M. 1988. *People and Folks: Gangs, Crime and the Underclass in a Rustbelt City*. Chicago: Lake View Press.

Huff, C. Ronald. 1989. "Youth Gangs and Public Policy." *Crime and Delinquency* 35 (4): 524-37.
————. 1996. "The Criminal Behavior of Gang Members and Nongang At-Risk Youth."
    Pp. 75-102 in *Gangs in America*, 2d ed., edited by C. Ronald Huff. Thousand Oaks, CA:
    Sage.
Joe, Karen A. and Meda Chesney-Lind. 1995. "Just Every Mother's Angel: An Analysis of
    Gender and Ethnic Variations in Youth Gang Membership." *Gender & Society* 9(4): 408-30.
Klein, Malcolm W. 1995. *The American Street Gang: Its Nature, Prevalence and Control*. New
    York: Oxford University Press.
Klein, Malcolm W. and Cheryl L. Maxson. 1989. "Street Gang Violence." Pp. 198-231 in *Violent
    Crime, Violent Criminals*, edited by Neil Weiner and Marvin Wolfgang. Newbury Park, CA:
    Sage.
LaLonde, Brent. 1995. "Police Trying to Contain Gang Problem." *The Columbus Dispatch*,
    September 3, p. 2A.
Lauderback, David, Joy Hansen, and Dan Waldorf. 1992. " 'Sisters Are Doin' It for Themselves':
    A Black Female Gang in San Francisco." *The Gang Journal* 1 (1): 57-70.
Lauritsen, Janet L. and Kenna F. Davis Quinet. 1995. "Repeat Victimization among Adolescents
    and Young Adults." *Journal of Quantitative Criminology* 11 (2): 143-66.
Lauritsen, Janet L., Robert J. Sampson, and John H. Laub. 1991. "The Link between Offending
    and Victimization among Adolescents." *Criminology* 29 (2): 265-92.
Lees, Sue. 1993. *Sugar and Spice: Sexuality and Adolescent Girls*. New York: Penguin.
Maher, Lisa and Richard Curtis. 1992. "Women on the Edge of Crime: Crack Cocaine and the
    Changing Contexts of Street-Level Sex Work in New York City." *Crime, Law and Social
    Change* 18:221-58.
Maxson, Cheryl L., Kristi Woods, and Malcolm W. Klein. 1995. Street Gang Migration in the
    United States. Final Report to the National Institute of Justice.
Mayhood, Kevin and Brent LaLonde. 1995. "A Show of Colors: A Local Look." *The Columbus
    Dispatch*, September 3, pp. 1-2A.
Messerschmidt, James W. 1993. *Masculinities and Crime: Critique and Reconceptualization of
    Theory*. Lanham, MD: Rowman and Littlefield.
Miller, Jody. 1996. "The Dynamics of Female Gang Involvement in Columbus, Ohio." Paper
    presented at the National Youth Gang Symposium, June, Dallas, TX.
Miller, Jody and Barry Glassner. 1997. "The 'Inside' and the 'Outside': Finding Realities in
    Interviews." Pp. 99-112 in *Qualitative Research*, edited by David Silverman. London: Sage.
Moore, Joan. 1991. *Going Down to the Barrio: Homeboys and Homegirls in Change*. Philadel-
    phia: Temple University Press.
Moore, Joan and John M. Hagedorn. 1996. "What Happens to Girls in the Gang?" Pp. 205-18
    in *Gangs in America*, 2d ed., edited by C. Ronald Huff. Thousand Oaks, CA: Sage.
Newburn, Tim and Elizabeth Stanko. 1994. *Just Boys Doing Business?: Men, Masculinities and
    Crime*. New York: Routledge.
Pesce, Rosario C. and Carol Gibb Harding. 1986. "Imaginary Audience Behavior and Its
    Relationship to Operational Thought and Social Experience." *Journal of Early Adolescence*
    6 (1): 83-94.
Rusk, David. 1995. *Cities without Suburbs*. 2d ed. Washington, DC: The Woodrow Wilson
    Center Press.
Sampson, Robert J. and William Julius Wilson. 1995. "Toward a Theory of Race, Crime, and
    Urban Inequality." Pp. 37-54 in *Crime and Inequality*, edited by John Hagan and Ruth D.
    Peterson. Stanford, CA: Stanford University Press.
Sanders, William. 1993. *Drive-Bys and Gang Bangs: Gangs and Grounded Culture*. Chicago:
    Aldine.

Short, James F. and Fred L. Strodtbeck. 1965. *Group Process and Gang Delinquency.* Chicago: University of Chicago Press.

Simpson, Sally. 1991. "Caste, Class and Violent Crime: Explaining Differences in Female Offending." *Criminology* 29 (1): 115-35.

Spergel, Irving A. and G. David Curry. 1993. "The National Youth Gang Survey: A Research and Development Process." Pp. 359-400 in *The Gang Intervention Handbook*, edited by Arnold P. Goldstein and C. Ronald Huff. Champaign, IL: Research Press.

Taylor, Carl. 1993. *Girls, Gangs, Women and Drugs.* East Lansing: Michigan State University Press.

Thornberry, Terence P., Marvin D. Krohn, Alan J. Lizotte, and Deborah Chard-Wierschem. 1993. "The Role of Juvenile Gangs in Facilitating Delinquent Behavior." *Journal of Research in Crime and Delinquency* 30 (1): 75-85.

Thorne, Barrie. 1993. *Gender Play: Girls and Boys in School.* New Brunswick, NJ: Rutgers University Press.

Wilson, William Julius. 1996. *When Work Disappears: The World of the New Urban Poor.* New York: Knopf.

Winfree, L. Thomas, Jr., Kathy Fuller, Teresa Vigil, and G. Larry Mays. 1992. "The Definition and Measurement of 'Gang Status': Policy Implications for Juvenile Justice." *Juvenile and Family Court Journal* 43:29-37.

[15]

MANAGING RETALIATION: DRUG ROBBERY AND INFORMAL SANCTION THREATS*

BRUCE A. JACOBS
VOLKAN TOPALLI
RICHARD WRIGHT
The University of Missouri-St. Louis
The National Consortium on Violence Research

The notion that informal sanction threats influence criminal decision-making is perhaps the most important contribution to neoclassical theory in the past 15 years. Notably absent from this contribution is an examination of the ways in which the risk of victim retaliation—arguably, the ultimate informal sanction—mediates the process. The present article addresses this gap, examining how active drug robbers (individuals who take money and drugs from dealers by force or threat of force) perceive and respond to the risk of victim retaliation in real-life settings and circumstances. The data's theoretical implications for deterrence and violence contagions are explored. Data were drawn from in-depth interviews with 25 currently active drug robbers recruited from the streets of St. Louis, Missouri.

Since its earliest days, criminology has sought to understand how the threat of official sanctions influences the behavior of would-be criminals (e.g., Beccaria, 1963 [1764]; Bentham, 1973 [1789]). Conventional wisdom holds that the more certain and severe the sanction, the less likely individuals will offend. "Informal" sanction threats also have attracted considerable scholarly attention, with particular emphasis placed on the role of shame and embarrassment (Blackwell et al., 1994; Grasmick and Bursik, 1990; Grasmick et al., 1993; Paternoster and Simpson, 1996). Initially attractive deviant actions, it is said, become decidedly less appealing when such conscience-linked variables are factored into the decision-making process. Some analysts have gone so far as to suggest that the extralegal consequences of offending may be the "real deterrent and that formal punishment is important only insofar as it triggers informal sanctions"

* This research was supported by Grant 98-1SDRP from the National Consortium on Violence Research. Points of view or opinions expressed in this document are those of the authors and do not necessarily reflect the position of the funding agency. We would like to thank Eric Baumer, Bob Bursik, Jennifer Jacobs, Rick Rosenfeld, and the anonymous referees for their helpful comments and criticisms on an earlier draft.

172   JACOBS ET AL.

(Bishop, 1984:405; see also Gibbs, 1989; Paternoster and Iovanni, 1986:769; Tittle, 1980:241; Williams, 1985:148).

The notion that informal sanction threats influence criminal decision-making is perhaps the most important contribution to deterrence theory in the past 15 years (see, e.g., Braithwaite, 1989; Grasmick et al., 1993; Williams and Hawkins, 1986). Notably absent from this contribution, however, is an examination of the ways in which the risk of victim retaliation—arguably, the ultimate informal sanction—mediates offender decisions. Indeed, we find it striking that the issue of deterrence has been discussed since the time of Beccaria and Bentham, yet retaliation has received so little attention from researchers (but see Black, 1983:39).

On its face, retaliation would appear to be a serious consequence of many offenses, especially those perpetrated against victims who themselves are involved in crime. Certainly the threat of retaliation is widely assumed in criminological discussions of organized crime (Arlacchi, 1987), gang violence (see, e.g., Decker and Van Winkle, 1996; Hagedorn, 1988), and drug dealing (see, e.g., Bourgois, 1995; Johnson et al., 1985). To hear criminologists talk, offenders who engage in these activities risk swift and potentially fatal consequences at the hands of their victims. Paradoxically, such discussions often are coupled with the observation that a major benefit of preying on fellow criminals is that they cannot go to the police (see, e.g., Wright and Decker, 1997). But why should offenders elect to reduce their chances of getting arrested at the cost of increasing their odds of being killed? What is it that allows them to accept this putatively greater risk?

Despite ample speculation on their part, criminologists lack any systematic empirical data on whether and, if so, how the threat of victim retaliation influences criminal behavior before, during, and after offenses. This lack of data represents a crucial gap in our understanding of both deterrence and of the contagion-like processes through which violence is contracted and contained (Loftin, 1986). If, as some have suggested, the spread of violence is a public health problem, then we must develop a better understanding of the precise mechanisms that facilitate or impede its transmission from one offense to another. To this end, the present paper examines how active drug robbers—individuals who take money and drugs from dealers by force or threat of force—perceive and respond to the risk of victim retaliation in real-life settings and circumstances.

CONCEPTUAL CONTEXT

Retaliation refers to an act of harm inflicted on another person in return for being wronged oneself. At its heart, retaliation is compensatory action designed to correct a perceived inequity. "Its hallmark is balance" (Black,

1993:91), and as such, it is grounded conceptually in the norm of reciprocity. This norm holds that persons will "respond to others in ways and to the degree that resembles that of the other person's initial [action]" (Craig, 1999:141; Gouldner, 1960). The greater the perceived imbalance, the more likely retributive responses become. Insofar as official channels of redress are either blocked or absent, the quest for payback will be especially strong (see also Barreca, 1995; Marongiu and Newman, 1987).

Like shame/embarrassment, retaliation is an informal sanction of both extralegal and moralistic character. Unlike its brethren, however, retaliation is unique in its ability to operate exclusively of formal sanctions. Shame and embarrassment, by contrast, tend to be triggered only after legal sanctions arise. As such, retaliation is capable of deterrence in its own right; to be sure, it may be the sole sanction offenders face.

Shame and embarrassment, moreover, have a middle class bias that retaliation typically lacks. As affective responses, they tend to influence only those with substantial stakes in conformity. Offenders, in general, and street offenders, in particular, often lack such stakes and therefore the "ability" to experience much of either emotion (see, e.g., Tittle, 1980). Indeed, failure to offend (e.g., by breaking the law to retaliate informally) can result in far more extreme forms of social disapproval: To endure in a world where only the strong survive, one must master the "ways of the badass" and control one's own destiny (see Katz, 1988). To do otherwise risks the label of weakling, inviting even more exploitation in the future.

The existence of retaliation necessarily means that the state and the self do not have a monopoly over sanction sources (see also Grasmick and Bursik, 1990). Its potential exists in every crime, though some offenses—like drug robbery—clearly are more conducive to it than others. The tactics designed to manage this threat—described in the present article—are not unlike "restrictively deterrent" behavior offenders use to evade formal sanction threats. The only difference lies in the intended target, offenders versus the police. Perhaps this is because "retaliation as social control" (see Black, 1983) more resembles a formal sanction—in its degree of threatened physical incapacitation, permanence, and external sourcing—than an informal one. Shame and guilt, by contrast, are *emotions* that deter *indigenously*.[1]

METHOD

The data for our study were obtained during in-depth interviews with 25 currently active drug robbers recruited from the streets of St. Louis, Missouri. Historically, St. Louis has had one of the largest illicit drug markets

---

1. Though embarrassment also is externally imposed, it means nothing unless or until it generates an emotive response within the psyche of the offender.

174   JACOBS ET AL.

in the Midwestern United States. In many neighborhoods, marijuana,
PCP, crack, and heroin are sold openly and available throughout the day.
St. Louis arrestees persistently have high rates of cocaine-, opiate-, and
marijuana-positive urine specimens; they are among the highest of the 24
cities measured in the Drug Use Forecasting program (now called Arres-
tee Drug Abuse Monitoring, or ADAM). Emergency room cases involving hard drugs mirror other large metropolitan areas and indicate a high
degree of street drug institutionalization.

Among the most socially distressed areas in the St. Louis metropolitan
area, the neighborhoods from which our offenders were recruited generally outrank other local sectors in the percentage of people living at or
below poverty, citizens unemployed or on welfare, school drop-outs, drug
arrests, and various other indicators of poor health. The neighborhoods
and contiguous blocks have all of the earmarks of "urban dead zones"
(Inciardi et al., 1993)—abandoned buildings, burned-out tenements, gar-
bage-strewn vacant lots, and graffiti-splashed walls.

The drug robbers were located through the efforts of two street-based
African-American field recruiters, both of whom were themselves active
members of the criminal underworld. One of these individuals had taken
part in a previous research project (see Jacobs, 1999b), and impressed us
as being more reliable than most of his colleagues. The second was his
associate, a person who quickly proved himself to be competent and
dependable. Each had extensive connections to networks of street offenders and, within those networks, enjoyed a solid reputation for integrity and
trustworthiness.

Trading on their trust, the field recruiters began by approaching relatives, friends, and acquaintances whom they knew to be active drug robbers. They explained our research objectives and told prospective
respondents that they would be paid $50 for participation. It is a cardinal
rule of street life that one should never do anything for nothing. Although
$50 may seem to be a substantial sum, it is important to remember that
most of these offenders could have earned much more through crime, and,
from their perspective, crime may have appeared to be less risky than talking to strangers about their law-breaking. Once the field recruiters' initial
source of active drug robbers was exhausted, they turned to referrals provided by earlier interviewees to further expand the sample.

Perhaps the greatest difficulty encountered by the field recruiters was
verifying that potential interviewees met the eligibility requirements for
project participation. To be considered an active drug robber, an offender
theoretically had to have (1) robbed at least one drug dealer in the last
three months and (2) committed at least three such robberies in the previous year. In practice, however, these criteria sometimes were difficult to

apply. Some offenders, whether because of heavy drug consumption, alcohol use, or circumspection, were initially unable or unwilling to recall the necessary information. Careful and sensitive questioning usually overcame this problem, but by that time, the offenders were sitting in front of us; those few who fell slightly outside the inclusion criteria could not safely be sent away empty-handed, and so we interviewed them anyway. From our perspective, this decision made perfect sense. Why turn away potentially valuable informants—individuals who regard themselves as active drug robbers and who are recognized by other offenders as active drug robbers—for the sake of adhering to what were, after all, somewhat arbitrary inclusion criteria in the first place?

The interviews, which typically lasted about an hour, were semistructured and conducted in an informal manner—thereby allowing offenders to respond freely and to introduce their own concepts and categories. Questions focused on the offenders' most recent drug robbery, but allowed for sufficient expansion to gauge whether this offense was executed in typical fashion. If it was not, additional questions were asked to determine the offenders' usual modus operandi. This strategy has been used successfully with active residential burglars (Wright and Decker, 1994), street robbers (Jacobs and Wright, 1999), and crack dealers (Jacobs, 1999a).

The drug robbers in our sample ranged in age from 15 to 46; the mean age was 29.6. All of them were African American; all but four were male. There is no way of knowing how well this sample represents the total population of active drug robbers, but it confidently can be said to overrepresent African-American offenders. No doubt the racial composition of our sample reflects the social chasm that exists between African Americans and whites in the St. Louis criminal underworld. These offender groups display a marked tendency to "stick to their own kind," seldom participating in overlapping criminal networks. The fact that both of our field recruiters were African American meant that they had few realistic opportunities to establish bonds of trust with white offenders; they simply had little day-to-day contact with them.

The internal validity of our data warrants comment. In an attempt to minimize lying and distortion, we promised the interviewees complete anonymity—we never asked for their real names—and assured them that what they told us would be held in strict confidence. The truthfulness of their responses was monitored by checking for and questioning inconsistent answers. This is not to suggest that the offenders never lied to protect themselves or embroidered their accounts to impress us; some of them may have done so. Nevertheless, we believe that undetected cases of distortion were sufficiently rare so as to not undermine the overall validity of

176   JACOBS ET AL.

our data.[2] Other researchers have assessed the quality of offender self-report data, concluding that semistructured interviews represent one of the best ways to obtain valid information about crime (see, e.g., Huizinga and Elliott, 1986). Using a sample of active street criminals similar to the one included here, Wright and Decker (1994) compared offenders' self-reports of arrest to official arrest records. They concluded that previous arrests were not underreported (see also West and Farrington, 1977).

Because drug robberies seldom are reported to the police, we could not check arrest records resulting from such offenses. That said, numerous opportunities developed during our research to verify that interviewees really were drug robbers and that what they said about their crimes was true. Six of them, for example, told us that they had been shot during one of their robberies and backed this claim by showing us their bullet wounds (some of which were in private places not normally visible to nonintimates). At least two of the offenders brought pistols to their interviews. On several occasions, we interviewed two or more offenders who had taken part in the same robbery. Although they were interviewed separately, often weeks apart, their descriptions closely matched one another.

Beyond this, we asked one of the field recruiters to sit in on several interviews relating to incidents of which he had direct knowledge. He said little during these interviews, although, on occasion, an interviewee asked him for help in recalling a precise location or exact address (something that we all have done in conversations with acquaintances). After the interviews, we debriefed the field recruiter to gauge the truthfulness of the drug robbers' accounts; in every case, he assured us that the interviewees had given us a broadly faithful description of the offense.

Finally, it could be argued that the field recruiters, in an effort to provide criminal acquaintances with easy cash, had somehow coached them to respond in a manner consistent with the goals of the project. In retrospect, this seems highly unlikely. First and foremost, the issue of retribution was never described or mentioned to recruiters as an empirical goal of the study. As such, they had no way of instructing interviewees how to respond "appropriately." In addition, one would assume that such coaching would have had to take our inclusion criteria into account (i.e., recruiters would instruct potential respondents to lie about their eligibility). Yet, a small number of respondents freely admitted falling outside these criteria, suggesting that they were not attempting to tailor their responses to our needs. Even if preinterview rehearsal were occurring, we would expect to obtain a rather homogeneous set of responses and

---

2. The only foolproof way to verify the details of offenses that are not reported to the police is to observe them in progress. We regard this as unacceptable for both practical and ethical reasons.

descriptions. This was not the case. Respondents described a variety of settings, locations, strategies, and circumstances, providing a diverse array of information inconsistent with premade scripts.

RETALIATORY THREAT MANAGEMENT

Although drug robberies are seldom reported to the police, those who commit them risk grave *extralegal* consequences. Victim dealers, unable to report the robbery to authorities, have a strong incentive to retaliate. To do otherwise risks being labeled a "mark," opening oneself up to even more exploitation. Street sellers, moreover, very often sell on consignment. To the extent that they must answer to someone else for lost cash and drugs, their need for retribution will be enhanced: The wrath of higher level suppliers can be swift and severe, and to chance it is unwise. Insofar as drug market participants are impulsive, short-run thinkers (Gottfredson and Hirschi, 1990; Walters, 1990), vengeance may become the only "proper" course of action. The drug robbers we interviewed well understood these issues and, in response, developed particular tactics to manage the threat. We present these tactics through a three-part typology consisting of intimidation, anonymity maintenance, and hypervigilance.

INTIMIDATION

First and foremost, the drug robbers wanted to choose dealers whose retributive potential was weak. Fundamentally, good targets were soft, bad ones were hard. By definition, soft targets are easily intimidated and unlikely to retaliate. Even a cursory review of the drug literature indicates that sellers make for pugnacious and formidable prey (see, e.g., Bourgois, 1995). Common sense suggests that they must be so to have any chance of survival in the cut-throat world of the streets. Yet, our offenders claimed that soft dealers were "everywhere." A reflection of drug market circumstances unique to St. Louis or of the particular experiences of our respondents, such comments highlight an important perception that guided their actions. As Ray Dog put it, "[D]ope dealers out here right now today man, are straight up chumps. They are chumps. They are punks...They are the weakest...." Do-dirty declared that dope dealers were "the most punk ass niggers in the world." Darnell used this stereotype to hone in on one particularly easy mark:

> He was a motherfucker that had all this dope and money but he was a bitch, real soft, you know what I'm saying? He was more like a little girl. He was the kind that did his feet and his hands, got his nails done, you know what I'm saying, had a couple of tough [friends] but he stayed by his self. Personally, I thought the motherfucker was gay but he wasn't, you know what I'm saying?

178   JACOBS ET AL.

As a general rule, streetcorner dealers were perceived to be softer than those who sold from houses (typically in larger quantities). Our respondents suggested that street dealers tended to be young and, surprisingly, unarmed—presumably to avoid the double sanction of drug and weapons possession.[3] We also know, from the literature, that curbside drug dealers often lack the organizational wherewithal required for even mundane retaliatory action. Their freelance, individualistic orientation simply is not conducive to focused payback (see, e.g., Decker and Van Winkle, 1996; Jacobs, 1999a). This is especially true for those who deal in high-volume, competitive sets (on which many of our offenders committed their drug robberies). Time spent seeking retaliation can better be spent making money, and for many, the opportunity cost of lost sales may be too high to justify the effort. As Blackwell put it, "I don't think I'm. . .gonna get retaliated back on by them cause they want to go back on they corner and sell drugs. That's what they do, sell drugs."

Targeting soft dealers, however, meant little in the absence of intimidation. Even the weakest sellers might be tempted to retaliate later if drug robbers failed to project a fierce enough persona during the offense. The goal, then, was to present a self so indomitable and trigger-happy that victims would not only hand over their possessions without hesitation (see, e.g., Luckenbill, 1981), but would think twice about seeking out perpetrators later. Menacing presentations were as much dramaturgical as indicative of the performer's "essential" character (see Shover, 1996). To the extent that such performances persuaded victims that the drug robbers' presented hardness was real, the drive for retaliation would weaken.

Both verbal and physical tactics were used toward this end. Expletive-loaded commands, such as (paraphrased here) "Get on the ground, don't move or you're dead motherfucker!," "Bitch, whore, asshole, motherfucker, up it or else!," and a host of others were reportedly voiced with a tone so fearsome as to leave no doubt that the perpetrator was not to be messed with, ever (see also Katz, 1988, on the ways of the "badass"). Pistol-whippings and warning shots drove this message home, underscoring the futility—and peril—of pursuit. "Sho[o]t. . .at the ground a few times," Darnell remarked, "let him know I [am] not bullshitting." Or as Kilo commented, "Hit him, hit him with the pistol, strike 'em. . .Just smack him with the butt of the gun, you know, in the back of the head somewhere. . . ." Buck took an even more menacing approach, grabbing his victims around the throat and then letting "them feel that cold steel [of the gun] on the back of they neck. [Cock the gun for] intimidation." Smoke

---

3. This suggests that the formal sanction threat of arrest outstrips that of being robbed, perhaps a testament to more vigorous policing, harsher weapons laws, or simply an underestimation of the real threat of drug robbery in this context.

MANAGING RETALIATION 179

Dog, similarly, pistol-whipped his victim, but only after seizing the booty—seemingly to make a point more than anything else. "I smacked him. . .so he grabbed his face and just laid on the ground. I guess he thought I was gonna go on and kill him or whatever but I walked on out. . .punk ass nigger." Lamont robbed a dealer of an eight-ball of crack (about three grams) and $100 outside an East St. Louis night club—shooting "less than lethal" shots before sprinting away. He made it clear, however, that preventing retaliation was very much on his mind:

> He could be having a gun on him too. I couldn't just walk away from him like that, just take that and walk away. He might have shot me in the back, shot me in the back of my head or something. . .I shot him to let him know I ain't playing with the .25, bing, bing, bing, bing. . . .I know he had a gun in his car and he messing around as soon as I walked away. He snuck in his car and might have run up behind me and shot me or something. So I shot him, bing, bing, I'm gonna leave him laying right here and I'm gonna make it to my car. Cause he gots to go to the hospital. Any person that you shot they got to go to the hospital unless you Superman or something, you can take these bullets, they bounce off you, you spit 'em out your mouth or something like Superman did. You a bad man if you can do that.[4]

Slim used the same approach, but took it to the next level, claiming he would return to his victims the "next fucking day." "[B]efore retaliation falls in," he explained, "I'm gonna retaliate first." He continued:

> I put that pistol in his mouth and I wanna know is there a problem?. . .find out what he want, what's on his mind. . . . See I have to go back. I got to go back. It's a must that I go back. If I don't he might slip up on me one day. . . . Either you [victim] can get the message or be laid out [killed]. . .'all right, now, if you got a problem with me, let me know now.' He say, 'no,' he ain't got no problem with me, 'all right.'

In nearly all cases, however, offenders endeavored to avoid seriously injuring or killing their victims. Lethal violence may be the best way to preempt retaliation, but it is the least desired. Bodies bring heat and negate the primary reason these offenders rob drug dealers in the first place: because they cannot go to the police. As V-O put it, "you kill somebody that's. . .14 years of your life [in prison]. You don't want. . .that." Establishing fear in the psyche of the victim, rather, is the name of the game. To

---

4. Lamont reportedly did not aim at his victim's head and used a .25 instead of his trusty .44 Magnum. "All guns hurt," he argued, "but a .25, that ain't nothing for real. Now if I'd have shot him with that .44 Magnum four times, he might have been dead. . .. He the fuck would have been dead right now or wearing a shit bag or something."

180   JACOBS ET AL.

instill it in would-be pursuers is to unnerve them and weaken their retributive resolve; as Lyman (1989:131) writes, "The wolf bares its teeth and the opposing wolf [bows its head] and slinks away."

ANONYMITY MAINTENANCE

Though choosing soft dealers and intimidating them into submission may be useful for shaping the "supply-side" of retribution, nothing eliminates the threat of reprisal in the way anonymity can: If victims never know who it is that robbed them, retaliation becomes moot. Nameless and faceless, drug robbers can move through the streets without worry or concern. This is not easy, however; significant effort is required to construct barriers around one's identity. Three particular strategies were used toward this end: stranger targeting, discretion, and disguises.

STRANGER TARGETING

Most of the offenders refused to target dealers with whom they were overly familiar. Acquaintanceships, no matter how weak or shallow, increase the odds of recognition and thus retribution. Preemptive lethal measures, which already have been identified as unattractive to the vast majority of our respondents, might be required as a result. The importance of attending to microstructure in "prequalifying" one's targets was thus undeniable. As Low Down emphasized:

> I ain't gonna rob nobody [I know]. If I rob [him], I'm pretty sure [he] would know my voice. . .if I be growing up with you all your life and I robbed you, I would be on the run. . .[you gonna be knowing me] since we was like this [younger]. . . .If I rob [an associate] I'll have to kill him cause he will know me and he'll be looking for me. . . .Then I being having to watch my back. . . .I'm not gonna come back and make like it never happened.

Three Eyes agreed:

> Like say for instance you are my friend. You are a drug dealer and I want to rob you but we been knowing each other about two or three years so I can't personally do it. If I do it I would actually have to kill you, see what I'm saying?. . . .Because he know me. . . .

Ray Dog insisted that the whole idea of robbing a friend was ridiculous, not because it violated basic loyalties (which are weak to begin with; see Klein, 1995), but because of its sheer impracticality. "I rob strangers better," he said, "because they don't know me. See friends know me, they know your voice, they know how you walk, how you talk, they know everything. . . .You can't [cover up] your face and go up there tell him, 'look nigger, up it.' 'Oh man, Ray, that you man,' you know."

This is not to suggest that known dealers were never targeted; some simply were too good to pass up. A number of drug robbers resolved the dilemma by enlisting a fellow offender, unknown to the mark, to commit the crime. Having accurate information of the dealer's movements, defensibility, support, and goods, the contracting offender would relay this intelligence to their proxy, who then did the job. Such ventures proved lucrative for both parties: Inside information produced a guaranteed and often considerable take that the two offenders would split; use of a surrogate, meanwhile, ensured continued anonymity for the offender who set up the scheme.

Innovations aside, there were important lessons to learn from those who failed to take interpersonal familiarity into account. Low Down, for example, witnessed the slaying of a partner who had robbed one acquaintance-dealer too many. This individual was killed after two prior retaliation attempts. "I stayed away from him," Low Down recalled. "I could have been riding with him and they seen me and thought I had something to do with it." Robbing a stranger-dealer more than once was misguided in a similar sense; anonymity could no longer be maintained or taken for granted. "You never go back and strike the same [victim]," Do-dirty warned, "never do that. . . .You rob a person one time then you go back a second time and try to rob them, they gonna be recognizing you." This, according to Lewis, would most assuredly result in a "gun down."

Familiarity, or the lack thereof, was also important in a geographic sense. Many offenders refused to commit drug robberies in or around the neighborhood where they spent most of their time. To do so risked almost certain exposure. As Slim asked, "Why would I rob somebody where I rest my head at? Why would I bring heat where I rest my head at, where I stay at? That don't make sense." YoYo concurred: "If I gonna do some dirt, I don't want [nobody] to know where I stay." Baby Doll put these sentiments into perspective:

> They [victims] know where you stay at, know where you hang out. . .[Doing a drug robbery in your "home neighborhood"] that's like putting your life on the line, you know what I'm saying. They can go on up and kill you. . . .I try to have a safe place to live, lay my head. When I go home I know I'm safe there, I ain't got to worry about nobody kicking my door in or chasing me, chasing me down, something like that you know.

The drug robbers plotted their activities accordingly. Slim, for example, restricted his offenses to St. Louis City, staying in objectively close, but perceptually distant, St. Louis County. "If I come out of this county and go down there and do my dirt down there I ain't bringing no dirt out here. Plus nobody don't know where I staying out here." Smoke Dog did the

182   JACOBS ET AL.

same, committing his robberies in the city and retiring to the safety of his "granny's" house in St. Louis county afterward:

> People riding around in the city looking for me, I'm out here chilling. . . .They ain't gonna find me. . . .You won't find that house unless I bring you to it and show you how to get there. We got so many ways to get to my house, we cool, you ain't gonna find it no type of way unless I show you. . . .You wouldn't believe, some of the guys down there [in the city], they don't even know where [the county] is man, they never even been out of the projects man for real.

The bottom line is that our offenders realized the importance of not "working" where they slept. Using one or more safe zones as a base of operation, they sought to establish separation between grounds intended for "hunting" and those geared toward habitation. In doing so, the offenders could enjoy an added layer of protection: Even if their anonymity somehow was blown, the likelihood of victims finding them remained small.

DISCRETION

Stranger targeting aside, anonymity maintenance also meant exercising discretion about what, or how much, one stole from victims. Flashing the spoils of a recent robbery—cash, expensive clothing, jewelry—was a sure-fire way to identify oneself as a "player" who needed to be taught a lesson. Showing off items that could be traced directly back to a specific victim was worse still. Both actions constitute affronts and serve as dangerous proclamations of one's "dirty work." This is especially problematic on the streets, where everybody knows everybody else's business and snitches are a ubiquitous feature of the social landscape. Spanky therefore refused to rip an expensive necklace off of his drug dealer-victim, fearing it would ultimately identify him as the perpetrator:

> I didn't want no chain cause the kind of chain he [victim] got, he had like a fat herringbone with a dagger on it and everybody know that's Bobo chain. [Bobo] seen with a size herringbone that big and if anybody else have it [others] would know it was his and they probably would have got hurt.

Subscribing to a policy of discretion might also call for taking "less." Darnell robbed a big-time house dealer of $10,000 in cash and several thousand dollars' worth of drugs, but left without taking all of the booty. This led him to claim that he really "didn't hurt [the victim] cause if I did, I could have gotten more out of the deal which I knew there was more there. . . .I see the guy to this day. He might smile. . . .And to this day, I don't think I really hurt him." Other offenders reported doing the same, settling for as much as they could get quickly, while leaving other valuable contraband behind. Though seemingly counterintuitive behavior for impulsive street offenders, it must be remembered that in these neighborhoods—and in the drug game in general—predation is so common as to be measured in degrees. To the extent that drug robbers moderate the amount they steal, victims might be more prone to chalk the experience up to the game, and move on.[5] Given the rapidity with which drugs and drug income can be replenished (at least by resourceful sellers), such a strategy may be well-grounded.

Perhaps the most vital component of discretion is postoffense silence. On the streets, word travels fast; there is no such thing as discussing a drug robbery in confidence. One never knows when, where, or to whom a story might be repeated. Postoffense boasting was perceived to be both dangerous and stupid. As June Bug explained:

> It don't make no sense to brag about it because see you could be bragging and ain't no telling this [person] might be somebody's cousin or relative, anybody, you see what I'm saying. So therefore you say to yourself why start bragging about shit? I'm not gonna get a bunch of motherfuckers here, 'I robbed this bitch you dig, and this you dig,' and just see what happened. Her cousin might be there, anybody's sister, brother, any motherfucker.

Ray Dog agreed, declaring that "You don't go around telling every motherfucker that you [did] that. That's how you get yourself killed." Or, as Buck put it, "Why would I tell on myself?. . . .I go to two or three [offender] funerals every year. . . .I don't want to get shot." Lewis and Slim concluded respectively:

> You don't put your goodies out in the street to everybody. . . .Everybody business ain't everybody business you know. . .just keep it to yourself then won't nobody know what you did. Only thing he can say, 'damn, somebody robbed me last night man!' that's it.

> There's nothing to brag about. See that's information. You don't brag about what you do. . . .Why would I tell these peoples about my business, what I'm doing. . . .Now if somebody else come up to them and tell them, 'damn, you know your partner robbed me last night.' He'll know for his self. But telling that there (inaudible) 'I knocked this fellow off last night for about $600, $700, $800 and 15, 16 rocks,' you know. Why would I brag to you about that there?

Loose talk risked having a price put on one's head. On the streets, snitches are a dime a dozen. To down-and-out drug users, even small

---

5. The same could be said of intimidating victims rather than killing them. Beyond the heightened risk of more severe formal sanctions, lethal violence also raises the odds of retribution—particularly when drug selling victims are gang-affiliated.

184   JACOBS ET AL.

offers of money or drugs can serve as powerful enticements to tattle. "Crack dealers. . .will pay a crackhead to tell [them], you know, where this person [drug robber] at," Baby Doll explained. "You don't let anybody know what you're doing." Three Eyes agreed: "[You tell and] the next person get jealous or get mad at you, turn you into the dope dealer for some money just for the information."

DISGUISES

As an anonymity maintenance device, few techniques trump the use of a good disguise. Recall that these offenders inhabit the same social world as their victims. Absent a disguise, they could easily be recognized later (even by stranger targets) or described to someone who knew their identity and whereabouts. "I don't never rob nobody without no mask," Low Down proclaimed, "because they'll [dealers] come back and kill me." "I don't want nobody to know me," Lewis added. "I might ride back down through the same street [sometime]. . .and he [past victim] might say,. . . 'damn, there goes the dude that robbed me right there.'. . . I would rather be safe than sorry." Ski masks were the cover of choice for most. As Smoke Dog observed:

> I'll wear a [ski] mask so they can't see my face. . . .[Some] of them, I be right in they faces laughing and they don't even know I'm the one that robbed them last night. . . .That's cold ain't it?. . . .I'm sitting here talking to you, riding in your car with you, you don't even know I'm the one that kicked in your house, put your baby's momma on the ground, you don't even know.

Other drug robbers donned ball caps and dark clothing, wrapped bandannas around their faces, shaved their beards or heads in particular ways, or used nighttime as natural camouflage. "I don't rob nobody in broad daylight," Low Down explained. "Too many people be out [and they can recognize you]." "You ride around, dark, you know," Do-dirty added. "Got some dark glasses on, you know, I might have a camouflage outfit on. I got a couple of camouflage outfits, army outfits, camouflage you know. What they call Ninja suits you know. . .put my glasses on with a cap." Ladybug claimed to dress like a street drug user, all in black, adding her "little hat" and "little glasses" to accessorize the look and make her less detectable. "I don't give a fuck if they [victims] see my face today or tomorrow," she boasted, "they don't know who the fuck I am [because I've changed my appearance since I robbed them]." She also claimed to wear a number of different wigs throughout a given week to ensure her continued anonymity. This strategy came in handy when she ran into a previous victim at a local White Castle (fast-food restaurant):

> This. . .dude ran up on me, pulled a gun, he was like, 'I remember

you!' [You robbed me!]. I said, 'you don't even know me. What's up?' 'Oh, I'm sorry,' [he said], 'I thought you was this other gal.' No I don't trip off these little punk ass niggers.

Failing to disguise one's identity could have fatal consequences. Smoke Dog neglected to do so on one occasion, with near disastrous results. "Dude. . .rolled down the city [later], started shooting at me and I started shooting back, me and my little partner. Started shooting back. He [drug robbery victim] jumped in his car and rolled off." Apparently, these gun battles continued well after the offense. "We was going to war," Smoke Dog declared. "Every time I see him he shoot at me, it's like that, we shoot at each other." The "war" stopped only when Smoke Dog's antagonist left town, which, of course, he claimed credit for: "I guess he got scared or whatever. . . .I broke him."

Disguises do possess a significant drawback, however; they make it difficult for drug robbers to capitalize on the element of surprise. A popular modus operandi among our respondents, for example, involved acting like customers who wished to purchase drugs. This allowed them to cover their true intentions until the last possible moment. Wearing a mask makes this impossible. "You don't come up out of the [neighbor]hood with no disguise on talking about can you cop [drugs]," Spanky explained. "'Cop what? Who are you?'. . .[That'll get you shot]."

HYPERVIGILANCE

No matter how effective their retaliatory management strategies, no single tactic or combination of tactics was foolproof. The effects of intimidation can wear off. Soft targets might enlist the services of a hit-man. Word of a drug robber's identity or whereabouts can leak. Anonymity might be breached by the most innocuous of chance encounters. The more recent a robbery, the more troublesome run-ins can become: Victims' memories are fresh, their sensitivity to interpersonal cues acute, and their thirst for revenge parching. Even with a mask, cues such as voice, demeanor, gait, size, and height remain tell-tale signs for especially attentive victims. Indeed, masks could draw only more attention to such factors during the robbery; essentially, they were the only things to attend to.

Our offenders thus devoted a significant portion of their day-to-day cognitive resources to minimizing the prospect of postoffense victim contact. Hypervigilance, the near obsessive attention to one's surroundings and the behavior of others, became the order of the day. As a general rule, offenders expected to be sought out by victims for hours, days, weeks, or even months after any given drug robbery. Measures had to be taken accordingly, given that dire consequences await those who let their guard down:

> You got to watch. I mean you could be inside some store, anybody
> walking behind you, you got to be like this here, man. You got to
> look around corners, you got to look around everywhere, you see
> what I'm saying? I mean even when I go to my mom's house some-
> times, I got to walk around through the back, go around to the back-
> yard, look around in the yard, see if anybody back there. . . .You stop
> coming outside during the day, you come out at nighttime. . . .Because
> during the day they notice you during the day. See at night it's dark.
> They might see you in a car or something. Then you change a
> lot. . . .You got to change your whole personality toward a lot of
> things. You got to change your attitude. (Ray Dog)

> You got to be cautious man. It's a job, man, all day long wherever
> you be at looking behind you. Cause one day, man, some
> motherfucker gonna get me. . . .You take $100,000 from a person,
> take it from him, you think he forget?. . . .Don't get me wrong. If they
> caught me tripping, man, I don't be here. If they was able to find out
> where they could actually get me or where I lay my head at night, I
> wouldn't be worth a god damn dime. (Curly)

To the middle-class observer, such behavior may seem paranoid. For drug
robbers, it is both functional and necessary. The threat of retaliation has a
long half-life, making it necessary for these offenders to keep their heads
up and their eyes open. Indeed, most of our respondents insisted that
attending to one's environment could never really be suspended, and as
the frequency and magnitude of their offenses increased, the need for sustained vigilance rose. "The more you rob," Do-dirty explained, "you
always gonna run into [victims] because St. Louis is too small. You bound
to run into him. Ain't no place you hide in the city of St. Louis at all." "I
see a lot of people that I done shit to," Darnell added. "I mean I laugh on
the inside [but] I always keep my eyes open. My uncle told me, 'you know
you've done a lot of wrong to these guys. Now that you're getting your life
together [getting off heroin], you really got to keep your head up. Cause
there is a time when all this shit might come back on you and when you
are ready to face it, then face it.'" YoYo claimed that such prospects tem-
pered the very attractiveness of drug robbery:

> [You] be taking a chance with your life everyday. . . .I mean you walk-
> ing around looking behind your back at every turn, every move you
> make, it ain't that easy, it's not that easy. [Drug robbery] sounds
> good, the money sounds good but it ain't that easy and that's the God
> honest truth, it's really not that easy. When you do dirt, you got to
> watch your back at all times cause you never know if somebody gonna
> get you. . .one day you can reap what you sow, you reap what you
> sow.

MANAGING RETALIATION   187

Decisions about whether, when, or how to return to the actual offense site
(or to contiguous areas) underscored the extent to which hypervigilance
constrained the drug robbers' postoffense movement patterns. Most interviewees steered clear of these locations for several weeks to several
months. "You give it three or four months before you roll back through
there," Do-dirty explained. "And even then, you don't be riding in your
car. . .[dude might see you and] he might tell his partner, 'man, that's the
dude that robbed me'. . . 'that's the dude that got you?' And his partners
come around the corner with a pistol and when you look up they gonna hit
you." Blackwell claimed to wait a "good four months" before returning.
By then, he argued, "they probably ain't worried about it." Baby Doll
insisted that she might never be able to go back to an area in which she
had done a drug robbery. Paradoxically, she recognized that her crack
habit was so powerful that she might have to go back:

> If I can't find no drugs in the area where I'm hanging out, shit, I say
> 'oh well,' I got to creep over this way [to a set where she had robbed].
> I got to do a little creeping you know. . . .I'll take a chance. . . .

Indeed, sometimes simply knowing that one had to "watch out" was not
enough to energize evasive conduct. Given the drug robbers' street-
focused lifestyle and frequent consumption of hard psychoactive drugs,
their decision-making abilities often were less than sharp. Drinking and
drug use are not conducive to clear thinking, and blunted judgment could
result in potentially fatal consequences. Baby Doll, for example,
recounted a revenge drug robbery in which she targeted a dealer who had
raped her a few months previously. The victim sought immediate retaliation, but was not successful: As Baby Doll put it, "He rolled around looking for us [that night] and he went and got I guess a couple of his partners
and stuff and they was on the streets. Shit, I had to stay off the street at
least about a good month, at least around in that area you know." Apparently, however, she went back too early—a decision no doubt influenced
by her drug-induced state of intoxication:

> There was one particular time, I was high, tripping, I was coming
> down Sarah [Street]. I didn't even think about it [the prospect of
> retaliation], you know, when you're high you forget about these
> things. [Her previous victim] pulled over and he had his little partner
> with him. . . .He jumped out of the car, his friend jumped out. I just
> took off running. I was running, I was running, running for dear
> life. . . .So one of them was riding around and the other one was on
> foot. So then his friend, they couldn't find me you know. . . .I hid
> down in this vacant building in the basement you know, underneath
> the steps. . . .I don't know, something just saved me but he didn't

188   JACOBS ET AL.

> catch me. . . .I waited there and it came to me, I said, I knew it [the
> drug robbery] would come back on me.

The task of hypervigilance was complicated by the drug robbers' nomadic
ways. Most of them claimed to never "lay their heads" in one place or
area for long, staying with kin, friends, girlfriends, and associates for small
intervals of time. "I'm a floater," Slim illustrated. "I can't believe in just
sitting there and letting roots grow up under my feet. I like to move, I like
to stay on the go."6 In one sense, the offenders' free-ranging lifestyles
gave them a much better chance at avoiding payback. Mobility allows
them to avoid "hot" areas (e.g., places where they have committed drug
robberies) and provides greater access to hiding places. In another, it carried significant risks of its own by increasing the odds of chance
encounters. This is especially true given the dense microstructure of the
streets. An encapsulated social world, the streets enmesh participants in
an expansive web of relations. The distance between ties is short. Weak
ties allow otherwise unconnected groups and networks to be bridged. Iso-
morphic lifestyles bring offenders and victims together (Lauritsen et al.,
1991). The more members of a network there are, and the denser that
network is, the more likely run-ins become. Bus stops, mini-malls, grocery
stores, bars, theaters, and fast-food restaurants emerge as contexts fraught
with potential risk.

One important and widespread response to this risk was to carry a firearm at all times. As Curly put it, "Never get caught without [your gun],
never. When I get out of the car I got it, man, I don't get out of the car
without it. Even if I'm getting out of the car to socialize, man, I got it
man." Lamont agreed, proclaiming that "I always have big magnum [.44]
with me. Big magnum is always with me. . . .I ride dirty every day, every
day, got to. . . .I'm strapped up, believe me, I'm strapped up. . . .That big
magnum gonna get busy. That's a quick loader too, he gonna get
busy. . . ." Ray Dog was even more emphatic, insisting that "You got to
sleep with your pistol, you got to eat with your pistol, you got to go to the
bathroom with your pistol, you got to take a shower with your pistol. . .everywhere you go you got to take your guns with you."

Bolstered by the confidence that only an ever-present firearm can provide, most offenders believed they could handle anything that came their
way:

> I'm the type of dude that, when you coming at me, I'm going back at
> you, you know. . . .I done put a lot of people to sleep. . .so hey, I ain't

---

6. Having safe zones to work out of and being mobile are not mutually exclusive.
Indeed, safe zones undoubtedly change over time as a direct consequence of mobility
patterns.

no joke. I'll tear a new hole in his ass just as quick as I'll tear one in any of these motherfuckers out here. . . .(Ray Dog)

Come with a gun. Come with your army,. . .cause it gonna take an army to take me down. . .you gonna kill me or I'm gonna kill you. . . .I come to a fight with a big old .45 because. . .when they see that big old .45 with a nine inch barrel on here, they bags up, they bags up. (Do-dirty)

Offenders with violent kin and friends were emboldened further by the knowledge that, even if they could not handle a particular situation personally, the slack could be taken up by others:

I got seven brothers, seven brothers and 13 youngsters, all of them straight up trigger-finger crazy. . .anything that happen to me, anything that goes down, I tell them where everything is, tell them where this is, this person did it. . . .That's a war, you know, that's a straight up war. (Ray Dog)

My little partners and them [get] down and dirty. . . .We're talking about hurt dudes. (Lamont)

If anybody come tripping,. . .they [my partners] already know what's up. . .they got my back. . .if I have any static, if any motherfuckers act like they gonna do something to me, [they get] trigger happy. (YoYo)

To some extent, comments such as these strain credulity. Street offenders hold each other in low esteem and relationships among them—even those who call each other "partner"—hinge on mutual distrust. Solidarity in the traditional sense of the term barely exists. Though some offenders seemed to recognize this contradiction, many held onto the belief that they somehow would be covered in the event of reprisal. Talk of being covered may provide all of the reassurance necessary; security comes in saying the words (cf. Fleisher, 1995).

DISCUSSION

Drug robbery is an offense with potentially grave extralegal consequences. Unable to report the crime to police, drug dealers have a strong incentive to retaliate. This article has examined how drug robbers perceive and respond to this threat. Three strategies were explored to this end: intimidation, anonymity maintenance, and hypervigilance. Intimidation deters dealer-victims from seeking retribution, anonymity maintenance prevents them from knowing whom to pursue, and hypervigilance reduces the likelihood that any given retaliatory strike will be successful. These tactics are depicted schematically in Figure 1.

Although the model has the appearance of a compartmentalized behavior set, it may not be so clear-cut. As the dotted lines and bidirectional arrows indicate, strategies might be implemented at various points in time

Figure 1.

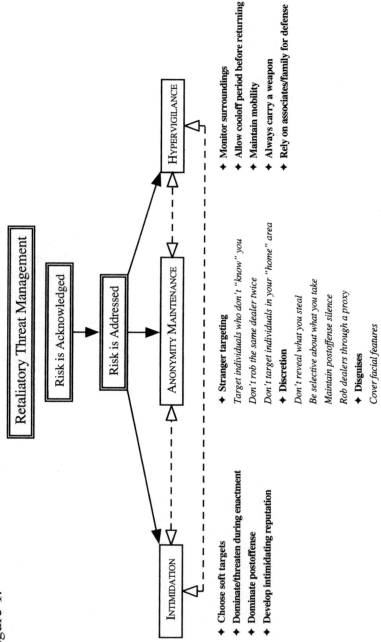

(before, during, and after the enactment of drug robbery). Strategies may also be used in degrees, in specific sequences, in concert, or in lieu of others. The weakest of intimidation attempts, for example, can be "covered" by remedial actions later. If anonymity maintenance fails, hypervigilance offers a countermeasure. Identity leakage is not nearly so damning if one can muster enough firepower to neutralize emergent threats, or can avoid those one has robbed. Over time, retaliatory threat management (RTM) tactics might even be suspended altogether. Bolstered by past successes, offenders may believe themselves invulnerable to attack (see Paternoster and Piquero, 1995, on direct experiences with punishment avoidance). Targets may be selected with less discretion, offenses enacted with less precision, and hypervigilance exercised with less urgency. Fatalism coupled with heavy drinking, hard drug use, and fiscal desperation—all of which characterize the vast majority of our offenders—only amplify these tendencies (see also Shover, 1996). Given that the risk of retaliation accumulates across offenses, RTM tactics may subjectively appear less necessary even as they become objectively more important.

Even if strictly adhered to, such tactics clearly are not foolproof. Some have a real potential for creating the opposite of their intended effect. Intimidation, for instance, may squelch within-offense resistance, but might also incite emasculated victims to seek reprisal with even greater resolve. Weapons provide protection, but can entice their carriers to (1) lay low for shorter periods of time, (2) travel to areas that otherwise would be considered off-limits, or (3) be less vigilant. Targeting "strange" drug sets ensures greater anonymity, but may confound a quick getaway (assuming escape routes are less known). Enlisting others to watch one's back engenders security, but exposes offenders to the hazards of gossip (particularly given the precarious loyalty and shifting alliances of the streets). Hypervigilance is functional, but also is emotionally draining. Ultimately, it may be suspended altogether in favor of a fatalistic, "fuck it" mentality (Walters, 1990) that emboldens offenders to commit even more crimes, or leads them to dismiss the importance of retaliatory threat management in favor of preemptive incapacitation (for an analogy, see Sherman, 1993, on the "defiance effect"; see also Brown et al., 1996, on the psychic costs of offending). Both function to increase the offenders' aggregate risk.

Pitfalls aside, one could argue that the tactics described in this paper have generic importance outside the realm of drug robbery. They may be part and parcel of a more general decision-making calculus reflected in all forms of victimizing behavior. The drug robbers' practice of intimidating dealers is not wholly unlike threats made against "ordinary" (noncriminal) victims to prevent pursuit. Disguises, discretion, and hypervigilance are

192   JACOBS ET AL.

analogous to the behavior of any prudent bank robber or street mugger seeking to elude those who might seek them out.[7] The difference is that law-abiding victims, almost by definition, are unlikely to retaliate. Typically, they lack the knowledge, skill, and disposition to do so, as well as the moral conviction to take the law into their own hands (and thus break it). Formal justice exists to shoulder their burden. Fortunately, for would-be offenders, the same tactics that discourage retaliation also may reduce the victim's willingness to seek official redress.

The point is that law cannot be useful if it is rendered perceptually unavailable. Such a possibility clearly exists. Certain offenses, for example, may be so violating or shaming that nothing short of personal retribution will do. Others may be so insignificant (i.e., to officialdom) that alerting authorities is not a viable option. Still others may ignite an acute, but intensely transitory need for official intervention that rapidly dissipates (e.g., road rage). Or, violations may lack sufficient evidence to justify anything beyond an informal response.

Law also can be unavailable because it is absent. War, civil unrest, and natural catastrophes periodically threaten a return to the Hobbesian state of nature, in which informal social control is the only kind available (see Black, 1983). Just the same, law may be present, but not granted legitimacy—such as when police are perceived as an occupying force, or when formal authority is judged to be capricious, random, and inequitable (see Sherman, 1993). Or, law may be present but not "usable"—perhaps because of status differences or social distance between complainants and offenders (Black, 1983). Finally, law may be unavailable because it is ineffectual. We know that the vast majority of offenses go undetected or unacted upon by police. Temporal gaps between detection, arrest, and conviction undermine the celerity of punishment. Bungled prosecutions sometimes result in the guilty going free. As confidence in the system wanes and skepticism rises, the perceived need to take matters into one's own hands increases. Retaliation becomes the only way to bring the swiftness, certainty, and severity of punishment back into deterrence.[8]

Illicit drug markets represent a context in which law is unavailable as a

---

7. Thanks go to Bob Bursik and an anonymous referee for bringing these points to our attention.

8. Recent legislative initiatives—harsh prison terms for minor offenses, mandatory minimum sentences, cries for corporal punishment (i.e., Singapore-style), and the reinvigoration of capital punishment—testify to a widespread perception that formal crime control mechanisms are too weak and need to be enhanced. Indeed, many state legislatures have gone so far as to allow ordinary citizens to carry concealed weapons (CCW), a policy with the ironic, if unintended, consequence of extending the retaliatory potential of criminal victims to law-abiding citizens. Behind such measures lies the notion that the threat of retaliation is a powerful deterrent. In this sense, CCW laws may represent an attempt to formalize informal deterrence.

matter of course (see also Black, 1983). As an underworld enterprise, it lacks formal regulation. Offenders and victims often are one in the same. Victims cannot truly be "innocent" and are therefore perceived to be undeserving of legal redress. This is far from saying, however, that victims of drug robbery will summarily shrug their shoulders and move on. On the streets, accepting one's victimization is an untenable proposition. To be exploited without fighting back is to be a punk, and to be a punk is to open oneself up to even more exploitation.

How the wrong gets "righted" is then the issue. We know that violence tends to be exchanged reciprocally (Singer, 1986:61). We also know that the motive behind such exchanges often is moralistic or normative in nature—a kind of "you got me so I have to get you back" mentality (see Black, 1983). If the tactics described in this paper work as effectively as our offenders suggest, reciprocal exchanges will be stifled. The better they work, the more unbalanced reciprocity becomes. Unable to exact revenge on those who robbed them and desperate to make back losses, victims might be prone to engage in unfocused retribution—predation displaced onto uninvolved third parties (see also Sherman, 1993 on "indirect defiance"). The crime-saturated drug sets in which predatory offenses like drug robbery are performed provide testimony. Such areas have a readily available group of potential victims in a discrete space whose lifestyle patterns render them easy and logical targets (see Lauritsen et al., 1991). This creates ideal conditions for violence to spiral beyond any given victim-offender dyad.

The extent to which this dynamic played into the historic levels of systemic instability and violence generated between 1984 and 1991—a major contemporary controversy in criminology—remains open to question. Though the emergence of crack cocaine seems to be the primary cause (Blumstein and Rosenfeld, 1998), unfocused "retribution" resulting from drug robberies may well have had a concomitant effect on the diffusion process. The threat of retaliation motivates widespread arming. Guns are acquired by individuals peripherally involved in the conflict. Weapons are used in an increasingly casual manner (see Blumstein and Rosenfeld, 1998). The ironic consequence is that, although retaliatory threat management tactics are geared toward impeding violence against drug robbers at the individual level, their implementation may create more violence on a systemic level.

Even if we accept the notion that retaliation is more successful than not and that predation is directly reciprocal, cycles of violence do not necessarily become less problematic. Retaliation can very well lead to counter-retaliation, which in turn can spawn even more violence as an increasing number of tangentially associated individuals get drawn into the conflict (see Goldstein, 1985). Given that formal social control on the streets is so

194   JACOBS ET AL.

lacking in effectiveness, credibility, and deterrent value (see, e.g., Paternoster, 1987; Paternoster and Piquero, 1995; Sherman, 1993), such diffusion is only to be expected. Indeed, street justice—once the modal form of dispute resolution—may be especially strong in this "vestigial context" because police often perceive such venues to be undeserving of formal intervention (see Klinger, 1997). Misfits and malcontents merit whatever fate befalls them. The more unstable the context, the more entrenched informal justice becomes, and the more likely formal authorities will "look the other way." This, in turn, engenders even greater instability, triggering a self-enclosed cycle of reinforcing behavior (cf., Lemert, 1953). Ultimately, whether such chaos is triggered by the diffusion of violence outward from some central point of origin (e.g., the original dealer-victim/drug robber dyad) or from microbursts of violence exploding across random nodes in the street-level microstructure (i.e., unfocused predation) makes little difference.

Undoubtedly, both dynamics are occurring at the same time, creating the tangled web of violence we see in so many high-crime urban locales across the country.

REFERENCES

Anderson, Elijah
    1990   Streetwise. Chicago: University of Chicago Press.

Arlacchi, Pino
    1987   Mafia Business. London: Verso.

Barreca, Regina
    1995   Sweet Revenge: The Wicked Delights of Getting Even. New York: Harmony.

Beccaria, Cesare
    1963   On Crimes and Punishments. Translated by Henry Paolucci. Indianapolis:
    (1764)   Bobbs-Merrill.

Bentham, Jeremy
    1973   Political Thought. New York: Barnes and Noble.
    (1789)

Bishop, Donna M.
    1984   Legal and extralegal barriers to delinquency: A panel analysis. Criminology 22:403–419.

Black, Donald
    1983   Crime as Social Control. American Sociological Review 48:34–45.
    1993   The Social Structure of Right and Wrong. San Diego: Academic Press.

Blackwell, Brenda S., Harold G. Grasmick, and John K. Cochran
    1994   Racial differences in perceived sanction threat: Static and dynamic hypotheses. Journal of Research in Crime and Delinquency 31:210–224.

MANAGING RETALIATION   195

Blumstein, Alfred and Richard Rosenfeld
   1998   Explaining recent trends in U.S. homicide rates. Journal of Criminal Law
           and Criminology 88(4):1175–1216.

Bourgois, Philippe
   1995   In Search of Respect: Selling Crack in El Barrio. Cambridge, U.K.: Cam-
           bridge University Press.

Braithwaite, John
   1989   Crime, Shame, and Reintegration. Cambridge, U.K.: Cambridge Univer-
           sity Press.

Brown, Stephen E., Finn-Aage Esbensen, and Gilbert Geis
   1996   Explaining Crime and Its Context. 2d ed. Cincinnati, Ohio: Anderson.

Craig, Kellina M.
   1999   Retaliation, fear, or rage: An investigation of African American and white
           reactions to racist hate crimes. Journal of Interpersonal Violence
           14:138–151.

Decker, Scott H. and Barrik Van Winkle
   1996   Life in the Gang. Cambridge, U.K.: Cambridge University Press.

Fleisher, Mark S.
   1995   Beggars and Thieves: Lives of Urban Street Criminals. Madison, Wisc.:
           University of Wisconsin Press.

Gibbs, Jack P.
   1989   Control: Sociology's Central Notion. Champaign, Ill.: University of Illinois
           Press.

Goldstein, Paul J.
   1985   The drugs/violence nexus: A tripartite conceptual framework. Journal of
           Drug Issues 15:493–506.

Gottfredson, Michael and Travis Hirschi
   1990   A General Theory of Crime. Palo Alto, Calif.: Stanford University Press.

Gouldner, Alvin W.
   1960   The norm of reciprocity: A preliminary statement. American Sociological
           Review 25:161–178.

Grasmick, Harold G. and Robert J. Bursik, Jr.
   1990   Conscience, significant others, and rational choice: Extending the deter-
           rence model. Law and Society Review 24:837–861.

Grasmick, Harold G., Brenda S. Blackwell, and Robert J. Bursik, Jr.
   1993   Changes in the sex patterning of perceived threats of sanctions. Law and
           Society Review 27:679–705.

Hagedorn, John M.
   1988   People and Folks. Chicago: Lake View Press.

Huizinga, David and Delbert S. Elliott
   1986   Reassessing the reliability and validity of self-report delinquency measures.
           Journal of Quantitative Criminology 2:293–327.

Inciardi, James A., Ruth Horowitz, and Anne E. Pottieger
   1993   Street Kids, Street Drugs, Street Crime. Belmont, Calif.: Wadsworth.

196 JACOBS ET AL.

Jacobs, Bruce A.
   1999a   Dealing Crack: The Social World of Streetcorner Selling. Boston: North-
           eastern University Press.
   1999b   Crack to heroin? Drug markets and transition. British Journal of Criminol-
           ogy 39:555–574.

Jacobs, Bruce A. and Richard Wright
   1999   Stick-up, street culture, and offender motivation. Criminology 37:149–173.

Johnson, Bruce D., Paul Goldstein, Edward Preble, James Schmeidler, Douglas S. Lipton, Barry Spunt, and Thomas Miller
   1985   Taking Care of Business: The Economics of Crime by Heroin Abusers. Lex-
           ington, Mass.: Lexington Books.

Katz, Jack
   1988   Seductions of Crime: Moral and Sensual Attractions in Doing Evil. New
           York: Basic Books.

Klein, Malcolm W.
   1995   The American Street Gang. Oxford, U.K.: Oxford University Press.

Klinger, David A.
   1997   Negotiating order in patrol work: An ecological theory of police response
           to deviance. Criminology 35:277–306.

Lauritsen, Janet L., Robert J. Sampson, and John H. Laub
   1991   The link between offending and victimization among adolescents. Criminol-
           ogy 29:265–291.

Lemert, Edwin
   1953   An isolation and closure theory of naive check forgery. Journal of Criminal
           Law, Criminology, and Police Science 44:296–307.

Loftin, Colin
   1986   Assaultive violence as a contagious social process. Bulletin of the New York
           Academy of Medicine 62:550–555.

Luckenbill, David
   1981   Generating compliance: The case of robbery. Urban Life 10:25–46.

Lyman, Stanford
   1989   The Seven Deadly Sins. Dix Hills, N.Y.: General Hall.

Marongiu, Pietro and Graeme Newman
   1987   Vengeance: The Fight Against Injustice. Totowa, N.J.: Rowman and Little-
           field.

Paternoster, Raymond
   1987   The deterrent effect of the perceived certainty and severity of punishment:
           A review of the evidence and issues. Justice Quarterly 4:173–217.

Paternoster, Raymond and Leann Iovanni
   1986   The deterrent effect of perceived severity: A reexamination. Social Forces
           64:751–777.

Paternoster, Raymond and Alex Piquero
   1995   Reconceptualizing deterrence: An empirical test of personal and vicarious
           experiences. Journal of Research in Crime and Delinquency. 32:251–286.

Paternoster, Raymond and Sally Simpson
  1996   Sanction threats and appeals to morality: Testing a rational choice model of corporate crime. Law and Society Review 30:549–583.

Sherman, Lawrence
  1993   Defiance, deterrence, and irrelevance: A theory of the criminal sanction. Journal of Research in Crime and Delinquency 30:445–473.

Shover, Neal
  1996   Great Pretenders: Pursuits and Careers of Persistent Thieves. Boulder, Colo.: Westview.

Singer, Simon I.
  1986   Victims of serious violence and their criminal behavior: Subcultural theory and beyond. Violence and Victims 1:61–70.

Tittle, Charles R.
  1980   Sanctions and Social Deviance. The Question of Deterrence. New York: Praeger.

Walters, Glenn
  1990   The Criminal Lifestyle. Newbury Park, Calif.: Sage.

West, Donald J. and David P. Farrington
  1977   The Delinquent Way of Life. London: Heinemann.

Williams, III, Frank P.
  1985   Deterrence and social control: Rethinking the relationship. Journal of Criminal Justice 13:141–151.

Williams, Kirk R. and Richard Hawkins
  1986   Perceptual research in general deterrence: A critical review. Law and Society Review 20:545–572.

Wright, Richard T. and Scott H. Decker
  1994   Burglars on the Job. Boston: Northeastern University Press.
  1997   Armed Robbers in Action: Stickups and Street Culture. Boston: Northeastern University Press.

Bruce A. Jacobs is Associate Professor of Criminology at the University of Missouri-St. Louis. His research explores street drug markets. He is author of the recently published book, *Dealing Crack: The Social World of Streetcorner Selling* (Boston: Northeastern University Press).

Volkan Topalli is NSF Postdoctoral Fellow with the National Consortium on Violence Research (NCOVR). His research focuses on experimental investigation of human aggression and offender decision-making.

Richard Wright is Professor of Criminology at the University of Missouri-St. Louis and a member of the National Consortium on Violence Research. His research explores offender decision-making. He is the co-author of *Armed Robbers in Action: Stick-ups and Street Culture* (Boston: Northeastern University Press).

Part V
Theoretical Explanations of Violence

[16]

ANNALS, *AAPSS*, 567, January 2000

Listening to What the Streets Say: Vengeance as Ideology?

By RALPH CINTRON

ABSTRACT: Based on 10 years of ethnographic fieldwork in Latino/a communities in northern Illinois, this article discusses violence and vengeance among mostly youths and gang members. Four points are made. First, violence and vengeance are attempts to establish order over escalating disorder. Vengeance often relies on a conviction regarding some higher moral order. Second, vengeance can operate as a kind of counter ideology when the values and beliefs of a legally based society seem hypocritical or unreliable. Third, when we consider vengeance as kind of ideology, we acknowledge the power of language to create a sense of what is real. Moreover, we acknowledge that ideological language always hides something from view. In short, vengeance hides pain, fear, and other vulnerabilities that lie at the root of violence. Fourth, in acknowledging these roots, the possibility of another ideology begins to take shape, that is, trust.

Ralph Cintron teaches in the Department of Rhetoric at the University of Iowa. In 1993-94, he was a Rockefeller Humanities Fellow at the State University of New York, Buffalo. He has published two books, one of which is Chero Ways, Gang Life, and Rhetorics of the Everyday *(1997), and is currently doing fieldwork in African American and Puerto Rican communities in the Chicagoland area.*

LISTENING TO WHAT THE STREETS SAY   43

"Thee Mystics rule," one of them yelled from the other side of the school fence. . . . I froze as the head-stomping came dangerously my way. But I was also intrigued. I wanted this power. I wanted to be able to bring a whole school to its knees and even make teachers squirm. All my school life until then had been poised against me: telling me what to be, what to say, how to say it. I was a broken boy, shy and fearful. I wanted what Thee Mystics had; I wanted the power to hurt somebody.

—Rodriguez (1993, 42)

Unlike most of the other articles in this volume on school violence, I will discuss experiences outside of school. I have spent considerable time ethnographically observing, talking to, and living with Latinos and Latinas as they try to make sense of their working-class lives. Accounts of violence and vengeance form only a small part of the talk that I have collected over the years. I discuss my broader interests in a recent publication (Cintron 1997). For this article, let me begin with a story of a scene experienced not so long ago.[1]

The setting is rural Illinois, Friday afternoon, October 1996, in the waiting room of a medium-security prison. Less than a mile away are next year's cornfields and soybeans. I am waiting with a group of mostly hefty women. Many come from Chicago. Most are African American or Latina (Mexican or Puerto Rican for the most part). Typically, these mothers, girlfriends, and wives come to the prison every other week. I come from a large public university, always on a Friday, not more than once a month. I am here to visit El Duque, a street gang leader who is about my age, late forties. Typically, the waiting, which usually lasts an hour or more, seems part of some vast system of punishment that imprisons us along with the convicted. Because this is one of my fieldwork days, I take notes on almost everything.

A young mother comes in holding a bassinet with a small baby inside. Her 4-year-old son, Willy, trails behind. Compared to the other women, this mother is stylish. She is wearing a suit coat with matching shorts. The outfit is made of shiny material. I am struck by Willy's fantastically sad eyes. Something has happened behind them, but, of course, I do not know what. Willy reaches into a bag that his mother has brought and pulls out a pair of toy handcuffs. He shuts his wrists inside them. "Look at me," he tells us. He shows his clasped hands to an occasional security guard walking through the waiting room: "Look at my handcuffs." He catches the attention of another boy, about his age, also waiting with his mother. "Let's play police," Willy tells him. "If you ever run away, I'll have to arrest you again." Willy's new prisoner flees and scurries around the crowded waiting room. The game begins to mirror too much of what these women know. One can feel the embarrassment and irritation mounting. Somebody has to stop their playing. Suddenly, the other boy's mother grabs her son and firmly places him in a chair. Game over.

Suddenly, I feel an electric surge of confirmation as one of the hefty women whom I have seen on a number of occasions has moved toward the front of the room and briefly turned so that I can read the words on her T-shirt: "Fear Is an Emotion/Bad Is an Attitude." After years of fieldwork in mostly Mexican or Puerto Rican neighborhoods in northern Illinois, those words label what I have come to understand about street life, its passion and special ideology. Those eight words on a T-shirt might neatly substitute for pages of data, analysis, speculation, and theory that I have been pulling together for years now.

The scene with Willy, the T-shirt—I scribble them hurriedly into my field book. One of the perverse thrills of the kind of research I do is that sometimes the theory that one has been crafting for a long time swoops down and becomes embodied in the events of everyday life. What I might otherwise look at with indifference acquires a certain import, a flash of recognition, as if yesterday's omen had materialized.

Suddenly, Willy's mother again: "Willy, pleeeeease stop your whining." But he does not. She is frazzled. She gives him a quick spank, and he lunges toward the floor with grand melodrama. He is going to stay there and turn himself into a furious spectacle to get back at his mother. The others in the room watch but do not watch. "Willy, pleeeeeeease don't do this to me." But he has suckered her into the drama, and now she cannot get out. She counters with exasperation, impatience, and anger in the dim hope of gathering everyone's attention and blame—and focusing it all, every bit of it, against him and deflecting it away from her.

For a fleeting moment, I marvel at how humans know so completely and yet so unconsciously how to pick at each other's vulnerabilities. It almost seems as if he knows what the floor means to her and others in this place that strips dignity from a person. "You can't lay on the floor like that," she screams. It is more than his defiance that is getting to her. He seems to know how to act out the symbols that shame her. She fights to recover some sort of order; he fights to disintegrate it. She is desperate to assert control, for, under the gazes of the tough women around her, her status as adult and parent is writhing on the floor. She screams ever more shrilly trying to trump his oversized scene with one of her own, "WILLYYYYYYYYYYYYY...." It is a long, long tussle, but they slowly move toward a momentary peace. She pulls him up to her lap and holds him, and there are moments of genuine affection now as they snuggle, but one realizes that there is misery here. They push and pull at each other, moving through a vast cycle of needs and resentments. Before I leave to visit El Duque, the cycle occurs at least two more times.

I am drawn to them. For me, all human dramas are deeply moving because they remind us of our own troubles. I want to pass my hand over their beings and give them whatever I can: some sort of respite, perhaps even love. I want someone to pass his or her hand over my being and to give me the same.

VIOLENCE VERSUS VENGEANCE

Shortly, I will make much of the T-shirt's "Fear Is an Emotion/Bad Is an Attitude," but for now I want to inquire into the central topic of this article, vengeance. Vengeance distinguishes itself from other forms of violence because it is often associated with a kind of justice. Vengeance seemingly entails a return to some moral order—or at least someone's perception of a moral order. Thus "vengeance" and its related terms— "revenge," "retribution," "just punishment," and so on—are exceptionally deceptive because they may hide their special brand of violence behind the aura of a return: a return to the way things were. Alternatively, these terms sometimes hide behind the aura of some future, idealized ought-to-be that will be wiped clean of current, wrongdoing antagonists. Sometimes these terms hide behind the conviction of right action in the name of some communal good by which avengers become convinced that their acts are good not only for themselves but for others as well. In all these possibilities, I want to point to the sort of moral conviction that may encourage someone to assume the role of a moral arbiter who acts quickly to reestablish a sense of right. In other words, vengeance is not just ordinary meanness. In many cases, it consists of an offended party who perceives authentic pain and then acts urgently to redress that pain. Unlike violence, then, which is often spontaneous, vengeance typically is more calculating. Indeed, much of the anthropological literature on small, remote (and some-

times not so remote) communities has told us for a long time that vengeance often functions in a complex system of deeply felt duty that, once performed, is rewarded with honor. Moreover, vengeance is sometimes shrouded in sacred dread and the need for ritual purification (Descola 1996). My point is that vengeance may be a particular species of violence insofar as it may operate in the name of some higher order.

But I want to be cautious here. It might well be that many acts of vengeance do entail a conception of some just, moral order that must be preserved, but is this true for all acts of vengeance? The recent killings of abortion doctors would seem, in part, to entail some sort of moral conviction, and Timothy McVay's Oklahoma bombing was amply described as getting back at the United States for its bungling of the Waco affair. So far so good. But I wonder about a whole set of other public events that seem similar but may not be. I am thinking of random shootings of people who are wholly unknown to the assailant and product tampering in which someone poisons a mass-distributed product that is, again, consumed by unknown people. When the targets of one's actions are this random and the higher causes behind them nebulous, can one describe them as acts of vengeance? When such actions are aimed against a generalized other instead of specifically known people, are they still vengeful? What about biological terrorism on the part of groups who do, indeed, see themselves as bearers of a truth? On one hand, such groups seem to have moral conviction; on the other hand, their targets are, again, anonymous. Acts of vengeance? Probably no grand theory of vengeance can contain all particular vengeances.

One last point needs to be made before proceeding. Earlier, I described vengeance as a species of violence, so it should prove helpful now to discuss briefly violence itself. It occurs to me that much of our violence is motivated by a desire to create order or to exert control over conditions that seem disordered. Although violence is typically imagined as a severe disruption, even eruption, in the midst of calm, I suspect that such calm is an illusion fabricated by some outside spectator. Violence has a tendency to escalate long before it crashes through the apparent surface of calm, and the intention behind each of those escalations may be to create order over a mounting disorder. In order to clarify this observation, consider my portrayal of the stuff roiling inside the heads of Willy and his mother. Both feared the escalating disorder and tried to trump it the best they knew how. Do we not yell this way in order to assert control or regain order over conditions that seem to be chaotic and escalating into greater chaos? Do we not slam lawsuits on the heads of offending parties when we feel that conditions have gone too far? (Even if these lawsuits are motivated by the desire for money, do they not have much to do with, say, mounting medical bills that are threatening?) Do we not undertake physical violence, if so disposed, when threatening disorder draws near?

If the answer to the preceding questions is yes, then we can understand that the violent impulse gets generated between these poles: an interpretation of disorder, an emotional need for order, and a sense of what order looks like. We might further acknowledge that different individuals or groups may interpret differently what is disordered versus what is ordered and may have different emotional needs regarding a state of order. An important point is that none of us is beyond the possible commission of violence. Indeed, we are all immersed in violence[2] but operate differently regarding what we think is ordered or disordered. At any rate, violence has something to do with the establishment of order, a calling to order, whereas vengeance would entail a special kind of ordering based on a moral and/or ethical conviction. Sometimes such convictions are based on hallucination, but, even in these instances, conviction remains an important ingredient.

Here is one of my central points: in legally based societies with centralized systems of government, vengeance is absorbed into one of the powers of the state and is, thereby, transformed into just (deserved) punishment. Under such conditions, those who continue to exercise serious vengeance outside the state become criminals. Herein lies a dilemma, for legally based societies do not homogeneously reproduce themselves; values, beliefs, and institutions do not replicate themselves evenly across a society's communities. Some pockets of a society may become fiercely attached to some aspects of the society, but other pockets are only partially introduced to that same ideology. A legally based society through its educational and governmental institutions may espouse the propriety of obeying laws X, Y, and Z, but different pockets of society may resist obeying all together, may adjust obeying in ad hoc fashion in order to meet actual circumstances, or may never have been exposed to that system of propriety (a central finding, by the way, of the Chicago school of sociology). So it is with vengeance. Serious acts of vengeance may persist in some communities or among some individuals according to a powerfully convincing logic—despite what the laws and institutions of a society recommend. Indeed, if a legally based society is perceived by such communities or individuals as fundamentally corrupt or anemic, vengeance, in contrast, might be perceived as not only an alternative logic but the only reliable one.

SOME ETHNOGRAPHIC CASES

I remember when I first became interested in vengeance. I had been hearing and tape-recording, as part of my research, a number of stories from young, school-age boys and girls. Some of the stories were about vengeance, and they seemed to have a pattern. The storytellers claimed that offensive words or actions had been aimed at them. In response, they felt compelled to "put things right" or "set things straight." The stories, typically, delineated the wrong and then justified the story-tellers' subsequent actions as "righting the wrong." In short, there was a kind of cause-and-effect relationship, a logic, that seemed to follow a fairly predictable sequence. Here is an example from someone who had just recently finished high school and who, with friends, had been arrested for selling narcotics. He claimed that his former buddies turned against him after their arrest and began to spread rumors that he had "set them up" with the help of the police in order to collect money from Crimestoppers:

So in the car, he [former friend] had a Alpine pull out, two Alpine amplifiers, one for each speaker with two 12-inch pyramid faze 3 pro series speakers and a kicker box and I had some guys take care of that, steal his shit out of the car, steal his alarm, and fuck up his car, in other words, key it up. They scratched his rims, they slashed his tires, they broke his windows, they fucked up the interior. . . . Because he kept insisting that, hey, number 1, that I had set them up because I wanted money [$1,000 from Crimestoppers for turning others in] and 2 . . . he was calling me a pussy, hey, you know, "Why you turning us in," this and that, "Why be a stool pigeon," you know, 'cause that is the kind of interpretation I took.

This story and others like it mobilized a certain ritualized language of the neighborhood, a language that functioned as kind of street ideology.[3] This language, brittle and predictable, was shared by both genders, and its key phrases often went like this: "So and so ain't showing me respect, no consideration"; "So and so's telling lies, talking trash; they ought to come talk to my face, and I'll set them straight"; "You gotta show 'em they can't fuck with you"; "I got my rights"; "No way so and so's going to take advantage of me." These phrases were the triggers, so to speak, for decision making. They assumed a clear, unambiguous offense (for instance, "telling lies, talking trash") and an equally clear offender. If the conditions were this clear, then the response was obvious, even commonsensical. The humiliation of the offended party called, automatically, without hesitation, for an equivalent humiliation of the offender. There was not much space here for ambiguity and tolerance. Its ethos was "an eye for an eye, a tooth for a tooth."

I puzzled over these stories. Why was there so much clarity regarding the nature of the offense and the intentions of the offender? The storytellers seemed not to doubt the facts of the situations as they perceived them, and they imagined that, by not taking action quickly, the rumor or humiliation would spread further or, worse yet, confirm their weaknesses in the eyes of others. These were authentic social pressures that might squeeze clarity out of situations that might otherwise have lacked such. But were there other things coursing through the community that might encourage this sort of clarity and urgency? As I looked at these stories and other instances of talk, I began to map a certain network of assumptions that ran through the community's talk and actions:

1. Life is tough.
2. Most people are not to be trusted.
3. Always be wary.

4. Defend yourself or get beaten up.
5. When a go-between reports the offensive remarks or actions of someone else, the go-between reports faithfully, without distortion.
6. Your enemies have simple motives: to hurt you.
7. Your enemies are basically lowlifes and not much else.
8. When wronged by your enemies, you occupy the moral high ground, a place of righteousness.
9. The wrongness of your enemies deserves punishment.
10. You always have the right to inflict such punishment.
11. You show more heart (honor, courage) when you take care of your own business.

IDEOLOGY OF VENGEANCE

We might summarize these assumptions by noting that the core worldview is one of distrust. The world is not a place that is abundant and gives of itself; rather, it is suspect and always ready to take from someone. Order is not a given, not something built into the fabric of human relationships. Rather, scarcity and the disorder that ensues are the givens. If order is to be made, one has to manufacture it and forcefully maintain it because it will always be threatened. Therefore, how can one rely on something as slow-moving, unpredictable, and abstract as a legally based society to deliver a regime of order? How can such an unpredictable entity right an injury committed by someone? The answer, of course, given the worldview outlined previously, is that it cannot.

The result is the emergence of the last assumption: one shows heart when taking care of one's own business.[4] This assumption means that the only reliable entity is the self operating independently outside the structures of a legally based society. Indeed, honor and dignity are awarded to such a self. In short, the act of vengeance becomes the tool of the righteous self putting order back into the world, a world inherently polluted by disorder.[5] We might call all this, then, the logic and ideology of vengeance. The problem for a legally based society is how to reinforce its own ideology in the face of a powerful, suspicious counter ideology. We might phrase this in a different way: a legally based society, as stated earlier, must find ways to reproduce itself across the entire range of its population, a population that is fragmented, according to the theories of ideology that inform this article, by an economy that distributes its wealth unevenly (class differences) and by a cultural capital that is similarly distributed unevenly (ethnic differences). Counter ideologies seem to flourish in those sites where a lack of those resources is most concentrated. (Readers here, however, might want to raise questions about Littleton, Colorado, and other sites of mass violence on the part of white youths in suburban and rural areas. Wealth and cultural capital seem more abundant in these areas than in my own fieldwork sites. One might speculate, however, that alienation is the connecting thread and that its different varieties may have different trajectories that end up in similar places.)

Let me put it this way: the vengeance stories contained language that seemed repetitious, ritualized, almost mantric. Vengeance thus seemed embedded so deeply that one might call it unconscious and ideological. As an ideology, it explained real events, feelings, and social conditions. Embedded in its talk was a very tight knot of emotion, worldview, and lived experience. Lived experience, in particular, served as evidence proving the correctness of the worldview. Lived experience represented a kind of realness that made the ideals and values preached by the educational institutions seem abstract, merely irrelevant, or, worse yet, hypocritical (because the practices of education were themselves seen as unjust; see the opening quotation from Rodriguez). In other words, this ideology made sense of "the way things are" and are expected to be. Moreover, it abstracted one's pain and dissatisfaction and placed it inside the nature of things. In short, it functioned as a kind of commonsense interpretation of street life. Creating another interpretation, cutting that knot, was no easy matter. Indeed, understanding life in some other way would have been difficult to imagine, for it would have entailed the making of a different common sense and, more profoundly, the making of a new psyche. The emergence of a new thought from within a frozen ideological interpretation entails a shake-up of old emotional patterns, and, more deeply, a new gut response to life itself. My experiences suggested that those who wagered certain life decisions on "the way things are" did not want to be proven wrong, indeed, would stubbornly resist the loss of that investment.

Like most ideologies, the ideology of vengeance hid its ideological character behind claims of being a real, a true, or a correct view. Ideologies, in general, occult themselves so thoroughly that a strenuous amount of reflexive thought is required to unpack how ideology insinuates itself inside communities and individual psyches. One way by which ideologies accomplish this occulting is through a process I call linguistic realism. The term refers to that most common supposition, namely, that speakers believe that they have the ability to say what they mean and, furthermore, that what they say is true. In other words, the supposition maintains that there is identity between the speaker, the words of the speaker, and what the words point to. For the most part, we really believe that what we say is really about reality. When we really, really believe—in short, when we have the conviction that the identity of speaker, word, and signified are most fused—we have an instance of authoritarianism. But we need not go this far in order to understand how all of us share in this conviction and how we ceaselessly gloss our propositions with very common expressions: "Here's the bottom line," "I'll stake my life on it," "You can bet your money on it," and "See, I told you so." The identity here between speaker, words spoken, and the world pointed to by the words, as described earlier, is so packed together that, as hearers, we forget that speakers speak from their perspectives, which are often incomplete or partial, and that their specific words materialize from a whole array of choices at, typically, the very moment of utterance. Indeed, when the identities seem convincingly packed together, it is as if we are hearing the very words that reality would speak if it had a voice. The partiality of the speaker gets occulted as does the fact of word choice, and, instead, reality seems to shine through. In other words, we forget that what is stated as real, true, or correct is a semblance. (Such a position, by the way, does not mean that some semblances are not better than others.) It is from the presumption of linguistic realism that conviction, decision, and action emerge—for better or worse. Moreover, it is via linguistic realism that ideologies hide their ideological character and, thus, endure.

But the maintenance of an ideology depends on more than linguistic realism. As I suggested earlier, there are emotional orientations and specific events that act as evidence of a worldview that must be synced with the ideological interpretation. When all three are synchronized, confirmation and conviction become more possible. As regards the emotional orientation, what was salient to me about the lives of those who told me stories of vengeance was a history of pain, fear, and anger. I never scaled and compared the examples of pain and fear that many of my interviewees, but not all, experienced when very young, but some sort of early injury to psyche was common enough. Indeed, one might examine some of these psyches as accumulating incidences of violence, small and large, incidences of violence that had metamorphosed from wounds to faint scars and then had metamorphosed further into a conviction that life is unstable or unjust. We might explain the emotional cycle in this way: the experience of pain generates the fear of some future pain, and one uses anger to protect oneself from pain—but anger, in turn, may destabilize the conditions around one and open the door again to a new round of pain. In other words, anxiety has captured such a life by the throat. Here we might remember the scene that opened this article and consider the difficulties of Willy and his mother. Of course, I cannot describe Willy's reality because I did not know him; much less can I predict his future. But what seemed to be happening in his life was consistent with the self-descriptions that I heard from others whom I knew fairly well. Life had become anxious, jittery. The possibility of disorder and its escalation was always near. Putting a stop to all that was paramount. In order to do that effectively, one squeezed clarity out of otherwise ambiguous events and responded decisively. The dense makeup of this ideology, then, included a history of anxiety, a set of assumptions about the nature of reality, actual life experiences that served as evidence proving those assumptions, and an able wielding of linguistic realism. This ideology inhabited individual psyches as well as street life's social imaginary as a kind of guiding ethos, in short, a sensible way (in some cases, a guaranteed way) to handle particular problems. In the end,

vengeance could not stop the spinning wheel of endless repetition, but it certainly answered deep-seated needs that were themselves forged and reinforced within the furnaces of this ideology.

CONCLUSION

I want to recall the T-shirt "Fear Is an Emotion/Bad Is an Attitude." Ultimately, I cannot know the intentions of the manufacturer or the wearer. Nevertheless, I think the T-shirt was consistent with a larger set of neighborhood meanings, and it is this consistency that I have been trying to lay out in this article. A short while after the scene with Willy and his mother, I asked El Duque what the T-shirt words might mean. El Duque was a powerful leader, famous in gang circles all over Illinois, and the one who called the shots for his organization at this particular prison. As a young boy, he had survived episodes of near torture inflicted by his father. As an adult, he was crafty, charismatic, and surprisingly legalistic in the handling of his organization; he had an intuitive grasp of others and a keen sense of what to do when. He described the meaning of the T-shirt this way: fear is something that one must hide; attitude is something that one acts out and that hides fear; one does not dare show fear because fear is a sign of weakness.

His words transformed into my own suggest the following: in an unreliable, aggressive world, showing weakness encourages others to take advantage of one. In contrast, badness as attitude hides fear, occults it behind a public persona of toughness that protects one from the challenges of others. The T-shirt, then, exposed an important dialectic in which the hiding of fear and emotion was paired against the display of badness and attitude. One way to cultivate badness and attitude was to acquire a reputation for violence and vengeance. Remember, for instance, the person I quoted earlier who faced down the challenge of being thought a "pussy" by destroying his rival's car.

But if we examine this dialectic closely, a conclusion to be drawn is that one side of the dialectic, say, badness and attitude, could not be mobilized without the other, that is, fear and layered pain. In other words, the public pose of badness and attitude was fragile at best, for the hidden world of emotion, fear, and layered pain that the public persona was paired to was dangerously close to the surface. Here in these spaces rendered dark by the sometimes hyperbolic performances of toughness, one might find the sorts of emotional experiences and anxiety that I tried to delineate in the story of Willy and his mother and that I have collected over time from El Duque and others. Indeed, this same dialectic was very much in evidence in the street corner poses of some gang members. With arms crossed over one's chest and the torso tilted slightly back (the street term for this pose, I learned later, was "gates locked"), the pose acted as a threat, a put-down, a sign of superiority, toughness, and attitude. In short, the pose signaled disrespect aimed against one's foes. As a communica-

tive system, it spoke most forcefully to those whose own histories of pain and humiliation were close to the surface. The put-down of gates locked, then, worked when it tapped someone else's terrain of anxiety. The fact that this second person might be seen at some later date signaling his own gates locked suggested that the dialectic was more than just part of the code of the streets. It also signaled the internalized tensions inside the individuals themselves, for gates locked rendered invisible a vast realm of difficulty, locked it away deep inside them. It would have taken a special courage to unlock the secret of the pose and to feel compassion for what was there. A person possessing such courage, however, might have been able to initiate a new kind of ideology, which, for lack of a better word, I would call trust. Such a logic, I am suggesting, might have had the chance of nudging out violence and vengeance, but how difficult it is to find such a logic in one's innerscape when the persistent outerscape has so thoroughly taught violence, large and small.

Notes

1. My research typically weaves analyses of economic and social conditions with analyses of the discourses of the people who inhabit those conditions. This article will concentrate on just the discourses. All names, including place names, are inventions in order to protect my sources.

2. I subscribe to an old Buddhist adage: physical and verbal violence are observable forms of violence, but thoughts, too, have form and therefore can be a species of violence.

3. Dictionary definitions of ideology, such as "a systematic body of concepts . . . about human life or culture" or "the integrated asser-

tions, theories, and aims that constitute a sociopolitical program," are not as significant to me as conceiving of ideology as a kind of sedimented common sense (Gramsci 1997; Althusser 1971; Roy 1994; Bourdieu and Passeron 1994; Hall 1996; Henry and Milovanovic 1996).

4. The word "heart" with this same meaning has a long history in the criminological literature. For instance, in *Delinquency and Drift* (1964, 76) David Matza reports its use in the context of delinquency, but undoubtedly it has an even older history. Incidentally, *Delinquency and Drift*, although a bit outdated in some senses, argues points similar to mine through Matza's concept of neutralization, especially his idea of the denial of the victim, meaning denial of a person's right to claim victim status for a harm because of past harms inflicted on the current offender (175). More generally, Matza argues, as I do, that violations of law are logical responses to what are seen as a legally based society's inadequacies. For instance, if one is faced with an affront, the law says that "if the police or citizenry are available, the coward's path is warranted" (76). My thanks to the editors of the present volume for pointing out the parallel.

5. I developed this interpretation of righteousness long before I read *Seductions of Crime* (1988), in which Jack Katz develops the concept of "righteous slaughter" to describe homicide resulting from attempts to correct injustices. My thanks to Stuart Henry for pointing me toward Katz's work.

References

Althusser, Louis. 1971. Ideology and Ideological State Apparatuses (Notes Towards an Investigation). In *Lenin and Philosophy and Other Essays*, ed. Ben Brewster. New York: Monthly Review Press.

Bourdieu, Pierre and Jean Claude Passeron. 1994. *Reproduction in Education, Society, and Culture*. Trans. Richard Nice. Thousand Oaks, CA: Sage.

Cintron, Ralph. 1997. *Chero Ways, Gang Life, and Rhetorics of the Everyday*. Boston: Beacon Press.

Descola, Philippe. 1996. *The Spears of Twilight: Life and Death in the Amazon Jungle*. Trans. Janet Lloyd. New York: New Press.

Gramsci, Antonio. 1997. *Selections from the Prison Notebooks*. Ed. and trans. Quintin Hoare and Geoffrey Nowell Smith. New York: International.

Hall, Stuart. 1996. The Problem of Ideology: Marxism Without Guarantees. In *Stuart Hall: Critical Dialogues in Cultural Studies*, ed. David Morley and Kuan Hsing Chen. London: Routledge.

Henry, Stuart and Dragan Milovanovic. 1996. *Constitutive Criminology: Beyond Postmodernism*. Thousand Oaks, CA: Sage.

Katz, Jack. 1988. *Seductions of Crime: Moral and Sensual Attractions in Doing Evil*. New York: Basic Books.

Matza, David. 1964. *Delinquency and Drift*. New York: John Wiley.

Rodriguez, Luis J. 1993. *Always Running, La Vida Loca: Gang Days in L.A.* Willimantic, CT: Curbstone Press.

Roy, Beth. 1994. *Some Trouble with Cows: Making Sense of Social Conflict*. Berkeley: University of California Press.

[17]

Annu. Rev. Sociol. 1996. 22:103–28
Copyright © 1996 by Annual Reviews Inc. All rights reserved

MASS MEDIA EFFECTS ON VIOLENT BEHAVIOR

Richard B. Felson

Department of Sociology, State University of New York at Albany, Albany, New York 12222

KEY WORDS: violence, aggression, exposure to television violence, media violence

ABSTRACT

The literature on the effect of exposure to media violence (including exposure to violent pornography) on aggressive behavior is critically reviewed. Evidence and theoretical arguments regarding short-term and long-term effects are discussed. Three points are emphasized: 1. Exposure to violence in laboratory and field experiments is as likely to affect nonaggressive antisocial behavior as it does aggressive behavior. The pattern is consistent with a sponsor effect rather than a modeling effect: an experimenter who shows violent films creates a permissive atmosphere; 2. the message that is learned from the media about when it is legitimate to use violence is not much different from the message learned from other sources, with the exception that illegitimate violence is more likely to be punished in media presentations; 3. the fact that violent criminals tend to be versatile—they commit nonviolent crimes as well—is inconsistent with explanations that emphasize proviolence socialization (from the media or other sources). I conclude that exposure to television violence probably does have a small effect on violent behavior for some viewers, possibly because the media directs viewer's attention to novel forms of violent behavior that they would not otherwise consider.

INTRODUCTION

Watching violence is a popular form of entertainment. A crowd of onlookers enjoys a street fight just as the Romans enjoyed the gladiators. Wrestling is a popular spectator sport not only in the United States, but in many countries in the Middle East. People enjoy combat between animals, e.g, cock fights in Indonesia, bull fights in Spain, and dog fights in rural areas of this country. Violence is frequently depicted in folklore, fairy tales, and other literature. Local news shows provide extensive coverage of violent crimes in order to increase their ratings.

104   FELSON

Technological advances have dramatically increased the availability of violent entertainment. The introduction of television was critical, particularly in making violent entertainment more available to children. More recently, cable systems, videocassette recorders, and video games have increased exposure. Hand-held cameras and video monitors now permit filming of actual crimes in progress. Economic competition for viewers, particularly young viewers, has placed a premium on media depictions of violence.

Not long after the introduction of television in American households, there occurred a dramatic increase in violent crime (Centerwall 1989). Some scholars and commentators see a causal connection. The most common argument is that children imitate the violence they see on television. The process of imitation is emphasized by social learning theory—a well-established approach in social psychology (Bandura 1983). For both practical and theoretical reasons, then, an interest developed in examining whether exposure to violence in the media affects the incidence of violence.

Violence usually refers to physical aggression. Aggression is usually defined as any behavior involving an intent to harm another person. Some studies of media effects, however, examine behaviors that do not involve an intent to harm. For example, a common procedure is to see whether children will hit a "Bobo" doll after observing an adult model do so or after being exposed to media violence. It seems unlikely that hitting a Bobo doll involves an intent to do harm (Tedeschi et al 1974). Other studies include measures of nonviolent criminal behavior, most of which do not involve an intent to do harm. Of course, it depends on what is meant by intent, a term most researchers do not define. Tedeschi & Felson (1994) define an intent to do harm as a behavior in which the actor expects the target will be harmed and values that harm.[1] Offenders who commit larceny and other nonviolent crimes know that the victim will be harmed, but in most cases they do not value that harm; harm is not their goal.

In the first section of this review, I discuss the empirical evidence regarding whether media violence has a causal effect on the aggressive behavior of viewers. I review the classic studies, the meta-analyses, and some more recent research. In the second section I examine the theoretical processes that might explain short-term effects, should they exist, and discuss relevant evidence. I do the same for long-term effects in the third section.[2]

---

[1] An alternative definition is that intentional harm involves deliberate harm or expected harm. However, teachers sometimes give low grades with the expectation that it will make their students unhappy, but their behavior should not be defined as aggressive, unless they also value that harm. Tedeschi & Felson (1994) substitute the term coercion for aggression and include coercive actions in which the actor values compliance as well as harm.

[2] This chapter borrows from Tedeschi & Felson (1994).

EMPIRICAL EVIDENCE REGARDING MEDIA EFFECTS ON AGGRESSION

The relationship between exposure to media violence and aggression has been examined using laboratory experiments, field experiments, natural experiments, and longitudinal analyses based on correlational data. I review some of the key research in each of these domains.

Laboratory Experiments

Laboratory experiments examine short-term effects of media violence. Most studies show that subjects in laboratory experiments who observe media violence tend to behave more aggressively than do subjects in control groups. A meta-analysis of these studies reveals consistent and substantial media effects (Andison 1977). However, research is inconsistent in showing whether it is necessary to provoke subjects before showing violence to get an effect (Freedman 1984). Thus, it is not clear whether media exposure acts as instigator of aggression in the laboratory or merely as a facilitator.

Researchers have raised questions about the external validity of laboratory experiments in this area (Freedman 1984, Cook et al 1983). They point out that the laboratory situation is very different from situations leading to violence outside the laboratory (e.g. Tedeschi & Felson 1994). For subjects to engage in aggressive behavior in the laboratory, the behavior must be legitimated. Subjects are told, for example, that the delivery of shocks is a teaching method or a part of a game. Subjects are then subjected to an attack by a confederate and given a chance to retaliate. Unlike aggressive behavior outside the laboratory, there is no possibility that this will be punished by third parties or subject them to retaliation from the target. It is unknown to what extent these differences limit the generalizability of experimental studies. Evidence suggests that aggression measures in many laboratory studies do involve an intent to harm (Berkowitz & Donnerstein 1982). Experimental subjects may not be so different from those who engage in violence outside the laboratory, who see their behavior as legitimate and who do not consider its costs.[3]

The demand cues in these studies are probably a more significant problem. Demand cues are instructions or other stimuli that indicate to subjects how the

---

[3] According to Freedman (1984), effects outside the laboratory are likely to be weaker than laboratory effects because violent programs are mixed with other types of programs. Friedrich-Cofer & Huston (1986) dispute this point, arguing that experimental research underestimates media effects. They claim that the stimuli used in experimental research are brief and often less violent than typical television programs and that the presence of experimenters inhibits subjects from engaging in aggressive behavior in laboratory settings.

106   FELSON

experimenter expects them to behave.[4] Experimenters who show violent films are likely to communicate a message about their attitudes toward aggression. A violent film may imply to subjects that the experimenter is a permissive adult or someone not particularly offended by violence. Just a few subjects aware of the demand and compliant could account for the mean differences in aggression found between experimental conditions.

The laboratory is a setting that exaggerates the effects of conformity and social influence (see Gottfredson & Hirschi 1993). The extent of compliance in laboratory settings is dramatically demonstrated in Milgram's (1974) well-known research on obedient aggression. Subjects' behavior is easily influenced for at least three reasons: (*a*) The standards for behavior are unclear and the situation is novel (Nemeth 1970); (*b*) subjects are influenced by the prestige of the experimenter and the scientific enterprise; (*c*) subjects want to avoid being perceived as psychologically maladjusted by the psychologist-experimenter (Rosenberg 1969).

Field Experiments

Concerns about external validity have stimulated researchers to employ field experiments. Field experiments retain the advantages of experimental design but avoid the problem of demand cues since subjects do not usually know they are being studied. A number of such studies have been carried out in institutionalized settings (Feshbach & Singer 1971, Leyens et al 1975, Parke et al 1977). In these studies, boys are exposed to either violent or nonviolent programming, and their aggressive behavior is observed in the following days or weeks. Each of the studies has some important methodological limitations (see Freedman 1984). For example, although the boys in each treatment lived together, the studies used statistical procedures that assumed that each boy's behavior was independent. Even if one overlooks the limitations, the results from these studies are inconsistent. In fact, one of the studies found that the boys who watched violent television programs were less aggressive than the boys who viewed nonviolent shows (Feshbach & Singer 1971).

The results of field experiments have been examined in at least three meta-analyses. Hearold's (1986) meta-analysis of a broad range of experimental studies revealed an effect for laboratory experiments but no effect for field experiments. A meta-analysis that included more recent studies, however, did find an effect for field experiments (Paik & Comstock 1994). Finally, Wood et al's meta-analysis (1991) was restricted to field studies of media violence

---

[4]Any cue that indicates which direction the experimenter prefers would be a demand cue. In their strongest form demand cues give away the experimenter's hypothesis to subjects, who then compliantly act to confirm the hypothesis. In their weaker form, demand cues simply guide behavior without creating awareness of the hypothesis.

on unconstrained social interaction.[5] In all of these studies children or adolescents were observed unobtrusively after being exposed to an aggressive or nonaggressive film. In 16 studies subjects engaged in more aggression following exposure to violent films, while in 7 studies subjects in the control group engaged in more aggression. In 5 of the studies there was no difference between control and experimental groups.

Natural Experiments: The Introduction of Television

These studies take advantage of the fact that television was introduced at different times in different locations. They assume that people who are exposed to television will also be exposed to a high dose of television violence. This is probably a reasonable assumption given the extremely high correlation between television viewing and exposure to television violence (Milavsky et al 1982).

Hennigan et al (1982) compared crime rates in American cities that already had television with those that did not. No effect of the presence or absence of television was found on violent crime rates in a comparison of the two kinds of cities. Furthermore, when cities without television obtained it, there was no increase in violent crime. There was an increase in the incidence of larceny, which the authors attributed to relative deprivation suffered by viewers observing affluent people on television.[6]

Joy et al (1986) examined changes in the aggressive behavior of children after television was introduced into an isolated Canadian town in the 1970s. The town was compared to two supposedly comparable towns that already had television. Forty-five children in the three towns were observed on the school playground in first and second grade and then again two years later. The frequency of both verbal and physical aggression increased in all three communities, but the increase was significantly greater in the community in which television was introduced during the study. Some of the results were not consistent with a television effect, however. In the first phase of the study, the children in the community without television were just as aggressive as the children in the communities that already had television. Without television they should have been less aggressive. The children in the community where television was introduced then became more aggressive than the children in the other communities in the second phase, when all three communities had television. At this point, the level of aggressive behavior in the three communities should have been similar. To accept the findings, one must assume that the community without television at the beginning of the study had more

[5] Some of the studies were in laboratory settings, but subjects did not know that their aggressive behavior was being observed as part of the study.

[6] The hypothesis that consumerism, promoted by advertising and the depiction of wealth on television, leads to more financially motivated crime has never been tested, to my knowledge.

108   FELSON

aggressive children than the other communities for other reasons, but that this effect was counteracted in the first phase by the fact that they were·not exposed to television. That assumption implies that there are other differences between the communities and thus casts doubt on the findings of the study.

Centerwall (1989) examined the relationship between homicide rates and the introduction of television in three countries: South Africa, Canada, and the United States. Television was introduced in South Africa in 1975, about 25 years after Canada and the United States. The white homicide rate increased dramatically in the United States and Canada about 15 years after the introduction of television, when the first generation of children who had access to television were entering adulthood. The white homicide rate declined slightly in South Africa during this time period. While Centerwall ruled out some confounding factors (e.g. differences in economic development), causal inference is difficult, given the many differences between the countries involved. In addition, Centerwall could not determine at the time he wrote whether the level of violence had increased 15 years after the introduction of television in South Africa; thus an important piece of evidence was missing.

Centerwall also examined the effect of the introduction of television in the United States. He found that urban areas acquired television before rural areas, and their homicide rates increased earlier. However, social changes in general are likely to occur in urban areas before they occur in rural areas. He also found that households of whites acquired television sets before households of blacks, and their homicide rates increased earlier as well. It is difficult to imagine an alternative explanation of this effect.

Still, the methodological limitations of these studies make it difficult to have confidence in a causal inference about media effects. The substantial differences between the comparison groups increase the risk that the relationship between the introduction of television and increases in aggression is spurious.

Natural Experiments: Publicized Violence

The effects of highly publicized violent events on fluctuations in homicide and suicide rates over time have been examined in a series of studies (see Phillips 1986 for a review). Phillips (1983) found an increase in the number of homicides after highly publicized heavyweight championship fights. Modeling effects were only observed when the losing fighter and the crime victims were similar in race and sex. The loss of prize fights by white fighters was followed by increases in deaths through homicide of white males on days 2 and 8. The loss of prize fights by blacks was followed by an increase in homicide deaths for black males on days 4 and 5. The rise in the homicide rate was not canceled out by a subsequent drop, suggesting that the prize fights affected the incidence and not just the timing of homicides.

Baron & Reiss (1985) attribute these effects to the fact that prize fights tend to occur during the week and homicides are more likely to occur on weekends. They were able to replicate Phillips' findings selecting weeks without prizefights and pretending that they had occurred. In response to this critique, Phillips & Bollen (1985) selected different weeks and showed that the weekend effect could not account for all of the findings. Miller et al (1991) replicated some of Phillips' results, but found that the effect only occurred on Saturdays following highly publicized fights.

Freedman (1984) has criticized Phillips' research on other methodological grounds, and Phillips (1986) has addressed these criticisms. There are still unresolved questions such as why effects tended to occur on different days for different races. In addition, experimental results suggest that watching boxing films does not affect the viewer's aggressive behavior. Geen (1978) found that, when provoked, college students were more aggressive after viewing vengeful aggression but not after viewing a boxing match (see also Hoyt 1970).

Longitudinal Surveys

Survey research demonstrates that the correlation between the amount of exposure to television violence and frequency of aggressive behavior generally varies between .10 and .20 (Freedman 1984, see Paik & Comstock 1994 for slightly higher estimates). There are good reasons to think the relationship is at least partly spurious. For example, children with favorable attitudes toward violence may be more likely to engage in violence and also more likely to find violence entertaining to watch. Also, children who are more closely supervised may be less likely to engage in violence and less likely to watch television. Intelligence, need for excitement, level of fear, and commitment to school are other possible confounding variables. Wiegman et al (1992) found that intelligence was negatively associated with both exposure to violence and aggressive behavior.

Longitudinal data has been used to examine whether viewing television violence produces changes in aggressive behavior. These studies statistically control for aggression at T1 in order to isolate causal effects on aggression at T2. Spuriousness is still possible if some third variable is associated with exposure to media violence and changes in aggressive behavior over time.

The main longitudinal evidence for a causal link between viewing violence and aggressive behavior has been provided by Eron, Huesmann, and their associates (Eron et al 1972, Huesmann & Eron 1986). In the first study, they examined the effect of children's exposure to television violence at age eight on aggressive behavior at age eighteen. A measure of viewing television violence at Time 1 was obtained by asking parents the names of their children's favorite television shows. These shows were coded for the level of violence depicted.

110   FELSON

Aggressive behavior at Time 2 was measured by ratings of aggressiveness by peers, self-reports, and the aggression subscale on the MMPI.[7] Effects of television violence were found only for boys and only on the peer nomination measure.

In addition to the inconsistent results, there are some measurement problems in this study (see Surgeon General's Report on Television Violence 1972, Freedman 1984). First, the aggression measure included items referring to antisocial behavior that do not involve aggression. Second, the measure of television exposure is based on parents' beliefs about the favorite programs of their children. Later research found that parental reports of their children's favorite programs are not strongly correlated to children's self-reports of total exposure (Milavsky et al 1982).

Three-year longitudinal studies of primary school children were later carried out in five countries: Australia, Israel, Poland, Finland, and the United States (Huesmann & Eron 1986). Aggression was measured by the same peer nomination measure as the one used in the earlier research. The children were asked to name one or two of their favorite programs and to indicate how often they watched them. Complex and inconsistent results were obtained. In the United States, television violence had a significant effect on the later aggressiveness of females but not males, a reversal of the effect found in their first study (Huesmann & Eron 1986). An effect of the violence of favorite programs on later aggression was found only for boys who rated themselves as similar to violent and nonviolent television characters. A similar conditional effect was found for males in Finland, but there was no effect of viewing television violence on later aggressiveness of females (Lagerspetz & Viemero 1986). In Poland a direct effect of violence in favorite programs was found on later aggressiveness for both males and females (Fraczek 1986). No effect of early viewing of television violence was found on subsequent aggressiveness for either males or females in Australia (Sheehan 1986), or among children living in a Kibbutz in Israel (Bachrach 1986). A television effect was found for city children in Israel when the measure of aggression was a single item asking "who never fights." But the effect did not occur on the same peer nomination measure that had been used in the other cross-national studies.

Negative evidence was obtained in a large-scale, methodologically sophisticated, longitudinal study carried out by Milavsky et al (1982). Their study was based on data collected from 3200 students in elementary and junior high schools in Fort Worth and Minneapolis. Students identified the programs they

---

[7] An important requirement of such studies is that they control for the aggressiveness of the viewer at the earlier time period, when looking at the effect of earlier exposure on later aggression. Eron & Huesmann do so in later reanalyses of their data.

had watched in the last four weeks and indicated how many times they had watched them; these were coded for violent content.[8] The authors refined the peer nomination measure of aggression used by Eron et al to include intentional acts of harm-doing, but not general misbehavior.

There was no evidence that any of the measures of exposure to television violence produced changes in aggressive behavior over time. The authors corrected for measurement error and used a variety of time lags, subsamples, and measures of exposure to television violence and aggressive behavior. In spite of a thorough exploration of the data, they found no evidence that exposure to violence on television affected the aggressive behavior of children. While the coefficients in most of the analyses were positive, they were all close to zero and statistically insignificant. The abundance of positive correlations led some critics to reject Milavsky et al's conclusion of no effect (e.g. Friedrich-Cofer & Huston 1986).

A more recent longitudinal study in the Netherlands also failed to find a media effect (Wiegman et al 1992). The children were surveyed in either the second or fourth grade and then again two years later. Peer nominations were used as a measure of aggressive behavior. The lagged effect of exposure on aggressive behavior was small and statistically insignificant.

It is difficult to reach a conclusion on the long-term effects of viewing television violence from these longitudinal studies. The studies that used better measurement failed to find an effect. In the studies where an effect was found, the relationship was between favorite show violence and subsequent aggression, rather than the amount of exposure to television violence, and Milavsky, et al did not replicate that effect. The findings reported in the cross-national studies were inconsistent and had as many negative findings as positive ones. Therefore one must conclude that longitudinal studies have not demonstrated a relationship between the amount of violence viewed on television and subsequent aggressive behavior.[9]

THEORETICAL EXPLANATIONS OF SITUATIONAL EFFECTS

The experimental results described above show that exposure to media violence can have at least a short-term effect on aggressive behavior. In this section, I

[8] Also included were parental reports of a child's favorite programs, and self-reports of children of their favorite programs. These measures of exposure to television violence were poor indicators of overall exposure.

[9] Valkenburg et al (1992) found that violent programming increased the level of aggressive-heroic fantasies found in a longitudinal analyses among Dutch children. However, nonviolent dramatic programming had the same effect.

consider theoretical reasons for expecting situational effects. I also review some of the evidence regarding these theoretical mechanisms.

Cognitive Priming

According to a cognitive priming approach, the aggressive ideas in violent films can activate other aggressive thoughts in viewers through their association in memory pathways (Berkowitz 1984). When one thought is activated, other thoughts that are strongly connected are also activated. Immediately after a violent film, the viewer is primed to respond aggressively because a network of memories involving aggression is retrieved. Evidence indicates that media violence does elicit thoughts and emotional responses related to aggression (Bushman & Geen 1990).

Huesmann (1982) makes a similar argument. He suggests that children learn problem-solving scripts in part from their observations of others' behavior. These scripts are cognitive expectations about a sequence of behaviors that may be performed in particular situations. Frequent exposure to scenes of violence may lead children to store scripts for aggressive behavior in their memories, and these may be recalled in a later situation if any aspect of the original situation—even a superficial one—is present.

The classic studies of these effects involve the exposure of subjects to the fight scene from a film, *The Champion,* starring Kirk Douglas. In one of these studies subjects were either shocked frequently or infrequently by a confederate, witnessed the fight scene, or viewed a neutral film, and then had an opportunity to shock the confederate, whose name was either Bob or Kirk (Berkowitz & Geen 1966). Subjects gave the confederate the most shocks in the condition when they had been provoked, had viewed the violent film, and the confederate had the same name as the film's star.

Tedeschi & Norman (1985) attribute the results from these studies to demand cues (see also Tedeschi & Felson 1994). They point out that experimenters mention the fact that the confederate's first name is the same as Kirk Douglas' in their instructions, and that they justify to subjects the beating that Kirk Douglas received. A series of studies have shown that it is necessary to provide this justification to get a violent film effect (Geen & Berkowitz 1967, Berkowitz 1965, Berkowitz et al 1962, Berkowitz & Rawlings 1963, Meyer 1972b).

Josephson (1987) examined the combined effects of exposure to a violent film and retrieval cues in a field experiment with second and third grade boys. The boys were exposed to either a violent film—in which a walkie-talkie was used—or a nonviolent film. The boys were also frustrated either before or after the film. Later they were interviewed by someone holding either a walkie-talkie or a microphone. After the interview, the boys played a game of field hockey and their aggressive behavior was recorded. It was predicted that boys who were exposed to both violent television and a walkie-talkie would be most aggressive in the game, since the walkie-talkie would lead them to retrieve scripts associated with the violent film. The hypothesis was confirmed for boys who were, according to teacher ratings, aggressive. Boys who were identified as nonaggressive inhibited their aggression when exposed to the walkie-talkie and the film. Josephson suggested that for these nonaggressive boys, aggression may be strongly associated with negative emotions such as guilt and fear which, when primed, may inhibit aggression. If we accept this post-hoc interpretation, it suggests that media violence may increase or inhibit the violent behavior of viewers depending on their initial predisposition. Such effects are likely to be short-term, and they may have no effect on the overall rate of violence.

Arousal from Pornography

According to Bandura (1973), emotional arousal facilitates and intensifies aggressive behavior. The facilitating effect of emotional arousal occurs only when the individual is already prone to act aggressively. If the individual is predisposed to behave in some other way, then emotional arousal will facilitate that behavior. Arousal energizes any behavior that is dominant in the situation.

Zillmann (1983) explains the facilitative effects of arousal in terms of excitation transfer. He has proposed that arousal from two different sources may combine with one another and be attributable to the same source. When the combined arousal is attributed to anger, the individual is likely to be more aggressive than would have been the case if only the anger-producing cue has been present.

Some research has examined whether the arousal produced by pornography facilitates aggressive behavior. A series of experiments have been carried out in which subjects are exposed to sexual stimuli and then allowed to aggress against another person, who may or may not have provoked them. The prediction is that arousal produced by pornography should increase aggression when a subject has been provoked. The message communicated by pornography and the gender of actor and target should not matter unless they affect the level of arousal.

Experiments that have examined the effects of arousal from pornography have produced mixed results. Some studies have found that erotic films increased the aggressiveness of subjects who had been provoked by the victim, while others have shown that pornography has an inhibitory effect (Zillman 1971, Meyer 1972a, Zillmann et al 1974, Baron & Bell 1973, 1977, Donnerstein et al 1975).

Researchers have developed hypotheses to provide explanations for the conditions under which opposite effects are obtained (Baron 1974, White 1979). Zillmann et al (1981) explained the contradictory findings using an arousal-affect hypothesis. They proposed that arousal has both an excitation component and an affective component. If arousal is accompanied by negative affect, it

114   FELSON

should add to the arousal produced by anger, and increase the level of aggression. If arousal is accompanied by positive affect, it should subtract from the arousal produced by anger, and decrease the level of aggression. The findings from research on the arousal-affect hypothesis are inconclusive (see Sapolski 1984, Tedeschi & Felson 1994 for reviews).

Even if these results are real, their significance for pornography effects outside the experimental lab seems trivial. They suggest, for example, that a man enjoying a pornographic film is less dangerous when provoked, while a man who dislikes the film, but is still aroused by it, is more likely to retaliate for a provocation. Perhaps the findings have more implications for the effects of arousal from other sources. For example, it is possible that arousal from the car chase in the Rodney King incident contributed to the violent behavior of the police.

It is difficult to manipulate arousal in the laboratory without also affecting the meanings subjects give to those manipulations (Neiss 1988). Experimenters who show pornographic films communicate information about their values and expectations and thus create demand cues. I discuss this issue in the next section.

Sponsor Effects

Demand cues provide a general explanation of short-term media effects in the experimental laboratory. Wood et al (1991) suggest that demand cues may be a type of "sponsor effect" that occurs outside the experimental laboratory as well:

> Viewers are likely to believe that the violent presentation is condoned by the media sponsor, whether it be an experimenter, one's family, the television networks or movie studios, or society in general.... Sponsor effects are not artifacts of laboratory procedures; they also occur in field settings (Wood 1991:373).

Wood et al's (1991) concept of sponsor effects appears to include both social learning and situational conformity. Social learning involves socialization and enduring effects on the viewer. Viewers may be more likely to internalize a media message if they think it is sponsored by someone they respect. A sponsor effect would enhance whatever message is being conveyed.

Field and laboratory experiments seem more likely to produce sponsor effects involving situational conformity. By showing a violent film, sponsors may communicate that they are not very strict or that they have a permissive attitude toward aggressive behavior. Young people, who are normally inhibited in front of adults, may engage in aggressive behavior if they think that they can get away with it. For example, students often misbehave when they encounter less experienced substitute teachers. According to this line of thinking, young people who are exposed to media violence should feel disinhibited and should be more likely to misbehave in a variety of ways, at least while adults are present. When the sponsors of the film are no longer present, the effects should disappear.

Meta-analyses show that exposure to violence is related to nonaggressive forms of antisocial behavior. Hearold (1986) performed a meta-analysis of experiments that included studies of effects of exposure to media violence on antisocial behavior generally. The effects of media violence on antisocial behavior were just as strong as the effects of media violence on violent behavior. A more recent meta-analysis that focused on all types of studies yielded similar results (Paik & Comstock 1994).

A study performed by Friedrich & Stein (1973) provides an example of an experiment showing general effects of exposure to media violence on antisocial behaviors. They found that nursery school children exposed to violent cartoons displayed more aggression during free play than children exposed to neutral films. However, they also found that children exposed to violence had lower tolerance for minor delays, lower task persistence, and displayed less spontaneous obedience in regard to school rules. These behaviors clearly do not involve an intent to harm.

Additional evidence for a sponsor effect comes from a study by Leyens et al (1975). They found that subjects delivered more shock to another person when they anticipated that the experimenter would show them violent films; it was not necessary for them to actually see the films. The investigators attributed this effect to priming, based on the assumption that the mere mention of violent films primes aggressive thoughts. It seems just as likely that sponsor effects were involved: an experimenter who is willing to show a violent film is perceived as more permissive or more tolerant of aggression.

The effects of exposure to television violence on antisocial behavior generally cast doubt on many of the theoretical explanations usually used to explain media effects on violence. Explanations involving cognitive priming or arousal cannot explain why those who view violence should engage in deviant behavior generally. Explanations that stress modeling (to be discussed) cannot explain this pattern of effects either. It is possible, however, that viewers imitate the low self-control behaviors of the characters they observe in television and films, rather than violence specifically. Children model the self-control behavior of adults in experimental situations (Bandura & Walters 1963), but it is not clear whether socialization or short-term situational effects are involved.

Sponsor effects may also explain the results of experimental studies involving exposure to pornography. Paik & Comstock's (1994) meta-analysis shows effects of both pornography and violent pornography on antisocial behavior

116   FELSON

in general. Experimenters who show pornography, especially violent pornography, may imply that they condone or at least are tolerant of taboo behavior (Reiss 1986). Subjects may be disinhibited in this permissive atmosphere and engage in more antisocial behavior.

In sum, these studies suggest that subjects may assume a more permissive atmosphere when they are shown a violent film, and their inhibitions about misbehavior generally are reduced. It is not yet clear whether their behavior reflects short-term conformity or longer-term socialization. Research is needed to determine whether subjects who view violent films in experiments engage in more aggression and other misbehavior in the absence of sponsors.

Television Viewing as a Routine Activity

According to the routine activity approach, crime should be less frequent when the routine activities of potential offenders and victims reduce their opportunities for contact (e.g. M Felson 1986). Any activity that separates those who are prone to violence from each other, or from potential victims, is likely to decrease the incidence of violence.

Messner uses this approach to argue that watching television can decrease the incidence of violence in society (Messner 1986, Messner & Blau 1987). Since people watch television at home, the opportunities for violence, at least with people outside the family, are probably reduced. When people watch television, they may also interact less often with other family members, so the opportunities for domestic violence may also be reduced. Messner found that cities with high levels of television viewing have lower rates of both violent and nonviolent crime (Messner 1986, Messner & Blau 1987). However, in an aggregate analysis of this type, one cannot determine the specific viewing habits of offenders or victims of criminal violence.[10]

The routine activities of young adult males are particularly important since they are most prone to use violence. Young adult males do not spend as much time as other groups watching television (Dimmick et al 1979). According to the routine activity approach, their level of violence would be lower if they did.

THEORETICAL EXPLANATIONS INVOLVING SOCIALIZATION

It is widely believed that people are more violent because they learn to be violent from their parents, their peers, and the mass media. These socialization effects

---

[10]Viewing violent television and viewing television are so highly correlated across cites that it does not matter which measure is used in analysis. The notion of catharsis provides an alternative explanation, but it cannot explain the negative relationship between exposure to television violence and the incidence of nonviolent crime.

tend to endure since they involve changes in the individual. The evidence on the versatility of criminal offenders casts doubt on the importance of this socialization process. Considerable evidence suggests that those who commit violent crime tend to commit nonviolent crime and other deviant acts as well. Studies of arrest histories based on both official records and self-reports show a low level of specialization in violent crime. For example, West & Farrington (1977) found that 80% of adults convicted of violence also had convictions for crimes involving dishonesty. Violent acts were also related to noncriminal forms of deviant behavior, such as sexual promiscuity, smoking, heavy drinking, gambling, and having an unstable job history.

The evidence that most offenders are versatile challenges the notion that violent offenders are more violent because of a special proclivity to engage in violence, due to exposure to media violence or any other factor. Individual differences in the propensity to engage in criminal violence reflect for the most part individual differences in antisocial behavior generally. Variations in the socialization of self-control and other inhibitory factors are probably important causal factors (Gottfredson & Hirschi 1990). Theories that emphasize specific socialization to violence are likely to be limited in their utility, since most violent offenders are generalists.

The versatility argument should not be overstated. Some people do specialize in violence, and exposure to media violence may play a role in their socialization. There are a variety of reasons one might expect viewers to learn aggressive behavior from the media. First, media depictions of violence may suggest novel behaviors to viewers that they otherwise might not have considered. Second, vicarious reinforcements and legitimation of violent actions may increase the tendency to model media violence. Third, viewers become desensitized about violence after a heavy diet of it on television. Finally, people may get a false idea of reality from observing a great deal of violence on television and develop unrealistic fears. I now examine each of the processes more closely.

Learning Novel Forms of Behavior

Bandura (1983) has argued that television can shape the forms that aggressive behavior takes. Television can teach skills that may be useful for committing acts of violence, and it can direct the viewer's attention to behaviors that they may not have considered. For example, young people may mimic karate and judo moves, or they may learn effective tactics for committing violent crime. This information may give direction to those who are already motivated to engage in aggression. Such a modeling process could lead to more severe forms of aggression. It could increase the frequency of violence if people who are motivated to harm someone choose a violent method they have observed on television.

118   FELSON

There is anecdotal evidence that bizarre violent events have followed soon after their depiction on television, suggesting a form of copycat behavior. In one widely reported case in Boston, six young men set fire to a woman after forcing her to douse herself with fuel. The scene had been depicted on television two nights before. In another instance, four teenagers raped a nine-year-old girl with a beer bottle, enacting a scene similar to one in the made-for-TV movie *Born Innocent*. Such incidents may be coincidental, but they suggest the possibility that unusual and dramatic behaviors on television are imitated by viewers who might never otherwise have imagined engaging in such behaviors.

Modeling can also be used to explain contagion effects observed for highly publicized violence, such as airline hijackings, civil disorders, bombings, and political kidnaping. The tendency for such events to occur in waves suggests that at least some viewers imitate real events that are reported on television. However, the central argument about the relationship of viewing violence on television and viewers' aggressive behavior focuses on fictional events.

Vicarious Reinforcement and Legitimations

Bandura (1983) also suggested that television may inform viewers of the positive and negative consequences of violent behavior. Audiences can be expected to imitate violent behavior that is successful in gaining the model's objectives in fictional or nonfictional programs. When violence is justified or left unpunished on television, the viewer's guilt or concern about consequences is reduced. Thus Paik & Comstock's (1994) meta-analysis found that the magnitude of media effects on antisocial behavior was greater when the violent actor was rewarded or the behavior was legitimated.

It is not at all clear what message is learned from viewing violence on television. In most plots, the protagonist uses violence for legitimate ends while the villain engages in illegitimate violence. The protagonist usually uses violence in self-defense or to mete out an appropriate level of punishment to a dangerous or threatening criminal. Television conveys the message that while some forms of violence are necessary and legitimate, criminal violence is evil.

The consequences of the illegitimate violence portrayed in fictional television and film are more negative than the consequences of illegitimate violence in real life. In real life violent people often evade punishment, while in television, the villain is almost always punished. Thus, one could argue that television violence might reduce the incidence of criminal violence, since crime doesn't pay for TV criminals. Another difference is in the appeal of those who engage in illegitimate violence. In fictional television, those who engage in illegitimate violence tend to lack any attractive qualities that would lead to sympathy or identification. In real life, illegitimate violence may be committed by loved ones or others who are perceived to have desirable qualities.

Other factors may limit the effects of any message about the legitimacy, or the rewards and costs of violence. First, the lessons learned from the media about violence may be similar or redundant to the lessons learned about the use of violence conveyed by other sources. In fact, most viewers probably approve of the violent behavior of the protagonists. The influence of television on viewers who already agree with its message would be weak at best. Second, the audience may not take the message from fictional plots seriously. Modeling is more likely to occur after viewing nonfiction than after viewing fiction (Feshbach 1972, Berkowitz & Alioto 1973).[11] Third, the violent contexts and provocations observed on television are likely to be very different from the contexts and provocations people experience in their own lives. Evidence suggests that viewers take context and intentions into account before they model aggressive behavior (Geen 1978, Hoyt 1970). Straus (Baron & Straus 1987), on the other hand, suggests that people are likely to be influenced by the violence they observe regardless of its context, message, or legitimacy. According to cultural spillover theory, violence in one sphere of life leads to violence in other spheres.

Finally, some young children may miss the more subtle aspects of television messages, focusing on overt acts rather than on the intentions or contexts in which such acts occur. Collins et al (1984) found that kindergarten and second grade children were relatively unaffected by an aggressor's motives in their understanding of a violent program. They focused more on the aggressiveness of the behavior and its ultimate consequences. However, even if young children imitate the violence of models, it is not at all clear that they will continue to exhibit violence as they get older. When they are older, and they pay attention to the intentions and context in violent television, their behavior is more likely to reflect the messages they learn. It is also at these later ages that violent behavior, if it should occur, is likely to be dangerous.

Creating Unrealistic Fear

Bandura (1983) claims that television distorts knowledge about the dangers and threats present in the real world. The notion that television viewing fosters a distrust of others and a misconception of the world as dangerous has been referred to as the "cultivation effect" (Gerbner & Gross 1976). Research shows that heavy television viewers are more distrustful of others and overestimate their chances of being criminally victimized (see Ogles 1987 and Gunter 1994 for reviews).[12] The assumption is that these fears will lead viewers to perceive

---

[11]In Paik & Comstock's (1994) meta-analyses the strongest effects were observed for cartoon programs. However, the subjects in these studies were children, and children may be more easily influenced.

[12]There is some evidence that the relationship is spurious; see Gunter's (1994) review.

120   FELSON

threats that do not exist and to respond aggressively. It is just as plausible that such fears would lead viewers to avoid aggressive behavior against others, if they feel it is dangerous, and might lead to victimization. Persons who fear crime may also be less likely to go out at night or go to places where they may be victimized. If viewing television violence increases fear, it might decrease the level of violence.

Desensitization

Frequent viewing of television violence may cause viewers to be less anxious and sensitive about violence. Someone who becomes desensitized to violence may be more likely to engage in violence. This argument assumes that anxiety about violence inhibits its use.

Desensitization has been examined indirectly using measures of arousal. Research shows that subjects who view violent films are less aroused by violence later on (Thomas et al 1977; see Rule & Ferguson 1986 for a review). In addition, heavy viewers of television violence tend to respond less emotionally to violence than do light viewers.

There is no evidence that desensitization produces lower levels of violent behavior.[13] Nor is it clear what effect should occur. Studies of desensitization measure arousal not anxiety, and arousal can facilitate violent behavior, according to the literature cited earlier (e.g. Zillmann 1983). If viewers are exposed to a heavy diet of television violence, one might argue that they will be less aroused by violence and therefore less likely to engage in violence. In addition, if viewers become desensitized to violent behavior on television, they may become indifferent to its message. Desensitization could thereby weaken the effect of a heavy diet of television violence.

Messages from Pornography

The discussion of situational effects of pornography on aggression focused on arousal as a mediating variable. Feminists have argued that pornography has special effects on violence against women because of the message it communicates (Dworkin 1981, MacKinnon 1984). Exposure to pornography supposedly leads to negative attitudes toward women which, in turn, affects the likelihood of rape and other forms of violence against women. It is argued, for example, that pornography leads male viewers to think of women as sex objects or as promiscuous (Linz & Malamuth 1993). Furthermore, some erotica portrays scenes of rape and sadomasochism. In such fictional forms the female victim may express pleasure during and after being raped, suggesting that women enjoy such treatment. Males who view such films may be induced to believe that

---

[13]Emergency room personnel may become desensitized to the consequences of violent behavior, but there is no evidence that they are more violent than other groups of people.

forceful sexual acts are desired by women. In addition, unlike illegitimate violence not associated with sex, violence in pornographic films rarely has negative consequences for the actor (Palys 1986, Smith 1976).

Evidence does not support the hypothesis that exposure to nonviolent pornography leads to violence toward women. Most experimental studies show no difference in aggression toward women between subjects exposed to pornographic films and control groups (for reviews, see Donnerstein 1984, Linz & Malamuth 1993). Research outside the laboratory has not demonstrated that exposure to pornography and violence toward women are even correlated, much less causally related. There is evidence that rapists report less exposure to pornography than controls, not more (see Linz & Malamuth 1993 for a review). Studies of the relationship between exposure to pornography and use of sexual coercion among college students yields mixed results (Demare et al 1993, Boeringer 1994).

Research using aggregate data has also failed to demonstrate a relationship between exposure to pornography and violence against women. Studies of the effect of changes in restrictions on pornography on rape rates show inconsistent results. States in which sex-oriented magazines are popular tend to have high rape rates (Baron & Straus 1987). However, it is questionable whether the state is a meaningful unit of analysis, given the heterogeneity within states. Gentry (1991) found no relationship between rape rates and circulation of sexually oriented magazines across metropolitan areas.

Effects of violent pornography have been reported in laboratory experiments, at least under certain conditions (see Linz & Malamuth 1993 for a review). Some studies show that an effect is obtained only if the sexual assault has positive consequences. In this case, subjects are told that the woman became a willing participant in the coercive sexual activities, and she is shown smiling and on friendly terms with the man afterwards (Donnerstein 1980). However, in a more recent study, exposure to a rape scene with positive consequences did not increase subjects' aggression toward women (Fisher & Grenier 1994).

The effects of exposure to violence with positive consequences have been examined in a field experiment. College students were exposed either to two films that showed women responding positively to men who had attacked them or to two neutral films (Malamuth & Check 1981). Subjects completed a survey that they thought was unrelated to the films several days later. Males who had viewed the violent films showed greater acceptance of violence against women. Note that these films did not involve pornography. Pornographic films in which the victim of sexual aggression is perceived as experiencing a positive outcome are quite rare (Garcia & Milano 1990).

122   FELSON

The experimental evidence is mixed concerning whether pornography or violent pornography affects male attitudes toward women, according to Linz's (1989) review of the literature. Evidence that men who have negative attitudes toward women are more likely to engage in violence against women is also inconsistent. Some studies find that men who engage in sexual coercion have different attitudes toward women and rape than do other men, while other studies do not (Kanin 1969, Malamuth 1986, Ageton 1983, Rapapport & Burkhart 1984). It may be that sexually aggressive men are more likely to have antisocial attitudes generally. Thus, convicted rapists are similar to males convicted of other offenses in their attitudes toward women and women's rights (e.g. Howells & Wright 1978) and in their belief in rape myths (Hall et al 1986).

The literature on violence and attitudes toward women is plagued by conceptual and measurement problems. Measures of belief in rape myths are problematic (Tedeschi & Felson 1994). In addition, traditional attitudes about gender roles do not necessarily involve negative attitudes toward women and may be negatively associated with violence toward women and exposure to pornography. Thus, rape rates are twice as high at private colleges and major universities than at religiously affiliated institutions (Koss et al 1987). Males who report greater exposure to pornography have more (not less) liberal attitudes toward gender roles (Reiss 1986). Finally, even if a correlation between certain attitudes regarding women and violence could be established, the causal interpretation would be unclear. For example, it may be that men express certain beliefs to justify coercive behavior already performed (Koss et al 1985).

One limitation on the impact of pornography or any media effect is selective exposure (McGuire 1986). Media effects are likely to be limited to the extent that viewers choose programming that already reflects their values and interests. The argument in regard to media violence is that violence is so pervasive on television that all viewers, including impressionable children, are exposed. In the case of pornography, particularly violent pornography, there is much more selective exposure, since those interested in viewing this material must make a special effort to do so. In addition, the viewers of pornography are usually adults, not children.

Pornography provides fantasies for masturbation. Viewers may select material depicting activities that they already fantasize about. When they substitute commercially produced fantasies for their own fantasies, the content is not necessarily more violent. Palys (1986) found that less than 10% of scenes in pornography videos involved some form of aggression. A study of college students revealed that approximately 39% of men and women reported that they had fantasized about forced sex (Loren & Weeks 1986).

The versatility evidence is also relevant to the literature on pornography and rape. Most rapists do not specialize in rape nor in violent crime (Alder 1984, Kruttschnitt 1989). Therefore, theories that emphasize socialization of rape-supportive attitudes, whether learned from the media or elsewhere, are going to have limited utility for understanding individual differences in the proclivity to rape.

In summary, some experimental research suggests that violent pornography that depicts women enjoying the event can lead male subjects to engage in violence against women in the laboratory. The effect of these films appears to be similar to the effects of violent films without a sexual theme. Demand cues provide an alternative explanation of these results as well (see Reiss 1986). The external validity of these studies is questionable given the rarity of these themes in pornography, and given selective exposure.

SUMMARY AND CONCLUSIONS

The inconsistencies of the findings make it difficult to draw firm conclusions about the effects of exposure to media violence on aggressive behavior. Most scholars who have reviewed research in the area believe that there is an effect (Friedrich-Cofer & Huston 1986, Centerwall 1989). Other scholars have concluded that the causal effects of exposure to television have not been demonstrated (Freedman 1984, McGuire 1989).

Given the pervasiveness of media violence, it would be surprising if it had no effect on viewers. I agree with those scholars who think that exposure to television violence probably does have a small effect on violent behavior (Cook et al 1983). The reason that media effects are not consistently observed is probably because they are weak and affect only a small percentage of viewers. These weak effects may still have practical importance since, in a large population, they would produce some death and injuries. However, it seems unlikely that media violence is a significant factor in high crime rates in this country. Changes in violent crimes mirror changes in crime rates generally. In addition, the people who engage in criminal violence also commit other types of crime. An explanation that attributes violent behavior to socialization that encourages violence cannot easily explain the versatility of most violent criminals.

It seems likely that some people would be more susceptible to media influence than others. Therefore it is puzzling that research has not shown any consistent statistical interactions involving individual difference factors and media exposure. The failure to find individual difference factors that condition the effects of media exposure on aggressive behavior contributes to skepticism about media effects.

124   FELSON

It seems reasonable to believe that the media directs viewers' attention to novel forms of violent behavior they might not otherwise consider. The anecdotal evidence is convincing in this area. There appear to be documented cases in which bizarre events on television are followed by similar events in the real world; the similarities seem too great to be coincidental. In addition, hijackings and political violence tend to occur in waves. Many parents have observed their children mimicking behaviors they've observed in films. Whether this process leads to a greater frequency of violence is unclear.

There is some evidence that the effects observed in laboratory experiments, and less consistently in field experiments, are due to sponsor effects. The fact that children who are exposed to violence tend to misbehave generally casts doubt on most of the other theoretical explanations of media effects. The issue has particular significance for laboratory research, where subjects know they are being studied and may be responding to demand cues. Research is needed in which sponsor effects are isolated and controlled. A field experiment in which subjects imitate violent behavior they have observed in the absence of the sponsor, but do not misbehave otherwise, would be convincing. Alternatively, there may need to be further development of the theoretical argument that self-control behavior is modelled.

It is not clear what lesson the media teaches about the legitimacy of violence, or the likelihood of punishment. To some extent that message is redundant with lessons learned from other sources of influence. The message is probably ambiguous and is likely to have different effects on different viewers. Young children may imitate illegitimate violence, if they do not understand the message, but their imitative behavior may have trivial consequences. Out of millions of viewers, there must be some with highly idiosyncratic interpretations of television content who intertwine the fantasy with their own lives, and as a result have an increased probability of engaging in violent behavior.

Literature Cited

Ageton S. 1983. *Sexual Assault Among Adolescents.* Lexington, MA: Lexington

Alder C. 1984. The convicted rapist: a sexual or a violent offender? *Crim. Justice Behav.* 11:157–77

Andison FS. 1977. TV violence and viewer aggression: a cumulation of study results: 1956–1976. *Public Opin. Q.* 41:314–31

Bachrach RS. 1986. The differential effect of observation of violence on kibbutz and city children in Israel. In *Television and the Aggressive Child: A Cross-National Comparison,* ed. LR Huesmann, LD Eron, pp. 201–38. Hillsdale, NJ: Erlbaum

Bandura A. 1973. *Aggression: A Social Learning Analysis.* Englewood Cliffs, NJ: Prentice-Hall

Bandura A. 1983. Psychological mechanisms of

aggression. In *Aggression: Theoretical and Empirical Reviews*, ed. RG Geen, EI Donnerstein, 1:1–40. New York: Academic

Bandura A, Walters RH. 1963. *Social Learning and Personality Development*. New York: Holt, Rinehart & Winston

Baron JN, Reiss PC. 1985. Same time next year: aggregate analyses of the mass media and violent behvaior. *Am. Sociol. Rev.* 50:347–63

Baron L, Straus MA. 1987. Four theories of rape: a macrosocial analysis. *Soc. Probl.* 34:467–89

Baron RA. 1974. The aggression-inhibiting influence of heightened sexual arousal. *J. Pers. Soc. Psychol.* 30:318–22

Baron RA, Bell PA. 1973. Effects of heightened sexual arousal on physical aggression. *Proc. 81st Annu. Conv. Am. Psychol. Assoc.* 8:171–72

Baron RA, Bell PA. 1977. Sexual arousal and aggression by males: effects of type of erotic stimuli and prior provocation. *J. Pers. Soc. Psychol.* 35:79–87

Berkowitz L. 1965. Some aspects of observed aggression. *J. Pers. Soc. Psychol.* 2:359–69

Berkowitz L. 1984. Some effects of thought on anti- and pro-social influences of media effects. *Psychol. Bull.* 95:410–27

Berkowitz L, Alioto JT. 1973. The meaning of an observed event as a determinant of its aggressive consequences *J. Pers. Soc. Psychol.* 28:206–17

Berkowitz L, Corwin R, Heironimus M. 1962. Film violence and subsequent aggressive tendencies. *Public Opin. Q.* 27:217–29

Berkowitz L, Donnerstein E. 1982. External validity is more than skin deep: some answers to criticism of laboratory experiments. *Am. Psychol.* 37:245–57

Berkowitz L, Geen RG. 1966. Film violence and the cue properties of available targets. *J. Pers. Soc. Psychol.* 3:525–30

Berkowitz L, Rawlings E. 1963. Effects of film violence: an inhibition against subsequent aggression. *J. Abnorm. Soc. Psychol.* 66:405–12

Boeringer S. 1994. Pornography and sexual aggression: associations of violent and nonviolent depictions with rape and rape proclivity. *Deviant Behav.* 15:289–304

Bushman BJ, Geen RG. 1990. Role of cognitive-emotional mediators and individual differences in the effects of media violence on aggression. *J. Pers. Soc. Psychol.* 58:156–63

Centerwall BS. 1989. Exposure to television as a cause of violence. In *Public Communication and Behavior*, ed. G. Comstock, 2:1–58. Orlando: Academic

Collins WA, Berndt TJ, Hess VL. 1984. Observational learning of motives and conse-

quences for television aggression: a developmental study. *Child Dev.* 45:799–802

Cook TD, Kendzierski DA, Thomas SV. 1983. The implicit assumptions of television: an analysis of the 1982 NIMH Report on Television and Behavior. *Public Opin. Q.* 47:161–201

Demare D, Lips HM, Briere J. 1993. Sexually violent pornography, anti-women attitudes, and sexual aggression: a structural equation model. *J. Res. Pers.* 27:285–300

Dimmick JW, McCain TA, Bolton WT. 1979. Media use and the life span. *Am. Behav. Scientist* 23:7–31

Donnerstein E. 1980. Aggressive erotica and violence against women. *J. Pers. Soc. Psychol.* 39:269–77

Donnerstein E. 1984. Pornography: its effect on violence against women. In *Pornography and Sexual Aggression*, ed. NM Malamuth, E Donnerstein, pp. 53–81. New York: Academic

Donnerstein E, Donnerstein M, Evans R. 1975. Erotic stimuli and aggression: facilitation or inhibition. *J. Pers. Soc. Psychol.* 32:237–44

Dworkin A. 1981. *Pornography: Men Possessing Women*. New York: GP Putnam's Sons

Eron LD, Huesmann LR, Lefkowitz MM, Walder LO. 1972. Does television violence cause aggression? *Am. Psychol.* 27:253–63

Felson M. 1986. Routine activities, social controls, rational decisions and criminal outcomes. In *The Reasoning Criminal: Rational Choice Perspectives on Offending*, ed. D Cornish, R Clarke. New York: Springer-Verlag

Feshbach S. 1972. Reality and fantasy in filmed violence. In *Television and Social Behavior*, ed. JP Murray, E Rubinstein, GA Comstock, pp. 318–45. Vol. 2: *Television and Social Learning*. Washington DC: US Govt. Printing Off.

Feshbach S, Singer R. 1971. *Television and Aggression*. San Francisco: Jossey Bass

Fisher WA, Grenier G. 1994. Violent pornography, antiwoman thoughts, and antiwoman acts: in search of reliable effects. *J. Sex Res.* 31:23–38

Fraczek A. 1986. Socio-cultural environment, television viewing, and the development of aggression among children in Poland. In *Television and the Aggressive Child: A Cross-National Comparison*, ed. LR Huesmann, LD Eron, pp. 119–60. Hillsdale, NJ: Erlbaum

Freedman JL. 1984. Effects of television violence on aggressiveness. *Psychol. Bull.* 96:227–46

Friedrich LK, Stein AH. 1973. Aggressive and prosocial television programs and the natural behavior of preschool children. *Monogr. Soc. for Res. in Child Dev.*, 38 4, Serial No. 151

126   FELSON

Friedrich-Cofer L, Huston AC. 1986. Television violence and aggression: the debate continues. *Psychol. Bull.* 100:364–71

Garcia LT, Milano L. 1990. A content analysis of erotic videos. *J. Law Psychiatry* 14:47–64

Geen RG. 1978. Some effects of observing violence upon the behavior of the observer. In *Progress in Experimental Personality Research,* Vol. 8, ed. B Maher. New York: Academic

Geen RG. 1983. Aggression and television violence. In *Aggression: Theoretical and Empirical Reviews,* ed. RG Geen, EI Donnerstein, 2:103–25. New York: Academic

Geen RG, Berkowitz L. 1967. Some conditions facilitating the occurrence of aggression after the observation of violence. *J. Pers.* 35:666–76

Gentry CS. 1991. Pornography and rape: an empirical analysis. *Deviant Behav.* 12:277–88

Gerbner G, Gross L. 1976. Living with television: the violence profile. *J. Commun.* 26:173–99

Gottfredson M, Hirschi T. 1990. *A General Theory of Crime.* Stanford: Stanford Univ. Press

Gottfredson M, Hirschi T. 1993. A control theory interpretation of psychological research on aggression. In *Aggression and Violence: Social Interactionist Perspectives,* ed. RB Felson, JT Tedeschi, pp. 47–68. Washington, DC: Am. Psychol. Assoc.

Gunter B. 1994. The question of media violence. In *Media Effects: Advances in Theory and Research,* ed. J. Bryant, D. Zillman, pp. 163–212. Hillsdale: Lawrence Erlbaum

Hall ER, Howard JA, Boezio SL. 1986. Tolerance of rape: a sexist or antisocial attitude. *Psychol. Women Q.* 10:101–18

Hearold S. 1986. A synthesis of 1043 effects of television on social behavior. In *Public Communication and Behavior,* ed. G. Comstock, 1:65–133. San Diego, CA: Academic

Hennigan KM, Del Rosario ML, Heath L, Cook TD, Wharton JD, Calder BJ. 1982. The impact of the introduction of television on crime in the United States. *J. Pers. Soc. Psychol.* 42:461–77

Howells K, Wright E. 1978. The sexual attitudes of aggressive sexual offenders. *Br. J. Crimnol.* 18:170–73

Hoyt JL. 1970. Effect of media violence 'justification' on aggression. *J. Broadcast.* 14:455–64

Huesmann LR. 1982. Television violence and aggressive behavior. In *Television and Behavior: Ten Years of Scientific Progress and Implications for the Eighties,* Vol. 2. *Technical Reviews,* ed. D Pearl, L Bouthilet, J Lazar eds, pp. 220–56. Washington, DC: Natl. Inst. Mental Health

Huesmann LR, Eron LD. 1986. The development of aggression in American children as a consequence of television violence viewing. In *Television and the Aggressive Child: A Cross-National Comparison,* ed. LR Huesmann, LD Eron, pp. 45–80. Hillsdale, NJ: Erlbaum

Josephson WL. 1987. Television violence and children's aggression: testing the priming, social script, and disinhibition predictions. *J. Pers. Soc. Psychol.* 53:882–90

Joy LA, Kimball MM, Zaback ML. 1986. Television and children's aggressive behavior. In *The Impact of Television: A Natural Experiment in Three Communities,* ed. TM Williams, pp. 303–60. New York: Academic

Kanin EJ. 1969. Selected dyadic aspect of male sex aggresssion *J. Sex Res.* 5:12–28

Koss MP, Gidycz CA, Wisniewski N. 1987. The scope of rape: incidence and prevalence of sexual aggression and victimization in a national sample of students in higher education. *J. Consult. Clin. Psychol.* 55:162–70

Koss MP, Leonard KE, Beezley DA, Oros CJ. 1985. Non-stranger sexual aggression: a discriminate analysis classification. *Sex Roles* 12:981–92

Kruttschnitt C. 1989. A sociological, offender-based, study of rape. *Sociol. Q.* 30:305–29

Lagerspetz K, Viemero V. 1986. Television and aggressive behavior among Finnish children. In *Television and the Aggressive Child: A Cross-National Comparison,* LR Huesmann, LD Eron, pp. 81–118. Hillsdale, NJ: Erlbaum

Leyens JP, Camino L, Parke RD, Berkowitz L. 1975. Effects of movie violence on aggression in a field setting as a function of group dominance and cohesion. *J. Pers. Soc. Psychol.* 32:346–60

Linz D. 1989. Exposure to sexually explicit materials and attitudes toward rape: a comparison of study results. *J. Sex Res.* 26:50–84

Linz D, Malamuth N. 1993. *Pornography.* Newbury Park: Sage

Loren REA, Weeks G. 1986. Sexual fantasies of undergraduates and their perceptions of the sexual fantasies of the opposite sex. *J. Sex Educ. Ther.* 12:31–36

MacKinnon C. 1984. Not a moral issue. *Yale Law Policy Rev.* 2:321–45

Malamuth NM. 1986. Predictors of naturalistic sexual aggression. *J. Pers. Soc. Psychol.* 50:953–62

Malamuth NM, Check JVP. 1981. The effects of mass media exposure on acceptance of violence against women: a field experiment. *J. Res. Pers.* 15:436–46

McGuire WJ. 1986. The myth of massive media impact: Savagings and salvagings. In *Public Communication and Behavior,* ed. G. Comstock, 1:175–257. Orlando: Academic

Messner SF. 1986. Television violence and violent crime: an aggregate analysis. *Soc. Probl.* 33:218–35

Messner SF, Blau JR. 1987. Routine leisure activities and rates of crime: a macro-level analysis. *Soc. Forces* 65:1035–52

Meyer TP. 1972a. The effects of sexually arousing and violent films on aggressive behavior. *J. Sex Res.* 8:324–31

Meyer TP. 1972b. Effects of viewing justified and unjustified real film violence on aggressive behavior. *J. Pers. Soc. Psychol.* 23:21–29

Milavsky JR, Stipp HH, Kessler RC, Rubens WS. 1982. *Television and Aggression: A Panel Study.* New York: Academic

Milgram S. 1974. *Obedience to Authority: An Experimental View.* New York: Harper & Row

Miller TQ, Heath L, Molcan JR, Dugoni BL. 1991. Imitative violence in the real world: a reanalysis of homicide rates following championship prize fights. *Aggressive Behav.* 17:121–34

Neiss R. 1988. Reconceptualizing arousal: psychobiological states in motor performance. *Psychol. Bull.* 103:345–66

Nemeth C. 1970. Bargaining and reciprocity. *Psychol. Bull.* 74:297–308

Ogles RM. 1987. Cultivation analysis: theory, methodology and current research on television-influenced constructions of social reality. *Mass Comm. Rev.* 14:43–53

Padget VR, Brislin-Slutz J, Neal JA. 1989. Pornography, erotica, and attitudes toward women: the effects of repeated exposure. *J. Sex Res.* 26:479–91

Paik H, Comstock G. 1994. The effects of television violence on antisocial behavior: a meta-analysis. *Comm. Res.* 21:516–45

Palys TS. 1986. Testing the common wisdom: the social content of video pornography. *Can. Psychol.* 27:22–35

Parke RD, Berkowitz L, Leyens JP, West S, Sebastian RJ. 1977. Some effects of violent and nonviolent movies on the behavior of juvenile delinquents. In *Advances in Experimental Social Psychology,* ed. L. Berkowitz, 10:135–72. New York: Academic

Phillips DP. 1983. The impact of mass media violence on U.S. homicides. *Am. Sociol. Rev.* 48:560–68

Phillips DP. 1986. The found experiment: a new technique for assessing the impact of mass media violence on real-world aggressive behavior. In *Public Communication and Behavior,* ed. G Comstock, 1:259–307. San Diego, CA: Academic

Phillips DP, Bollen KA. 1985. Same time last year: selective data dredging for unreliable findings. *Am. Sociol. Rev.* 50:364–71

Rapaport K, Burkhart BR. 1984. Personality and attitudinal characteristics of sexually coercive college males. *J. Abnorm. Psychol.* 93:216–21

Reiss IL. 1986. *Journey into Sexuality: An Exploratory Voyage.* Englewood Cliffs, NJ: Prentice

Rosenberg MJ. 1969. The conditions and consequences of evaluation apprehension. In *Artifacts in Behavioral Research,* ed. R Rosenthal, R Rosnow. New York: Academic

Rule BG, Ferguson TJ. 1986. The effects of media violence on attitudes, emotions, and cognitions. *J. Soc. Issues* 42:29–50

Sapolsky BS. 1984. Arousal, affect, and the aggression-moderating effect of erotica. In *Pornography and Sexual Aggression,* ed. NM Malamuth, E Donnerstein, pp. 83–115. New York: Academic

Sheehan PW. 1986. Television viewing and its relation to aggression among children in Australia. In *Television and the Aggressive Child: A Cross-National Comparison,* ed. LR Huesmann, LD Eron, pp. 161–200. Hillsdale, NJ: Erlbaum

Smith DD. 1976. The social content of pornography. *J. Comm.* 29:16–24

Straus N. 1991. Discipline and divorce: physical punishment of children and violence and other crime in adulthood. *Soc. Probl.* 38:133–54

Surgeon General's Scientific Advisory Committee on Television and Social Behavior. 1972. Television and growing up: the impact of televised violence. *Rep. to the Surgeon General, US Public Health Serv. HEW Publ. No. HSM 72–9090.* Rockville, MD: Natl. Inst. Mental Health, USGPO

Sykes G, Matza D. 1961. Juvenile delinquency and subterranean values. *Am. Sociol. Rev.* 26:712–19

Tedeschi JT, Felson RB. 1994. *Violence, Aggression, and Coercive Actions.* Washington, DC: Am. Psychol. Assoc.

Tedeschi JT, Norman N. 1985. Social mechanisms of displaced aggression. In *Advances in Group Processes: Theory and Research,* ed. EJ Lawler, Vol. 2. Greenwich, Conn.: JAI

Tedeschi JT, Smith RB III, Brown RC Jr. 1974. A reinterpretation of research on aggression. *Psychol. Bull.* 89:540–63

Thomas MH, Horton RW, Lippincott EC, Drabman RS. 1977. Desensitization to portrayals of real-life aggression as a function of exposure to television violence. *J. Pers. Soc. Psychol.* 35:450–58

Valkenburg PM, Vooijs MW, Van der Voort TH. 1992. The influence of television on chil-

128   FELSON

dren's fantasy styles: a secondary analysis. *Imagination, Cognition, Pers.* 12:55–67

West DJ, Farrington DP. 1977. *The Delinquent Way of Life.* London: Heinemann

White LA. 1979. Erotica and aggression: the influence of sexual arousal, positive affect, and negative affect on aggressive behavior. *J. Pers. Soc. Psychol.* 37:591–601

Wiegman O, Kuttschreuter M, Baarda B. 1992. A longitudinal study of the effects of television viewing on aggressive and antisocial behaviors. *Br. J. Soc. Psychol.* 31:147–64

Wood W, Wong FY, Chachere JG. 1991. Effects of media violence on viewers aggression in unconstrained social interaction. *Psychol. Bull.* 109:371–83

Zillman D. 1971. Excitation transfer in communication-mediated aggressive behavior. *J. Exp. Soc. Psychol.* 7:419–34

Zillman D. 1983. Arousal and aggression. In *Aggression: Theoretical and Empirical Reviews,* ed. RG Geen, EI Donnerstein, 1:75–101. New York: Academic

Zillmann D, Bryant J, Comisky PW, Medoff NJ. 1981. Excitation and hedonic valence in the effect of erotica on motivated intermale aggression. *Eur. J. Soc. Psychol.* 11:233–52

Zillmann D, Hoyt JL, Day KD. 1974. Strength and duration of the effect of aggressive, violent, and erotic communications on subsequent aggressive behavior. *Comm. Res.* 1:286–306

[18]

Annu. Rev. Sociol. 1998. 24:291–311

ALCOHOL, DRUGS, AND VIOLENCE

Robert Nash Parker and Kathleen Auerhahn

Presley Center for Crime and Justice Studies, and Department of Sociology,
University of California, Riverside, California 92521; e-mail: robnp@aol.com,
auerhahn@wizard.ucr.edu

KEY WORDS: selective disinhibition, intoxication and aggression, tripartite framework,
alcohol availability, psychopharmacological, economic compulsive, systemic

ABSTRACT

A review of the scientific literature on the relationship between alcohol and
violence and that between drugs and violence is presented. A review and
analysis of three major theoretical approaches to understanding these relationships are also presented. A number of conclusions are reached on the basis of these efforts. First, despite a number of published statements to the
contrary, we find no significant evidence suggesting that drug use is associated with violence. Second, there is substantial evidence to suggest that alcohol use is significantly associated with violence of all kinds. Third, recent
theoretical efforts reviewed here have, despite shortcomings, led to significant new understanding of how and why alcohol and drugs are related to violence. Fourth, these theoretical models and a growing number of empirical
studies demonstrate the importance of social context for understanding violence and the ways in which alcohol and drugs are related to violence. Fifth,
the shortcomings of these theoretical models and the lack of definitive empirical tests of these perspectives point to the major directions where future
research on the relationship between alcohol and violence, and between
drugs and violence, is needed.

INTRODUCTION

That the United States leads the industrialized nations in rates of interpersonal
violence is a well-documented fact (National Research Council 1993). Examples of this can be seen in the extraordinarily high rates of violent crimes such

292   PARKER & AUERHAHN

as homicide, robbery, and rape in the United States (National Research Council 1993, Parker & Rebhun 1995); an additional and disturbing fact that has come to light in recent years is the increasing rate of youth violence, particularly lethal violence (Blumstein 1995; Alaniz et al 1998).

During the last decade, interest has grown in the relationship between alcohol, drugs, and violence. In addition to the mostly misguided attention in mass media and in political circles to the relationship between illegal drugs and violence, a number of empirical studies have attempted to disentangle the associations between alcohol, drugs, and violence. Several studies have attempted to organize this knowledge into a comprehensive theoretical framework. This chapter synthesizes this body of work to assess the state of the art in thinking about the relationships between psychoactive substances and violent behavior.

Defining and understanding the complex relationships among alcohol, drugs, and violence require that we examine issues of pharmacology, settings, and larger social contexts to understand the mechanisms that associate substance use and violence in individuals. In addition to this, we must also consider not only the ways in which individuals are nested within larger social contexts, but also the ways in which these contexts themselves may create conditions in which violent behavior takes place, for example, the ways in which availability of substances, while itself conditioned to some degree by larger social forces, contributes to the spatial distribution of crime and violence.

We do not attempt to review the growing literature on the biological aspects of violence. Despite increased interest in this area of research, no credible scientific evidence currently exists that demonstrates any significant link between biological characteristics and violence (National Research Council 1993). Future research may reveal complex interactions among biological, pharmacological, psychological, and contextual aspects of alcohol- and drug-related violence, but no conclusive evidence exists to support this idea at present.

In addition to trying to understand the ways in which alcohol and drug use may contribute to violent behavior, it is also important to consider the ways that alcohol and other drugs relate to human behavior in general. Some advances have been made in the study of psychological expectancies concerning alcohol's effect on behavior (Brown 1993, Grube et al 1994), the relationship between alcohol and cognitive functioning (Pihl et al 1993), the impact of alcohol on aggressive behavior (Leonard & Taylor 1983), and the dynamic developmental effects of early exposure to alcohol and violence among young people (White et al 1993) and among women who have been victimized as children and as adults (Miller & Downs 1993, Widom & Ames 1994, Roesler & Dafler 1993).

Similar work has attempted to understand the links between illicit drugs and behavior, although due to the attention focused on the illegality of these substances, this body of work tends to be most concerned with illegal behaviors that might be associated with drugs. Examples from this literature include examinations of the links between drug use and delinquent behavior among juveniles (Watts & Wright 1990, Fagan 1993, Fagan et al 1990); relationships between substance use and domestic violence (Bennett 1995, Bennett et al 1994, Roberts 1987, Blount et al 1994); the ways in which the use and distribution of illicit drugs are related to all types of crime, particularly nonviolent property offenses (Ball et al 1982, Ball 1991, Baumer 1994, Greenberg 1976, Johnson et al 1994, Klein & Maxson 1985, McCoy et al 1995, Meiczkowski 1994, Feucht & Kyle 1996); and the impact of drug use on the ability to maintain interpersonal relationships (Joe 1996, Fishbein 1996, Lerner & Burns 1978).

A fairly common problem specific to theoretical and empirical investigations of the relationship between drugs and violence is the tendency—largely ideological—to lump all illicit drugs together, as if all drugs might be expected to have the same relationship to violent behavior. Different drugs certainly do have different pharmacological effects, which may or may not influence the user's tendency toward violence; this should be treated as a prominent empirical question, rather than as an afterthought usually addressed only when results are disaggregated by drug type. Another problem specific to the analysis of the impacts of illicit drugs on behavior that hinders our understanding of the relationship between drugs and violence in real-world (as opposed to laboratory) settings was cogently pointed out by one researcher—that the degree of both impurity and deception in the illicit drug market "makes any direct inferences between drug-taking and behavior seem almost ludicrous" (Greenberg 1976, p. 119; see also Johnson 1978). Evidence of the greater likelihood of polydrug use among more violent research subjects also confuses any causal inferences that can be made with respect to particular drugs (e.g. Spunt et al 1995, Inciardi & Pottieger 1994).

DRUGS, ALCOHOL, AND VIOLENCE AT THE INDIVIDUAL LEVEL

A rather fragmented research literature attempts to identify links between alcohol, drugs, and violence at the individual or pharmacological level. This work is discussed briefly below, mainly as a prelude to theoretical models developed in light of these empirical findings.

Evidence of an individual level association between alcohol and violence is widespread. For example, Collins (1981) reviewed a number of studies in which alcohol and violence were associated among individuals. Experimental studies have also shown a consistent relationship at the individual level between alcohol use and aggressive behavior, especially in the presence of social cues that would normally elicit an aggressive response; the consumption of alcohol increases the aggressiveness of this response (Taylor 1983, Gantner &

Taylor 1992, Pihl et al 1993). Roizen (1993, pp. 4–5) reports that in nearly 40 studies of violent offenders, and an equal number of studies of victims of violence, alcohol involvement was found in about 50% of the events and people examined. Although most individual-level studies assume that alcohol has a potentially causal role, an argument supported by the experimental studies cited here, some have argued variously that the relationship is spurious (Collins 1989), that both are caused by third factors (Jessor & Jessor 1977), or that aggression and violence precede alcohol and drug abuse (White et al 1987).

In general, little evidence suggests that illicit drugs are uniquely associated with the occurrence of violent crime. While respondents of the 1991 National Criminal Victimization Survey perceived more than one fourth of violent criminal assailants to be under the influence of alcohol, less than 10% of these assailants were reported by victims to be under the influence of illicit drugs. Of these, more than half were reported to be under the influence of both alcohol and drugs (Bureau of Justice Statistics 1992a). These percentages are supported by urinalysis data for persons arrested for violent offenses, which yield the finding that in 1990, only 5.6% of violent offenders were under the influence of illicit drugs at the time of their offense (US Bureau of Justice Statistics 1992b).

Studies of the drug and alcohol involvement of homicide offenders and victims also support the notion that alcohol is, overwhelmingly, the substance most frequently implicated in this particular form of violence (Abel 1987, Spunt et al 1994, 1995, Wieczorek et al 1990, Yarvis 1994, Fendrich et al 1995, Goldstein et al 1992). Interview studies with homicide offenders as well as toxicology studies of homicide victims consistently report that approximately half of all homicide offenders are intoxicated on drugs or alcohol at the time of the crime; similar percentages of homicide victims test positive for substance use as well (Abel 1987, Langevin et al 1982, Ray & Simons 1987, Fendrich et al 1995, Spunt et al 1994, 1995, Wieczorek et al 1990, Kratcoski 1990, Welte & Abel 1989, Garriott 1993, Tardiff et al 1995). Some evidence suggests that alcohol is the substance most frequently implicated in other violent events as well (Buss et al 1995, US Bureau of Justice Statistics 1992a).[1]

---

[1]Difficulties inherent in trying to assess the involvement of alcohol relative to other drugs in violent events are largely the result of the way in which the research agenda surrounding the relationship between drugs, alcohol, and violence has been constructed. The majority of data collection efforts seem to be focused either on one particular substance (e.g. cocaine) and its relationship to or involvement in violent episodes or on comparisons between alcohol and illicit drugs in general, thereby hindering comparisons not only between alcohol and other drugs, but between different illicit drugs as well. A recent example is the National Institute of Justice report entitled *Drugs, Alcohol, and Domestic Violence in Memphis* (1997), which details research conducted to determine the role of substance use in incidents of domestic violence. At no point in the report are alcohol and drug use separated into distinct phenomena, making it impossible to determine what substances may be associated with domestic violence.

A shortcoming common to much of the work that has attempted to disentangle the individual-level relationships between drugs, alcohol, and violence is that many researchers fail to make a theoretical and/or empirical distinction between different types of drugs. For this reason, a short review of the literature concerning the links between violence and specific types of illicit drugs is presented below in the hope that some general conclusions can be drawn about the nature and magnitude of the relationship between illicit drugs and violence.

Heroin

Evidence to support a link between heroin and violence is virtually nonexistent. While there is some evidence that heroin users participate in economically motivated property crimes (see Kaplan 1983, pp. 51–58 for a thoughtful and critical discussion of this issue), the work of Ball and his colleagues (Ball et al 1982, Ball 1991) fails to uncover persuasive evidence for a link between heroin use and violent crime. Although no specific measures for violent crime are reported in the analysis of self-reported criminality (validated by official records) from a sample of 243 heroin addicts in Baltimore, only 3% of the sample reported committing, on a daily basis, any crime other than theft; the figures for the weekly and "infrequent" commission of crimes other than theft are 3% and 9%, respectively (Ball et al 1982). A later, more comprehensive analysis undertaken to determine whether or not "common forces attributable to heroin addiction are of primary etiological importance with respect to crime" (Ball 1991, p. 413) compares addict samples from three major Eastern cities. Echoing the results of the 1982 study, involvement in violent crime was negligible, accounting for between 1.5% and 5.6% of all addict criminality across cities (Ball 1991, p. 419).

Amphetamines

Considerable investigation has been made into a possible pharmacological link between amphetamines and violence. Some evidence indicates that in rare cases, either sustained periods of heavy use or extremely high acute doses can induce what has variously been called "toxic psychosis" or "amphetamine-induced psychosis," a reaction that is virtually indistinguishable from schizophrenia (Ellinwood 1971, Fukushima 1994). Aside from these extremely rare cases, some evidence may speak to a link between violent behavior and amphetamine use in ethnographic samples (Joe 1996) and in case-study research (Ellinwood 1971). One researcher notes, however, that this link may result from situational influences: "several...subjects seem to have lost intellectual awareness because they lived alone and had little chance to cross-check their delusional thinking. A long-term solitary lifestyle seems particularly significant in fostering this effect" (Ellinwood 1971, p. 1173).

296   PARKER & AUERHAHN

The importance of context and situation for the association between amphetamine use and violent behavior is supported by animal studies as well; Miczek & Tidey (1989) report that the social relationship between experimental animals significantly influences the level and type of violent behavior that they manifest when on amphetamines (Miczek & Tidey 1989, p. 75). Additionally, the baseline rate of violent or aggressive behavior prior to amphetamine administration was an important predictor of violent behavior after drug administration. The authors conclude from this review of animal studies that:

> Among the most important determinants of amphetamine effects on aggressive and defensive responses are the stimulus situation, species, prior experience with these types of behavior, and...dosage and chronicity of drug exposure. (Miczek & Tidey 1989, p. 71)

Cocaine

Some evidence suggests that cocaine use and violent behavior may be associated (Miller et al 1991, Budd 1989, Inciardi & Pottieger 1994); one of the most widely reported pharmacological effects of cocaine in users is feelings of paranoia (Goode 1993, Miller et al 1991). At least one group of researchers suggest that cocaine-associated violence "may in part be a defensive reaction to irrational fear" (Miller et al 1991, p. 1084).

The route of administration may influence the likelihood of violent behavior in users, with methods delivering the most intense and immediate effects being most closely associated with some forms of violent behavior. Users who smoked the drug in the form of "crack" were most likely to engage in violence proximate to cocaine use, followed by users taking the drug intravenously. Users who "snorted" the drug were found to be least likely to engage in violence (Giannini et al 1993).[2] However, these researchers also reported that forms of violence "requiring sustained activity" (defined by the authors to include such acts as rape and robbery) were not associated with route of administration of cocaine. Because of this, the authors conclude that "circumstance and situation may be as important as route of administration" (Giannini et al 1993, p. 69).

The greater influence of social rather than pharmacological factors on the cocaine-violence relationship has also been reported elsewhere. Goldstein et al (1991) found that the relationship of violence to volume of cocaine use varied according to gender, with only male "big users" of cocaine contributing disproportionately to the distribution of violent events reported by the sample as a

---

[2]Miller et al (1991) failed to find any such relationship between route of administration and violence; however, the authors point out that this lack of finding may be explained by the use of a treatment sample of users who were likely using cocaine in such high dosage and frequency as to blur any distinction between acute toxicity effects specific to route of administration (Miller et al 1991, p. 1084).

whole (Goldstein et al 1991, p. 354). Additional evidence for the importance of context can be found in ethnographic research, which reports that a great deal of violent behavior experienced by crack-using women arises as a result of their involvement in prostitution, which is related circumstantially, although not pharmacologically, to their drug use (Mieczkowski 1994, Johnson et al 1994).

An issue of research design has emerged in the extensive literature surrounding cocaine use and violence. Chitwood & Morningstar (1985) report systematic differences between samples of cocaine users in and out of treatment programs, with samples from those in treatment characterized by greater cocaine use in both frequency and volume. This difference has been reported elsewhere (e.g. Miller et al 1991); Inciardi & Pottieger (1994) also report that a comparison of cocaine users in treatment to users not in treatment reveals that treatment users were substantially more likely to be polydrug users and to engage in violence. These findings are important in that the type of sample used may, at least in the case of cocaine, greatly influence the findings about a drug-violence association.

Phencyclidine

Phencyclidine (PCP) is widely believed to be associated with violence; this conclusion is based almost exclusively on case study research, often of individuals with psychiatric disturbances (e.g. Lerner & Burns 1978, McCarron et al 1981). Ketamine, a drug pharmacologically quite similar to PCP, has enjoyed increasing popularity in recent years (Dotson et al 1995). PCP and Ketamine are classified as "dissociative anaesthetics" because they diminish awareness not only of pain but also of the environment in general. Delusions, paranoia, and (in rare cases) psychosis are among the most commonly reported effects of these drugs by users and clinicians (Marwah & Pitts 1986, Lerner & Burns 1978, McCarron 1986, Dotson et al 1995). However, one researcher concludes that "emotionally stable people under the influence of PCP probably will not act in a way very different from their normal behavior" (Siegel 1978, p. 285).

Official crime statistics fail to show conclusive evidence for a unique link between PCP use and violent crime; arrestees who were not under the influence of illicit drugs (according to urinalysis) were more likely to be charged with assault than were persons testing positive for PCP (Wish 1986). Among PCP-positive arrestees, the conditional distribution of offenses is influenced toward a greater likelihood of robbery charges, but Wish (1986) notes that this may be an artifact of demographic coincidence; PCP users tend to be younger than the average user of illicit drugs and thus coincide with the age group that dominates robbery arrests (Wish 1986, Maguire et al 1993).

298   PARKER & AUERHAHN

Summary

This review of the evidence concerning the relationship between the use of various illicit drugs and violence makes it clear that support for such linkages is absent. At best, we can characterize the available results as inconclusive. The strongest evidence is for a link between cocaine use and violence; however, the conclusions of researchers whose findings support this idea universally highlight a social rather than a pharmacological basis for this link. At present, no compelling evidence exists to support an association between violence and amphetamines, Phencyclidine/Ketamine, or heroin. While there is some evidence that some of these drugs may induce psychosis, this reaction is exceedingly rare; virtually all research on this phenomenon consists of case studies, making it impossible to even estimate the frequency of such reactions in the population.

   The most extensive research literature concerning drugs and violence is that of investigations of the relationship between cocaine use and violence. A search through *Sociological Abstracts* reveals that this literature has grown concurrently with concern about, if not use of, cocaine (see White House Office of National Drug Control Policy 1997 for use statistics). Between 1970 and 1980, only four articles with "cocaine" or "crack" in the title are indexed, while between 1980 and 1990 there are approximately 75; in the 1990s, this figure is at nearly 200 before the decade's end. However, even in the face of this profusion of research interest, we are still unable to say with any certainty that cocaine use and violent behavior are related. In part this may be attributable to the limitations inherent in ideologically driven research (e.g. Inciardi & Pottieger 1994); it may also indicate that such a link really does not exist, and that any amount of looking will continue to fail to uncover it. At this point in the state of our knowledge, it is clear that we must look beyond the level of the individual user in order to adequately understand and characterize the relationship (if any) between illicit drugs and violence.

THEORETICAL APPROACHES

We have identified four recent attempts to specify and/or explain the linkages among drugs, alcohol, and violence that are worthy of discussion, either for the fact of their prominence in the research literature or for the promise of greater understanding that they afford. Three of these four approaches have associated with them at least some empirical tests of the theories; these are discussed along with the explication of the theories. Each is discussed in turn, with attention then passing to the commonalities between these theories, to determine whether a useful synthesis can be made.

Fagan's Approach: Intoxication, Aggression, and the Functionality of Violence

Jeffrey Fagan has produced several attempts to formulate a comprehensive theory of the relationship between the use of psychoactive substances, violence, and aggression (Fagan 1990, 1993, Fagan et al 1990). In addition, he has also been part of a joint effort to further our understanding of youth violence in general (Fagan & Wilkinson 1998); this work is discussed here briefly vis-à-vis its complementarity with Fagan's formulations of the relationship of alcohol, drugs, and violence.

Above all, Fagan and his colleagues argue for the use of hierarchical or "nested contexts" models if we are to gain any understanding of the etiology of violence in general and of the relationships between substance use and violence (Fagan 1993, 1990). In his most recent work Fagan has argued for a "situated transactions" framework as the most promising way to understand youth violence (Luckenbill 1977).

In assessing the relationships between alcohol, drugs, and violence, Fagan (1990) has reviewed research and theoretical arguments from biological and physiological research, psychopharmacological studies, psychological and psychiatric approaches, and social and cultural perspectives in an attempt to present a comprehensive model of this relationship. He argues that the most important areas of consensus from these different perspectives are that intoxication has a significant impact on cognitive abilities and functioning, and that the nature of this impact varies according to the substance used but is, in the last instance, moderated by the context in which behavior takes place. For example, social and cultural meanings of how people function under the influence of alcohol, understandings about the impact of intoxication on judgment, the ability to perceive social cues, and the ability to focus on long- as well as short-term outcomes and desires are all extremely important factors in determining the outcome of a social situation in which drugs or alcohol are present and whether that situation will result in violence. The nature of the setting in which interaction takes place and the absence or presence of formal and informal means of social control are also important factors whereby intoxication influences aggression. Fagan also posits that intoxicated individuals tend to have limited response sets in situations of social interaction (1990, pp. 299–300); Fagan & Wilkinson (1998) extend this view to a general analysis of the etiology of youth violence.

To date, no empirical tests of this model exist. Fagan's approach leads to a very general theoretical model that would require substantial revision to permit empirical testing. For example, the outcome measure, aggression, is hardly the same thing as violence, although there is certainly some relationship between these concepts. Further theoretical explanation is needed to establish the transition from aggression to violence, as well as the linkages between the antecedents of aggression and aggression itself.

Fagan & Wilkinson propose a general model of youth violence that is relevant to this discussion. They propose that youth violence is "a functional, purposive behavior that serves definable goals within specific social contexts" (Fagan & Wilkinson 1998, p. 2). Fagan & Wilkinson argue that one of the most important benefits that accrue to youth from the use of violence is the attainment of status, something to which youths have limited access. The social world in which adolescents operate places an increasingly high premium on status and reputation; broader contextual influences such as technology (in the form of weapons) are important in "raising the stakes" of potentially violent situations, which may change the meanings attributed to different behaviors (Fagan & Wilkinson 1998). Another factor that may influence the meanings attributed to the actions of others is the consumption of drugs or alcohol, due to the behavioral expectancies that may be associated with them. These potentially violence-producing combinations in meaning-assignment may be particularly significant when considered in the context of the cognitive limitations of the developmental stage of adolescence (Leigh 1987). Dating violence may be a particularly relevant phenomenon to examine within this framework, given the highly charged adolescent expectancies surrounding alcohol consumption and sexuality (George et al 1988, Corcoran & Thomas 1991) as well as the heightened importance of sexuality to status attainment at this developmental stage (Fagan & Wilkinson 1998).

Selective Disinhibition: Parker's Approach

Parker (1993) and Parker & Rebhun (1995) attempt to specifically link alcohol and violence in an overall conceptual model, utilizing rates of homicide as the indicator of violent behavior. Parker & Rebhun (1995) advance a sociological approach to the relationship between alcohol and violence that is much different from earlier, biologically based formulations of this relationship (see Room & Collins 1983 for a review of that literature and the widespread criticisms applied to this notion). In these earlier conceptualizations, alcohol was conceived as a biochemical agent that had a universal effect on social behavior, despite substantial evidence from cross-cultural studies that alcohol has a differential impact on behavior depending on the social and cultural contexts in which it is consumed (see Marshall 1979 for a number of examples of this point).

Noting this limitation of previous formulations, Parker & Rebhun (1995) advance a social disinhibition approach, which tries to explain why normatively proscribed behavior is "disinhibited" in relatively few cases. Alcohol selectively disinhibits violence depending on contextual factors specific to the situation, the actors involved and their relationships to one another, and the impact of bystanders. In US society, norms about the appropriateness of violence in solving interpersonal disputes argue both for and against such behavior (Parker 1993). The theory proposes that individuals are constrained from engaging in certain behaviors in a social situation by the norms that they have internalized; however, people do violate norms and may have conflicting sets of norms to draw on in some situations. It is possible that norms that have the least institutional support are more likely to be disinhibited in a situation, all else being equal (Parker 1993, p. 118).

To explain how choices are made between these conflicting normative structures, Parker & Rebhun (1995, p. 34–35) introduce the tandem concepts of active and passive constraint. In potentially violent situations, it takes active constraint—a proactive and conscious decision not to use violence to "solve" the dispute—to preclude violence. In some of these cases, alcohol may disinhibit norms that usually prevent or constrain individuals from engaging in violent behavior. Thus, the selective nature of alcohol-related homicide is dependent upon the interaction of an impaired rationality and the nature of the social situation. The nature of the social situation, or the context in which behavior takes place, is of paramount importance in determining the outcome of a potentially violent situation. This is indicated by the fact that most alcohol-involved interpersonal disputes do not result in violence and homicide, but a few of these situations do (Parker & Rebhun 1995; see also Wilbanks 1984).

Parker & Rebhun (1995) further refined and specified their theoretical model of the ways in which alcohol consumption and homicide rates might be related at the aggregate level by incorporating into the model control variables suggested by previous literature on the etiology of homicide, such as subcultural theories (e.g. Wolfgang & Ferracuti 1976), social bonds theory (e.g. Hirschi 1969, Krohn 1991), deterrence theory, routine activities (Cohen & Felson 1979), and, taking a cue from strain and social disorganization theories (e.g. Merton 1949, also Wilson 1987), controls for economic inequality and poverty rates.

A test of this particular specification of the theory was reported by Parker (1995). Cross-sectional analysis of state-level data was undertaken for five different types of homicide, differentiated by circumstances of crime and/or victim-offender relationship (e.g. robbery homicide, family homicide). Alcohol consumption was a significant predictor of family intimate and primary nonintimate homicide, or those homicides involving the closest interpersonal relationships. These results suggest that norms prohibiting violence in resolving interpersonal disputes in close or intimate relationships may be weaker than such norms prescribed in other interactions; alcohol consumption would appear to contribute to the "selective disinhibition" of an already weak normative apparatus. Parker (1995, p. 27) also reported that the impact of poverty on robbery and other felony homicides was stronger in states with above average rates of alcohol consumption; the deterrent effect of capital punishment on homicide rates was strongest in states that had below average rates of alcohol consumption, providing further support for the importance of the interplay between alcohol consumption and contextual and social situational factors in the disinhibition of active constraint.

Parker & Rebhun (1995) also report the results of two tests of this approach that utilize longitudinal research designs. The first, using city-level data, yielded evidence that increases in alcohol availability help to explain why homicide nearly tripled in these cities between 1960 and 1980. This study also found some evidence for mediating effects of poverty, routine activities, and a lack of social bonds on the relationship between homicide and alcohol availability at the city level.

In an examination of the general hypothesis that alcohol has a causal impact on homicide, Parker & Rebhun (1995, p. 102–17) conducted a dynamic test of the impact of increases in the minimum drinking age on youth homicide at the state level. Using data from 1976 through 1983, Parker & Rebhun (1995) estimated a pooled cross-section and time series model in which two general types of homicide, primary and nonprimary (based on the prior relationship between victim and offender), in three age categories (15–18, 19–20, and 21–24) were analyzed. In the presence of a number of important predictors, the rate of beer consumption was found to be a significant predictor of homicide rates in five of the six age-homicide type combinations, and increases in the minimum drinking age had a negative and significant impact on primary homicides in all age categories.

Violence Across Time and Space: The Cultural Consequences of Availability

In another theoretical formulation that attempts to explain the links between alcohol availability and violence, Maria Luisa Alaniz, Robert Nash Parker, and others (1998, 1999) propose some mechanisms by which the spatial distribution of alcohol outlets and the targeted advertising of alcohol to particular communities—in both the spatial and demographic sense—may mediate this relationship.

The work of Alaniz et al (1998, 1999) focuses on the relationship of youth violence to alcohol availability. Given the recent increases in youth violence, including the increasing proportional contribution to overall rates of lethal violence (Blumstein 1995), this appears to be a very fruitful line of research to pursue, if one of the ultimate goals of such research is the prevention and reduction of the incidence of violence. Additionally, these authors propose that due to the differences in cultural and legal status for alcohol and drugs (even taking into account the illegality of alcohol to minors), the relationship between illicit drugs and violence is more likely to stem from properties of the illicit distribution system (see Goldstein 1985), while the relationship between alcohol and violence would be expected to be more related to ingestion of the substance, whether due to the effects of pharmacology, cultural expectancies surrounding alcohol's use, or both (Parker 1995, Alaniz et al 1998).

The authors propose two pathways by which alcohol availability may be related to youth violence. The first of these is largely grounded in Parker & Rebhun's (1995) selective disinhibition approach, in specifying the ways in which norms proscribing violence may be overcome (disinhibited) given the particular characteristics of a social situation, including the presence of alcohol. The second considers the distribution of alcohol outlets in physical space and the ways in which this distribution may produce "great attractors" (Alaniz et al 1998, p. 14), areas where social controls of all kind are diminished, if not completely absent; such areas have also been conceptualized as "hot spots" (Sherman et al 1989, Roncek & Maier 1991) and "deviance service centers" (Clairmont & Magill 1974). Alaniz et al theorize that in this kind of "anything-goes" atmosphere (1998, p. 15), active constraint may be more likely to become disabled. Add to this the kinds of circumstances in which youths usually drink; due to the illegal status of alcohol for minors, youths must usually consume alcohol in "semi-private" spaces, such as cars or deserted public parks, "thus [further] limiting the effectiveness of most external forms of social control" (Alaniz et al 1998, p. 13)

Alaniz et al (1999) also highlight the role of advertising in helping to articulate the link between outlet density and youth violence that is particularly relevant in minority communities, which bear a disproportionate share of all types of violence, including youth violence. This aspect of the theory is further explicated by Alaniz & Wilkes (1995), who undertook a semiotic analysis of alcohol advertising targeted at Latino communities. The authors argue that such attempts to target minority communities are very effective because, for minority groups in the United States,

> ...the state exhibits indifference or hostility to claims of citizenship; the market openly embraces the same people...components of Latino cultural armature are appropriated by advertisers, reinvented, and returned...[;] this form of reinvention constructs a symbolic system that builds alcohol consumption into an idealized lifeworld of its constituents. (Alaniz & Wilkes 1995, p. 433)

While this process of transforming cultural symbols into the commodity form is relevant for all sorts of products and services, it is especially relevant in the case of alcohol, given the highly charged nature of cultural expectancies surrounding its use (Brown et al 1987). In support of this thesis, Alaniz et al (1999) found that the density of alcohol advertising using sexist and demeaning images of minority women was associated, at the neighborhood level, with rates of sexual violence against females aged 12–18.

The importance of context and the cultural effects of advertising on youths is demonstrated particularly well by the findings of researchers who initially set out to study links between illicit drugs and delinquency among Latino youth populations; these researchers found that tobacco use was significantly related to violent delinquency, while the use of alcohol and illicit drugs was not found to be so related. The authors explain this finding thus:

> Youngsters who use tobacco act out tobacco-associated identities available in the media and popular culture. They express a range of symbols about themselves that suggest being independent, adult, adventuresome, and tough. These values are also associated with drug use and violent delin-quency. (Watts & Wright 1990, p. 152)[3]

Goldstein's Tripartite Framework

In 1985, Paul J Goldstein made an explicit attempt to develop a theoretical framework to describe and explain the relationship between drugs and vio-lence. Goldstein developed a typology of three ways in which drug use and drug trafficking may be causally related to violence.

"Psychopharmacological violence" is violence that stems from properties of the drug itself. In Goldstein's framework, this can be violence associated with drug ingestion by the victim, the perpetrator, or both. "Economic compul-sive violence" is violence associated with the high costs of illicit drug use. This type of violence does not stem directly from the physiological effects of drugs but is motivated by the need or desire to obtain drugs. Based on the capacity to induce physical dependency, the drugs one would expect to be most often as-sociated with economic compulsive violence would be opiates (particularly heroin) and cocaine, due to the capacity of these to produce strong physical and psychological dependencies in users. "Systemic violence" is defined by Gold-stein as that type of violence associated with "traditionally aggressive patterns of interaction within the system of drug distribution and use" (Goldstein 1985, p. 497). Goldstein maintains that the risks of violence are greater to those in-volved in distribution than to those who are only users (Goldstein et al 1989).

In the years since Goldstein's original formulation, a fairly large number of empirical studies have been undertaken using this framework. Nearly all of them have been produced by researchers associated with Narcotic and Drug Research, Inc. as part of one of two major research initiatives; these are the

---

[3]It should be pointed out that the majority of the variance in violent delinquency is explained by prior incarceration; however, tobacco use also emerges as a significant, albeit weaker, predictor of violent delinquency, thus highlighting the importance of social context in the links between substance use and violent behavior.

Drug Relationships in Murder (DREIM) and the Drug Related Involvement in Violent Episodes/Female Drug Related Involvement in Violent Episodes (DRIVE/FEMDRIVE) projects.

The DREIM project involved extensive interviews with 268 homicide offenders incarcerated in New York State correctional facilities. One of the purposes of this project was to gain a more extensive understanding than that afforded by official police records of the role that drugs and alcohol play in homicide.

The DREIM project data indicated that the substance most likely to be used by homicide offenders on a regular basis as well as during the 24 hours directly preceding the crime was, overwhelmingly, alcohol. Marijuana and cocaine were the second and third most frequently implicated drugs in the lives of homicide offenders as well as in the offense itself (Spunt et al 1994, 1995).

Other empirical investigations that rely on the Goldstein framework have attempted to classify the relationship between drugs and all types of violence, under the auspices of the DRIVE/FEMDRIVE research initiative. The data collection for this project consisted of interviews with 152 male and 133 female subjects concerning both drug and alcohol use and also their participation in violent events, over an eight week period. In one analysis, Spunt et al (1990) reported that violent events are drug-related if any of the participants report drug use proximate to the incident; similarly, if there is no link to drug distribution or robbery, these "drug-related events" are classified as psychopharmacological. These researchers fail to identify any mechanism by which these psychopharmacological effects of drugs manifest themselves in violent behavior. For example, they conclude that "heroin and methadone were the [illicit] drugs most likely to be associated with psychopharmacological violence" (Spunt et al 1990, p. 299), despite the fact that virtually no evidence exists to support individual-level associations between opiate use and violence (Kaplan 1983, Ball et al 1982, Ball 1991).

Goldstein et al (1989) reported the results of research that was concerned primarily with the effect of the "crack epidemic" on homicide. Utilizing data from official police reports of homicides supplemented by an observational instrument designed by Goldstein and his research team, the authors concluded that slightly over half of the 414 New York City homicides sampled were drug-related. Evidence from official records indicated that 65% of these drug-related homicides involved crack cocaine as the primary substance, while another 22% were related to other forms of cocaine; combined, nearly 90% of drug-related homicides in the sample involved cocaine. Of these, the overwhelming majority (74.3% of all drug-related homicides) were classified as "systemic" by the researchers. Interestingly, all homicides in which alcohol was the primary substance involved were classified as psychopharmacological.

Another example of the use of the Goldstein typology is the analysis of nine female homicide offenders, reported by Brownstein et al (1994). This analysis provides further evidence that alcohol is the substance most commonly associated with homicide. The authors also conclude from these data that the use of alcohol or drugs by either perpetrator or victim proximate to the homicide makes the homicide primarily drug- or alcohol-related (Brownstein et al 1994, p. 110) despite the fact that the authors report, in some cases, long histories of spousal abuse on the part of the homicide victim, which another researcher might consider at least as important a causal factor as the fact of drug or alcohol consumption in leading up to the homicide.

A central problem that characterizes all the work that utilizes the Goldstein tripartite framework is that it is not treated as a set of testable propositions but rather as a set of assumptions about the nature of drug- and alcohol-related violence. Because of this, studies guided by this set of assumptions do not address the task of explaining mechanisms by which violent events might be related to the presence or use of drugs or alcohol; additionally, all of these studies fail to provide a detailed explanation of the way in which study events come to be classified into one type or another. Another problem with Goldstein's classificatory scheme is that the categories are not mutually exclusive. For example, many of the situations coded by researchers as events of systemic violence are economic in nature. Robbery of a drug dealer would seem to be an economically motivated crime but is classified as systemic in this framework, based on drug trafficking involvement of the victim and/or perpetrator. In short, the Goldstein framework seems biased toward support of the systemic model of drug-effected violence, which also limits the utility of the framework for explaining the relationship between alcohol—the substance most frequently implicated in violent events of all kinds—and violence. Additionally, the rigidity and inherently descriptive nature of the classification scheme fails to take into account the possibility of interactions between social context, individuals, and pharmacology.

CONCLUSIONS

Several clear conclusions can be drawn from this extensive review of the literature concerning drugs, alcohol, and violence. One is the overwhelming importance of context in any relationship that may exist between substance use and violent behavior. Our review of the literature finds a great deal of evidence that the social environment is a much more powerful contributor to the outcome of violent behavior than are pharmacological factors associated with any of the substances reviewed here.

The other consistent finding that we can report from this review of the empirical evidence is that when violent behavior is associated with a substance, that substance is, overwhelmingly, alcohol. Study after study indicates that, even in samples containing relatively high baseline rates of illicit drug use, violent events are overwhelmingly more likely to be associated with the consumption of alcohol than with any other substance. In fact, a review of the literature concerning rates of co-occurrence of violent crimes with the use of illicit substance fails to provide any support whatsoever for a link. The 1991 Criminal Victimization Survey indicates that less than 5% of violent assailants were perceived by their victims to be under the influence of illicit drugs; the corresponding figure for alcohol is more than four times that.

The consensus among the authors of previous reviews of research on alcohol, drugs, and violence (Roizen 1993, Collins 1981, Pernanen 1991) was that evidence existed for an association especially between alcohol and violence, but that the research base would not support any stronger conclusions. These and other reviews would invariably end with a call for more and better research to address the issue of whether evidence about a causal relationship between alcohol, drugs, and violence could be found. What was missing from those reviews, however, was a full recognition of the importance of theoretical development in the search for evidence about causality. Until the last ten years, such efforts were largely absent; a number of the studies cited here would replicate associational findings and end with this same lament about the absence of causal evidence. However, recent developments, especially the work of Goldstein and colleagues, Fagan, and Parker and colleagues, have led to an increased conceptual and theoretical base from which questions of causality can be better assessed. None of these approaches has succeeded in fully theorizing the potential relationships among alcohol, drugs, and violence, and none of these perspectives has provided definitive empirical tests of these theoretical models. Indeed, all of these approaches need more theoretical development as well as better data and methodological approaches to advance the state of knowledge about these relationships. However, at least it is reasonable to claim that research on alcohol, drugs, and violence demonstrates some promising theoretical approaches and some useful empirical studies based on those approaches. Much work is yet to be done, but the prospects for greater understanding of how and why alcohol and drugs contribute to violence have never been brighter.

ACKNOWLEDGMENTS

We would like to acknowledge the support of the University of California, Riverside; Raymond Orbach, Chancellor; David Warren, Vice Chancellor; Carlos Velez-Ibanez, Dean of the College of Humanities, Arts and Social Sciences; Linda Brewster Stearns, Chair, Sociology Department; as well as the State of California, for their support of the Presley Center for Crime and Justice Studies, which supported the authors during the completion of this article.

308 PARKER & AUERHAHN

Literature Cited

Abel EL. 1987. Drugs and homicide in Erie County, New York. *Int. J. Addictions* 22(2):195–200

Alaniz ML, Parker RN, Gallegos A, Cartmill RS. 1998. Immigrants and violence: the importance of context. *Hispanic J. Behav. Sci.*. 20(2): In press

Alaniz ML, Parker RN, Gallegos A, Cartmill RS. 1999. Ethnic targeting and the objectification of women: alcohol advertising and violence against young Latinas. In *Currents in Criminology*, ed. RN Parker.

Alaniz ML, Wilkes C. 1995. Reinterpreting Latino culture in the commodity form: the case of alcohol advertising in the Mexican American community. *Hispanic J. Behav. Sci.* 17(4):430–51

Ball JC, Rosen L, Flueck JA, Nurco DN. 1982. Lifetime criminality of heroin addicts in the United States. *J. Drug Issues* 12: 225–39

Ball JC. 1991. The similarity of crime rates among male heroin addicts in New York City, Philadelphia, Baltimore. *J. Drug Issues* 21:413–27

Baumer E. 1994. Poverty, crack, crime: a cross-city analysis. *J. Res. Crime Delinq.* 31:311–27

Bennett LW. 1995. Substance abuse and the domestic assault of women. *Soc. Work* 40: 760–71

Bennett LW, Tolman RM, Rogalski CJ, Srinivasaraghavan J. 1994. Domestic abuse by male alcohol and drug addicts. *Violence Victims* 9:359–68

Blount WR, Silverman IJ, Sellers CS, Seese RA. 1994. Alcohol and drug use among abused women who kill, abused women who don't, their abusers. *J. Drug Issues* 24(2):165–77

Blumstein A. 1995. Youth violence, guns, the illicit drug industry. *J. Crim. Law Criminol.* 86(1):10–36

Brown SA. 1993. Drug effect expectancies and addictive behavior change. *Exp. Clin. Psychopharmacol.* 1(Oct):55–67

Brown SA, Christiansen BA, Goldman MS. 1987. The alcohol expectancy questionnaire: an instrument for the assessment of adolescent and adult alcohol expectancies. *J. Stud. Alcohol* 48(5):483–91

Brownstein HH, Spunt BJ, Crimmins S, Goldstein PJ, Langley S. 1994. Changing patterns of lethal violence by women: a research note. *Women Crim. Justice* 5: 99–118

Budd RD. 1989. Cocaine abuse and violent death. *Am. J. Drug Alcohol Abuse* 15: 375–82

Bureau of Justice Statistics. 1992a. *Drugs and Crime Facts. 1992.* Washington, DC: USGPO

Bureau of Justice Statistics. 1992b. *Drugs, Crime, the Justice System.* Washington, DC: USGPO

Buss TF, Abdu R, Walker JR. 1995. Alcohol, drugs, violence in a small city trauma center. *J. Substance Abuse Treat.* 12:75–83

Chitwood DD, Morningstar PC. 1985. Factors which differentiate cocaine users in treatment from nontreatment users. *Int. J. Addictions* 20:449–59

Clairmont DH, Magill D. 1974. *Africville: The Life and Death of a Canadian Black Community.* Toronto: McClelland & Stewart

Cohen LE, Felson M. 1979. Social change and crime rate trends: a routine activities approach. *Am. Sociol. Rev.* 44:588–607

Collins JJ Jr. 1981. Alcohol use and criminal behavior: an empirical, theoretical, methodological overview. In *Drinking and Crime: Perspectives on the Relationship between Alcohol Consumption and Criminal Behavior,* ed. JJ Collins Jr, pp. 288–316. New York: Guilford

Collins JJ Jr. 1989. Alcohol and interpersonal violence: less than meets the eye. In *Pathways to Criminal Violence,* ed. NA Weiner, ME Wolfgang, pp. 49–67. Newbury Park, CA: Sage

Corcoran KJ, Thomas LR. 1991. The influence of observed alcohol consumption on perceptions of initiation of sexual activity in a college dating situation. *J. Appl. Soc. Psychol.* 21:6:500–7

Dotson JW, Ackerman DL, West LJ. 1995. Ketamine abuse. *J. Drug Issues* 25:751–57

Ellinwood EH Jr. 1971. Assault and homicide associated with amphetamine abuse. *Am. J. Psychiatry* 127:1170–75

Fagan J. 1993. Interactions among drugs, alcohol, violence. *Health Affairs* 12(4):65–79

Fagan J. 1990. Intoxication and aggression in drugs and crime. In *Crime and Justice: A Review of Research*, ed. M. Tonry, JQ Wilson, 13:241–320. Chicago: Univ. Chicago Press

Fagan J, Wilkinson DL. 1998. The functions of adolescent violence. In *Violence in American Schools*, ed. DS Elliott, KR Williams, B Hamburg. Cambridge Univ. Press

Fagan J, Weis JG, Cheng Y. 1990. Delinquency and substance use among inner-city students. *J. Drug Issues* 20(3): 351–402

Fendrich M, Mackesy-Amiti ME, Goldstein P, Spunt B, Brownstein H. 1995. Substance involvement among juvenile murderers: comparisons with older offenders based on interviews with prison inmates. *Int. J. Addictions* 30(11):1363–82

Feucht TE, Kyle GM. 1996. *Methamphetamine Use Among Adult Arrestees: Findings from the Drug Use Forecasting (DUF) Program*. Washington, DC: Natl. Inst. Justice

Fishbein DH. 1996. Female PCP-using jail detainees: proneness to violence and gender differences. *Addictive Behav.* 21(2): 1:55–172

Fukushima A. 1994. Criminal responsibility in amphetamine psychosis. *Jpn. J. Psychiatr. Neurol.* 48(Suppl.):1–4

Gantner AB, Taylor SP. 1992. Human physical aggression as a function of alcohol and threat of harm. *Aggressive Behav.* 18:(1) 29–36

Garriott JC. 1993. Drug use among homicide victims: changing patterns. *Am. J. Forensic Med. Pathol.* 14(3):234–37

George WH, Gournic SJ, McAfee MP. 1988. Perceptions of postdrinking female sexuality: effects of gender, beverage choice, drink payment. *J. Appl. Soc. Psychol.* 18(15):1295–1317

Giannini AJ, Miller NS, Loiselle RH, Turner CE. 1993. Cocaine-associated violence and relationship to route of administration. *J. Substance Abuse Treatment* 10:67–69

Goldstein PJ. 1985. The drugs/violence nexus: a tripartite conceptual framework. *J. Drug Issues* 15:493–506

Goldstein P, Brownstein HH, Ryan PJ, Belluci PA. 1989. Crack and homicide in New York City 1988: a conceptually based event analysis. *Contemp. Drug Problems* Winter: 651–87

Goldstein P, Brownstein HH, Ryan PJ. 1992. Drug-related homicide in New York: 1984 and 1988. *Crime Delinq.* 38(4):459–76

Goldstein PJ, Bellucci PA, Spunt BJ, Miller T. 1991. Volume of cocaine use and violence: a comparison between men and women. *J. Drug Issues* 21:345–67

Goode E. 1993. *Drugs in American Society*. New York: McGraw-Hill. 4th ed.

Greenberg SW. 1976. The relationship between crime and amphetamine abuse: an empirical review of the literature. *Contemp. Drug Probl.* 5:101–30

Grube J, Ames GM, Delaney W. 1994. Alcohol expectancies and workplace drinking. *J. Appl. Soc. Psychol.* 24(7):646–60

Hirschi T. 1969. *Causes of Delinquency*. Berkeley: Univ. Calif. Press

Inciardi JA, Pottieger AE. 1994. Crack-cocaine use and street crime. *J. Drug Issues* 24:273–92

Jessor R, Jessor SL. 1977. *Problem Behavior and Psychosocial Development: A Longitudinal Study of Youth*. New York: Academic

Joe KA. 1996. The lives and times of Asian-Pacific American women drug users: an ethnographic study of their methamphetamine use. *J. Drug Issues* 26:199–218

Johnson BD, Natarajan M, Dunlap E, Elmoghazy E. 1994. Crack abusers and noncrack abusers: profiles of drug use, drug sales, nondrug criminality. *J. Drug Issues* 24: 117–41

Johnson KM. 1978. Neurochemical Pharmacology of Phencyclidine. In *Phencyclidine (PCP) Abuse: an Appraisal, NIDI Research Monograph No. 21*, ed. RC Petersen, RC Stillman, pp. 44–52. Rockville, MD: Dep. Health Human Serv.

Kaplan J. 1983. *The Hardest Drug: Heroin and Public Policy*. Chicago: Univ. Chicago Press

Klein MW, Maxson CL. 1985. 'Rock' sales in central Los Angeles. *Sociol. Soc. Res.* 69: 561–65

Kratcoski PC. 1990. Circumstances surrounding homicides by older offenders. *Criminal Justice Behav.* 17(4):420–30

Krohn MD. 1991. Control and deterrence theories. In *Criminology: A Contemporary Handbook*, ed. J Sheley, pp. 295–314. Belmont, CA: Wadsworth

Langevin R, Paitich D, Orchard B, Handy L, Russon A. 1982. The role of alcohol, drugs, suicide attempts, situational strains in homicide committed by offenders seen for psychiatric assessment. *Acta Psychiatr. Scand.* 66(3):229–42

Leigh BC. 1987. *Drinking and unsafe sex: background and issues*. NIMH/NIDA Workshop, Women and AIDS: Promoting Healthy Behaviors. Washington, DC

Leonard KE, Taylor SP. 1983. Exposure to pornography, permissive and nonpermissive cues, male aggression toward females. *Motivation Emotion* 7(3):291–99

Lerner SE, Burns RS. 1978. Phencyclidine use

310   PARKER & AUERHAHN

among youth: history, epidemiology, and acute and chronic intoxication. See Johnson 1978, pp. 66–118

Luckenbill DF. 1977. Criminal homicide as a situated transaction. *Social Probl.* 25: 176–86

Maguire K, Pastore AL, Flanagan TJ, eds. 1993. *Sourcebook of Criminal Justice Statistics 1992.* US Dep. Justice, Bur. Justice Statist. Washington, DC: USGPO

Marshall M, ed. 1979. *Beliefs, Behaviors, Alcoholic Beverages: A Cross-Cultural Survey.* Ann Arbor: Univ. Mich. Press

Marwah J, Pitts DK. 1986. Psychopharmacology of phencyclidine. In *Phencyclidine: An Update, NIDA Res. Monogr. No. 64,* ed. DH Clout, pp. 127–35. Rockville, MD: Dep. Health Human Serv.

McCoy HV, Inciardi JA, Metsch LR, Pottieger AE. 1995. Women, crack, crime: gender comparisons of criminal activity among crack cocaine users. *Contemp. Drug Probl.* 22:435–51

McCarron M. 1986. *Phencyclidine intoxication.* In *Phencyclidine: an Update, NIDA Res. Monogr. No. 64,* ed. DH Clout, pp. 209–217. Rockville, MD: Dep. Health Human Serv.

Merton RK. 1949. *Social Theory and Social Structure.* Glencoe, IL: Free

Miczek KA, Tidey JW. 1989. Amphetamines: aggressive and social behavior. In *Pharmacology and Toxicology of Amphetamine and Related Designer Drugs,* ed. K Asghar, E Souza, pp. 68–100. Washington, DC: USGPO

Mieczkowski T. 1994. The experiences of women who sell crack: some descriptive data from the Detroit Crack Ethnography Project. *J. Drug Issues* 24:227–48

Miller BA, Downs WR. 1993. The impact of family violence on the use of alcohol by women: research indicates that women with alcohol problems have experienced high rates of violence during their childhoods and as adults. *Alcohol Health Res. World* 17(2):137–42

Miller NS, Gold MS, Mahler JC. 1991. Violent behaviors associated with cocaine use—possible pharmacological mechanisms. *Int. J. Addictions* 21:1077–88

National Institute of Justice. 1997. *Drugs, Alcohol, Domestic Violence in Memphis: Research Preview.* Natl. Criminal Justice Ref. Serv.

Parker RN. 1995. Bringing 'booze' back in: the relationship between alcohol and homicide. *J. Res. Crime Delinquency* 32 (1):3–38

Parker RN. 1993. Alcohol and theories of homicide. In *Advances in Criminological Theory,* ed. F Adler, W Laufer, 4:113–42. New Brunswick, NJ: Transaction

Parker RN, with LA Rebhun. 1995. *Alcohol and Homicide: A Deadly Combination of Two American Traditions.* Albany: State Univ. NY Press

Pernanen K. 1991. *Alcohol in Human Violence.* New York: Guilford

Pihl RO, Peterson JB, Lau MA. 1993. A biosocial model of the alcohol-aggression relationship. *J. Stud. Alcohol* 11(Sept):128–39 (Suppl.)

Ray MC, Simons RL. 1987. Convicted murderers' accounts of their crimes: a study of homicide in small communities. *Symbolic Interact.* 10(1):57–70

Reiss AJ Jr, Roth JA, eds. 1993. *Understanding and Preventing Violence.* Washington, DC: Natl. Acad. Press

Roberts AR. 1987. Psychosocial characteristics of batterers: a study of 234 men charged with domestic violence offenses. *J. Family Violence* 2:81–93

Roesler TA, Dafler CE. 1993. Chemical dissociation in adults sexually victimized as children: alcohol and drug use in adult survivors. *J. Substance Abuse Treatment* 10: 537–43

Roizen J. 1993. *Issues in the Epidemiology of Alcohol and Violence in Alcohol and Interpersonal Violence: Fostering Multidisciplinary Perspectives, Natl. Inst. on Alcohol Abuse and Alcoholism Res. Monogr. No. 24,* ed. SE Martin. Washington, DC: Natl. Inst. Health

Roncek DW, Maier PA. 1991. Bars, blocks, crimes revisited: linking the theory of routine activities to the empiricism of 'hot spots'. *Criminology* 29:725–54

Room R, Collins G, eds. 1983. *Alcohol and Disinhibition: Nature and Meaning of the Link.* Washington, DC: *Natl. Inst. Alcohol Abuse and Alcoholism, Res. Monogr. No. 2.*

Sherman LW, Gartin PR, Buerger ME. 1989. Hot spots of predatory crime: routine activities and the criminology of place. *Criminology* Vols. 27–56

Siegel RK. 1978. Phencyclidine, criminal behavior, the defence of diminished capacity. In *Phencyclidine (PCP) Abuse: An Appraisal,* ed. RC Petersen, RC Stillman, pp. 272–88. Rockville, MD: Dep. Health Human Serv.

Spunt B, Brownstein H, Goldstein P, Fendrich M, Liberty HJ. 1995. Drug use by homicide offenders. *J. Psychoactive Drugs* 27(2):125–34

Spunt B, Goldstein P, Brownstein HH, Fen-

ALCOHOL, DRUGS, AND VIOLENCE 311

drich M, Langley S. 1994. Alcohol and homicide: interviews with prison inmates. *J. Drug Issues* 24(1):143–63

Spunt BJ, Goldstein PJ, Belluci PA, Miller T. 1990. Race, ethnicity and gender differences in the drugs-violence relationship. *J. Psychoactive Drugs* 22:293–303

Stets JE. 1990. Verbal and physical aggression in marriage. *J. Marriage Family* 43: 721–32

Tardiff K, Marzuk PM, Leon AC, Hirsch CS, Stajik M, et al. 1995. Cocaine, opiates, ethanol in homicides in New York City: 1990 and 1991. *J. Forensic Sci.* 40(3): 387–90

Taylor SP. 1983. Alcohol and human physical aggression. In *Alcohol, Drug Abuse, Aggression*, ed. E Gottheil, KA Druley, TE Skoloda, HM Waxman. Springfield, IL: Thomas

Watts WD, Wright LS. 1990. The drug use–violent delinquency link among adolescent Mexican-Americans. In *Drugs and Violence: Causes, Correlates, Consequences, NIDA Res. Monogr. No. 103,* ed. M De La Rosa, EY Lambert, B Gropper, pp. 136–159. Washington, DC: USGPO

Welte JW, Abel EL. 1989. Homicide: drinking by the victim. *J. Stud. Alcohol* 50(3): 197–201

White HR, Hansell S, Brick J. 1993. Alcohol use and aggression among youth. *Alcohol Health Res. World* 17(2):144–50

White HR, Pandina RJ, LaGrange RL. 1987. Longitudinal predictors of serious substance abuse and delinquency. *Criminology* 25(3):715–40

White House Office of National Drug Control Policy. 1997. *Fact Sheet: Drug Use Trends. National Criminal Justice Reference Service.* Available online at http://www.ncjrs.org

Widom CS, Ames MA. 1994. Criminal consequences of childhood sexual victimization. *Child Abuse Neglect* 18(4):303–18

Wieczorek W, Welte J, Abel E. 1990. Alcohol, drugs, murder: a study of convicted homicide offenders. *J. Criminal Justice* 18: 217–27

Wilbanks W. 1984. *Murder in Miami.* Lantham, MD: Univ. Press Am.

Wilson WJ. 1987. *The Truly Disadvantaged: The Inner City, the Underclass, Public Policy.* Chicago: Univ. Chicago Press

Wish ED. 1986. PCP and crime: just another illicit drug? In *Phencyclidine: An Update. NIDA Res. Monogr. No. 64,* ed. DH Clout, pp. 174–89. Rockville, MD: Dep. Health Human Serv.

Wolfgang ME, Ferracuti F. 1976. *The Subculture of Violence: Towards an Integrated Theory in Criminology.* London: Tavistock

Yarvis RM. 1994. Patterns of substance abuse and intoxication among murderers. *Bull. Am. Acad. Psychiatry Law* 22(1):133–44

[19]

Personality and Social Psychology Review
1999, Vol. 3, No. 3, 210–221

The Intrinsic Appeal of Evil: Sadism, Sensational Thrills, and Threatened Egotism

Roy F. Baumeister and W. Keith Campbell

Department of Psychology
Case Western Reserve University

Three main sources of intrinsic appeal and satisfaction from performing violent acts are described. First, sadism involves deriving pleasure directly from the suffering of the victim. An opponent-process model is suggested. Second, the quest for thrilling sensations to escape from boredom can produce violent acts, including many in which the harmful consequences were not intended. Third, threatened egotism entails that one's favorable view of self (or public image) has been attacked, and violent responses are directed toward the source of this attack. Relevant individual differences (respectively, low guilt, high sensation seeking, and narcissism) moderate these patterns. Analyzing the intrinsic appeal of evil acts is a useful complement to analyzing situational determinants of violence.

Violence, oppression, exploitation, cruelty, and other evil actions have fascinated mankind for centuries. To the social scientist, and to many a layperson as well, they pose a compelling question: How can people bring themselves to do such shocking, heinous things?

Yet this question is misleading. The notion that people must bring themselves to do shocking, heinous things assumes that the perpetrators recognize the acts as shocking and heinous and hence must force themselves to overcome the revulsion (both moral and visceral) with which those acts are regarded. This assumption is quite plausibly wrong. Acts that seem heinous to victims and in retrospect may be experienced quite differently by perpetrators at the time. Evil is defined largely by the victim's perspective, insofar as the victim's suffering constitutes the evil consequence of the action (Baumeister, 1997). Perpetrators, however, may see things quite differently. In the victim's perspective, the enormity of the crime is central (especially because one's own suffering is almost impossible to ignore), and the victim's question is either whether the perpetrator is so depraved as to actually enjoy inflicting harm or, at best, if the perpetrator has somehow managed to conceal the evil of the actions from himself or herself. To the perpetrator, however, the act may be of far less importance, and engaging in it at all may be guided more by positive attractions than the overcoming of

barriers and inhibitions. In some cases, conceivably, the perpetrator may regard the victim's suffering as trivial and as irrelevant to the perpetrator's goals and satisfactions.

The purpose of this article is to explore the positive appeal that may make the performance of evil deeds attractive. There is not likely to be a single source of this appeal, and so we offer three different models. They are not mutually exclusive, and indeed, we suggest that each applies to a different subset of perpetrators.

Our focus is on the intrinsic appeal of violence, and by defining the problem that way, we screen out several other (i.e., extrinsic) reasons for performing evil acts. These others include using violence as a means of accomplishing material or other ends, such as in attacking someone to take possession of that person's land or money. They also include the category of idealistic evil, in which people may perform acts of great harm and even mass murder in the service of positive ideals, group values, or utopian projects. For example, the highest body counts in history were achieved in the Stalinist and Maoist purges, each of which is currently estimated at having caused more than 20 million deaths. These killing campaigns, however, were shaped and sustained by an idealistic vision of creating a utopian society based on equality, shared wealth, and dignity for all. Because the killing was largely performed as a regrettable step toward a desirable goal, it qualifies as extrinsic, and therefore, it lies outside our focus.

We proceed as follows. First, we offer a working definition of evil, which requires some appreciation for the discrepancy between victim and perpetrator per-

Requests for reprints should be sent to Roy F. Baumeister, Department of Psychology, Case Western Reserve University, 10900 Euclid Avenue, Cleveland, OH 44106–7123. E-mail: rfb2@po.cwru.edu.

INTRINSIC APPEAL OF EVIL

spectives, and so we also summarize some essential aspects of that discrepancy. Next, we turn to the problem of sadism, which involves direct pleasure in harming others, and we offer a theoretical account of how that pleasure may arise. Then, we consider other forms of pleasure in harm, such as relief of boredom and the attainment of thrills. Last, we consider rage based on threat to self-esteem and the consequent desire to harm others who have humiliated the perpetrator.

Victims and Perpetrators of Evil

Although many writers may prefer to reserve the term *evil* for very limited categories of wrongdoing, we use the term in a broad and inclusive sense. One explanation for this is that there is reason to think that such grand heinous acts may actually conform to similar patterns and principles as relatively minor transgressions, and therefore, studying the smaller ones may offer valuable guidelines to the understanding of large-scale evil. Another reason is that some restrictive definitions may necessarily rest on the victim's perspective, which, although important to understand in its own right, may hamper free inquiry into understanding how the perpetrator (who may see things quite differently) could perform such acts.

Indeed, a particular problem with defining evil in terms of the magnitude of the harm is that perpetrators and victims often have strikingly different views on that magnitude. After reviewing an interdisciplinary literature on violence, aggression, crime, and other transgressions, Baumeister (1997) proposed that there is generally a *magnitude gap* between victims' and perpetrators' perceptions of the same act. The essence of the magnitude gap is that the victim loses more than the perpetrator gains. As examples, the amount of money for which a thief can sell stolen property is generally less than the replacement cost to the victimized owner. Rape victims may suffer anxiety, nightmares, and impaired sexual functioning for years, in contrast to the fleeting and feeble pleasure gained by the rapist. Murder costs the victim his or her life, plus inflicts considerable grief and suffering on the victim's social network, whereas nothing the murderer gains by the act can match that value.

Among other things, the magnitude gap explains why longstanding disputes and vendettas may be so difficult to resolve. Each violent act increases the discrepancy between the two perspectives. Just when one side may regard the score as settled, because in its view the other's suffering matches its own, the other side is likely to see a huge imbalance calling for violent redress.

For the purposes of this article, the key point is that the magnitude of an act may be much less in the perpe-trator's than in the victim's perspective, and therefore, to understand the psychology of perpetrators, it may be necessary to distance oneself from the victim's view. The question with which we began this article, namely, how someone could bring himself or herself to perform an enormously evil action, is often inappropriate, because the perpetrator failed to see it as enormous.

Other differences between victim and perpetrator perspectives are also relevant. Based on a study of relatively minor interpersonal transgressions (Baumeister, Stillwell, & Wotman, 1990; see also Mikula, 1994), these differences can be summarized as follows.

First, victim accounts tend to have longer, more inclusive time spans than perpetrator accounts. Victim accounts often integrate the transgression into a prior history of problems and a set of subsequent effects, often extending to the present. In contrast, perpetrator accounts tend to deny connections between the past transgression and the present situation. Transgressions clearly fade into irrelevant "ancient history" much more rapidly for perpetrators than for victims. Outside the laboratory, similar patterns are evident: Slavery and reconstruction in the United States, the Holocaust and religious massacres in Europe, and the Crusader invasions of the Middle East remain much fresher and more relevant to the present in the view of the victims' descendants than in the view of the perpetrators' descendants.

Second, victim accounts tend to see stark moral issues with clear lines, whereas perpetrator accounts see many more gray areas in the relevant moral judgments. Perpetrators often acknowledge some wrongdoing but also see extenuating circumstances, provocations by the eventual victims, and some degree of legitimate justification for some of their actions, but victims judge perpetrators much more harshly and unambiguously. Victims rarely acknowledge any causal or provoking role to themselves, whereas perpetrators often perceive the victims as having contributed to the conflict, even if the perpetrators acknowledge that their own responses were excessive.

Third, perpetrators usually have reasons and explanations for their actions, whereas many victims describe the perpetrator's actions as utterly gratuitous. A victim may emphasize that the perpetrator's action was for no reason at all, or in other cases, victims describe perpetrators as acting out of sheer malice. Sadistic pleasure and sadistic motivations thus figure centrally in victims' pictures of perpetrators. Perpetrators rarely describe themselves in those terms, however.

Sadism

Sadism, defined as the direct achievement of pleasure from harming others, is the most obviously intrinsic appeal of evil acts. Insofar as people get sadistic pleasure from hurting or killing others, there is little need to develop further explanations of evil. People do it because it feels good; enough said.

Does Sadistic Pleasure Exist?

Yet, sadism is an elusive, puzzling phenomenon. Accounts and memoirs by perpetrators do not commonly claim that inflicting harm was a source of pleasure or joy (e.g., Arlacchi, 1993; Browning, 1992; Sereny, 1983). More commonly, they emphasize uncertainty, fear, awkwardness, and some struggle with guilt.

A further obstacle to constructing a theory of sadism is that the well-documented reactions of perpetrators and harmdoers indicate that, far from being pleasant or satisfying, harming others leads most perpetrators to suffer physical and emotional distress. Thus, accounts by participants in the massacre at My Lai, in which American soldiers killed Vietnamese civilians, emphasize that many soldiers were crying while carrying out their orders, and some shot themselves as a way of getting excused from the work of killing (Kelman & Hamilton, 1989). Although posttraumatic stress disorder is often understood as deriving from the sufferings and fears of being in combat, one study of Vietnam veterans in such therapy found that 30% of them were suffering from problems caused by their own violent acts (as cited in Gibson & Haritos-Fatouros, 1986). Likewise, a psychiatrist who dealt with German soldiers assigned to shoot civilians early in World War II estimated that 20% of the soldiers on such duty suffered psychiatric problems such as anxiety, depression, and sleep disorder, and many others suffered physical complaints such as vomiting and other gastrointestinal disturbances (see Lifton, 1986).

One of the best studies of perpetrators is Browning's (1992) work *Ordinary Men,* which explored the subjective experiences of a group of middle-age reserve German policemen who were assigned occupation duty in Poland and rather unexpectedly received assignments to execute groups of civilians. Browning's evidence made clear that the initial reactions were extremely aversive and encompassed nightmares as well as emotional distress. Browning emphasized that the courtroom testimony of these men might have been expected to be self-serving by phrasing the distress in terms of moral qualms and guilt, but such responses were largely absent. Instead, the men described their negative reactions in terms of physical disgust, such as the horrific sound of screams, the revolting sensation of being splattered with blood and brains from shooting someone at close range, and the simple fact that it feels profoundly unpleasant to kill someone. Indeed, many men were unable to bring themselves to shoot the person and would repeatedly "fire past" or miss the victim even at point-blank range.

Professional torturers suffer similar problems. A study of Greek torturers was conducted after the repressive military regime ended, and they, too, reported many problems and sufferings connected with their cruel work. These afflictions included nightmares, depression, and severe irritability (Gibson & Haritos-Fatouros, 1986).

At a much less severe level, and much closer to home, participants in Milgram's (1963) obedience studies appeared to have suffered substantial distress over the seemingly minor act of pressing a button to deliver electric shock to another participant who was not even directly visible. In his initial article, Milgram boasted that the distress of his participants far exceeded what is observed in the majority of psychology experiments, which in his view attested to the subjective power and experimental realism of his procedures. He also observed that some participants engaged in fits of nervous laughter during the procedure, which "seemed entirely out of place, even bizarre" and which in several cases reached the point of "full-blown, uncontrollable seizures" (p. 375).

The laughter is important because it undoubtedly contributes to some of the discrepancies between victim and perpetrator accounts of crimes. Victims tend to focus on perpetrator laughter (e.g., Nordland, 1996), whereas perpetrator accounts hardly ever mention laughter. Moreover, victims take the perpetrators' laughter as a compelling sign that the perpetrators were enjoying themselves and hence as a sign of evil, sadistic pleasure. As Milgram's (1963) observations made clear, however, reluctant harmdoers may laugh out of discomfort. Milgram knew that his research participants were not enjoying themselves, even if they were laughing, but one may forgive victims of violence for failing to make such subtle attributional adjustments regarding the laughter by their tormentors.

Still, one should not overstate the negative attitude toward violence. People do at least seem to enjoy watching violence, as shown by the immense revenues generated by violent movies and television shows. This is also not an exclusively modern phenomenon: In bygone eras, hangings and other public executio: . frequently attracted large crowds of spectators. Likewise, the "autos-da-fé," public burnings of heretics during the Spanish Inquisition, often were timed to coincide with public celebrations and attracted huge numbers of people, many of whom traveled great distances to see the spectacle. Bullfights, and even the ancient Roman spectacles of feeding Christians to the lions, were less motivated by the desire to get rid of bulls (or Chris-

INTRINSIC APPEAL OF EVIL

tians) than by the wish to provide entertainment to the spectators.

More to the point, perpetrators' accounts and other observations often do acknowledge that occasional individuals (not usually the writer himself, though) did develop a capacity to enjoy cruel or hurtful activities (e.g., Arlacchi, 1993; Bing, 1991; McCall, 1994; Pakenham, 1979, 1991; Wyden, 1983). Toch's (1969/1993) influential study of violent men concluded that around 6% of his sample found pleasure in harming or bullying others and went out of their way to be unfair, unmerciful, and violent. Groth's (1979) influential study of rapists concluded that about 5% of rapists derived their principal pleasure and satisfaction from the victim's suffering. Jankowski's (1991) important study of gang members concluded that most of them disliked violence and fighting and sought to avoid it, but a few of them did enjoy it. Zimbardo's (1972) prison simulation likewise noted that, although the majority of students assigned to play the guard role fell into either the gentle, sympathetic category or the tough-but-fair category, a minority did become sadistic in that they seemed to delight in tormenting the helpless, vulnerable prisoners.

A last aspect of the puzzle of sadism, at least on extensive anecdotal evidence, is that it seems to emerge only gradually. Comments by the violent men in Toch's (1969/1993) study or the rapists in Groth's (1979) study suggest that the person slowly develops the habit of inflicting harm, and indeed, some explicitly compared it to an addiction (see Scully, 1990, p. 158). Even in Browning's (1992) work on the German reserve police, the instances of cruelty and gratuitous violence appeared to increase with the later killing operations rather than the first one.

Among professional torturers, one might predict that novices would occasionally get carried away and be excessively cruel, whereas old hands would remain in control and conform to proper procedures and limits. However, there is some evidence that the opposite is the case. In other words, novice torturers remain hesitant and tentative, but the old hands are more likely to commit excessive acts (Stover & Nightingale, 1985). (Some may object that all torture is "excessive," and we are inclined to agree. Still, from the point of view of the oppressive regime, torture is typically a means of interrogation, and therefore, when the infliction of harm becomes so severe that victims become unable to reply, such as when they pass out or die, the torture is counterproductive. It is these instances to which we refer here as excessive, insofar as even the torturers themselves recognize them as mishaps.)

Sexual sadism is also perhaps useful as a guide to how people may derive pleasure from hurting others. Evidence suggests that actual sadists are quite rare, and even in the community of sadomasochistic practitioners, people desiring to play the submissive role far outnumber those wishing to play the dominant one (e.g., Scott, 1983). Among those who qualify as sadists, it appears that this enjoyment emerges only gradually, and indeed, most people (even professionals) who play the dominant role typically started out as submissives (see Baumeister, 1989). Thus, evidence from sexual sadism converges with what we find from violent sadism: It emerges gradually and in only a minority of cases.

Based on these observations, we can outline the following requirements for an adequate psychological account of sadism. First, the initial reaction to hurting others (at least among adults) appears to be quite aversive, and the distress seems to be at a visceral level rather than a moral or abstract one. Second, the distress one experiences over inflicting harm appears to subside over time. Third, the pleasure in harming others also seems to emerge gradually over time and is described by some as comparable to an addiction. Fourth, the majority of perpetrators do not seem to develop sadistic pleasure or a feeling of addiction.

Opponent Processes and Sadism

Opponent-process theory offers one promising way to account for sadistic pleasure. Opponent-process theory was first proposed by Solomon and Corbit (1974; also see Solomon, 1980), based on physical homeostasis. It holds that each response that takes the body away from its stable, resting state must be followed by an internal process that returns the body to its normal state. Furthermore, they contended that the initial, departing (the A process) response is often strong at first, whereas the restorative B process is relatively inefficient, but over time (i.e., through many similar experiences), the B process becomes increasingly efficient and powerful, whereas the A process becomes weaker. In effect, the B process comes to dominate.

For example, when someone unaccustomed to strenuous exercise runs up a flight of stairs, the body responds by pumping the heart faster and increasing the tempo of breathing. These A processes are necessary responses to adapt to the unusual circumstance of exertion. They are followed, however, by a B process that returns heart rate and breathing to their normal rates (otherwise, the person would continue breathing fast forever). The first time this is done, the B process may seem to work rather poorly, and it will take the person a long time to return to normal. After many days of running up that same flight of stairs, however, the A processes (such as the increment in heart rate) will diminish, whereas the B process will become increasingly efficient, so that the person quickly recovers his or her normal state.

This theory provides a good fit to what was observed about sadism. As noted, the initial reaction to inflicting harm on another human being is severe distress that is typically of a visceral rather than an apparently moral nature. Novice perpetrators may feel quite ill. Over time, these upset reactions diminish in power, so that presumably killing one's hundredth victim is far less upsetting than killing the first.

Meanwhile, a B process is necessary to end the aversive, distressed response, and it would likely have a fairly pleasant, positive quality. Initially this might be quite slight and weak, so that the person's overall experience of hurting or killing would have a predominantly negative tone (consistent with most reports). Over time, however, the B process may come to predominate, in the sense that it would become more powerful, efficient, and subjectively salient. Because the B process would involve a pleasurable feeling—indeed, something approaching euphoria would be the most effective antidote to the severe disgust and distress engendered by the initial acts of harmdoing—the overall quality of violent acts would take on a positive, pleasant nature.

Indeed, the occurrence of laughter among harmdoers could conceivably be one indication of the opponent (B) process. When one is shocked by one's own actions into remorse and disgust, the response of seemingly involuntary, bizarre laughter may reflect the body's efforts to counteract the distress with a response that is normally pleasant and happy.

The habit-forming or pseudoaddictive quality of harmdoing, which has been suggested by some perpetrators, would be readily explained in opponent-process terms. People would be held back from committing harm, in part, by the initial A reaction, which is highly upsetting, but over time, this would become less powerful, and therefore, the main restraint on behavior would diminish and even disappear. Meanwhile, the slow improvement of the B process would gradually make the episodes of hurting increasingly pleasant. Performing the same harmful actions over and over, however, eventually would cease to have much effect at all (just as running up the flight of stairs every day would cease to produce much reaction at all), insofar as the A reaction becomes so weak that only a small B process is needed to overcome it. Hence, the individual might gradually indulge in escalating acts of cruelty to activate the full power of his or her B response in the quest for euphoria or satisfaction.

Guilt as Moderator

The most apparent flaw in this theory is that it should hold true for everyone, and hence, all perpetra-

tors should turn into sadists—whereas the data suggest that only a small minority of perpetrators take that step. It is necessary, therefore, to postulate some substantial moderator variable that prevents most people from evolving into full-blown sadists when they perform repeated acts of harm.

A likely candidate for this moderator is guilt. People are taught to feel guilty when they inflict harm on others, and guilt, therefore, would be a deterrent to embracing sadistic pleasure. We assume that guilt is a highly socialized emotion that depends on cognitive processing, and therefore, the innate mechanisms of the body would not likely have prepared an opponent process that would produce euphoria in response to guilt. Guilt is also based strongly on empathy (Baumeister, Stillwell, & Heatherton, 1994; Hoffman, 1982; Leith & Baumeister, 1998; Tangney, 1991), and empathizing with a victim's distress would make empathic perpetrators feel bad themselves. For these reasons, guilt will make most harmdoing aversive, thereby effectively spoiling the potential enjoyment. Only the small minority of people who manage to avoid guilt and empathic distress could benefit from the opponent process that gradually would render harmdoing pleasant. This would fit the empirical evidence that only a small minority of perpetrators evolve into sadists.

Thus, we suggest that most people are sufficiently socialized to feel guilty when they harm others, and therefore, they would not allow themselves to notice or accept any pleasant aspects of an opponent process reaction that would accompany inflicting harm. The operation of guilt would be aided by the fact that, initially, the B process is likely to be weak and inefficient, and therefore, guilt feelings could combine with the physical disgust to make the person reject the entire harmdoing episode.

One way to test the moderator hypothesis would be to see whether people more readily come to enjoy inflicting harm when guilt is minimized. Some evidence suggests that people can more readily come to enjoy violence when they do not feel guilty. For example, hunting is regarded in many circles as morally acceptable, and even if hunters initially have the disgust reaction to killing prey, they might strive to overcome these reactions. It does seem that many more hunters enjoy the activity than the 6% figures we noted previously for people who learn sadistic enjoyment of killing people. Thus, in a context in which killing animals is morally acceptable, guilt is prevented, and people can enjoy the activity.

By the same token, sexual sadism is morally acceptable in many circles, especially insofar as the activity is undertaken with the consent (and often eager initiative) of the masochistic partner. (The term *victim* seems inappropriate for consensual sadomasochistic

INTRINSIC APPEAL OF EVIL

activity.) If people who take the dominant role in sex come to enjoy it at a higher rate than the 5% or 6% figure, this, too, would suggest that sadistic pleasure in actual interpersonal harm is restrained by guilt.

Other spheres in which morality is less opposed to harmdoing include police work, military combat, and officially sanctioned torture. If people who perform those roles learn to derive pleasure and satisfaction from their work at higher rates than those in morally questionable activities (such as criminal violence), then, again, one tentatively could conclude that guilt is indeed an important moderator of sadistic pleasure. Even the widespread rates of enjoyment of violent movies and violent entertainments could suggest that guilt-free violence can become pleasant.

Still, we acknowledge that the amount of evidence presently available is not adequate to permit a clear or strong conclusion that sadistic pleasure derives from opponent processes moderated by guilt. This model provides a good fit to what is known, but further research is needed.

Seeking Thrills, Reducing Boredom

Sadism is undoubtedly the prototype of intrinsic enjoyment of evil, but it is necessary to recognize that many violent acts may be enjoyed in a different, shallower way. For many people—especially, perhaps, undersocialized male adolescents—the quest for thrills and excitement is a frequent experience, arising perhaps from the sense that most of life is boring (Larkin, 1979; Pfefferbaum & Wood, 1994). Acts of violence and aggression can provide such thrills, and therefore, in an important sense, evil acts can be fun.

The emphasis on the thrill of illegal activity was the focus of work by Katz (1988). For example, he collected a set of personal narratives of shoplifting. Although one might assume that shoplifting is motivated primarily by a desire for particular goods, he found that many narratives indicated a low desire for the stolen item. In fact, he said, many people reported that the item for which they had risked detection and criminal prosecution was quickly discarded or forgotten. Instead, the narratives focused on what Katz called "sneaky thrills": the forming of a plan, the concealment of the item, the high suspense of leaving the store with the stolen item, and the euphoric sense of having gotten away with it.

To be sure, shoplifting is in most cases a small-scale crime hardly worthy of the label "evil." However, as we have suggested, there is a continuity between small-scale and large-scale crimes, especially insofar as perpetrators themselves regard many of their acts as relatively small and inconsequential even when victims consider them much more momentous. The quest for such thrills can undoubtedly lead to severe consequences in some cases.

From Boredom to Unintended Evil

In many cases, the perpetrator may not even be seeking or intending to cause harm. The goal is to find something arousing and enjoyable, and this could be reached by a broad variety of excitement such as pranks or diversions. Exuberant, risky, physically stimulating activities are sought. The outcome may seem evil to the person who unfortunately ends up being harmed by the acts, but it is very possible that evil was the farthest thing from the perpetrator's mind prior to the event.

For example, a group of adolescents might find sitting at home to be insufferably boring, and they would prefer to drive around together. Perhaps driving fast is more fun than driving in a slow, cautious, law-abiding fashion. Perhaps they do not own a car and must borrow one, even perhaps without actually getting permission, or perhaps even temporarily taking possession of a stranger's car with the assumption that they will return it eventually. Alcohol intoxication is also fun and could be combined with the activity. All these pleasures may relieve boredom and provide fun, and the legal technicalities (grand theft auto, driving while intoxicated, and speeding or reckless driving) may be kept far from awareness, as opposed to the laughter and pleasant, alcohol-enhanced sensations of speed. If no one is hurt and the car returned without damage, the episode can end before almost anyone would describe the activity as evil. However, if the speeding, stolen car with its drunk-driving teenage boys happens to run over a pedestrian or crash into another car, killing and maiming a family, the episode quickly takes on the label of evil, and the boys will find themselves mumbling inadequately into the television cameras that they never intended to hurt anyone.

Apter (1992) described the seductive appeal of risky behavior as an escape from boredom. In one memorable passage, Apter related the story of an 18-year-old man who worked as a railroad signalman in an isolated part of England. The job required little effort and, indeed, the endless boredom was only slightly relieved by watching trains go by. One day he began to stack cement building blocks on the train tracks. The next train collided with the blocks, knocking them into the air and making a huge grinding sound. The man found this stimulating and began to repeat and refine the cement block procedure, until eventually he was caught. He was quite fortunate that his amusement never derailed a train, which would have resulted in death and injury to innocent people—a result that easily could have happened and most likely would have occurred had he continued this hobby. The young man does not appear to have thought about these potential consequences, however, and he also did not regard his actions as evil. He was simply trying to relieve the boredom.

A far more destructive and historically important example of the drift from bored fun-seeking into evil is provided in the history of the Ku Klux Klan (Wade, 1987). The organization was founded by a small group of young men in an acutely boring situation: In the American South right after the Civil War had been lost, most economic, military, and social activity had come to a standstill, and several jobless ex-Rebels with absolutely nothing to do formed a club whose express purpose was only and explicitly to "have fun, make mischief, and play pranks on the public" (Wade, 1987, p. 34). To make costumes, they raided the linen closet of the home where they stayed and had to make do with white bedsheets, which were serviceable as ghost disguises. They began to play pranks on the community and found the former slaves to be excellent targets, especially insofar as the freedmen were largely uneducated and superstitious and hence gullible enough to believe in ghosts.

Later, of course, the Klan was notorious for its violence, and to many it has become one of the leading embodiments of evil in the United States. Murder, rape, assault, and destruction of property have been repeatedly attributed to Klansmen. Much of its violence has sprung from racial and religious antagonism, and these patterns of victimizing helpless individuals on the basis of race or religion are particularly central to the perception of the Klan as evil. Even so, it continues to attract new members, often far more explicitly on the basis of offering fun as well as its programs of charitable good works than on the basis of its use of racial and religious violence (Wade, 1987).

Such instances suggest that the search for initially innocent fun can lead into violent, evil acts. In these cases, the perpetrators did not initially set out to hurt anyone, but over time or in unforeseen ways, the amusing activities did gradually lead to harmful, destructive outcomes.

Violent Thrills

A more important and disturbing category of evil thrills finds the violence explicitly enjoyable. Damaging buildings or inflicting harm is likely to be arousing and can perhaps be pleasant, too. As such, it is certainly an antidote to boredom. At the extreme, it shades into sadism, but in many cases, it probably represents merely a use of violent acts to entertain the self and relieve the boredom of life.

A recent incident reported by Kornblut, Rutenberg, and McFarland (1997) illustrated this form of evil as boredom relief. Two young men, aged 17 and 18, were unable to find anything stimulating to do in the very small town in rural New Jersey where they lived. They walked around, hung out near the bowling alley, and generally felt they had exhausted the meager opportunities to stimulate themselves. They hit on the plan of telephoning pizza places until they found one that would make a late-night delivery to the address they gave, which was an abandoned house in a remote area. When the pizza delivery arrived, the boys shot the drivers to death. They made no effort to rob the pizza employees, and they did not even eat the pizza but simply threw it around.

The seemingly pointless, senseless violence had no purpose other than to relieve the boys' boredom. It does not conform to the patterns we saw for sadism, in which there is a gradual development of the capacity to gain pleasure from the harm suffered by others. The act itself was simply exciting, and, as such, it provided a welcome escape from boredom. These cases do not, perhaps, conform to the opponent-process model we identified (although empathy and guilt presumably would prevent most people from getting enjoyment from such an act). It is thus more closely related to the fun-seeking activities we describe in this section than to the sadistic pleasures we discussed previously.

Sensation Seeking

The desire for excitement that, we argue, can lead to evil acts in certain circumstances has been termed *sensation seeking* (e.g., Zuckerman, 1979). Individuals who are high on this trait actively search for adventure, act impulsively, and dislike boredom. Sensation seeking is related to a host of acts that sometimes can result in evil. Examples include drunk driving, drug use, and assault.

Teenagers drink and drive for several reasons. Often, it is because it is the only way they can think of to get home. Some teenagers, however, drink and drive more than others. Those teenagers are often high in sensation seeking (Arnett, 1990, 1996). Driving can be fun, especially when one is a novice driver, and this fun aspect of driving may be enhanced when one is intoxicated. To a young person, both drinking and driving are forbidden activities until a certain age, and in combination, they are of course illegal at any age. The rebellious adolescent may find that breaking the rules enhances the fun

INTRINSIC APPEAL OF EVIL

even further (see Brehm, 1966). None of this will seem evil—unless or until the drunk driver happens to cause an accident that harms an innocent victim.

Sensation seeking also is related to drug and alcohol use more generally. A large part of the motivation for consuming drugs or alcohol seems to be driven by the need to find excitement or reduce boredom (Arnett, 1996; La Grange, Jones, Erb, & Reyes, 1995; Tang, Wong, & Schwarzer, 1996). Yet, alcohol and some drugs seem to impair self-control and increase tendencies to respond aggressively to perceived provocations (e.g., Bushman & Cooper, 1990), and therefore, they increase violent acts. In fact, alcohol is implicated in a majority of the violent crimes in the United States (National Research Council, 1993). Indeed, when violence is desired, alcohol is often used to increase the willingness to aggress. The doctors and guards in the Nazi concentration camps, for example, typically used heavy amounts of alcohol to make their jobs more bearable (e.g., Lifton, 1986). More generally, serving alcohol rations to troops just prior to battle has been a standard military practice for many centuries (Keegan, 1976).

Although other drugs have less bloodstained records than alcohol, this may be largely due to the greater availability of alcohol throughout history and the greater amount of research done on alcohol than other drugs. There is no reason to assume that alcohol is unique in its capacity to promote violence. Some (although certainly not all) recreational drugs are undoubtedly as dangerous as alcohol.

Thus, one path may lead from sensation seeking to violence, even though that result was neither intended nor foreseen. Sensation seekers are vulnerable to boredom, and one escape from boredom is to get drunk. Once drunk, the person is more likely to engage in violent acts. Moreover, the alcohol does not appear to lead directly to violence, but rather it makes the person respond violently when he (or, less often, she) believes himself to have been provoked or insulted by someone else. Taylor, Gammon, and Capasso (1976) showed that intoxication did not produce higher levels of aggression in a reciprocal electric shock paradigm—unless the person felt provoked, in which case intoxicated students escalated to higher levels of aggression than sober ones.

From the clinical perspective, certain elements of sensation seeking, specifically boredom intolerance and impulsivity (although not necessarily adventure seeking), can be seen in individuals with *antisocial personality disorder*. Individuals with this disorder, which is very similar to what used to be referred to as *psychopathy*, are known for drug use, drunk driving, sexual impulsivity, and aggressiveness and violence. It is not necessarily that antisocials commit violent acts only for fun, but they likely are motivated by an intolerance for boredom coupled with a mean streak (American Psychiatric Association, 1994).

Are these sensation-seeking acts likely to result in criminal prosecution? There is some evidence that sensation seeking is linked to criminality more generally. In their influential theory on crime, Gottfredson and Hirschi (1990) argued that low impulse control and boredom intolerance are important elements in understanding criminals. The typical burglary, for example, involves an adolescent boy who wanders into an unlocked dwelling within a mile of his residence. The adolescent then takes anything easily available (cash, stereo equipment, alcohol). During the crime, the individual may spend some time in the entered dwelling drinking alcohol, eating food, or listening to music. Clearly, there is an element of thrill seeking and boredom relief in this kind of behavior, and this may help account for the finding that prisoner populations are higher than nonincarcerated normals on sensation seeking (Haapasalo, 1990). Furthermore, there is speculation that sensation seeking may be a particularly potent factor in adolescence (Baldwin, 1985), which may, in part, account for the large proportion of crime committed by youth. Vandalism, for example, is higher among adolescents who score high in sensation seeking than among other adolescents (Arnett, 1996).

Sensation seeking itself is hardly evil. Plenty of individuals manage to relieve boredom and find thrills through innocuous, legal means. Navy divers, for example, report elevated scores on some elements of sensation seeking (Biersner & LaRocco, 1983). Many people get the same satisfactions from activities that bring risks only to themselves. The problem is simply that some violent and interpersonally dangerous activities offer comparable thrills, and therefore, some sensation seekers will find their satisfactions in these ways.

In short, this pathway into violence primarily is used by a certain group of individuals who are characterized by high sensation seeking and low self-control. They are prone to feeling bored, and they seek to escape this aversive state by engaging in arousing activities. Such activities likely include things that break rules and are physically stimulating, as well as substance abuse. The low self-control means that these people do not always think ahead to the potential consequences of their actions (see Baumeister, Heatherton, & Tice, 1994; Leith & Baumeister, 1996), and therefore, they may be extra willing to perform actions that could cause harm to others. These perpetrators are unlikely to regard themselves and their actions as evil, but of course, their victims may see things quite differently.

Threatened Egotism

The third and final form of intrinsic appeal that evil acts enjoy involves threatened egotism. More precisely, when people feel that their favorable self-images or reputations have been impugned by someone, they may become motivated to attack that person in a violent or aggressive fashion.

Whether to label such aggression as intrinsically or extrinsically motivated is difficult. They are not engaging in aggression for the pleasure of aggressing, and the enjoyment of the other's suffering depends on the context (i.e., the other may have insulted them), which could be described as extrinsic. Still, the insult does create a state that seeks satisfaction in causing harm to the other, and the aggression is not genuinely extrinsic in the sense that it is a means toward some further end.

As a parallel, research on the overjustification effect can be invoked. Early studies established a powerful distinction between doing an activity for its own sake (intrinsic) and doing it to gain some exterior goal (extrinsic); these findings established that intrinsic rewards sustained motivation, whereas extrinsic rewards undermined intrinsic motivation (Deci, 1971; Lepper, Greene, & Nisbett, 1973). Still, this distinction became somewhat blurred when self-esteem became involved. Rosenfeld, Folger, and Adelman (1980) showed that, when rewards carried a symbolic message affirming the performer's competence, intrinsic motivation was not reduced. Rewards involving self-esteem thus resembled intrinsic rather than extrinsic rewards in their consequences and should perhaps be considered a quasi-intrinsic form of reward.

By the same token, then, aggression that derives from self-esteem concerns also can be considered as having a form of intrinsic or quasi-intrinsic appeal. In support of this argument, Brown (1968) found that people will sacrifice extrinsic rewards (in that case, their own money) to gain revenge on someone who had caused them to lose face.

The view that threatened egotism is a major source of aggression runs contrary to conventional wisdom in psychology, however. A longstanding tradition has held that aggression is caused by low self-esteem. Although it is quite difficult to locate an original or authoritative statement of that theory, many authors do mention low self-esteem as a cause of violence, as if this were common knowledge (e.g., Anderson, 1994; Gondolf, 1985; Levin & McDevitt, 1993; Long, 1990; MacDonald, 1975; Oates & Forrest, 1985; Renzetti, 1992; Schoenfeld, 1988; Staub, 1989; Wiehe, 1991).

Contrary to that view, Baumeister, Smart, and Boden (1996) reviewed considerable evidence and concluded that aggressors tend to have quite favorable views of self. Thus, the highest scores on a hos-

tility scale are achieved by people who show high but unstable self-esteem (Kernis, Grannemann, & Barclay, 1989). Psychopaths, who are responsible for a high number of violent and exploitative crimes, have grandiose views of their own superiority (Hare, 1993). Many convicted rapists likewise show grandiose, inflated concepts of themselves as well as remarkably self-flattering distortions of events (Scully, 1990). Violent groups such as the Nazis and Ku Klux Klan generally operate from a basic assumption of their own innate superiority over others. In *bipolar disorder*—in which a person's self-esteem oscillates between extreme highs and lows—aggressive and violent acts generally are performed during the manic stage, in which self-esteem is very high (Goodwin & Jamison, 1990). Alcohol intoxication, which generally is accepted as an important cause of a great many violent acts and crimes, tends to bring about an elevation in self-esteem (Banaji & Steele, 1989; National Research Council, 1993).

However, such findings did not lead Baumeister et al. (1996) to conclude that high self-esteem per se causes violence (which would be the direct opposite of the traditional view). Although violent people tend to have high self-esteem, there are other people with high self-esteem who are exceptionally nonviolent. For example, we already reported that Kernis et al. (1989) found the highest scores on aggression and hostility among people with high but unstable self-esteem; the other side of the coin is that the lowest hostility scores were attained by people with high but stable self-esteem.

Threatened egotism, however, did provide a good fit to the evidence reviewed by Baumeister et al. (1996). People with favorable views of self who felt these views were being questioned, undermined, or attacked were the most likely to behave aggressively in response. This may explain why Kernis et al. (1989) found that hostility scores were so low among people with high and stable self-esteem: The stability indicates that nothing threatens their high self-esteem.

Likewise, the domestic violence literature seems best explained by the concept of threatened egotism. An early view held that abusive men had low self-esteem (Walker, 1979), but subsequent controlled studies have failed to confirm that theory (see Baumeister et al., 1996, for a review). More recent work has abandoned the low self-esteem view in favor of the concept of status inconsistency, which was introduced by Hornung, McCullough, and Sugimoto (1981). They found, for example, that the most violent men were those who had radical inconsistencies between their educational level and their occupational achievements, such as the PhD who drives a taxi.

Yet, the notion of status inconsistency failed to fit the full pattern of data, even in Hornung et al.'s (1981)

INTRINSIC APPEAL OF EVIL

own study. Indeed, they did find high violence among men with high-status backgrounds and low-status occupations. They found exceptionally low violence, however, among men with low-status backgrounds but highly successful careers. Both groups have status inconsistency. Only the violent group seems to suffer from threatened egotism, however, insofar as the high-status background (such as education) creates expectations of life success, and an unsuccessful career would be a severe blow to one's ego. In contrast, the men whose careers had succeeded beyond their wildest dreams would not feel their egos threatened.

Thus, the findings in research on domestic violence suggest that only some forms of status inconsistency lead to violence—and these forms seem to be the ones most likely to produce threatened egotism.

Laboratory tests of the link between self-appraisals and aggression were largely lacking from the literature reviewed by Baumeister et al. (1996). Bushman and Baumeister (1998) conducted a pair of studies to examine links between self-esteem, narcissism, and aggression. Their results confirmed the threatened egotism view: The highest levels of aggression were exhibited by narcissists who had been insulted. Moreover, this aggression was directed only toward the source of the insult. Narcissists were not made generally aggressive by the insult, as shown by their lack of aggression toward an innocent third person. Self-esteem yielded no significant effects on aggression at all, either by itself or in interaction with other variables.

Narcissism thus deserves attention as the most relevant self-concept variable for studying aggression. Narcissism is defined by highly favorable, even grandiose views of self, as well as the desire to be admired by others. Hence, when others evaluate them negatively, narcissists are extremely upset and prone to respond in an aggressive or violent manner.

Conclusions

Much human violence may be attributed to instrumental or ideological motives. In those cases, the attitude of the perpetrator toward the actual harmdoing may be neutral or even regretful, and certainly the evidence supports the view that some instances of aggression involve perpetrators who regard their own violent acts as distasteful and unfortunate. The contribution of those actions to the toll of human misery is immense.

This article, however, has focused on instances in which people find harmful, destructive acts to be satisfying. Three distinct sources of satisfaction have been identified, and available evidence suggests that they all exist. We also have sought to offer theoretical explana-

tions for how these satisfactions arise, and the data are consistent with those explanations, although further research is needed.

The first source of satisfaction is sadism. Ample observations from many sources and contexts suggest that some people (although usually only a small minority of harmdoers) get pleasure directly from causing their victims to suffer. We proposed an opponent-process explanation for sadistic pleasure: Over time, the initially unpleasant response to causing harm is outweighed by the opponent process of pleasure and euphoria. This only occurs in individuals with a weak sense of guilt, because guilt will only prevent people from accepting and recognizing the pleasure.

The second form of appeal involves seeking thrills and reducing boredom by means of performing risky, potentially destructive acts. Vigorous physical activity may provide pleasant sensations, perhaps especially when it involves breaking or defying some rules. The causing of harm may be incidental to the perpetrators, such as being a side effect of the quest for sensations, and often, it may be unintended or at least not premeditated. Our account of this appeal invoked the desire to escape from boredom and to achieve intense, thrilling sensations, as well as low self-control.

The third form of satisfaction involves affirming the self by harming someone who has threatened or attacked one's favorable view of self (or public image). Such aggression defends the favorable self-image and discourages others from questioning it, and people who are strongly invested in sustaining a favorable image may be especially prone toward such violence. It can operate at either the group or the individual level.

Although, in principle, these satisfactions are available to almost anyone, in practice they are each likely to appeal only to a small category of individuals with particular predispositions. First, sadism depends on being undeterred by guilt and empathy so that one can gradually embrace the acquired pleasure that is the natural bodily response to the distasteful act of harming someone. Second, violent thrills may appeal especially to adolescent boys who have high sensation-seeking tendencies and low self-control. Third, the violent response to threatened egotism may characterize individuals (or groups) who have both a strong emotional investment in being superior to others and a deep concern with having this favorable self-image validated by others. Narcissism, rather than high self-esteem per se, is the predisposing factor for this third path to violence.

Social psychologists long have been interested in the situational forces that induce people to perform acts of which they disapprove (e.g., Milgram, 1963). Undoubtedly, some evil acts are performed by reluctant individuals who feel unable to resist situational pressures. On the other hand, many other evil acts are performed because of the positive, intrinsic appeal that they offer. By elucidating both the situational push and the intrinsic pull of violence, the field may yet attain a balanced understanding of the roots of evil.

References

American Psychiatric Association. (1994). *Diagnostic and statistical manual of mental disorders* (4th ed.). Washington, DC: Author.

Anderson, E. (1994, May). The code of the streets. *Atlantic Monthly, 273*, 81–94.

Apter, M. J. (1992). *The dangerous edge: The psychology of excitement.* New York: Free Press.

Arlacchi, P. (1993). *Men of dishonor: Inside the Sicilian Mafia* (M. Romano, Trans.). New York: Morrow. (Original work published 1992)

Arnett, J. (1990). Drunk driving, sensation seeking, and egocentrism among adolescents. *Personality and Individual Differences, 11*, 541–546.

Arnett, J. J. (1996). Sensation seeking, aggressiveness, and adolescent reckless behavior. *Personality and Individual Differences, 20*, 693–702.

Baldwin, J. D. (1985). Thrill and adventure seeking and the age distribution of crime: Comment on Hirschi and Gottfredson. *American Journal of Sociology, 90*, 1326–1330.

Banaji, M. R., & Steele, C. M. (1989). Alcohol and self-evaluation: Is a social cognition approach beneficial? *Social Cognition, 7*, 137–151.

Baumeister, R. F. (1997). *Evil: Inside human violence and cruelty.* New York: Freeman.

Baumeister, R. F. (1989). *Masochism and the self.* Hillsdale, NJ: Lawrence Erlbaum Associates, Inc.

Baumeister, R. F., Heatherton, T. F., & Tice, D. M. (1994). *Losing control: How and why people fail at self-regulation.* New York: Academic.

Baumeister, R. F., Smart, L., & Boden, J. M. (1996). Relation of threatened egotism to violence and aggression: The dark side of high self-esteem. *Psychological Review, 103*, 5–33.

Baumeister, R. F., Stillwell, A. M., & Heatherton, T. F. (1994). Guilt: An interpersonal approach. *Psychological Bulletin, 115*, 243–267.

Baumeister, R. F., Stillwell, A., & Wotman, S. R. (1990). Victim and perpetrator accounts of interpersonal conflict: Autobiographical narratives about anger. *Journal of Personality and Social Psychology, 59*, 994–1005.

Biersner, R. J., & LaRocco, J. M. (1983). Personality characteristics of US Navy divers. *Journal of Occupational Psychology, 56*, 329–334.

Bing, L. (1991). *Do or die.* New York: HarperCollins.

Brehm, J. (1966). *A theory of psychological reactance.* New York: Academic.

Brown, B. R. (1968). The effects of need to maintain face on interpersonal bargaining. *Journal of Experimental Social Psychology, 4*, 107–122.

Browning, C. R. (1992). *Ordinary men: Reserve police battalion 101 and the final solution in Poland.* New York: HarperCollins.

Bushman, B. J., & Baumeister, R. F. (1998). Threatened egotism, narcissism, self-esteem, and direct and displaced aggression: Does self-love or self-hate lead to violence? *Journal of Personality and Social Psychology, 75*, 219–229.

Bushman, B. J., & Cooper, H. M. (1990). Effects of alcohol on human aggression: An integrative research review. *Psychological Bulletin, 107*, 341–354.

Deci, E. L. (1971). Effects of externally mediated rewards on intrinsic motivation. *Journal of Personality and Social Psychology, 18*, 105–115.

Gibson, J. T., & Haritos-Fatouros, M. (1986, November). The education of a torturer. *Psychology Today, 20*, 50–58.

Gondolf, E. W. (1985). *Men who batter.* Holmes Beach, FL: Learning Publications.

Goodwin, F. K., & Jamison, K. R. (1990). *Manic–depressive illness.* New York: Oxford University Press.

Gottfredson, M. R., & Hirschi, T. (1990). *A general theory of crime.* Stanford, CA: Stanford University Press.

Groth, A. N. (1979). *Men who rape: The psychology of the offender.* New York: Plenum.

Haapasalo, J. (1990). Sensation seeking and Eysenck's personality dimensions in an offender sample. *Personality and Individual Differences, 11*, 81–84.

Hare, R. D. (1993). *Without conscience: The disturbing world of the psychopaths among us.* New York: Simon & Schuster.

Hoffman, M. L. (1982). Development of prosocial motivation: Empathy and guilt. In N. Eisenberg (Ed.), *The development of prosocial behavior* (pp. 281–313). New York: Academic.

Hornung, C. A., McCullough, B. C., & Sugimoto, T. (1981). Status relationships in marriage: Risk factors in spouse abuse. *Journal of Marriage and the Family, 43*, 675–692.

Jankowski, M. S. (1991). *Islands in the street: Gangs and American urban society.* Berkeley: University of California Press.

Katz, J. (1988). *Seductions of crime: Moral and sensual attractions in doing evil.* New York: Basic Books.

Keegan, J. (1976). *The face of battle.* New York: Military Heritage Press.

Kelman, H. C., & Hamilton, V. L. (1989). *Crimes of obedience: Toward a social psychology of authority and responsibility.* New Haven, CT: Yale University Press.

Kernis, M. H., Grannemann, B. D., & Barclay, L. C. (1989). Stability and level of self-esteem as predictors of anger arousal and hostility. *Journal of Personality and Social Psychology, 56*, 1013–1022.

Kornblut, A. E., Rutenberg, J., & McFarland, S. (1997, April 23). Pizza thrill-kill accused seen on camera. *New York Daily News.* Retrieved August 26, 1999 from the World Wide Web: http://www.nydailynews.com

La Grange, L., Jones, T. D., Erb, L., & Reyes, E (1995). Alcohol consumption: Biochemical and personality correlates in a college student population. *Addictive Behaviors, 20*, 93–103.

Larkin, R. W. (1979). *Suburban youth in cultural crisis.* New York: Oxford University Press.

Leith, K. P., & Baumeister, R. F. (1996). Why do bad moods increase self-defeating behavior? Emotion, risk taking, and self-regulation. *Journal of Personality and Social Psychology, 71*, 1250–1267.

Leith, K. P., & Baumeister, R. F. (1998). Empathy, shame, guilt, and narratives of interpersonal conflicts: Guilt-prone people are better at perspective taking. *Journal of Personality, 66*, 1–37.

Lepper, M. R., Greene, D., & Nisbett, R. E. (1973). Undermining children's intrinsic interest with extrinsic reward: A test of the "overjustification" hypothesis. *Journal of Personality and Social Psychology, 28*, 129–137.

Levin, J., & McDevitt, J. (1993). *Hate crimes: The rising tide of bigotry and bloodshed.* New York: Plenum.

Lifton, R. J. (1986). *The Nazi doctors: Medical killing and the psychology of genocide.* New York: Basic Books.

Long, D. E. (1990). *The anatomy of terrorism.* New York: Free Press.

MacDonald, J. M. (1975). *Armed robbery: Offenders and their victims.* Springfield, IL: Thomas.

McCall, N. (1994). *Makes me wanna holler: A young black man in America.* New York: Random House.

INTRINSIC APPEAL OF EVIL

Mikula, G. (1994). Perspective-related differences in interpretations of injustice by victims and victimizers: A test with close relationships. In M. Lerner & G. Mikula (Eds.), *Entitlement and the affectional bond: Justice in close relationships* (pp. 175–203). New York: Plenum.

Milgram, S. (1963). Behavioral study of obedience. *Journal of Abnormal and Social Psychology, 67,* 371–378.

National Research Council. (1993). *Understanding and preventing violence.* Washington, DC: National Academy Press.

Nordland, R. (1996, April 15). Death of a village. *Newsweek, 127,* 52–57.

Oates, R. K., & Forrest, D. (1985). Self-esteem and early background of abusive mothers. *Child Abuse and Neglect, 9,* 89–93.

Pakenham, T. (1979). *The Boer War.* New York: Random House.

Pakenham, T. (1991). *The scramble for Africa: White man's conquest of the dark continent from 1876 to 1912.* New York: Avon Books/Random House.

Pfefferbaum, B., & Wood, P. B. (1994). Self-report study of impulsive and delinquent behavior in college students. *Journal of Adolescent Health, 15,* 295–302.

Renzetti, C. M. (1992). *Violent betrayal: Partner abuse in lesbian relationships.* Newbury Park, CA: Sage.

Rosenfeld, D., Folger, R., & Adelman, H. F. (1980). When rewards reflect competence: A qualification of the overjustification effect. *Journal of Personality and Social Psychology, 39,* 368–376.

Schoenfeld, C. G. (1988). Blacks and violent crime: A psychoanalytically oriented analysis. *Journal of Psychiatry and Law, 16,* 269–301.

Scott, G. G. (1983). *Erotic power: An exploration of dominance and submission.* Secaucus, NJ: Citadel.

Scully, D. (1990). *Understanding sexual violence.* London: HarperCollins Academic.

Sereny, G. (1983). *Into that darkness: An examination of conscience.* New York: Vintage/Random House.

Solomon, R. L. (1980). The opponent-process theory of acquired motivations: The costs of pleasure and the benefits of pain. *American Psychologist, 35,* 691–712.

Solomon, R. L., & Corbit, J. D. (1974). An opponent-process theory of motivation: I. Temporal dynamics of affect. *Psychological Review, 81,* 119–145.

Staub, E. (1989). *The roots of evil: The origins of genocide and other group violence.* New York: Cambridge University Press.

Stover, E., & Nightingale, E. O. (Eds.). (1985). *The breaking of bodies and minds: Torture, psychiatric abuse, and the health professions.* New York: Freeman.

Tang, C. S. K., Wong, C. S. Y., & Schwarzer, R. (1996). Psychosocial differences between occasional and regular adolescent users of marijuana and heroin. *Journal of Youth and Adolescence, 25,* 219–239.

Tangney, J. P. (1991). Moral affect: The good, the bad, and the ugly. *Journal of Personality and Social Psychology, 61,* 598–607.

Taylor, S. P., Gammon, C. B., & Capasso, D. R. (1976). Aggression as a function of alcohol and threat. *Journal of Personality and Social Psychology, 34,* 938–941.

Toch, H. (1993). *Violent men: An inquiry into the psychology of violence.* Washington, DC: American Psychological Association. (Original work published 1969)

Wade, W. C. (1987). *The fiery cross: The Ku Klux Klan in America.* New York: Simon & Schuster.

Walker, L. (1979). *The battered woman.* New York: Harper & Row.

Wiehe, V. R. (1991). *Perilous rivalry: When siblings become abusive.* Lexington, MA: Heath.

Wyden, P. (1983). *The passionate war: The narrative history of the Spanish Civil War.* New York: Simon & Schuster.

Zimbardo, P. G. (1972). *The Stanford prison experiment* [Slide/tape presentation]. (Available from P. G. Zimbardo, Inc., P.O. Box 4395, Stanford, CA 94305)

Zuckerman, M. (1979). *Sensation seeking: Beyond the optimal level of arousal.* Hillsdale, NJ: Lawrence Erlbaum Associates, Inc.

[20]

Community Cohesion and Violent Predatory Victimization: A Theoretical Extension and Cross-national Test of Opportunity Theory*

MATTHEW R. LEE, *Mississippi State University*

Abstract

This study extends the research on the opportunity theory of criminal victimization. Specifically, it is proposed that living in a cohesive community directly reduces the likelihood of experiencing violent predatory criminal victimization. Tightly knit communities have higher levels of informal guardianship, and members of such communities are more active in intervening in public deviant or criminal activities, thus limiting opportunities for the commission of violent crimes. This theoretical model is tested with a sample of more than 19,000 respondents to national-level victimization surveys from 15 countries. A replication is also performed with data from over 10,000 respondents to city level surveys in another 12 countries. The results provide strong support for the hypothesis that people who live in communities which they perceive to be cohesive have a lower likelihood of violent victimization. The data indicate that net of relevant socioeconomic, demographic, lifestyle, and neighborhood status characteristics, community cohesion consistently reduces the likelihood of robbery and assault near the home, and robbery and assault near the home by strangers. The consistency of the results suggests that community cohesion may be a major determinant of victimization risk.

Although it has long been known that community characteristics are associated with their levels of crime, the bulk of the research investigating this link has focused on explaining *neighborhood differences in offending frequency*. In the last twenty years, criminologists have broadened their focus to develop theories explaining a different phenomenon: individual differences in victimization.

* Direct correspondence to Matthew R. Lee, Department of Sociology, Anthropology, and Social Work, Mississippi State University, P.O. Box C, Mississippi State, MS, 39762. E-mail: lee@soc.msstate.edu.

684 / *Social Forces* 79:2, December 2000

Most research examining the correlates of individual violent victimization has focused on individual level factors. These studies have been framed within the opportunity (e.g., routine activities/lifestyle) theoretic tradition. The principal theorem of these perspectives states that when motivated offenders are in proximity to attractive targets and there is a lack of informal guardians, the probability of a crime occurring is maximized. In their original statement of the scope of the routine activities version of opportunity theory, Cohen and Felson (1979:589) note that it applies only to "direct contact predatory violations."

A substantial body of research has tested the central precepts of the opportunity framework (see review in Meier & Miethe 1993). These studies have collectively identified several factors which are important in explaining individual variation in the likelihood of violent victimization. These factors can be classified as socioeconomic/demographic characteristics and lifestyle characteristics. Age, marital status, gender, and socioeconomic status generally appear as control variables in multivariate tests. Younger people, the unmarried, males and the economically disadvantaged tend to have daily activity patterns placing them in proximity to motivated offenders in an unguarded environment more frequently than people with other socioeconomic/ demographic profiles.

In contrast to these varied socioeconomic and demographic attributes of individuals, the principle measure tapping lifestyle characteristics has been the frequency with which individuals go out in the evening for leisure activities (see Miethe and Meier 1990; Sampson and Lauritsen 1990; Miethe, Stafford and Long 1987). The rationale behind this measure is that individuals who go out more frequently in the evening to eat, go to bars, go to the movies, or engage in other activities have a higher probability of being victimized because they are likely to be carrying portable valuables such as cash or jewelry, are traveling under cover of darkness which limits guardianship capacity, and are generally more likely to encounter motivated offenders. In these models, the presence of motivated offenders is usually not directly measured but rather assumed.

Although it is clear that certain demographic, socioeconomic, and lifestyle differences between individuals may explain part of their victimization risk, it is less clear what role neighborhood characteristics play in determining differential victimization risk. Only a few studies have examined the effects of contextual factors on victimization risk. For example, Sampson and Lauritsen (1990) demonstrate that individuals who live in neighborhoods with a high level of violent victimization also have a greater victimization risk because of proximity to motivated offenders. Similarly, Miethe and McDowall (1993) report that living in a neighborhood characterized by numerous 'busy public places' and poor socioeconomic conditions elevates individual risk of violent victimization, again because of exposure to motivated offenders.

These studies are important because they highlight the contextual nature of criminal victimization. That is, aside from the attributes of individuals, there are identifiable characteristics of their communities independently contributing to the variation in risk of victimization observed among individuals.

One dimension of community structure which may influence individual victimization risk is the degree of community cohesion. Community cohesion is defined here as the residents of a given community helping each other out when in need. Although social disorganization theory has long relied on similar concepts (i.e., local network strength and density) to explain neighborhood differences in offending patterns, seldom has it been applied to explaining individual victimization. But, as discussed below, there are strong theoretical reasons to expect community levels of cohesion to explain part of the social differentiation in victimization risk. Centering on the idea that community cohesion is a direct indicator of guardianship, I test whether this factor reduces individual victimization risk using data from nationally representative victimization surveys in 15 countries. A replication is also undertaken using victimization surveys collected only in cities in another 12 countries. The results suggest that being embedded in a tightly knit community may directly reduce the objective risk of becoming the victim of a violent predatory crime.

Background

There are several variants of opportunity theory currently available which are designed to explain differential victimization risk across individuals and social groups. The two most prominent, lifestyle/exposure and routine activities have a degree of overlap, but are sufficiently distinct to warrant separate treatment.

Routine activities as formulated by Cohen and Felson (1979) is primarily concerned with changes in the structural features of social groups which effectively alter the normal everyday routines of most group members. The overriding concern here is that certain social changes will covary with crime rate trends. A considerable amount of research has tested this theory and advanced our understanding of the macrodynamic forces driving national crime trends (see Cohen & Felson 1979; Cohen, Felson & Land 1980; Messner & Blau 1987; Miethe, Hughes & McDowall 1991).

In contrast to this macrolevel perspective, the lifestyle/exposure model posits that certain characteristics of individuals and their lifestyles result in a higher victimization risk for the individual. The lifestyle model was first introduced by Hindelang, Gottfredson, and Garafolo (1978) and was an attempt to draw together the variety of findings these authors had empirically derived from the then relatively new NCVS. The fundamental proposition from lifestyle theory is that the relationship between the typical demographic profile and victimization risk can largely be accounted for by differential lifestyle activity. And so it follows that single, young, low income males have the highest victimization risk because they exhibit lifestyle activity patterns which are most likely to bring them into contact with potential offenders in an unguarded environment.

The concept of guardianship occupies a central position in both the lifestyle/ exposure and routine activities perspectives. Over the last twenty years guardianship has come to take on several distinct meanings. For example, it can refer to guardianship over one's own property such as the home. It can also refer to target hardening devices such as door and window locks, outdoor lighting, bars over windows and car alarms. Finally, guardianship can refer to surveillance over individuals by third parties. Examples of this latter form include neighborhood watch programs and community policing, but especially unorganized forms of guardianship which arise from extensive neighboring and participation in community affairs.

This final form of guardianship, local informal guardianship, is of particular interest to the present research. Although the notion that strong informal associations within a community can reduce crime has been a mainstay of social disorganization theory, rarely is this idea discussed in terms of opportunities to commit crime. Below I draw on the literature from the systemic model of community attachment and develop a conceptual argument suggesting that strong community ties are evidence of high levels of guardianship, and hence lower victimization risk.

Community Cohesion

In what way might living in a cohesive community reduce the likelihood of being the victim of a violent crime? Recent research on social disorganization theory has focused on fully integrating the systemic model of community attachment into the traditional social disorganization model to explain neighborhood differences in offending prevalence (e.g., Bursik 1999). The basic premise of the community attachment model as first formulated by Kasarda and Janowitz (1974) is that the length of residence in a community contributes to local social bonds, such as the number of friends in the neighborhood and the prevalence of informal social activities. These mediating factors in turn lead to community attachment and cohesion. Community attachment and cohesion are posited to reduce offending within neighborhoods because high degrees of local integration foster the development and realization of common values and goals, the primary goal being to keep the neighborhood safe (Bürsik & Grasmick 1993). Implicit in this is a socialization argument, where children raised in cohesive communities are essentially socialized into behaviors that do not violate community standards. At face value, this framework reveals little about how community cohesion reduces the likelihood of victimization.

Community Cohesion and Violent Victimization / 687

Nevertheless, in a recent empirical test of this model, Sampson and Groves (1989) employed the 1982 and 1984 waves of the British Crime Surveys to investigate the role that community cohesion plays in reducing victimization. They found that their community cohesion measures (local friendship ties and organizational participation) actually mediate the role of traditional social disorganization variables (poverty, heterogeneity, population turnover, and family disruption). Specifically, community cohesion was reported to directly reduce the incidence of mugging and street robbery, stranger violence, and total levels of victimization *at the neighborhood level.*

The logic of this argument conforms well to traditional macro-level thinking, and provides a preliminary indication that the factors explaining offending may also actually explain victimization. This observation is further reinforced by the fact that victims and offenders mirror each other (demographically) almost completely. Hence, Sampson and Lauritsen (1990) report that prior offending behavior is a strong predictor of victimization risk using the same data as Sampson and Groves (1989). With some modification, the concept of community cohesion may also lend itself to explaining variation in individual victimization risk. The key to making this link lies in conceptualizing community cohesion as a central element of opportunity theory — guardianship. A recent study by Sampson, Raudenbush, and Earls (1997) advances our understanding substantially here.

Using data from the Project on Human Development in Chicago Neighborhoods, these authors construct a measure derived from survey responses of 'collective efficacy'. This measure reflects both community level cohesion and informal self-help social control (see Black 1983 for more on the latter). The results of this multilevel study indicate that 'collective efficacy' reduces the incidence of violence because the residents of cohesive neighborhoods tend to intervene in public deviant or criminal activities on behalf of the collective good (Sampson Raudenbush, and Earls 1997). Thus guardianship appears to be the central explanatory element in the systemic model. The active use of informal social control (or guardianship) as measured by intervention in public deviant activities by the residents of some neighborhoods therefore has important implications for individual level formulations of opportunity theory.

Specifically, these recent findings provide evidence that community cohesion directly reduces neighborhood victimization levels because guardianship is strong. Most extant research has measured guardianship in terms of individual level characteristics, such as whether respondents live alone, and target hardening devices such as whether they own a gun or a house alarm (Miethe and Meier 1990). Yet these factors fail to capture the broader community context in which individuals are embedded. Guardianship is not simply an individual level phenomenon, but in fact refers to the constellation of networks and social interactions with other individuals and groups external to the individual.

688 / *Social Forces* **79:2, December 2000**

Some research has evaluated whether local community interaction reduces individual victimization risk. Massey, Krohn and Bonati (1989) use data from 6 neighborhoods in Atlanta collected in 1979 to test whether their measures of local social ties reduce the likelihood of property victimization. These data are unique in that they contain extensive information on neighborhood networks. Unfortunately, the results from this study do not provide evidence that strong local networks reduce victimization. Caution should be exercised though in making definitive statements about the findings from this study for several reasons. First, the universe from which the data are drawn is extremely limited, focusing on the residents of a handful of communities in one American city. Second, the sample size for the study is also rather small, with a total of 523 respondents. Because victimization is generally a statistically unusual event, most studies rely on much larger samples (e.g., Miethe, Stafford & Long 1987; Miethe & Meier 1990). Third, as the authors acknowledge, their sample is representative of their neighborhoods of interest, but not of the general population. The ability to draw meaningful inferences from their study is therefore unclear.

In light of the limitations of that study, and given the theoretical appeal of the idea that living in a strong community should reduce the likelihood of being the victim of a crime because guardianship levels are high, this study revisits opportunity theory. The following analysis extends the research on opportunity theory by investigating the role that community cohesion plays in determining individual violent victimization risk. The working hypothesis is that individuals living in what they perceive to be cohesive communities will have a lower victimization risk due to the high levels of guardianship and active social control community cohesion entails.

Most tests of opportunity theory or various theoretical extensions thereof have used data from the U.S. (the NCVS) or Great Britain (the BCS). These countries, although quite different in many cultural aspects, are quite similar along other dimensions. For instance both countries are highly industrialized democratic welfare states. Aside from these two countries and Canada (see Kennedy and Ford 1990), few countries have committed the resources necessary to carry out victimization surveys and collect the data necessary to test the generalisability of opportunity theory. Those which have generally have not constructed their victimization survey instruments in a way that fosters comparability across countries. Only recently have data been systematically collected allowing for the kind of rigorous cross-national testing a general theory should be able to withstand. The following analysis therefore also extends the research on opportunity theory by utilizing data from nationally representative victimization surveys carried out in 15 countries, and replicating the analysis with victimization survey data from city level surveys conducted in another 12 countries.

Data and Measures

The data employed to test the proposed conceptual framework are drawn from the 1992 wave of the International Victimization Survey. The survey instrument was developed by the United Nations Interregional Crime and Justice Research Institute and was designed to provide an alternative crime index to official police counts. Although the survey instrument was developed by the United Nations Institute, each country which participated was required to provide the money to fund the data collection effort within their own country. These data are considered some of the highest quality international crime data available, and are unique in that they contain *systematically comparable* information on victimization, the characteristics of the victims, the perceived neighborhood characteristics of victims, and the location of the actual crime itself for a reasonably diverse sample of countries. Information on a number of standard serious crimes are included in the data archive including robbery and assault. Overall, national level victimization surveys were carried out in seventeen countries in 1992.

Each country was counseled to collect 1,500 to 2,000 interviews. This modest sample size was suggested so as to encourage as many countries as possible to participate. Interviews were conducted using the CATI telephone interviewing system when possible (which was most instances), and face-to-face interviews when this was not possible, with a randomly chosen member of the household 16 years or older based on the composition of the household (The Troldahl-Carter method). There was no substitution of the respondent that was initially selected for interview allowed. The average response rate for the 1992 wave was 61% (van Dijk and Mayhew 1993:7)

The usual caveats that apply to the telephone survey technique apply here as well (see Czaja & Blair 1996; Schuman & Presser 1996). For instance, when asking about victimization, respondents may forget to mention incidents which occurred in the relevant time frame, and telescoping may also occur where incidents occurring before the relevant time frame are reported. Further, the propensity to report certain types of victimization (such as rape) may vary by cultural/national context. As the directors of the study note, there is no real way to determine if these types of bias vary across countries or if they are a constant (van Dijk & Mayhew 1993). While there are some limitations associated with these data, they still essentially amount to the best data available for a cross-national test. Fortunately, data are also available for a full replication (discussed below), providing a form of external validation.

Key Independent Variable

The key exogenous concept measured here is the degree of perceived *community cohesion*. The survey instrument for this study employs a question measuring community cohesion in a rather straightforward manner. The specific question states: "Now I would like to ask you some questions about your area and about your opinion of crime in your area. In some areas people do things together and try to help each other, while in other areas people mostly go their own way. In general, what kind of area would you say you live in. Is it one where people mostly help each other, or where people mostly go their own way?" The response options for the interviewers for this question were: (1) Mostly help each other, (2) Mostly go their own way. This variable has been coded into a dichotomous measure with 1 indicating communities in which people mostly help each other out and 0 for all others. With the variable coded in this way I expect a negative statistical relationship. Communities that are more cohesive — measured as helping each other out — should present fewer opportunities for the successful completion of crimes because of the higher levels of guardianship entailed by community cohesion.

It is important to note here that this measure taps the respondents perception of the degree of community cohesion and not the objective degree of community cohesion. One might argue that a given respondent has an unrealistic view of how tightly integrated the community actually is. However, the advantage of this measure is that the question is worded in such a way as to force the respondent to simplify their evaluation of the neighborhood. The nature of the response options leaves little room for offering an evaluation that would be diametrically opposed to that reached through some other, more objective method. Similarly, because no middle category is explicitly offered, respondents cannot drift into an essentially neutral category as easily, again forcing them to make an assessment that may be closer to an actual objective assessment.

Dependent Variables

Several dependent variables are constructed which permit testing the main effects of community cohesion and the control variables under a variety of conditions. Cohen and Felson (1979) indicate that the opportunity framework applies most directly to criminal events involving direct contact between the offender and the victim. Following this suggestion, two forms of victimization are measured, robbery and assault. The logic of the theoretical model also specifies that the guardianship effect derived from living in a cohesive community should only reduce the likelihood of victimization within the community in which the respondent lives. Hence each of the response variables takes into account the location of the reported incident. Further, some have suggested that the opportunity model applies most directly to crimes perpetrated by strangers (Miethe, Stafford & Long 1987). Some of the dependent variables are therefore constructed to take into account the victim-offender relationship.

Neighborhood robbery is constructed from respondents' reports that they were the victim of a robbery near their home in this year or last. Violent victimization is a rather rare event, resulting in a dichotomous distribution. Consequently, this variable is measured as a dichotomy, with those who have been victimized near the home receiving a score of 1, and all others 0. Constructing the response variable in this manner is consistent with most research testing opportunity theory.

Stranger-neighborhood robbery takes into account the location of the criminal event and the victim offender relationship simultaneously. This variable is also measured as a dichotomy, with respondents reporting being the victim of a robbery near the home by a stranger receiving a score of 1, and all others 0.

Analogous measures of assault victimization have been constructed for respondents who reported being the victim of an assault near the home and being the victim of an assault near the home by a stranger. These are labeled *neighborhood assault* and *stranger-neighborhood assault.*

Controls

Several standard control variables are included in the multivariate analysis as well. Age of respondent is measured as a grouped interval level variable starting with the age of 16. This measure is expected to have an inverse association with rates of victimization because younger people are victims (as well as perpetrators) of violent crime at much higher rates than are older people (Hindelang, Gottfredson & Garafolo 1978). Sex is measured as a dichotomy with males being coded as 1 and females 0 because males also have much higher rates of involvement in violent crime as both victims and offenders than do females. A measure of marital status, being single, is constructed as a dichotomy with those who are never married and not cohabiting receiving a score of 1 and all others 0. Being single may influence one's risk of victimization because of the fact that single individuals spend less time under the guardianship and watchful eye of others. Socioeconomic status is also measured as a dichotomy with respondents who report having an income below the 50th percentile in their country receiving a score of 1, and all others 0. It is expected that a lower socioeconomic status will be associated with a higher victimization risk.

A measure of lifestyle/leisure activities is also constructed. Consistent with many other studies, this is measured as a dichotomy, coded 1 if the respondent goes out in the evening almost every night for leisure activities and 0 otherwise (e.g., Miethe, Stafford & Long 1987).

692 / *Social Forces* 79:2, December 2000

TABLE 1: Variable Coding and Descriptive Statistics, National Level Surveys

	Variable Coding	Percentage
Dependent Variables		
Neighborhood robbery	1 = victim	.9
	0 = not victim	99.1
Neighborhood assault	1 = victim	2.5
	0 = not victim	97.5
Neighborhood-stranger robbery	1 = victim	.6
	0 = not victim	99.4
Neighborhood-stranger assault	1 = victim	1.2
	0 = not victim	98.8
Independent Variables		
Age	1 = 16-19	4.4
	2 = 20-24	7.7
	3 = 25-29	9.7
	4 = 30-34	12.0
	5 = 35-39	11.8
	6 = 40-44	10.9
	7 = 45-49	8.4
	8 = 50-54	7.6
	9 = 55-59	6.2
	10 = 60-64	7.0
	11 = 65-70	6.1
	12 = 70 +	8.2
Male	1 = male	48.4
	0 = female	51.6
Single	1 = single	20.0
	0 = all other	80.0
Low income	1 = income below median	48.5
	0 = all other	51.5

The two final variables are added as controls, one due to the nature of the national level sampling frames and one due to the neighborhood level orientation of the main exogenous predictor, community cohesion. City size is measured as an interval level variable because some countries are more highly urbanized than others, and because crimes such as robbery are primarily an urban as opposed to rural phenomenon. Controlling for this should account for possibly spurious relationships that may emerge without it present. Respondents perceptions of the status of their neighborhoods is also controlled for and is measured as a three category variable with 1 =low status, 2=middle status, and 3=high status. This is a

TABLE 1: Variable Coding and Descriptive Statistics, National Level Surveys
(Continued)

	Variable Coding	Percentage
City Size	0 = 0 (no town)	13.0
	1≤ 10,000	25.9
	2 = 10-50,000	22.9
	3 = 50-100,000	9.2
	4 = 100-500,000	15.0
	5 = 500-1,000,000	6.3
	6 = 1,000,000+	7.6
Neighborhood status	1= low status	11.5
	2 = middle status	66.2
	3 = high status	22.3
Night time activity	1 = goes out almost every night	9.9
	0=all other	90.1
Community cohesion	1 = high neighborhood cohesion	45.9
	0=low neighborhood cohesion	54.12

potentially important control because respondents may confuse the fact that they live in a wealthy or high status neighborhood with the degree of community cohesion. But certainly not all high status neighborhoods have strong community ties, just as all low status neighborhoods do not have weak community ties. Controlling for this will help tease out these possibly empirically related but conceptually distinct phenomenon.

With missing data removed for all indicators, the final sample size for the national level analysis is 19,180 respondents representing 15 countries. The United State and Indonesia omitted certain questions, resulting in all of their respondents being excluded. The fifteen countries included in this final sample are England and Wales, the Netherlands, Belgium, Finland, Sweden, Italy, Canada, Australia, New Zealand, Poland, Czechia, Slowakia, Georgia, Estonia and Costa Rica.

Table 1 provides a summary of the variable definitions and coding procedures, as well as basic descriptive summary statistics in the form of percentages falling into each category. As the percentages for the dependent variables generally indicate, violent victimization is a comparatively rare phenomenon. Slightly less than 1% of the respondents indicated that they had been the victim of a robbery near the home, and the figure for victims of a robbery near the home by a stranger is even smaller. Similar proportional differences are observed for the measures of neighborhood assault and stranger-neighborhood assault. Assault is also a more

TABLE 2:   Percentage of Respondents Victimized by Degree of Neighborhood
           Cohesion, National Level Surveys

	Neighborhood Robbery	Neighborhood Assault	Stranger-Neighborhood Robbery	Stranger-Neighborhood Assault
Low neighborhood cohesion	1.1	3.0	.7	1.6
High neighborhood cohesion	.7	1.8	.5	.7
Raw difference	.4	1.2	.2	.9
Percentage difference	57.14	66.66	40.00	128.57

frequent occurrence than robbery, as can be observed in the higher values for these measures.

Age is a rather normally distributed variable, with the bulk of the respondents appearing in the middle age ranges of 30 years old to the mid-40's. Almost half of the sample (48.4%) is male, and one-fifth of the respondents are single. Income, measured here as a dichotomy, also appears rather evenly distributed, with 48.5% of the sample reporting that they earn below the average income for their country (the value of which was provided by interviewers during the interview). Sixty percent of the sample lives in towns of 100,000 or less, which, by US standards, are not generally considered large cities. A solid two-thirds of the sample also reports living in neighborhoods that are of a middle status, but another one-fifth report living in a high status neighborhood and only 11.5% view their local areas as low status.

Only a small percentage (9.9%), go out almost every evening for leisure activities such as going to pubs, out to eat, or to the movies. As lifestyle/exposure theory has generally been formulated, this should be a major factor explaining victimization risk. Victimization may be comparatively rare because going out frequently in the evening is comparatively rare.

Finally, it is quite interesting to note while almost half of the respondents indicated that people in their own neighborhood tend to help each other out (45.9%), over half indicated that their neighborhood is not tightly knit, but in fact quite the opposite - people tend to go about their own business. This stands in interesting contrast to the neighborhood status measure, which, although allowing three categories rather than two, indicated that more view their neighborhood as high status rather than low. This may provide some evidence that neighborhood status and community cohesion are distinct phenomenon. The empirical evidence also supports this, as the bivariate correlation between the two measures is only $r = .068$.

Analysis

The first stage of the analytical strategy involves examining the distribution of victimization by level of neighborhood cohesion. The results of this stage for the national level surveys are presented in Table 2. What is most striking here is that for all types of victimization, respondents in neighborhoods with low cohesion report victimization at higher levels.

For example, only .7% of respondents living in neighborhoods which they perceive to be cohesive report being the victim of a robbery near the home, whereas 1.1% of those living in neighborhoods which they do not perceive to be cohesive were the victims of a robbery near their home. While the raw difference here is rather small, the percentage difference is substantial, 57.14%. Similar differences across levels of perceived community cohesion are evident for the other measures of victimization. In fact, for all forms of victimization, the percentage difference is 40% or greater. This gives a clear initial indication that violent victimization is more prevalent in neighborhoods with low levels of cohesion.

The second phase of the analytical strategy pursued here employs multivariate regression models. Due to the dichotomous nature of the dependent variables, the chief estimator is logistic regression. Logistic regression is preferable to log linear methods in this case because it allows some of the independent variables (such as age and city size) to be measured at the interval level.

Multivariate Results

The results of the multivariate logistic regression models are presented in Table 3. There are four models contained in this table, with each one predicting one of the dependent variables. The goal of these models is to assess the independent partial effect of community cohesion on the risk of various forms of individual victimization near the home. Following Miethe and Meier (1990) and Miethe and McDowall (1993), coefficients that are significant at the $p < .10$ level are reported. Generally speaking, these models provide consistent support for the expectation that living in a cohesive community directly reduces the likelihood of being the victim of a violent predatory crime. The coefficients for the community cohesion variable are negative and statistically significant for each model. The odds ratios are also rather substantial, with the smallest being .754 for the measure of neighborhood robbery. In plain terms this suggests that living in a cohesive neighborhood reduces the odds of being the victim of a violent crime substantially, net of the demographic, socioeconomic, and lifestyle characteristics of individuals. Note that this is also net of the relatively consistent performance of the neighborhood status indicator, which suggests that living in higher status communities directly reduces all forms of victimization, but is especially relevant to reducing robbery.

696 / *Social Forces* 79:2, December 2000

TABLE 3: Logistic Regression Models Predicting Victimization Measures Using National Level Victimization Surveys for 15 Countries, 1992

	Neighborhood Robbery	Neighborhood Assault	Stranger-Neighborhood Robbery	Stranger-Neighborhood Assault
Age	-.068*	-.110**	-.060†	-.061*
	.933	.896	.941	.941
Male	.344*	.090	.384*	.245†
	1.411	1.094	1.468	1.277
Single	.235	-.124	.115	-.037
	1.266	.884	1.121	.964
Low income	.225	.087	.208	.039
	1.253	1.091	1.231	1.040
City size	-.004	.075**	-.047	.124**
	.996	1.078	.953	1.132
Neighborhood status	-.454**	-.212**	-.521**	-.190†
	.634	.809	.593	.827
Frequency of night activity	.254	.428**	.326	.332†
	1.290	1.534	1.386	1.394
Community cohesion	-.281†	-.448**	-.396†	-.857**
	.754	.639	.691	.425
Constant	-3.641**	-2.722**	-3.834**	-3.865**
Model χ^2	43.912**	111.849**	32.041**	71.396**
-2 Log likelihood	1929.605	4337.926	1363.877	2384.472

Note: First row is logistic regression coefficient. Second row is odds ratio.

† $p < .10$ * $p < .05$ ** $p < .01$

Several of the control variables also exhibit the expected association with the dependent variables. For example, as age increases, the likelihood of experiencing victimization of any type near the home decreases. Males are also more likely to be the victims of both types of robbery near the home. Individuals with low-income have no greater likelihood of being a victim of either type of robbery or assault when other factors are accounted for, but those who live in big cities are more likely to experience assault, as are those who go out almost every evening for leisure activities. Each of these findings are also consistent with expectations derived from the theoretical model and are consonant with the findings of previous research using different data sets.

Overall, these models provide rather consistent support for the expectation that living in a cohesive community directly reduces the likelihood of being the victim of a violent crime. The models predict the assault measures better than robbery, but the results for the robbery models are consistent with each other in and of themselves.

Replication and External Validation

Although the results from this analysis are compelling and lend substantial credence to the hypothesis that people living in cohesive communities have lower victimization risk, there is the possibility that the observed results are an artifact of measurement error. Further, there is also another substantial limitation to the national level surveys. Due to the fact that the sampling frames are designed to be representative of entire nations, the data represent a mix of urban and rural residents. This can potentially be problematic because it remains unclear whether opportunity theory, especially in its lifestyle/exposure form, is generalizeable to rural populations. Although the models above did control for respondents city size, the nature of routine lifestyle and evening activities is substantially different in rural areas. Respondents may not live in neighborhoods at all, and may have quite different notions of what constitutes their 'local community'. In essence, opportunity theory seems to apply mostly to urban and suburban populations.

To assess the reliability of these results then, a full scale replication has also been undertaken using surveys carried out in cities for another 12 countries. These surveys were collected independently using an almost identical survey instrument to that employed in the national level surveys. The main difference is that the city level surveys did not ask respondents the size of their city, presumably because within countries there would be no variation across respondents. The countries which only collected data from cities were Russia, Slovenia, Uganda, Brazil, Philippines, Egypt, Argentina, India, South Africa, Tanzania, Tunisia, and China. In general the samples from the city level surveys are slightly smaller with most having total samples of around 1000 respondents. Like the national level surveys, the key concern here is that violent victimization is a rare event, and so it is necessary to pool the data into one large data set in order to achieve cell sizes with reliable frequencies. The analytic strategy is to provide a complete replication where possible of the models examined using the national level survey data. With missing data removed on all of the variables of interest, the final sample size for the city level surveys is 10,781.

As noted above, all of the variables of interest employed in the national level surveys are available in the city level surveys except 1, city size. And so while an exact replication is not possible, it is very close to exact. Each of the variables are measured in the same manner as in the national level surveys, and the descriptive statistics and coding scheme are presented in Table 4.

Considering first the dependent variables, it is apparent from the percentage distributions that victimization near the home in cities is substantially more prevalent than that observed when national sampling frames are utilized. For instance 3.8% of the respondents to the city level surveys indicated being the victim of a robbery whereas only .9% of the respondents to the national level surveys did. Similar differences are observed for the other forms of victimization as well.

Most of the control variables are distributed quite similarly to those in the national level sample, except for neighborhood status. In this case, three times as many respondents in the city level sample indicate that they reside in a low status neighborhood as reported so in the national level sample. The similarity in the percentage of respondents reporting living in a cohesive community is also evident, with those reporting living in a neighborhood with high community cohesion differing by less than 2% between samples.

Table 5 reports the percentage of respondents victimized according to their perceived level of neighborhood cohesion. The results here again are also quite similar to those which emerged in the national level sample. For every form of victimization, neighborhoods with low neighborhood cohesion have higher percentages of their residents reporting being the victim of a crime. What is also evident though is that the percentage difference between neighborhoods by type of victimization is generally less than observed in the national level sample. Yet the differences by level of neighborhood cohesion are quite striking, with the prevalence of victimization being at least 23% higher for residents of neighborhoods which they perceive to have a low degree of cohesion.

Turning to Table 6, the results of the logistic regression models predicting each form of victimization are presented. The main finding from this table which mirrors the findings from the analogous models using the national level sample (Table 3)is that the community cohesion variable is negative and statistically significant in each instance. That is, individuals who live in neighborhoods which they perceive to be cohesive have a lower likelihood of experiencing any of these forms of victimization. The absolute magnitude of these effects also closely parallel that reported in the analysis of the national level surveys. This close consistency suggests that the findings are relatively reliable and robust.

The performance of several of the control variables are also consistent with their performance in the national level sample. For two of the four models, the age measure is statistically significant and in the expected direction. Being male also elevates the likelihood of being the victim of a robbery as was observed in the national level sample, but in the city level sample also elevates the risk of both forms of assault. Individuals with low income only have a higher likelihood of neighborhood robbery, but those who go out almost every night for leisure activities have a higher risk of experiencing both robbery and assault in their neighborhood,

Community Cohesion and Violent Victimization / 699

TABLE 4: Variable Coding and Descriptive Statistics, City Level Surveys

	Variable Coding	Percentage
Dependent variables		
Neighborhood robbery	1= victim	3.8
	0=not victim	96.2
Neighborhood assault	1= victim	3.7
	0=not victim	96.3
Neighborhood-stranger robbery	1= victim	2.8
	0= not victim	97.2
Neighborhood-stranger assault	1= victim	1.8
	0= not victim	98.2
Independent variables		
Age	1= 16-19	5.7
	2= 20-24	12.5
	3= 25-29	13.6
	4= 30-34	15.7
	5= 35-39	14.0
	6= 40-44	12.0
	7= 45-49	7.6
	8= 50-54	6.1
	9= 55-59	4.2
	10= 60-64	3.9
	11= 65-70	2.6
	12=70+	2.1
Male	1= male	48.9
	0= female	51.1
Single	1= single	23.5
	0= all other	76.5
Low income	1= income below median	57.6
	0= all other	42.4
Neighborhood status	1= low status	34.9
	2= middle status	50.4
	3= high status	14.7
Night time activity	1= goes out almost every night	10.7
	0= all other	89.3
Community cohesion	1= high neighborhood cohesion	47.5
	0= low neighborhood cohesion	52.5

700 / *Social Forces* 79:2, December 2000

TABLE 5:   Percentage of Respondents Victimized by Degree of Neighborhood
           Cohesion, City Level Surveys

	Neighborhood Robbery	Neighborhood Assault	Stranger-Neighborhood Robbery	Stranger-Neighborhood Assault
Low neighborhood cohesion	4.2	4.4	3.2	2.2
High neighborhood cohesion	3.4	3.0	2.3	1.3
Raw difference	.81	.4	.9	.9
Percentage difference	23.53	46.66	39.13	69.23

though not by strangers. Those who live in high status neighborhoods have a lower
likelihood of being victimized, but again, not by strangers. There are some
departures from expectations here, mostly in the form of statistical insignificance.
Most instances of this occur when predicting stranger-neighborhood robbery and
stranger neighborhood assault, the two models with the weakest fit. Overall though,
the findings for the main variable of interest, community cohesion, are consistent
and expected.

Discussion

These results lend substantial support to the notion that neighborhood context,
specifically the degree of community cohesion, is an important determinant of
victimization risk. Each of the 8 models presented above indicate that individuals
residing in communities where they perceive the residents to help each other out
have a lower victimization risk. This study has departed from prior research on
victimization and community level processes in several ways, and provides some
unique insight into the forces driving crime, not in the U.S., but in other countries
around the world.

The relationship between community context and crime has traditionally been
the domain of social disorganization theorists. Opportunity theory has only
effectively linked community context to individual victimization by arguing that
living in a community with a high crime rate elevates individual victimization
risk through increased exposure to crime (Sampson & Lauritsen 1990). This study
has attempted to advance our understanding of the multi-dimensional role of
neighborhood context in victimization by emphasizing an alternative facet of
community context, guardianship.

This study has also taken a somewhat unusual approach to the problem of
community context and victimization because community cohesion is measured
not as an objective feature of neighborhoods but rather as a perceptual

Community Cohesion and Violent Victimization / **701**

TABLE 6: Logistic Regression Models Predicting Victimization Measures Using
City Level Victimization Surveys for 12 Countries, 1992

	Neighborhood Robbery	Neighborhood Assault	Stranger-Neighborhood Robbery	Stranger-Neighborhood Assault
Age	-.054*	-.069**	-.041	-.045
	.947	.934	.959	.956
Male	.251*	.271**	.317**	.377*
	1.286	1.311	1.373	1.459
Single	-.222	.158	-.385*	-.069
	.800	1.171	.680	.933
Low income	.259*	-.053	.194	.156
	1.295	.948	1.215	1.168
Neighborhood status	-.182*	-.287**	-.133	.125
	.833	.751	.874	1.133
Frequency of night activity	.246†	.345*	.269	.210
	1.280	1.412	1.309	1.234
Community cohesion	-.256*	-.404**	-.351**	-.463**
	.773	.667	.7035	.629
Constant	-2.782**	-2.443**	-3.175**	-4.133**
Model χ^2	33.864**	61.619**	28.384**	24.126**
-2 log likelihood	3470.598	3371.172	2733.535	1894.892

Note: First row is logistic regression coefficient. Second row is odds ratio.

† p < .10   * p < .05   ** p < .01

phenomenon. That is, the measurement of community cohesion here is based on
respondents' personal evaluations of whether or not they believe that people in their
local community mostly help each other out. This is at odds with most community
level research, which tries to measure objectively the degree of community cohesion
by asking respondents how many friends they have in the local neighborhood, how
many organizations they belong to, and how frequently they interact with others
in their neighborhood (see Bellair 1997; Kasarda & Janowitz 1974; Sampson &
Groves 1989). But as Sampson, Raudenbush, and Earls (1997:919) note, "Even if
personal ties are strong in areas of concentrated disadvantage, they may be weakly
tethered to collective actions". Although the present study does not address
concentrated neighborhood disadvantage, the same general principal is relevant.
Namely, that people may know many residents of their neighborhood, but also be
aware of the fact that the residents are not unified in a way that promotes

guardianship. Consequently, there may be a substantial degree of merit in the approach taken here.

It is reasonable to assume that the objective degree of community cohesion is important in determining the level of community offending behavior. This is especially true if one takes into consideration the 'reasoning criminal' perspective, which suggests that offenders do evaluate the likelihood of successfully completing a crime based on the observable guardianship capacity of a community, among other things (see Cornish & Clarke 1986). It may also be the case that studies which evaluate the determinants of community levels of victimization can similarly benefit from objective measures of community cohesion. However, theoretically, individual victimization risk is a different beast, and may require different explanatory foci.

First, there is no reason to believe that communities are more cohesive than the individuals which reside in them perceive them to be. Even if this assumption were to be made, the leisure activities of a given individual hinge on, if anything, their subjective evaluation of the sociospatial context in which they are embedded. As such, the expectation would be that individual victimization risk is determined more in part by subjective evaluations of the degree of community cohesion because that is what the decision to engage in leisure activities is based on.

Second, especially given the dichotomous nature of the response options for the measure of community cohesion used here, it is likely that individual evaluations of the degree of community cohesion are more accurate than not. If this variable were measured as a continuum, it would probably be the case that a substantial degree of measurement error would be introduced. But it is unlikely that a person resides in a highly cohesive community and does not know it, and it is also unlikely that a person resides in a highly fragmented community but perceives it as highly cohesive. As such, it appears reasonable to assume that respondents evaluations in this case are relatively accurate. Even allowing for some measurement error in this variable, the fact that the results were completely replicable provides some degree of ex ante evidence that the observed relationship is not due to random measurement error. It does appear that people who live in communities where they perceive people to mostly help each other out have lower probabilities of being the victim of a violent crime near the home.

Conclusions

This study has attempted to develop a theoretical extension of opportunity theory by arguing that community context is an important determinant of individual victimization risk. Drawing on the community attachment literature, I have argued that well integrated communities actually lower the risk of violent victimization

Community Cohesion and Violent Victimization / 703

among individuals because such communities tend to exhibit active social control. That is, they tend to be characterized by high levels of informal guardianship because the residents of said communities are more likely to intervene in public deviant and criminal activities. This basic concept has been referred to as 'collective efficacy' (see Sampson, Raudenbush & Earls 1997). This theoretical extension was tested using comparable data collected from national level sampling frames on the victimization experiences of more than 19,000 individuals in 15 countries.

A complete replication was also undertaken with comparable data from more than 10,000 more respondents gleaned from city level sampling frames in another 12 countries. The results from both analyses are consistent and appear to be robust across different forms of victimization. In sum, living in a community which one evaluates to be cohesive appears to substantially reduce the individual risk of violent victimization within that community. Note that this conclusion is not drawn from a survey of respondents in a single country, but from surveys of residents in 27 countries. This lends substantial support to the idea that community context is important in explaining victimization not just in the U.S. or Britain, but in various social, cultural, political, and economic contexts.

Future research should continue to focus on guardianship as a key to understanding the likelihood of individual violent victimization. Although most research on opportunity theory conceptualizes guardianship in terms of target hardening or informal surveillance, the role of the police in acting as guardians should not be neglected. Although some specialized data sets do contain information on the presence of police for local communities (e.g., Massey, Krohn & Bonati 1989), most large scale victimization surveys contain no such information. Those that do are also limited in that they contain information on the number of police per capita, a measure which does not tap the construct of interest — how frequently individuals actually see the police patrolling their local community.

Another potentially profitable line of inquiry would be to examine the cross-cultural relationship between fear of crime and individual routine activities. Little is known about how fear of being the victim of a crime actually alters the lifestyles of individuals. It may be the case that fear of crime deteriorates community cohesion- possibly increasing victimization risk, but at the same time reduces the willingness of individuals to venture out of doors- elevating guardianship over ones own property. This effectively creates a paradox which criminologists should attempt to disentangle. Until recently the cross-national investigation of these types of issues has been severely undermined by the lack of standardized and comparable data from an appreciable sample of countries. As the U.S. and other countries progress towards a more globally based and unified system, data collection efforts will continue to improve and the opportunities for research on these and other important issues will be enhanced.

704 / *Social Forces* 79:2, **December 2000**

Notes

1. Attempts or threats excluded from all victimization measures.

2. Another demographic control that may be associated with victimization risk is race. This is especially true for the risk of robbery, but the extant evidence does not indicate that there is a strong relationship between race and assault (see Sampson & Lauritsen 1994). The present data set does not contain information on the race of the respondent. As Tonry (1997) notes, some European countries consider it unethical to collect information on the race of their citizens. But, in addition, as Neapolitan (1997) argues, race is essentially a socially constructed category rendering its meaning across nations and cultures ambiguous.

3. The original formulation of lifestyle theory by Hindelang, Gottfredson, and Garafolo (1978) did suggest that not just night-time activities would be instrumental in determining victimization risk, but that daytime acitivities were important as well. Miethe, Stafford and Long (1987) examined this and found no effect of daytime activity patterns such as work or school on violent victimization in their U.S. sample.

A second issue in the measurement of lifestyle activity, specifically with regard to going out in the evening for leisure activities, is that some activities are clearly more conducive to criminal victimization than others. For example, Sampson and Lauritsen (1990) find that going out in the evening drinking substantially elevates victimization risk in their analysis of the British Crime Survey data, as do Kennedy and Ford (1990) in their analysis of the Canadian Urban Victimization Survey. A recent survey of college students reported in Mustaine and Tewksbury (1998) reports that numerous activities away from the home results in an increased risk of larceny theft victimization. And so the research evidence does seem to support the conclusion that certain activities away from the home are especially conducive to victimization risk. Unfortunately, the current survey does not contain detailed information on lifestyle acitvities away from the home (and, in fact, most victimization surveys do not). Consequently, the measure of going out in the evening is somewhat crude and certainly less desirable than a more detailed measure. This shortcoming is not considered extremely detrimental because the actual focus of the study is not what people are doing when away from their home in the evenings.

4. Analogous models were examined for a combined index of robbery and assault victimization. The results regarding the main indicator of interest, community cohesion were substantively similar and so are not reported in tabular format to avoid redundancy.

5. Extensive probing for contextual effects were undertaken for all of the models reported above. To assess whether hte effects of community cohesion on any of the measures of violent victimization varied by national context, dummy variables for each country were calculated and interacted with the community cohesion meaure. In nearly every case the interaction terms were not statistically significant, and there certainly were no consistent patterns evident. It appears therefore that there is little in the way of contextual variability in these data, which seems to further support the generality of the main hypothesis.

Community Cohesion and Violent Victimization / 705

Interaction models were also examined to assess whether the effects of community cohesion varied by neighborhood status. These models are not reported in tabular format because no statistically significant interactions emerged. See Meithe and McDowall (1993) for similar findings regarding contextual effects in models of violent victimization.

6. The contextual models described in note 4 were also examined using the city-level data, but again no substantive contextual effects were revealed.

References

Bellair, Paul E. 1997. "Social Interaction and Community Crime: Examining The Importance of Neighbor Networks." *Criminology* 35:677-701.

Black, Donald. 1983. "Crime as Social Control." *American Sociological Review.* 38:34-45.

Bursik, Robert J. 1999. "The Informal Control of Crime Through Neighborhood Networks." *Sociological Focus* 32:85-97.

Bursik, Robert and Harold Grasmick. 1993. *Neighborhoods and Crime: The Dimensions of Effective Community Control.* Lexington Books.

Cohen, Lawrence and Marcus Felson. 1979. "Social Change and Crime Rate Trends: A Routine Activity Approach." *American Sociological Review* 44:588-608.

Cohen, Lawrence E., Marcus Felson, and Kenneth C. Land. 1980. "Property Crime Rates in the Unites States: A Macrodynamic Analysis 1947-77 with Ex Ante Forecasts for the Mid-1980's." *American Journal of Sociology* 86:90-118.

Cornish, Derek B. and Ronald V. Clark. 1986. *The Reasoning Criminal: Rational Choice Perspectives on Offending.* Springer-Verlag.

Czaja, Ronald and Johnny Blair. 1996. *Designing Surveys: A Guide to Decisions and Procedures.* Pine Forge Press.

Hindelang, Michael J., Michael R. Gottfredson, and James Garafolo. 1978. *Victims of Personal Crime: An Empirical Foundation for a Theory of Personal Victimization.* Cambridge Mass: Ballinger Publishing Company.

Kasarda, John and Morris Janowitz. 1974. "Community Attachment in Mass Society". *American Sociological Review* 39:328-39.

Kennedy, Leslie W. and David R. Forde. 1990. "Routine Activities and Crime: An Analysis of Victimization in Canada." *Criminology* 28:137-51.

Massey, James L., Marvin D. Krohn, and Lisa M. Bonati. 1989. "Property Crime and the Routine Activities of Individuals." *Journal of Research in Crime and Delinquency* 26:378-400.

Meier, Robert F. and Terance D. Miethe. 1993. "Understanding Theories of Criminal Victimization." Pp. 459-99 in *Crime and Justice: A Review of Research, Volume 17.* Edited by Michael Tonry. University of Chicago Press.

Messner, Steven F. and Judith R. Blau. 1987. "Routine Leisure Activities and Rates of Crime: A Macro-level Analysis." *Social Forces* 65:1035-52.

Miethe, Terance D., Michael Hughes, and David McDowall. 1991. "Social Change and Crime Rates: An Evaluation of Alternative Theoretical Approaches." *Social Forces* 70:165-85.

706 / *Social Forces* **79:2, December 2000**

Miethe, Terance D., and David McDowall. 1993. "Contextual Effects in Models of Criminal Victimization." *Social Forces* 71:741-59.

Miethe, Terance D. and Robert F. Meier. 1990. "Opportunity, Choice, and Criminal Victimization: A Test of a Theoretical Model". *Journal of Research in Crime and Delinquency* 27:243-66.

Miethe, Terance D., Mark C. Stafford, and J. Scott Long. 1987. "Social Differentiation in Criminal Victimization: A Test of Routine Activities/Lifestyle Theories." *American Sociological Review* 52:184-94.

Mustaine, Elizabeth Ehrhardt and Richard Tewksbury. 1998. "Predicting Risks of Larceny Theft Victimization: A Routine Activity Analysis Using Refined Lifestyle Measures." *Criminology* 36:829-57.

Neapolitan, Jerome. 1998. "Cross-National Variation in Homicides: Is Race a Factor?" *Criminology.* 36:139-56.

Sampson, Robert J., and W. Byron Groves. 1989. "Community Structure and Crime: Testing Social-Disorganization Theory." *American Journal of Sociology* 94:774-802.

Sampson, Robert J., and Janet L. Lauritsen. 1990. "Deviant Lifestyles, Proximity to Crime, and the Offender-Victim Link in Personal Violence." *Journal of Research in Crime and Delinquency* 27:110-39.

Sampson, Robert J., and Janet L. Lauritsen. 1994. "Violent Victimization and Offending: Individual-, Situational-, and Community-Level Risk Factors." Pp. 1-114 in *Understanding and Preventing Violence: Volume 3, Social Influences.* Edited by Albert J. Reiss and Jeffrey A. Roth. Washington D.C.: National Academy Press.

Sampson, Robert J., Stephen W. Raudenbush, and Felton Earls. 1997. "Neighborhoods and Crime: A Multilevel Study of Collective Efficacy." *Science* 277:918-24.

Schuman, Howard and Stanley Presser. 1996. *Questions and Answers in Attitude Surveys: Experiments on Question Form, Wording, and Context.* Thousand Oaks: Sage Publications.

Tonry, Michael. 1997. "Ethnicity, Crime, and Immigration". Pp 1-30 in *Ethnicity, Crime, and Immigration: Comparative and Cross-National Perspectives. Crime and Justice, A Review of Research, Volume 21.* Edited by Michael Tonry. University of Chicago Press.

van Dijk, Jan J. M., and Patricia Mayhew. 1993. "'Criminal Victimization in the Industrialized World: Key Findings of the 1989 and 1992 International Crime Surveys." Pp. 1-49 in *Understanding Crime: Experiences of Crime and Crime Control.* Edited by Anna Alvazzi del Frate, Ugljesa Zvekic, and Jan J.M. van Dijk.Rome: United Nations.

[21]

Boys Against Girls

The Structural and Interpersonal Dimensions
of Violent Patriarchal Culture in the
Lives of Young Men

BERNARD SCHISSEL
University of Saskatchewan

This article contends that male youth violence against female youth is a formidable social problem that originates largely within the confines of patriarchal/profit-driven culture. Many factors that cause young men to be aggressive and abusive to young women originate within cultures of achievement such as sports, where aggression is equated with success and where girls and women are literally and figuratively relegated to exploited or denigrated positions. Using both an empirically based causal analysis of youth in Canada and a more descriptive analysis of several male contexts, the author tests and describes how personal and interpersonal experiences influence aggression toward young women and how these experiences often arise in contexts that are both ideological and profit driven.

The study of male youth violence against female youth is important for at least three reasons. First, such behavior physically and emotionally injures both young victims and offenders (Makepeace, 1986; Miedzian, 1991). Second, male attitudes that foster sexism and women abuse are likely set in the formative years, and such attitudes grow as male youth and men come to believe in their inherent right to power over women (DeKeseredy & Schwartz, 1998). In fact, abused women often report that their first encounters with male violence were in adolescent dating situations, especially in their early teens (Simons, Lin, & Gordon, 1998). Third, the athletics/military-based and education-based subcultures largely responsible for constructing masculinities and femi-

AUTHOR'S NOTE: I am indebted to the Social Sciences and Humanities Research Council of Canada, grant number 41-095-1532 for funding for the Saskatchewan Youth Attitudes Survey (1997).

VIOLENCE AGAINST WOMEN, Vol. 6 No. 9, September 2000   960-986

ninities in young people largely go unchallenged for the potential damage they do to girls and boys (Miedzian, 1991).

The study of how young males orient themselves toward masculinity within these subcultures tells us something very valuable about the nature of society and how it is structured. Much of the traditional literature on young male violence, however, avoids such larger structural issues regarding patriarchy and political economy in lieu of more popular psychological or family-based explanations, some of which I discuss and test in this article. In this regard, the focus of this article is on the larger issues that provide the context of youth male violence. Given this, it is somewhat difficult to discuss issues of treatment and policy. However, given that communities, cultures, and subcultures do affect the way that young men and women orient themselves toward one another, it is reasonable to assume that policy actions, especially at the community and subcultural levels, can ameliorate the sexist contexts of the political, social, and economic worlds. Individual and collective actions obviously can have an immediate impact on redressing sexism. Still, they also have long term effects on changing the context in which boys and girls come to see each other as stereotypical. I will discuss some of these collective actions within this article.

A recurrent explanation for male youth violence against female youth is that orientations toward the opposite sex are learned in the family of origin. The reasoning is that if parents are predisposed toward violence, especially toward each other or toward their children, their behavior provides lessons that legitimate violence among their offspring (Straus, Gelles, & Steinmetz, 1980; Straus & Smith, 1990). The legitimation perspective suggests that young people who are the targets of their parents' aggression, in the forms of both corporal punishment and spontaneous violence, tend to assume that violence is sometimes a necessary strategy for maintaining stability and discipline in intimate relationships. The spontaneous violence argument is reasonable, although the corporal punishment argument is debatable (Foo & Margolin, 1995; Riggs & O'Leary, 1996). The counterargument is that because corporal punishment is premeditated, it is less destructive than the more spontaneous acts of violence that are subsumed under the rubric of child abuse.

The criminological literature has broadened the work on youth violence and interpersonal relationships by suggesting that dating violence, as the most common forum for potential dysfunction in boy-girl interactions, is associated with a general orientation toward criminality that is manifested in other forms of deviant behavior. The logic is that aggression in dating situations is indicative of a larger antisocial behavior patterning that involves aggression in other contexts and in high risk behavior (Farrington, 1991; Patterson & Yeorger, 1993). The types of behavior associated with this antisocial orientation likely include violent peer group behavior, low-level criminality, and substance abuse. Male youth who are typified in these various types of high-risk behaviors are prone to use aggression in dating situations. The use and abuse of substances as a typical form of high-risk behavior may produce chemically-induced effects that exacerbate violence (Eron, Gentry, & Schlegel; 1994; Norris, George, Cue Davis, Martell, & Leonesio, 1999).

How an antisocial orientation arises is a matter of continuing debate. The psychological literature focuses on the pathology of violence and suggests, in concert with media accounts and commonsense perceptions, that violence against girls and women is perpetrated by essentially "sick" individuals (Eron et al., 1994). This sickness paradigm is hard to sustain completely because there is such a substantial number of male youth and adults who are abusive. The conventional criminological wisdom, on the other hand, focuses on high-risk and aggressive orientations as the result, in part, of ineffective, indifferent parenting. The argument is not so much that children model themselves after aggressive parents, but that lack of involvement and support by parents is a risk factor for violent behavior in dating relationships for males especially, because young boys who have conflictual relationships with their parents suffer relatively high levels of masculine role conflicts and stresses (Fischer & Good, 1998). They, in turn, suffer from perceived intellectual inferiority and physical inadequacy and may "bolster their vulnerable sense of masculinity by externalizing their inner conflicts through traditionally masculine activities such as sports, sexual conquest, and substance abuse" (Fischer & Good, 1998, p. 350). The identity and behavior problems that ineffective parenting creates in male children are often manifested in unhealthy and dangerous conduct toward female peers. The extended argument is that indifferent or antisocial parents who create antisocial children are also more likely to engage in interspousal aggression, child abuse, and corporal punishment (Simons et al., 1998).

The conventional criminological literature supports the general position that ineffective parenting leads to aggressive behavior in male-female interactions while downplaying the damaging influences of corporal punishment or of physical child abuse. In other words, within conventional paradigms such as social process theory, once parenting quality is taken into account in explaining youth dating behavior, the influences of family violence and corporal punishment are secondary to family attachment (Farrington, 1991; Rosen, 1985). A related argument is that violence is a manifestation of the relative powerlessness that some youth feel, especially in a family context. The logic is that if young men feel disempowered in other life situations, they will tend to use abusive power in dating contexts. Feminist literature argues that when men struggle to access or maintain power, they do so primarily against women and, in doing so, they maintain their social advantage over women (Bowker, 1998; Dobash, Dobash, Wilson, & Daly, 1992). Applied to youth, the thesis is that young men who are disempowered, or who at least feel that they have little control over their lives, will act out the fantasy of empowerment by being aggressive and affrontive in interactions with young females.

An accompanying hypothesis to the disempowerment argument is that youth who feel generally alienated from society also feel greater levels of depression than their more well-adjusted counterparts. The link to violence is twofold: Greater levels of depression may result in higher levels of both inward and outward violence, and, as a corollary, involvement in violent situations may result in higher levels of depression (Durant, Cadenced, Pendergrast, Slavens, & Linder, 1994). The concept of male depression is becoming increasingly recognized as a marker of danger, especially self-destructive danger (Seidler, 1989) and involvement with the criminal justice system (Kupers, 1999). Decades of work on clinical depression determined that depression is largely a female phenomenon and that men are somehow relatively impervious or resilient to psychic trauma. Recent research on men and health has shown quite clearly that men are traumatized by depression and manifest that depression in various ways, from self-destructive lifestyles to overt manifestations of inward and outward violence (Eron et al., 1994; Nichols, 1999).

The last and probably most vital part of a discussion of male youth violence against female youth deals with how patriarchal ideologies come to be part of the lives of young males. Feminist theories have been especially important in helping us understand how and why males in general, and young men especially, come to hold distorted views about gender. For example, the male peer support thesis combines elements of the powerlessness argument with issues involving male peer group support and patriarchal belief systems. The logic is that men or male youth who are especially under stress or who experience feelings of relative powerlessness in dating relationships tend to congregate or seek out the support of other males who likely are experiencing the same types of pressures or inadequacies. The associations with like-minded peers may, under the right conditions, encourage violence against outsiders, especially female youth and women (DeKeseredy, 1988; DeKeseredy & Schwartz, 1998). This argument combines the dynamics of dating and social stress with the broader social forces that contribute to sexism. Male youth peer groups do tend to isolate from female youth, and the lack of knowledge of femaleness and the larger forces that disadvantage women and girls (manifested in the media, through sports and the world of work) combine to create sexist male youth cultures (Miedzian, 1991).

To extend this argument about the world of patriarchy, feminist studies have alerted us to the forces of patriarchy (including the masculine control of women and female youth in the areas of labor and sexuality), which circumscribe the ways that young men come to view women. Despite upbringing, substance abuse, or emotional orientation, male youth will tend to express control over female youth. One manifestation of this is violence in interpersonal relationships. In a final section in this article, I explore several contexts in which sexist violence is created and maintained. These contexts are defined broadly as communities, and understanding them as places in which violence against female youth by male youth is sanctioned helps us understand the role that cultural teaching and community can have in deterring male youth violence. First, however, the empirical section of this article explores issues raised in the introduction, to parcel out the

TABLE 1
Percentage Distributions of Violence Against Girls
by 13 to 19-Year-Old Boys (N = 1,132)

	Number of Times Reported			
Type of Violent Act	*Never*	*1 to 4*	*4 to 20*	*More than 20*
Hit, kicked, or bit	90.2	6.0	2.1	1.7
Threw something	55.6	28.9	9.0	6.5
Slapped	90.6	6.8	1.6	1.1
Pushed or shoved	84.3	11.6	2.6	1.5
Swore at	53.6	29.9	11.7	4.9

relative effects of family violence, substance use, criminality, attachments to conventional institutions, personal and structural powerlessness, and ethnocultural and geographical communities on young male violence toward female youth.

PREDICTING MALE YOUTH VIOLENCE: EMPIRICAL ANALYSIS

The empirical part of this article is based on the Saskatchewan Youth Attitudes 1997 Survey, which was administered to 2,605 high school students throughout the province of Saskatchewan, Canada. Thirty-five schools in 18 communities participated in the research project. Of the 2,605 students who participated, 1,179 (47.2%) were male and 1,317 (52.8%) female. Twenty percent of the respondents defined themselves as either Aboriginal or Métis. I use the data gathered from this sample to test a model of youth male violence against female youth in a dating context. The concept of violence is measured by a series of self-report questions dealing with different dimensions of aggression by boys against girls in any type of encounter including dating, athletics, and other social settings. Table 1 illustrates the types of aggression included in the construct of violence and the frequency that young men report.

The table is self-explanatory, but it is important to mention that the severe forms of aggression, including hitting and slapping, exist in rather unexpected numbers. For example, approximately 4% of male youth hit female youth four or more times in their middle and high school years, and almost 3% have slapped a female youth four or more times. A small percentage in both categories have done so 20 or more times. A much larger proportion of young males have thrown something at someone of the opposite sex (15.5% in both the 4 to 20 and more than 20 categories) and have sworn in anger at female youth (16.6% in both 4 to 20 and more than 20 categories). Although the data may not be indicative of an epidemic of violence by male youth against female youth, they do suggest that verbal aggression is quite common and that more serious forms of physical violence are persistent for a small but significant proportion of male youth. I use these measures of intergender violence together as a construct of male violence against females. The construct is the dependent variable in the following regression model, which is designed to investigate why these violent acts occur. The regression format allows us to judge the relative impact that sociodemographic, behavioral, and psychological traits have on the perpetration of violence against female youth.

First, I test the differential effects of corporal punishment and child abuse on dating violence by incorporating dual measures of parental violence: whether respondents had been spanked by parents while they were growing up and how often they had been hit in anger by their parents while they were growing up. Both questions included Likert-type categories ranging from "a lot" to "never," and are intended to distinguish the singular effects of premeditated disciplinary violence against spontaneous abuse. These variables are accompanied by a scale that measures the respondent's attachments to and satisfaction with his family. This tactic allows us to test the isolated effect of violence against young males on their future violence by eliminating how closely the youth is attached and committed to his family. An extension of this exposure to violence argument is that youth who have a relatively criminogenic lifestyle have an antisocial orientation that is manifested in aggression and abusive behavior. I measure the degree of a criminogenic orientation by combining questions that measure the amount of violent physical assault, fighting, and taking something by physical force (see Appendices A through E).

Second, and consistent with some of the more conventional literature in youth studies focusing on attachment and commitment to conventional activities (Agnew, 1985; Hirschi, 1969; Samuelson,

Hartnagel, & Krahn, 1990), I have incorporated several other attachment/commitment variables in the model, including school and friends. The indicators that make up the scales are listed and explained in Appendices B, C, and D and all scales are constructed on the basis of factor analyses of a series of questions focusing on a range of issues within each concept, the results of which are also included in the appendices.

Third, again, a considerable body of literature documents the relationship between substance abuse and violence among youth (Eron et al., 1994; Norris et al., 1999). The conventional wisdom is that excessive drug and alcohol abuse may be at once indicative of a poorly adjusted youth who is disposed to anger and reaction as a consequence of his life circumstances. Also, substance use has a psychochemical effect on behavior during both inebriation and withdrawal. In this research, I illustrate the varying effects of drug and alcohol use on male violence toward female youth using a composite of all typical available drugs and a composite of beer and hard liquor use (both scales measure days used per year).

Fourth, I analyze the influences of both personal powerlessness and structural powerlessness. The personal powerlessness variable is a composite measure based on a factor analysis of items in a powerlessness scale. (See the appendices for the questions and factor analysis.) Structural powerlessness is measured by income adequacy. This self-report estimate of family income relative to others is arguably the best way of assessing socioeconomic standing for youth, especially given that youth rarely know family income, or, if they do, they rarely report it.

Fifth, the inclusion of depression in a prediction model of violence is in deference to the psychomedical research that suggests that even mild levels of depression foster desperate behavior, either self-destructive or destructive of others. The depression scale is based on a series of questions that tap how the respondent feels about himself and the world around him. (The questions and factor analysis are included in Appendix E.)

The demographic variable age is self-explanatory. I have included, in addition, a rural-urban dichotomous variable (based on schools in communities that are 3,000 people or less) to test the degree to which violence is culturally normative, at least with respect to cultures circumscribed by large open communities or small closed communities. The arguments are that rural societies

Predetermined Variables		Regression Coefficients	
Substance abuse	Alcohol use	.200	$(.138)^a$
	Drug use	.090	$(.491)^a$
Conventional attachments	School	.022	$(.031)$
	Family	−.019	$(−.014)$
	Friends	−.039	$(−.035)$
	Peer group size	.024	$(.008)$
Demographic	Age	.000	$(.000)$
	Race	.067	$(.469)^b$
	Rural/urban	−.012	$(−.073)$
Family violence	Parents spanked	−.006	$(−.015)$
	Parents hit	.076	$(.421)^b$
Criminal orientation		.083	$(.113)^b$
Personal/psychological	Times in love	.074	$(.413)^a$
	Depression	.101	$(.081)^a$
Powerlessness	Powerlessness	.061	$(.046)^b$
	Income adequacy	−.009	$(−.026)$

NOTE: $R^2 = .240$, $N = 1,129$. Race (nonaboriginal coded 0, Aboriginal coded 1), Rural/urban (rural coded 0, urban coded 1). All coefficients are ordinary least squares regression coefficients. Unstandardized coefficients are in parentheses. Dependent variable is logged, as are drug use, criminal orientation, parents hit, and times in love.
a. Significant beyond .01
b. Significant beyond .05

may provide a more male-oriented context in which violence is collectively tolerated than do urban societies (Bergman, 1992). But, it may be that rural societies are not more tolerant of violence; instead, there is an ethos that intimate violence is a private matter and is not to be discussed or pursued as a social problem (Schissel & Robertson, in press). Furthermore, there is a growing body of important work that seeks to understand the effects that years of colonialist oppression have had on Aboriginal peoples in Canada, especially with respect to violence among First Nations communities. Therefore, I incorporate a dichotomous race variable in the following regression analysis to test whether being of Aboriginal ancestry has an effect on dating violence.

Table 2 presents the regression analysis testing the simultaneous effects of the previously discussed influences on dating violence for male youth. The table is constructed so that the variables are grouped according to the logical categories of substance use, attachments to conventional institutions, family violence, criminality, powerlessness, and psychoemotional influences.

Quite clearly, the most obvious influences on dating violence involve substance abuse. Alcohol consumption, with a standardized regression coefficient of .20, has the greatest influence of any of the variables in the model, and, as expected, the greater the alcohol use, the higher the levels of dating violence. A similar, yet weaker influence occurs for drug use (beta .090). For the variables that measure attachment to conventional activities, it is interesting that none of these influences is significant, in contradiction to the literature based on social control theory that argues that these attachments are fundamental to prosocial, well-adjusted personalities and behaviors. It should also be noted that none of the background variables is significant, with the exception of the race variable. The positive coefficient (.067), although relatively weak, suggests that violence in a dating context is more common for Aboriginal than non-Aboriginal youth. This suggests, as Aboriginal leaders have argued for years, that the historical and contemporary oppression of First Nations has left a legacy of violence and dysfunction (Monture-Angus, 1999; York, 1990).

As for the variables tapping experiences of violence, corporal punishment has no statistically significant effect on dating violence, but whether the respondent experienced being hit by a parent does. In effect, these variables help us understand the impact that violence against children has on future offending by indicating that it is the unpremeditated, nondisciplinary violence by parents or caregivers that has the substantial impact on a youth's future violent behavior, at least in a dating context. I do not mean to suggest that corporal punishment does not create an atmosphere of childhood trauma, but the results of my research do suggest that unpremeditated violence is more damaging than the premeditated, disciplinary form. It is important to realize here as well that the analysis has essentially controlled for parenting quality through the operationalization of family attachment (which includes variables on closeness to parents and affinity with family).

The criminal orientation variable illustrates quite clearly that those male youth who have broken the law and been caught are disposed to higher levels of violence against female youth. This suggests, as discussed previously, that there may be an antisocial orientation for male youth who have engaged in criminal behavior that is part of a behavior pattern that includes violence against women. It is also conceivable that youth learn violence as they are processed and confined in the legal/welfare system. The data, however, are based on self-report criminal activity and not on experiences in the legal system, so it is difficult to parcel out the iatrogenic effect of the justice system.

The last four variables provide some insight into the psychological context of intergender violence and are intended to study how a young man's psychological state affects how he acts toward the opposite sex. The variable "times in love," for example, indicates, in part, the respondent's perception of the affection involved in the dating relationship. The literature on intimate violence against women is quite clear in its insistence that the revolving door of intimate violence is ironically often perceived by the offender and victim as a deeply loving relationship (Mcleod, 1987; Walker, 1984). Here, we see that the number of times in love does have a significant impact (.074) on violence, and, as expected, the more times a male youth is in love (by self-declaration), the more that youth engages in intergender violence. It could be merely that the more in love a person is, the greater the opportunities for violence are. However, given that the model controls for age and other sociodemographic variables, it is defensible that the variable also largely measures self-perceptions of the degree of romantic involvement. Consistent with the literature on battering, this research suggests that the perception of being in love seems to be related to violence in intimate relationships.

The variables measuring depression and powerlessness show that damaging psychological states contribute to aggressive behavior. For example, the higher the levels of depression for male youth, the greater the degree of violence toward young women, controlling for psychic, social, and behavioral factors (.101). Similarly, the greater the degree of powerlessness, the greater the amount of violence against female youth. This is consistent with the literature on intimate violence, which suggests that men who feel relatively powerless tend to express their frustration and vengefulness in sexual relationships (Bowker, 1998; Dobash et al., 1992).

Overall, the foregoing prediction model provides a relatively clear picture of the origins of young male violence against young females. Abusive young men seem to have relatively high alcohol and drug use, they were damaged as children by their parents' unpremeditated violence toward them, they are involved in a criminal lifestyle, they express themselves as being in loving relationships with their victims, and they are psychically disposed to depression and powerlessness. The next part of this article looks at the types of communities in which young men learn their attitudes toward violence against young women.

PATRIARCHAL COMMUNITIES AND THE CULTURE OF VIOLENCE

The community sets the standards of tolerance and fosters a collective belief system that either lets sexism flourish or thwarts its growth and prevents its damage. If communities blame victims, they not only do not provide for the victims of assault, but they also foster a patriarchal ideology that privileges men and endangers women. If communities hold offenders responsible, they create the framework for the most effective violence prevention strategy: high demand for nonviolent behavior. I explore several examples of communities of youth, which create and foster sexism and violence against female youth, and examples of microcommunities that practice zero tolerance with extraordinary success.

The first example is based on Canadian and U.S. work on violence in sports. This work sees sport as a community that endangers, both physically and ideologically, the lives of girls and women. For example, Robinson (1998) documents the world of junior hockey and argues that organized hockey, from the age of eight to junior level, is a culture of misogyny and violence that has resulted in extremely violent sexual acts against young women that for the most part go unreported and/or unprosecuted. She documents gang rapes and single acts of sexual violence accompanied by death threats. The same "conspiracies of violence" have been documented in American football:

> Many big-time schools designate one coach or faculty member to protect the young athlete from the law. . . . Not surprisingly, several of our most famous athletes have found themselves involved in ugly scandals when whole segments of a team have engaged in gang-rape, a jovial college version of *jus primae noctis* in which the football hero expects to be accorded seignorial rights while

the local sheriff stands guard. (Michener, 1976; quoted in Miedzian, 1991).

Robinson (1998) explains these essentially conspiratorial violations of criminal law as the result of a combination of culture of masculinity and corporatism that is functional to men and highly profitable. Violence is contrived and controlled by marketing experts who "reduce young men to commodities that are bought and sold on the whim of older men who stand to make money by signing or trading the right player" (p. 2). The connection between corporate greed and the commodification of young male players is furthermore exemplified by the lengths to which owners and managers go in order to make sure that the players' crimes are never prosecuted. Essentially, she shows that "players are turned into products, commodified as youthful masculinity" (p. 11). Consequently, they grow up lacking essential skills, such as shopping, signing a chequebook, and budgeting, but more importantly, they come to have little sense of gender sensitivity and gender equity. They are essentially indifferent or misogynistic toward women.

Messner and Sabo (1994) discuss organized American athletics and document how the "culture of masculinity" filters through to the society in general. Their work shows that institutionalized masculine and feminine roles come to frame both the participation and the watching of sports. Organized sports is a social setting where children and youth learn not only gender roles but also sexual identity. Football, for example, has always juxtaposed the potent male athlete—aggressive, violent, and competent—and the provocative female cheerleader—adoring, sexual, and subservient. The language and the ethos of sports such as football promote and privilege the lone male, the one most valuable player. Messner and Sabo (1994) contend that this often "prevents male athletes from understanding women and their life experiences. Though women's voices may reach men's ears from the sidelines and grandstands, they remain distant and garbled by the clamor of male competition" (p. 39).

This distance between men and women, and girls and boys is the result of the historical exclusion of females from the male sport arena. Girls have been excluded from playing alongside boys. Witness the almost universal segregation in school physical education classes. The segregated context is accompanied by the language and practice of male sports that equate toughness and prowess within a male discourse; failure, kindness, and fairness, on the other hand, constitute a feminized discourse. Especially through the discourse of male athletics, girls and women are seen as "the other," in effect, the opponent or the enemy. It is conceivable that many young men engaged in or affected by watching athletics develop a view of the opposite sex as a thing to be feared and conquered. The "ya throw like a girl" mentality becomes part of a popular belief system, which, although seemingly innocuous, is about disdain and indifference.

This sexist belief system, although not exclusive to schools, is probably most covertly and overtly influential in the education system. Schools do not intend to produce masculinities and femininities, but the construction of student identity occurs through negotiation in a context that circumscribes behavior and discourse. If the school football team is held up as the epitome of achievement and participation, then how a student orients himself or herself to the school subculture of football determines popularity, social involvement, and ultimately social and academic success. By privileging "male, aggressive" sports, schools are actively involved in producing masculinities. By rewarding masculinist activities, schools covertly encourage male aggression in sports as a substitute for legitimate academic achievement. Males, especially working class males, find a substitute for academic failure in the masculine world of school sports. For example,

> Masculinity is organized on the macro-scale around social power. Social power in terms of access to higher education, entry to professions, command of communication, is being delivered to the boys who are academic "successes." The reaction of the "failed" is likely to be a claim to other sources of power, even other definitions of masculinity. Sporting prowess, physical aggression, sexual conquest may do. (Connell, 1989, p. 295)

The pursuit of masculine forms of identity serves to empower when more mainstream forms of empowerment are blocked. It is important, therefore, to restate the importance of powerlessness in conceptualizing an explanatory model of male violence.

A body of literature and research extends the study of masculine sports both metaphorically and literally in the context of war and conscription. The main focus of this research is that war, like sports, constructs an idealized view of what it means to be a man. The masculinities of soldiers, much like the masculinities of male athletes, are enveloped by an ethos of absolute victory, of the enemy as a feminized other, and of the currency of rage and violence (McBride, 1995). War is about men and about excluding women, but more importantly, it is about gendering a world in which male activity—as normal—is adjudicated on the bases of the efficiency and the duty of violence, whether violence is against the enemy male, the enemy's women, or women in general. Importantly, the military and sports culture influence extends well beyond war and the arena into "for example, organizational culture where military and warlike metaphors are used by managers, of at least the post-war generation, to describe their work experiences" (Peterson, 1998, p. 55).

The masculinist paradigm of war and sports extends well beyond this to the world of entertainment in which youth idols are most often seen as variations of Rambo, Hulk Hogan, or the Terminator, a vicarious world in which male youth acquire much of their information about heroism and masculinity (Miedzian, 1991). Karner's (1998) work, based on oral histories of Vietnam veterans, illustrates how an ethos of masculinity framed within a paradigm of patriotism, racism, and sexism quickly converts to a world of unbridled cruelty and destruction, especially in a wartime context. She describes how the young male's search for male identity became pathological:

> Their quest for manhood initially led them to the military and into combat, which in turn left them with a continuing need to find acceptance as men, which has led them to participate in what I have elsewhere called "toxic masculinity"—aspects of the gendered culture that influenced the veteran's behaviors in detrimental and pernicious ways. (1998, p. 231)

Another example of communities that foster sexist violence against women and girls is based on a study by Schissel and Robertson (in press) that investigated male violence against women in an agrarian-based rural community. They focused on women who were abused by their husbands, but the overall research studied a culture of masculinity that is tied to the patriarchal and patrilineal nature of traditional and modern-day prairie agriculture. The findings are indicative of the linkages between patriarchy, economy, and culture, for the nature of spousal violence in rural areas reflects the geographic and sociocultural nature of the rural community.

For example, on average, rural women stay in abusive relationships 5 to 7 years longer than their urban counterparts. The reasons they remain are complex and involve farm/business ownership issues and family legacies (women, in many cases, are blamed for the discord and ultimately for the threat to the family-based economic unit), the stigma of a close-knit community, physical isolation, lack of financial alternatives, and lack of programs for victims of abuse. Furthermore, rural family violence is typical in that high rates of alcohol abuse are involved (about 70% of all cases of abuse involve alcohol). Abuse is also more prevalent in bad economic times, and a culture of denial exists in rural communities that tends to hide the reality of family violence by fostering an ethos of privacy and individual mother/wife responsibility. Lastly, traditionally rural peoples rely on family and friends for support more than do urban people; as a consequence, when families/social networks are disrupted (primarily through economic upheavals), rural residents are especially vulnerable to interpersonal violence. This reality occurs in a context in which rural victims of violence generally do not rely on professional support (given the tremendous stigma attached to abuse), and, when this support is available, it is often based on an urban model of care that is insensitive to the cultural and economic needs of rural peoples.

Finally, as rural areas experience increasing depopulation, and rural economies become increasingly tenuous, families become further isolated and vulnerable. What is left, then, is a culture and a physical context in which young children observe violence, observe the privacy and stigma attached to wife and child abuse, and observe violence as a way of dealing with socioeconomic problems, especially acute in modern-day agrarian communities.

The cultural practices of farming and lineage support the patriarchal nature of family life in rural areas. Farms, traditionally and contemporarily, are passed on from fathers to sons, and the wealth passed on is tremendous. Many women who are abused in farm family situations are caught between asserting their rights to property and input and facing proscription from husband and family. When abuse occurs, the woman as wife and mother is often isolated from the owning family, and when violence ensues, she is often blamed for the discord (Schissel & Robertson, in press). Young males who are raised in a context in which their lineage and financial heritage are paramount and in which women as mothers are subdued and abused, have little room but to grow up believing that such domineering patriarchal behavior is the norm.

A poignant case-study example that illustrates the foregoing contention is based on the Colin Thatcher murder of his former wife, JoAnn Wilson, in 1984. Siggins (1985) chronicles the story of the murder but more importantly illustrates the culture in which the violence occurred and in which the sons of Colin Thatcher, as inheritors of the agricultural and political legacy of the Thatcher political name, came to view their mother and her inherent right to the family wealth as dishonorable. The culture of men described by Siggins is an example of how sexist masculinities grow in a political-economic context. As socialist feminists suggest, patriarchy and political economy are inextricably joined.

FOSTERING A NONSEXIST, NONVIOLENT SOCIETY

This article offers several visions for understanding and dealing with young male violence against females. The empirical analysis indicates that young male violence, in part, rests in the psychosocial domain in which feelings of powerlessness and depression increase the likelihood of young men using violence against women. Furthermore, this world of psychosocial trauma is often a world in which alcohol and drug abuse exacerbate the problems of violence and in which a criminal history is relatively likely. Importantly, it is also a world in which parental violence, especially in an unpremeditated form, is responsible for a young man's predisposition to violence against women. The social policy implications are clear: Programs addressing violence must account for the historical import of family violence, substance abuse, and psychic trauma.

I have also presented descriptions of a male cultural milieu in which women are devalued, both structurally and linguistically. Also, as we have seen in the case of both sports and agricultural communities, the patriarchal culture is strongly associated with the culture of making money; the welfare of both the abused and the abuser is subordinate to the pursuit of profit. In the world of organized youth athletics, for example, the sexist language and treatment of girls and boys denigrates both and advantages those who see young male athletes as potentially valuable commodities. Similarly, farming, because heritage and business are so closely tied with ownership, profit, and male privilege, is a context in which women are often discarded both economically and physically. Men comply through their own patriarchal ascriptions or because they too are damaged by the economic culture. Again, global economics and politics have created an agricultural environment in which farms and farmers are disappearing, and the trauma that farmers suffer is astonishing as evidenced by the increasing incidence of suicide and mental health problems among Canadian farmers. Ironically, as male farmers endure inordinate stress, they attack those with whom they are closest, damaging their intimate relationships. The patriarchal culture of agriculture, for the most part, allows this disease to go untreated, and generations of men grow up believing that the trauma of farming is normal, or at least necessary, and that violence against girls and women is justified because girls and women pose an ostensible threat to the intact farm.

There are, however, places and institutions that are able to deal with the ravages of patriarchal cultures and organizations. Importantly, in the examples that follow, the baseline rule of zero-tolerance of violence is unwavering, and the nongendered treatment of boys and girls living through and experiencing the same things is axiomatic. Schools are the places where issues of gender tolerance should be encouraged without exception within academic, social, and sport pursuits. Schools that actually do this are rare; the following descriptions provide examples of what can be accomplished.

Joe Duquette Alternative High School is an inner-city school in Saskatoon, Canada. Its students are primarily Aboriginal and in the final three grades of their high school years. Many students do not "fit" in the "regular" education system and could be said to be "high risk" in that they are unattached to families or communities and quite susceptible to confrontations with the law. The school's policy on violence, especially intergender violence, is formal and unequivocal. When someone abuses someone else, either verbally or physically, he or she has two choices. The student can either leave the school or take the option of apologizing and making reparation by taking it on him or herself to ensure that the person abused feels secure during the remainder of the school year. Simply put, abusing students are responsible, as much as possible, for protecting their original victim from verbal and physical abuse. This accomplishes two fundamentally important things: It creates protracted empathy between the abuser and the abused, and, in cases of males abusing females, it provides a context in which boys and girls are able to interact as people rather than as genders. This philosophy of gender equality occurs in a school context in which healthy lifestyles are discussed in relation to Aboriginal spirituality and healing (Haig-Brown, Hodgson-Smith, Regnier, & Archibald, 1997). The resulting belief system is one in which respect for others, especially gendered, sexualized, and racialized others, is closely tied to culture/spirituality. Thus, when young men learn respect for young women, they do so as part of a general respect for all the earth and its inhabitants.

The Aboriginal community of LaRonge in Northern Saskatchewan has taken similar steps in its community sports program in reaction to the sexism and violence that was characteristic of the community hockey program. The town council decided that, based on the principles of respect and caring, the community hockey program needed to change in three fundamental ways. First, the community did away with contact in the game and replaced the hard traditional hockey puck with a soft, safe alternative puck. Second, the town directors declared that all hockey teams would have both boys and girls playing on the same team. Third, they declared that all community members would have access to ice time with preference to no group. The community addressed, in a very basic way, the deficits and dangers inherent in organized hockey, which were previously described in this article.

The most important example of school-based programs that directly confront the problems of gendered abuse, however, is that of Princess Alexandria Elementary School in Saskatoon (Schissel, 1997). Princess Alexandria School in Saskatoon is a community-based elementary school situated in one of the poorer inner-city areas and is characterized by a relatively high marginalized and transient population. Both the school and the community deal with issues typical of communities that are relegated to the margins of society, including street crime, drug and alcohol abuse, and family dysfunction. Many of the students, as a result, are highly disadvantaged when they enter their school years.

The school has taken upon itself the task of creating a healing and nurturing environment in which violence and punishment have no place. The school's philosophy of mutual respect and responsibility is a direct attempt to address violence and abuse in a forthright and nonstigmatizing way. For example, when confronted with abusive situations, the school meets as a community of children and adults in an open forum. When an 11-year-old girl had been sexually assaulted outside the school, the teachers, all the children, a social worker, and an elder met to discuss issues of assault and abuse in an open environment with the expressed purpose of destigmatizing the victim and promoting understanding between male and female students, especially with respect to gendered victimizations. The overall purpose of such activity is to deal with specific traumatic incidents by placing them in the context of general issues of safety, security, and gender sensitivity. As a result, the trauma of the victim is shared by the school community. Such efforts permit the student to return to school in an atmosphere of understanding and not a gendered atmosphere of pity and fear. The school also deals with issues of sexual exploitation and sexually transmitted diseases—other dimensions of gendered violence—in the same community context. The result is an education program that is essentially an ongoing forum about issues of gender and respect.

Classroom-based violence prevention programs in school are important because they provide exposure to the issues surrounding sexism and violence, especially with respect to the abandonment of sexual violence myths (Macgowan, 1997). Other programs have detected short-term changes in attitudes among male students, although they are somewhat hesitant to argue for long-term change (Avery-Leaf, Cascardi, O'Leary, & Cano, 1997; Hilton, Harris, Rice, Krans, & Lavigne, 1998). The problem with classroom-based programs is that they may teach and preach, but they do little to create a real-life atmosphere in which males and females gain empathy for one another. The school programs described above go well beyond instruction by creating a gestalt in which mutual respect and experience-based understanding should preclude not only gender violence but all violence.

When schools and communities mandate that male and female children and youth participate together (e.g., in sports), they create the potential conditions under which sexist stereotypes break down (Messner & Sabo, 1994). The problem remains, however, that giving girls equal opportunity to boys and putting them in the same "arena" may do nothing to break down stereotypes or to create empathy. If the institution is based on an ethic of domination and submission (e.g., winning at all costs and aggression as valuable)—and many competitive sports seem to embrace such an ethos—then the environment, although integrated, is still disabling. That is why school-based programs that get at the heart of intolerance by creating a "community" (for at least several hours a day) that functions with an ethos of gender integration are important and revolutionary.

Finally, on this issue of community, I hearken back to the discussions surrounding agricultural communities and patriarchal violence. Although men and women work side-by-side in agriculture, even to the extent that women are owners and operators, the fact that violence against women as spouses persists in rural areas suggests that the culture frames the socialization of boys and girls. The prevailing belief is that violence is a family matter and, therefore, a private matter. The perception that patrimony is vital to family farming and that somehow the community will miraculously care for its victims reveals that there are alarmingly dysfunctional gendered relationships in rural areas. Certainly, programs for men who batter are part of the solution for dysfunctional men, but it would seem that men, especially in farming communities, could deal with sexism through voluntary activities including coaching, boys and girls clubs, and service organizations. How the sensitivity to gender and nonviolence filter to all men in isolated communities, however, is a fundamental problem. The solution must lie, in part, in collective and individual strategies that men generate and sustain.

For rural communities, shelters, crisis centers, and antiviolence programs in schools are badly needed short-term solutions, but they fall short of providing a living context in which sexual egalitarianism becomes the norm and not the exception. Programs to fight male violence against females—especially for children and youth—must get at the need for mutual experience. Nonsexist, nonviolent communities do not foster the segregation of the sexes, but rather they encourage an atmosphere in which males and females are naturally together. The best alternative schools do just that as do some of the more progressive school and community sports programs; moreover, the best of their programs start to sensitize children to gender equity at a very early age.

Finally, I wish to address the overarching theme of what men can do to prevent violence. Although the focus of this article has been on the structural context in which young men learn sexist attitudes and transfer learned violence to women, the initiatives I have described, which attempt to redress contexts of violence, provide ample opportunity for men to participate collectively and individually in positive social transformation. For example, within the context of sports, coaches, trainers, and teachers who are conscious of the inherent sexism in sports can make a considerable difference as they make concerted efforts to avoid sexist language and prohibit sexist behavior among players and spectators, engage girls as well as boys in the same activities, encourage participation rather than domination and, most importantly, work to rid sports of deliberate violence. Coaches are in a very powerful position as mentors and role models, and male coaches work in a context in which they have considerable potential to address both the immediate and long term consequences of violence (especially gendered violence) within and without sports.

The same argument could easily be made for men in positions of authority in other gendered contexts: the school, the community, and especially the family. The family context is important as it addresses several of the important issues presented in the empirical section of this article. For example, the overwhelming influence of substance abuse on dating violence suggests that drug use and especially alcohol use, as learned behaviors, are the results of children and youth emulating adult behavior. Although there are proscriptions against drinking for children and youth, such proscriptions are placed against cultural representations that value the connection between alcohol and the good life: athletic prowess, manliness, hard work, and dating success. It would be logical to assume that if men provide the role models for drinking, they could and should also be role models for abstinence or sensible substance use. The empirical analyses in this article also illustrate the consistently damaging effects of family violence; once again, the importance that men, as fathers, have in stopping the generational transmission of violence cannot be overstated.

How young men come to observe and emulate compassionate male role models is the important social policy question. Within the best alternative schools, many of the initiatives that deal with substance abuse and violence tend to avoid punitive strategies and attempt to provide adult role models, especially men, who do not drink or use drugs and who never resort to punishment or any form of verbal or physical chastisement. The strategy is that adult mentoring and role modeling are much more sensible and efficient than moralizing or proscriptions. Given that many of the youths in alternative schools have been exposed to a great deal of violence and substance abuse in both familial and nonfamilial contexts, the strategy of mentoring seems to work very well in providing substitute father figures. Although this research indicates the need for family-based programs that deal with constructive, gender-sensitive fathering, in the absence of such programs, good schools seem to provide a substitute family context that works in redressing sexist, aggression-based socialization. The responsibility lies not only with institutions that provide for youth, but also with individual men in positions of respect who have profound opportunities to make immediate and long-term changes to gendered and nongendered violence.

APPENDIX A
Factor Analysis on the Items Used to Generate the Scale for the Construct *Violence Toward Female Youth*

Question	Common Factor Unrotated Matrix
Pushed, grabbed, or shoved a girlfriend	.796
Slapped a girlfriend	.727
Kicked, hit, or bit a girlfriend	.714
Insulted/swore at your girlfriend	.693
Threw, hit, or kicked something	.534

NOTE: Questions based on a five response Likert-type scale. Eigenvalue = 4.234, percent of variation = 35.3, and Cronbach's alpha = .852

APPENDIX B
Factor Analysis on the Items Used to Generate the Scale for the Construct *Family Attachment*

Question	Common Factor Unrotated Matrix
My family gets along well together	.660
My family is better than most	.622
My parents treat me fairly	.623
I enjoy being at home with my family	.828
I like spending time with my family	.743

NOTE: Questions based on a five response Likert-type scale. Eigenvalue = 3.19, percent of variation = 39.9, and Cronbach's alpha = .834.

APPENDIX C
Factor Analysis on the Items Used to Generate the Scale for the Construct *Attachment to Friends*

Question	Common Factor Unrotated Matrix
My friends are nice to me	.785
My friends will help me if I need it	.705
My friends are mean to me (reverse coded)	.689
I wish I had different friends (reverse coded)	.616
I have enough friends	.370

NOTE: Questions based on a five response Likert-type scale. Eigenvalue = 2.77, percent of variation = 25.2, and Cronbach's alpha = .776.

APPENDIX D

Items Used to Generate the Scale for the Construct *Attachment to School*
 1. Are you satisfied with your grades (never, seldom, sometimes, often, a lot)?
 2. Do you take part in school activities such as sports teams, clubs, music, art, and so forth (never, seldom, sometimes, often, a lot)?

Items Used to Generate the Scale for the Construct *Criminal Orientation*

How many times in the past year have you
 1. used physical force to get money or things?
 2. attacked someone with a weapon or fists, to the point at which the person needed medical attention?
 3. got into a fight just for the hell of it?

APPENDIX E
Factor Analysis on the Items Used to Generate the Scale for the Construct *Depression*

Question	Common Factor Rotated Matrix
How often in the past few months have you	
felt depressed?	.686
felt lonely?	.632
felt like people were unfriendly?	.521
talked less than usual?	.508
felt happy (reverse coded)?	.429

NOTE: Questions based on a five response Likert-type scale. Eigenvalue = 3.27, percent of variation = 27.2, and Cronbach's alpha = .700.

REFERENCES

Agnew, R. (1985). Social control theory and delinquency: A longitudinal test. *Criminology, 23,* 47-61.

Avery-Leaf, M., Cascardi, M., O'Leary, K., & Cano, A. (1997). Efficacy of a dating violence prevention program on attitudes justifying aggression. *Journal of Adolescent Health, 21,* 11-17.

Bergman, L. (1992). Dating violence among high school students. *Social Work, 37,* 21-27.

Bowker, L. H. (Ed.). (1998). *Masculinities and violence.* Thousand Oaks, CA: Sage.

Connell, R. W. (1989). Cool guys, swots and wimps: The interplay of masculinity and education. *Oxford Review of Education, 15,* 291-303.

DeKeseredy, W. S. (1988). *Woman abuse in dating relationships: The role of male peer support.* Toronto: Canadian Scholars Press.

DeKeseredy, W. S., & Schwartz, M. D. (1998). *Woman abuse on campus: Results from the Canadian national survey.* Thousand Oaks, CA: Sage.

Dobash, R., Dobash, R. E., Wilson, M., & Daly, M. (1992). The myth of sexual symmetry in marital violence. *Social Problems, 39,* 71-91.

Durant, R., Cadenced, C., Pendergrast, R., Slavens, G., & Linder, C. (1994). Factors associated with the use of violence among urban Black adolescents. *American Journal of Public Health, 84,* 612-617.

Eron. L., Gentry, J., & Schlegel, P. (1994). *Reason to hope: A psychological perspective on violence and youth.* Washington, DC: American Psychological Association.

Farrington, D. (1991). Childhood aggression and adult violence: Early predictors and later life outcomes. In D. Pepler & K. Rubin (Eds.), *The development and treatment of childhood aggression* (pp. 5-30). Hillsdale, NJ: Erlbaum.

Fischer, A., & Good, G. (1998). Perceptions of parent-child relationships and masculine role conflicts of college men. *Journal of Counseling Psychology, 45,* 346-352.

Foo, L., & Margolin, G. (1995). A multivariate investigation of dating aggression. *Journal of Family Violence, 10,* 351-377.

Haig-Brown, C., Hodgson-Smith, K., Regnier, R., & Archibald, J. A. (1997). *Making the spirit dance within: Joe Duquette High School and an Aboriginal community.* Toronto: Lorimer.

Hilton, N. Z., Harris, G., Rice, M., Krans, T., & Lavigne, S. (1998). Anti-violence education in high schools. *Journal of Interpersonal Violence, 13,* 726-742.

Hirschi, T. (1969). *Causes of delinquency.* Berkeley: University of California Press.

Karner, T. X. (1998). Engendering violent men: Oral histories of military masculinity. In L. H. Bowker (Ed.), *Masculinities and violence* (pp. 197-232). Thousand Oaks, CA: Sage.

Kupers, T. (1999). *Prison madness: The mental health crisis behind bars and what we must do about it.* San Francisco: Jossey-Bass.

Macgowan, M. (1997). An evaluation of a dating violence prevention program for middle school students. *Violence and Victims, 12,* 223-235.

Makepeace, J. (1986). Gender differences in courtship violence victimization. *Family Relations, 35,* 383-388.

McBride, J. (1995). *War, battering, and other sports: The gulf between American men and women.* Atlantic Highlands, NJ: Humanities Press.

McLeod, L. (1987). *Battered but not beaten.* Ottawa: Canadian Advisory Council on the Status of Women.

Messner, M., & Sabo, D. (1994). *Sex, violence and power in sports: Rethinking masculinity.* Freedom, CA: Crossing Press.

Michener, J. A. (1976). *Sports in America.* New York: Random House.

Miedzian, M. (1991). *Boys will be boys: Breaking the link between masculinity and violence.* New York: Doubleday.

Monture-Angus, P. (1999). Standing against Canadian law: Naming omissions of race, culture, and gender. In E. Comack (Ed.), *Locating law: Race, class, gender connections* (pp. 76-288). Halifax: Fernwood.

Nichols, M. (1999, February 22). Men's health. *Maclean's,* 29-39.

Norris, J., George, W., Cue Davis, K., Martell, J., & Leonesio, R. J. (1999). Alcohol and hypermasculinity as determinants of men's empathic responses to violent pornography. *Journal of Interpersonal Violence, 14,* 683-700.

Patterson, G., & Yeorger, K. (1993). Development models for delinquent behavior. In S. Hodgin (Ed.), *Mental disorder and crime* (pp. 140-172). Newbury Park, CA: Sage.

Peterson, A. (1998). *Unmasking the masculine: Men and identity in a sceptical age.* London: Sage.

Riggs. D., & O'Leary, K. (1996). Aggression between dating partners: An explanation of a causal model of courtship aggression. *Journal of Interpersonal Violence, 11,* 519-540.

Robinson, L. (1998). *Crossing the line: Violence and sexual assault in Canada's national sport.* Toronto: McClelland and Stewart.

Rosen, L. (1985). Family and delinquency: Structure or function. *Criminology, 23,* 553-573.

Samuelson, L., Hartnagel, T., & Krahn, H. (1990). Crime and social control among high school dropouts. *Journal of Crime and Justice, 18,* 129-161.

Schissel, B. (1997). *Blaming children: Youth crime, moral panics and the politics of hate.* Halifax, NS: Fernwood.

Schissel, B., & Robertson, A. (in press). Rural sustainability and violence against women: Public and private jeopardy. *Health and Canadian Society.*

Seidler, V. (1989). *Rediscovering masculinity: Reason, language, and sexuality.* London: Routledge.

Siggins, M. (1985). *A Canadian tragedy: Joann and Colin Thatcher: A story of love and hate.* Toronto: Macmillan.

Simons, R., Lin, K. H., & Gordon, L .C. (1998). Socialization in the family of origin and male dating violence: A prospective study. *Journal of Marriage and the Family, 60,* 467-478.

Straus, M. A., Gelles, R. J., Steinmetz, S. K. (1980). *Behind closed doors: Violence in the American family.* New York: Anchor Books.

Straus, M. A., & Smith, C. (1990). Violence in Hispanic families in the United States: Incidence rates and structural interpretations. In M. A. Straus & R. J. Gelles (Eds.), *Physical violence in American families: Risk factors and adaptions to violence in 8,145 families* (pp. 341-368). New Brunswick, NJ: Transaction.

Walker, L. (1984). *The battered woman syndrome*. New York: Springer.

York, G. (1990). *The dispossessed: Life and death in native Canada*. Toronto: Little Brown.

Bernard Schissel is professor of sociology at the University of Saskatchewan. He has published articles in Youth and Society, Social Science Research, *and* Social Justice. *He is also the author of* Blaming Children: Youth Crime, Moral Panics and the Politics of Hate *and* The Social Dimensions of Canadian Youth Justice.

Part VI
Explanations of Violence as Socially Constructed

[22]

'The Violence We Have Lost'? Body Counts, Historians and Interpersonal Violence in England

John E. Archer[*]
Edge Hill University College

Late Victorian commentators felt able to congratulate themselves on the growing civility of English society. Hard evidence for this decline in lawlessness was to be found in the decline of interpersonal violence, especially homicide and murder in particular, as recorded in the annual parliamentary criminal statistics between the 1850s and 1914. Historians have located this decline as belonging to a much longer term drop in homicides, which can be traced back to the Middle Ages. This essay will argue that historians' approaches to the subject of violence have been restricted both in terms of methodology and content. In the former case they have shown an over-reliance on the veracity of statistical data and have restricted themselves in the main to studies of the most extreme form of interpersonal violence, murder. These two interrelated limitations, the reliance on statistics and the focus on murder, have recently been placed under critical scrutiny by Howard Taylor in his seminal study which places homicide and murder in a whole new perspective[1]. The decline in murder experienced by England and Wales, he concludes, may have been statistical rather than real. This essay proposes to examine the histo-

---

[*] This paper is based on examples drawn from a project on 'Violence in the North West with Special Reference to Liverpool and Manchester 1850-1914' funded by the Economic and Social Research Council (award number L133251004) as part of the *Violence Research Programme.* My thanks are extended to Jo Jones, the project research officer, for the newspaper references and to Andrew Davies for his helpful advice.
[1] Howard TAYLOR, 'Rationing Crime: the Political Economy of Criminal Statistics Since the 1850s', in *Economic History Review,* LI, 3, 1998, pp. 569-590.

[*Memoria y Civilización* 2, 1999, 171-190]

riography of the study of interpersonal violence and provide evidence, mainly taken from the North West of England, in support of a qualitative approach to violence.

The most frequent approach adopted by historians to the study of criminal behaviour has been in the form of broad historical surveys which have utilised statistics and quantification. Gatrell and Hadden, in their pioneering work 27 years ago, were more than aware of the many pitfalls in counting crime[2]. In spite of all these drawbacks the statistical analytical approach was, in their opinion, worth pursuing. This appeared to be confirmed when Gatrell published his seminal and influential study on the decline of theft and violence between 1850 and 1914[3]. In this essay he persuasively argued that the rate of trials for indictable crime declined and that furthermore this decline was real or actual for a number of reasons. First, the nature, quality and accuracy of governmental statistics became more detailed and fuller from 1857 and were further refined in 1892. Second, England and Wales became fully policed as a result of the 1856 County and Borough Policing Act. Consequently the state was able to increase its surveillance and control over a population which increasingly came to accept the presence and role of the police. Arising from this fact was the implication that the working classes along with other social groups were prepared to report and prosecute crimes of violence. As a result Gatrell was able to conclude that 'the rate of recorded crime crept ever closer to the rate of actual crime' and that all forms of interpersonal violence, with the exception of sexual violence, declined in the second half of the nineteenth century[4].

This important conclusion was examined in more focused studies which analysed long-term trends in crimes of violence. Gurr, whilst

---

[2] V.A.C. GATRELL and T. B. HADDEN, 'Nineteenth-Century Criminal Statistics and their Interpretation, in E.A. WRIGLEY (ed.), Nineteenth-Century Society: Essays on the Use of Quantitative Methods for the Study of Social Data, Cambridge, Cambridge University Press, 1972.

[3] V.A.C. GATRELL, 'The Decline of Theft and Violence in Victorian and Edwardian England', in V.A.C. GATRELL, BRUCE LENMAN and GEOFFREY PARKER (eds.), *Crime and the Law: the Social History of Crime in Western Europe Since* 1500, London, Europa, 1980.

[4] V.A.C. GATRELL, 'Decline...', pp. 250-251, 286.

acknowledging the unknowable but large 'dark figure' of unreported crime, contended murder has been the most widely and accurately reported crime because it was the most difficult to conceal and gave rise to most public anger[5]. Moreover as a criminal act it was probably prosecuted more fully than other crimes not only because of its seriousness but also, as most historical studies have shown, because the victim was frequently known to the offender who consequently was more liable to arrest and prosecution. Two other important factors lend homicide and especially murder to historical analysis. First, murder has left its mark in official records well before the advent of police forces. Sudden deaths and most especially violent deaths became the subject of official scrutiny in the coroner's court by the Middle Ages. Second, murder, being the most serious of crimes, has been subject to less definitional and legal change than other forms of criminal actions which have been reclassified, redefined and downgraded in seriousness. For historians the main distinctions within the homicide category have been murder, manslaughter and infanticide and so long as these were recognised and allowed for, historians have been willing to identify long-term movements. Gurr, for example, has been able to conclude that English homicide rates have declined dramatically from about 1200 and that rates of violent crime were 'probably 10 and possibly 20 or more times higher' in medieval and early Modern England than in the twentieth century[6].

This decline continued so that by the sixteenth and seventeenth centuries the homicide rate had dropped to five and 10 times higher than the 1980s, which led Stone to conclude confidently; 'it is hard to see how it is possible to challenge the weight of evidence for a great secular decline of homicide, the most serious of all crimes of violence, over five centuries, especially rapid between about 1660 and 1800[7]. The idea that England had enjoyed a peaceful bygone era was, in Stone's opinion, a nonsense. In his response to Stone, Jim

---

[5] T.R. GURR, 'Historical Trends in Violent Crime: A Critical Review of the Evidence', in *Crime and Justice: An Annual Review of Research,* III, 1981, pp.296-298. This can also be found in T.R. GURR (ed.), *Violence in America, Vol. 1,* New York, F. A. Praeger, 1969.

[6] T.R. GURR, 'Historical Trends...', p.312.

[7] L. STONE, 'Interpersonal Violence in English Society 1300-1800', in *Past and Present,* 101, 1983, see especially p.25 and p.32.

Sharpe accepted the downward trend but he introduced a new note of caution in so far as the measurement of homicide rates per 100,000 of the population failed to tell us about how violence was perceived by society. Were the Tudors, for example, conscious of living in a violent age? In joining what he termed as 'the violence we have lost' debate, Cockburn has provided the most detailed evidence for the decline in the homicide rate. Based on his study of Kent between 1560 and 1980 he has shown that the decline has not been constant, there being a period of stagnation in the eighteenth century, followed by a slow and steady fall from 1800 when the rate was 1.6/100,000 of the population to 0.3/100,000 in 1971. Nationally the homicide rate displays a similar trend, the decline being from 1.8/100,000 in 1841 to 0.3/100,000 in 1951[8]. Thus a consensus has been reached among historians, namely that there has been a long-term decline in homicides and most importantly for the purposes of this essay, both the homicide and murder rates continued to fall in the nineteenth century.

Why this decline in homicides occurred has presented historians with a harder question which has not as yet been satisfactorily answered. Explanations, which have remained largely general in tone and detail, have identified a number of possibilities, not least the 'civilising effects' of religion, education and environmental reform', the convergence of an increasingly policed society and a society which found violence unacceptable, the growth of the market economy in which crimes against property as opposed to the person predominated. This growing sensitisation and the change in popular manners were arguably responsible for both a decline in violence and an absolute decline in murder[9].

---

[8] J. A. SHARPE, 'The History of Violence in England: Some Observations', in *Past and Present*, 108, 1985, pp.206-215. This and the 'Rejoinder' from L. STONE, *Past and Present*, 108, 1985, pp.216-224, took on an increasingly ill-tempered tone. A moderating voice came from J.S. COCKBURN, 'Patterns of Violence in English Society: Homicide in Kent 1560-1985', in *Past and Present*, 130, 1991, pp.70-106.

[9] All the explanations to date have been vague see, for example, V.A.C. GATRELL, 'Decline...', pp. 293-294 and T. R. GURR, 'Historical Trends...', p. 300.

This then was the 'social fact' of the nineteenth century which Howard Taylor chose to examine, dissect and challenge. He too, like his predecessors, chose a statistical quantitative approach to his analysis. In his paper 'Rationing crime: the political economy of criminal statistics since the 1850s', Taylor noted how the criminal statistics of England and Wales developed a peculiar pattern after the mid-nineteenth century. Criminal trials in the upper law courts had, he observed, risen seven-fold between 1805 and 1842 but thereafter the growth had stopped and stagnated until about 1925. Crimes known to the police varied by only 20% either side of the mean and, most importantly and pertinently for this study, the pattern for murder was identical. The number of reported murders hovered 20% either side of the average of 150 a year between 1880 and 1966[10]. By identifying this pattern Taylor has challenged not only Gatrell's original and influential essay on the decline of theft and violence, he has also fundamentally brought into question the accuracy of the 'gold standard' of English criminal statistics, the annual recorded number of murders.

His explanations for this stagnation and even decline in both crime in general and murder in particular are mundane and persuasive. Prosecution costs, which were falling increasingly on the police and local authorities after the stopping of the Treasury Grant in 1887, forced the police to downgrade some crimes so that they could be dealt with more cheaply in the lower courts where convictions would also result in lighter and hence cheaper prison sentences. Moreover police efficiency in the second half of the nineteenth century was now measured in terms of declining crime figures within the police authorities' areas. The police therefore had a strong disincentive not to enter crimes into their statistics and, arising from that, not to detect and prosecute all crimes[11].

When Taylor's argument addresses the specific issue of murder his revelation with regards to the stagnation in the annual number of murders is in reality quite shocking and it dispels any lingering myths about the English being civilised, and by implication, more civilised

---

[10] Howard TAYLOR, 'Rationing Crime...' p.569.
[11] *Ibidem*, pp. 574-580.

than the rest of the world. He found that the average number of murders recorded annually for quarter century periods between 1875-1899 and 1925-1949 ranged between 149.32 and 148.76, and between 1862 and 1966 recorded murders only rose above 179/year or fell below 120/year on just five occasions. The investigation of murder, it would seem, was subject to financial considerations like everything else. Consequently the police solved easy to prove obvious murders which were comparatively cheap to prosecute. They may well have downgraded other cases to assaults and manslaughter, or accepted the verdicts of coroners' courts juries which found accidental deaths or suicides. Interestingly suicides rose sharply from 1314 in 1856 to 4054 by 1925[12]. Taylor was able to conclude that 'most murders and suspicious deaths went uninvestigated'[13].

His main arguments have not, as yet, been challenged nor too have they been accepted. Taylor has certainly forced historians to consider the prosecution process in the second half of the nineteenth century. A theme which warrants further investigation and analysis. He has also brought into sharp focus the possible naivety of the historical profession which blithely assumed that the murder figures were the least corrupted because of the seriousness of the charge. Whatever the costs of detection and prosecution it was assumed that murder was always thoroughly investigated by the police, at least that is what they told society and that is what we have always believed. Taylor has moreover forced crime historians to examine in a little more detail both how criminal statistics were constructed and, in the case of murder, other homicides and sudden deaths, the crucial role played by the coroner's court.

However certain lingering doubts and questions remain before Taylor's thesis can be embraced unequivocally[14]. At present his ar-

---

[12] *Ibidem*, pp. 583-588 deal specifically with murder and violent deaths. His findings came as a surprise and a shock to those who were present when he delivered a paper at The European Centre for the Study of Policing at the Open University seminar, February 1998.

[13] *Ibidem*, p.588.

[14] I owe a debt of gratitude to the North-West Historians of Crime and Policing who met at Liverpool University in October 1998 and discussed the implications of Taylor's article. Present at the meeting were Andrew Davies,

gument is portrayed in the broadest of terms; regional and local studies would need to be conducted to see if murders varied greatly. Murders in some of the larger towns and cities probably did fluctuate 20% either side of the average, but was there someone in the Director of Public Prosecutions' office who kept tight control of the figures so that they remained within the confines of the national norm? This would almost suggest some kind of conspiracy in which many officials, head constables, coroners *et al.*, were implicated. We must also ask whether the disproportionate rise in suicides necessarily reflected the stagnation or decline in murders; are the two related, in other words? There also appears an internal contradiction within the argument, for Taylor has stated that there were on average 150 murders a year because the funding allowed for that many. This implies that the cost of prosecuting each murder was approximately the same. Surely some murders were more costly and expensive to prosecute in terms of witnesses, forensic expertise and so forth, and this would have had important repercussions on the annual budget. Taylor might well counter this criticism by arguing that the varying costs in prosecuting murders would account for the fluctuations in the number of murders either side of the average. However we must be wary of providing monocausal explanations for the murder figures. All kinds of explanations can and have been provided for the downgrading of homicides, especially domestic disputes in the period prior to 1850, none of which were based on financial considerations[15].

Does Taylor provide enough documentary evidence in a sufficiently chronologically persuasive manner? His evidence seems to flit freely from the 1850s to the 1930s. The clinching evidence for Taylor's thesis must be the discovery of dead bodies which, to all intents and purposes, were those of murder victims but which were never counted as such; what Martin Wiener called 'smoking guns', which in the context of nineteenth-century England, were more likely to have been those who had been poisoned or suffocated.

Shani D'Cruze, Barry Godfrey, Helen Johnston, Jo Jones, John Locker, Frank Neal, Kate Newham, Phil Riley, John Walton, whilst Mike Winstanley sent his comments via the e-mail.

[15] Homicides were downgraded or ignored outright in duelling incidents and boxing matches. See J. M. BEATTIE, *Crime and the Courts in England 1660-1800*, Oxford, Clarendon Press, 1986, pp.97-98.

Unfortunately, from this distance in time, it is not only impossible but also mistaken for historians to take on the role of murder detectives. We cannot solve crime with our imperfect knowledge but we can at least identify and locate suspicious deaths that lend credence to Taylor's argument.

There seems little doubt that Taylor has identified a pattern of order and constancy in the figures relating to murder which suggests they have been manipulated. Nor would it necessarily require a conspiracy of policemen, coroners and public prosecutors to engineer or construct such figures. Rather Taylor has been describing a bureaucratic process in which the individual authorities were aware of only their own individual budgets and who were, moreover, mindful of how they portrayed themselves to their ratepayers and to the police inspectorate through their annual crime statistics. In such an environment it does not seem unreasonable to hypothesise that if the police found a dead body which went unclaimed by relatives or friends they would not necessarily have rigorously investigated the circumstances surrounding the death of that individual. Obviously it would be helpful to find evidence of the kind that Conley has provided[16]. This concerned a corpse found on Ramsgate beach in 1859. Both the magistrate and coroner felt it was that of foreigner and hence not worth the taxpayers' expense of an investigation. The verdict of suicide passed by the coroner's jury seems strange given that the corpse had stab wounds in its back.. It would appear that just a few weeks later another body was found naked at the foot of some cliffs at Ramsgate. In this case the German had been staying at a local hotel where a porter recalled seeing him with a heavily bandaged left hand. This fact led some to argue that: his death was suicide, and that 'in a fit of frenzy, [he] first chopped off his hand and then stabbed himself to the heart'. In this state, it was claimed, he then threw himself off the cliff. The local doctor favoured a finding of murder[17]. The decision in the

---

[16] Carolyn A. CONLEY, *The Unwritten Law: Criminal Justice in Victorian Kent,* New York, Oxford University Press, 1991, p. 55.

[17] *Manchester Courier, 16* May 1859. This case appears very similar to the one cited by Conley above. However more research is required to see if they are one and the same case. There are differences, for example in Conley's case the injuries are different and the reports date from 16 to 23

former case, if indeed they are separate cases, actually caused questions to be asked in the House of Commons which raises, perhaps, an additional query regarding Taylor's thesis. If murders were being rationed, why is it that the public did not find out and cause a stir? It does seem somewhat surprising that the newspaper press of the day never picked up on statements made in the annual *Judicial Statistics* which suggested murders were not being thoroughly investigated[18].

However there was one group of victims who have historically always been vulnerable to homicide, infants under one year of age. The Act of 1624 relating to infanticide was harsh in that it carried a capital punishment and, furthermore, it demanded that the onus of proof of innocence fell upon the unmarried mother for whom the law was specifically designed. Married mothers were charged with murder. With the passing of time juries became increasingly reluctant to convict and often sought out evidence which suggested the mothers had made preparations for their children through the purchase or making of baby linen[19]. In recognition of this reluctance the law was changed in 1803 so that, in future, the prosecution had to prove the murder in the same manner all other murders were proved and, in addition, if they so wished the jury could find the defendant guilty of concealment of birth which carried the relatively mild sentence of two years.

Crime statistics from the nineteenth century suggest a continued reluctance on the part of the police and coroners to investigate closely the sudden death of infants. Moreover there can at times appear many

---

April 1859. In the latter case the Manchester newspaper reported that: it had occurred 'on Monday'.

[18] Howard TAYLOR, 'Rationing Crime...', p. 586. 'It was', he writes, 'an open secret that most murders went: uninvestigated'.

[19] The following studies on infanticide are useful: J.M. BEATTIE, *Crime and the Courts in England* 1660-1800, Oxford, Clarendon Press, 1986, pp. 113-124; M. JACKSON, *New-Born Child Murder: Women, Illegitimacy and the Courts in Eighteenth-Century England*, Manchester, Manchester University Press, 1996; R.W. MALCOLMSON, 'Infanticide in the Eighteenth Century', in COCKBURN (ed.), *Crime in England*, London, Methuen, 1977; Lionel ROSE, *Massacre of Innocents: Infanticide in Great Britain 1800-1939*, London, RKP, 1986.

180   *John E. Archer*

contradictions and discrepancies in the official documents. In one
parliamentary return on infant deaths it was shown that only 224
verdicts of wilful murder were recorded by coroners' juries out of a
total of 5547 sudden deaths in England and Wales over an 18-month
period between 1861 and 1862. There were, in addition, 697 open
verdicts of 'found dead' and 956 cases of suffocation[20]. With regard
to the latter form of death one Liverpool journalist, although not
regarding suffocation as murder, was sufficiently angered by the fact
that 81 children in that borough had been smothered 'accidently' by
drunken parents on Saturday nights and early Sunday mornings. A
law, he maintained, should be passed to punish such careless and
irresponsible behaviour[21]. The same journalist, Hugh Shimmin, made
the unsubstantiated claim that the smothering of children was not
simply found in the poorest homes. Quoting an article from the
Athenaeum Shimmin wrote that it was 'rife' among the middle and
upper classes. The respectability, wealth and status of such privileged
parents however ensured the coroner's office never became
involved[22]. Hammick in his study of criminal statistics noted the wide
variation between police returns for murder and the verdicts of
coroners' inquests. In 1865 the former returned 135 murders whereas
the latter returned 227, leading Hammick to the supposition 'that,
according to the police view of the matter, infanticide is not
murder'[23]. In his footnotes, however, he observed that police and
coroners returns differed, the former counted such deaths as concealment of births, whereas the latter carried a heading for infanticide[24].

---

[20] *Times*, 25 July 1863, see also:
http://wsrv.clas.virginia.edu/~cjr2q/victorian/times.072563.html
     It is worth noting that recent research on cot deaths or SIDS(sudden
infant death syndrome) indicates that some of them were more than likely
homicides, see *The Guardian*, 8 January 1999.
     [21] John L. WALTON and Alastair WILCOX (eds.), *Low Life and Moral
Improvement in Mid-Victorian England: Liverpool Through the Journalism
of Hugh Shimmin*, Leicester, Leicester University Press, 1991. See pp. 134-
145.
     [22] *Ibidem*, p. 143.
     [23] James T. HAMMICK, 'On the Judicial Statistics of England and Wales,
with Special Reference to the Recent Returns Relating to Crime' in *Journal
of the Statistical Society*, XXX, pt.111, September 1867, p.384.
     [24] *Ibidem*, p.384, see his footnote.

This explanation for the disparity in the figures does not account for the wide regional and annual variations in the returns on the murder or the concealment of children under one year of age. If one examines the Manchester chief constables' annual reports between 1847 and 1913 the figures make for some strange reading. Between 1847 and 1859 one person only was arrested for infanticide and 14 for concealment of birth. Despite the change in the headings and the methods in counting, the figures after 1857 are surprisingly low. The worst years for murder of under one year olds were 1886 and 1888 when just four cases each were recorded. Yet the coroners' inquests for 1886 found 124 children dead in bed[25]. Whether such deaths were accidental, overlaying and suffocation, or not was difficult to discern even at that time. Some coroners were clearly of the opinion that 'most' children had not been killed accidently by careless parents, rather they had been murdered[26].

This becomes all too apparent with the appointment of Edwin Lankester to the post of coroner to the central division of Middlesex. The number of infanticides in the county was seven in 1862, or 5.6% of the national total of infanticides, but in the first year of Lankester taking up his post the number had risen to 40 cases or 24% of the national total. On the basis of his district's findings Lankester believed there were 1000 child murders a year in England and Wales. Other districts of the country failed to match his rather shocking returns. Lancashire for example returned 12 infanticides for the entire county as against the central division of Middlesex with 71. The coroners in the former county returned 506 'found dead' decisions and yet central Middlesex returned just nine[27]. The expertise and the concerns of the coroner could, it would appear, have an important bearing on the number of homicides. Murder it seems was to some

---

[25] David JONES, *Crime, Protest, Community and Police in Nineteenth-Century Britain,* London, Routledge and Kegan Paul, 1982, p. 153. See also *Criminal and Miscellaneous Statistical Returns of the Manchester Police,* Manchester Library Local History Unit (MLLHU), 352.2.M1.

[26] George K. BEHLMER, 'Deadly Motherhood: Infanticide and Medical Opinion in Mid-Victorian England', in *Journal of the History of Medicine and Allied Science,* vol.34, 1979, pp.409-410.

[27] *Ibidem.,* pp.424-425. Also see L. ROSE, *op. cit.,* chapter 7 on the variable quality of coroners and the less than rigorous inquest system.

extent a construct not of the law necessarily but of medical knowledge and regional cultural practices. If one wants to search for 'smoking guns' to add weight to Taylor's arguments then one might well start with infants under one year of age. Since in Manchester, for example, under the 'found dead' open verdict anything between 50 and 60% related to children under 12 months old[28].

More detailed scrutiny of the coroners' registers, where they exist, may cast light on those open verdicts. A cursory glance at the Liverpool Coroners Court does raise one's suspicions that murders of infants were being subsumed under such headings. For example on 8 August 1854 the court reached an open verdict on an unknown infant that had been found exposed as indeed did the jury at Newton near Warrington[29]. In the latter case the body of an 18-month-old female child was found under a bush close to the turnpike road but as the coroners court had been unable to trace anyone to 'the supposed infanticide', they brought an open verdict[30]. Yet in other not dissimilar cases, such as the discovery of a two-day-old baby girl. tied up in a bundle in Manchester, the coroner's jury arrived at its decision having taken the lead from the surgeon who had conducted the *post mortem*. In this case death as a result of desertion was their conclusion[31]. However no such doubts could have existed in the case of the two-year old boy found floating, naked but for socks, in the canal at Stretford. The *post mortem* revealed a serious cut at the back of his head and a splintered skull which indicated violence rather than drowning had been the cause of death[32]. In another case a new-born infant found floating in a brook with string tied tightly around its neck the jury returned a verdict of murder against a person or persons unknown[33]. In attempting to assess the number of homicides historians would also need, if possible, to try and determine what happened to cases like the death of Arthur Ellis, an infant who had been left in a door entry in Liverpool. His mother, Mary Ann Allen

---

[28] See tables relating to coroners' inquests in *The Criminal and Miscellaneous Statistics* for Manchester (MLLHU).

[29] Liverpool record Office (LRO), 347COR1.

[30] *Manchester Courier,* 13 July 1861.

[31] *Manchester Courier,* 18 February 1860.

[32] *Manchester Courier,* 11 February 1860.

[33] *Manchester City News,* 21 January 1871.

was charged with manslaughter but was acquitted at the assizes[34]. Did the police as the recorders of crime alter their statistics as a result of the court case?

Whilst suffocation and, in some instances, drowning were and are suspicious causes of death in open verdict cases one tends to ignore cases where the deceased were burnt to death since children were very vulnerable to open fires which often went unguarded in poorer homes. The figures for such deaths could be quite sizeable; in Westminster 10 of the 91 inquests on infants under two years of age involved burns and scolds in 1861, and in Southwark there were nine deaths by burns out of 84 inquests[35]. Were all such deaths accidental? In one case, (whether this is unique or not is too early to say), Margaret Blakey of Burnley was charged with throwing her two-year old daughter onto a fire. In what appears to have been a bitter custody fight with her husband she claimed that 'she would put it on the fire' rather than let him have the girl. Fortunately the child was dragged from the flames severely 'but not dangerously' burnt[36].

Although Taylor's thesis of the engineered number of murders per annum covers the period from 1862 to 1966 it is possible to discern the presence of suspicious adult deaths prior to the early 1860s. The River Mersey for example would have provided ample opportunity to dispose of the dead. Mystery surrounded the body of a 21 -year- old woman found on the beach 'with discoloration about her eyes' and last seen alive with a group of intoxicated sailors[37]. The coroners court also carried open verdicts which may or may not have been cases of natural deaths like 60-year-old Elizabeth Graham found dead in a barrel of water in Green Street, Liverpool, or 39-year-old John Murray who had suffocated to death at Waterloo Dock. In the latter case this does not appear to have been an industrial accident as the

---

[34] *Manchester Courier,* 16 August 1862.
[35] *Parliamentary Papers* 1862, A Return of the Verdicts of Coroners' Inquests in the Metropolis on Infants Under Two Years of Age During the Year 1861, cited on:
  http://wsrv.clas.virginia.edu/~cjr2q/victorian/times.072563.html.
[36] *Manchester Courier,* 23 May 1859. Blakey was imprisoned for six months with hard labour.
[37] *Liverpool Mercury,* 2 July 1850.

coroner's court received no evidence of the particulars of the death[38]. In the same year the coroner's register recorded five deaths between January and May in which the bodies had marks of injury upon them but the court was unable to determine how they had been received. Among them was 18-year-old Thomas Regan who died in North Hospital, an unknown man found in the River Mersey and 30-year-old Margaret Loftus[39]. Coroners' registers where they exist, may well offer historians hints, no more than that, of homicides which were not recorded as such at the time. Although this kind of evidence is based on supposition to a large extent, it does at least give some credence to Taylor's thesis of the rather static murder figures which by implication disguised the actual or real amount of murder.

If under-reporting affected the most serious crimes like murder and manslaughter then it may be reasonable to assume that many less serious forms of violence went unreported, uninvestigated or unrecorded in the annual police statistics. Cases of domestic violence offer the best examples of under-reporting. When the annual criminal returns of persons apprehended for aggravated assaults on women and children are examined the figures are remarkably low. In Manchester for example, with a population of 462,000 in 1881 there were only 64 cases[40]. Whilst it is recognised that assaults on women were often prosecuted as common assaults, thus making it very difficult to estimate even the official size of the problem, the figures suggest domestic violence was declining during the final decades of the nineteenth century. This view was endorsed by Nancy Tomes in her pioneering study of violence to women in London[41]. More recent studies have been less confident in accepting a real decline in domestic violence. Hammerton, for example, has concluded that magistrates' court records for estimating the level of wife beatings cannot be relied on because these very same courts attempted to deal

---

[38] LRO 347COR1, Graham on 31 May 1854, Murray on 7 November 1854.

[39] LRO 347COR1, Regan on 13 November 1854, Loftus on 15 May 1854.

[40] *Criminal and Miscellaneous Statistical Returns*, 1881, 352.2 M1 (MLLHU).

[41] Nancy TOMES, 'A "Torrent of Abuse": Crimes of Violence between Working-Class Men and Women in London, 1840-75', in *Journal of Social History*, 11, 1977-78.

with such cases not by convicting but by conciliating men and women either through the granting of maintenance and separation orders or reconciliation with occasional home visits from police court missionaries[42]. Legislation such as the Matrimonial Causes Act (1878), Married Women (Maintenance in Case of Desertion) Act (1886) and the Summary Jurisdiction (Married Women) Act (1895) helped reduce the number of summary convictions.

In Hammerton's excellent study of nineteenth-century marital conflict he argues that newspaper reports of wife beatings are unhelpful in determining the decline in such incidents. This is hard to dispute since press reportage of assaults and the number of prosecutions coming up in the courts bore little or no relationship to one another[43]. The press however can offer insights into the incidence and scale of domestic violence and other kinds of interpersonal violence which the police and the courts ignored or overlooked. Hugh Shimmin, the radical Liverpool journalist mentioned earlier, who left the *Liverpool Mercury* to establish his own paper, *The Porcupine,* was a well informed and, from what 1 can judge, an honest observer of events in spite of prejudices which were overtly stated. In a series of fascinating articles which offer some of the best eye-witness accounts of day to day policing Shimmin accompanied a patrol on night duty in the, Vauxhall Road neighbourhood. 'There were,' he wrote, 'symptoms of disorder and disquiet in nearly all the narrow side streets and courts' which the police ignored until the patrol met up with a young mother with a child in her arms. Her drunken and violent husband had, she claimed, turned her out. In seeking the police's help to return inside her own home, the constable replied that 'it was, not a case which they could interfere' since their intervention would only make the situation worse[44]. This lack of interference could have fatal consequences. Only ten years later Shimmin, who by now was a highly critical observer of the Liverpool police, reported the 'shocking story' of the murder of 32-year-old Dinah Quigley. In all five police constables came to the close where her husband Thomas

---

[42] A. James HAMMERTON, *Cruelty and Companionship: Conflict in Nineteenth-Century Married Life,* London, Routledge, 1992.

[43] *Ibidem,* pp.41-42.

[44] *Liverpool Mercury,* 10 August 1857, chapter XX.

was in the process, by all accounts a lengthy one, of kicking, stamping and jumping on his wife. They appeared to have had only a little conversation with Quigley and only one of them took the trouble to look inside the house, and even then only on the urgings of a female neighbour. The woman, Dinah, lay in a heap on the floor and was, according to her husband, drunk. Soon after the police departed so too did Quigley, leaving his neighbours to take his wife to hospital where she died soon afterwards. The moral of this incident for Shimmin was that he feared that 'police officers think a husband has a prescriptive right to beat his wife as often as he likes, so long as he does not actually break her limbs or knock her brains out...' In Dinah Quigley's case the doctor found seven fractured ribs, a fractured leg and bruising over her entire body[45].

For many people, not only female victims of domestic assaults, medical attention for their wounds was provided at local dispensaries where for a penny their injuries or sickness were attended to by a trained doctor. More serious cases were transferred to hospitals. In Liverpool there were by the 1880s three dispensaries treating upwards of 60,000 patients a year. In one two-hour visit to the East Dispensary in that town on a Saturday night between 11.00pm and one o' clock in the morning, a local journalist noted that most patients had received their injuries not as a result of accidents but in street brawls. He further noted that very few of these street assaults would ever end in the magistrates' court the following Monday morning. It appeared that the dispensary and the police had, in previous years, between them operated a bureaucratic system whereby victims on receiving their treatment would be handed a 'note' which stated 'that they had been more or less severely injured by a knife, or poker, or some other thing', and which the police received and acted upon by arresting the accused person. However with the stopping of the 'note' the police refused to prosecute and, as a consequence, left the individuals, often 'of the very lowest class: idle, lawless, dissolute, and dirty' to take out private summonses which, given their poverty, they were unable to afford. 'This will probably explain', the *Review* claimed, 'the apparent falling off in aggravated and violent assaults on the person.' The report continued:

---

[45] *The Porcupine*, 4 January 1868.

Under circumstances like these, the public may easily be lulled into a state of false security -and gulled into believing that crimes of violence are dying out. No, my friend, I am sorry to say that brutality and lawlessness are very rife in some quarters of the town, and that knives and pokers are resorted to on the slightest provocation, or no provocation at all. Scores of men and women are struck down with some dangerous weapon; struck down bleeding and insensible in the streets of Liverpool every Saturday night -and the public never never hear word about it all. The dispensary doctor knows about it; the victims and their friends are, of course, fully aware of the wrong which has been done; the policeman hears about it -but takes no action without "the note"- and the street rowdy gets off scot free[46].

This article illustrates both the importance of qualitative evidence in that it describes unreported violence, it also points to the dangers of relying too heavily on quantitative records in so far as an administrative practice within a doctor's surgery could affect the numbers being arrested and prosecuted in the police court the following Monday morning. Police and judicial statistics may well contain serious flaws but we need not necessarily agree with J.J. Tobias who concluded that 'criminal statistics have little to tell us about crime and statistics in the nineteenth century[47]. Despite their many drawbacks they can and do serve useful purposes for historians of crime, not least in alerting us to sudden increases in particular crimes. In Jennifer Davis' study of garotting in London in 1862, which is a fine example of such a phenomenon, she convincingly argued that the rise in prosecutions for street violence reflected not a real increase in garotting but a 'moral panic'. Herein lies the importance of statistical evidence, Victorians, who were great quantifiers, often reacted to what they thought was happening and crime statistics created their perceptions of crime and could also frame their responses to what they thought was happening[48].

---

[46] *Saturday Review, 18 July 1891.* The journalist's visit occurred on the evening of 13 July a time of sectarian fighting in Liverpool. This may have made the dispensary unusually busy. The 'note' continued to be given but only in 'really serious cases'.

[47] J.J. TOBIAS, *Crime and Industrial Society in the Nineteenth Century,* Penguin, Harmondsworth, 1967, p.25.

[48] This viewpoint has been put forward most recently by Rob SINDALL, *Street Violence in the Nineteenth Century: Media Panic or Real Danger?,*

The flesh of historical detail needs to be put on the bones of nine-teenth-century annual criminal returns. In my opinion the best sources for historians working on crime in the nineteenth century are the local newspapers. They are a rich source and provide, most crucially, detail and context which may not be found anywhere else. Where court registers provide only the bare details of a case; for example the defendant's name, charge, court decision etc., the press can provide all sorts of incidental detail, not least neighbourhood reactions to crimes of violence, and by extension their relations with and expectations of the police in investigating such incidents. More recently feminist historians, among others, have subjected press reports to close textual analysis and from this can be extracted evi-dence of prevailing attitudes towards women and violent crime[49].

News reports help clarify what would be a very misleading picture if one were to rely solely on annual statistical returns. If we return to the issue of domestic violence to women it has been pointed out how few men were prosecuted under legislation specifically drawn up to criminalise that offence. Prosecutions in Manchester rarely exceeded 90 a year before 1890, this low figure can, however, be partly ex-plained when one investigates reports of common assaults cases in the police courts. This particular charge covered a variety of acts of interpersonal violence from verbal insults in which no physical injury occurred, pub brawls, child abuse and even some serious sex offences[50]. Moreover and perhaps more importantly for historians press reports actually uncover cases in which defendants are found not guilty even though acts of violence have taken place. In a case heard at Birkenhead Police Court, Francis Leonard was charged with

---

Leicester, Leicester University Press, 1990, ch.2, pp. 16-28. J. DAVIS, 'The London Garotting Panic: a Moral Panic and the Creation of a Criminal Class', in V.A.C. GATRELL, B. LENMAN and G. PARKER (eds.), *op. cit.*

[49] For example see Shani D' CRUZE, *Crimes of Outrage: Sex, Violence, and Victorian Working Women*, London, UCL Press, 1998.

[50] The number of people tried for common assaults in the lower courts ranged between 1500-2000 a year in Manchester between 1857-1880, there-after dropping off. This charge did not include cases of assault on the police or aggravated assault. See also C. A. CONLEY, *op. cit.*, for examples of downgrading of sexual assault cases, pp. 82-84.

assaulting his mother and threatening her with a poker. Before sentencing the magistrate made enquiries into the family. It was stated:

> Detective Inspector Moore... found the mother to be a drunken and dissipated woman. She was drunk throughout her husband's last illness, drunk while he was dying and drunk very frequently after his death. It was by no means surprising the young man had picked up a poker; she called the dead father foul names though he was a good man. The prisoner gave her a guinea last Saturday and yet the young children were almost without food ... A fellow workman of the father was called and he bore out the assessment of the police officers. The woman used to pawn everything although her husband used to give her large wages and her children were sometimes days without food. Mr. Preston (magistrate) now called the complainant before him and she boldly protested that every word derogatory to her was a falsehood and said she had suffered a lifetime of martyrdom during her husband's life and since. ..He then discharged the young man and communicated to the complainant the opinion he entertained of her conduct[51].

This article provides an insight into the problems confronting women attempting to prosecute male assailants, As the case develops it becomes clear that it is Mrs. Leonard rather than her son, Francis, who was on trial. Consequently her behaviour as a mother and homemaker, which falls far short of what the magistrate expects, is enough to dismiss the charges of assault against her son. The actual incident with the poker appears to have been ignored by both the magistrate and the press which suggests that a level of violence directed at women was still tolerated and condoned.

Whilst the newspapers cannot measure accurately, in quantifiable terms, the rise and fall of violence, they can uncover and differentiate between acts of petty and serious violence which may come under the same legal heading in statistical returns. They can also offer us clues as to attitudes and tolerance limits of both the public and the police. Through the reporting of court cases historians can gain important insights into working-class attitudes both to crimes of interpersonal

---

[51] The report which originally appeared in the *Liverpool Courier* has been taken from the *Manchester Evening News*, 26 June 1875. My thanks to Jo Jones for providing me with this example.

violence and their acceptance of the police. Their presence as prosecution witnesses for example, may suggest that they not only tolerated the police but also expected them to intervene in physical disputes. Thus an approach using qualitative evidence will be able to
arrive at more nuanced and subtle conclusions than one utilising and
analysing police statistics. The latter approach, however, should not
be discarded altogether for Taylor's important work has made crucial
discoveries which could only have been arrived at through statistical
analysis.

[23]

Hazel May

Who killed whom?: victimization and culpability in the social construction of murder

ABSTRACT

Based on in-depth interviews with relatives of people convicted of murder, this article examines the ways in which everyday understandings of 'murder' are socially constructed, as revealed by the narratives of murderers' relatives. To this end, interviewees' explanations of the killings are analysed and a distinction is drawn between interviewees who understood the killings committed by their relatives as manslaughter and those who accepted the murder verdict. In defining the offences in this way, interviewees identified the significance of victimization and culpability to understandings of interpersonal violence. Through the analysis of interview data, it is possible to examine the ways in which 'murder' is seen to have occurred only when particular criteria of victimization and culpability are met.

KEYWORDS: murder; victimization; culpability

INTRODUCTION

By examining a range of scenarios, it is possible to argue that there is no single social meaning attached to the killing of one person by another. During war, for example, killing the 'enemy' is not only legalized, but can also be a source of others' respect, both for the killer and the killer's family. Alternatively, the killing of a young man by another during a consensual fight may be interpreted as tragic yet within acceptable behavioural boundaries for young men (Polk 1997). In contrast, the killing of a toddler by two young boys – as in the killing of James Bulger[1] – suggests, not simply action outside acceptable behavioural boundaries for children, but also the victimization of a weaker being (Jackson 1995). That these different killing scenarios generate different meanings can also be witnessed in the form and content of media coverage. For example, James Bulger's killing received a broad range of local, national and international media attention, yet the killing of a young man by another after a 'pub brawl' may not even be on the front page of a local newspaper. These examples reveal that there is no singular interpretation of a killing, and our social world constructs the

British Journal of Sociology Vol. 50 No. 3 (September 1999) pp. 489–506
ISSN 0007-1315 © London School of Economics 1999

killing of a toddler as more shocking, more horrific, more tragic and less intelligible than the killing of the young man in a pub brawl. For the purposes of this paper, one implication to be drawn from this is that being related to the killers of James Bulger also carries different connotations and experiences than being related to the young man who 'won' the pub brawl.

The social meanings attached to acts of violence – as described above, for example – seem to revolve around notions of culpability and victimization, mediated by interpretations of what is deemed to be appropriate behaviour for the social actors. In law,[2] culpability for murder is complex, dependent upon a potentially ambiguous combination of intent, recklessness and what could reasonably expected to be the outcome. If it can be proven that one's intention was to cause harm to another, that death could be seen to be a probable outcome of one's violence, and that one recklessly disregarded this probable outcome, there is sufficient evidence to 'constitute the mental element for murder' (Clarkson and Keating 1990: 589). The ambiguity lies in the difficulty of proving this crucial combination and herein lies a blurred boundary between murder and voluntary manslaughter.

What reinforces such ambiguity is the range of legally acceptable defences. Insanity and self-defence are absolute defences to the charge of murder, but a murder charge can be reduced to the lesser charge of voluntary manslaughter if the accused successfully claims provocation. In legal terms, 'provocation' refers to a victim's actions which would have pushed any 'reasonable man' [*sic*] to lose control. This is open to divergent interpretation, as legal outcomes have shown: a 'reasonable man' may be pushed to lose control in the face of an adulterous wife (Rock 1998b) or in a panic response to a perceived 'homosexual advance' (Toolis 1995) and yet a 'reasonable woman' would not be pushed beyond control by long term abuse by a male partner (Maynard and Winn 1997). In these contexts, culpability and victimization can be seen to be inextricably bound: a wife's adultery and a man's homosexuality can mitigate their victim status, which in turn can mitigate the killers' culpability.

These gendered and sexualized interpretations of the legal defence of 'provocation' are significant to the social definitions of killings (Richardson and May 1999). The 'law' does not exist in a vacuum, but both shapes, and is shaped, by everyday understandings of culpability and victimization. Thus the gendered and sexualized interpretations embedded within legal precedence are dimensions of wider social processes and normative assumptions. This paper focuses on how such social definitions of victimization and culpability inform everyday understandings of homicide, as revealed in the interpretations made by killers' relatives.

METHODOLOGY

Fourteen in-depth interviews were carried out, involving sixteen relatives of eight offenders convicted of murder, as part of a research project which, in the absence of any previous research into the lives of murderers' relatives, sought to explore commonalities of experience amongst this population.[3] Each interview lasted between two and five hours and most interviewees were interviewed twice.[4] The first interviews were unstructured and exploratory, concerned with the general circumstances of the killings and their impact upon interviewees' lives. Based on a preliminary analysis of emergent data and concepts it was possible to develop a semi-structured interview guide for the second round of interviews.

Whilst there were many differences between interviewees – reflecting, perhaps, the unusualness of homicide as a crime in England and Wales – there were similarities: interviewees felt angry with their relatives yet, confusingly, also loving and protective of them; they experienced stigmatization and felt isolated and vulnerable in their communities; they grieved their loss of social status and mourned for their relative – lost to incarceration. They were no longer in control of their lives because of the actions of another and they felt like victims – victims that nobody cared about or sympathized with. This is consistent with other manifestations of traumatic loss experienced by, for example, relatives of suicide victims (Silverman, Range and Overholser 1995) and those who develop chronic physical or mental illnesses (Brown and Powell-Cope 1993; Solomon and Draine 1996). Aspects of murderers' relatives' experiences also appear to mirror those of the relatives of homicide victims (Rock 1998b; Rynearson 1996).

Potential interviewees were only included in the research if they had defined themselves as related to the killer at the time of the offence. Most interviewees were women: five mothers, five sisters, one aunt and one niece took part in the research. In addition two fathers, one brother and one male cousin agreed to be interviewed. Significantly, it was the women who arranged the interviews and acted as the point of contact between their families and the researcher – reproducing a gendered pattern of familial communication with the offenders themselves.

Reaching interviewees was problematic, reflecting both the sensitive nature of the research and the 'hidden' nature of the research population, who have no statutory relationship with any organization. As outlined above, and discussed in more detail elsewhere (May 1997), key commonalities in murderers' relatives' experiences were bereavement, stigmatization and vulnerability to exposure. The combination of these factors rendered the collection, holding and dissemination of the families stories 'problematic', thus conforming to Renzetti and Lee's definition of a 'sensitive research topic' (1993: 5). Others have discussed ways of reaching similarly hidden, stigmatized and potentially vulnerable populations, but have relied ultimately upon networks of people (Lee 1969) or common use of place (Humphreys 1970). One common 'place' for vulnerable hidden populations might be self-help groups. Indeed, there are several support groups for offenders' families. But at the time of seeking access (1994–5) there was only one support group for the families of serious offenders:[5] Aftermath. (Since completing the fieldwork a new organization, Serious Offenders'

Families Association, has been established). None the less, most families of serious offenders do not turn to Aftermath for help and by its own calculation the group claims to have helped only a small proportion of the families with a member who is serving, or has served, a prison sentence for a serious offence (Aftermath 1995).

Why more people have not sought assistance from Aftermath is not easy to answer and there are a number of factors which may be involved. Importantly, many of those that have been helped found out about the organization by happenstance – there is no system of referrals as there is to Victim Support, for example. More generally, other research suggests that those who join support groups have fewer avenues of social support compared with those who do not join (Reif et al. 1995); additionally, those who join bereavement support groups tend to report higher levels of depression, anger and stress than those who do not join (Rynearson 1995). When these factors are combined with a perception amongst joiners and non-joiners that attending such groups is evidence of a lower self-sufficiency and something to be ashamed of (Levy and Derby 1992), it is possible to see joining a support group as a desperate act of last resort.

The combination of seeking a 'hidden' population in order to carry out 'sensitive' research meant that it took a total of twenty one months to reach and interview members of eight families, three of whom had sought help from Aftermath. Two families were reached directly through Aftermath. The other six families were reached through South Yorkshire and Inner London Probation Services and the Prison Service; these organizations allowed access to the offenders only, whose permission to approach their families was required. As a result, the access process involved two layers of gatekeepers within the organizations (management and prison/probation officers) and a third gatekeeper: the offenders themselves. The low response to interview requests (one hundred offenders were approached) reflected the convoluted process by which it was made possible to approach the killers' relatives, the shame and stigmatization experienced by the killers' relatives and the problems long term prisoners have in maintaining contact with their families of origin. Contact is often lost because it is likely that the victims were also family members (over 40 per cent of homicides occur within the family Criminal Statistics, (1993a)), because their families have rejected them as a result of their crimes, or simply because the distance between 'home' and prison, can be prohibitive to sustained familial contact.

There are implications stemming from this process for the representativeness of the sample. Interviewees represented a particular sub-group of killers' relatives in that they all had good relations with their offending relatives; were likely to have good relationships with their relatives' prison and probation officers who implicitly selected 'suitable' offenders and their families for inclusion; and none of these interviewees or their families had prior criminal records. Excluded, then, were families in which the victims were also members (the largest group of homicide survivors), who had lost contact for other reasons and/or were more familiar with criminality and violence amongst its members. These factors may be significant to the processes by which killers' relatives understand the killings themselves.

There are also issues of representativeness which relate to the offenders themselves. Statistics on offenders identify three relevant age groups: 14–16, 17–20 and 21+. Between 75–78 per cent of all murders are committed by those aged over twenty one in any given year yet 14–16 year olds are responsible for only 1–3 per cent of annual murders (Criminal Statistics, 1993b).[6] Of the eight offenders in this research, six were over twenty one – which 'fits' with national distribution – but there is an 'over-representation' of very young offenders: two of the eight were aged 14–16 at the time of the killings. Additionally, although women are responsible for approximately 3–7 per cent of all murders in England and Wales they are predominantly aged over twenty one. The one woman offender, whose relatives participated in this research, was not only unusual because of her gender, but also because she was aged 14–16. The predominant youth of the offenders, combined with the fact that all but two offenders still lived in the family home at the time of the offence, may additionally influence how interviewees came to make sense of their relatives' violence.

Clearly, the sample size and make up renders problematic a generalization to the whole population of murderers' relatives. However, as an exploratory project, offering a conceptual framework and agenda for future research, this paper is significant because there is no other literature which examines the social and interactional significance of being related to a serious offender. Whilst there is research which addresses the experiences of the families of general prisoners, this has tended to focus on the implications on the maintenance of intra-familial communication (Light 1992), economic standards (Shaw 1992) and emotional and educational development of prisoners' children (Fishman 1982; Matthews 1983). Where texts have addressed serious offenders, the concern has been with the offenders' – not their relatives' – experiences of altered relationships, of stigma and of leaving prison on licence (Coker and Martin 1985; Parker 1990). Research specifically addressing the experiences of family members of killers is extremely limited. Cooney (1994) found that relatives of many people convicted of homicide were vulnerable to negative and violent responses from others, but did not examine the social meanings attached to the killings. Bailey (1996) identified the emotional devastation experienced by the families of adolescents who murder, but this was an adjunct to his/her main concern of identifying factors within the families which contributed to the killing.

This paper therefore reveals new stories of homicide. Different audiences offer different narratives of homicide; for example, professionals within the criminal justice system, criminologists and relatives of homicide victims may all construct different narratives of the crime (Rock 1998a). Killers themselves may construct yet different accounts (Ray and Simons 1987). What offenders' families say about their relatives' crimes provides another dimension of homicide narratives and contributes to a fuller understanding of the wider social process and normative assumptions upon which assessments of inter-personal violence and appropriate behaviour rest.

EXPLAINING HOMICIDE

In seeking to examine interviewees' understandings of their relatives' crimes, it is important to ask the general question: how *can* we understand homicide? Rock (1998a) would argue that this depends upon one's audience status. While there is an abundance of fictional, non-fictional and 'factional' sources of homicide 'scripts' available through various media forms (Cameron and Frazer 1987), Rock (1998a) juxtaposes a traditional criminology of homicide with the experiences of victims' families. The former has historically constructed homicide as a 'duet': an ongoing interactional situation which has the outcome of death of one of the players. In contrast, victims' families have been shown to experience homicide suddenly: the 'duet' may have been ongoing, but they may have known nothing of it – or at least of its potential deadly consequences – until the moment of death. For the victims' families, the death has no historical genealogy; instead it represents sudden trauma and loss.

Murderers' relatives interviewed also experienced the killings as moments of sudden trauma and loss. They had seen themselves and their families as 'respectable': hardworking and non-criminal. The killings committed by their relatives shattered this self-perception and were therefore problematic to the maintenance of social reality (Berger and Luckmann 1967). Their social worlds were thrust into disarray – what they had taken for granted could no longer be relied upon; who and what they 'knew' themselves to be was no longer 'true'. They now defined themselves as 'murderers relatives' – and assumed others did so too. This was a problematic social status, partly because it represented their losses, but mainly because they understood 'murder' as the purposive seeking and killing of an 'innocent' victim and 'murderers' as evil, cold-blooded and predatory

> *Mother.* Murderers are these people who just walk about and beat somebody senseless and to a pulp, walk away and do it again to somebody else. Because they're murderers, they're evil.

To be a 'murderer' therefore obliterated all other dimensions of the person and interviewees routinely referred to Peter Sutcliffe (The 'Yorkshire Ripper'), Myra Hindley (one of the 'Moors Murderers') and the Kray twins (London gangsters) as examples of this master status. But interviewees could not see their relatives as 'murderers', even if they had killed someone. They had too much social and individual knowledge of their offending relatives to apply such a stereotype – they were still 'our kid'. In order to cope with the dissonance between 'our kid' and 'murderer' they had to understand why the killing took place. As in other examples of traumatic and sudden events, struggles to build understanding 'explode into obsessive reviews' (Weber et al. 1992: 267). Details of the past were scrutinized for early warning signs and influences – as one mother asked of herself 'I smacked him . . . did I teach him violence?'.[7] But this did not resolve their seeming inability to make sense of their relatives' crimes, for, as Weber et al. (1992) argue, latching onto simplistic answers to complex problems serves to highlight, rather than fill, gaps in understanding.

In common with others who have had traumatic experiences (Plummer 1995), interviewees constructed explanatory accounts of the killings and their relatives' actions.[8] In attempting to explain negatively received behaviour we appeal to culturally acceptable inferences about the causes of events and the roles, goals and expectations of various actors. Such 'vocabularies of motive' are socially situated and activated by well known culturally-specific 'scripts' (Mills 1940). For the purposes of this paper, it is possible to identify two dominant account 'clusters' amongst murderers' relatives interviewed: accounts which accepted the legal definition of murder ascribed to their relatives' crimes and accounts which did not. Of the eight families who participated in this research four believed their relatives should have been found guilty of manslaughter. Significantly, the three families who had also been involved in Aftermath accepted the murder verdict. Interviewed members of the eighth family held conflicting views regarding what their relative had been found guilty of – ranging from murder through manslaughter to accessory after the fact – but were all convinced of his innocence. The account offered by these interviewees is not the subject of this paper.

This paper will now go on to examine the differences between the 'manslaughter accounts' and the 'murder accounts'. At this point, it is important to acknowledge that by referring to 'clusters', an analytical illustration of responses, interpretations and experiences is made. In reality, the borders between such 'clusters' are blurred with overlaps and contradictions. These 'clusters' are neither fixed nor exclusive, but reflect, none the less, different explanatory emphases.

ACCOUNTS OF MANSLAUGHTER

Account givers who rejected their relatives' murder verdicts accepted that their relatives had killed the victims but argued the offenders' actions had been misinterpreted and that the crimes should be considered as manslaughter. For the accounts to be coherent, these interviewees had to explain both the violence and the legal verdicts of murder and so appealed to 'vocabularies of motive' that serious offenders, such as rapists (Scully and Marolla 1984) and murderers (Ray and Simons 1987), have also been shown to draw upon. Firstly, vocabularies of excuse: in appealing to cultural scripts of accident and illness, offenders sought to mitigate culpability for their crimes. Secondly, offenders drew on vocabularies of justification which established some degree of offender victimization through provocation and/or injustice. In this way, manslaughter account givers sought to mitigate both the offenders' culpability and the deceaseds' victimization.

EXPLANATIONS OF EXCUSE

Explanations of excuse 'attempt to weaken the association between the actor and certain undesired events by trying to reduce personal responsibility . . . by portraying the undesirable behaviour as being uncontrollable and irregular' (Sheer and Weigold 1995: 593–4). Explanations of excuse, therefore, accounted for the offences by focusing upon factors which mitigated offenders' culpability.

The first factor identified as mitigating offenders' culpability was the perceived uncontrollable and aberrant nature of the violence: the offenders acted out of character and without agency

> *Father.* I think he just went berserk. I think he just lost all sense of control, which he admitted himself, afterwards. He said 'I just don't know what made me do it Dad . . . everything went blank'.

> *Sister.* But he's not the sort of person to let fly . . . I think something must have flipped inside him.

This is similar to rapists' (Scully and Marolla 1984) murderers' (Ray and Simons 1987) accounts which have pointed to intoxication and/or a temporary break from their 'real' (i.e. non-violent) personalities to explain their actions. This notion of 'diminished responsibility', however temporarily it was perceived to exist (and regardless of the legal irrelevance to the formal defence of 'diminished responsibility'), enabled the manslaughter account givers of this paper to distinguish between 'murder' and the actions of their relatives.

This distinction was reinforced because these interviewees also drew upon a narrative of accidental and non-intentional killing

> *Mother.* To me, it's murder when they go out deliberately to do it. Our Matthew didn't go out purposely to kill anyone.

The intention contained in the violence was crucial to the meanings interviewees ascribed to the killings. If the perpetrator was acting out of control and out of character, if the violence was not planned and the intended outcome of the violence was not death, they argued, the perpetrator should not be seen to be responsible for 'murder' – despite the fact that this is at odds with the legal definition of culpability for murder. By appealing to cultural scripts of accident and abberation these interviewees located their relatives' culpability within the more socially acceptable parameters of manslaughter. A crucial aspect of these manslaughter accounts, therefore, was the identification of factors which pointed to the mitigation of offenders' culpability.

EXPLANATIONS OF JUSTIFICATION

Explanations of justification 'focus on changing an audience's perception of the event itself . . . by appealing to an alternative set of rules that might transform the act' (Sheer and Weigold 1995: 594). The explanations of justification offered by interviewees accounted for the killings by identifying aspects of the victims' behaviour (provocation) and the legal process (injustice) which went some way to produce a degree of victimization in the offenders. Consequently, as will be demonstrated, both the violence and the murder conviction were constructed as intelligible.

In constructing their relatives' violence as intelligible, interviewees sought to explain the violence in terms of the context in which it occurred. Winch (1958) argues that different social contexts offer various frameworks by which events can be seen to be intelligible, expressed through acceptable vocabularies of motive (Mills 1940). The specific context these interviewees were keen to emphasize was that of provocation: the victims were seen to have had a significant role in the chain of events leading to their deaths. This reflects Stanko's (1990) argument that there are social rules which guide appropriate behaviour and when these are contravened the consequences are seen to be the responsibility of the rule breaker

> If people frequent places that are known to be dangerous or they do not follow exactly the rules for precaution then we implicitly hold them responsible for whatever happens to them (Stanko 1990: 49).

Of significance to this paper is the gendered and sexualized nature of these spatialized rules. In everyday life as well as in contexts of violence, heterosexual women, gay men and lesbians must conform to particular constructions of what is deemed socially appropriate behaviour and they have 'behavioural responsibility' to ensure they are not victimized (Richardson and May 1999). For example, women who have been raped are commonly called upon to 'prove' – socially, if not legally – their sexual 'innocence' for their victimization to be heard. Similarly, whilst gay men and lesbians have achieved greater social acceptance in the past thirty years, in certain circumstances it may be possible to argue that this acceptance is contingent upon their conformity to heterosexualized rules and a willingness to remain non-visible in public heterosexualized space. Those that trespass these boundaries may be seen to provoke a threat to the authority of heteronormativity and punishments, in the form of harassment, verbal abuse and homophobic violence, may be meted out to non-conformers (Mason and Palmer 1996).

'Appropriate' behaviour is, then, defined within a context of gendered and sexualized occupation of spatial and temporal locations. That such gendered and sexualized assumptions may be embedded within normative interpretations of homicidal 'provocation' can be seen in the justificatory accounts of interviewees which located the offenders in 'victimized' positions. For example, the father of one offender believed his son's fatal violence towards a naked man in the street was an understandable response; the victim's nakedness represented a sexual danger, reinforced by the posthumous discovery of 'pornographic literature' in his home and convictions for 'indecent exposure'. This father understood the violence as the direct result of the victim's own activities and the offender was therefore a victim of this 'sexual deviance'

> *Father.* [My son] came round the corner and he was confronted by this naked man. Some words were exchanged between them . . . [he then] came towards [my son] with his arm outstretched. [My son] panicked. I think basically what [he] intended was to give him a good hiding, but it went too far . . . they knew about [this man], why didn't they do more to help him and stop [my son], or any young man, being put in that position?

Similarly, gender played an important role in the interpretation of offenders' and victims' actions. For example, the interviewees quoted below constructed their relative as emotionally vulnerable and his estranged wife, whom he killed, as sexually promiscuous and manipulative. The victim's seeming refusal to comply with gendered notions of heterosexual expression was seen as the catalyst to her estranged husband's violence

> *Sister.* When they'd split up, they decided that he'd go to The Red Lion and she'd go to The Bull. But then she'd walk in where she wasn't supposed to go, with another man . . . I think at the end, he couldn't have her, so that's what happened. I think she just enticed him. She just drove him to the end and he snapped.

> *Niece.* I think it was her, she made him do it.

In appealing to gendered and sexualized notions of appropriate behaviour, the interviewees who presented accounts of manslaughter believed their relatives had been placed in vulnerable positions by the victims' own actions. Because the victims' behaviour was seen to be sexually threatening and because it is 'understandable' that the offenders would feel threatened by such behaviour, the provoked responses of violence were constructed as intelligible. Similar to the rapists in Scully and Marolla's research, who 'attempted to discredit and blame the victims while presenting their own actions as justified in the context' (Scully and Marolla 1984: 537), interviewees in my research questioned their relatives' culpability for murder by pointing to the mitigated victim status of those who had been killed.

In order to maintain internal coherence of their manslaughter stories, interviewees in the first 'cluster' needed also to explain the murder verdict. They constructed the murder verdicts as marginal, by pinpointing identifiable factors which, if different, could have altered the trial outcomes. Justice was assessed as unpredictable: dependent on the whims and biases of a variety of key players within the legal process of defining crimes. These key players were, firstly, the jury who were believed to have ultimate control over the trial outcome, yet could make decisions based on their own agendas

> *Father:* We say out of a population of half a million, we had the wrong twelve people on the jury. If we'd gone the following week we'd have had a different jury who probably would have looked at it with a different light.

Secondly, there was concern about the role of the judge, seen to direct the jury and provide an overall view of the case. For example, one sister believed the judge's summary at the end of the hearing rejected what she saw to be the popular construction of the killing

> But the judge, I didn't like the way he summed up afterwards . . . He was summing up for the prosecution. To hear how this thing happened, everyone knows it was an accident.

Finally, all of the families in the first 'cluster' questioned the quality of the legal advice they received and the in-court advocacy provided

> *Sister:* The solicitors . . . were just going through the motions. Because they were Legal Aid, they didn't put themselves out.

Trial outcome was therefore understood to be determined less by the 'facts' of the case and more by the vagaries of the legal system and the relative power positions of those key to its operation at any given time. To support their interpretation, interviewees in this 'cluster' made comparisons with other cases, based upon perceived intention and harshness of verdict, and identified other killers who were seen to have intentionally killed yet were found guilty of manslaughter, not murder – thus revealing the capricious nature of legal outcomes. Rock (1998b) has shown that homicide victims' relatives also experience justice as arbitrary – particularly because of the defences' scope for plea bargaining. This suggests that the two 'sides' of vested familial interest symbolically compete to control the meanings ascribed to killings and this can occur in two arenas: the trial court itself and informal accounts. In seeking to minimize the legal significance of the killings, the defence may 'constant[ly] blur . . . causal and moral boundaries for pragmatic end' (Rock 1998b: 81). These claims feed into the informal extra-legal accounts that offenders and their supporters construct. The factors seen to have prevented the success of such claims may appear to the lay defence as rooted in legal happenstance: the peculiarities of legal key players. By locating trial outcomes within a context of unpredictable (in)justice, then, offenders' relatives interviewed were able to define the killings in terms of 'manslaughter' yet coherently account for the murder verdicts.

ACCOUNTS OF MURDER

The second 'clustering' of interviewees identified in this research reflects an acceptance of their relatives' culpability for murder. Explanations arising from this acceptance 'admit blameworthiness [and] acknowledge that valued prescriptions for conduct have been violated' (Sheer and Weigold 1995: 594). In contrast to accounts of manslaughter – which focused upon the actions of both offenders and victims in the lead up to the violence – accounts of murder were more likely to focus upon the outcomes of the violence: the deaths themselves. Although social and legal differences between murder and manslaughter were acknowledged, these differences were not significant to the accounts of murder because both crimes were, as one mother said, 'the worst crimes [you] could commit: murder, manslaughter, whatever you want to call it'.

As a consequence – and in common with victims' relatives (Rock 1998b) – the second 'cluster' of interviewees retained a notion of absolute culpability. Unlike intent-laden interpretations of culpability made by the relatives in the previous cluster, this notion of absolute culpability focused on the outcome of perpetrators' actions. Factors which others may have presented in mitigation of culpability were rejected in the assessments of the violence made by the relatives in the second cluster. For example, one offender was diagnosed as schizophrenic at the time of the killing, which could have been appealed to in developing an illness based excuse for the violence, but his aunt refused to detract from the fatal results of the violence

> The killing of that man was dreadful. And for some people in a way it's easier to come to terms with: 'Oh yes, so and so killed because he was mentally ill at the time', because that's an OK reason to do that. But it isn't really an OK reason. I understand how it happened, but the man is dead.

In addition to accepting their relatives' full culpability, interviewees in the second 'cluster' also retained a notion of absolute victimization. This was also similar to the perception of innocence amongst victims' relatives (Rock 1998b). The victims were not constructed as having any role in the killings and others' attempts to devalue their victimization were also rejected

> *Mother.* I don't think anyone deserves to die in that manner. People have said that at least it was an old lady and not a child, that she'd lived a life. But I don't agree with that. No-one, however young however old or whatever they've done in their life deserves to die a violent death.

> *Aunt:* [The Police said] at least it was somebody who was a drug dealer, a pimp and a fence. But really, at the end of the day, it doesn't make any difference, because that man is dead. His life has gone.

In conceding the blameworthiness of their relatives, the interviewees in the second 'cluster' faced a particular problem in making sense of their relatives' crimes. Whilst they rejected manslaughter-based explanations of excuse or justification, they could not accept explanations of murder based upon the stereotype of 'evil' cold-blooded predatory killer. Although they shared with victims' relatives a dialect of victimization and culpability, they could not share victims' relatives' absolute hatred and rejection of the perpetrators themselves (Rock 1998b). In trying to find an alternative explanation, interviewees in this 'cluster' sought various forms of help from a range of individuals and organizations, including Victim Support, family therapy and counselling. Of significance was their common involvement in the support group Aftermath, which provided a framework for understanding violent crimes that was different to both the 'manslaughter' and 'evil murderer' models they had rejected. There were two processes by which this was possible.

First, through Aftermath, the interviewees in this second 'cluster' came to understand the stereotypical social category of 'murderer' as problematic. Aftermath encouraged those who sought the group's help to believe that their relatives' crimes should not be considered to be the sum of their personalities

> *Mother:* Even though I detest what he's done, even though we hate the crime, it is possible to still love the person.

> *Father:* You've got to divorce the person from the crime. He is still that person, the same person he's always been, it's just that something has happened.

This is akin to western Christian traditions of 'loving the sinner, but not the sin'. Parents of offspring who come out as gay, but cannot accept this in their daughters and sons, have also been shown to make a similar distinction (Griffin et al. 1990). In differentiating between 'being' and 'doing', interviewees were 'allowed' to acknowledge their relatives' culpability and yet not seeing them as 'evil murderers'.

Second, to reinforce the distinction between 'someone who had killed' and 'evil murderer' interviewees sought to explain the killings within a context of 'blame management' (McGraw 1991). In appealing to explanatory caveats to offenders' culpability interviewees were able to contain their relatives' blameworthiness as the actions of a 'sad' person, rather than an 'evil murderer'. The Aftermath narrative reveals two key explanatory caveats of 'blame management' which interviewees in this cluster drew upon: firstly, violence is connected to offenders' life experiences and secondly, offenders' families are part of these experiences. These are illustrated in the following comments of Aftermath's founding Director[9]

Without exception, there is always a pattern to the offence. A murder, for instance, you get a woman walking down the road and she's murdered and the police say 'Ooh, an awful motiveless crime'. There is no such thing as a motiveless crime. The motive is in the man who did it. (Or woman, but mostly men). So therefore, that innocent woman walking along the road, it's nothing to do with her whatsoever. And the man who murdered her is building up and building up and building up until that day something triggers him and it's vomited over her, everything that happened to him since the moment he was born, she becomes the tragic recipient of the lot. And in the tapestry of life a family may not be responsible, but they're part of the weave that comes off the loom.

All interviewees who presented accounts of murder identified factors in their relatives' lives which could help explain the killings. Some relatives, for example, identified childhood experiences which, they came to believe, shaped all later experiences of their offending relatives, whilst others recounted a catalogue of more recent contributory factors. The themes of these interviewees' narratives were rejection, difference and emotional vulnerability; the offenders were perceived as individuals who were not socially competent to deal with the circumstances in which they found, or had placed, themselves. None of these factors 'made' the offenders kill. They were, however, understood to have affected offenders' perceived choices and contributed significantly to their decisions to act violently.

In addition, interviewees who sought the Aftermath's support examined the role of familial interaction and communication on offenders' life experiences and their social and emotional competency. In particular, the Aftermath narrative suggested that only people with low self-esteem will have so little respect for others that they can act violently and that such low self-esteem is rooted in intra-familial relationships. Accepting this argument, all interviewees took some responsibility for generating these familial conditions but also marked a clear delineation between this and offenders' responsibilities for the killings

> *Mother:* I've made mistakes. But when all's said and done whatever I have done I didn't stand at the back of David when he killed that old lady and say 'You do that'.

> *Father:* Basically I am to blame for him not being emotionally competent to deal with that situation he was in . . . It wasn't my fault, the act, but how he felt at the time can be traced back to me not teaching him properly . . . I must accept some responsibility.

> *Aunt:* I don't actually believe we are not part of what Jonathon's done. I am sure that as a family, somewhere along the line we have to take our respective responsibilities for this, but not for what he's done.

Aftermath's analytical framework revealed to these interviewees familial environments which, they came to believe, did not recognize their relatives' emotional incompetency and so reinforced insecurities experienced. While they were clear that much of these experiences stemmed from, and were reinforced within families, they drew clear boundaries around the responsibility they were willing to accept, and did not believe their relatives to be any less culpable for the killings as a result. In managing the accepted blameworthiness of their relatives, interviewees were able to accept them as solely responsible for the deaths – leaving the victims' status intact – without recourse to the 'evil murderer' script which they had rejected as meaningless.

CONCLUSION

In focusing on the previously unresearched issue of being related to a convicted murderer, this paper reveals a number of social processes important in making sense of violence. In particular, the accounts of the murderers' relatives interviewed reveals the problematic nature of the killings for the maintenance of social reality. The killings challenged interviewees' understanding of their relatives as non-violent and 'murder' as the predatory and purposeful act of an 'evil' person. In seeking to explain their relatives' crimes, interviewees offered accounts of manslaughter – involving explanations of excuse and justification – and murder, in which offenders' blameworthiness was acknowledged yet managed. Although drawing different implications, all the accounts reflected interviewees' attempts to regain control over the social – and to some extent legal – meanings attached to their relatives' offences.

However, the narrow base of the research sample reflects, as discussed earlier, problems of accessing a hidden, vulnerable research population for the purposes of carrying out sensitive research. Because of these methodological problems, there are limits to the generalizability of this paper. However, the primary value of this paper rests on the conceptual framework it offers for further research and policy and practice. Of particular interest is the seemingly interconnected relationship between notions of victimization and culpability in the social interpretations made of the killings. Who killed whom appears central to the assessment of victimization and culpability and, therefore, social definitions of the crime itself. The claim for 'murder' appears to be socially justified on the premise of a wholly innocent victim and wholly culpable offender. This can be seen in both the 'murder' and 'manslaughter' accounts described above. Whilst interviewees offering 'manslaughter' accounts sought to blur the moral distinction between victims' and perpetrators' responsibility, those offering 'murder' accounts retained interpretations of absolute victimization and culpability. Absolute victimization and culpability can also be found in the murder accounts of homicide victims' relatives (Rock 1998a).

Significantly, it seems that interpretations of victimization and culpability are structured by wider normative assumptions; for example, 'common-sense' constructions of gender and sexuality can be seen in the interpretations made by interviewees. This raises questions for further research into the social definitions ascribed to inter-personal violence and homicide. It is important to fully explore the structured relationship between everyday understandings of victimization and culpability and the factors which mediate their assessments. In addition to gender and sexuality, there are other factors which mediate these social definitions: class, 'race' and age remain under-researched and deserving of further exploration. Moreover, the intersecting complexities of such mediating factors, crucial in the social definitions of homicide, need to be centrally located in theorizing violence in future research.

A second area of interest is that amongst the small number of interviewees those who offered accounts of murder had all been involved in the support group Aftermath. This suggests that an important area of future study should be the examination of the work of support groups with offenders' families and these organizations' relationship with other agencies – such as the police and prison and probation services. At the time of the field research, it became clear through conversations with probation officers and members of the support group Aftermath that a certain degree of distrust existed on both 'sides'. Yet there seem to be significant parallels between the work of both Aftermath and prison and probation services: to encourage offenders and their families to acknowledge perpetrators' responsibility in the killings. Families can be important significant others in offenders' own social reality and meaning attribution; how they understand the violence may impact upon offenders' own interpretation. It is important to explore, therefore, how the work of support groups such as Aftermath may be able to complement and enhance probation and prison services' work with offenders in understanding, and developing pathways away from, violence.

(Date accepted: February 1999)

Hazel May
Department of Sociology and
Social Policy
University of Leeds

NOTES

1 Two year old James Bulger was killed in 1993 by Jon Venables and Robert Thompson, both aged ten, in Liverpool, UK.

2 For a comprehensive and up-to-date review of the English and Welsh law on, and incidence of, homicide see Chapter One in Rock (1998b).

3 The field work was carried out as part of a doctoral thesis and supported by ESRC funding, award number R00429334225.

4 One family did not want to be interviewed again and the interviewed member of another family, although willing, was too ill to be re-interviewed for the duration of this research.

5 In the UK, the term 'serious' is used in reference to violent offences: homicide, armed robbery and rape.

6 Because homicide is a relatively rare crime in Britain, a single year should not

be given too much prominence. Therefore, it is best to understand the age of convicted murderers in terms of a percentage range.

7 Such examination of the past was confined primarily – though not exclusively – to parents, who felt, and are seen by others, to have responsibility for offspring's discipline and personality. However, this is also a gendered process, reflecting normative interpretations of maternal responsibility as greater than paternal (Richardson 1993).

8 Arguably, the interviews offered opportunities to rehearse and 'concretise' (Riches and Dawson 1996) these narratives.

9 Comments made in conversation with the author.

BIBLIOGRAPHY

Aftermath 1995 *For The Other Victims – The Families Of Serious Offenders*, Sheffield: Aftermath.

Bailey, S. 1996 'Adolescents Who Murder', *Journal of Adolescence* 19(1): 19–39.

Berger, P. L. and Luckmann, T. 1967 *The Social Construction of Reality: A Treatise on the Sociology of Knowledge*, Middlesex: Penguin.

Brown, M. A. and Powell-Cope, G. 1993 'Themes of Loss and Dying in Caring for a Family Member with AIDS', *Research in Nursing and Health* 16: 179–91.

Cameron, D. and Frazer, E. 1987 *The Lust To Kill: A Feminist Investigation of Sexual Murder*, Cambridge: Polity Press.

Clarkson, C. M. V. and Keating, H. M. 1990 *Criminal Law: Test and Materials* (Second Edition), London: Sweet and Maxwell.

Coker, J. B. and Martin, J. P. 1985 *Licensed to Live*. Oxford: Basil Blackwell.

Cooney, M. 1994 'The Informal Control of Homicide', *Journal of Legal Pluralism and Unofficial Law*, 34: 31–59.

Criminal Statistics 1993a *Chapter Four: Homicide. Table 4.4: Offences Currently Recorded as Homicide by Relationship of Victim to Principle Suspect and Sex of Victim*, London: HMSO.

—— 1993b *Supplementary Tables: Persons Convicted of Homicide England and Wales 1950–1993*, London: HMSO.

Fishman, S. H. 1982 'The Impact of Incarceration on Children of Offenders', *Journal of Children in Contemporary Society* 15(1): 89–99.

Griffin, C. W., Wirth, M. J. and Wirth, A. G. 1990 *Beyond Acceptance: Parents of Lesbians and Gays Talk About Their Experiences*, New York: St Martin's Press.

Humphreys, L. 1970 *Tea-Room Trade: A Study of Homosexual Encounters in Public Places*, London: Duckworth.

Jackson, D. 1995 *Destroying the Baby in Themselves: Why Did The Two Boys Kill Jamie Bulger?*, Nottingham: Mushroom.

Lee, N. H. 1969 *The Search For An Abortionist*, Chicago: Chicago University Press.

Levy, L. H. and Derby, J. F. 1992 'Bereavement Support Groups – Who Joins – Who Does Not – And Why', *American Journal of Community Psychology* 20(5): 649–62.

Light, R. 1992 *Prisoners' Families: Keeping In Touch.*, Bristol: Bristol Centre for Criminal Justice.

Mason, A. and Palmer, A. 1996 *Queer Bashing: A National Survey of Hate Crimes Against Lesbians and Gay Men*, London: Stonewall.

Matthews, J. 1983 *Forgotten Victims*, London: NACRO.

May, H. 1997 *An Exploration into the Experiences of Convicted Murderers' Relatives*, Unpublished doctoral thesis, University of Sheffield.

Maynard, M. and Winn, J. 1997 'Women, Violence and Male Power', in V. Robinson and D. Richardson (eds) *Introducing Women's Studies*, London: Macmillan.

McGraw, K. M. 1991 'Managing Blame: Experimental Test of the Effects of Political Accounts', *American Political Science Review* 85: 1135–57.

Mills, C. Wright 1940 'Situated Action and Vocabularies of Motive', *American Sociological Review* 5(6): 904–13.

Parker, T. 1990 *Life After Life*, London: Secker & Warburg.

Plummer, K. 1995 *Telling Sexual Stories: Power, Change and Social Worlds*, London: Routledge.

Polk, K. 1997 'A Re-examination of the Concept of Victim-Precipitated Homicide', *Homicide Studies: An Interdisciplinary and International Journal* 1(2): 141–68.

Ray, M. C. and Simons, R. L. 1987 'Convicted Murderers' Accounts of their

Crimes: A Study of Homicide in Small Communities', *Symbolic Interaction*, 10(1): 57–70.

Reif, L. V., Patton, M. J. and Gold, P. B. 1995 'Bereavement, Stress and Social Support In Members of a Self-Help Group', *Journal of Community Psychology* 23: 292–306.

Renzetti, C. M. and Lee, R. 1993 'Problems of Researching Sensitive Topics: An Overview and Introduction', in C. M. Renzetti and R. M. Lee (eds) *Researching Sensitive Topics*, London: Sage.

Richardson, D. 1993 *In the Club: Women, Motherhood and Childrearing*. Hampshire: Macmillan.

Richardson, D. and May, H. 1999 'Gender and Sexuality as Mitigating Factors in the Social Construction of Violence', *Sociological Review* 47(2): 308–31.

Riches, H. and Dawson, P. 1996 ' "An Intimate Loneliness": Evaluating the Impact of a Child's Death on Parental Self-Identity and Marital Relationships', *Journal of Family Therapy* 18: 1–22.

Rock, P. 1998a 'Murderers, Victims and "Survivors": The Social Construction of Deviance', *British Journal of Criminology* 38(2): 185–200.

—— 1998b *After Homicide: Practical and Political Responses to Bereavement*, Oxford: Clarendon Press.

Rynearson, E. K. 1995 'Bereavement After Homicide: A Comparison of Treatment Seekers and Refusers', *British Journal of Psychiatry* 166: 507–10.

Scully, D. and Marolla, J. 1984 'Convicted Rapists' Vocabularies of Motive: Excuses and Justifications', *Social Problems* 31(5): 530–44.

Shaw, R. 1992 *Prisoners' Children: What Are The Issues?* London: Routledge.

Sheer, V. C. and Weigold, M. F. 1995 'Maintaining Threats of Identity: The Accountability Triangle and Strategic Accounting', *Communication Research* 22(5): 592–611.

Silverman, E., Range, L. and Overholser, J. 1995 'Bereavement From Suicide as Compared to Other Forms of Bereavement', *Omega – Journal of Death and Dying* 30(1): 41–51.

Solomon, P. and Draine, J. 1996 'Examination of Grief Among Family Members of Individuals With Serious and Persistent Mental-Illness', *Psychiatric Quarterly* 67(3): 221–34.

Stanko, E. A. 1990 *Everyday Violence: How Women and Men Experience Sexual and Physical Danger*, London: Pandora.

Toolis, K. 1995 'A Queer Verdict', in the *Guardian: Weekend Section*, 25.1.95.

Weber, A. L., Harvey, J. H. and Orbuch, T. L. 1992 'What Went Wrong: Communicating Accounts of Relationship Conflict', in M. L. McLaughlin, M. J. Cody and S. J. Read (eds) *Explaining Oneself to Others: Reason Giving in a Social Context*, Hillside, NJ: Lawrence Erlbaum Associates.

Winch, P. 1958 *The Idea of a Social Science*, London: Routledge and Kegan Paul.

[24]

THE ROLE OF VICTIM CHARACTERISTICS IN THE DISPOSITION OF MURDER CASES*

ERIC P. BAUMER**
University of Missouri-St. Louis

STEVEN F. MESSNER***
University at Albany

RICHARD B. FELSON****
The Pennsylvania State University

Using data from prosecutors' files in a sample of 33 U.S. counties, we examine how victims' conduct and victims' demographic characteristics affect the disposition of murder cases at various stages of the criminal justice process. We find that victims' age and past conduct do not significantly influence legal outcomes in murder cases, but their race, gender, and conduct at the time of the incident do so. Although these effects vary across the criminal justice decision-making stages considered, they generally are consistent with the claim that killings of disreputable or stigmatized victims tend to be treated more leniently. We also find some evidence that the effects of victim characteristics are stronger in jury proceedings than in bench proceedings, and that the influence of a victim's race on the disposition of murder cases is conditioned by the racial composition of the county in which the case is processed.

   * We thank three anonymous *Justice Quarterly* reviewers for helpful comments.

   ** Eric P. Baumer is an assistant professor of criminology and criminal justice at the University of Missouri-St. Louis and a member of the National Consortium on Violence Research (NCOVR). His research focuses on spatial and temporal urban crime patterns, the effects of neighborhood characteristics on the behavior of individuals, and cross-cultural analyses of crime and punishment.

   *** Steven F. Messner is a professor of sociology at the University at Albany, SUNY. His research has focused on the relationship between social organization and crime, with emphasis on criminal homicide. He has also studied crime in China and the situational dynamics of violence. In addition to his publications in sociological and criminological journals, Professor Messner is co-author of *Crime and the American Dream* (Wadsworth), *Perspectives on Crime and Deviance* (Prentice-Hall), and *Criminology: An Introduction Using ExplorIt* (MicroCase), and co-editor of *Theoretical Integration in the Study of Deviance and Crime* (SUNY Press). He is also a member of the National Consortium on Violence Research (NCOVR).

   **** Richard B. Felson is a professor of crime, law, and justice in the Department of Sociology at The Pennsylvania State University. His recent research is concerned with situational and contextual factors in interpersonal violence. Currently he is writing a book on violence against women.

JUSTICE QUARTERLY, Vol. 17 No. 2, June 2000
© 2000 Academy of Criminal Justice Sciences

The pursuit of criminal justice involves a large number of individuals making a series of complex decisions. In most jurisdictions, this process includes decisions by law enforcement officials about whether to investigate a crime and make an arrest, pre- and post-indictment charging decisions by prosecutors, the decision regarding the nature of the adjudication (trial versus plea), the decision about whether to convict or acquit, and the decision regarding the nature and severity of the punishment to be imposed (e.g., Samaha 1994). Although decisions made at each stage of the criminal justice process are restricted by substantive and procedural criminal law, a considerable amount of discretion remains in the decisions made and in the factors that may influence each of these decisions (e.g., Albonetti 1986; Black 1989; Lundsgaarde 1977).

Researchers have considered a broad range of factors that influence outcomes for persons accused of crime. Among the most commonly considered factors are the seriousness of the offense, the characteristics of the defendant, and the characteristics of the case (see, e.g., Albonetti 1991; Myers and Talarico 1987; Sampson and Lauritsen 1997; Williams 1976).

The present research focuses on the effect of victim characteristics on legal outcomes in murder cases. We examine how the conduct of victims during the incident, their prior criminal record, and their demographic characteristics affect legal outcomes at five stages of the criminal justice process: the initial prosecutorial screening, indictment, post-indictment prosecutorial screening, the nature of the disposition (i.e., plea versus trial), and the outcome of the trial. In the discussion below we outline the ways in which victim characteristics might affect outcomes in criminal cases at each of these stages. We then describe the specific hypotheses addressed in our research, and the data and methods used to test these hypotheses.

Victims' Conduct and Legal Outcomes

The conduct of crime victims may influence judges' and jurors' decisions in three ways. First, victims are often key witnesses; their conduct is an important consideration in whether they will be viewed as credible (Holstrom and Burgess 1978; Stanko 1981). Victims who have engaged in some form of disreputable behavior are more likely to be viewed as untrustworthy and dishonest, which may decrease the likelihood of indictment and conviction (Elwork, Sales, and Suggs 1981; Frohmann 1991; Myers and Hagan 1979; Sales 1981).

Second, victims' conduct may influence judges' and jurors' decisions by affecting the level of blame attributed to the defendant.

According to attribution theory, the attribution of blame for an outcome depends in part on attributions of internal and external causality (e.g., Heider 1958; Weary, Stanley, and Harvey 1989). The more an outcome is attributed to external forces, the less the assignment of internal causality and blame. In the case of a crime, the greater the causality attributed to the victim (an external force), the less the causality attributed to the defendant (an internal force) (see Jones and Aronson 1973; Landy and Aronson 1969; Walster 1966; Whatley 1996). In a criminal justice system in which the defendant's guilt must be proved beyond a reasonable doubt, even the slightest tilt in the balance of blame toward the victim (and away from the defendant) may affect judges' and jurors' adjudication decisions (Kalven and Zeisel 1966). Thus a defendant may be less likely to be indicted and convicted, and may face a lesser charge, if the victim is perceived as blameworthy.

Third, victims' conduct may affect judgments of the amount of harm done. A crime against an upstanding citizen may be perceived by judges and jurors as a greater harm, and thus as a more serious offense, than a crime against a disreputable person (e.g., Black 1989). In addition, sympathy for the victim within the community, and anger toward the defendant, are likely to be greater when the victim is someone who is considered reputable. If this is so, the demand for punishment may be weaker in cases involving victims who have engaged in disreputable conduct; judges and jurors may be less likely to indict or convict defendants in such cases.

If the victim's conduct affects the decisions of judges and jurors, it is also likely to be an important consideration for prosecutors (Frohmann 1991; Mather 1979; Stanko 1981; also see Albonetti 1987; Myers and Hagan 1979; Spears and Spohn 1997). As Albonetti (1986, 1987) points out, prosecutors often face strong organizational pressure to win cases, and victory is defined primarily in terms of obtaining a conviction at trial. In response to this pressure, prosecutors may reject or drop cases when they are uncertain about the likelihood of conviction (Albonetti 1987, 1991; Frohmann 1991; Mather 1979; Spears and Spohn 1997; Stanko 1981).

Prosecutors' judgments of the likelihood of conviction are based largely on such factors as the nature and seriousness of the crime, the quality of evidence associated with the case, whether there were aggravating circumstances, and the previous criminal record (if any) of the accused (Albonetti 1986; Miller 1970; Neubauer 1974; Swigert and Farrell 1977). In estimating the likelihood of conviction, however, prosecutors also consider "how judge and jury will assess a victim's life-style and moral character" (Stanko 1981: 229, also see Frohmann 1991; Miller 1970). If prosecutors are less confident about winning cases that involve disreputable victims, they may be more likely to reject these cases at first screening, to drop those which are indicted via a *nolle prosequi* motion, or to push for plea negotiations rather than proceeding to trial.

In summary, the victim's past and present conduct may influence the decisions of judges, jurors, and prosecutors by affecting assessments of credibility, attributions of blame, and perceptions of the amount of harm done. In murder, the offense considered here, the victim's credibility as a witness is generally not a factor.[1] Victims' conduct should have an influence because of its effect on attributions of responsibility and perceptions of the amount of harm done.

Demographic Characteristics of The Victim

The victim's race, gender, and age also may affect criminal justice decisions if they influence attributions of responsibility and harm (e.g., Spears and Spohn 1997; Stanko 1988; Williams 1976). In regard to race, Hawkins (1987:726) argues that "the lives and persons of whites are more valued than those of blacks in American society" (also see Garfinkel 1949; LaFree 1980; Myrdal 1944). If nonwhites are devalued, then homicides in which the victim is nonwhite may be perceived as involving less harm. In addition, stereotypes about black crime may lead officials to assign more blame to black victims. Both of these processes may lead to more lenient treatment of defendants when the victim is nonwhite.

The victim's gender also may influence legal outcomes, although contradictory predictions can be advanced. Criminal justice decision makers may attribute more blame to male than to female victims, based on gender differences in violence. In addition, research shows that violence against women is perceived more negatively than violence against men (Harris 1991; for a review, see Felson 1996). These processes would lead to more severe treatment of defendants who are accused of killing a woman. On the other hand, theories of gender conflict suggest that females are devalued in comparison with males (see Chesney-Lind 1988; Daly 1989; Edwards 1988). If this is so, defendants accused of victimizing females may receive less severe sanctions.

Expectations about the effect of the victim's age on legal outcomes are also unclear. On the one hand, killing a young person

---

[1] In murder cases, victims obviously can play a "witness" role only at a very early stage of the processing, perhaps by identifying the defendant before their demise.

may be perceived as more harmful than killing an older person because more years of life are lost. This reasoning implies more severe outcomes for defendants who victimize young persons. On the other hand, victims in age groups associated with high rates of criminal violence (e.g., 18 to 29) may be viewed as more likely to have done something to provoke the attack. This attribution would result in a lower likelihood of conviction and a lower penalty for defendants when the victim is a young adult.

Statistical Interactions

Theoretical discussions suggest that the effect of victim characteristics on legal outcomes may be conditioned by case characteristics, especially the seriousness of the case and the nature of adjudication. Kalven and Zeisel (1966) argue that criminal justice decision makers use more discretion and thus are more willing to consider extralegal factors in situations in which they are "liberated" from the strict letter of the law (also see Black 1989; Estrich 1987; Kalven and Zeisel 1966; Reskin and Visher 1986; Spears and Spohn 1997). The seriousness of the case has been identified as important in determining whether decision makers are likely to be liberated from the law and to consider extralegal characteristics. As Spears and Spohn (1997:504) observe, in "less serious cases the appropriate disposition is not obvious; criminal justice officials and jurors therefore have more discretion, and thus more opportunities to take legally irrelevant factors into account." This suggests that victim characteristics may be more influential in murder cases that are perceived as less serious (e.g., second-degree versus first-degree murder).

Extending the liberation hypothesis, Kalven and Zeisel (1966) also suggest that jurors are more likely than judges to consider extralegal characteristics. Black (1989) derives similar conclusions, arguing that jurors are influenced less than judges by legal standards and more by extralegal factors because they tend to be closer in social status to defendants (also see Elwork et al. 1981). These arguments suggest that legally irrelevant victim attributes should affect legal outcomes more strongly in jury proceedings than in bench proceedings.

Some scholars also believe that racial discrimination in legal outcomes is likely to vary across communities: it is more likely to occur in communities containing relatively few nonwhite residents (Blalock 1967; Myers and Talarico 1987). In communities with a sizable nonwhite population, nonwhites have more political power and more influence on the legal system, which should lessen racial discrimination. Following this line of reasoning, we predict that

Violence

crimes against nonwhite victims are more likely to be treated leniently in communities with relatively few nonwhite residents.

PREVIOUS RESEARCH

Prior research on the influence of victim characteristics on legal outcomes focused primarily on prosecutors' initial screening decision and on the likelihood of conviction. With some exceptions (e.g., Albonetti 1986, 1991), this research suggests that provocation by the victim reduces the likelihood of prosecution (Albonetti 1987, 1991; Spears and Spohn 1997; Stanko 1981; Williams 1976) and conviction (LaFree 1980; LaFree, Reskin, and Visher 1985), and leads to less severe punishment (Kruttschnitt 1985; Myers 1979, 1980; Williams 1976; Wolfgang 1967). The literature also suggests that cases involving evidence of disreputable conduct by the victim at the time of the offense (e.g., drinking, using drugs, engaging in criminal behavior) are less likely to be prosecuted both at initial screening (Frohmann 1991; Spears and Spohn 1997; Stanko 1981; Williams 1976) and at post-indictment screening (Albonetti 1986). Offenders in these cases also are less likely to be convicted if prosecuted (Williams 1976), and are assigned significantly less guilt by trial jurors (see LaFree 1980, 1989; LaFree et al. 1985).

Support is less consistent for the influence of the victim's past behavior on legal outcomes. Williams (1976) and Boris (1979) report that evidence of a criminal record and history of alcohol or drug abuse do not significantly affect prosecutorial screening decisions in murder, robbery, and assault cases. Spears and Spohn (1997) and Williams (1976), however, report that prosecutors are less likely to file official charges in sexual assault and rape cases if the victim's past conduct was disreputable. Similarly, LaFree (1989) and Estrich (1987) report that jurors tend to assign less guilt to defendants accused of victimizing persons known to have engaged in morally disreputable conduct in the past (also see LaFree 1980; LaFree et al. 1985); Williams (1976) reports that such cases are less likely to result in a conviction. Finally, Myers' (1979) findings indicate that defendants convicted of victimizing individuals who had a criminal record are significantly less likely to be sentenced to prison than defendants who are convicted of victimizing individuals with no criminal record.

Some researchers also have examined the effect of victims' demographic characteristics on legal outcomes. In general, the research suggests that defendants tend to receive less severe punishment when they victimize nonwhites, especially in capital murder cases (e.g., Hawkins 1987; Kleck 1981). Several researchers (e.g., Baldus, Pulaski, and Woodworth 1983; Bowers and Pierce 1980;

Gross and Mauro 1984; Paternoster 1984) report that defendants indicted for murder are significantly less likely to receive death sentences when the victim is nonwhite than when the victim is white. Further, Boris (1979) reports that persons accused of murdering white victims are more likely to be prosecuted than those accused of murdering nonwhite victims. Beaulieu and Messner (1999) find that conviction is more likely for persons indicted for murdering whites than for those indicted for murdering blacks.

Various studies suggest that the effect of the victim's race on legal outcomes is conditioned by the defendant's race (e.g., Bowers and Pierce 1980; LaFree 1980; Spohn and Spears 1996). The most consistent finding is that cases involving white victims result in a more severe sentence when the defendant is black than when the defendant is white (Baldus et al. 1983; Bowers and Pierce 1980; Garfinkel 1949; Johnson 1941; Paternoster 1984; Spohn and Spears 1996). Furthermore, Myers (1979, 1980) reports that felony cases involving white victims are more likely to result in conviction when the defendant is black than when the defendant is white. In a fairly recent study, Spohn and Spears (1996) observe that prosecution is more likely and prison sentences more severe in sexual assault cases involving a white victim when the defendant is black than when the defendant is white. Spohn (1994) also observes that sexual assault crimes involving a white victim result in a greater likelihood of incarceration when the defendant is black. This effect, however, is not observed for other crimes, including murder.

Several studies have also examined the effects of victim's gender on legal outcomes. Myers (1979, 1980) observes that a prison sentence is more likely if the victim is a woman; Beaulieu and Messner (1999) report that defendants who murder females are less likely to receive a charge reduction than those who murder males. In contrast, Spohn (1994) finds victim's gender is not significantly related to the likelihood of incarceration for persons convicted of a felony, and Beaulieu and Messner (1999) observe no significant effect of victim's gender on the likelihood of conviction.

The few studies that have considered the victim's age also report mixed findings. The most consistent finding is that the victim's age is not significantly related to outcomes of criminal cases. Myers (1979, 1980) observes that victim's age is not significantly related to the seriousness of the conviction nor to the length of the sentence imposed in felony cases. Similarly, Boris (1979) finds no significant effect of victim's age on the likelihood of prosecution in murder cases; Paternoster (1984) observes no effect of victim age on prosecutors' decisions to seek the death penalty; and Spohn and Spears

(1996) report no effect of victim's age on the likelihood of prosecution, conviction, or incarceration, nor on the severity of prison sentence, in sexual assault cases. Studies reporting significant effects of victim's age suggest that its effects are complex, and may vary by crime type and by the stage of the criminal justice process studied. Williams (1976) finds that defendants accused of murdering victims over age 60 are less likely to be prosecuted; Spears and Spohn (1997) report that sexual assault cases involving victims age 13 and older are more likely than other cases to result in prosecution. Finally, Myers (1980) reports that defendants convicted of victimizing older persons are more likely to receive a prison sentence.

A few studies have considered whether the effects of victim characteristics are moderated by indicators of case seriousness or by the type of trial proceeding. Kalven and Zeisel's (1966) findings suggest that jurors' perceptions about the victim's conduct in the moments leading up to the crime are more likely to influence the verdict in less serious cases. In keeping with Kalven and Zeisel's general argument, Paternoster (1984) finds that the victim's race exerts a stronger effect on the decision to seek the death penalty in murder cases that involve fewer aggravating circumstances. Spears and Spohn (1997), however, report that the strength or seriousness of the case does not moderate the effects of victim's character, conduct, and relationship to the defendant on prosecutors' charging decisions in sexual assault cases.

Finally, we see some evidence that the effects of victim characteristics on trial outcomes are conditioned by the type of trial proceeding. Kalven and Zeisel's (1966) findings suggest that jurors are less likely than judges to follow the strict letter of the law, especially in cases in which jurors felt that the victim shared some of the blame and when the consequences of a guilty verdict (i.e., the punishment) were severe (also see Elwork et al. 1981).

THE PRESENT RESEARCH

We extend prior research on the influence of victim characteristics on legal outcomes in several ways. First, much of the research on the influence of victim characteristics has focused on rape and sexual assault. With some notable exceptions (Boris 1979; Myers 1979; Spohn 1994; Williams 1976), that research has not examined the effects of victim characteristics on legal outcomes of murder cases. Murder is one of the most serious crimes of which a defendant may be accused; prosecutors, judges, and jurors are likely to face intense public (and moral) pressure to apply "the strict letter of the law" in these cases. The inherent seriousness of murder cases may restrict the discretion that prosecutors, judges, and jurors are willing and able to reserve for considering factors such as victim's conduct, race, age, and sex. Thus, focusing on murder cases provides a stringent test of the hypothesis that victim characteristics influence the decisions of prosecutors, judges, and jurors.

Second, we examine the influence of victim characteristics on legal outcomes at several stages of the criminal justice process. Despite some exceptions (e.g., Albonetti 1986; 1990; Spohn and Spears 1996; Williams 1976), most of the research on the effects of victim characteristics on legal outcomes has focused on the initial prosecutorial screening decision, the outcome of the trial, or the severity of the sentence imposed. Victim characteristics also may influence decisions at other stages of the criminal justice process, including the indictment stage and the type of adjudication (trial versus plea) (Black 1989). Indeed, some evidence suggests that the effects of victim characteristics on legal outcomes may vary at different stages of the criminal justice process; the most salient effects are observed during prosecutorial screening (Williams 1976). Although this seems reasonable when we consider that prosecutors enjoy far greater discretion than other criminal justice decision makers (Albonetti 1986), few studies have formally and directly examined the effects of victim characteristics across outcomes at multiple stages of the criminal justice process. As we elaborate below, our research examines the effects of several victim characteristics at five key stages of criminal justice decision making. This approach allows us to assess whether the effects of victim characteristics vary across these stages.

Finally, most studies of the influence of victim (and other) characteristics on criminal case processing rely on data drawn from one or only a few jurisdictions. In contrast, our research is based on a random sample of murder cases processed in 33 counties that are representative of the 75 largest urban U.S. counties. This sample allows us to generalize our results to a much larger geographic area than did previous studies. In addition, unlike previous researchers, we can examine whether a county's racial composition influences legal outcomes in murder cases and whether it moderates the effects of victim's race on these outcomes.

HYPOTHESES

As noted, we focus on the role of victim characteristics in legal outcomes at five key decision making stages in the processing of murder cases: the initial screening of murder cases by prosecutors, the indictment or preliminary hearing stage, post-indictment prosecutorial screening, the nature of the disposition (i.e., plea versus trial), and the trial outcome.

290   ROLE OF VICTIM CHARACTERISTICS

We address four empirical questions at each of these stages. First, we explore whether the victim's conduct influences legal outcomes in murder cases. We hypothesize that legal outcomes are less severe when the victim physically provoked the defendant, engaged in other disreputable conduct at the time of the incident, or had engaged in disreputable behavior in the past. These cases should be less likely to be prosecuted, less likely to be indicted, and less likely to be carried forward if indicted. Also, the uncertainty associated with these types of victims may make prosecutors reluctant to proceed to trial (that is, they may be more likely to negotiate a guilty plea) and less likely to obtain a conviction in cases that result in a trial.[2]

Second, we explore whether the victim's demographic characteristics influence legal outcomes. On the basis of prior theory and research, we predict that defendants accused of murdering white victims and female victims receive more severe treatment. We make no predictions regarding the effects of the victim's age.

Third, we examine statistical interactions involving the victim's race. On the basis of prior research and theory, we predict that leniency toward defendants in cases involving nonwhite victims is less likely when the defendant is nonwhite and in cases processed in counties in which nonwhites make up a larger fraction of the total population.

Finally, we examine whether the effects of victim characteristics on legal outcomes are conditioned by the nature of the adjudication and the seriousness of the case. Kalven and Zeisel's (1966) liberation hypothesis suggests that victim characteristics will have a stronger effect in jury proceedings than in bench proceedings, and in less serious cases than in more serious cases.

DATA AND ANALYTIC STRATEGY

As stated above, we address these questions with data on murder cases adjudicated in a probability sample of 33 counties that are representative of the 75 largest urban counties in the United States (U.S. Department of Justice 1996).[3] Data were collected for 2,539 murder cases that included 3,119 defendants and 2,655 victims. A random sample of murder cases in which one or more defendants

---

[2] Although the uncertainty of these types of cases may make prosecutors reluctant to proceed to trial, it may encourage defendants (and their attorneys) to forgo plea negotiations and take their chances at trial.

[3] This data file was obtained from ICPSR, Study 9907, *Murder Cases in 33 Large Urban Counties in the United States, 1988* (U.S. Department of Justice 1996). The original collector of the data (ICPSR) and the relevant funding agency bear no responsibility for our use of this data collection, nor for our interpretations or inferences based on the data.

had been arrested for murder at any time during or before 1988, and in which a final disposition had been reached during 1988, was drawn from prosecutors' case files in each county included in the study.[4] Following prior research, we limit our analyses to cases with a single victim and a single defendant to avoid ambiguities in classifying incidents with multiple victims and defendants (see Beaulieu and Messner 1999; Williams and Flewelling 1988). By imposing this restriction and removing cases with missing values on the explanatory variables, we obtain a maximum sample of 1,990 murder cases for our analyses.[5]

Dependent Variables

We assess the effects of victim characteristics on five dependent variables. First, we examine whether victim characteristics influence the decision to prosecute (coded 1) or reject (coded 0) (*Prosecution*). Second, for cases that result in an initial decision to prosecute, we examine whether the judge or grand jury hands down an indictment (coded 1) or dismisses the charges (coded 0) (*Indictment*). Third, in cases resulting in an indictment, we consider prosecutors' post-indictment screening decisions: in other words, whether the case is carried forward (coded 1) or dropped (coded 0) (*Carried Forward*). Fourth, for cases carried forward for prosecution, we contrast those cases which are adjudicated at trial (coded 1) with those disposed through a guilty plea negotiation (coded 0) (*Trial*). Fifth, for cases that proceed to trial, we examine the effects of victim characteristics on the legal outcome at trial. Here, unlike the other four outcomes, which are measured as dichotomous dependent variables, we construct an ordinal dependent variable that captures three possible trial outcomes of murder cases: acquittal (*Acquittal*) conviction for a reduced charge (*Conviction on Reduced Charge*), and conviction for the most serious indictment charge (*Conviction on Most Serious Indictment Charge*).

Independent Variables

We are interested primarily in examining whether these outcomes are influenced by the victim's conduct and the victim's race, age, and sex. We include two measures of the victim's conduct during the incident, and one measure of the victim's past conduct. The first indicator of victim's conduct is whether the victim physically

---

[4] A random sample of 200 eligible cases was selected from each county included in the study. All eligible cases were sampled in counties containing fewer than 200 eligible cases.

[5] The 33-county murder data set includes 2,160 cases that involve a single victim and a single defendant. We exclude 170 of these cases because of missing data on explanatory variables.

292   ROLE OF VICTIM CHARACTERISTICS

provoked the defendant. This variable is coded 1 if the prosecutors' case files contain evidence that the victim was the first to physically attack or threaten the defendant with a weapon; it is coded 0 if there was no evidence of such provocation (*Physical Provocation*).

The second indicator of victim's conduct taps whether the victim was behaving in a disreputable manner at the time of the incident. This variable is constructed from two items available in the data used for our research: whether the victim possessed a weapon, and why the victim was on the scene of the crime. Specifically, disreputable conduct on the part of the victim is coded 1 if the victim possessed a weapon or if the victim was on the scene to seek confrontation with the defendant, to purchase, sell, or use drugs, or to engage in some other form of criminal behavior; it is coded 0 if the victim did not possess a weapon and was not at the murder scene for these reasons (*Disreputable Conduct*).

Past disreputable conduct on the victim's part is a dichotomous measure indicating whether the prosecutors' case files contained evidence that the victim ever had been convicted of a crime (1 = yes; 0 = no) (*Disreputable Past Conduct*).[6]

The remaining independent variables refer to victim's demographic characteristics. Victim's race (*Victim Nonwhite*) is coded 1 for nonwhite victims; 0 for white victims; victim's gender (*Victim Male*) is coded 1 for male victims and 0 for female victims. Finally, victim's age is measured with three dummies that distinguish victims under age 18 (*Victim under 18*), victims between ages 18 and 29 (*Victim 18 to 29*), and victims age 30 and older; the latter category serves as the reference group.

Control Variables

To isolate the effects of these victim characteristics on legal sanctioning at each of the five stages of the criminal justice process considered, we include many of the defendant, offense, and case characteristics shown in previous research to be related to outcomes in criminal cases. The measurement of defendant's race (*Defendant Nonwhite*), gender (*Defendant Male*), and age (*Defendant under 18, Defendant 18 to 29*) corresponds to the measurement of victim's race, gender, and age as described above.

---

6 U.S. courts have adopted a general rule that permits an accused person to introduce evidence of a pertinent trait of a crime victim's character. For example, the accused may present evidence of the victim's propensity toward criminal behavior (e.g., evidence of a criminal record) to prove that the victim was the aggressor (see Mueller and Kirkpatrick 1995).

We also include indicators of defendant characteristics such as whether the defendant has a criminal record, and offense characteristics such as the seriousness of the offense and whether the offense is accompanied by aggravating circumstances (see Albonetti 1992; Spears and Spohn 1997). Defendant's prior criminal record (*Defendant Prior Conviction*) is measured with a dummy variable scored 1 if the defendant has such a conviction and scored 0 if the defendant does not have such a conviction (Welch, Gruhl, and Spohn 1984). As a control variable we include an indicator of whether the defendant was arrested on the scene on the day of the murder (coded 1) or later (coded 0) (*Defendant Arrested on Scene*). In general, the defendant's involvement in the murder is perceived as more certain by prosecutors, judges, and jurors when the defendant was arrested on the scene (e.g., Albonetti 1986; Lizotte 1978).

Prior research suggests that crimes between nonstrangers are less likely than those between strangers to be prosecuted (Albonetti 1987; Bernstein, Kelly, and Doyle 1977; LaFree 1980; Radelet and Pierce 1985), less likely to result in an indictment (Lundsgaarde 1977; Vera Institute 1977), less likely to result in continued prosecution if indicted (Albonetti 1986), and less likely to result in a conviction (Myers 1980; Spohn and Spears 1996; Vera Institute 1977; Williams 1976). Following prior research, we measure relationship between the victim and the defendant as a dichotomy, coded 1 for cases in which the prosecutors' files contained evidence that the victim and the defendant were nonstrangers (i.e., spouses, ex-spouses, other family relations, or friends) and coded 0 for those who were strangers (*Defendant and Victim Nonstrangers*).

In accordance with previous research (Albonetti 1992), we include as a measure of aggravating circumstances a dummy variable that distinguishes murders committed with a firearm (coded 1) from those that did not involve a firearm (*Gun Murder*). Although all members of our sample were arrested for murder, a serious offense, we include two dummy variables that tap differences in the legal seriousness of the murder for which defendants in our sample were accused. These dummy variables refer to the specific offense for which the members of our sample were arrested (*Murder 1 Arrest Charge*) and indicted (*Murder 1 Indictment Charge*). Both of these dichotomous variables distinguish defendants charged with first-degree murder (coded 1) from those charged with second-degree murder or manslaughter (coded 0). As noted above, we use these indicators not only as important controls, but also to explore whether the effects of victim characteristics are conditioned by case seriousness, as suggested by the liberation hypothesis.

294   ROLE OF VICTIM CHARACTERISTICS

The liberation hypothesis also implies that the effects of victim characteristics will exert stronger effects in jury proceedings than in bench proceedings. To test this hypothesis at the adjudication stage, we include a dummy variable in our analyses of trial outcomes, coded 1 for jury trials and 0 for bench trials (*Jury Trial*), and we explore interactions between this variable and the victim attributes described above.

The primary data source used for our research does not include a similar indicator at the indictment stage. Thus we cannot identify whether cases that proceed to the indictment phase were resolved by a grand jury proceeding or a preliminary bench hearing. Using data from the National Prosecutors Survey (U.S. Department of Justice 1997), however, we include a dummy variable in our analysis of outcomes at the indictment stage; this is coded 1 if the case was processed in a county in which more than three-quarters of indictments in felony cases were obtained by grand jury, and coded 0 otherwise (*Grand Jury Proceeding*).[7] We employ this variable to control for variation across jurisdictions in the type of legal proceeding used to obtain indictments in felony cases (Eisenstein, Flemming, and Nardulli 1988), and to explore whether the effects of victim attributes on the likelihood of indictment are conditioned by type of indictment proceeding, as suggested by the liberation hypothesis.

Finally, our analysis includes the racial composition of the county in which the case was processed, measured as the proportion of the county population that is nonwhite (*Proportion Nonwhite in County*).[8]

---

[7] The National Prosecutors Survey (NPS) is a biennial survey of chief prosecutors in 300 U.S. counties that includes information on prosecutors' offices, policies, and practices. A public-use version of this data set is freely available through the Inter-University Consortium for Political and Social Research (ICPSR, Study 9579; U.S. Department of Justice 1997). The public-use version, however, does not include the geographic identifiers of the counties represented by the prosecutors in the sample. ICPSR and the Bureau of Justice Statistics granted us access to a private-use version of the 1989-1990 NPS that included county identifiers. Using this data set, we were able to compute the fraction of all felony cases processed by a grand jury for 27 of the 33 counties included in our sample of murder cases. For the six counties not included in the NPS, we computed the fraction of all felony cases processed by a grand jury in the four counties adjacent to these counties. After merging this variable to our primary data source, we created a dummy variable identifying murder cases processed in counties in which indictments were sought by the grand jury in three-quarters or more of felony cases.

[8] County racial composition, which we obtained from the *County and City Data Book, 1994* (U.S. Bureau of the Census 1994), refers to the proportion of the population of each county that was nonwhite in 1990. Although the timing of the measurement of this variable does not correspond precisely to our data on murder cases (which were collected in 1988-1989), racial composition is likely to be quite stable over such a short period; therefore this discrepancy is not likely to introduce serious bias.

Analytical Strategy

Our dependent variables at initial prosecutorial screening, indictment, post-indictment prosecutorial screening, and the nature of adjudication are dichotomous. Accordingly we use binary logistic regression to estimate the effects of victim characteristics at these stages. Our dependent variable at the trial outcome stage is trichotomous; thus we use multinomial logit regression to model the effects of victim characteristics on this variable. Multinomial logit regression is an extension of the binary logistic equation that allows for the comparison of two or more contrasts (see Clogg and Shihadeh 1994). In the analyses presented below, we estimate adjacent category contrasts and equations of trial outcomes.[9] Specifically, the multinomial logit equations presented for trial outcome represent the contrasts of the log-odds of conviction for the most serious indictment charge relative to conviction for an intermediate (reduced) charge and the log-odds of conviction for an intermediate charge relative to acquittal.[10]

RESULTS

Before reporting results of the multivariate analyses, it is instructive to examine the percentage distributions for the dependent and independent variables. The results displayed in Table 1 reveal that only a small fraction of murder cases are rejected by prosecutors, dismissed during the indictment or preliminary hearing phase of the criminal justice process, or dropped by prosecutors after indictment. In the great majority of murder cases presented for prosecutorial screening (92%), prosecutors filed official charges of murder. Most of these cases (97%) resulted in an indictment or

---

[9] We estimated these equations using the CATMOD procedure in SAS. We also estimated ordinal cumulative logit equations (with the LOGISTIC procedure) in which the slopes associated with different cumulative log odds were assumed to be parallel. The results of these analyses (not shown) indicated that the assumption of proportional odds was not satisfied with the outcomes examined in this research. Therefore, separate equations must be reported for the respective category contrasts.

[10] Our analytic design entails the examination of decisions at multiple stages, which raises the highly controversial issue of sample selection bias. Some researchers favor the computation of "correction factors" to control for selection bias (e.g., Albonetti 1991; Berk 1983; Dubin and Rivers 1994). Others caution that such procedures can do more harm than good (Clogg and Shihadeh 1994; Lillard, Smith, and Welch 1986; Stolzenberg and Relles 1990, 1997). In supplemental analyses, we used Heckman's (1976) two-stage estimation procedure and added the resulting correction factors to our equations for indictment, carried forward, nature of disposition, and trial outcome. With the exception of trial outcome, the results of the equations including the correction factor were very similar to those reported below. The coefficients and standard errors for the model of trial outcome were severely inflated, but also led to conclusions substantively similar to those obtained from the model presented without the correction factor. In view of the lack of consensus on appropriate remedies for censored sampling, we report results without the correction factor. (Results of equations including the correction factor are available from the first author.)

Table 1. Percentage Distributions for Variables Included in Analysis of the Effects of Victim Characteristics on the Severity of Sanctioning in Murder Cases

Variables	Percentage
Dependent Variables	
Prosecutor's initial screening[a]	
Prosecute	92.0
Reject	8.0
Indictment/preliminary hearing[b]	
Indictment	96.7
Dismissal	3.3
Prosecutor's post-indictment screening[c]	
Carried Forward	95.9
Dropped Charges	4.2
Nature of adjudication[d]	
Trial	52.3
Plea	47.7
Trial outcome[e]	
Conviction on most serious indictment charge	41.8
Conviction on reduced charge	38.5
Acquittal	19.7
Victim Characteristics	
Physical provocation	19.3
Disreputable conduct	31.5
Disreputable past conduct	7.0
Victim nonwhite	58.5
Victim male	76.9
Victim under 18	7.2
Victim 18 to 29	37.1
Victim 30 and older	55.7
Control Variables	
Defendant nonwhite	63.1
Defendant male	87.8
Defendant under 18	3.3
Defendant 18 to 29	48.3
Defendant 30 and older	48.4
Defendant prior conviction	34.6
Defendant and victim nonstrangers	38.4
Gun murder	56.4
Defendant arrested on scene	52.5
Murder 1 Arrest Charge	73.4
Second degree murder or manslaughter arrest charge	26.6
Murder 1 Indictment Charge	61.7
Second degree murder charge or manslaughter indictment charge	38.3
Proportion nonwhite in county (mean)	.358

[a]The percentages for initial prosecutorial screening and those for all victim characteristics and control variables are based on 1,990 cases.

[b]Based on the 1,831 cases in which official charges were filed; 33.8 percent of these represent cases processed in jurisdiction in which the grand jury was the dominant mode of assessing probable cause.

[c]Based on 1,757 cases in which an indictment resulted.

[d]Based on 1,684 cases carried forward by prosecutors.

[e]Based on 880 cases adjudicated at trial; 68 percent of these were jury trials and 32 percent were bench trials.

were bound over for trial, and prosecutors carried forward 96% of murder cases that resulted in indictment. Slightly more than half (52%) of murder cases carried forward by prosecutors were adjudicated at trial; the remaining cases were disposed via a guilty plea negotiation. Finally, only about one-fifth of the murder cases that proceeded to trial resulted in an acquittal. The most common outcome at trial was conviction on the indictment charge (42%), followed by conviction on a reduced charge (39%).

In regard to the indicators of victims' conduct and demographic characteristics, physical provocation was present in about one-fifth of the murder cases. Disreputable behavior on the victim's part at the time of the murder (i.e., victim possessed a weapon, was selling, purchasing, or using drugs, or was engaged in criminal behavior) was observed in just under one-third of the cases. About 7% of the victims were known to have engaged in disreputable conduct in the past, as reflected in a prior conviction. Finally, 59% of the victims were nonwhite, 77% were male, 7% were under age 18, 37% were between ages 18 and 29, and 56% were age 30 or older. (We also report percentage distributions for the control variables in Table 1, but to conserve space we do not discuss them.)

The Effect of Victim Characteristics

The multivariate regression results, presented in Table 2, show that victim's conduct has the predicted effects on several of the legal outcomes considered here. Incidents in which the victim provoked the defendant are less likely to be prosecuted, less likely to lead to indictment, and more likely to lead to conviction on a reduced charge. Incidents during which the victim engaged in other disreputable conduct are less likely to be carried forward and more likely to result in conviction on a reduced charge.[11] In contrast, past disreputable conduct has no significant effect on any of the legal outcomes.

---

[11] We also estimated a binary logit equation (results not shown) with the dependent variable coded 1 for conviction on any charge and coded 0 for acquittal. Unlike the results shown in equations (5) and (6), the results of this equation indicate that disreputable conduct by the victim is not related significantly to the odds of conviction. In addition, although the effect of provocation was significant in this equation, the magnitude was less than half of the magnitude of the coefficient for provocation shown in equation (5). Thus our analysis of trial outcome as a trichotomous variable reveals important effects of victim characteristics (provocation and disreputable conduct) that would have been masked by the more common measurement strategy of conviction versus acquittal.

Table 2. Logistic Regressions of the Effect of Victim Characteristics on Pre- and Post-Indictment Prosecutorial Screening, Indictment, Nature of Disposition, and Trial Outcomes

	Binary Logistic Regressions								Multinomial Logistic Regressions			
	(1) Prosecution		(2) Indictment		(3) Carried Forward		(4) Trial		(5) Conviction on Indictment Charge vs. Reduced Charge		(6) Conviction on Reduced Charge vs. Acquittal	
	Beta	SE	Beta	SE	Beta	SE	Beta	SE	Beta	SE	Beta	SE
Victim Characteristics												
Physical provocation	-1.06*	.21	-.78*	.35	.14	.34	.18	.15	-1.06*	.29	-.31	.25
Disreputable conduct	-.19	.20	-.43	.32	-.65*	.27	-.23*	.12	-.43*	.21	.23	.23
Disreputable past conduct	.37	.38	.37	.63	-.06	.45	.13	.20	.33	.35	-.51	.35
Victim nonwhite	.23	.28	-.05	.46	-.53	.39	-.02	.16	-.57*	.26	-.22	.32
Victim male	-.59*	.27	.20	.37	.65*	.31	-.17	.13	-.45*	.21	-.36	.27
Victim under 18	.04	.38	.49	.76	.41	.63	.29	.21	-.20	.33	.20	.38
Victim 18 to 29	-.21	.19	-.03	.30	.03	.26	-.02	.11	-.04	.19	.21	.22
Control Variables												
Defendant nonwhite	.10	.29	.58	.46	.75*	.39	.15	.16	.30	.27	.04	.32
Defendant male	.43	.26	-.08	.51	.90*	.37	.01	.17	.74*	.33	-.19	.30
Defendant under 18	-.01	.43	1.13	1.05	-.34	.66	-1.19*	.32	-.04	.61	1.16	.82
Defendant 18 to 29	.30*	.19	.58*	.30	.10	.26	-.32*	.11	.03	.18	.20	.21
Defendant prior conviction	1.09*	.23	1.16*	.36	.13	.27	-.27*	.11	.53*	.18	.46*	.23
Defendant and victim nonstrangers	.05	.21	.48	.35	.82*	.31	-.54*	.12	-.11	.21	.18	.23
Gun murder	-.30*	.19	-.45	.31	-.74*	.28	-.10	.11	-.10	.18	.22	.20
Defendant arrested on scene	.74*	.19	.88*	.30	.20	.25	-.04	.11	-.44*	.18	.07	.20
Proportion Nonwhite in county	-2.04*	.69	.79	1.19	.04	.99	1.72*	.43	-1.37*	.73	1.13	.88
Murder 1 arrest charge	-1.24*	.25	-.34	.34								
Grand jury proceeding			-.21	.30								
Murder 1 indictment charge					.04	.26	.67*	.11	-.76*	.19	.50*	.21
Jury trial									1.23*	.20	-.06	.21
N	1,990		1,831		1,757		1,684		880		880	
Model Chi-Square	139.83*		48.44*		32.40*		93.99*					
Likelihood Ratio									1564.51		1564.51	

*p < .05, one-tailed test.

The victim's demographic characteristics generally have few effects. Defendants accused of killing nonwhite victims are less likely to be convicted on the most serious indictment charge, as expected. Also in line with predictions, defendants accused of killing female victims are more likely to be prosecuted and more likely to be convicted on the most serious indictment charge. Contrary to expectations, however, defendants accused of killing female victims are less likely to have their cases carried forward. Finally, the victim's age has no influence on any of the legal outcomes.[12]

Effects of Control Variables

Evidence of discrimination based on the defendant's race is apparent at only one stage of the legal process: cases involving nonwhite defendants are more likely to be carried forward, independent of other variables in the equation. The defendant's gender and age also exert some significant effects on legal outcomes. Male defendants are more likely to have their case carried forward, and are less likely to benefit from a reduced charge. Defendants under 18 are less likely to go to trial than defendants over 30 (the reference category). Young adults (ages 19-29) are more likely to be prosecuted and indicted than older defendants, and less likely to go to trial.

Not surprisingly, defendants with a prior conviction receive harsher treatment at multiple stages of the legal process.[13] Such defendants are more likely to be prosecuted and indicted, more likely to plead guilty, more likely to be convicted on the most serious charge, and less likely to be acquitted. Victim-offender relationship yields two significant effects: defendants indicted for killing a nonstranger are *more* likely to have their cases carried forward and less likely to go to trial. Somewhat unexpectedly, gun murders are less likely to be prosecuted and less likely to be carried forward. When the defendant is arrested on the scene, prosecution and indictment are more likely, whereas conviction on the original charge rather than on a reduced charge is less likely.

---

[12] Following recent research on the effects of defendant characteristics on sentencing outcomes (see Steffensmeier, Ulmer, and Kramer 1998), we tested for interactions between victim's age, race, and sex. These analyses revealed no statistically significant two- or three-way interactions between these demographic characteristics.

[13] The defendant's prior criminal history may be highly prejudicial and is often excluded from evidence at the adjudication stage, especially in jury trials (Mueller and Kirkpatrick 1995). Yet, because this information is made known in some trials, we retain this variable in our equations for trial adjudication. We obtained substantively similar results after excluding defendant's criminal history from equations (5) and (6).

300   ROLE OF VICTIM CHARACTERISTICS

In addition to the effect of defendant's race noted above, racial composition is a significant determinant of selected legal outcomes. Murder cases in counties with higher proportions of nonwhites are less likely to be prosecuted, more likely to go to trial, and less likely to lead to conviction on the most serious charge. Also, first-degree murder cases are less likely than those with a less serious charge to be prosecuted and to result in conviction on the most serious indictment charge, but also are less likely to result in an acquittal. This pattern probably reflects the stringent legal requirements for conviction on first-degree murder and the relatively generous "wiggle room" for reducing charges from first-degree murder. Finally, grand jury proceeding has no effect on the likelihood of indictment, and a jury trial increases the chance that the defendant is convicted on the most serious charge rather than on a reduced charge.[14]

Statistical Interactions

To examine interactions, we reestimated the equations shown in Table 2 after adding the appropriate product terms. Coefficients for these product terms are presented in Table 3.

We first explored interactions involving race. We observe no statistically significant interactions between victim's and defendant's race in the disposition of murder cases.[15] Our analyses, however, reveal that the county's racial composition moderates the effect of victim's race on the likelihood of indictment and on the nature of adjudication (i.e., trial adjudication vs. plea negotiation). As predicted, the negative effects, on indictment and trial adjudication, of murdering nonwhite victims are weakened as the relative size of the county's nonwhite population increases.

We next examined whether the effects of victim characteristics on legal outcomes vary by the seriousness of the murder charge

---

[14] The exclusion of direct measures of the presence or amount of evidence (not available in the data used for our research) may introduce specification bias into the equations shown in Table 2. Prior research, however, suggests that such bias may not be severe. Some studies report that the presence of evidence does not significantly affect legal outcomes when defendant, victim, and case characteristics are controlled (e.g., Spears and Spohn 1997; Spohn and Spears 1996). Others report significant effects for indicators of evidence (e.g., Albonetti 1986, 1987, 1991), but the victim characteristics considered in these studies (e.g., provocation) also tend to exert the expected effects, net of the effects of evidentiary measures.

[15] We also tested for a more specific form of statistical interaction between victim's and defendant's race by adding to the equations in Table 2 dummy variables that represent all possible victim/defendant race combinations (white offender/white victim was the omitted category). These analyses reveal no statistically significant interactions between victim's and defendant's race. Also, following recent research on legal outcomes in sexual assault cases (Spohn and Spears 1996), we tested for three-way interactions between victim's race, defendant's race, and victim-defendant relationship, and between victim's race, defendant's race, and the victim's conduct at the time of the crime. Contrary to Spohn and Spears (1996), we found no evidence of statistically significant interactions between these variables.

(first-degree murder versus second-degree murder or manslaughter). Our analyses reveal three findings consistent with the liberation hypothesis. First, disreputable conduct by the victim at the time of the incident has a stronger negative effect on the likelihood of indictment in less serious cases. Second, provocation by the victim exerts a stronger negative effect on the odds of continued prosecution in cases in which the indictment charge is less serious. Third, defendants indicted for murdering males are more likely to receive an acquittal in less serious cases. These effects support the prediction that the strict letter of the law is less likely to be followed in less serious cases.

Most of the product terms involving victim characteristics and the seriousness of the murder charge are not statistically significant, however. In addition, one finding is in the opposite direction to that predicted by the liberation hypothesis: the "leniency effect" of murdering males on conviction for the most serious charge (relative to conviction on a reduced charge) is greater in more serious cases than in less serious murder cases.

We also tested the hypothesis that victim characteristics should exert stronger effects on convictions in jury proceedings than in bench trials. Three significant findings emerge for indictment. In keeping with the liberation hypothesis, the negative effects of physical provocation, disreputable conduct, and murdering a male are stronger in grand jury proceedings than in preliminary hearings. We find three additional statistically significant interactions at other stages of criminal processing; each is consistent with the liberation hypothesis. The negative effects of provocation by the victim and of murdering a male on conviction for a more serious charge are stronger in jury trials than in bench trials. In addition, the tendency towards acquittal in cases with nonwhite victims is more pronounced in jury than in bench trials.

SUMMARY AND CONCLUSIONS

We have examined here how victims' conduct and characteristics affect the disposition of homicide cases at various stages of the criminal justice system. We hypothesized that offenders who kill disreputable victims or victims from stigmatized groups are likely to receive more lenient treatment from criminal justice authorities and juries. These hypotheses are based on two underlying processes: (1) disreputable or stigmatized victims are more likely to be perceived as blameworthy, and this blame should detract from the blame attributed to the offender; and (2) offenders who kill disreputable or stigmatized victims are perceived as having committed less harm.

Table 3. Regression Coefficients for Product Terms of Interactions of Victim Characteristics with Race, Charge Seriousness, and Type of Legal Proceeding.

| | Binary Logistic Regressions | | | | | | | | Multinomial Logistic Regressions | | | |
| | (1) Prosecution | | (2) Indictment | | (3) Carried Forward | | (4) Trial | | (5) Conviction on Indictment Charge vs. Reduced Charge | | (6) Conviction on Reduced Charge vs. Acquittal | |
	Beta	SE	Beta	SE	Beta	SE	Beta	SE	Beta	SE	Beta	SE
Interactions with Race												
Victim nonwhite x Defendant nonwhite	.54	.56	-.01	.92	-1.27	.97	.10	.34	.69	.60	.18	.62
Victim nonwhite x nonwhite in county	-1.24	1.41	4.18*	2.29	-.52	2.02	1.37*	.83	-1.26	.97	1.25	1.09
Interactions with Murder 1[a]												
Physical provocation	.59	.52	.59	.67	.94*	.44	.16	.27	-.80	.57	-.21	.46
Disreputable conduct	.34	.50	1.71*	.75	.51	.51	-.25	.23	.06	.40	.44	.44
Disreputable past conduct	.30	.88	-.21	1.31	.69	1.25	.14	.39	-.90	.74	.25	.74
Victim nonwhite	.05	.51	-.67	.66	.18	.52	-.08	.21	-.48	.38	.28	.45
Victim male	.82	1.07	1.20	1.11	-.10	.57	.09	.25	-1.08*	.41	1.37*	.57
Victim under 18	-.32	1.11	-.54	1.42	-.24	1.30	.62	.41	-1.67*	.76	1.22	.83
Victim 18 to 29	-.04	.52	-.84	.70	.44	.52	.33	.22	-.62	.39	.60	.45
Interactions with Jury Proceeding[b]												
Physical provocation			-1.68*	.64					-.73*	.36	-.26	.44
Disreputable conduct			-1.83*	.63					.12	.47	-.59	.43
Disreputable past conduct			-1.02	1.31					.20	.77	-.74	.68
Victim nonwhite			-.70	.58					.03	.40	-1.09*	.41
Victim male			-1.50*	.85					-.99*	.44	-.03	.50
Victim under 18			.45	.90					.28	.70	-.44	.73
Victim 18 to 29			.20	.60					-.61	.41	.49	.42

[a]Coefficients for product terms between each victim characteristic and a dichotomous variable, coded 1 for cases in which the most serious charge was first-degree murder and coded 0 for cases in which the most serious charge was second-degree murder or manslaughter.
[b]Coefficients for product terms between each victim characteristic and a dichotomous variable, coded 1 for cases processed via jury proceeding and coded 0 for cases processed via bench proceeding.
*p < .05, one-tailed test.

We find evidence that the victim's conduct does affect legal outcomes. Offenders who kill the victim in response to a physical attack are less likely to be prosecuted; if they are prosecuted, they are less likely to be indicted; and if they are indicted, they are less likely to be convicted of the most serious indictment charge rather than a reduced charge. The effects of the victim's physical provocation on decisions early in the processing of cases (e.g., prosecution and indictment) are not surprising, given that statutes recognize self-defense as a legal justification for violence. It seems unlikely, however, that self-defense in the technical sense plays a role in the effect of physical provocation at the stage of conviction on the most serious charge versus a reduced charge. Presumably, self-defense cases already should have been adjudicated before this stage. We suspect that the more lenient treatment observed here occurs because the first use of violence by the victim results in the attribution of less blame to offenders, even if this violence did not constitute an "imminent threat" to the offender.

The victim's disreputable activity at the time of the incident (other than physical provocation) apparently has no effect on early decisions. In other words, an offender who kills someone engaged in disreputable activity is not able to avoid prosecution or indictment. At the three later decision points, however, the victim's misconduct matters. Offenders who have killed people engaged in disreputable activity are less likely to have their cases carried forward (i.e., they are more likely to have their cases dropped), are less likely to go to trial, and are more likely to be convicted on a reduced charge.

The remaining indicator of victim's conduct — prior conviction — exhibits no significant effects at any stage of criminal processing. Offenders receive no more lenient treatment if they kill someone with a criminal record than if they kill someone with a "clean" record. These findings show that legal outcomes are affected by victims' conduct at the time of the incident, not by their past conduct. Apparently, decision making in murder cases reflects attributions of responsibility for the event, rather than beliefs about the degree of harm based on the victim's general character. If the victim's character mattered, then past behavior as well as current behavior would be influential.

We also examined the effect of victims' demographic characteristics on legal outcomes. The victim's age has no significant effects. The victim's gender has significant effects, but they are inconsistent. As predicted, offenders who kill females are more likely to be prosecuted and more likely to be convicted on the most serious charge. Offenders who kill females, however, are *less* likely to have the charge carried forward.

304   ROLE OF VICTIM CHARACTERISTICS

We also find some evidence of racial discrimination. A main effect of victim's race is observed at one stage of processing: offenders who kill nonwhite victims are less likely to be convicted on the most serious indictment charge (i.e., more likely to receive a charge reduction). In addition, we observe two instances of statistical interactions involving the county's racial composition. The negative effects associated with murdering a nonwhite victim on indictment and on trial adjudication become weaker as the nonwhite proportion of the population increases. In other words, racial discrimination is less likely in counties containing relatively large numbers of nonwhites. Nonwhites presumably have greater influence on the legal system in these counties.

We find mixed support for the "liberation hypothesis" — that is, the hypothesis that extraneous factors are likely to play a greater role in less serious cases and in cases adjudicated by juries. The significant statistical interactions between victim characteristics and case seriousness, and between victim characteristics and jury trials, are generally in the predicted direction. These interaction effects must be interpreted cautiously, however, because most of the interactions are not statistically significant, and one is opposite to predictions.

In sum, our analyses indicate that victim characteristics affect the processing of murder cases. The effects are modest but are consistent with the general claim that killings of disreputable or stigmatized victims tend to be treated more leniently by the criminal justice system. In addition, our results underscore the complexity of the processing of murder cases. Predictors sometimes exhibit different (and, in a few cases, opposite) effects at distinct decision points. Moreover, our findings reaffirm previous research on the potential role of contextual factors such as racial composition (Myers and Talarico 1987). A full understanding of legal outcomes thus requires consideration of a wide range of factors, including offender, victim, and contextual characteristics, and calls for assessment of the effects of these factors at multiple stages of adjudication.

REFERENCES

Albonetti, C.A. 1986. "Criminality, Prosecutorial Screening, and Uncertainty: Toward a Theory of Discretionary Decision Making in Felony Case Processing." *Criminology* 24:623-44.

———. 1987. "Prosecutorial Discretion: The Effects of Uncertainty." *Law and Society Review* 21:291-312.

———. 1990. "Race and the Probability of Pleading Guilty." *Journal of Quantitative Criminology* 6:315-34.

———. 1991. "An Integration of Theories to Explain Judicial Discretion." *Social Problems* 38:247-65.

———. 1992. "Charge Reduction: An Analysis of Prosecutorial Discretion in Burglary and Robbery Cases." *Journal of Quantitative Criminology* 8:317-33.

Baldus, D., C. Pulaski, and G. Woodworth. 1983. "Comparative Review of Death Sentences: An Empirical Study of the Georgia Experience." *Journal of Criminal Law and Criminology* 74:661-753.

Beaulieu, M. and S.F. Messner. 1999. "Race, Gender, and Outcomes in First Degree Murder Cases." *Journal of Poverty* 3:47-68.

Berk, R.A. 1983. "An Introduction to Sample Selection Bias in Sociological Data." *American Sociological Review* 48:386-98.

Bernstein, I.N., W.R. Kelly, and P.A. Doyle. 1977. "Societal Reactions to Deviants: The Case of Criminal Defendants." *American Sociological Review* 42:743-55.

Black, D. 1989. *Sociological Justice*. New York: Oxford University Press.

Blalock, H. 1967. *Toward a Theory of Minority-Group Relations*. New York: Wiley.

Boris, S.B. 1979. "Stereotypes and Dispositions for Criminal Homicide." *Criminology* 17:140-58.

Bowers, W.J. and G.L. Pierce. 1980. "Arbitrariness and Discrimination under Post-*Furman* Capital Statutes." *Crime and Delinquency* 26:563-635.

Chesney-Lind, M. 1988. "Girls in Jail." *Crime & Delinquency* 34:150-68.

Clogg, C. C. and E. S. Shihadeh. 1994. *Statistical Models for Ordinal Variables*. Thousand Oaks, CA: Sage.

Daly, K. 1989. "Neither Conflict nor Labeling nor Paternalism Will Suffice: Intersections of Race, Ethnicity, Gender, and Family in Criminal Court Decisions." *Crime & Delinquency* 35:136-38.

Daly, K. and R. Bordt. 1995. "Sex Effects and Sentencing: A Review of the Statistical Literature." *Justice Quarterly* 12:143-77.

Dubin, J. A. and D. Rivers. 1990. "Selection Bias in Linear Regression, Logit and Probit Models." Pp. 410-42 in *Modern Methods of Data Analysis*, edited by J. Fox and J. S. Long. Newbury Park, CA: SAGE.

Edwards, A. 1988. *Regulation and Repression*. Winchester, MA: Allen and Unwin, Inc.

Eisenstein, J., R. B. Flemming, and P. F. Nardulli. 1988. *The Contours of Justice: Communities and their Courts*. Boston, MA: Little, Brown.

Elwork, A., B. D. Sales, and D. Suggs. 1981. "The Trial: A Research Review." Pp. 1-68 in *The Trial Process* edited by B. D. Sales. New York: Plenum Press.

Estrich, S. 1987. *Real Rape*. Cambridge, MA: Harvard University Press.

Felson, R. B. 1996. "Violent Disputes and Calling the Cops: The Role of Chivalry and Social Relationship." Paper presented at the Annual Meetings of the American Sociological Association, Chicago, November, 1996.

Frohmann, L. 1991. "Discrediting Victims' Allegations of Sexual Assault: Prosecutorial Accounts of Case Rejections." *Social Problems* 38:213-26.

Garfinkel, H. 1949. "Research Note on Inter- and Intra-Racial Homicides." *Social Forces* 27:369-81.

Gross, S. R. and R. Mauro. 1984. "Patterns of Death: An Analysis of Racial Disparities in Capital Sentencing and Homicide Victimization." *Stanford Law Review* 37:27-153.

Harris, M. B. 1991. "Effects of Sex of Aggressor, Sex of Target, and Relationship on Evaluations of Physical Aggression." *Journal of Interpersonal Violence* 6:174-86.

Hawkins, D. 1987. "Beyond Anomalies: Rethinking the Conflict Perspective on Race and Criminal Punishment." *Social Forces* 65:719-45.

Heckman, J. J. 1976. "The Common Structure of Statistical Models of Truncation, Sample Selection, and Limited Dependent Variables and a Simple Estimator for Such Models." *Annals of Economic and Social Measurement*: 5:475-92.

Heider, F. 1958. *The Psychology of Interpersonal Relations*. New York: Wiley.

Holstrom, L. and A. W. Burgess. 1978. *The Victim of Rape: Institutional Reactions*. New York: Wiley.

Johnson, G. B. 1941. "The Negro and Crime." *Annals of the American Academy of Political and Social Sciences* 271:93-104.

Jones, C. and E. Aronson. 1973. "Attribution of Fault to a Rape Victim as a Function of Respectability of the Victim." *Journal of Personality and Social Psychology* 26:415-19.

Kalven, H. and H. Zeisel. 1966. *The American Jury*. Boston, MA: Little, Brown.

Kleck, G. 1981. "Racial Discrimination in Criminal Sentencing: A Critical Evaluation of the Evidence with Additional Evidence on the Death Penalty." *American Sociological Review* 46:783-805.

306   ROLE OF VICTIM CHARACTERISTICS

Kruttschnitt, C. 1985. "Are Businesses Treated Differently? A Comparison of the Individual Victim and the Corporate Victim in the Criminal Courtroom." *Social Problems*:225-38.

LaFree, G. D. 1980. "Variables Affecting Guilty Pleas and Convictions in Rape Cases: Toward a Social Theory of Rape Processing." *Social Forces* 58:833-50.

———. 1989. *Rape and Criminal Justice: The Social Construction of Sexual Assault.* Belmont, CA: Wadsworth Publishing Co.

LaFree, G. D., B. F. Reskin, and C. A. Visher. 1985. "Jurors' Responses to Victims' Behavior and Legal Issues in Sexual Assault Trials." *Social Problems* 32:389-405.

Landy, D. and E. Aronson. 1969. "The Influence of the Character of the Criminal and His Victim on the Decisions of Simulated Jurors." *Journal of Experimental Social Psychology* 5:141-52.

Lillard, L, J.P. Smith, and F. Welch. 1986. "What Do We Really Know About Wages?: The Importance of Nonreporting and Census Imputation." *Journal of Political Economy* 94:489-506.

Lizotte, A. J. 1978. "Extra-legal Factors in Chicago's Criminal Courts: Testing the Conflict Model of Criminal Justice." *Social Problems* 25:564-80.

Lundsgaarde, H. P. 1977. *Murder in Space City: A Cultural Analysis of Houston Homicide Patterns.* New York: Oxford University Press.

Mather, L. 1979. *Plea Bargaining or Trial?* Lexington, MA: Lexington Books.

Miller, F. 1970. *Prosecution: The Decision to Charge a Suspect with a Crime.* Boston, MA: Little Brown.

Mueller, C.B. and L.C. Kirkpatrick. 1995. *Evidence.* New York: Little, Brown.

Myers, M. A. 1979. "Offended Parties and Official Reactions: Victims and the Sentencing of Criminal Defendants." *Sociological Quarterly* 20:529-40.

———. 1980. "Personal and Situational Contingencies in the Processing of Convicted Felons." *Sociological Inquiry* 50:65-74.

Myers, M. A. and J. Hagan. 1979. "Private and Public Trouble: Prosecutors and the Allocation of Court Resources." *Social Problems* 26:439-52.

Myers, M. A. and S. Talarico. 1987. *The Social Contexts of Criminal Sentencing.* New York: Springer-Verlag.

Myrdal, G. 1944. *An American Dilemma: The Negro Problem and Modern Democracy.* New York: Harper and Brothers.

Neubauer, D. 1974. "After the Arrest: The Charging Decision in Prairie City." *Law & Society Review* 8:475-517.

Paternoster, R. 1984. "Prosecutorial Discretion in Requesting the Death Penalty: A Case of Victim-Based Racial Discrimination." *Law & Society Review* 18:437-78.

Radelet, M. L. and G. L. Pierce. 1985. "Race and Prosecutorial Discretion in Homicide Cases." *Law & Society Review* 19:587-621.

Reskin, B. and C. A. Visher. 1986. "The Impacts of Evidence and Extralegal Factors in Jurors' Decisions." *Law & Society Review* 20:423-38.

Sales, B. D. (ed.). 1981. *The Trial Process.* New York: Plenum Press.

Samaha, J. 1994. *Criminal Justice.* 3rd Edition. St. Paul, MN: West Publishing.

Sampson, R. J. and J. L. Lauritsen. 1997. "Racial and Ethnic Disparities in Crime and Criminal Justice in the United States." In M. Tonry (ed.), *Ethnicity, Crime, and Immigration: Comparative and Cross-National Perspectives.* Chicago, IL: University of Chicago Press.

Spears, J. and C. C. Spohn. 1997. "The Effect of Evidence Factors and Victim Characteristics on Prosecutors' Charging Decisions in Sexual Assault Cases." *Justice Quarterly* 14:501-24.

Spohn, C. C. 1994. "Crime and the Social Control of Blacks: Offender/Victim Race and the Sentencing of Violent Offenders." In *Inequality, Crime, and Social Control,* G. S. Bridges and M. A. Myers (eds.). Boulder, CO: Westview Press.

Spohn, C. C. and J. Spears. 1996. "The Effect of Offender and Victim Characteristics on Sexual Assault Case Processing Decisions." *Justice Quarterly* 13:649-79.

Stanko, E. A. 1981. "The Impact of Victim Assessment on Prosecutor's Screening Decisions: The Case of the New York District Attorney's Office." *Law & Society Review* 16: 225-39.

———. 1988. "The Impact of Victim Assessment on Prosecutors' Screening Decisions: The Case of the New York County District Attorney's Office." Pp. 169-80 in G. Cole (ed.), *Criminal Justice: Law and Politics.* Pacific Grove, CA: Brooks/Cole.

Steffensmeier, D., J. Ulmer, and J. Kramer. 1998. "The Interaction of Race, Gender, and Age in Criminal Sentencing: The Punishment Cost of Being Young, Black, and Male." *Criminology* 36:763-93.

Stolzenberg, R. M. and D. A. Relles. 1990. "Theory Testing in a World of Constrained Research Design: The Significance of Heckman's Censored Sampling Bias Correction for Non-experimental Research." *Sociological Methods and Research* 18:395-415.

———. 1997. "Tools for Intuition About Sample Selection Bias and Its Correction." *American Sociological Review* 62:494-507.

Swigert, V. and R. A. Farrell. 1977. "Normal Homicides and the Law." *American Sociological Review* 42:16-32.

U.S. Bureau of the Census. 1994. *County and City Data Book, 1994.* Washington, DC: U.S. Department of Commerce.

U.S. Department of Justice, Bureau of Justice Statistics. 1996. *Murder Cases in 33 Large Urban Counties in the United States, 1988* [Computer file]. Conducted by U.S. Dept. of Commerce, Bureau of the Census. ICPSR ed. Ann Arbor, MI: Inter-University Consortium for Political and Social Research [producer and distributor].

———. 1997. *National Prosecutors Survey, 1990* [Computer file]. Conducted by U.S. Dept. of Commerce, Bureau of the Census. ICPSR ed. Ann Arbor, MI: Inter-University Consortium for Political and Social Research [producer and distributor].

Vera Institute of Justice. 1977. *Felony Arrests: Their Prosecution and Disposition in New York City's Courts.* New York: Vera Institute of Justice.

Walster, E. 1966. "Assignment of Responsibility for an Accident." *Journal of Personality and Social Psychology* 3:73-79.

Weary, G., M. A. Stanley, and J. H. Harvey. 1989. *Attribution.* New York: Springer-Verlag.

Welch, S., J. Gruhl, and C. Spohn. 1984. "Sentencing: The Influence of Alternative Measures of Prior Record." *Criminology* 22:215-27.

Whatley, M. A. 1996. "Victim Characteristics Influencing Attributions of Responsibility to Rape Victims: A Meta-Analysis." *Aggression and Violent Behavior* 1:81-95.

Williams, K. M. 1976. "The Effects of Victim Characteristics on the Disposition of Violent Crimes." Pp. 177-213 in *Criminal Justice and the Victim*, edited by W. F. McDonald. Beverly Hills, CA: Sage.

Williams, K. R. and R. L. Flewelling. 1988. "The Social Production of Criminal Homicide: A Comparative Study of Disaggregated Rates in American Cities." *American Sociological Review* 53:421-31.

Wolfgang, M. E. 1967. *Patterns of Criminal Homicide.* New York: Wiley.

[25]

Moral Tales: Representations of Child Abuse in the Quality and Tabloid Media

Ania Wilczynski
Keys Young

Kate Sinclair
University of Sydney

Although child abuse is a favourite topic for media stories, there has been little research on how the media portrays such issues. The present research examined the media construction of child abuse in a comprehensive sample of all 1302 reports on the subject during 1995 in a representative quality and tabloid newspaper in NSW. It was found that: the focus was on 'hard news' reports of individual cases and the most atypical and sensational 'child abuse horror stories'; irony or incongruity between the offence and the offender was emphasised; child abuse was popular as a topic for 'soft news' (human interest) media stories; criminal justice agencies were the predominant sources used for the stories; child abusers were individualised and demonised by the press and used to promote 'law and order' agendas; and there was little coverage of the social causes of abuse and prevention issues. Although both the quality and tabloid press demonstrated these features, there were some marked differences between the coverage in the two sources, such as a much greater emphasis on individual cases in the tabloid press.

"Priest jailed for seven years over child sex spree" (M. Cowley, *Daily Telegraph Mirror*, 16th June 1995, p. 38)

"The Devil's advocates: How Australia became obsessed with satanic abuse" (R. Guilliatt, *Sydney Morning Herald*, 31st August 1996, p. 1 *Spectrum*)

Headlines such as these are common fare in our newspapers. We regularly read stories about children being battered to death, 'perverts' sexually molesting children, and inept agencies failing to protect children. But what do these stories tell us about how child abuse is constructed as a social problem?

There is a strong body of criminological literature examining how the media portrays crime. Three key themes in this literature are: the concept of 'moral panic' in explaining media reporting of crime; the identification of factors which make crime stories 'newsworthy'; and the emphasis on strong 'law and order' messages.

Address for correspondence: Dr Ania Wilczynski, Keys Young, PO Box 252, Milsons Point NSW 2061, Australia. Email: ania_wilczynski@optusnet.com.au

First, 'moral panic' theories have been frequently used to analyse the media portrayal of crime (see, for example, Goode & Ben-Yehuda, 1994). The 'deviancy amplification' cycle associated with 'moral panic' involves: experts defining a social issue as a problem (particularly one perceived to threaten traditional values); the identification of proposed solutions; continued distortion and dramatisation by the media to create stereotypes; and increased deviance and confirmation of stereotypes (Cohen, 1980, p. 199). 'Folk devils' are also identified for the purpose of scapegoating so that attention is diverted from more fundamental social ills. These 'folk devils' provide "visible reminders of what we should not be" (1980, p. 10).

Secondly, the literature indicates that the 'newsworthiness' of a crime event is determined by a matrix of 'news values', or what Ericson *et al* (1987, pp. 133–38) term a "vocabulary of precedents". These values result in crime stories which: concentrate on individual offences of a more unusual nature, such as 'violent and predatory street crime'; are constructed primarily from official criminal justice sources; and place little emphasis on the social causes of crime (Surette, 1992, pp. 59, 63–4). Katz also argues that crime stories are used as a powerful ritual form of 'moral tale' to highlight broader social pressures which readers must face in everyday life (1987, pp. 56, 67, 70). Crime reports therefore focus on offences perceived to threaten traditional moral values such as the sanctity of the family, and often involve victims perceived as 'innocent' such as children (Grabosky & Wilson, 1989, p. 13).

Thirdly, the media often plays a powerful role in reflecting and reinforcing punitive criminal justice policies. As Brown and Hogg (1998) demonstrate, the media has played a key role in promoting the theme of 'law and order commonsense' which has come to strongly influence criminal justice policy and debate in NSW, elsewhere in Australia, and overseas jurisdictions such as America. This 'commonsense' theme portrays crime as of ever-increasing gravity and requiring urgent and punitive policies, such as tougher penalties and increased police powers, and as a result does not facilitate informed debate about effective, long-term crime control strategies (1998, pp. 4, 18–44). A key strand in these 'law and order' debates has been the concept of 'dangerousness', focusing on the identification, isolation and punishment of dangerous offenders (Craze & Moynihan, 1994; Pratt, 1997).

Prior Research

Despite the considerable literature that exists on crime stories, there is nonetheless a paucity of research on the presentation of child maltreatment by the media, either as a criminal matter or as a more general social issue. This presents a stark contrast to the vast amount of literature produced on child abuse generally since the 1960s.

What literature there is suffers from some key limitations. First, most researchers have used very selective samples which concentrate on the most extreme and sensational instances of either: one or a small number of more sensational maltreatment cases in the media, such as the 'Children of God' satanic abuse case in Victoria and New South Wales (Goddard, 1994); sub-groups of child maltreatment, such as satanic or ritual abuse (Rowe & Cavender, 1991); or media criticism of the actions of child protection workers in maltreatment cases (Hillman, 1988; Franklin & Parton, 1991).

Secondly, the literature is predominantly British or American; there is negligible Australian literature (Vinson, 1987; Hodge, 1990; Carment, 1987; Goddard & Liddell, 1995).

Thirdly, prior studies do not systematically address the important differences between quality and tabloid media coverage. For instance, compared to the quality media, tabloid coverage tends to be more sensational (Roshier, 1981), to promote more conservative 'law and order' agendas (Garkawe, 1995, p. 431), and to have more 'entertainment' than 'serious' news material (Sparks, 1991, p. 64) and more 'circumscribed content' (Ericson et al., 1991, p. 46).

Fourthly, many studies in this area lack interdisciplinary analysis, which is vital since the topic lies at the intersection of a number of different fields such as criminology, child abuse, media studies, social work practice, legal sociology and the study of social problems.

The present study attempts to address the issues raised above. It analysed a complete and representative dataset of *all* the coverage of *all* forms of child abuse in a quality and tabloid newspaper in New South Wales (NSW) over a specific and relatively long time-frame, as this appears to provide the most reliable form of data (see, for example, Johnson, 1989). This included an analysis of the similarities and differences between the quality and tabloid press in the way in which child abuse was addressed.

This paper reports a selection of some of the key themes to emerge from the analysis[1]: child abuse as 'hard news' (the focus on individual cases); the 'child abuse horror story'; the emphasis on irony or incongruity; child abuse as 'soft news' (the human interest story); the reliance on official criminal justice sources; the individualisation and demonisation of child abusers, with an emphasis on the appropriateness of punitive criminal justice responses; and the lack of attention paid to the social causes of and prevention of abuse. These themes demonstrate that the traditional criteria for 'newsworthiness' in crime reporting generally (described above) are applied to the press representation of child maltreatment, and that 'law and order' themes feature strongly.

Methodology

Sample

The sample consisted of all the coverage of child maltreatment during a 12-month period (January–December 1995) in the following newspapers:

- A quality newspaper — the Monday–Saturday editions of *The Sydney Morning Herald* (SMH), and the Sunday paper by the same publisher (Fairfax), the *Sun-Herald* (SH) (which has a more tabloid style than the SMH). The SMH articles were identified by two electronic SMH indexes. One search was based on a large number of key words such as 'child abuse', 'child sexual abuse', 'physical abuse', 'emotional abuse' and 'neglect'. The other search was based on a scan of a comprehensive list of all SMH headlines to locate stories which fit our criteria but were not indexed under child abuse topics. The SMH articles were retrieved in electronic form; however, where it was noted that the articles were accompanied by illustrations, the original paper copies were obtained. The SMH was the only paper in the sample for which an index was available; therefore a comprehensive manual search was conducted for the *SH*.

- A tabloid newspaper — the Monday–Saturday editions of *The Daily Telegraph Mirror* (*DTM*) (renamed *The Daily Telegraph* in 1996), and its Sunday version by the same publisher, the *Sunday Telegraph* (*ST*). Articles in these papers were identified by extensive manual search of every edition for the year.

The papers selected all have a wide circulation (Audit Bureau of Circulation, 1995) and readership (Roy Morgan Research Centre, 1995). In this article, in the discussion of differences by paper (quality versus tabloid), '*SMH*' refers to the *SMH* and *SH*, and '*DTM*' to the *DTM* and *ST*.

Definitions

There is no standard definition of 'child abuse' accepted by professionals (Parton, 1985, p. 133), and as Clapton points out, "terminology becomes a terrain on which a classic struggle for social and political meaning takes place" (1993, p. 9). Moreover, the researcher plays an important and complex role in constructing a "theoretically informed sample" of media coverage (Altheide, 1996, p. 19). For instance, some articles included in the sample did not explicitly use words such as 'child abuse' to refer to the behaviour being discussed. This occurred because our selection of data was influenced by our knowledge of current professional literature and practice in child protection at a particular historical moment (the time of data collection). To illustrate, in 1993 domestic violence became grounds for notification to the NSW Department of Community Services (DOCS) — the agency with statutory responsibility for child protection in NSW — and was included in the sample where its impact on children was discussed.

The definition of maltreatment adopted in the study also extended beyond that used in a legal context, since to use a legal definition would have provided a narrow and misleading impression of how the *media* constructs child abuse issues. The following types of maltreatment were included:

- homicide
- physical abuse, including corporal punishment
- sexual abuse, including 'ritual' abuse
- emotional abuse, including reports about children who witnessed or were exposed to crimes committed on others such as domestic violence, children being coerced and supported to commit a crime by adults, and the forcible State removal of Aboriginal children from their families (which has become known as the 'stolen generation')
- neglect, including child labour, street children and abandoned children
- missing and abducted children
- custody disputes where the emotional trauma caused to children was evident (on occasion also accompanied by other more direct forms of abuse such as sexual)
- 'home invasions' (robberies of people's homes where children were involved), and
- the incidental mention of child abuse in articles primarily about other topics.

Several forms of child abuse were excluded from the study: the physical, sexual and emotional abuse and neglect of children in war zones, and crimes by children against children (except where the age difference between the victim and alleged offender exceeded 10 years).

'Child' was defined as aged up to 18 years; unborn children were also included where they had been injured as a result of assaults on or by their mothers in the final months of pregnancy.

Data Analysis

The sample consisted of 1302 articles — 431 in the *SMH* and 871 in the *DTM*. Throughout the paper reference is made both to *articles* (ie media stories) and *cases* (ie specific instances of maltreatment discussed). Obviously there could be a number of stories on one case, and not all articles mentioned cases.

A combination of qualitative and quantitative methodology was used (the latter using the statistical package SPSS). The coverage was coded on the following variables: the newspaper; location (Australian versus overseas); article size; page number; the subject of any illustrations; whether the headline immediately indicated (a) that the article was about child abuse and (b) the sex of the perpetrator; category of coverage (news story, editorial or other); type of abuse; scene of the abuse; primary source of information for the article; primary focus of the article; perpetrator number and sex; victim number, sex and age; and the relationship between perpetrator and victim.

On several variables (such as the type of abuse), many reports could have been coded into multiple categories. As a result the guiding selection principle adopted was the predominant portrayal in each report (see Hughes, 1994, p. 45, citing Strauss, 1987, p. 45). The coding was carried out simultaneously by both authors in the same setting, with frequent cross-checking to ensure inter-rater reliability.

Key themes in the analysis were identified in two ways: first, through the recording of detailed analytical notes and discussion between the two authors throughout the data coding process; and secondly, by extensive analysis of the quantitative data (particularly using cross-tabulations by paper).

Limitations

There are five limitations to the study. First, only print media coverage is included; samples of other sources such as radio and/or television may have produced somewhat different results (see Ericson et al., 1991, p. 20–40).

A second potential limitation is that two different methods were used for identifying the sample articles: an electronic index for the *SMH*, and manual search for the *SH*, *DTM* and *ST*. As Soothill and Grover (1997) point out, these two methods can produce different results. The *SMH* portion of the sample may be somewhat *less* comprehensive than those from the other papers in some ways, in that it largely relies on the quality of the indexing and may omit some items which should have been included (Soothill & Grover, 1997, p. 593). Nonetheless, given that a large number of keywords were used and that a database of all *SMH* headlines was also scanned, it would appear unlikely that this difference would be great. On the other hand, the *SMH* sample may be *more* comprehensive than those from the other papers in other respects, since reports which were not clearly about child abuse on initial appearance but contained words directly concerning 'child abuse' may be more likely to have been included in the *SMH* indexes. A further limitation of using electronic indexes is that most of the *SMH* articles were retrieved in electronic form; although the limitations of this were partially remedied by obtaining the original paper copies of articles with illustrations, the significance of spacing issues in the layout of the article was lost for the remaining articles (see Soothill & Grover, 1997, p. 592).

Thirdly, whereas the *ST* is very similar in style and content to the *DTM*, the *SH* is somewhat more tabloid in nature than the *SMH*. The amalgamation of the two latter papers together for the *SMH* sample may have produced somewhat different results than if the *SMH* was analysed alone. However, it is unlikely these differences would have been marked.

A fourth limitation is related to having to prioritise the primary focus of each report, particularly where multiple issues are mentioned in a story.

Finally, the analysis of media texts by themselves does not necessarily tell us how audiences receive and use these sources of information. As the body of literature on 'reception analysis' demonstrates, various individuals may interpret the same media item in different ways (Jensen, 1991, pp. 135, 137–8). These issues are addressed in more detail elsewhere (Wilczynski & Sinclair, 1999).

Child Abuse as 'Hard News': The Focus on Individual Cases

An important finding was that the emphasis in the sample was on 'hard news' stories which dealt with individual cases of child maltreatment as crime news (Nelson, 1984, pp. 57–8). As Osmer (1980, p. 254) points out, this approach to child abuse tends to be of a 'hit and run' nature, describing only the most immediate details of the case. This does not facilitate an analysis of the broader social and systemic context of abuse.

The focus on individual cases is demonstrated by a number of findings: the proportion of reports discussing individual cases; the number of cases reported overall in the sample; and the depictions of individuals in illustrations accompanying the stories. This focus on individual cases, which is consistent with other research (Kitzinger & Skidmore, 1995, p. 48), was a much more marked feature of the *DTM* rather than *SMH* coverage.

Coverage of Individual Cases

As can be seen from Table 1, the majority of the stories (58.2%) primarily focused on reporting an individual abuse case. One example is the article headlined "Father beat children, court told" (*DTM*, 5th June 1995, p. 8).

In 12.9% of the articles, the primary focus of the story was not on abuse (for example, coverage where child abuse was mentioned in passing as a risk factor for a variety of other social problems; see further discussion below). In over a third (35.7%) of these 168 reports the discussion of abuse issues was again primarily focused on an individual case.

ANIA WILCZYNSKI AND KATE SINCLAIR

TABLE 1

Focus on Specific Cases by Paper

	Daily Telegraph Mirror (%)	Sydney Morning Herald (%)	Total (%)
Primary focus on specific cases	72.1	30.2	58.2
Partial focus on specific cases	7.9	14.8	10.2
General reports not linked to specific cases	14.7	26.7	18.7
Abuse the non-primary focus of the article	5.3	28.3	12.9

There was a dramatic difference between the papers in that the *DTM* articles were much more likely than the *SMH* reports to have their primary focus on specific cases (see Table 1). This difference was highly statistically significant (χ^2 = 0.00000 i.e. < 0.001). The *SMH* was more likely than the *DTM* to have reports which either focused partially on individual cases in the context of more general stories, or were more general reports about abuse. Such reports were more likely to provide some broader context for the discussion of abuse issues. Overall, the *SMH* demonstrated markedly more interest in 'systemic' issues rather than individual cases. These findings indicate the *DTM*'s more sensational tabloid reporting.

Number of Cases Reported

Those reports which discussed specific instances of abuse reported a large number of cases — 430 — overall. Again there was a marked difference by paper, with three and a half times the number in the *DTM* (361) compared to the *SMH* (106). It is of note, however, that the quality and tabloid press primarily 'picked up' different incidents of maltreatment to report: only 8.6% of the cases were discussed in both papers. This is consistent with the finding that 73% of the (adult and child) sexual assaults examined by Soothill and Walby (1991, p. 27) were not reported in more than one paper.

Illustrations

The emphasis on individual cases was also demonstrated by the subject material of illustrations which accompanied the coverage. Of the 545 reports (41.9%) with pictures, the majority of the illustrations (71.1%) were related to an alleged individual victim or perpetrator of abuse. This was a much more common feature of the *DTM* coverage rather than that in the *SMH* (82.3% versus 49.8% of the reports with pictures).

The 'Child Abuse Horror Story'

Not only did the print media focus on individual instances of abuse, but it also concentrated on only certain *types* of case. In contrast to what might be described as the mundane and undramatic nature of the vast majority of child abuse cases (Johnson, 1989, p. 13), the most common maltreatment story in the study was, as found in other research, the 'child abuse horror story'. This is the report of the specific abuse case involving unusual, dramatic or bizarre injuries and evoking strong negative emotions of horror, anger, revulsion, anger and/or tragedy (Johnson, 1989, pp. 7, 8). An example is an article headlined "Toddler who paid with her life", which reported a case where an eighteen-month-old girl who had soiled her nappy was plunged into a bath of scalding water up to her chest by her mother's immature, violent partner (who was in drug withdrawal) (A. Horin, *SMH*, 25th September 1995, p. 2).

Consistent with the dramatic and revulsive themes, the report details how the girl was screaming in pain, her skin was peeling off, and large amounts of fluid were oozing from her body. However, the man and the child's mother only applied some ointment and wrapped the child in nappies. The child lost consciousness and was only taken to hospital by the couple three hours later. She took 2 months to die. The child was known to DOCS, and it was alleged that the department had failed to provide adequate support to the family. The story was accompanied by large photographs of the child (with her eyes blacked out for confidentiality reasons) after her admission to hospital.

The emphasis on the 'child abuse horror story' was reinforced by another finding: that the print media gave disproportionate coverage to the more severe and/or atypical forms of abuse. This was found for both the tabloid and quality press on many of the variables[2] on which the sample findings were compared to official statistics. The official figures used were primarily for substantiated notifications to DOCS in the financial year 1995–96 for children aged up to 18 years (DOCS, 1996a, 1996b). 'Notifications' are primarily reports of suspected child abuse made to DOCS by professionals or members of the public (DOCS, 1996a, p. 5); 'substantiated notifications' are those where an investigation by DOCS has determined that maltreatment is 'highly probable' (DOCS, 1996a, p. 37).

These findings are reported in detail elsewhere (Wilczynski and Sinclair, 1998). An illustration of the findings is that, compared to the official figures, the press *over*-reported homicides and sexual assaults, non-familial abuse (for example perpetrated by strangers), and abuse occurring outside the home. For instance, homicides constituted 28.4% of the sample coverage but only 0.06% of the DOCS substantiated notifications in 1995/96.[3] Similarly, 22.6% of the sample reports concerned abuse by strangers compared to only 4% in the DOCS statistics (DOCS, 1996a: Table 6.2). Conversely, the press *under*-reported emotional abuse, neglect, abuse inside the home and maltreatment committed by family members. Even given that the DOCS figures may disproportionately exclude certain types of case (for example, cases such as homicides and abuse by strangers may be more likely to be referred directly to police), this is unlikely to account for such dramatic disparities between the sample findings and DOCS figures. For example, 8 homicides are reported in the DOCS figures for 1995. When this figure is compared to the 10 homicides of children under 15 years reported to police in 1995/96, the difference is not marked.[4]

The press' tendency to concentrate on the most atypical cases was heightened by its propensity to favour cases with unusual (even bizarre) facts. This was a particularly marked feature of the *DTM* coverage, especially of overseas cases. Examples include the American mother charged after placing her two-year-old daughter in a school cafeteria oven, thereby causing her second-degree burns (*DTM*, 7th

November 1995, p. 17). Another illustration consistent with more sensational tabloid coverage was an American murder-kidnapping where it was alleged that two men and a woman shot and stabbed a mother and her two children and cut the dead woman's unborn child from her stomach (*DTM*, 20th December 1995, p. 43).

Emphasis on Irony or Incongruity

The emphasis on the more atypical and sensational cases is also heightened by two other common techniques used in media stories: the concentration on features which indicate "ironic contrast and structural incongruity" (Johnson, 1989, p. 9) between the offence and the offender. This incongruity could be based on a variety of factors, such as age, sex and gender, class, occupation, and physical appearance. As Katz points out in relation to crime reporting generally, this concentration on the 'unexpected' is used "for its normative value in articulating the normatively expected" (1987, pp. 62–3).

An example is the popularity of stories about 'respectable' abusers in non-familial authority situations. The coverage given to this group of offenders was vastly disproportionate to the official statistics: non-familial authority figures were the subject of 21.7% of the sample articles about specific cases, but none of the substantiated notifications to DOCS in 1995/96 (DOCS, 1996a, Table 6.2).

These findings are supported by prior research which indicates that the media gives disproportionate attention to 'white collar' criminals compared to 'common' offenders (Katz, 1987, p. 58). As Katz argues, the crimes of such people in authority situations are 'unexpected' and therefore newsworthy, because we feel we should trust and defer to them due to their legitimate power in society (1987, pp. 54, 62, 69). Whilst in a child abuse context this can divert attention from the more usual abuse within the family home, it also has some benefits. This is because research indicates that those who are more 'respectable' (for instance, being from a higher social class) are less susceptible to allegations of maltreatment due to their less extensive contact with professional agencies (Gelles, 1987), greater resistance to intervention (Ogden, 1991, p. 9), and lower likelihood of being labelled as abusive due to stereotypical assumptions about abusers (Dingwall, 1989a, pp. 161–3).

Abusers in authority situations were particularly common in the sample articles about cases of sexual abuse: they constituted 47.2% of such offenders. These cases featured, for example, priests, teachers, police officers, scoutmasters, politicians, lawyers, film directors, child protection workers, and celebrities such as Michael Jackson and basketball star Kendall Pinder. Often the authority status of the offender was emphasised, such as in cases headlined "Scoutmaster lured children" (*DTM*, 11th February 1995, p. 6) and "Priest 'fondled girl's breasts' in blessing" (*DTM*, 11th March 1995, p. 11).

These examples also demonstrate the tendency for the tabloid paper (*DTM*) to describe child sexual abuse cases in a sexually titillating manner. An example is the extensive descriptions of the sexually explicit 'love letters' written by a schoolgirl to her much older barrister lover John Bryson (who was accused of sexual assault) (C. Wockner, *DTM*, 4th March 1995, p. 28) and his request when going on holiday for her to wear her school uniform during sex "because it was 'naughty' " (B. Clifton, *DTM*, 21st June 1995, p. 23). This 'titillating' coverage is consistent with Soothill and Walby's observations in relation to the tabloid portrayal of sex crime generally (1991, p. 22). Thus it could be argued that some sexual abuse cases can become just another — only slightly more subtle — version of the tabloid 'Page Three' girl (see Matheson, 1991; and Hay, Soothill & Walby, 1980, cited in Soothill & Walby, 1991, p. 22).

This finding also illustrates another theme from the study: the undermining of female abuse victims. It was primarily only in the sexual abuse cases — and here only with older girls — that many victims were perceived as tainted 'Lolitas' who were in some way to blame for their abuse. The division of female sexual abuse victims into 'good' and 'bad', based on their conformity to gender stereotypes, is well-documented in the literature on the maltreatment of girls (Kitzinger, 1988, pp. 79, 80) and adult women (Benedict, 1992; Bumiller, 1990).

The credibility of female sexual abuse victims was also undermined in another important way: it was primarily only in their cases that claims of 'False Memory Syndrome' (FMS) were raised. Articles about FMS intimated that 'repressed' memories of abuse which were allegedly 'recovered' (typically many years after the abuse) were fabricated or unreliable; this theme was particularly evident in a series of prominent articles by Richard Guilliatt in the *SMH* (see, for example, R. Guilliatt, *SMH*, 26th August 1995, pp. 1, 6, A *Spectrum*). The only case associating a *male* with FMS involved an allegation of sibling abuse in a primarily female family. By implicitly portraying FMS as a 'female problem', the commonly noted stereotype that females are prone to making false allegations of sexual assault (Bumiller, 1991, p. 140) was reinforced.

Child Abuse as 'Soft News': The Human Interest Story

Although the literature often discusses the media presentation of child abuse in the context of 'hard news' reflecting the values of crime reporting generally, it is rarely explicitly acknowledged that child abuse is popular as a 'soft news' — that is, 'human interest' — topic as well. Nelson identifies two forms of such reports — the traditional form of 'interesting' story, and the 'research-related' story — and argues that their addition to the standard 'hard news' child abuse story helps explain the popularity of child abuse as a media topic (1984, pp. 57–8, 66). Both of these report types were found in the sample.

The Traditional Human Interest Story

A popular form of the traditional 'human interest' story in the sample was the 'victim success story'. Such reports constituted 0.8% of the sample articles, and were a feature of both papers (0.9% of the *SMH* coverage versus 0.8% of the *DTM* coverage). These 'feel good' stories were usually about individual teenagers or adults — often celebrities or well-known public figures — who had been abused as children but had made successes of their lives. However, some of these cases give the impression that those who have been abused at times have their victim status 'paraded' by the press like a badge.

For example, both the *SMH* and *DTM* featured large articles on 26-year-old actress Traci Lords, the theme of which was 'bad girl makes good' (S. Chenery, *SMH*, 15th July 1995, p. 3 *Spectrum*; K. McCabe, *DTM*, 5th August 1995, p. 33). The

SMH article is headlined "After the fall". It described Lords' history of "family dysfunction", with an "alcoholic, bullying, raging father" and "timid, cowering mother". She "became a fallen woman while she was still a child": running away from home at 13, abusing and overdosing on hard drugs, being "exploited" as a child "porn queen" between the ages of 15 and 18, and making suicide attempts. (The *DTM* article also describes the sexual assault of Lords at the age of 11 by an older boy). This is then contrasted with her process of "recovery" and "rehabilitation", and how today she represents "a mainstream, albeit tarnished icon" who embodies "American Success, and the extremes from which it springs: tragedy and survival".

The article opens with the conclusion that Lords' attempt to establish herself as a "legitimate actress" is bound to succeed because "America loves ...bad blonde [girls]" who have reputations "with a capital R" and "Pasts" for which "they never apologise". The 'good girl'/'bad girl' dichotomy is emphasized by a quote from Lords that "There is, you see, the old Traci and the new Traci. Two separate lives", and the journalist's description of Lords as having a "devastating mixture of tensile strength, pure sexuality and angelic innocence".

In contrast to the popularity of the 'victim success story', only one of the articles in the sample (0.1%) — in the *DTM* — was a 'victim failure' story. This result should be interpreted cautiously, since as noted above an important type of report in the sample was that in which child abuse was not the primary focus, but was linked in passing as a risk factor for a whole range of social problems, such as alcohol and drug abuse, suicide and mental disorder. For example, one article reported that "Those who have been sexually abused and were binge drinkers were 6.5 times more likely to have tried to commit suicide" (*DTM*, 27th July 1995, p. 16). 3.1% of the sample articles were of this nature, but formed a higher proportion of the articles in the *SMH* rather than *DTM* (4.2% versus 2.6%). In short, a number of articles implicitly describing the negative impact of abuse were coded in this latter category. However, unlike the 'victim success stories', these were usually general reports about the particular social problem under discussion, rather than detailed case histories of individuals. The rarity of individual 'negative impact' stories may reflect a stereotypical perception that the abused child who develops later problems is to be expected, but that those who make a success of their lives are more the 'exception' and thus more 'newsworthy'.

The value of both the 'victim success' and 'victim failure' stories in encouraging in-depth understanding of abuse issues is very mixed. On the one hand the detailed case histories often provide graphic illustrations of the nature of child abuse, its often devastating long-term consequences, and its causative links with other social problems. In a context in which there are very few positive portrayals of young people in the press (Australian Centre for Independent Journalism, 1992, pp. 1–2; Young Media Australia, 1996, p. 2), the 'victim success' stories also counteract the common view that abused children are 'damaged' for life and provide positive role models of them as being able to control and make successes of their lives. They also lend support to the Australian Centre for Independent Journalism's (AICJ) observation that as "victims, young people are sometimes given a definite voice" in the press (1992, p. 41).

Despite providing a platform of communication, however, this 'voice' is only permitted expression within narrowly confined limits. While 'victim success' stories counteract stereotypes in some ways, they reinforce them in others. For instance, the Lords case is a very clear illustration of the 'bad' female victim of sexual abuse discussed above. Further, as the AICJ found in relation to print media images of young people generally, positive role models "are rarely genuine or realistic", and often focus on the lives of the beautiful and famous, whose experiences are very distant from those of most young people (1992, p. 1). Again this illustrates the print media's under-emphasis on 'regular' abuse in 'average' homes. A rare example of a more 'realistic' 'victim success' story was a story headlined "State ward now a top young chef" which opens:

> Ricky Fitzgerald is a living testament to the power of love and courage.
>
> The once painfully withdrawn, difficult and untrusting State ward has blossomed into a confident young man, with a promising career as a chef at a top hotel, thanks to the undying support from foster parents and welfare workers.

The article describes Fitzgerald's unhappy and unstable childhood with a total of 8 foster placements, and the "grit, guts, determination and courage" which led him to undertake a catering certificate at technical college and voluntary catering work at a club which eventually gave him an apprenticeship and started his career (S. Houeweling, *DTM*, 4th June 1995, p. 5).

The 'victim success' and 'victim failure' stories can also reinforce stereotypes in other ways. Both types of story tend to portray abused children as dysfunctional, damaged individuals with numerous 'problems' (even if they manage to overcome them 'against the odds' in the 'victim success' stories). This was one of the most common images of abused children in the sample as a whole, as the ACIJ found in their study of print media images of children more generally (1992, pp. 1, 17; see also Merlock Jackson, 1986, p. 184). This 'troubled' image can produce a negative view of young people as being inevitably associated with problems (ACIJ, 1992, p. 11). Furthermore, this image of weakness is rarely accompanied by any analysis of children's structural powerlessness in society which is largely responsible for these difficulties (see Kitzinger, 1988, p. 81).

The Research-related Story

The second form of human interest story is the 'research-related story'. This focuses on reporting the findings of professional research in the child abuse field (Nelson, 1984, p. 57, 66). These stories were relatively few, and were predominantly in the *SMH* rather than *DTM*. They tended to receive less prominent coverage than the 'hard news' stories — for example they rarely had illustrations or were front-page news.

In the *SMH*, the 'research-related' stories were more likely than the 'hard news' stories to be written by specialist journalists with a particular interest in child abuse — for example, Adele Horin in the *SMH*. One of Horin's articles critically contrasts two findings from a National Child Protection Council (NCPC) study: the high level of community acceptance of corporal punishment by parents, and the fact that "most believe child abuse in Australia is widespread". The first finding is contrasted with the dismissive response by the then Minister for Family Services, Senator Crowley, to the recommendations of another major NCPC report commissioned by the Federal Government on strategies to reduce corporal punishment that it was "not the view of the Federal Government to impose a view, let alone laws..." (A. Horin, *SMH*, 5th September 1995, p. 6). The clear message of the article is that this government policy decision is harmful and runs counter to the research evidence.

The *DTM* was markedly less likely than the *SMH* to cite research findings. Even when it did so, on occasion these were dismissed or trivialised. A *DTM* article reporting the release of the study by the NCPC into corporal punishment can be contrasted with the Horin article described above. The article is headlined "A Slap in the Face of Common Sense" and reports an American case in which a mother who slapped her nine-year-old son across the face in a public place and reprimanded him for inappropriate behaviour was charged with causing him "excessive physical and mental pain". The husband cashed in his retirement account to raise $30,000 bail and to hire a lawyer. This provides the lead-in story to the discussion of the NCPC report:

> It was only last week that an *Australian outfit calling itself the National Child Protection Council* was calling for legislation to outlaw the physical punishment of children at home and at school, *alleging* that such punishment was a breach of human rights and caused aggression and amorality in adulthood (emphasis added).

In contrast to the treatment given to Senator Crowley's comments by the *SMH*, the *DTM* article cited these views with approval. Rather than maintaining a research focus, the American case is used to indicate that it cannot be assumed that "commonsense will prevail" on the issue. It is then stated that

> No one condones child abuse. But it seems that many *so-called experts* confuse *genuine child abuse* with *everyday discipline* (A. Jones, DTM, 18th June 1995, p. 133; emphasis added).

Therefore, even though the article cites the NCPC report, the Council and its research findings — and indeed the whole issue of corporal punishment — is nonetheless sensationalised and trivialised and the child protection system itself denigrated. The article also demonstrates how the media tends to focus on the most extreme abuse cases, and portray maltreatment as a problem which is far removed from the behaviour of 'normal' parents. Another common theme in the *DTM* coverage is also illustrated: a deep suspicion of government intervention in 'the family' (see Sinclair, 1995, p. 166). Reports such as these tend to discourage rather than promote public dialogue and debate, and invite readers to react to such issues in an emotional manner rather than objectively assessing the research evidence.

Reliance on Official Criminal Justice Sources

The Primary Sources Used for the Reports

A further theme was the predominance of criminal justice agencies as sources for stories. Again this is consistent with prior research (Hodge, 1990, p. 12). The majority of coverage used legal sources as the primary source of information (63.2%), for

TABLE 2
Primary Sources for the Articles by Paper

Primary Source of Information for the Article	Daily Telegraph Mirror (%)	Sydney Morning Herald (%)	Total (%)
Legal	72.8	43.9	63.2
Criminal Court Cases	51.3	19.7	40.9
Government Sources	4.8	8.6	6.1
Non-government Sources	3.9	6.0	4.6
Academic Sources	2.0	5.1	3.0
Media-generated Investigation	16.5	36.4	23.1

the most part criminal court cases (see Table 2). Other legal sources included, for instance, data from the Attorney-General's department or parliament. The concentration on legal sources was a particularly marked feature of the *DTM* coverage.

The reports usually focused on one or more of the following stages of the criminal process: the notification of the offence to the police; charging by police; committal proceedings (where the prosecution's evidence is initially tested); and the trial itself, particularly the conviction and sentencing stages.

The strong emphasis on criminal court cases underlines the press' attention to the less typical abuse cases discussed above, since very few abuse cases result in criminal proceedings. For instance, only 28.5% of cases notified to DOCS are even referred to or jointly investigated by the police (DOCS, 1996b, p. 54). There is also a high rate of 'attrition' throughout the criminal justice process (see, for example, Oates et al., 1995, p. 127; Gallagher et al., 1997, p. 11).

While the focus of media attention in child abuse reporting is clearly on individual criminal cases, it should be noted that there are practical constraints on reporting data on abuse from other sources. For instance, confidentiality requirements prevent DOCS discussing the facts of individual cases in the media. These constraints arise due to legal duties to maintain confidentiality — under s68 of the *Children (Care and Protection) Act* 1987 (NSW)[5] — and professional ethical responsibilities to protect client families from media intrusion (Young, 1998). This places a limit both on the type of case which journalists can report upon, and DOCS' capacity to respond to allegations of practice failure by the Department (DOCS, undated p. 83). However when these 'constraints' are considered from a media perspective, 'confidentiality' can be seen to be misused by State welfare departments to prevent exposure of systemic inadequacy (Hechler, 1993).

The Primary Focus of the Articles
In line with the finding that the most commonly-used source of information in the sample was criminal justice agencies, by far the most common primary focus of the articles was on legal issues and proceedings (43.2%). This "fixation on procedural justice" in the media is partly explained by Ericson et al. as:

the primary means by which the news media and law join in helping to constitute the legitimacy of institutions, including their own (1991, p. 343; see also Welch et al., 1997, p. 484).

Child protection 'system' issues were also popular amongst the sample articles (11.1%). Stories focusing on the experiences of child abuse victims (11.6%) and perpetrators (9.2%) were common as well — for the most part in individual cases.[6]

Consistent with the *DTM*'s (often brief) attention to specific court cases, that paper was more likely than the *SMH* to have the primary focus of its reports as legal issues or proceedings (50.7% versus 28.1%), and the history of the perpetrator or the victim and/or their family (10.8% versus 6.0%). Conversely, the *SMH* had a higher proportion of reports dealing with child protection 'system' issues (18.8% versus 7.3%).

The Individualisation and Demonisation of Child Abusers

It has been demonstrated above that the press tends to concentrate on specific criminal cases of a very severe nature without providing details of the social context within which abuse occurs. It is therefore not surprising that the predominant image presented of abusers in the sample was in simplistic and at the same time sensationalised terms, as 'bad' (evil), 'mad' (mentally disturbed) or 'sad' (inadequate) individuals whose actions are divorced from any social causes. This is consistent with the previous research on the official portrayals of child-killers (Wilczynski, 1997, p. 424) and media images of child abusers (see Johnson, 1989, p. 15).

Cases involving offenders viewed as 'bad' received by far the most prominent coverage. These cases were often used as barometers of "the state of the nation" (Soothill & Walby, 1991, p. 27), and it was here that the function of media narratives as 'moral tale' became most explicit (Katz, 1987, p. 70). An example was Roger Cheney, convicted of abducting two girls from their beds and sexually assaulting them. The case was described in a front-page article headlined "A monster jailed for 30 years". The sentencing judge's comments provided the lead-in to the story: Cheney was described as an "evil sexual predator" who had performed "evil crimes against these children" and represented a "true menace to the community" who was "totally unrepentant, totally without remorse...and without any prospect of rehabilitation" (B. Clifton, *DTM*, 23rd June 1995, p. 1). While there is no doubt that the crimes committed are monstrous, this is a classic example of the pathological 'sex beast' — a common typification of sex offenders as primitive monsters which has received increased prominence in more modern times (Soothill & Soothill, 1993, p. 19).

The above case also illustrates the way that child abuse cases were used in the sample to promote criminal justice policies such as longer sentences, greater restrictions on the release of offenders from prison, and capital punishment. This was particularly marked in the tabloid paper (the *DTM*), which as noted above is a finding reported in the literature on the media reporting of crime generally (Garkawe, 1995, p. 431).

Cases in which this 'law and order' approach were advocated drew on the strong appeal of children as 'innocent' victims (Grabosky & Wilson, 1989, pp. 13–14), and often used highly emotive language. This was especially prominent in the homicide cases: as Grabosky and Wilson point out, the killing of a child represents a breach of fundamental social values, and thus its reporting in the media allows the ideal opportunity for the public to share its outrage and reaffirm such values (1989, p. 12).

For example one *DTM* article headlined "Hang the bastard" reports the initial court appearance of Paul Osborne, charged with the murder of two schoolgirls. It features a large photograph of the father of one of the victims, Alby Oliver, smiling as he hangs up a noose out of his car window outside the court. This is flanked by two smaller photos of the victims underneath. The article focuses on the "wild protests" which "erupted inside and outside" the court by members of the public, calling for the death penalty (M. Jones, *DTM*, 2nd November 1995).

This case also helps to illustrate the way in which the views of victims or their families (and photos of them) were given particular prominence in arguing for harsher criminal justice responses. Whilst not denying that many victims and society in general are concerned about apparently lenient sentences, and that such coverage may represent the views of some victims at least, it also demonstrates the way in which concern for crime victims has been harnessed to further conservative 'law and order' agendas which do not necessarily advance the interests of victims (Garkawe, 1995). Promotion of this theme is connected with the failure by the media to address the causes and prevention of crime.

Causation and Prevention

Child abuse prevention (particularly of a primary rather than a tertiary nature) received relatively little coverage. Prior findings were also confirmed in the lack of attention to the social causes of child abuse (Carment, 1987) such as poverty, social isolation, gender inequality and socialisation, and the social acceptance of corporal punishment. The absence of discussion about such issues is noteworthy in the face of research which has clearly established the crucial importance of these factors in precipitating child maltreatment (Cole, 1985).

Overall, causation issues were the primary focus of only 0.2% of the articles. However as noted above, child abuse was quite often linked in passing with a whole range of other social problems. In short, while the direction of the stories was primarily linking child abuse as a causative factor in other social problems, there was much less emphasis on these other social problems as causative factors for precipitating child abuse. Where there was such linkage, it was rarely tied to the analysis of the individual abuse cases reported.

The coverage of child abuse issues is therefore generally superficial. In part this reflects the fact that child abuse media reports are usually not written by specialists in the topic, as noted elsewhere (Skidmore, 1995, p. 89). For instance the sample reports were often written by generalist journalists or, less frequently, by those in a diverse range of specialty areas such as crime.

This is not to say that all press coverage of child abuse is negative and superficial. There were certainly notable exceptions to this in the sample, particularly in the *SMH*. For example, Adele Horin's "Lost Children" series provided a more in-depth understanding of child maltreatment with its coverage of issues such as the complicated and resource-starved nature of child protection work. The series also included an article which described how two families had been helped by child abuse intervention programs, in order to argue that "the earlier intervention occurs, the better" (*SMH*, 25th September 1995, p. 1 and p. 2; 26th September 1995, p. 2 and p. 13; 27th September 1995, p. 1 and p. 6). However, it is important to note that this series appeared in the context of a media scandal about child deaths and criticism of DOCS for failing to prevent 19 deaths over the previous two and a half years. These more in-depth articles were also the exception rather than the rule.

Moral Panic: Dangerousness and the Media

As the Glasgow University Media Group points out, the discourse produced by the media is "a sequence of socially manufactured messages, which carry many of the dominant assumptions of our society" (1995, p. 41). If we "unpack the coding" (Glasgow University Media Group, 1995, p. 41) embedded in the media narratives about child abuse presented above, what are these assumptions and implicit ideological messages?

The sample findings confirmed that the print media coverage of child abuse is largely stereotyped and superficial (Kitzinger & Skidmore, 1995; Franklin & Parton, 1991; Johnson, 1989), and that there is a lack of coverage of issues of social causation and prevention (Surette, 1992, pp. 59, 64, 68). The reinforcement of gender stereotypes was also evident, with the press portrayal of female sex abuse victims as "seductive, liars, vindictive, [and] hysterical" (Carmody, 1992, p. 13). Many of the above trends intensified in the period following the sample (1996–97), with the concentration on non-familial homosexual child sexual assault by the Royal Commission into the NSW Police Service inquiry into paedophilia (Carrington, 1997, pp. 141–43).

The tendency for the tabloid press to report crime issues in a more sensational manner than the quality press (Roshier, 1981) was also confirmed by the results. For instance, the tabloid press primarily reported individual cases drawn from criminal trials. Conversely, the quality press used a more diverse range of material, had a marked interest in systemic issues, and gave greater — and more even-handed — coverage to research findings. Nonetheless, there were some key areas of similarity between the quality and tabloid papers, primarily in their concentration on the more extreme forms of abuse such as homicide, and the lack of coverage given to educational issues such as prevention and the social causes of abuse.

Theories of moral panic, which have provided a popular lens for analysing the media portrayals of child abuse (Jenkins, 1992; Edwards & Lohman, 1994), are clearly useful in explaining some of the above findings. One of the key indicators of 'moral panic' is the notion of 'disproportionality' — that is, that the perception of the threat posed by the behaviour in question is not commensurate with the objective facts (Goode & Ben-Yehuda, 1994, p. 36). This is certainly true of the perception of danger presented by certain types of abusers — such as the stranger-killer and the 'evil' or 'mad' molester or killer. These 'folk devils' reinforce dominant social stereotypes about maltreatment, and hamper rather than assist our understanding of the causes, incidence and prevention of abuse.

Nonetheless, care should be taken not to apply the concept of moral panic to child abuse as a more general phenomenon. As Atmore (1997, pp. 124,127) points out, the media 'obsession' with child abuse has in some instances led to a "panic about panics" by commentators, and a view that child abuse is " 'over-rated' as an issue of social concern" (see also Johnson, 1997, p. 1515). This can reinforce the arguments made by the 'backlash' movement, which has sought to discredit the child protection system and claims made by abuse victims (Sinclair, 1995; Myers, 1994). These views were evident in the current study, particularly in a series of articles on FMS by Richard Guilliatt in the *SMH* (see, for example, Richard Guilliatt, SMH, 26th August 1995, pp. 1, 6, A *Spectrum*). Social acceptance of these arguments can potentially undermine arguments by feminists and others who wish to highlight the seriousness of child abuse and work towards its prevention (Atmore, 1997, p. 128).

Moral panic theories also highlight the fact that "alarmist reactions to crime... contribute to the escalating *vocabulary of punitive motives*" which is then used to promote harsh criminal justice responses as the solution to crime (Welch et al, 1997, pp. 484, 486; emphasis in original). The study supports these findings to the extent that child abuse cases became powerful vehicles for promoting "law and order commonsense" (Brown & Hogg, 1998, pp. 18–44).

In addition to the linkages with moral panic, the concept of 'dangerousness' in particular was found to be a key aspect of the 'law and order commonsense' theme portrayed by the print media in maltreatment cases. As Craze and Moynihan argue (in developing the work of Foucault), such concepts rely on identifying, separating and punishing the "transgressive Other" and fostering fear of the danger which is symbolised. Thus,

> ... representations of violence have been given a centred position in delivering both the meanings of contemporary social life and the role and character of law within it (1994, pp. 30–31).

Therefore certain abusers — such as the non-familial paedophile — become "textual outlaws" in the media, to be "put under surveillance, punished, contained, constrained" and "symbolically sacrificed" (Young, 1996, p. 9). These 'outlaws' provide a focal point for public anxiety and are subjected to what some might term a high-tech 'lynching'. As Pratt (1997) demonstrates, in the modern era this anxiety about dangerousness has centred on recidivist violent and/or sexual offenders, and has been used to justify a raft of criminal justice policies to ostensibly protect the community from threatening outsiders.

To conclude, the large amount of media coverage of child maltreatment provides something of a 'smokescreen': the large *quantity* of media reports is certainly not in most instances an indication of *quality*. The media focuses largely on individual cases, criminal justice sources (at a superficial level), the most extreme and less common forms of abuse, and gives little attention to the social causes of maltreatment and prevention issues. It therefore presents a powerfully stereotyped view of child abuse which enforces social norms by labelling abusers as defective and in some cases dangerous individuals to be cast out of society. Thus whilst the focus on deviance and dangerousness in media debates may help to sell newspapers and incite public outrage and horror, it does little to encourage an in-depth understanding of child abuse, child abusers or child abuse victims. Without such understanding, society is ill-equipped to respond to the maltreatment of children. Public assumptions about what is 'real' child abuse will remain unchallenged, and in this context debates about child abuse will continue to be played out in trivial and distorted terms.

ANIA WILCZYNSKI AND KATE SINCLAIR

Acknowledgments

This research was made possible by two grants each under the Law Foundation of New South Wales Legal Scholarship Support Fund within the Faculty of Law, University of Sydney, and the University Research Grant Scheme within the University of Sydney. The research was conducted whilst the first author was a Lecturer at the Faculty of Law, University of Sydney and a Visiting Fellow at the Social Policy Research Centre, University of NSW (January–May 1998). Earlier versions of parts of this paper were presented at: the Social Policy Research Centre, University of NSW, 24th March 1998; the 'Kids First — Agenda for Change' Conference, Melbourne Convention Centre, Mebourne, 2nd–3rd April 1998; the School of Social Science and Policy, University of NSW, 20th April 1998; and the NSW Child Protection Council State Conference, 'Building Partnerships ... From Rhetoric to Reality', Masonic Centre, Sydney, 4th–5th May 1998. We are grateful for the helpful comments made by the participants at those presentations and the following people who commented on earlier drafts of this paper: Professor Terry Carney, Dr Don Bross, Professor Tony Vinson, the Editor of this journal (Dr John Pratt), and two anonymous reviewers. We also wish to thank Dr Bronwyn Naylor for helpful discussions concerning analysis of media texts, and the following for their efficient research assistance: Lynne Barnes for help with literature searches, SPSS data entry, and preliminary data analyses; Fran Smithard for her assistance with SPSS data entry and photocopying; and Simon Keizer for a variety of tasks in the final stage of the project.

Endnotes

1. Other findings of the study are reported elsewhere (Wilczynski & Sinclair, 1999).
2. The variables examined included: the type of abuse; the scene of the abuse; the relationship between victim and perpetrator; the number of perpetrators and their sex; and the number of victims.
3. Calculated from unpublished data on substantiated notifications during the financial year 1995/96 obtained from the Information and Research Unit, DOCS. Note that the official DOCS figures categorise physical abuse and homicide together (DOCS, 1996a, Table 5.2).
4. Unpublished data obtained from the Homicide Monitoring Program, Australian Institute of Criminology, Canberra.
5. This Act will be replaced by the *Children and Young Persons (Care and Protection) Act 1998* (NSW) in 1999. However, a similar section (s105) appears in the new Act.
6. Only the most common topics which formed the primary focus of the articles are reported here.

References

Altheide, D.L. (1996). *Qualitative media analysis*, Thousand Oaks, California: Sage.

Atmore, C. (1997). Rethinking moral panic and child abuse for 2000. In J. Bessant, & R. Hil (Eds.), *Youth, crime and the media: Media representations of and reaction to young people in relation to law and order*, Hobart: National Clearinghouse for Youth Studies.

Audit Bureau of Circulation. (1995). *Circulation summary January–June 1995*, Sydney: Audit Bureau of Circulation.

Australian Bureau of Statistics. (1997). *Population by age and sex, Australian states and territories, June 1992–June 1997*, Canberra: Australian Bureau of Statistics.

Australian Centre for Independent Journalism. (1992). *Youth and the media: A report into the representation of young people in the New South Wales print media,* Sydney: Australian Centre for Independent Journalism.

Benedict, H. (1992). *Virgin or vamp: How the press covers sex crimes,* New York: Oxford University Press.

Best, J. (1990). *Threatened children: Rhetoric and concern about child-victims,* Chicago: University of Chicago Press.

Brown, D., & Hogg, R. (1998). *Rethinking law and order,* Annandale, Sydney: Pluto Press.

Bumiller, K. (1990). Fallen angels: The representation of violence against women in legal culture, *International Journal of the Sociology of Law, 18,* 125–42.

Carment, A. (1987). The media and the 'discovery' of child abuse: Bringing the monster back home, *Australian Journal of Law and Society, 4,* 7–41.

Carmody, M. (1992). Uniting all women: A historical look at attitudes to rape. In J. Breckenridge, & M. Carmody (Eds.), *Crimes of violence: Australian responses to rape and child sexual assault,* North Sydney, Sydney: Allen and Unwin.

Carrington, K. (1997). Representations of young women as victims of sexual violence. In J. Bessant, & R. Hil (Eds.), *Youth, crime and the media: Media representations of and reaction to young people in relation to law and order,* Hobart: National Clearinghouse for Youth Studies.

Clapton, G. (1993). *The satanic abuse controversy: Social workers and the social work press,* London: University of North London Press.

Cohen, S. (1980). *Folk devils and moral panics: The creation of the mods and the rockers* (2nd ed.). Oxford: Martin Robertson.

Cole, S.G. (1985). Child battery. In C. Guberman, & M. Wolfe (Eds.), *No safe place — Violence against women and children,* Toronto, Canada: Women's Press.

Craze, L., & Moynihan, P. (1994). Violence, meaning and the law: Responses to Garry David, *Australian and New Zealand Journal of Criminology, 27,* 30–45.

Department of Community Services (DOCS) (Information and Planning Group, Child and Family Services Directorate). (1996a). *Trends in the child protection program: Profiles for financial years 1991/92 – 1995/96,* Sydney: DOCS.

Department of Community Services (Child and Family Services Directorate). (1996b). *Review of Intake to the child protection program: review of 253 case files,* Sydney: DOCS.

Department of Community Services (n.d.). *NSW Department of Community Services: Annual report 1996–1997,* Sydney: DOCS.

Dingwall, R. (1989). Labelling children as abused or neglected. In W.S. Rogers, D. Hevey, & E. Ash (Eds.). *Child abuse and neglect: Facing the challenge,* London: Batsford in association with The Open University.

Edwards, S.S.M., & Lohman, J.S.S. (1994). The impact of 'moral panic' on professional behavior in cases of child sexual abuse: An international perspective, *Journal of Child Sexual Abuse, 3,* 103–26.

Ericson, R.V., Baranek, P.M., & Chan, J. (1987). *Visualising deviance: A study of news organisation,* Toronto: University of Toronto Press.

Ericson, R.V., Baranek, P.M., & Chan, J. (1991). *Representing order: Crime, law and justice in the news media,* Milton Keynes: Open University Press.

Franklin, B. (1989). Wimps and bullies: Press reporting of child abuse. In P. Carter, T. Jeffs, & M. Smith (Eds.), *Social welfare and social policy yearbook 1,* Milton Keynes: Open University Press.

Franklin, B., & Parton, N. (1991). Media reporting of social work: A framework for analysis. In B. Franklin, & N. Parton (Eds.), *Social work, the media and public relations,* London: Routledge.

Gallagher, P., Hickey, J., & Ash, D. (1997). *Child sexual assault: An analysis of matters determined in the District Court of New South Wales during 1994,* Sydney: Judicial Commission of New South Wales.

Garkawe, S. (1995). Victims of crime and law and order ideology: A critical analysis, *Australian Journal of Social Issues, 30*, 424–44.

Gelles, R. (1987). *Family violence*, Newbury Park, California: Sage.

Glasgow University Media Group. (1995). Reviewing the news. In J. Eldridge (Ed.), *Glasgow media group reader, volume 1*, London: Routledge.

Goddard, C. (1994). Governing the 'family': Child protection policy and practice and the 'Children of God', *Just Policy, 1*, 9–12.

Goddard, C., & Liddell, M. (1993). Child abuse and the media: Victoria introduces mandatory reporting after an intensive media campaign, *Children Australia, 18*, 23–7.

Goddard, C., & Liddell, M. (1995). Child abuse fatalities and the media: Lessons from a case study, *Child Abuse Review, 4*, 356–64.

Goode, E., & Ben-Yehuda, N. (1994). *Moral panics: The social construction of deviance*, Oxford: Blackwell.

Grabosky, P., & Wilson, P. (1989). *Journalism and justice*, Sydney: Pluto Press.

Hay, A., Soothill, K., & Walby, S. (1980). Seducing the public by rape reports, *New Society, 53*, 214–15.

Hechler, D. (1993). Damage control, *Child Abuse and Neglect, 17*, 703–8.

Hillman, J. (1988). When social workers are used as scapegoats, *Social Work Today, 19*, 18–19.

Hodge, R. (1990). Mass media and the problem of child sexual abuse. In T. Minchin, & M. Lee (Eds.), *Proceedings of a symposium on child sexual abuse organised by the Western Australian branch of the Australian Psychological Society held in March 1989 at the Churchlands Campus of the Western Australian College of Advanced Education*, Nedlands, Western Australia: Australian Psychological Society.

Hughes, C. (1994). From field notes to dissertation: Analyzing the stepfamily. In A. Bryman, & R. G. Burgess (Eds.), *Analyzing qualitative data*, London: Routledge.

Jenkins, P. (1992). *Intimate enemies: Moral panics in contemporary Great Britain*, New York: Aldine de Gruyter.

Jensen, K.B. (1991). Reception analysis: Mass communication as the social production of meaning. In K.B. Jensen, & N.W. Jankowski (Eds.), *A handbook of qualitative methodologies for mass communication research*, London: Routledge.

Johnson, J. (1989). Horror stories and the construction of child abuse. In J. Best (Ed.), *Images of issues: Typifying contemporary social problems*, New York: Aldine de Gruyter.

Johnson, N.R. (1997). [Review of the book *Moral panics: The social construction of deviance*]. *Social Forces, 75*, 1514–5.

Katz, J. (1987). What makes crime news?, *Media, Culture and Society, 9*, 47–75.

Kitzinger, J. (1988). Defending innocence: Ideologies of childhood, *Feminist Review, 28*, 77–87.

Kitzinger, J., & Skidmore, P. (1995). Playing safe: Media coverage of child sexual abuse prevention strategies, *Child Abuse Review, 4*, 47–56.

Matheson, A. (1991). Violence against women: Pornography as news?, *Refractory Girl, 38*, 7–10.

Merlock Jackson, K. (1986). *Images of children in American film*, Metuchen, New Jersey: Scarecrow Press.

Myers, J.B. (Ed.). (1994). *The backlash: Child protection under fire*, Thousand Oaks: Sage.

Nelson, B. (1984). *Making an issue of child abuse: Political agenda setting for social problems*, Chicago: University of Chicago Press.

Oates, R.K., Lynch, D.L., Stern, A.E., O'Toole, B.I., & Cooney, G. (1995). The criminal justice system and the sexually abused child: Help or hindrance?, *The Medical Journal of Australia, 162*, 126–130.

Ogden, J. (1991). Class distinctions, *Social Work Today, 17th January*, 9.

Osmer, M. (1980). Responsibility to sources. In G. Gerbner, C.J. Ross, & E. Zigler, (Eds.), *Child abuse: An agenda for action*, New York: Oxford University Press.

Parton, N. (1985). *The politics of child abuse*, Houndmills, Hampshire: Macmillan Education.

Pratt, J. (1997). *Governing the dangerous: Dangerousness, law and social change*, Sydney: Federation Press.

Roshier, B. (1981). The selection of crime news by the press. In S. Cohen, & J. Young (Eds.), *The manufacture of news: Social problems, deviance and the mass media*, (2nd ed.). Beverly Hills, CA: Sage.

Rowe, L., & Cavender, G. (1991). Cauldrons bubble, Satan's trouble, but witches are okay: Media constructions of Satanism and Witchcraft. In J.T. Richardson, J. Best, & D.G. Bromley (Eds.), *The Satanism scare*, New York: Aldine de Gruyter.

Roy Morgan Research Centre. (1995). *Readership survey, 12 months to June 1995*, Melbourne: Morgan Research Centre.

Sinclair, K. (1995). Responding to abuse: A matter of perspective, *Current Issues in Criminal Justice, 7*, 153–175.

Skidmore, P. (1995). Telling tales: Media power, ideology and the reporting of child sexual abuse in Britain. In D. Kidd-Hewitt, & R. Osborne (Eds.), *Crime and the media: The post-modern spectacle*, London: Pluto Press.

Smith, B.E. (1995). *Prosecuting child physical abuse cases: A case study in San Diego*, Washington: National Institute of Justice, US Department of Justice.

Soothill, K., & Grover, C. (1997). Research note: A note on computer searches of newspapers, *Sociology, 31*, 591–96.

Soothill, K., & Soothill, D. (1993). Prosecuting the victim? A study of the reporting of barristers' comments in rape cases, *The Howard Journal, 32*, 12–24.

Soothill, K., & Walby, S. (1991). *Sex crime in the news*, London: Routledge.

Sparks, C. (1991). Goodbye, Hildy Johnson: The vanishing 'serious press'. In P. Dahlgren, & C. Sparks (Eds.), *Communication and citizenship: Journalism and the public sphere in the new media age*, London: Routledge.

Strauss, A.L. (1987). *Qualitative analysis for social scientists*, Cambridge and New York: Cambridge University Press.

Surette, R. (1992). *Media, crime, and criminal justice*, Pacific Grove, California: Brooks/Cole Publishing Company.

Vinson, T. (1987). Child abuse and the media. In Institute of Criminology (Ed.) *Proceedings of a seminar on media effects on attitudes to crime*, Sydney: Institute of Criminology, Faculty of Law, Sydney University.

Welch, M., Fenwick, M., & Roberts, M. (1997). Primary definitions of crime and moral panic: A content analysis of experts' quotes in feature newspaper articles on crime, *Journal of Research in Crime and Delinquency, 34*, 474–94.

Wilczynski, A. (1997). Mad or bad? Child-killers, gender and the courts, *British Journal of Criminology, 37*, 419–36.

Wilczynski, A., & Sinclair, K. (1999). *Fractured images: Child maltreatment in the news*. Manuscript submitted for publication.

Young Media Australia. (1996). *Youth media images: Report from the Youth Media Images Forum on Media Coverage of Youth and Media Issues held at Headlines Theatre, Adelaide, 29 February 1996*, Adelaide: Young Media Australia.

Young, A. (1996). *Imagining crime: Textual outlaws and criminal conversations*, London: Sage.

Young, T. (1998). *Debunking the bunker mentality*. Paper presented at the NSW Child Protection Council State Conference, 'Building Partnerships ... From Rhetoric to Reality', Masonic Centre, Sydney, 4th–5th May.

Part VII
Political Violence

[26]

The utilitarian justification of torture

Denial, desert and disinformation

ROD MORGAN
University of Bristol, UK

Abstract

Torture is prohibited by customary international law. Yet the practice widely persists. Beneath the rhetoric of human rights talk the utilitarian justification of torture commands a good deal of support among police and security agencies and is detectable between the lines of the discourse of denial. Can torture be justified on utilitarian grounds? Close examination of Bentham's defence of torture, and the reasoning of the Landau Report in support of 'moderate physical pressure' in Israel, suggests that it cannot. The practice of torture will arguably best be countered by confronting the subterranean utilitarian justifications of torture on their own terms: in the long term it does not work but, rather, undermines the legitimacy of the state itself.

Key Words

Bentham · human rights · terrorism · torture · utilitarianism

INTRODUCTION

The enforcement of legal systems in all modern states relies ultimately on the use of force. The police are generally defined in terms of their monopoly of the legitimate use of force, on which they may rely to apprehend and detain suspected offenders. Punishment, which involves the deliberate imposition of pain, is generally regarded as the just deserts of convicted offenders. The amount of force employed or punishment imposed is ideally proportionate to the harm threatened or proven (Ashworth, 1998) and it is generally agreed that it should be the minimum necessary. But this begs the question as to what is necessary and thus what scale should apply. Various international law norms have been established in order to limit, on human rights grounds, the amount of force used (restricting, for example, the period during which the police may

181

detain suspects prior to their being brought before a court) or punishment imposed (attempts to abolish capital and corporal punishment, for example). But consensus has not been achieved and dissenting states go their own way or enter reservations regarding international treaties that they have ratified. On one issue, however, there *appears* to have been established general agreement: 'no one shall be subjected to torture' (Article 5 of the Universal Declaration of Human Rights). This prohibition is the most well attested in the entire human rights calendar. Yet the prohibition has given rise to a paradox. Though the proscription of torture is now part of customary international law, and though the domestic law of most states either explicitly prohibits torture or deems invalid evidence collected through its use, torture widely persists and in certain situations torture, or near-torture, is regarded by many practitioners to be a practical necessity. It is justified on utilitarian grounds. But the justifications are subterranean. Such is the strength of the legal prohibition and the discourse of human rights that these dissenting utilitarian opinions are seldom voiced or the practices justified by them admitted. Denial of torture is the order of the day and euphemisms are employed to cover its tracks (Cohen, 1993). This article has four purposes. First, to illustrate the persistence of torture. Second, to consider the utilitarian justifications offered for its use. Third, to assess whether the use of torture can be justified on solely utilitarian grounds. And, fourth, to show that torture and apologias for torture thrive best in conditions where there are deep social conflicts and an absence of democratic accountability.

THE PERSISTENCE OF TORTURE

Books like Krousher's *Physical interrogation techniques* (1985) are fortunately rare. Krousher offers advice supplementary to the US Army Field Manual, which prohibits force as an aid to the interrogation of hostile subjects. Krousher says that he does not advocate the use of torture but considers that if a 'commmander feels he *must* use torture . . . he should understand the techniques available to him, and especially understand the dangers inherent in each technique' (1985, 2–3, emphasis added). His book (written in appalling English) comprises a detailed catalogue of practical advice on how subjects can be made vulnerable and humiliated, and how pain can best be inflicted without leaving marks or causing permanent damage or resulting in death. Thus the chapter on electricity is introduced with the observation:

> The equipment is commonly available. It can be conducted with relatively little training or special skill. It can be easily varied from mildly unpleasant to excruciatingly agonizing. With a few relatively simple precautions, it leaves no marks and does little or no lasting damage. (Krousher, 1985: 63)

The latter is an important consideration because: 'Often it is necessary that no signs of "force" be visible on the subject when he is released, visited by neutral parties, or when his body is examined' (1985: 6). Krousher's message is clear. There *will* be situations when interrogators *must* resort to torture, but it is imperative that no one be able to prove that they have done so.

Krousher's book is in every sense so crude that it might be dismissed as the extravagant product of extremist American fringe publishing, of little or no relevance for the analysis of the policies of states. That might be the case were it not for the fact that the methods Krousher describes have been and are widely practised in several countries whose military or law enforcement personnel have been trained by American special forces. Consider the case of Turkey, a country in which torture is prohibited by law, is officially condemned and yet is extensively employed. Turkish discourse on torture illustrates a common configuration: general denial, but concessions by politicians that it may occasionally happen; condemnation, but appeal to special extenuating circumstances; commitment to purge the practice, but the suggestion that the remedy actually lies in the hands of those who regularly accuse the authorities of employing torture and who are allied to groups who threaten the integrity of the Turkish state.

The facts regarding the situation in Turkey are well known and can briefly be summarized. There are deep-seated conflicts within Turkey, ideological conflicts (between secularism and Islamic fundamentalism) and regional/ethnic conflicts (notably between sections of the Kurdish minority and the dominant Turkish population) and the democratic tradition is fragile there. There have been repeated periods of military rule, the most recent in the early 1980s. An armed struggle, involving the use of terror tactics by both sides, has long been waged between the militant Kurdish PKK (though in September 1999 they announced a cease-fire) and the Turkish military and police authorities. The international human rights NGOs have long been critical of the Turkish human rights record, accusing the Turkish authorities, inter alia, of the extensive use of torture (see, for example, Amnesty International, 1989, 1996; Human Rights Watch, 1993; Physicians for Human Rights, 1996). Human rights NGOs within Turkey agree (HRFT, 1996). Turkey has seven times been visited by the Strasbourg-based European Committee for the Prevention of Torture and Inhuman or Degrading Treatment or Punishment (the CPT), a Committee established by a European Convention of the same name to which Turkey, along with 41 other European states, is a signatory (for a general review, see Evans and Morgan, 1998). The CPT, unlike the international NGOs, has right of access without warning to all places within which persons are held in custody on the authority of the state. In the absence, until recently (Council of Europe, 1999), of Turkish willingness to publish CPT reports (the only Council of Europe member state to adopt this stance for an extended period and *not* subsequently to authorize publication of the CPT reports produced within that period) the CPT has twice issued public statements of what the Committee has found in Turkey (Council of Europe, 1992, 1996). The findings are clear, namely, that the use of torture is 'widespread' and that ordinary criminal suspects, as well as persons suspected of engaging in terrorism, or being members of groups supporting such acts, are the victims. This accords with locally collected evidence: there were said by one Turkish human rights organization to be 19 deaths in custody, 94 disappearances following arrest and 1292 cases of torture in 1995 alone (HRFT, 1996). The practices described by the CPT are well within the definitional limits of torture in international law:

> suspension by the arms; suspension by the wrists, which were fastened behind the victim (so-called 'palestinian hanging', a technique apparently employed in anti-terror departments); electric shocks to sensitive parts of the body (including the genitals); squeezing of the testicles; beating of the soles of the feet ('falaka'); hosing with pressurised water; incarceration for

> lengthy periods in very small, dark and unventilated cells; threats of torture or other forms of serious ill-treatment to the person detained or against others; severe psychological humiliation. (Council of Europe, 1992, para. 5)

That is, the methods involve great pain, are used purposefully to elicit information or confessions, and constitute an aggravated form of inhuman or degrading treatment.

What have the Turkish authorities to say regarding this evidence? First, the authorities *largely* deny what is alleged: torture is not *widespread* or *systematic*, though it *may* be *sporadic*. The Turkish Ambassador to the UN has said that his country has 'never denied the fact that sporadic cases of torture may occur in Turkey'. But in his opinion it was 'almost impossible to completely eliminate torture in a struggle against a savage terrorism' (quoted in Gemalmaz, 1999). Mr Yilmaz, the Turkish Prime Minister, reportedly said to the CPT during their visit in 1996: 'Even though we pay great attention, because of our struggle against terrorism cases of torture unfortunately still occur. However, a cessation of the state of emergency regime will decrease torture cases' (Gemalmaz, 1999: 16). Second, the '*cases*' of torture that 'unfortunately still occur' are explained by terrorism. 'Cases of torture ... occur, *because* of our struggle against terrorism'. Indeed, because of terrorism it is '*impossible*' to rid Turkey of torture, the implication being either that torture is *necessitated* by the need to combat terrorism or the practice is *excused* by the threat of terrorism. Third, again by implication, torture will decrease or be eliminated when the state of emergency, and the opposition to the state which gives rise to the state of emergency, ceases. Denial, justification and blame are thus subtly fused by the Turkish authorities. The authorities will take strenuous steps to stop torture when the terrorists, and the apologists for the groups engaged in terrorism, cease their activities.

There is more than a hint in all this of just deserts and proportionality. Extreme harm is being met, and will continue to be met, with extreme harm. The conjunction of terrorism and torture is either a fact of life, something which civilian politicians are powerless to change (which given the longstanding power of the military authorities in Turkey, may substantially be true), or constitutes a moral equation that they are unwilling to upset.

The Turkey case study illustrates a broader theme, namely that though torture is *absolutely* prohibited in customary international law (Article 2[2] of the UN Convention Against Torture makes clear that 'No exceptional circumstances whatsoever, whether a state of war or a threat of war, internal political instability or any other political emergency, may be invoked as a justification of torture'), torture continues, particularly in states riven by internal conflict, and is widely seen to be a justified or excusable response to those conflicts. The official Turkish discourse is less than honest in this respect, but fortunately there is another better articulated contemporary statement of the same connections on which we can draw, namely the report of the Landau Commission in Israel. Here also there is a deep-seated conflict and extensive well-attested use of torture by the Israeli security services against Palestinians (B'Tselem, 1991, 1992). The Israeli authorities also deny that they employ torture. But they have admitted to and have justified using '*moderate physical pressure*', the forms of which, some commentators consider, amount to torture and which, whether they do or do not,

MORGAN   The utilitarian justification of torture

all the evidence suggests, spill over into practices which, to the extent that they occur, *everyone* agrees are torture.

THE LANDAU COMMISSION

The background to the Israeli Landau Commission is as follows. In the mid-1980s two scandals relating to the actions of the Israeli General Security Services (GSS) led to the establishment, under Mr Justice Moshe Landau, a former Supreme Court President, of an official inquiry into the investigative methods employed by the GSS against alleged terrorists. The resulting report came in two parts. The first part, which was published (Landau Commission, 1987), presented findings as to what had happened in the precipitating incidents, outlined the threat to Israel presented by Arab terrorism, described the dilemmas confronting the Israeli security services in their efforts to combat terrorism and presented the case for the GSS being able to use investigatory methods involving '*moderate physical pressure*' subject to the approval of a Ministerial Committee. The second part of the report, outlining the approved interrogation methods, was not published and remains secret. The remarkable aspect of the Landau Inquiry is that it was held and that any of its findings were published. The Landau text represents the state putting its head above the parapet to reveal a debate and practices that generally remain entirely secret.

The Landau argument can briefly be summarized as follows. Israel is confronted by several organizations dedicated to its destruction. These organizations are made up of highly professional personnel who employ terrorist methods which make no distinction between civilian and military targets. These organizations command widespread support within their own Arab communities, but they are also ruthless with regard to critics and informants. The threat they pose is therefore potent and difficult to counter. The primary role of the GSS, unlike the Israeli police, is not to bring individual offenders to justice (which requires the collection of valid evidence by means of approved methods), but to infiltrate these organizations, gather intelligence and neutralize the threat they pose. The GSS task is to protect the 'very existence of society and the State' (Landau Commission, 1987: para. 2.18). Further, the GSS have to rely on sources that cannot usually be disclosed: their work is secretive because it has to be. Thus when they used officially disapproved interrogation methods to obtain information and it was discovered: 'They simply lied', and their perjury was explicitly approved by their departmental superiors (Landau Commission, 1987: para. 2.27). This was the logical consequence of the nature of their work.

The Landau Commission accepted GSS contentions both regard to the effectiveness and necessity of GSS methods. And, in spite of the lies that GSS personnel were found to have told and admitted, the Commission also accepted the integrity of GSS officers: they found, in effect, that officers had been engaged in *noble cause corruption*. GSS personnel felt they had a '*sacred mission*' and the Landau Commission accepted that they had only used those *moderate* methods of physical pressure which the Commission subsequently endorsed. They also accepted that, because of the legal constraints to which they were then subject, GSS officers had had no alternative but to lie about their methods.

GSS personnel felt their *sacred* mission justified 'the means, any means' (Landau Commission, 1987: para. 2.40). The Landau Commission agreed that the emergency situation justified the adoption of special measures, but did not go quite so far. In

185

coming to their conclusion they discussed the aprochyphal ticking bomb scenario (though see Horne's [1987: 204] account of an actual incident in the Algerian War). A bomb has been placed in a crowded, but unidentified, public place and could explode at any moment. The perpetrator, or a knowledgeable collaborator, is captured. What methods is the interrogator justified in using in order to obtain information as to the whereabouts of the bomb? The Commission put the issue thus:

> The deciding factor is not the element of time [the imminence of the danger], but the comparison between the gravity of the two evils – the evil of contravening the law as opposed to the evil which will occur sooner or later . . . [W]eighing these two evils, one against the other, must be performed according to the concept of morality implanted in the heart of every decent and honest person. To put it bluntly, the alternative is: are we to accept the offence of assault entailed in slapping a suspect's face, or threatening him, in order to induce him to talk. . . . and thereby prevent the greater evil which is about to occur? The answer is self-evident. (Landau Commission, 1987: para. 3.15)

Interrogators, the Commission argued, are justified in using force – it is a self-defence necessity – but they should not have carte blanche to decide the level of force. That would irreparably pervert 'the image of the State' – note the *image*, not the *reality*, of the state – 'as a law-abiding polity which preserves the rights of the citizen' (Landau Commission, 1987: para. 3.16). The force used should not be disproportionate: it should 'never reach the level of physical torture or maltreatment' and the choice of measures should be weighed against the level of danger anticipated. Moreover, the permitted methods of physical and psychological force should be defined and regulated, though in order that the methods remain effective (i.e. be not easily countered), their character should remain secret.

Before considering this line of reasoning we should consider Jeremy Bentham's utilitarian defence of torture to which the Landau deliberations bear a striking similarity.

BENTHAM'S DEFENCE OF TORTURE

Bentham's article on torture was not published in his lifetime but he wrote it in the period 1777–9 after having read Beccaria's seminal text *On crimes and punishments* (see Bellamy, 1995) in which, inter alia, Beccaria argued against the practice of judicial torture. Bentham admired Beccaria's article and agreed with most of it. He was concerned, however, that 'the delusive power of words' might lead 'the extensive considerations of utility' to be overridden by the 'first impressions of sentiment' (Bentham, 1777–9: 308). He was not persuaded that Beccaria had logically disposed of the utilitarian arguments under which torture might be used. He was 'inclined to think there are a very few cases in which for a very particular purpose, Torture might be made use of with advantage' (Bentham, 1777–9).

Bentham asked, if torture 'is where a person is made to suffer any violent pain of body in order to compel him to do something or to desist from doing something which done or desisted from the penal application is immediately made to cease', and if the 'community has an interest in his doing' it and he 'having it in his power to do it . . . is obstinate and in despite of Justice persist in refusing to do it . . . where is the harm done' in using torture to make him do it? (Bentham, 1777–9: 309–12). Indeed Bentham suggests that if by torture we could be certain that the subject would do that which it is in the public interest to make him do, then the utilitarian justification for torture would be more secure than that for judicial punishment because, in the case of punishment, the utilitarian justification for which lies in deterrence or reformation, there is always a risk, the future being uncertain, that more punishment will be used than is necessary. With torture, he suggests, there is no such risk. The torture stops immediately the subject complies. The difficulty with torture lies in being *certain* that the subject *can* comply – that is, that he has the information which it is in the public interest to obtain. This is the difficulty that Bentham seeks to tame. Can we formulate rules for cases 'in which Torture may with propriety be applied' (Bentham, 1777–9: 309–12)? Bentham thought he could and his rules are in several respects similar to those proposed by the Landau Commission.

First, torture ought not to be applied 'without good proof of its being in the power of the prisoner to do what is required of him'. The investigator should be as certain as he can be – Bentham referred to the quality of evidence sufficient to convict for a serious crime – that the suspect is an offender and has the information regarding the offence (the identity of co-offenders, the location of hidden objects, or whatever) which is sought. Second, torture should only be used 'in cases which admit of no delay'. It has to be certain, or very probable, that harm will be done unless the information sought is obtained with urgency. Third, the harm to be averted, even in urgent cases, must be great. The use of torture must be proportionate to the harm prevented – though how the harm of employing so 'extreme' a remedy as torture is to be measured against other harms is not explained. Where, however, it is not absolutely certain that the offender knows the information sought, torture 'ought not to be employed but where the safety of the whole state may be endangered for want of that intelligence' and the decision to employ torture in these circumstances should be vested in such persons as 'are best qualified to judge of that necessity'. Fourth, the use of torture should be regulated and limited by law. Fifth, the type of torture used should cause pain sufficiently acute in the short term to achieve its purpose, but it should be of the sort where the 'pain goes off the soonest', that is, it should have as little long-term effect as possible (Bentham, 1777–9: 313–5).

Thus though Bentham, with Beccaria, was adamant that he would abolish torture as it was routinely employed in some European jurisdictions in his day (see Langbein, 1977; Peters, 1996; Evans and Morgan, 1998: ch. 1), he favoured its retention, if limited to the circumstances he set out. As to methods, they should be the most effective available: it would be illogical *not* to use whatever degree of pain was necessary to get the information required, providing the test of proportionality was satisfied.

Bentham illustrated his case:

Suppose an occasion, to arise, in which a suspicion is entertained, as strong as that which would be received as a sufficient ground for arrest and commitment as for felony – a suspicion that at this very time a considerable number of individuals are actually suffering, by illegal violence inflictions equal in intensity to those which if inflicted by the hand of justice, would universally be spoken of under the name of torture. For the purpose of rescuing from torture those hundred innocents, should any scruple be made of applying equal or superior torture, to extract the requisite information from the mouth of one criminal, who having it in his power to make known the place where at this time the enormity was practising or about to be practised, should refuse to do so? To say nothing of wisdom, could any pretence be made so much as to the praise of blind and vulgar humanity, by the man who to save one criminal, should determine to abandon a 100 innocent persons to the same fate? (1777–9: 347)

However, far from supporting his case this scenario arguably exposes its flaws. Bentham simply glosses over what he has identified as the key problem for the utilitarian advocate of torture. He simply asserts that the suspect *knows* that which his interrogators wish to know and that we *know* what the suspect and his accomplices intend. But how do we know that he knows? And how do we know what they intend? Bentham's answer is that that issue can be decided in the same way that we decide the guilt of an offender pleading not guilty: 'Perfect certainty ... is an advantage scarce permitted to human kind' (1777–9: 317). The issue must be decided by a judge or jury weighing the evidence in exactly the same way that courts decide guilt, the outcome of which decisions may be punishments as severe as anything contemplated in the name of pre-trial torture. But today, if not in Bentham's day, an examination the equivalent of a full trial of the facts where guilt is contested is scarcely consistent with the urgent circumstances which Bentham stipulates must prevail for torture to be justified – the ticking bomb, the imminent massacre of the innocents. Any urgent examination would literally have to be conducted in crisis circumstances where judgements would scarcely be unclouded and judgements calmly arrived at. The examination would have to be cursory, the evidence untested, the protective safeguards of representation and independent examination lacking. That is to say, it would involve granting a judge, or more likely the police, precisely the unaccountable power which Bentham elsewhere argues would likely lead to tyranny (as discussed later). Beccaria provided the reason as to why Bentham's illustration is not propitious:

> No man may be called guilty before the judge has reached his verdict; nor may society withdraw its protection from him until it has been determined that he has broken the terms of the compact by which that protection was extended to him. (Bellamy, 1995: 39)

Indeed, it is not at all clear why the process that Bentham advocated is logically different from the elaborate jurisprudence recommended to interrogators for using torture to elicit confessions within the Romano-canonical tradition to which Bentham objected (see Peters, 1996; Evans and Morgan, 1998: ch. 1). If the suspect undergoing torture confessed to the crime the torture was to be stopped and the suspect's account of what happened checked: was the weapon to be found where he said he left it? were the wounds consistent with his description of the attack? and so on. The time necessary for this process would scarcely be compatible with the imminent crisis which Bentham argued would alone justify the use of torture. That is, the circumstances in which Bentham was prepared to justify torture cannot easily be reconciled with his own premises.

CONTEMPORARY JUSTIFICATIONS FOR THE USE OF TORTURE AND NEAR-TORTURE EXAMINED

Bentham's rules for the use of torture are in several respects similar to those proposed by the Landau Commission for use of *moderate physical pressure*. Other policing agencies have adopted guidelines, official or unofficial, reflecting the same approach. In 1931, for example, the American Wickersham Commission found that in Newark, New Jersey, 'third degree' methods were used,

> but subject to control ... kept within bounds ... It seems to be the fact that uniformed policemen obey their orders not to question or maltreat suspects and that pressure is applied by the detectives at headquarters. The questioning by the detective force is not invariably accompanied by violence. The decision to employ force is made ... only after a protracted period of questioning without violence has failed to 'break' a man. This long questioning may involve two or three nights of wakefulness, with more or less constant pressure upon the suspect by relays of detectives. There is reason to believe that food is sometimes denied, and that threats are made during the process. The detectives are reported as being careful that they are not subjecting an innocent man to rough methods, this being determined by them before the stage of violence is reached. The danger of a mistake by an unintelligent questioner is given as a reason for safeguarding the process by entrusting the use of force to a few selected detectives and forbidding it to others. (Chaffee et al., 1931: 110–11)

These *working practices* – the unequivocally illegal 'third degree methods' which the Wickersham Commission typified as torture – had, it seems, to be approved by senior officers qualified to judge the seriousness of the threat to be countered. There was, the American police argued, a new breed of organized gangster abroad: the police were literally engaged in a *war* to protect the *American way of life*. The force used against these serious offenders, who detectives *knew* to be guilty, was far less severe than the gangsters were prepared to employ against their victims (Chaffee et al., 1931: 174–80). These 1930s police justifications can readily be transposed into late 20th century discourse regarding international drug traffickers against whom, in many jurisdictions, the police now enjoy specially extended powers of detention. The only one of Bentham's ingredients lacking here is the urgency of the cause, something not omitted from the Landau recommendations.

Bentham insisted that the use of torture be regulated and in Israel, it appears, the use of *moderate physical pressure* has been regulated.[1] However, the day-to-day judgements remain a secret affair left in the hands of the GSS: the regulations are not public. The Landau Commission insisted that the pressures applied to suspects are moderate, less severe than those employed by the British in Northern Ireland in the 1970s (the events leading to the controversial judgment of the European Court of Human Rights in *Ireland* v *UK* – see Evans and Morgan, 1998: ch. 2). There is allegedly no question of extracting false confessions from suspects and great care is said to be taken to apply pressures only in cases where existing intelligence satisfies the investigators that the suspect *knows* whatever it is that the authorities need to know. In all this Landau was prepared to trust the integrity of GSS personnel subject to the supervision recommended.

But Landau's detailed 'lesser evil' proposals are as flawed as those sketched by Bentham. First, Landau justified the systematic use of physical pressure by the state on the basis of the criminal law defence of necessity. This, as several commentators have argued, is a highly questionable use of the concept of necessity in criminal law. The defence of necessity in individual cases rests on the unique, isolated and extraordinary character of the situation which makes it an exception to the rule ... [whereas] The granting of power to an authority is an integral part of the legal system, and the exercise of that power in accordance with rules is studied, institutionalized and normal. (Kremnitzer, 1989: 237)

Necessity, as the old adage has it, knows no law. It is the most 'lawless of legal doctrines ... an emergency measure', designed to fill lacunae, 'not suited to situations which recur over long periods of time ... especially so when the claimant to the benefits of the defense is a state agency (or its members)' (Dershowitz, 1989: 196–7). To justify a regular state practice on this basis means standardizing allegedly compelling circumstances incapable of standardization. It means, to take us back to Bentham – a link which none of the contributors to the Israeli debate at the time of Landau made – granting GSS personnel a general discretion to use physical pressure: where, in an individual case, there is no necessary urgency; where no specific harm prevented by gathering intelligence from that particular suspect can precisely be identified; where the guilt of the suspect has not been proved; and where the suspect's capacity to provide information about the alleged threat is assumed, possibly reasonably, but not independently tested. It is, in short, a recipe for precisely the abuse of power which Landau found *had* been perpetrated in one of the scandalous cases which led to the appointment of the Landau Commission (Landau Commission, 1989: para. 2.7).

Second, even if a genuine 'ticking bomb' situation were to arise, and force were to be used by the GSS (or any other security force) in order to obtain information to dispel the imminent threat, and even were that conduct by the security forces subsequently to be excused, that would not mean that the evidence derived from the exercise should be capable of being used, as Landau proposed, in criminal proceedings for a past crime. There is a difference between averting a future harm and punishing an old one. To allow evidence collected by force to be used in criminal proceedings would be to create an incentive *routinely* to apply coercive means to *all* suspects resisting interrogation (see Zuckerman, 1989: 364). It would also mean allowing the police to treat suspects in a way which, if done by others, would constitute a criminal offence – the objection which Lord Donaldson had to the interrogation methods used by the British army against terrorist suspects in Northern Ireland in the early 1970s (Parker Report, 1972). It would mean licensing the police to use the very practices which the criminal law and the criminal justice system is ostensibly designed to prevent. That could only mean bringing the system generally into contempt. For, were the use of force to be allowed to the police against citizens subject to the presumption of innocence and wishing to preserve their right to remain silent, it would no longer be clear to citizens that their security was being safeguarded by the system. How would the behaviour of the security forces be distinguishable from that of criminals?

Third, there is something rather odd about utilitarian attempts to erect upper limits to the use of pressure, pressure justified on the utilitarian grounds of the necessity of gaining unwilling compliance. Bentham, as we have seen, set no upper limits. He imposed a proportionality rule. But the pain imposed had to be sufficient to achieve compliance thereby to prevent the greater harm to the public interest. Of course we *can* conceive a utilitarian basis for setting upper limits. Compliance with international legal obligations and the preservation of the state's international reputation in a world in which, misguidedly the utilitarian may argue, certain human rights norms prevail, is one criterion. The Landau Commission argues, unconvincingly its critics maintain, that the interrogation methods they recommend do fall short of torture and are consistent with Israel's international obligations. Another possible criterion is the approval of public opinion, though it is difficult to see how this test could be applied given the prevailing conditions of secrecy. But it is conceivable that an afeared public might favour the application against some *other* of extreme investigatory methods. A third possible test could be that the evidence elicited be reliable. But such a test is manifestly implausible. There is now a sufficient corpus of research and case study evidence to demonstrate that even the mildest pressure – pressure so mild that the ordinary citizen might not even interpret it to be pressure – is capable of eliciting a false confession or misleading information from a vulnerable or suggestible subject (Royal Commission, 1981: 25–6; Gudjonsson, 1996). This danger the Landau Commission appeared blithely to ignore. Any upper limit established on this basis would rule out the possibility of even detaining a suspect in custody for the purpose of questioning let alone granting the sort of powers likely to be considered necessary in an emergency.

One is forced to conclude, therefore, that any upper limit established on these grounds would be entirely self-defeating and impractical. Is it seriously to be suggested that trained terrorists who, if discovered to have co-operated with the authorities risk the ultimate penalty at the hands of their own organizations – a factor well acknowledged in the Algerian, Northern Ireland, Turkish and Israeli conflicts – would succumb to moderate pressures applied by their avowed enemies? Is it plausible that the upper limits could remain secret – a condition repeatedly said by Landau to be essential – when scores of suspects are subject to the permitted methods, the details of which they are bound to report back to their organizations? And if surprise or uncertainty is held to be an essential element in the methods employed, what does this say about the measure of discretion permitted to the security services by the guidelines? Or to logically extend this point: is it credible that security services, operating largely in secret and subject to minimal public accountability, licensed now to employ coercive methods the justification of which is the breaking down of detainees' resistance, will abide by whatever upper limits are set when those methods repeatedly fail to break down the resistance of suspects? The evidence is clear. From the Northern Ireland and Israeli case studies it is apparent that in these circumstances the security forces go further. Much further. That near-torture spills over into actions that unequivocally comprise torture, however that term is defined. Krousher (1985: 8–9), in his manual for torturers, makes the point clear. What he describes as *self-torture* – requiring the subject to do something that is painful (such as standing for long periods in a stress position, one of the five techniques which the British used in Northern Ireland and which the Israelis have clearly made extensive use of) only works if the torturer is prepared to use violence to enforce compliance with the *self-torture*.

Lowering the psychological threshold for the use of force almost inevitably leads the dam to be swept away. 'If a suspect's body is no longer taboo, what is one blow relative to the sanctity of the cause?' (Kremnitzer, 1989: 254). The pressure on the interrogator to succeed is effectively increased and there is almost bound to be an escalation of resistance and pressure to wear down that resistance in tandem. In these circumstances any quantitative distinction between torture, maltreatment and moderate physical

PUNISHMENT AND SOCIETY 2(2)

pressure is likely to prove illusory. The qualitative Rubicon will have been crossed of regarding the suspect no longer as a subject but as an object, not a person but a body, not a citizen but an alien, a reservoir of information to be tapped, a means to an end (see Scarry, 1984). What begins with clean and tidy utilitarian references to the public interest and the greater good ends with dirty, unregulated and personalized contests of will waged in secret by unaccountable police officials against demonized *others* whose *assumed* inhumanity means that they do not count in a calculus where almost anything goes.

CONCLUSION: DELIGITIMATION AND DISINFORMATION

Bentham's utilitarian defence of torture was flawed, which is possibly why he never published it. But there is one additional aspect of his article which is of interest for the beginning of the new millennium. Bentham was acutely aware of the dangers of torture, the principal of which he considered to be its efficacy:

> The efficacy is so great, that by the help of it a few weak lights will commonly be sufficient to enable the magistrate *of himself* to unravel the most intricate and fine-spun thread of delinquency, whether consummated or projected ... Thus armed he has power enough *within himself* to punish every act which the Law has pronounced to be punishable. (Bentham, 1777–9: 334, emphasis added)

Why did Bentham consider this dangerous? Because, under ordinary circumstances, the magistracy (or the police) are dependent on the willingness of the citizenry to provide the evidence which enable crimes to be proved and offenders convicted. And there are many reasons why citizens may be unwilling to provide such evidence including, inter alia, 'a partiality in favour of the offence ... a dislike of the law which punishes it ... [and] a dislike of the legislator who enacted the Law which punishes it' (Bentham, 1777–9: 335). Armed with torture, therefore, the magistracy (and the police) could dispense with public co-operation and enforce the law without reference to the wishes of the people. They could

> in spite of the people give execution to laws repugnant to the interests as well as to the affections of the people ... the magistrate, in short, may find the same facility [in] the establishment of tyranny or usurpation as in the maintenance of a beneficent and rightful government. (Bentham, 1777–9: 336)

That is, Bentham reasoned that torture was least justified with respect to political or politically motivated crimes, precisely the crimes against which torture is most likely to be used in the late 20th century. We should not stretch Bentham's argument beyond its historical limits. When referring to political crimes he had in mind sedition, libel and the protest movements of his day (see Bentham, 1777–9: 337), not the 20th-century phenomenon of terrorism. Furthermore, he overstated the relative effectiveness of torture given the investigative and surveillance capacities of modern states. But his reasoning is nonetheless salutary. Effective policing should ultimately rest on the legitimacy of the law and the co-operation of the people. Placing powerful tools in the hands of the police so that they can dispense with the wishes of the people, or a significant proportion of the people, invites tyranny.

This objection can be linked to a more longstanding debate regarding torture. The ancient Greek term for torture was *basanos*, the same word as the touchstone used to test gold for purity. Gold, the metal least liable to corruption, became emblematic of human integrity and *basanos*, as torture, the test for purity or truth. The Greeks applied torture only to slaves. In theory no test was necessary for citizens: they could be relied on to tell the truth. The word of slaves, however, could be relied on only if they were put to the torture. The problem with this doctrine, as many commentators, including Aristotle, pointed out, was that it made no distinction between natural slaves (those who do not possess reason) and legal slaves (citizens captured in war and enslaved) and thus, as duBois (1991: 125) has argued, two notions of truth competed in ancient Athens. One was a fixed version of truth, traditional, legal, oracular, immutable, constraining, truth that lies within and which can be revealed as gold can be tested for purity. The other was a negotiated truth, contextual, time and place-specific, relative, derived through understanding and argument and the democratic process. Torture, duBois argues, is the servant of oracular truth and the enemy of negotiated truth. It is

> motivated by control, the domination of an unpalatable truth . . . this truth, located in the body of the revolutionary, the student, the dissident, must be rooted out, extracted, dominated, in the process of torture. Torture flourishes in intolerance of difference, inability to permit democratic exchange. (1991: 149–50)

At the end of the late 20th century torture thrives most in societies characterized by gross inequalities of power or where one ethnic or religious community seeks to repress, through force, the interests of another. Where the *other*, the person or category eligible for torture, does not *count* and, thus, is not incorporated in the imperative that one should do as one should be done by. In these campaigns torture is employed as a terror tactic. The knock on the door, the taking of a suspect into custody, becomes the enemy of civil society itself (Millet, 1994).

The ultimate utilitarian objection to torture, therefore, is that it corrosively deligitimizes the state. The torturer's most potent threat to the captive and isolated subject may be 'No one can hear your screams. No one cares what happens to you. No one will ever know'; but denial by state authorities ultimately never succeeds. The facts always leak out, as they have done in Turkey and Israel and as they did in Algeria and Northern Ireland. When the truth emerges the repercussions go beyond citizens asking themselves whether there is an essential difference between the threat posed to persons subject to the presumption of innocence at the hands of the state and the threat posed by criminals against whom the state purports to offer a defence. Moreover, even if popular prejudices initially support the proposition that there is a definable *other* against whom the state may legitimately deploy extreme measures, the *other* is ultimately never capable of precise definition and identification in practice. Moral, religious, ethnic, sexual or nationality categories are never so clear cut: individuals stray across or are ambiguously related to them, families and communities are artificially divided by them, persons of good conscience make sacrificial leaps across them. Once the venom is unleashed ultimately all begin to feel vulnerable. This process is aided and abetted by counter-state

PUNISHMENT AND SOCIETY 2(2)

groups into whose hands the authorities have placed, through the torture of innocents, false confessions and mistaken identities, the weapon of mistrust. Thereafter counter-state groups are able to train their members to allege, with the reasonable prospect that they will be believed, that they have been tortured whenever they are released from custody. And because members of counter-state groups now allege that they have been tortured whenever they are released from custody, whether they have been tortured or not, police authorities are tempted to resort to torture either because any subsequent allegations can effectively be attributed to a pattern of disinformation, or because they might as well be hung for a sheep as a lamb. If there are no limits, and the state is engaged in dirty tricks, why should trust be invested and authority granted to officialdom? There is no safe haven about which we can be certain.

That is, there is set in train a cycle of denial, disinformation, cynicism and mistrust which only years of official integrity can begin to put right. During the Algerian War of Independence the French appear in the short term to have used torture effectively to break FLN terrorism in the Battle of Algiers (Horne, 1987; Maran, 1989; Evans and Morgan, 1998: ch. 2). But in the long term they lost by these same means the respect of the Arab population and left Algeria in ignominy. In the Basque country and Northern Ireland the Spanish and British authorities once thought that they could solve a conflict through repression (including torture) of minority community members and by whittling away, on the basis of short-term utilitarian calculations, the due process rights of the citizenry. It has taken years to rebuild the bridges that were thrown down. In Israel and Turkey the denial of Palestinian and Kurdish rights, and the use of torture in an attempt to break Arab and Kurdish resistance, has not given peace and security to the Israeli and Turkish peoples. Nor will it.

Note

1   Has been, because the Israeli Supreme Court ruled on 6 September 1999 (*Public Committee Against Torture in Israel*) that certain physical pressures to aid interrogation which the state did not deny the GSS used – sleep deprivation, enforced stress positions, shaking, hooding and the playing of loud music – were not lawful and could not be governed by the use of general directives of the sort that were secretly employed. It should be noted, however, that GSS personnel were reassured that the defence of necessity remained available to them and that an interrogator might 'find refuge under the "necessity" defence's wings (so to speak), provided this defence's conditions are met by the circumstances of the case' (25).

References

Amnesty International (1989) *Turkey: torture and deaths in custody*. London: Amnesty International, International Secretariat.

Amnesty International (1996) *Turkey: no security without human rights*. London: Amnesty International, International Secretariat.

Ashworth, A. (1998) *The criminal process: an evaluative study*. Oxford: Clarendon Press.

Bellamy, R. (1995) *Beccaria: on crimes and punishments and other writings*, trans. Richard Davies. Cambridge: CUP.

Bentham, J. (1777–9) 'Of torture', previously unpublished manuscript edited by

Twining & Twining in 'Bentham on torture', *Northern Ireland Legal Quarterly* (1973) 24(3): 307–56.

B'Tselem (1991) *The interrogation of Palestinians during the Intifada: ill-treatment, 'moderate physical pressure' or torture?* Jerusalem: B'Tselem.

B'Tselem (1992) *The interrogation of Palestinians during the Intifada: follow-up to March 1991 B'Tselem report.* Jerusalem: B'Tselem.

Chaffee, Z., Pollock, W.H. and Stern, C.S. (1931) 'The third degree: report on lawlessness in law enforcement', National Commission on Law Observance and Enforcement, Vol. IV, no. II. Washington, DC: Government Printing Office.

Cohen, S. (1993) 'Human rights and crimes of the state: the culture of denial', *Australian and New Zealand Journal of Criminology* 26: 87.

Council of Europe (1992) *Public statement on Turkey.* CPT, Strasbourg: Council of Europe.

Council of Europe (1996) *Public statement on Turkey.* CPT, Strasbourg: Council of Europe.

Council of Europe (1999) *Report to the Turkish government on the visit to Turkey carried out by the European Committee for the Prevention of Torture and Inhuman or Degrading Treatment or Punishment (CPT) from 5–17 October 1997.* CPT, Strasbourg: Council of Europe.

Dershowitz, A. (1989) 'Is it necessary to apply "physical pressure" to terrorists – and to lie about it?', *Israeli Law Review* 24: 192–200.

du Bois, P. (1991) *Torture and Truth.* New York: Routledge.

Evans, M. and Morgan, R. (1998) *Preventing torture: a study of the European Convention for the Prevention of Torture and Inhuman or Degrading Treatment or Punishment.* Oxford: Clarendon Press.

Gemalmaz, M.S. (1999) 'The CPT and Turkey', in R. Morgan and M. Evans (eds) *Protecting prisoners: the standards of the Committee for the Prevention of Torture in Context.* Oxford: Clarendon Press.

Gudjonsson, G. (1996) 'Custodial confinement, interrogation and coerced confessions', in D. Forrest (ed.) *A glimpse of hell: reports on torture worldwide.* London: Amnesty International UK.

Horne, A. (1987) *A savage war of peace: Algeria 1954–62.* London: Macmillan.

Human Rights Foundation of Turkey (HRFT) (1996) *Turkey human rights report 1995.* Ankara: HRFT.

Human Rights Watch (1993) *The Kurds in Turkey: killings, disappearances and torture.* New York: Human Rights Watch.

Kremnitzer, M. (1989) 'The Landau Commission report: was the security service subordinated to the law, or the law to the "needs" of the security service?', *Israeli Law Review* 24: 216–79.

Krousher, W. (1985) *Physical interrogation techniques.* Port Townsend, WA: Loompanics.

Landau Commission (1987) *Report of the Commission of Inquiry into the methods of investigation of the general security service regarding hostile terrorist activity, part one.* Jerusalem: Israeli Government.

Langbein, J.H. (1977) *Torture and the law of proof.* Chicago, IL: Chicago University Press.

PUNISHMENT AND SOCIETY 2(2)

Maran, R. (1989) *Torture: the role of ideology in the French Algerian war*. New York: Praeger.

Millet, K. (1994) *The politics of cruelty: an essay on the literature of political imprisonment*. London: Viking.

Parker Report (1972) *Report of the Committee of Privy Counsellors appointed to consider authorised procedures for the interrogation of persons suspected of terrorism* (Chairman, Lord Parker), Cmnd 4981, London: HMSO.

Peters, E. (1996) *Torture*. Pennsylvania, PA: University of Pennsylvania Press.

Physicians for Human Rights (1996) *Torture in Turkey and its unwilling accomplices*. Boston, MA: Physicians for Human Rights.

Royal Commission (1981) *Report of the Royal Commission on criminal procedure*. London: HMSO.

Scarry, E. (1984) *The body in pain*. New York: Oxford University Press.

Zuckerman, A. (1989) 'Coercion and judicial ascertainment of truth', *Israeli Law Review* 24: 357–74.

ROD MORGAN is Professor of Criminal Justice in the Faculty of Law, University of Bristol, UK and Director of the Bristol Centre for Criminal Justice. He is an advisor to Amnesty International and the Council of Europe on police powers and procedures and custodial conditions. He is the co-author (with Malcolm Evans) of two recent books on the subject of torture and inhuman or degrading treatment: *Preventing torture* (1998) and *Protecting prisoners* (1999), both published by Oxford University Press, Oxford.

Annu. Rev. Sociol. 1998. 24:423–52

ETHNIC AND NATIONALIST VIOLENCE

Rogers Brubaker

Department of Sociology, University of California, Los Angeles, 264 Haines Hall, Los Angeles, California 90095-1551; e-mail: brubaker@soc.ucla.edu

David D. Laitin

Department of Political Science, University of Chicago, 5828 S. University Avenue, Chicago, IL 60637; e-mail: d-laitin@uchicago.edu

KEY WORDS: ethnicity, nationalism, conflict

ABSTRACT

Work on ethnic and nationalist violence has emerged from two largely non-intersecting literatures: studies of ethnic conflict and studies of political violence. Only recently have the former begun to attend to the dynamics of violence and the latter to the dynamics of ethnicization. Since the emergent literature on ethnic violence is not structured by clearly defined theoretical oppositions, we organize our review by broad similarities of methodological approach: (*a*) Inductive work at various levels of aggregation seeks to identify the patterns, mechanisms, and recurrent processes implicated in ethnic violence. (*b*) Theory-driven work employs models of rational action drawn from international relations theory, game theory, and general rational action theory. (*c*) Culturalist work highlights the discursive, symbolic, and ritualistic aspects of ethnic violence. We conclude with a plea for the disaggregated analysis of the heterogeneous phenomena we too casually lump together as "ethnic violence."

INTRODUCTION

The bloody dissolution of Yugoslavia, intermittently violent ethnonational conflicts on the southern periphery of the former Soviet Union, the ghastly butchery in Rwanda, and Hindu-Muslim riots in parts of India, among other dispiriting events, have focused renewed public attention in recent years on ethnic and nationalist violence as a striking symptom of the "new world disorder."

To be sure, measured against the universe of possible instances, actual instances of ethnic and nationalist violence remain rare. This crucial point is obscured in the literature, much of which samples on the dependent variable (Fearon & Laitin 1996) or metaphorically mischaracterizes vast regions (such as post-communist Eastern Europe and Eurasia in its entirety or all of sub-Saharan Africa) as a seething cauldron on the verge of boiling over or as a tinderbox, which a single careless spark could ignite into an inferno of ethnonational violence (Bowen 1996, Brubaker 1998). Ethnic violence warrants our attention because it is appalling, not because it is ubiquitous.

Nonetheless, although measurement and coding problems prevent confident calculations, two general features of the late modern, post–Cold War world—in addition to the particular traumas of state collapse in the Soviet and Yugoslav cases—have probably contributed to a recent increase in the incidence of ethnic and nationalist violence and have certainly contributed to an increase in the share of ethnic and nationalist violence in all political violence—that is, to what might be called the ethnicization of political violence. The first could be called "the decay of the Weberian state": the decline (uneven, to be sure) in states' capacities to maintain order by monopolizing the legitimate use of violence in their territories and the emergence in some regions—most strikingly in sub-Saharan Africa—of so-called quasi-states (Jackson 1990, Jackson & Rosberg 1982), organizations formally acknowledged and recognized as states yet lacking (or possessing only in small degree) the empirical attributes of stateness.

The end of the Cold War has further weakened many third world states as superpowers have curtailed their commitments of military and other state-strengthening resources, while the citizenries—and even, it could be argued, the neighbors—of Soviet successor states are more threatened by state weakness than by state strength (Holmes 1997). Such weakly Weberian states or quasi-states are more susceptible to—and are by definition less capable of repressing, though not, alas, of committing—violence of all kinds, including ethnic violence (Desjarlais & Kleinman 1994). Meanwhile, the stronger states of the West are increasingly reluctant to use military force—especially unilaterally, without a broad consensus among allied states—to intervene in conflicts outside their boundaries (Haas 1997). As a result, weakly Weberian third world states can no longer rely on an external patron to maintain peace as they could during the Cold War era.

The second contextual aspect of the post–Cold War world to highlight is the eclipse of the left-right ideological axis that has defined the grand lines of much political conflict—and many civil wars—since the French Revolution. From the 1950s through the early 1980s, violence-wielding opponents of existing regimes could best mobilize resources—money, weapons, and political and logistical support—by framing their opposition to incumbents in the language of the grand ideological confrontation between capitalism and communism. Incumbents mobilized resources in the same way. Today, these incentives to frame conflicts in grand ideological terms have disappeared. Even without direct positive incentives to frame conflicts in ethnic terms, this has led to a marked ethnicization of violent challenger-incumbent contests as the major non-ethnic framing for such contests has become less plausible and profitable.

Moreover, there may be positive incentives to frame such contests in ethnic terms. With the increasing significance worldwide of diasporic social formations (Clifford 1994, Appadurai 1997), for example, both challengers and incumbents may increasingly seek resources from dispersed transborder ethnic kin (Tambiah 1986, Anderson 1992). And a thickening web of international and nongovernmental organizations has provided greater international legitimacy, visibility, and support for ethnic group claims (normatively buttressed by culturalist extensions and transformations of the initially strongly individualist human rights language that prevailed in the decades immediately following World War II). This institutional and normative transformation at the level of what Meyer (1987) calls the "world polity" provides a further incentive for the ethnic framing of challenges to incumbent regimes. To foreshadow a theme we underscore later: Ethnicity is not the ultimate, irreducible source of violent conflict in such cases. Rather, conflicts driven by struggles for power between challengers and incumbents are newly ethnicized, newly framed in ethnic terms.

Ethnicity, Violence, and Ethnic Violence

Attempts to theorize ethnic and nationalist violence have grown from the soil of two largely nonintersecting literatures: studies of ethnicity, ethnic conflict, and nationalism on the one hand, and studies of collective or political violence on the other. Within each of these large and loosely integrated literatures, ethnic and nationalist violence has only recently become a distinct subject of inquiry in its own right.

In the study of ethnicity, ethnic conflict, and nationalism, accounts of *conflict* have not been distinguished sharply from accounts of *violence*. Violence has generally been conceptualized—if only tacitly—as a *degree* of conflict rather than as a *form* of conflict, or indeed as a form of social or political action in its own right. Most discussions of violence in the former Yugoslavia, for example, are embedded in richly contextual narratives of the breakup of the state

(Glenny 1992, Cohen 1993, Woodward 1995). Violence as such has seldom been made an explicit and sustained theoretical or analytical focus in studies of ethnic conflict [though this has begun to change with Lemarchand's (1996) work on Burundi, and Tambiah's (1996), Brass's (1997) and Horowitz's (forthcoming) work on ethnic riots].

In the study of collective or political violence, on the other hand, ethnicity figured (until recently) only incidentally and peripherally. In a number of influential studies (e.g. Gurr 1970, Tilly 1978) ethnicity figured scarcely at all. Revealingly, Gurr used the general term "dissidents" to describe nongovernmental participants in civil strife. Although the empirical significance of ethnicity was recognized, its theoretical significance was seldom addressed explicitly; it was as if there was nothing analytically distinctive about ethnic (or ethnically conditioned or framed) violence. Ethnicity thus remained theoretically exogenous rather than being integrated into key analytical or theoretical concepts.

In recent years, to be sure, a pronounced "ethnic turn" has occurred in the study of political violence, paralleling the ethnic turn in international relations, security studies, and other precincts of the post–Cold War academic world. But this sudden turn to ethnicity and nationality too often has been external and mechanical (Brubaker 1998). Although ethnicity now occupies a central place in the study of collective and political violence, it remains a "foreign body" deriving from other theoretical traditions. It has yet to be theoretically digested, or theorized in a subtle or sophisticated manner.

This suggests two opportunities for theoretical advance today—and in fact significant work is beginning to emerge in these areas. On the one hand, it is important to take violence as such more seriously in studies of ethnic and nationalist conflict. It is important, that is, to ask specific questions about, and seek specific explanations for, the occurrence—and nonoccurrence (Fearon & Laitin 1996)—of violence in conflictual situations. These questions and explanations should be distinguished from questions and explanations of the existence, and even the intensity, of conflict. We lack strong evidence showing that higher levels of conflict (measured independently of violence) lead to higher levels of violence. Even where violence is clearly rooted in preexisting conflict, it should not be treated as a natural, self-explanatory outgrowth of such conflict, something that occurs automatically when the conflict reaches a certain intensity, a certain "temperature." Violence is not a quantitative degree of conflict but a qualitative form of conflict, with its own dynamics. The shift from nonviolent to violent modes of conflict is a phase shift (Williams 1994:62, Tambiah 1996:292) that requires particular theoretical attention.

The study of violence should be emancipated from the study of conflict and treated as an autonomous phenomenon in its own right. For example, to the extent that ethnic entrepreneurs recruit young men who are already inclined toward or practiced in other forms of violence, and help bestow meaning on that violence and honor and social status on its perpetrators, we may have as much to learn about the sources and dynamics of ethnic violence from the literature on criminology (Katz 1988) as from the literature on ethnicity or ethnic conflict.

At the same time, the strand of the literature that grows out of work on political violence and collective violence should take ethnicity and nationality more seriously. This does not mean paying more attention to them; as noted above, there has already been a pronounced ethnic turn in the study of political violence and collective violence. *That* political violence can be ethnic is well established, indeed too well established; *how* it is ethnic remains obscure. The most fundamental questions—for example, how the adjective "ethnic" modifies the noun "violence"—remain unclear and largely unexamined. Sustained attention needs to be paid to the forms and dynamics of ethnicization, to the many and subtle ways in which violence—and conditions, processes, activities, and narratives linked to violence—can take on ethnic hues.

Defining the Domain

In reviewing emerging work in anthropology, political science, and to a lesser extent other disciplines as well as sociology, we immediately face the problem that there is no clearly demarcated field or subfield of social scientific inquiry addressing ethnic and nationalist violence, no well-defined body of literature on the subject, no agreed-upon set of key questions or problems, no established research programs (or set of competing research programs). The problem is not that there is no agreement on *how* things are to be explained; it is that there is no agreement on *what* is to be explained, or *whether* there is a single set of phenomena to be explained. Rather than confronting competing theories or explanations, we confront alternative ways of posing questions, alternative approaches to or "takes" on ethnic and nationalist violence, alternative ways of conceptualizing the phenomenon and of situating it in the context of wider theoretical debates. In consequence, this review specifies the contours and attempts a critical assessment of an emergent rather than a fully formed literature.

What are we talking about when we talk about ethnic or nationalist violence? The answer is by no means obvious. First, despite its seemingly palpable core, violence is itself an ambiguous and elastic concept (Tilly 1978:174), shading over from the direct use of force to cause bodily harm through the compelling or inducing of actions by direct threat of such force to partly or fully metaphorical notions of cultural or symbolic violence (Bourdieu & Wacquant 1992:167–74). But the difficulties and ambiguities involved in characterizing or classifying violence (which we shall understand here in a narrow

428   BRUBAKER & LAITIN

sense) as ethnic or nationalist[1] are even greater. Although these difficulties have yet to receive—and cannot receive here—the full exploration they deserve, a few summary points can be made:

1. The coding of past, present, or feared future violence as ethnic is not only an analytical but a practical matter. Violence is regularly accompanied by social struggles to define its meaning and specify its causes, the outcome of which—for example, the labeling of an event as a pogrom, a riot, or a rebellion—may have important consequences (Brass 1996b).
2. Coding practices are influenced heavily by prevailing interpretive frames. Today, the ethnic frame is immediately and widely available and legitimate; it imposes itself on, or at least suggests itself to, actors and analysts alike. This generates a coding bias in the ethnic direction. A generation ago, the coding bias was in the opposite direction. Today, we—again, actors and analysts alike—are no longer blind *to* ethnicity, but we may be blinded *by* it. Our ethnic bias in framing may lead us to overestimate the incidence of ethnic violence by unjustifiably seeing ethnicity at work everywhere and thereby artifactually multiplying instances of "ethnic violence" (Bowen 1996). More soberingly, since coding or framing is partly constitutive of the phenomenon of ethnic violence, not simply an external way of registering and coming to terms with it intellectually, our coding bias may actually increase the incidence (and not simply the perceived incidence) of ethnic violence.
3. With these caveats in mind, we define ethnic violence on first approximation as violence perpetrated across ethnic lines, in which at least one party is not a state (or a representative of a state), and in which the putative ethnic difference is coded—by perpetrators, targets, influential third parties, or analysts—as having been integral rather than incidental to the violence, that is, in which the violence is coded as having been meaningfully oriented in some way to the different ethnicity of the target.

This preliminary definition allows us to exclude the violence between Germans and Frenchmen on the Marne in 1914. Similarly, it allows us to exclude the assassination of Robert F. Kennedy, since the shooting was not interpreted in ethnoreligious terms as a Catholic being shot by a Muslim. But the definition hardly allows us to define a focused domain of research. A great profusion of work—only a small fraction of which is engaged by most contemporary analysts of ethnic violence—is related in one way or another to ethnic vio-

---

[1]To avoid cumbersome repetition, we refer simply to "ethnic" rather than to "ethnic or nationalist." But we understand "ethnic" broadly as including "nationalist" (insofar as this latter term designates ethnic or ethnocultural forms of nationalism, as opposed to purely "civic" or state-centered forms of nationalism).

lence. The range and heterogeneity of this work compel us to be highly selective in our review. We have had to exclude many pertinent literatures, or at best
touch on them only in passing. These include literatures on pogroms (Klier &
Lambroza 1992) and genocides (Dobkowski & Wallimann 1992); on antisemitism (Langmuir 1990), Nazism (Burleigh & Wippermann 1991), fascism,
and the radical right (Rogger & Weber 1965); on racial violence (Horowitz
1983), race riots (Grimshaw 1969), and policing in racially or ethnically mixed
settings (Keith 1993); on slavery (Blackburn 1997), colonialism (Cooper &
Stoler 1997), third-world nationalist revolutions (Chaliand 1977, Goldstone et
al 1991), and state formation [especially in contexts of encounters with aboriginal populations (Bodley 1982, Ferguson & Whitehead 1992)]; on separatism (Heraclides 1990), irredentism (Horowitz 1991b), and the formation of
new nation-states (Brubaker 1996); on xenophobia and anti-immigrant violence (Björgo & Witte 1993), "ethnic unmixing" (Brubaker 1995, Hayden
1996), forced migration (Marrus 1985), and refugee flows (Zolberg et al
1989); on religious violence (Davis 1973); on terrorism (Stohl 1983, Waldmann 1992), paramilitary formations (Fairbanks 1995), and state violence
(van den Berghe 1990, Nagengast 1994); on conflict management (Azar &
Burton 1986) and peace studies (Väyrynen et al 1987); on the phenomenology
or experiential dimensions of violence (Nordstrom & Martin 1992); and on
rage (Scheff & Retzinger 1991), humiliation (Miller 1993), fear (Green 1994),
and other emotions and psychological mechanisms (e.g. projection, displace-
ment, identification) implicated in ethnic and nationalist violence (Volkan
1991, Kakar 1990).[2] Clearly, this would be an unmanageable set of literatures
to survey. Moreover, most of these are well-established, specialized literatures
addressing particular historical forms and settings of ethnic or nationalist violence, whereas we have interpreted our task as that of bringing into focus a
newly emerging literature addressing ethnic violence as such. For different
reasons, we neglect the theoretically impoverished policy-oriented literature
on conflict management, and for lack of professional competence, we neglect
the psychological literature.

Since the emerging literature we survey is not structured around clearly defined theoretical oppositions, we organize our review not by theoretical position but by broad similarities of approach. We begin by considering a variety
of inductive analyses of ethnic and nationalist violence that build on statistical
analysis of large data sets, on the extraction of patterns from sets of broadly
similar cases, on controlled comparisons, and on case studies. We next consider clusters of theory-driven work on ethnic violence deriving from the realist

---

[2]Citations here are merely illustrative; we have tried to cite relatively recent, wide-ranging, or
otherwise exemplary works, in which ample citations to further pertinent literature can be found.

430   BRUBAKER & LAITIN

tradition in international relations, from game theory, and from rational choice theory. We conclude by examining culturalist analyses of ethnic violence.

We recognize the awkwardness of this organizing scheme: It is logically unsatisfactory, combining methodological and substantive criteria. It lumps theoretically and methodologically heterogeneous work under the loose rubric "inductive." It risks implying, incorrectly, that inductive work is not theoretically informed, and that culturalist approaches are neither inductive nor theory driven. We nonetheless adopt this scheme in an effort to mirror as best we can the emerging clusters of work.

INDUCTIVE APPROACHES

Without questioning the truism that all research—and all phases of research (including data collection)—is theoretically informed, we can characterize the work grouped under this heading as primarily data-driven rather than theory-driven. This work seeks to identify the regularities, patterns, mechanisms, and recurrent processes comprising the structure and texture of ethnic violence in inductive fashion through the systematic analysis of empirical data. The data in question range from large sets of highly aggregated data through small-n comparisons to single case studies. Methods of analysis range from statistical analysis and causal modeling to qualitative interpretation. We organize our discussion by level of aggregation.

Large Data Sets

Gurr has been a leading figure in the study of political violence for three decades and a pioneer in the statistical analysis of large data sets in this domain (1968). His first major work (1970) outlined an "integrated theory of political violence" as the product of the politicization and activation of discontent arising from relative deprivation. Although ethnicity played no role in his early work, it has become central to his recent work (1993a, 1993b, 1994, Harff & Gurr 1989, Gurr & Harff 1994). This work has been built on a large-scale data set surveying 233 "minorities at risk" that have (*a*) suffered (or benefited from) economic or political discrimination and/or (*b*) mobilized politically in defense of collective interests since 1945. For each of these "nonstate communal groups"—classified as ethnonationalists, indigenous peoples, ethnoclasses, militant sects, and communal contenders—Gurr and associates have assembled and coded on ordinal scales a wide array of data on background characteristics (such as group coherence and concentration), intergroup differentials and discrimination, and group grievances and collective action. They then seek to explain forms and magnitudes of nonviolent protest, violent protest, and rebellion through an eclectic synthesis of grievance and mobilization variables.

This work sensitizes us to the sharply differing dynamics, configurations, and magnitudes of ethnic violence across regions. This comparative perspective is crucial, since violence in Northern Ireland or in the Basque region, while unsettling in the context of post–World War II Europe, can be placed in more benign perspective when compared to Burundi, Rwanda, Sri Lanka, or post–Cold War Bosnia, where killing is measured not in the hundreds and thousands but in the tens or even hundreds of thousands (Heisler 1990). The standardized data set built by Gurr and associates gives us little reason to believe that the processes and mechanisms generating violence in Northern Ireland are the same as those that drive the violence in Sri Lanka. It is not even clear, as we shall suggest in the conclusion, that these are both instances of the same thing (i.e. ethnic violence).

If for Gurr the unit of analysis is the group, for Olzak (1992), Tarrow (1994), and Beissinger (1998), the unit is the event. Assembling data on ethnic and racial confrontations and protests in the United States in the late nineteenth and early twentieth century, Olzak uses event history analysis and ecological theories of competition and niche overlap to show that the breakdown of ethnic and racial segregation, by increasing economic and political competition, triggers exclusionary collective action, including ethnic and racial violence. Beissinger, constructing a database on violent collective events in the disintegrating Soviet Union and its incipient successor states, analyzes the highly clustered incidence of nationalist violence in the context of a larger cycle of nationalist contention. He shows that nationalist struggles turned increasingly violent (and increasingly assumed the form of sustained armed conflict) late in the mobilizational cycle, in connection with the contestation of republican (and incipient state) borders at a moment when effective authority (to the extent it existed at all) was passing from the collapsing center to the incipient successor states. In part, Beissinger echoes the findings of Tarrow (1994, Della Porta & Tarrow 1986) concerning the tendency for violence in Italy to occur toward the end of a mobilizational cycle. Although not directly concerned with ethnicity, Tarrow's work—notably his finding that violence does not map directly onto protest—has implications for the study of ethnic violence. In Italy, violence appears to increase when organized protest weakens. As mobilization wanes, violence is practiced by splinter groups as the only way to cause disruption. Although the dynamics of the two cases differ, both Beissinger and Tarrow analyze violence as a phase in a mobilizational cycle rather than as a natural expression of social conflict or social protest.

Case-Based Pattern Finding

For the analysis of ethnic conflict and violence in postcolonial Africa and Asia, Horowitz (1985) remains the classic text. Seeking to extract patterns from sets of broadly comparable cases, he stresses the social psychological and cogni-

432   BRUBAKER & LAITIN

tive underpinnings as well as the richly elaborated symbolic dimensions of violent ethnic conflict, giving particular emphasis to comparative, anxiety-laden judgments of group worth and competing claims to group legitimacy.[3] At the same time, Horowitz has given systematic attention to the effects of institutions—notably electoral systems, armed forces, and federalist arrangements—in fostering or preventing violent ethnic conflict (1985:Parts 3–5, 1991c). His arguments concerning institutional design—notably the design of electoral systems—in the context of post-apartheid South Africa (1991a) have led to a lively debate with Lijphart (1990).

More recently, Horowitz (forthcoming) has returned to an earlier (1973, 1983) concern with ethnic riots. He analyzes the morphology and dynamics of the "deadly ethnic riot," building inductively from detailed reports on a hundred riots, mainly since 1965, in some 40 postcolonial countries. Arguing for a disaggregated approach to ethnic violence, Horowitz distinguishes the deadly ethnic riot—defined as mass civilian intergroup violence in which victims are chosen by their group membership—from other forms of ethnic (or more or less ethnicized) violence such as genocide, lynchings, gang assault, violent protest, feuds, terrorism, and internal warfare. The deadly ethnic riot is marked by highly uneven clustering in time and space, relatively spontaneous character (though not without elements of organization and planning), careful selection of victims by their categorical identity, passionate expression of intergroup antipathies, and seemingly gratuitous mutilation of victims.

Using broadly similar inductive approaches, other scholars have addressed ethnic riots in recent years, chiefly in the South Asian context (Freitag 1989; Das 1990a; Spencer 1990; Pandey 1992; Jaffrelot 1994; Brass 1996a, 1997). The most sustained contribution in this genre is Tambiah's (1996) richly textured, multilayered account. While distancing himself from a simplistic instrumentalist interpretation of ethnic riots as the joint product of political manipulation and organized thuggery, Tambiah devotes considerable attention to the routinization and ritualization of violence, to the "organized, anticipated, programmed, and recurring features and phases of seemingly spontaneous, chaotic, and orgiastic actions" (p. 230), the cultural repertory and social infrastructure [what Brass (1996b:12) calls "institutionalized riot systems"] through which riots are accomplished. At the same time, however, reworking Le Bon, Canetti, and Durkheim, Tambiah seeks to theorize the social psychological dynamics of volatile crowd behavior.

Other works in the pattern-finding mode address not particular forms of ethnic violence (such as the deadly ethnic riot) in their entirety but rather (like

---

[3]Working within a broadly similar theoretical tradition, Petersen (1998) argues that structurally induced resentment, linking individual emotion and group status, best accounts for ethnic violence in a broad range of East European cases.

Horowitz 1985) general mechanisms and processes that are implicated in ethnic violence. As Blalock (1989) notes in a different context, such mechanisms and processes, although not the immediate or underlying cause of violent conflicts, do causally shape their incidence and modalities. Here we restrict our attention to one class of such mechanisms and processes (albeit a large and important one): to the ways in which *inter*-ethnic violence is conditioned and fostered by *intra*-ethnic processes.[4]

One such mechanism involves in-group policing. As analyzed by Laitin (1995a), this involves the formal or informal administration of sanctions, even violent sanctions, within a group so as to enforce a certain line of action vis-à-vis outsiders (who may be defined not only in ethnic terms but in religious, ideological, class, or any other terms). Practices such as "necklacing" in South African townships, "kneecapping" by the IRA, the execution of Palestinians alleged to have sold land to Israelis, and the killing of alleged "collaborators" in many other settings have attracted notoriety as techniques used by ethnonationalist radicals to maintain control over in-group followers. Pfaffenberger (1994), for example, shows how members of the dominant Tamil separatist group in Sri Lanka, the Liberation Tigers, have prevented young male Tamils from leaving Jaffna and murdered leaders of rival Tamil groups, dissidents within their own ranks, and civilian Tamils suspected of helping the Sinhalese.

A second intragroup mechanism—and a classical theme in the sociology of conflict (Simmel 1955, Coser 1956)—involves the deliberate staging, instigation, provocation, dramatization, or intensification of violent or potentially violent confrontations with outsiders. Such instigative and provocative actions are ordinarily undertaken by vulnerable incumbents seeking to deflect within-group challenges to their position by redefining the fundamental lines of conflict as inter- rather than (as challengers would have it) intragroup; but they may also be undertaken by challengers seeking to discredit incumbents.

Gagnon's (1994/1995) analysis of the role of intra-Serbian struggles in driving the bloody breakup of Yugoslavia is the most theoretically explicit recent contribution along these lines. Gagnon argues that a conservative coalition of party leaders, local and regional elites, nationalist intellectuals, and segments of the military leadership, threatened in the mid-1980s by economic crisis and strong demands for market-oriented and democratic reforms, provoked violent ethnic confrontation—first in Kosovo and then, more fatefully, in the Serb-inhabited borderland regions of Croatia—in a successful attempt to define ethnicity (specifically the alleged threat to Serb ethnicity) as the most

---

[4]General mechanisms may, of course, be specified in a deductive as well as an inductive manner. Although most of the work cited in the rest of this subsection is broadly inductive, we also cite here for reasons of convenience a few deductive works. Deductive theorizing about general mechanisms implicated in ethnic violence is considered in more sustained fashion in the next section.

pressing political issue and thereby to defeat reformist challengers and retain their grip on power. Although Gagnon's empirical analysis is one-sided in its exclusive focus on the Serbian leadership (partially similar points could be made about the Croatian leadership), his theoretical argument on the within-group sources of intergroup conflict is valuable. In a broader study of nationalism and democratization, Snyder (1998) argues that such strategies of provocation are particularly likely to occur, and to succeed, in newly democratizing but institutionally weak regimes. Other instances of such cultivated confrontations arising from intragroup dynamics are found in Deng's (1995) study of the Sudan and Prunier's (1995) study of Rwanda.

A third important intragroup mechanism is ethnic outbidding (Rabushka & Shepsle 1972, Rothschild 1981, Horowitz 1985:Chapter 8, Kaufman 1996). This can occur in a context of competitive electoral politics when two or more parties identified with the same ethnic group compete for support, neither (in particular electoral configurations) having an incentive to cultivate voters of other ethnicities, each seeking to demonstrate to their constituencies that it is more nationalistic than the other, and each seeking to protect itself from the other's charges that it is "soft" on ethnic issues. The outbidding can "o'erleap itself" into violent confrontations, dismantling the very democratic institutions that gave rise to the outbidding. This is a powerful mechanism (and a general one, not confined to *ethnic* outbidding). *How* it works is theoretically clear, and *that* it sometimes works to intensify conflict and generate violence was classically, and tragically, illustrated in Sri Lanka (Horowitz 1991c, Pfaffenberger 1994).

Yet outbidding does not always occur, and it does not always pay off as a political strategy when it is attempted. Contrary to many interpretations, Gagnon (1996) argues that the violent collapse of Yugoslavia had nothing to do with ethnic outbidding. In his account, Serbian elites instigated violent conflict, and framed it in terms of ethnic antagonism, not to mobilize but to demobilize the population, to forestall challenges to the regime. When they needed to appeal for public support during election campaigns, elites engaged not in ethnic outbidding but in "ethnic underbidding," striving to appear more moderate rather than more radical than their opponents on ethnic issues. Further work needs to be done (following Horowitz 1985) in specifying the conditions (e.g. different types of electoral systems) in which such outbidding is more or less likely to occur, and more or less likely to pay off.

A fourth intragroup mechanism concerns the dynamics of recruitment into gangs, terrorist groups, or guerrilla armies organized for ethnic violence. Although most ethnic leaders are well educated and from middle-class backgrounds, the rank-and-file members of such organizations are more often poorly educated and from lower or working class backgrounds (Waldmann 1985, 1989; Clark 1984). Considerable attention has been focused on the intergroup dynamics that favor recruitment into such organizations. For example, interviewing IRA members, White (1993:Chapter 4) finds that many working-class Catholics joined the IRA after experiencing violence in their neighbor-hoods at the hands of British security forces and loyalist paramilitaries. We have little systematic knowledge, however, about the social and psychological processes within groups that govern the recruitment of young men (and, much more rarely, women) into disciplined, ethnically organized violence-wielding groups—processes such as the distribution of honor, the promising and provision of material and symbolic rewards for martyrs, rituals of manhood, the shaming of those who would shun violence, intergenerational tensions that may lead the impetuous young to challenge overcautious elders, and so on.

"Small-N" Comparisons

Controlled comparisons have been relatively few, especially those comparing regions suffering from ethnic violence with regions in which similar ethnic conflicts have not issued in violence. The Basque/Catalan comparison is a natural in this respect and has been explored by Laitin (1995b), who focuses on linguistic tipping phenomena and the differential availability of recruits for guerrilla activity from rural social groups governed by norms of honor, and by Díez Medrano (1995), who focuses on the social bases of the nationalist move-ments. Varshney (1997) compares Indian cities that have similar proportions of Muslim and Hindu inhabitants and that share other background variables, yet have strikingly divergent outcomes in terms of communal violence. He ar-gues that high levels of "civic engagement" between communal groups ex-plain low levels of violence between Muslims and Hindus. Waldmann (1985, 1989) compares the violent ethnic conflicts in the Basque region and Northern Ireland to the (largely) nonviolent conflicts in Catalonia and Quebec, and ex-plains the transition from nonviolent nationalist protest to violent conflict in the former cases in terms of the loss of middle-class control over the nationalist movement. Friedland and Hecht (1998) compare the violent conflicts for con-trol of sacred places in Jerusalem and the Indian city of Ayodhya. In both cases, they show, struggles over religious rights at sacred centers claimed by two religions—Jews and Muslims in Jerusalem, Hindus and Muslims in Ayodhya—have been closely bound up with struggles to establish, extend, or reconfigure nation-states.The comparison of Rwanda and Burundi is compel-ling because of stunning violence in both cases despite quite different histori-cal conditions. This comparison has not been analyzed systematically, but Le-marchand (1996) suggestively discusses the multiple ways in which the two cases have become intertwined. To be sure, the idea of controlling all relevant variables through a "natural experiment" is illusory. But Laitin (1995b) de-fends the exercise as worthwhile because it compels us to focus on specific processes under differing conditions, setting limits to overgeneralized theory.

Case Studies

In this domain as in others, "cases" continue to be identified generally with countries. Thus substantial literatures have formed around key cases such as Northern Ireland (McGarry & O'Leary 1995; Feldman 1991; Bruce 1992; Bell 1993; White 1993; Aretxaga 1993, 1995); Yugoslavia (Woodward 1995, Cohen 1993, Glenny 1992, Denich 1994, Gagnon 1994/1995); Sri Lanka (Kapferer 1988; Tambiah 1986; Kemper 1991; Pfaffenberger 1991, 1994; Spencer 1990; Sabaratnam 1990); and Rwanda and Burundi (Lemarchand 1996, Prunier 1995, Malkki 1995). The identification of case with country, however, is a matter of convention, not logic. Ethnic or nationalist violence in a country is treated as a case when the violence is portrayed as a single processual whole. If the violence is instead construed as a set of separate (though perhaps interdependent) instances, then it becomes a case set, suitable for controlled comparison or even for a large-*n* study. In Olzak's (1992) study of confrontations and protests, for example, the United States is not a case but the location for a large-*n* study of events. The breakup of Yugoslavia has most often been treated as a single complex interconnected case, but if we had adequately disaggregated data, it could be studied as a set of cases (for example, of recruitment to unofficial or quasi-official violence-wielding nationalist militias or gangs).

Most case studies are organized around a core argumentative line. In Woodward's 1995 analysis of Yugoslavia, for example, the cumulative effect of economic crisis, a weakening central state, and external powers' recognition of constituent "nations" that were incapable of acting like states created a security dilemma for minorities in the newly recognized states. For Deng (1995), the attempt by the North to identify the Sudanese nation as an Arab one could lead only to rebellion from the South, which had been enslaved by Arabs but never assimilated into an Arab culture. For Kapferer (1988), Sinhalese Buddhist myths and rituals—rooted in an embracing cosmology and "ingrained in the practices of everyday life" (p. 34)—provided a crucial cultural underpinning for a radically nationalizing Sinhalese political agenda and for anti-Tamil violence in Sri Lanka. In Prunier's 1995 analysis of Rwanda, an externally imposed ideology of sharp difference between Hutus and Tutsis, and postcolonial claims to exclusive control of the state on both sides of this colonially reified group difference, created a security dilemma favoring preemptive violence.

At the same time, authors of these and other case studies recognize that the explanatory lines they highlight are partial, and they consequently embed these arguments in richly contextualized narratives specifying a web of intertwined supporting, subsidiary, or qualifying arguments. As a result, one cannot evaluate these works on the same metric as one would the statistical or even the small-*n* studies. The rhetorical weight in case studies tends to be carried by the richness and density of texture; although a major argumentative line is almost always identifiable, the argument takes the form of a seamless web rather than a distinct set of explanatory propositions. Attempts to extract precise propositions from such case studies often reduce the original argument to the point of caricature. [5] However, close reading of such works can yield rich material on microsocial processes at low levels of aggregation that macro theories miss.

THEORY-DRIVEN RATIONAL ACTION APPROACHES

The main clusters of theory-driven work on ethnic violence have employed models of rational action, drawing in particular from the realist tradition in international relations, from game theory, and from rational choice theory in general.[6] Although "rational action" (or "strategy," the preferred term of international relations and game theory) is understood differently in these traditions (referring in international relations to the grand designs of states engaged in power politics, in game theory to the fully specified plan for playing a particular game, and in rational choice theory in general to individual action oriented to the maximization of subjective expected utility), ethnic violence in all three traditions is seen as a product of rational action (rather than emotion or irrationality), though structural background conditions are seen as crucially shaping the contexts of choice.

International Relations Approaches

International relations scholars of the realist school (Jervis 1978) posit the existence of a "security dilemma" under conditions of anarchy in which even nonaggressive moves to enhance one's security, perceived as threatening by others, trigger countermoves that ultimately reduce one's own security. While formulated to explain interstate wars, the security dilemma has been applied to intrastate ethnic violence as well.

A line of argument initiated by Posen (1993) focuses on the windows of opportunity—and vulnerability—occasioned by the collapse of central authority in multiethnic empires (see also Carment et al 1997). In such circumstances, especially given an historical record of serious intergroup hostilities (amplified and distorted, of course, in the retelling), groups are likely to view one another's nationalist mobilization as threatening. These perceived threats may create incentives for preemptive attack (or at least for countermobilization that will in turn be perceived as threatening by the other group, engendering a mo-

---

[5]Blalock (1989:14) notes the degradation of propositional conflict that typically occurs once case studies get taken up in the literature and involved in theoretical controversy.

[6]These clusters are not, of course, mutually exclusive. For example, Lake & Rothchild (1996) draw on elements from all three.

bilization spiral that can lead to violence, especially since violent action can be undertaken autonomously, under conditions of state breakdown, by small bands of radicals outside the control of the weak, fledgling successor states).

To be sure, the international relations perspective on ethnic violence has its weaknesses. Ethnic conflict differs sharply from interstate conflict (Laitin 1995c). States are distinct and sharply bounded entities [though to treat them as unitary actors, as international relations scholars commonly do (Van Evera 1994), is problematic (Mann 1993:Chapters 3, 21)]. In contrast, ethnic groups are not "given" entities with unambiguous rules of membership, as is well known from a generation of research (Barth 1967, Young 1965). Rarely is a single leader recognized as authoritatively entitled to speak in the name of the group. As a result, ethnic groups generally lack what states ordinarily possess, namely, a leader or leaders capable of negotiating and enforcing settlements (Paden 1990, Podolefsky 1990). Moreover, ethnic group membership is fluid and context-dependent. Relatively high rates of intermarriage (as in the former Yugoslavia) mean that many people, faced with interethnic violence, are not sure where they belong. Boundary-strengthening, group-making projects *within* ethnic groups are almost always central to violent conflicts *between* groups, but these crucial intragroup processes are obscured by international re-lations–inspired approaches that treat ethnic groups as unitary actors.

Game Theoretic Approaches

In examining ethnic violence, game theorists subsume the issue as part of a general theory of social order (Kandori 1992, Landa 1994). With specific ref-erence to ethnic violence, however, game theorists seek to understand the ra-tionale for the choice to use violence, assuming that violence will be costly to both sides in any conflict (Fearon 1995). They are not satisfied with theories, especially psychological ones (Tajfel 1978), that can account for conflict or mistrust but not for violence. Game theorists seek to provide a specific account of violence rather than accept it as an unexplained and unintended byproduct of tense ethnic conflicts.

There is no unitary or complete game theory of ethnic violence. Rather, game theorists have identified certain general mechanisms that help account for particular aspects of the problem of ethnic violence. Here we review game-theoretic accounts of three such mechanisms, associated with problems of credible commitments, asymmetric information, and intragroup dynamics, re-spectively.

Fearon (1994) has developed a model of the problem of credible commit-ments and ethnic violence. In this model, the problem arises in a newly inde-pendent state dominated by one ethnic group but containing at least one power-ful minority group as well. The model focuses on the inability of an ethnicized state leadership to "credibly commit" itself to protect the lives and property of subordinate ethnic groups, who, as a result, have an interest in fighting for independence immediately rather than waiting to see if the leadership honors its commitment to protect them. Once a war breaks out, as Walter (1994) shows, settlement is extremely difficult, because neither side will want to disarm without full confidence that the agreement will be adhered to; but no one will have such confidence unless the other side disarms. Weingast (1998) shows that individuals who are told by their group leaders that they are targets for extermination would rationally take up arms even if the probability is negligible that their leaders' prognostications are accurate, since a low probability event with drastic consequences has a high expected disutility. Therefore ethnic war can emerge from a commitment problem even if only vague suggestions of repression exist, or if only a maniacal wing of the ruling group has genocidal intentions. Weingast's work is sensitive to the importance of institutions such as the consociational ones described by Lijphart (1977) that enhance the credibility of commitments. In the absence of such institutions, ethnic violence is more likely to occur.

Some scholars discount the credible commitments problem, arguing that many states do not even seek to make such commitments to protect their minorities. Rothchild (1991) shows that ethnic violence in Africa is associated strongly with regimes that show no interest in bargaining with disaffected groups. In many cases violence results neither from fear nor from failed coordination but from deliberate policy. However, if violence of this type were not reciprocated, and carried few costs for its perpetrators, it would be, in game-theoretic terms, a dominant strategy for leaders of ethnocratic regimes; and researchers must then explain why this sort of violence is not more common than it is.

Concerning the problem of information asymmetry, Fearon & Laitin (1996) suggest, with Deutsch (1954), that ethnic solidarity results from high levels of communication. As a result, in everyday interaction within an ethnic group, if someone takes advantage of someone else, the victim will be able to identify the malfeasant and to refuse future cooperation with him or her. High levels of interaction and of information about past interaction make possible the "evolution of cooperation" (Axelrod 1984) within a community. Interethnic relations, however, are characterized by low levels of information; the past conduct of members of the other ethnic group, as individuals, is not known. Under such conditions, an ethnic incident can more easily spiral into sustained violence, if members of each group, not being able to identify particular culprits, punish any or all members of the other group. This unfortunate equilibrium, Fearon and Laitin show, is not unique. They describe an alternate equilibrium, one that helps explain why violent spiraling, although gruesome, is rare. They find that even under conditions of state weakness or breakdown, ethnic cooperation can be maintained by local institutions of in-group policing—where leaders of one group help identify and punish the instigators of the violence against members of the other group—and intergroup mediation. The in-group policing equilibrium is one in which interethnic violence can be cauterized quickly.

Concerning in-group dynamics, game theory can help to clarify the microfoundations for the intragroup processes discussed previously in the section on case-based pattern finding. Game theoretic approaches, attuned to the individual level of analysis, do not assume—as do many theorists of ethnic conflict—that members of ethnic groups share a common vision or common interests. Kuran (1998a, 1998b) assumes that people have distinct preferences for some combination of ethnically marked and generic, ethnically indifferent consumption (including not only goods but activities, modes of association, policies, and so on). Ethnic entrepreneurs, who will be more successful to the extent that their constituents favor ethnic over generic consumption, try to induce the former at the expense of the latter. Such pressures, and constituents' interdependent responses to them, can trigger ethnification cascades—sharp and self-sustaining shifts from ethnically neutral to ethnically marked activities that divide once integrated societies into separate ethnic segments between whom violence is much more likely to flare up, and spread, than between the same individuals before the "cascade." Laitin (1995b) uses a cascade model similar to that of Kuran. He assumes that ethnic activists, in the context of a national revival, will use tactics of humiliation to induce co-nationals to invest in the cultural repertoires of the dormant nation. But when humiliation fails, and when activists fear that no cascade toward the national revival is possible, they will consider the possibility of inducing both intra- and interethnic violence.

Rational Action Theory

Rational action perspectives on ethnicity and nationalism have proliferated in recent years (Rogowski 1985, Meadwell 1989, Banton 1994). Yet despite an abundance of informal observations concerning the strategic, calculated, or otherwise instrumental dimensions of ethnic or nationalist violence, few systematic attempts have been made (apart from the international relations and game-theoretic traditions mentioned above) to analyze ethnic and nationalist violence as such from a rational action perspective. One exception is Hechter (1995), who claims that "nationalist violence can best be explained instrumentally." Hechter argues that while the dispositions linked to emotional or expressive violence are distributed randomly in a population, and thus have no effect at the aggregate level, the dispositions underlying instrumental violence are clustered systematically and thus are decisive at the aggregate level. This argument presupposes that the dispositions underlying emotional or expressive violence are idiosyncratic individual characteristics, yet surely such powerful violence-fostering emotions as rage or panic-like fear may be clustered systematically at particular places and times and thus may be significant at the aggregate level. But Hechter does stake claim to territory into which rationalists—for all their expansionist inclinations—have so far hesitated to tread. He also clearly states a series of propositions about the relation between group solidarity, state strength and autonomy, and oppositional nationalist violence. Another exception is Hardin (1995), who applies broadly rational choice perspectives (following Olson 1975) to the formation of ethnic groups and their development of exclusionary norms and then relies on an informal game model to explain how groups with such norms can "tip" toward violence.

Blalock's general theory of power and conflict (1989), though not specifically addressed to ethnic or nationalist violence, analyzes structures, mechanisms, and processes that are often implicated in such violence. These include the small, disciplined "conflict groups" specifically organized to carry out violence and the mechanisms through which protracted conflicts are sustained or terminated. He adopts a modified rational-actor persepective—modified in emphasizing structures of power and dependency and allowing for non-economic goals and the the role of misperception, deception, ideological bias, and so on in shaping the subjective probabilities on the basis of which action is undertaken.

CULTURALIST APPROACHES

Culturalist analyses of ethnic and nationalist violence reflect the broader "cultural turn" the social sciences have taken in the past 20 years. Although such analyses are extremely heterogeneous, they generally characterize ethnic violence as meaningful, culturally constructed, discursively mediated, symbolically saturated, and ritually regulated. Some culturalist analyses expressly reject causal analysis in favor of interpretive understanding (Zulaika 1988) or adopt a stance of epistemological skepticism (Pandey 1992, Brass 1997). Yet for the most part, culturalist accounts do advance explanatory claims, although the status and precise nature of the claims are not always clear. Here we sketch a few clusters of recurring themes in culturalist analyses.

The Cultural Construction of Fear

Like the rational action approaches just considered, culturalist approaches seek to show that even apparently senseless ethnic violence "makes sense" (Kapferer 1988) in certain contexts. Yet while they claim to discover a "logic" to ethnic and ethnoreligious violence (Spencer 1990, Zulaika 1988, Juergensmeyer 1988) and reject representations of it as chaotic, random, meaningless, irrational, or purely emotive, culturalists claim that such violence makes sense not in instrumental terms but in terms of its meaningful relation to or resonance with other elements of the culturally defined context.

442   BRUBAKER & LAITIN

Culturalist analyses construe the relevant context in different ways. One major focus of attention has been on the cultural construction of fear, on the rhetorical processes, symbolic resources, and representational forms through which a demonized, dehumanized, or otherwise threatening ethnically defined "other" has been constructed. The social construction of fear, to be sure, is not a new theme in analyses of ethnic violence. It was central to Horowitz (1985:175–184), who in turn drew on a generation of work in social psychology. Yet while Horowitz sought to elaborate a universal "positional group psychology" to account for cross-cultural regularities in patterns of ethnic antipathy and anxiety, recent culturalist accounts have tended to emphasize particular features of individual cultural contexts; they have emphasized the cultural and historical rather than social psychological grounding of ethnic fear. A literature has emerged on the construction of fearful Hindu beliefs about Muslims in India (in the context of opposed ethnoreligious idioms and practices, religiously justified social segregation, and the rise of militant Hindu nationalism) (Gaborieau 1985, Pandey 1992, Hansen 1996); of Sinhalese beliefs about Tamils in Sri Lanka (in the context of an ethnocratic Sinhalese state, Tamil terrorism, state repression, and unchecked rumor) (Spencer 1990); and of Serbian beliefs about Croats in disintegrating Yugoslavia (in the context of a nationalizing Croatian successor state symbolically linked to, and triggering memories of, the murderous wartime Ustasha regime) (Glenny 1992, Denich 1994). Once such ethnically focused fear is in place, ethnic violence no longer seems random or meaningless but all too horrifyingly meaningful.

Without using the term, culturalist analyses have thus been concerned with what we discussed above as the security dilemma—with the conditions under which preemptive attacks against an ethnically defined other may "make sense." Unlike the international relations approaches to the security dilemma, however—and unlike political and economic approaches to ethnic violence in general—culturalist approaches seek to specify the manner in which fears and threats are constructed through narratives, myths, rituals, commemorations, and other cultural representations (Atran 1990). Culturalist analyses thus see security dilemmas as subjective, not objective, and as located in the realm of meaning and discourse, not in the external world. Many cultural analyses (e.g. Tambiah 1996, Bowman 1994) acknowledge the crucial role of ethnic elites in engendering ethnic insecurity through highly selective and often distorted narratives and representations, the deliberate planting of rumors, and so on. But the success of such entrepreneurs of fear is seen as contingent on the historically conditioned cultural resonance of their inflammatory appeals; cultural "materials" are seen as having an inner logic or connectedness that makes them at least moderately refractory to willful manipulation by cynical politicians.

Although such accounts may be plausible, even compelling "on the level of meaning" (Weber 1968:11), they have two weaknesses. The first is evidentiary: It is difficult to know whether, when, where, to what extent, and in what manner the posited beliefs and fears were actually held. How do we know that, in India, the most "rabid and senseless Hindu propaganda," "the most outrageous suggestions" about the allegedly evil, dangerous, and threatening Muslim "other," have come to be "widely believed," and to constitute "a whole new 'common sense'" (Pandey 1992:42–43, Hansen 1996)? How do we know that, in Sri Lanka in 1983, Tamils were believed to be "superhumanly cruel and cunning and, like demons, ubiquitous" (Spencer 1990:619) or "agents of evil," to be rooted out through a kind of "gigantic exorcism" (Kapferer 1988:101)? How do we know that, in the Serb-populated borderlands of Croatia, Serbs really feared Croats as latter-day Ustashas? Lacking direct evidence (or possessing at best anecdotal evidence) of beliefs and fears, culturalist accounts often rely on nationalist propaganda tracts (Pandey 1992:43, Lemarchand 1996:Chapter 2) but are unable to gauge the extent to which or the manner in which such fearful propaganda has been internalized by its addressees. [Malkki (1995) has attempted to document the extent of such internalization in her fieldwork among Hutu refugees from Burundi, but because this work concerns the victims of near-genocidal violence, not the perpetrators, it speaks most directly to the consequences rather than to the causes of ethnic violence—although consequences of past violence can become causes of future violence in the course of a long-term cycle of intractable violent conflict (Lemarchand 1996, Atran 1990)].

The second problem is that such accounts (though culturalist accounts are not alone in this respect) tend to explain too much and to overpredict ethnic violence. They can not explain why violence occurs only at particular times and places, and why, even at such times and places, only some persons participate in it. Cultural contextualizations of ethnic violence, however vivid, are not themselves explanations of it.

Framing Conflict as Ethnic

In southern Slovakia in 1995, a pair of Hungarian youths were pushed from a train by Slovakian youths after a soccer match. Although one of the youths was seriously injured, and although the incident occurred after the Hungarians had been singing Hungarian nationalist songs, the violence was interpreted as drunken behavior by unruly soccer fans rather than as ethnic violence, and even the nationalist press in Hungary made no attempt to mobilize around the incident (Brubaker field notes). Similarly, the burning down of an Estonian secondary school in a predominantly Russian region of Estonia in 1995 was interpreted as a Mafia hit, even on the Estonian side, and no mobilization occurred, even though no one could suggest why the Mafia might have been interested in a secondary school (Laitin field notes). These incidents illustrate what we alluded to in the introduction as the constitutive significance of coding or framing processes in ethnic violence. The "ethnic" quality of ethnic violence is not intrinsic to the act itself; it emerges through after-the-fact interpretive claims. Such claims may be contested, generating what Horowitz (1991a:2) has called a metaconflict—a "conflict over the nature of the conflict" that may, in turn, feed back into the conflict in such a way as to generate (by furnishing advance legitimation for) future violence (Lemarchand 1996:Chapter 2, McGarry & O'Leary 1995). Such social struggles over the proper coding and interpretation of acts of violence are therefore worth studying in their own right (Brass 1996a, 1997; Abelmann & Lie 1995) as an important aspect of the phenomenon of ethnic violence.

Gender

Like other forms of violence and war, and like the phenomena of ethnicity and nationhood in general (Verdery 1994), ethnic and nationalist violence is strongly gendered. The Basque ETA and the Irish Republican Army (IRA), for example, are overwhelmingly male (Waldmann 1989:154, Zulaika 1988:182), although Aretxaga (1995:138) discusses women's efforts to be recognized as full members of the IRA rather than of its women's counterpart. As victims of ethnic violence, women are sometimes deliberately spared, at other times deliberately targeted [for example, in the notorious mass rapes of Bosnia Muslim women by Bosnian Serbs (Korać 1994)]. More research is needed on the specific roles that women may play in certain ethnic riots, not necessarily as direct perpetrators but, for example, in shaming men into participating (Hansen 1996:153). Katz (1988) argues that while women as well as men are susceptible to the "seductions of crime," the characteristic modalities of women's criminal activities are different; we might expect the same to be true of ethnic violence.

The representation of ethnic violence is also strongly gendered. Recent research on nationalism shows that in many settings, prospective threats to (as well as actual attacks on) "the nation" are construed as a feared or actual violation or rape of an "innocent, female nation" by a brutal male aggressor (Harris 1993:170, Verdery 1994:248–249). To defend or retaliate against such threats or attacks, conspicuously masculinist virtues may be asserted in compensatory or overcompensatory fashion. In India, for example, Hindu nationalist organizations offer a "way of recuperating masculinity" to their recruits, enabling them to "overcome the [stereotypically] 'effeminate' Hindu man and emulate the demonized enemy, the allegedly strong, aggressive, militarized, potent and masculine Muslim" (Hansen 1996:148, 153).

Ritual, Symbolism, Performance

A number of analysts—echoing themes from the Manchester school of social anthropology (Gluckman 1954, Turner 1969)—have underscored the ritualized aspects of ethnic violence. Gaborieau (1985) highlights "rituals of provocation," which he describes as "codified procedures" of deliberate disrespect, desecration, or violation of sacred or symbolically charged spaces, times, or objects—in India, for example, the killing of cows by Muslims, or the disturbance of Muslim worship by noisy Hindu processions (on noise as a cultural weapon in ethnoreligious struggles, see Roberts 1990). Marches and processions through space "owned" by another group have triggered violence in Northern Ireland and India with sufficient regularity and predictability to warrant calling these too rituals of provocation (Feldman 1991:29–30, Jaffrelot 1994, Tambiah 1996:240). Even without deliberate provocation, conflicting claims to the same sacred spaces (Ayodhya, Jerusalem) or sacred times (when ritual calendars overlap) may provide the occasion for ethnic violence (Van der Veer 1994; Tambiah 1996:Chapter 9; Das 1990b:9ff; Friedland & Hecht 1991, 1996). Freitag (1989) and Tambiah (1985:Chapter 4, 1996:Chapter 8) have applied what the latter calls a semiotic and performative perspective on rituals and public events to ethnic confrontations, disturbances, and riots in South Asia. Performance and ritual are also emphasized in Zulaika's (1988) study of the cultural context of violence in a Basque village. Van der Veer (1996) sees riots as a form of ritual antagonism expressing an opposition between the self and an impure, alien, or demonic "other." Following Davis's (1973) analysis of the "rites of violence" in the religious riots of sixteenth-century France, analysts of ethnic riots have called attention to the ritualized nature and symbolic resonance of the seemingly gratuitous forms of mutilation often involved (e.g. hacking off of body parts, desecration of corpses).

Feldman's (1991) study of Northern Ireland is the most sustained discussion of the symbolic dimension of ethnic violence. Feldman focuses on the ethnically charged symbolism of urban space in Belfast, the increasing ethnic partitioning of which is both a consequence of ethnic violence and a reinforcing cause of future violence. He also analyzes the equally charged symbolism of the body. Ironically, given his critique of instrumental analyses of ethnic violence, Feldman devotes a great deal of attention to the body as an instrument, as a weapon deployed by those (in his case, IRA prisoners) for whom it is the only resource. Of course, as he shows in rich detail, this instrumentalization of the body through the "dirty protest" (in which prisoners denied special political status refused to wear prison clothing and smeared feces on the walls) and the subsequent hunger strike (in which 10 prisoners died) was achieved in symbolically resonant form [analyzed also by Aretxaga (1993, 1995), the latter piece focusing on female prisoners' own "dirty protest," centered on the display of menstrual blood].

It should be emphasized that no serious culturalist theory today argues that violence flows directly from deeply encoded cultural propensities to violence or from the sheer fact of cultural difference. In this salutary sense, there are no purely culturalist explanations of ethnic violence; and it is difficult to simply classify as culturalist a work such as Tambiah (1996), in which cultural, economic, political, and psychological considerations are deftly interwoven. By considering separately culturalist approaches, we do not imply that they are or ought to be segregated from other approaches. We suggest, rather, that such approaches highlight aspects of ethnic violence—discursive, symbolic, and ritualistic aspects—that should ideally be addressed by other approaches as well.

CONCLUSION: A PLEA FOR DISAGGREGATION

The temptation to adopt currently fashionable terms of practice as terms of analysis is endemic to sociology and kindred disciplines. But it ought to be resisted. The notion of "ethnic violence" is a case in point—a category of practice, produced and reproduced by social actors such as journalists, politicians, foundation officers, and NGO representatives, that should not be (but often is) taken over uncritically as a category of analysis by social scientists. Despite sage counsel urging disaggregation (Snyder 1978, Williams 1994, Horowitz forthcoming), too much social scientific work in this domain (as in others) involves highly aggregated explananda, as if ethnic violence were a homogeneous substance varying only in magnitude. To build a research program around an aggregated notion of ethnic violence is to let public coding—often highly questionable, as when the Somali and Tadjikistani civil wars are coded as ethnic—drive sociological analysis.

The paradigmatic instances of ethnic and nationalist violence are large events, extended in space and time. Moreover, they are composite and causally heterogeneous, consisting not of an assemblage of causally identical unit instances of ethnic violence but of a number of different types of actions, processes, occurrences, and events. For example, it is evident from the case literature that in Sri Lanka "ethnic violence" consists of episodic riots on the one hand and more continuous low-level terrorism (and state violence in response to the terrorism) on the other, all occurring against the background of the "cultural violence" perpetrated by a series of ethnocratic Sinhalese governments. Not only do the riots, terrorism, and state violence involve sharply opposed mechanisms and dynamics (in terms of degree and mode of organization, mode of recruitment and involvement of participants, affective tone, symbolic significance, contagiousness, degree and modality of purposeful rationality, and so on), but within each category there is also a great deal of causal heterogeneity. Thus an ethnic riot typically involves at one level deliberate manipulation and organization by a small number of instigators but also, at other levels, turbulent currents of crowd behavior governed by powerful emotions and compelling collective representations requiring social psychological and cultural modes of analysis.

ETHNIC AND NATIONALIST VIOLENCE 447

There is no reason to believe that these heterogeneous components of large-scale ethnic violence can be understood or explained through a single theoretical lens. Rather than aspire to construct a theory of ethnic and nationalist violence—a theory that would be vitiated by its lack of a meaningful explanandum—we should seek to identify, analyze, and explain the heterogeneous processes and mechanisms involved in generating the varied instances of what we all too casually lump together—given our prevailing ethnicizing interpretive frames—as "ethnic violence." This can be accomplished only through a research strategy firmly committed to disaggregation in both data collection and theory building.

ACKNOWLEDGMENTS

The authors wish to thank John Bowen, James Fearon, and Timur Kuran for their comments on earlier drafts and Joan Beth Wolf for her able assistance in compiling a preliminary bibliography.

Literature Cited

Abelmann N, Lie J. 1995. *Blue Dreams: Korean Americans and the Los Angeles Riots.* Cambridge, MA: Harvard Univ. Press

Anderson B. 1992. *Long-distance nationalism: world capitalism and the rise of identity politics.* Wertheim Lecture 1992, Center for Asian Studies, Amsterdam

Appadurai A. 1997. *Modernity at Large.* Minneapolis: Univ. Minn. Press

Aretxaga B. 1993. Striking with hunger: cultural meanings of political violence in Northern Ireland. In *The Violence Within: Cultural and Political Opposition in Divided Nations*, ed. KB Warren, pp. 219–53. Boulder, CO: Westview

Aretxaga B. 1995. Dirty protest: symbolic overdetermination and gender in Northern Ireland ethnic violence. *Ethos* 23(2): 123–48

Atran S. 1990. Stones against the iron fist, terror within the nation: alternating structures of violence and cultural identity in the Israeli-Palestinian conflict. *Polit. Soc.* 18(4):481–526

Axelrod R. 1984. *The Evolution of Cooperation.* New York: Basic

Azar EE, Burton JW, eds. 1986. *International* *Conflict Resolution: Theory and Practice.* Sussex and Boulder: Wheatsheaf and Lynne Rienner

Banton M. 1994. Modeling ethnic and national relations. *Ethnic Racial Stud.* 17(1): 1–19

Barth F, ed. 1967. *Ethnic Groups and Boundaries: The Social Organization of Cultural Difference.* Boston: Little Brown

Beissinger MR. 1998. Nationalist violence and the state: political authority and contentious repertoires in the former USSR. *Comp. Polit.* In press

Bell JB. 1993. *The Irish Troubles: A Generation of Violence 1967–1992.* New York: St. Martin's

Björgo T, Witte R, eds. 1993. *Racist Violence in Europe.* New York: St. Martin's

Blackburn R. 1997. *The Making of New World Slavery: From the Baroque to the Modern 1492–1800.* New York: Verso

Blalock HM Jr. 1989. *Power and Conflict: Toward a General Theory.* Newbury Park, CA: Sage

Bodley J, ed. 1982. *Victims of Progress.* Palo Alto, CA: Mayfield. 2nd ed

Bourdieu P, Wacquant LJD. 1992. *An Invita-*

448   BRUBAKER & LAITIN

tion to Reflexive Sociology. Chicago, IL: Univ. Chicago Press

Bowen JR. 1996. The myth of global ethnic conflict. *J. Democr.* 7(4):3–14

Bowman G. 1994. Ethnic violence and the phantasy of the antagonist: the mobilisation of national identity in former Yugoslavia. *Polish Sociol. Rev.* 106:133–53

Brass PR, ed. 1996a. *Riots and Pogroms.* New York: New York Univ. Press

Brass PR. 1996b. Introduction: discourse of ethnicity, communalism, and violence. See Brass 1996a, pp. 1–55

Brass PR. 1997. *Theft of an Idol: Text and Context in the Representation of Collective Violence.* Princeton, NJ: Princeton Univ. Press

Brubaker R. 1995. Aftermaths of empire and the unmixing of peoples: historical and comparative perspectives. *Ethnic Racial Stud.* 18(2):189–218

Brubaker R. 1996. *Nationalism Reframed: Nationhood and the National Question in the New Europe.* Cambridge and New York: Cambridge Univ. Press

Brubaker R. 1998. Myths and misconceptions in the study of nationalism. In *The State of the Nation: Ernest Gellner and the Theory of Nationalism,* ed. John Hall. Cambridge and New York: Cambridge Univ. Press. In press

Bruce S. 1992. *The Red Hand: Protestant Paramilitaries in Northern Ireland.* Oxford: Oxford Univ. Press

Burleigh M, Wippermann W. 1991. *The Racial State: Germany 1933–1945.* New York: Cambridge Univ. Press

Carment D, Rowlands D, James P. 1997. Ethnic conflict and third party intervention. In *Enforcing Cooperation: Risky States and Intergovernmental Management of Conflict,* ed. G Schneider, P Weitsman, pp. 104–32. New York: MacMillan

Chaliand G. 1977. *Revolution in the Third World.* New York: Viking

Clark R. 1984. *The Basque Insurgents: ETA, 1952–1980.* Madison: Univ. Wisc. Press

Clifford J. 1994. Diasporas. *Cult. Anthropol.* 9(3):302–38

Cohen L. 1993. *Broken Bonds: The Disintegration of Yugoslavia.* Boulder, CO: Westview

Cooper F, Stoler AL, eds. 1997. *Tensions of Empire: Colonial Cultures in a Bourgeois World.* Berkeley: Univ. Calif. Press

Coser L. 1956. *The Functions of Social Conflict.* New York: Free

Das V, ed. 1990a. *Mirrors of Violence: Communities, Riots, and Survivors in South Asia.* Oxford and New York: Oxford Univ. Press

Das V. 1990b. Introduction: communities, riots, survivors—the South Asian experience. See Das 1990a, pp. 1–36

Davis NZ. 1973. The rites of violence: religious riot in sixteenth-century France. *Past Present* (59):51–91

Della Porta D, Tarrow S. 1986. Unwanted children: political violence and the cycle of protest in Italy, 1966–1973. *Eur. J. Polit. Res.* 14:607–32

Deng FM. 1995. *War of Visions: Conflict of Identities in the Sudan.* Washington, DC: Brookings Inst.

Denich B. 1994. Dismembering Yugoslavia: nationalist ideologies and the symbolic revival of genocide. *Am. Ethnol.* 21(2): 367–90

Desjarlais R, Kleinman A. 1994. Violence and demoralization in the new world order. *Anthropol. Today* 10(5):9–12

Deutsch K. 1954. *Nationalism and Social Communication.* Cambridge, MA: MIT Press

Diez Medrano J. 1995. *Divided Nations.* Ithaca, NY: Cornell Univ. Press

Dobkowski MN, Wallimann I. 1992. *Genocide in Our Time: an Annotated Bibliography with Analytical Introductions.* Ann Arbor, MI: Pierian

Fairbanks CH Jr. 1995. The postcommunist wars. *J. Democr.* 6(4):18–34

Fearon JD. 1994. *Ethnic war as a commitment problem.* Paper presented at Annu. Meet. Am. Polit. Sci. Assoc., New York

Fearon JD. 1995. Rationalist explanations for war. *Int. Organ.* 49:379–414

Fearon JD, Laitin DD. 1996. Explaining interethnic cooperation. *Am. Polit. Sci. Rev.* 90(4):715–35

Feldman A. 1991. *Formations of Violence: The Narrative of the Body and Political Terror in Northern Ireland.* Chicago, IL: Univ. Chicago Press

Ferguson RB, Whitehead NL, eds. 1992. *War in the Tribal Zone: Expanding States and Indigenous Warfare.* Santa Fe, NM: School Am. Res. Press

Freitag SB. 1989. *Collective Action and Community: Public Arenas and the Emergence of Communalism in North India.* Berkeley: Univ. Calif. Press

Friedland R, Hecht RD. 1991. The politics of sacred place: Jerusalem's Temple Mount/ al-haram al-sharif. In *Sacred Places and Profane Spaces: Essays in the Geographics of Judaism, Christianity, and Islam,* ed. J Scott, P Simpson-Housley, pp. 21–61. New York: Greenwood

Friedland R, Hecht RD. 1996. Divisions at the center: the organization of political violence at Jerusalem's Temple Mount/*al-*

haram al-sharif—1929 and 1990. See Brass 1996a, pp. 114–53

Friedland R, Hecht RD. 1998. Profane violence at the sacred center: the case of Jerusalem and Ayodhya. Unpublished manuscript, Depts. of Sociology and Religious Studies, Univ. Calif., Santa Barbara

Gaborieau M. 1985. From Al-Beruni to Jinnah: idiom, ritual and ideology of the Hindu-Muslim confrontation in South Asia. *Anthropol. Today* 1(3):7–14

Gagnon VP. 1994–1995. Ethnic nationalism and international conflict: the case of Serbia. *Int. Secur.* 19(3):130–66

Gagnon VP. 1996. *Ethnic conflict as demobilizer: the case of Serbia.* Inst. European Stud. Working Paper No. 96.1. Inst. European Stud., Cornell Univ.

Glenny M. 1992. *The Fall of Yugoslavia: The Third Balkan War.* London: Penguin

Gluckman M. 1954. *Rituals of Rebellion in South-East Africa.* Manchester, UK: Manchester Univ. Press

Goldstone JA, Gurr TR, Moshiri F, eds. 1991. *Revolutions of the Late Twentieth Century.* Boulder, CO: Westview

Green L. 1994. Fear as a way of life. *Cult. Anthropol.* 9(2):227–56

Grimshaw A. 1969. *Racial Violence in the United States.* Chicago, IL: Aldine

Gurr TR. 1968. A casual model of civil strife: a comparative analysis using new indices. *Am. Polit. Sci. Rev.* 62(4):1104–24

Gurr TR. 1970. *Why Men Rebel.* Princeton, NJ: Princeton Univ. Press

Gurr TR. 1993a. *Minorities at Risk: A Global View of Ethnopolitical Conflicts.* Washington, DC: US Inst. Peace

Gurr TR. 1993b. Why minorities rebel: a global analysis of communal mobilization and conflict since 1945. *Int. Polit. Sci. Rev.* 14(2):161–201

Gurr TR. 1994. Peoples against states: ethnopolitical conflict and the changing world system. *Int. Stud. Q.* 38:347–77

Gurr TR, Harff B. 1994. *Ethnic Conflict in World Politics.* Boulder, CO: Westview

Haas EB. 1997. *Nationalism, Liberalism and Progress.* Ithaca, NY: Cornell Univ. Press

Hansen TB. 1996. Recuperating masculinity: Hindu nationalism, violence and the exorcism of the Muslim "Other." *Crit. Anthropol.* 16(2):137–72

Hardin R. 1995. *One for All: the Logic of Group Conflict.* Princeton, NJ: Princeton Univ. Press

Harff B, Gurr TR. 1989. Victims of the state: genocide, politicides and group repression since 1945. *Int. Rev. Victimol.* 1:23–41

Harris R. 1993. The "Child of the Barbarian": rape, race and nationalism in France during the First World War. *Past Present* 141: 170–206

Hayden RM. 1996. Imagined communities and real victims: self-determination and ethnic cleansing in Yugoslavia. *Am. Ethnol.* 23(4):783–801

Hechter M. 1995. Explaining nationalist violence. *Nations Natl.* 1(1):53–68

Heisler M. 1991. Ethnicity and ethnic relations in the modern West. See Montville 1991, pp. 21–52

Heraclides A. 1990. Secessionist minorities and external involvement. *Int. Organ.* 44(3):341–78

Holmes S. 1997. What Russia teaches us now: how weak states threaten freedom. *Am. Prospect* 33:30–39

Horowitz DL. 1973. Direct, displaced, and cumulative ethnic aggression. *Comp. Polit.* 6:1–16

Horowitz DL. 1983. Racial violence in the United States. In *Ethnic Pluralism and Public Policy: Achieving Equality in the United States and Britain,* ed. N Glazer, K Young, pp. 187–211. Lexington, MA: Lexington/Heinemann Educ.

Horowitz DL. 1985. *Ethnic Groups in Conflict.* Berkeley: Univ. Calif. Press

Horowitz DL. 1991a. *A Democratic South Africa?: Constitutional Engineering in a Divided Society.* Berkeley: Univ. Calif. Press

Horowitz DL. 1991b. Irredentas and secessions: adjacent phenomena, neglected considerations. In *Irredentism and International Politics,* ed. N Chazan. pp. 9–22. Boulder, CO: Lynne Rienner/Adamantine

Horowitz DL. 1991c. Making moderation pay: the comparative politics of ethnic conflict management. See Montville 1991, pp. 451–75

Horowitz DL. Forthcoming. *Deadly Ethnic Riots.*

Jackson RH. 1990. *Quasi-States: Sovereignty, International Relations and the Third World.* New York: Cambridge Univ. Press

Jackson RH, CG Rosberg. 1982. Why Africa's weak states persist: the empirical and juridical in statehood. *World Polit.* 35(1): 1–24

Jaffrelot C. 1994. *Processions Hindoues, stratégies politiques et émeutes entre Hindous et Musulmans.* In *Violences et Non violences en Inde,* ed. D Vidal, G Tarabout, E Meyer, pp. 261–87. Paris: École Hautes Étud. Sci. Soc.

Jervis R. 1978. Cooperation under the security dilemma. *World Polit.* 30(2):167–214

Juergensmeyer M. 1988. The logic of religious violence: the case of the Punjab. *Contrib. Indian Sociol.* 22(1):65–88

Kakar S. 1990. Some unconscious aspects of

450   BRUBAKER & LAITIN

ethnic violence in India. See Das 1990a, pp. 135–45

Kandori M. 1992. Social norms and community enforcement. *Rev. Econ. Stud.* 59:63–80

Kapferer B. 1988. *Legends of People, Myths of State: Violence, Intolerance, and Political Culture in Sri Lanka and Australia.* Washington, DC: Smithsonian Inst. Press

Katz J. 1988. *Seductions of Crime: Moral and Sensual Attractions in Doing Evil.* New York: Basic

Kaufman SJ. 1996. Spiraling to ethnic war: elites, masses, and Moscow in Moldova's civil war. *Int. Secur.* 21(2):108–38

Keith M. 1993. *Race, Riots and Policing: Lore and Disorder in a Multi-Racist Society.* London: UCL

Kemper S. 1991. *The Presence of the Past: Chronicles, Politics, and Culture in Sinhala Life.* Ithaca, NY: Cornell Univ. Press

Klier JD, Lambroza S, eds. 1992. *Pogroms: Anti-Jewish Violence in Modern Russian History.* New York: Cambridge Univ. Press

Korać M. 1994. Representation of mass rape in ethnic conflicts in what was Yugoslavia. *Sociologija* 36(4):495–514

Kuran T. 1998a. Ethnic dissimilation and its international diffusion. In *Ethnic Conflict: Fear, Diffusion, and Escalation,* ed. DA Lake, D Rothchild, pp. 35–60. Princeton, NJ: Princeton Univ. Press

Kuran T. 1998b. Ethnic norms and their transformation through reputational cascades. *J. Legal Stud.* 27: In press

Laitin DD. 1995a. Marginality: a microperspective. *Rational. Soc.* 7(1):31–57

Laitin DD. 1995b. National revivals and violence. *Arch. Eur. Sociol.* 36(1):3–43

Laitin DD. 1995c. *Ethnic cleansing, liberal style.* Paper presented to the Harvard-MIT Transnational Security Project seminar on Intergroup Conflict, Human Rights, and Refugees, November 20, 1995

Lake DA, Rothchild D. 1996. Containing fear: the origins and management of ethnic conflict. *Int. Secur.* 21(2):41–75

Landa JT. 1994. *Trust, Ethnicity and Identity.* Ann Arbor: Univ. Mich. Press

Langmuir GI. 1990. *Toward a Definition of Antisemitism.* Berkeley: Univ. Calif. Press

Lemarchand R. 1996. *Burundi: Ethnic Conflict and Genocide.* New York/Cambridge: Woodrow Wilson Center Press/Cambridge Univ. Press

Lijphart A. 1977. *Democracy in Plural Societies.* New Haven, CT: Yale Univ. Press

Lijphart A. 1990. The alternative vote: a realistic alternative for South Africa? *Politikon* 18(2):91–101

Malkki L. 1995. *Purity and Exile: Violence, Memory, and National Cosmology Among Hutu Refugees in Tanzania.* Chicago, IL: Univ. Chicago Press

Mann M. 1993. *The Sources of Social Power: The Rise of Classes and Nation-States, 1760–1914,* Vol. II. New York: Cambridge Univ. Press

Marrus MR. 1985. *The Unwanted: European Refugees in the Twentieth Century.* New York: Oxford Univ. Press

McGarry J, O'Leary B. 1995. *Explaining Northern Ireland: Broken Images.* Oxford: Blackwell

Meadwell H. 1989. Ethnic nationalism and collective choice theory. *Comp. Polit. Stud.* 22:139–54

Meyer JW. 1987. The world polity and the authority of the nation-state. In *Institutional Structure: Constituting State, Society, and the Individual,* ed. GM Thomas, JW Meyer, FO Ramirez, pp. 41–70. Newbury Park, CA: Sage

Miller WI. 1993. *Humiliation.* Ithaca, NY: Cornell Univ. Press

Montville J, ed. 1991. *Conflict and Peacemaking in Multiethnic Societies.* Lexington, MA: Lexington

Nagengast C. 1994. Violence, terror, and the crisis of the state. *Annu. Rev. Anthropol.* 23:109–36

Nordstrom C, Martin J, eds. 1992. *The Paths to Domination, Resistance, and Terror.* Berkeley: Univ. Calif. Press

Olson M. 1975. *The Logic of Collective Action: Public Goods and the Theory of Groups.* Cambridge, MA: Harvard Univ. Press

Olzak S. 1992. *The Dynamics of Ethnic Competition and Conflict.* Stanford, CA: Stanford Univ. Press

Paden JN. 1991. National system development and conflict resolution in Nigeria. See Montville 1991, pp. 411–32

Pandey G. 1992. In defense of the fragment: writing about Hindu-Muslim riots in India today. *Representations* 37:27–55

Petersen R. 1998. *Fear, Hatred, Resentment: Delineating Paths to Ethnic Violence in Eastern Europe.* Unpublished manuscript, Dept. of Political Science, Washington Univ., St. Louis

Pfaffenberger B. 1991. Ethnic conflict and youth insurgency in Sri Lanka: the social origins of Tamil separatism. See Montville 1991, pp. 241–58

Pfaffenberger B. 1994. The structure of protracted conflict: the case of Sri Lanka. *Humboldt J. Soc. Relat.* 20(2):121–47

Podolefsky A. 1990. Mediator roles in Simbu conflict management. *Ethnology* 29(1):67–81

Posen BR. 1993. The security dilemma and ethnic conflict. *Survival* 35(1):27–47

Prunier G. 1995. *The Rwanda Crisis 1959–1994: History of a Genocide.* London: Hurst

Rabushka A, Shepsle KA. 1972. *Politics in Plural Societies: A Theory of Democratic Instability.* Columbus, OH: Merrill

Roberts M. 1990. Noise as cultural struggle: tom-tom beating, the British, and communal disturbances in Sri Lanka, 1880s–1930s. See Das 1990a, pp. 240–85

Rogger H, Weber E, eds. 1965. *The European Right: a Historical Profile.* Berkeley: Univ. Calif. Press

Rogowski R. 1985. Causes and varieties of nationalism—a rationalist account. In *New Nationalisms of the Developed West: Toward Explanation,* ed. EA Tiryakian, R Rogowski. pp. 87–108. Boston: Allen & Unwin

Rothchild D. 1991. An interactive model for state-ethnic relations. In *Conflict Resolution in Africa,* ed. FM Deng, IW Zartman. Washington, DC: Brookings Inst.

Rothschild J. 1981. *Ethnopolitics, a Conceptual Framework.* New York: Columbia Univ. Press

Sabaratnam L. 1990. Sri Lanka: the lion and the tiger in the ethnic archipelago. See van den Berghe 1990, pp. 187–220

Scheff TJ, Retzinger SM. 1991. *Emotions and Violence: Shame and Rage in Destructive Conflicts.* Lexington, MA: Lexington

Simmel G. 1955. *"Conflict" and "The Web of Group-Affiliations,"* trans. KH Wolff, R Bendix. New York: Free

Snyder D. 1978. Collective violence: a research agenda and some strategic considerations. *J. Confl. Resol.* 22(3):499–534

Snyder J. 1998. *Nationalist Conflict in the Age of Democracy.* New York: Norton. In press

Spencer J. 1990. Collective violence and everyday practice in Sri Lanka. *Mod. Asia Stud.* 24(3):603–23

Stohl M, ed. 1983. *The Politics of Terrorism.* 2nd ed. New York: Marcel Dekker

Tajfel H, ed. 1978. *Differentiation Between Social Groups.* London: Academic

Tambiah SJ. 1985. *Culture, Thought, and Social Action : An Anthropological Perspective* Cambridge, MA: Harvard Univ. Press

Tambiah SJ. 1986. *Sri Lanka: Ethnic Fratricide and the Dismantling of Democracy.* Chicago, IL: Univ. Chicago Press

Tambiah SJ. 1996. *Leveling Crowds: Ethnonationalist Conflicts and Collective Violence in South Asia.* Berkeley: Univ. Calif. Press

Tarrow S. 1994. *Power in Movement.* Cambridge, UK: Cambridge Univ. Press

Tilly C. 1978. *From Mobilization to Revolution.* Reading, MA: Addison-Wesley

Turner V. 1969. *The Ritual Process.* London: Routledge

Väyrynen R, Senghaas D, Schmidt C, eds. 1987. *The Quest for Peace: Transcending Collective Violence and War Among Societies, Cultures and States.* Beverly Hills, CA/London: Sage/Int. Soc. Sci. Counc.

van den Berghe PL, ed. 1990. *State Violence and Ethnicity.* Niwot, CO: Univ. Press Colo.

van der Veer P. 1994. *Religious Nationalism: Hindus and Muslims in India.* Berkeley: Univ. Calif. Press

van der Veer P. 1996. Riots and rituals: the construction of violence and public space in Hindu nationalism. See Brass 1996a, pp. 154–76

van Evera S. 1994. Hypotheses on nationalism and war. *Int. Secur.* 18(4):5–39

Varshney A. 1997. Postmodernism, civic engagement and ethnic conflict: a passage to India. *Comp. Polit.* 30(1):1–20

Verdery K. 1994. From parent-state to family patriarchs: gender and nation in contemporary Eastern Europe. *East Eur. Polit. Soc.* 8(2):225–55

Volkan V. 1991. Psychoanalytic aspects of ethnic conflicts. See Montville 1991, pp. 81–92

Waldmann P. 1985. Gewaltsamer Separatismus. Am Beispiel der Basken, Franko-Kanadier und Nordiren. *Kölner Z. Soziol. Sozialpsychol.* 37(2):203–29

Waldmann P. 1989. *Ethnischer Radikalismus: Ursachen und Folgen gewaltsamer Minderheitenkonflikte am Beispiel des Baskenlandes, Nordirlands und Quebecs.* Opladen: Wesdeutscher

Waldmann P. 1992. Ethnic and sociorevolutionary terrorism: a comparison of structures. *Int. Soc. Mov. Res.* 4:237–357

Walter B. 1994. *The resolution of civil wars: why negotiations fail.* Ph.D thesis, Polit. Sci. Dept., Univ. Chicago

Weber M. 1968. *Economy and Society,* ed. G Roth, C Wittich. Berkeley: Univ. Calif. Press

Weingast B. 1998. Constructing trust: the politics and economics of ethnic and regional conflict. In *Institutions and Social Order,* ed. V Haufler, K Soltan, E Uslaner. Ann Arbor: Univ. Mich. Press. In press

White RW. 1993. *Provisional Irish Republicans: An Oral and Interpretive History.* Westport, CT: Greenwood

Williams RM Jr. 1994. The sociology of ethnic conflicts: comparative international perspectives. *Annu. Rev. Sociol.* 20:49–79

452   BRUBAKER & LAITIN

Woodward SL. 1995. *Balkan Tragedy: Chaos and Dissolution After the Cold War*. Washington, DC: Brookings Inst.

Young C. 1965. *Politics in the Congo*. Princeton, NJ: Princeton Univ. Press

Zolberg A, Suhrke A, Aguayo S. 1989. *Escape From Violence: Conflict and the Refugee Crisis in the Developing World*. New York: Oxford Univ. Press

Zulaika J. 1988. *Basque Violence: Metaphor and Sacrament*. Reno: Univ. Nevada Press

[28]

Interpretations of Political Violence in Ethnically Divided Societies

KATHLEEN A. CAVANAUGH

This article challenges traditional interpretations of political violence in Northern Ireland. Based on a series of ethnographic studies undertaken in republican and loyalist communities in Belfast, Northern Ireland, I argue that it is the question of state legitimacy, not materialism, culture or religion, that is core to understanding the underpinnings and history of political violence in Northern Ireland. Research findings suggest that communal support for and tolerance of paramilitary groups and their tactics are underpinned by security-related concerns and a crisis of legitimacy which renders the state unable to claim a monopoly on the use of force. In contradistinction to counter-insurgency theorists, I argue that the basis for paramilitarism *is not* created by fear of reprisal or intimidation. Rather, intra-communal fears of identity loss and threats (both perceived and real) from the outgroup have created a space for republicanism and loyalism in both its political and paramilitary forms.

Unpacking the causes of political violence is a complex task; language becomes codified and terminology emotively laden. Definitions of violence are often designed to either condemn or support its use. Organized violence by the state is often set in contradistinction to acts of violence against the state. At the root of all discourse concerning the use of violence are questions of justification and legitimacy.

Weber distinguishes the state by its 'capability of monopolizing the *legitimate* [my emphasis] use of violence within a given territory ... [finding] its ultimate sanction in the claim to the monopoly of force ...'.[1] Often state use of 'formal collective violence ... is frequently privileged as legitimate and excepted from studies of violence'.[2] Yet challenges to the legitimacy of state violence frame political discourse. Western political thought accepts that political violence, in certain circumstances, may be used by both the state (in order to protect state security and maintain order) and non-state agents (when opposing tyranny). Rebel violence is often based upon the idea that violence must counter violence (at times, structural) in order to be free from violence (*Est autem vis legem simulans*).[3]

The absence of national state legitimacy is central to understanding the use of violence in Northern Ireland. This article will address why the absence of state legitimacy has fostered support for both loyalist and republican initiatives in Northern Ireland. I will explore two primary

Terrorism and Political Violence, Vol.9, No.3 (Autumn 1997), pp.33–54
PUBLISHED BY FRANK CASS, LONDON

questions: what sustains violence by militant agents; and what underpins communal support for, and restraint on, paramilitant activities?[4] Before turning to this task, I will provide a brief look at the history and composition of paramilitant groups in Northern Ireland.

History and Composition

Although there are three agents of political violence in Northern Ireland: nationalist paramilitaries; loyalist paramilitaries; and state security forces, I will discuss ideologies of loyalist and republican paramilitant groups only.

Republicanism and Republican Paramilitaries

There are a number of nationalist paramilitaries. Two smaller groups have emerged, faded and then re-emerged. The Irish National Liberation Army (INLA; on occasion employs the *nom de guerre*, Catholic Reaction Force), an offshoot from the Official IRA (OIRA), was most active between 1975 and 1986. INLA's political counterpart is the Irish Republican Socialist Party (IRSP). Its writings are Marxist in leaning but, unlike the OIRA, INLA/IRSP believes that the unity of the working class is possible only after national liberation. Smaller and less disciplined than PIRA, INLA was wracked by internal feuding that led to the formation of a splinter group, the Irish People's Liberation Organisation (IPLO). An unsuccessful attempt by IPLO to dissolve INLA led to a feud between the two groups which resulted in twelve deaths. A truce was eventually brokered in March 1987. The two organizations continued to exist and from 1987 to date, both IPLO and INLA have claimed responsibility for a number of violent acts. In 1996, renewed INLA feuding led to the death of a number of its members including Gino Gallagher, the reputed leader of INLA,[5] as rival factions vie for control of the organization.

The largest and most significant of nationalist paramilitary groups is the Provisional Irish Republican Army (PIRA).[6] PIRA emerged in 1969 after a split occurred between the more traditional 'physical force' republicans and the more Marxist 'Official' membership. After a brief armed campaign (1969–72), the OIRA declared a cease-fire, maintaining that violence was driving a wedge through the working class.[7] Some analysts of Irish republicanism, bolstered by Irish republican rhetoric, attempt to establish a continuity of ideology, goals and discourse. The lineage of PIRA, according to this thesis, can be traced to the birth of the United Irishmen in the 1790s and the failed 1916 Easter Rising. Critics of this thesis have quite rightly noted that republicanism has, in fact, experienced a 'discontinuity', with notable shifts in republican ideology (with concomitant economic and social programmes) and tactics. As sociologist Munck has noted, 'No single

POLITICAL VIOLENCE IN ETHNICALLY DIVIDED SOCIETIES   35

unbroken thread from Wolfe Tone to the 'Provos' can explain the fabric of Irish republicanism'. Munck's interpretation of republicanism, echoed by Anthony McIntyre, is that it '... must be read within its own terms of references'.[8] The development and change of republican ideology and tactic since 1970 is marked. There are four fundamental changes in republican strategy with concomitant ideological shifts. I will explore each briefly in turn.

From 1970 to 1977 a military campaign by PIRA was aimed at British withdrawal. PIRA emerged from the Official/Provisional split, to re-embrace the physical force tradition. During this phase, republicans were committed to a military strategy or 'politics by other means'. From 1977 to 1987 republican strategy and ideology entered a second phase. After a 1975 reorganization, the republican movement's power and leadership base shifted north. The political and electoral success of the Hunger Strikes added a new dimension to the republican campaign; military tactics were complemented with a politics of propaganda.[9] Sinn Féin's role in the republican movement began to take form. Shadings of left-wing ideology in republican discourse emerged.[10] Republicans were now committed not only to an Ireland free from British rule, but to creating a 32-county socialist republic. Given its loosely woven theoretical base, republicanism continued to evolve, shed and change its ideological wrappings.

Up until this point, republican analysis of the British government, the SDLP and the Protestant population was unidimensional. The British were imperialists, the SDLP was a co-collaborator[11] and the Protestant population was little more than 'dupes' of the British government. Beginning with the Hume–Adams dialogue in 1987–88 and Peter Brooke's 1990 speech, once again republican ground shifted. Republicans were faced with a failed military campaign and an increasingly sophisticated British intelligence. Sinn Féin's electoral appeal hit a ceiling. A new realism began to emerge in republican discourse. While traces of traditional republican thinking remained, a new strategy began to take form[12] and a more accommodating and inclusive definition of nationalism was adopted. Republicans sought to cooperate with the SDLP and southern nationalists. Writings from prominent republicans revealed a change in republican perceptions of unionism.[13] A reassessment of Britain's role in Ireland recast the British as 'persuaders' of unionism. Dialogue between the republican movement, the British government and the SDLP ensued.

Following the 1994 IRA cease-fire, the republican movement again entered a new arena with new challenges, demands and adaptations. The current republican strategy is, to a large extent, merely an extension of a process which began with Hume–Adams in 1987. However, the inclusion of Sinn Féin into the political process following the IRA's cessation of

Violence

violence brought an essentially fringe party from the periphery to the core. The transition has not been smooth. With the breakdown of the IRA cease-fire in February 1996, republicanism is at a crossroads. Inclusion into the core demands that republicanism once again redefine itself; what will emerge from this process remains to be seen. The contradictions and limitations that emerge through analysis of republican discourse resurface in republican explanations of political violence.

Loyalism and Loyalist Paramilitaries

Unlike nationalist paramilitaries, which boast a smattering of Protestant members, loyalist paramilitants are drawn exclusively from the Ulster Protestant population. Loyalist paramilitaries, until quite recently, have been primarily (though not consistently) reactive. They see themselves as protectors of the Union. Trying to provide a number and accurate listing of all loyalist paramilitary groups proves difficult as many were small, localized, ineffectual and short-lived. The largest of loyalist paramilitaries are the Ulster Volunteer Force (UVF) and the Ulster Defence Association (UDA) which, on occasion, have operated jointly.

First established in 1971, the Ulster Defence Association (UDA) is the largest Protestant paramilitary organization which had, during its peak in 1972, some 40,000 members. By the mid-1980s, its membership was estimated at only 10,000.[14] Despite its alleged ties to militant groups, the UDA remained a legal organization until it was proscribed in August 1992. Because of its legal status, assassinations, bombing campaigns and other acts of violence were attributed to a group called the Ulster Freedom Fighters (UFF; references to the UFF first appeared in 1973), which was simply a cover name for the UDA. The UDA's greatest 'success' was its involvement with the Ulster Workers' Council in May 1974 which facilitated the collapse of the Sunningdale initiative. As an organization consistently in transition, the UDA's history is a mix of militant, political and criminal elements. Under the leadership and direction of Andy Tyrie and John McMichael, a proposal for an independent Northern Ireland was launched in 1979 through a newly created UDA think-tank, the New Ulster Political Research Group (NUPRG). NUPRG would have an unsuccessful run at politics and in 1981 was transformed into the Ulster Loyalist Democratic Party (now known as simply the Ulster Democratic Party and led by McMichael's son, Gary). As part of the Combined Loyalist Military Campaign (CLMC), the UDA together with the UVF declared a cease-fire in October 1994. Since the cease-fire, UDA militant groups have been responsible for drug-trafficking, punishment beatings and intimidation. Rumours persist that factions within the UDA are currently involved in an internal struggle for control of the organization.[15]

Established by Gusty Spence[16] in 1966, the Ulster Volunteer Force (UVF) was responsible for some of the earliest sectarian killings.[17] At its peak in 1972, the UVF was reported to have 1,500 members. The UVF has also operated under various cover names including the Red Hand Commandos (Loyalist Retaliation and Defence Group), Ulster Protestant Action Group and the Protestant Action Group. By the mid- to late 1980s, the UVF had been wracked by internal dissent, touting and the testimony of Supergrass Joseph Bennett, although it continued to claim responsibility for a number of assassinations until the 1994 cease-fire. The UVF has strong ties to the Progressive Unionist Party (PUP), a party which stresses the importance of working class solidarity. Both the PUP and UDP have been on the 'cutting edge' of attempts by loyalists to project a positive, dynamic face. Their electoral appeal, thus far, has been marginal.[18] Ostensibly, the leadership of both the PUP and UDP have closer ties to grassroots loyalists than either of the two main unionist parties. In fact, however, the progressive message from PUP and UDP spokespersons, particularly in the post-cease-fire environment, has out-stepped loyalist working class sentiments.

Interpretations of Violence: Militant Agents in Northern Ireland

There are a number of conflicting theories offered to interpret participation in political violence by non-state agents. Some researchers have found a positive relationship between levels of economic deprivation and the level of political violence. Alternative interpretations are offered by rational choice theorists using resource mobilization, collective action and political processes arguments. In ethnic conflict situations, explanations of violence by militant agents often focus on culture or religion, and suggest that contestants are predisposed to antagonisms. Each of these hypotheses lends itself to testing on an empirical, comparative or normative basis. I will examine each in turn.

'Insurgency of the Deprived'

One traditional interpretation of political violence posits that an event generates a perceptual difference between anticipated and realized goals that, in turn, fuels discontent, grievance and aggression, which frequently leads to violence.[19] This model has found favour with a number of researchers who have linked political violence in Northern Ireland to institutionalized socioeconomic inequalities.[20] Another related theory posits that 'feelings of injustice' are based on determinations of inequity.[21] This thesis, commonly referred to as *equity theory*, suggests that equity exists if two people entering an exchange relationship receive benefits proportionate

38   TERRORISM AND POLITICAL VIOLENCE

to the investment made. If, however, the relationship is not equitable, aggrieved individuals may turn to violence as a means to restore equity.[22]

When applied to Northern Ireland, deprivation arguments lend themselves to both empirical and comparative testing, and, at first glance, appear to have merit. A review of economic performance indicators reveals that Northern Ireland has the highest unemployment rate (13.9 per cent) and the lowest per capita GDP (only 81.3 per cent of the UK average) of all the UK regions. The unemployment rate for those living in public sector housing is 50 per cent, and male unemployment for six Belfast and six Derry City Council Area wards was more than 50 per cent.[23] However, if we are to accept that economic factors underlie the use of violence, we would expect to find the following:

- those engaged in the use of violence would be from economically deprived backgrounds;

- a causal link between the use of violence and the levels of economic growth or decline; a decline in living standards should necessarily see a rise in political violence;

- class, not nationalist cleavages, would characterize the conflict in Northern Ireland;

- on a comparative basis, we would expect to see similar violent patterns or tendencies present in other economically deprived areas in the UK and Ireland;

- finally, we should be able to argue the converse; the use of political violence could be averted through distributive justice and equitable fulfillment of grievances.

The most compelling argument in this thesis rests with the class composition of paramilitants and their supporters. It is true that most members of paramilitary groups are from republican and loyalist working class communities where unemployment is high.[24] It is also true that economic deprivation may have influenced initial outbreaks of violence in the early stages of civil rights protest. However, the socio-economic status of paramilitary members is not uniform[25] and cannot account for the patterns or persistence of violence in Northern Ireland. When examining the link between the use of violence and the overall levels of economic growth or decline, studies undertaken in Northern Ireland by Robert White reveal that higher levels of economic deprivation, as indexed by changes in the rate of unemployment, were not related to increased violence, contrary to what deprivation arguments suggest.[26] O'Leary and McGarry's examination of paramilitary killings against the rates of male unemployment yield similar

POLITICAL VIOLENCE IN ETHNICALLY DIVIDED SOCIETIES 39

results. They compared rates of Catholic unemployment against Republican violence and Protestant unemployment against Loyalist violence from 1981 to 1991. Their findings do not support any causal relationship and, moreover, 'if anything suggests that increasing unemployment is an effective way of reducing violence!'[27]

Results from a series of interviews I conducted with loyalist and republican paramilitants also yield only limited support for frustration-deprivation arguments. Recognition of socioeconomic factors, at times cited by paramilitants as contributing to the use of political violence in Northern Ireland, was often part of a politicization and education process that occurred *after* joining paramilitary groups. The results of interviews with paramilitants suggest that it was experience with state repression and threats (perceived or real) from the outgroup that were the most important determinants in their paramilitary involvement.[28] Activism for both loyalists and republicans (and with few exceptions) was underpinned by a perceived, collective victimization. Respondents referred to a sense of being collectively rather than individually threatened (references to 'my community' rather than 'myself' or 'my family') when marking the transition from passive to active involvement. In recounting personal experiences, a number of senior members of the republican movement marked internment as the beginning of their politicization which moved some from non-involvement (or supporting peaceful protest) to involvement as paramilitants. Internment, intended to crush the republican movement, had backfired. Men who, allegedly, 'never had much time for politics', and who had been on the fringe of protest had, as a result of repressive state measures, felt victimized. Recognition of the collective victimization for many turned to protest, activism and, for some, military engagement. Most younger republican members did not mark a certain event to explain their engagement, rather a sense of alienation, apartness, victimization and even communal responsibility.

Paramilitant involvement assures repeated encounters with security forces, thereby reinforcing and recycling justifications. Paramilitarism defines movement, community, family relationships[29] and privacy. Communal cohesion is strong within republican areas. Security-related fears have created an interdependency between paramilitants and community members.[30] Paramilitants depend on their community for protection, discretion and financial support. Maintaining security requires maintaining control and keeping order. In turn, the community members demand defense and protection – from loyalists, security forces and the hoods.[31] A number of paramilitants described a strong sense of communal responsibility (to defend and protect) which either underpinned their decision to engage or sustained their involvement.

Among senior loyalists many related early, paramilitary involvement to a sense of having simply 'fallen in'. Most loyalist paramilitant members interviewed, however, were in the 19–25 age group. With few exceptions, those interviewed had lived all their lives in all Protestant neighborhoods.[32] They grew up with Protestants, went to state schools with Protestants and socialized with Protestants. Most of the younger paramilitants indicated that their decision to engage was based on political and communal pressures. One UDA member stated that he was 'tired of being pushed around'.[33] Perceptions that they were left to 'their own devices' and were being 'sold out' were prevalent. Respondents rejected rational economic interpretations of loyalist paramilitarism and much like republicans, loyalist paramilitants expressed the security-related fears of the wider loyalist community. Amidst an often contradictory mix of bravado and self reflection, political violence was most often explained as reactive and necessary. Like many of the younger paramilitants interviewed, a senior loyalist activist indicated that loyalists were most likely to use violence when they felt threatened. He argued that loyalist paramilitaries had a core of active support and that support within the greater loyalist and unionist populations would be activated if 'the Protestant people continued to be pushed to the edge'.[34] These findings, in concert with White's earlier analysis, suggest that levels of republican violence are most affected by organized and unorganized state repression, while loyalist violence is most affected by republican violence and most likely to escalate when loyalists feel 'threatened'.[35]

Deprivation arguments also fail on comparative testing. We do not see analogous levels of violence or unrest in other areas of the UK and Ireland which experience similar or, in some cases, higher levels of economic deprivation.[36] Perhaps most damaging to the proponents of the deprivation thesis is that the conflict in Northern Ireland is waged along nationalist, not class divisions. It would be difficult to argue, then, that amelioration of economic disparities and improvement in the overall economic health of Northern Ireland without addressing the national question will bring an end to the use of political violence. In fact, survey data indicate that unionists/loyalists have consistently opposed unification with the Republic of Ireland, *even if their economic conditions remain the same or improve.* Members of the nationalist/republican community remain committed to unification,[37] while at the same time acknowledging that economic conditions may deteriorate and that higher taxes may result.[38] Results from my ethnographic studies are consistent with survey data. As one member of a loyalist community stated, 'right – if all these things [socio-economic conditions] were put on the same basis as the UK in Southern Ireland, I still would not feel any more inclined toward a united Ireland'.[39]

POLITICAL VIOLENCE IN ETHNICALLY DIVIDED SOCIETIES 41

Contact Hypothesis: Segregation, Dehumanization and Violence

One interpretation that has found a great deal of support specific to the Northern Irish case posits that conflict can be ascribed to the level of segregation. The protractedness of the conflict, together with the polarizing use of violence, serves to define an individual's in and outgroup, thereby furthering segregation and polarization and establishing a 'pattern of interaction among contestants'.[40] At the outcome stage, distinct conditions emerge that serve to 'generate' and reinforce the conflict,[41] what Gallagher has referred to as mechanisms which reproduce and maintain the *integrity* of the conflict.[42] Among the conditions to emerge is the *ossification* of conflict that entails:

> ...a vicious cycle of fear and hostile interactions among communal contestants. With the continued stress of such conflict, attitudes, cognitive processes and perceptions become set and ossified. War culture and cynicism dominate. Meaningful communication between or among conflicting parties dries up, and the ability to satisfy communal acceptance needs is severely diminished.[43]

At this stage, a process of negation or dehumanization of outgroup members occurs.

The ossification of a conflict is often accompanied, and indeed facilitated, by segregation. In the case of Northern Ireland, segregation along ethno-religious lines has permeated civil society. Residential segregation in Northern Ireland is endemic. From Social Attitudinal Survey data we know that an individual living in Northern Ireland is most likely to have relatives, friends and neighbors who are of the same religion. A recent survey found that cross-community contact was 'quite low in most areas of social life' and there existed a 'high level of endogamy'.[44] Paul Compton's recent review of the 1991 Continuous Household Survey found that mixed marriages in Northern Ireland account for only 3.7 per cent to 4.6 per cent of the total.[45] Given the strong sense of local economy and fear of 'travel to work', it was unsurprising that the survey also found marked segregation in the workplace. Forty-four per cent of Catholics and 42 per cent of Protestants surveyed indicated that their co-workers were of the same religion.[46] The organization *All Children Together* estimates that educational segregation in Northern Ireland at both the primary and secondary levels is pervasive with *less than* 2 per cent attending integrated school systems. Segregation in primary and secondary education provides an environment that fosters stereotyping and negative imaging of outgroup members.[47]

Political segregation, which is party membership divided along ethno-religious lines, is also strong in Northern Ireland. Following Partition, the political party system in Northern Ireland formed (and largely remains) along confessional lines. In a recent article, William Hazleton correctly observes that, 'cultural identity, particularly religion, and not social class, acts as the principal mobilizing agent in Northern Ireland elections'.[48] While this tendency, as Donald Horowitz has noted,[49] is not particular to Northern Ireland, strong ethnic cleavages in voting patterns have left bi-confessional parties, such as the Alliance Party of Northern Ireland (APNI), the Workers Party (WP) and the Northern Ireland Conservative Party, politically weak. Since 1981 electoral support for the APNI in local government elections, for example, has held between 7 to 9 per cent of the total vote.[50]

Based on these divisions in education, residence, social activities, political voting patterns and attitudes – cut neatly across ethno-religious lines – scholars have ascribed the conflict to the level of segregation within Northern Ireland (with particular emphasis on the education system), and support integrationist approaches to conflict management. But if we are to accept that segregation underpins conflict and the use of political violence in Northern Ireland then, logically, it should follow that the converse is also true; integration should reduce or eliminate these manifestations. Yet, empirical data not only run contrary to this conclusion, but some studies indicate that the converse may actually be true.

If we look at the question of voting patterns and behaviour, for example, it follows that stronger biconfessional parties would create cross-cutting cleavages which, in turn, would lead to moderation. However, in a review of party competition in ethnically divided societies, Paul Mitchell effectively challenges this premise:

> The idea that ethnic exclusivity may not be such a negative factor challenges one of the pluralist articles of faith: namely, that cross-cutting cleavages lead to moderation, whereas reinforcing cleavages engender extremism.[51]

Instead, Mitchell argues, the key to successful conflict resolution strategies may lie in creating 'ethnically exclusive but *stable* [emphasis in original] party segments'.[52] Evidence also suggests that far from increasing levels of violence, segregation may actually serve to reduce intercommunal violence. In his 1986 study, John Darby asked not, why the conflict in Northern Ireland was so violent, but rather what are the elements which restrain it? Darby argues that 'control mechanisms', which he identifies as *avoidance, controlled contact* and *functional integration*, act as an 'effective control on the spread of violence'.[53] Rosemary Harris' seminal study of the rural community of 'Ballybeg' conducted in the 1950s also challenges contemporary integrationist approaches to ethnic conflict. Despite a high degree of residential integration and repeated contact between Protestant and Catholic community members, Harris' findings reveal almost complete social segregation and strong ingroup/outgroup identification.[54]

My research suggests that conflict and the use of political violence in Northern Ireland cannot be ascribed to segregation. However, as John Whyte suggests, segregation does provide a structural base for sectarianism and allows for the development and perpetuation of stereotyping, myth-building and a perceptual denial of outgroup members, 'in a situation where other reasons for conflict exist'.[55]

Cultural Essentialism, Religion and Political Violence

Other internal explanations of political violence in Northern Ireland include cultural or religious interpretations. Religious interpretations are based on theocratic doctrines[56] or draw inference from the degree of religious segregation, communal self-identification as either Protestant and Catholic,[57] high levels of church attendance[58] and extremist rhetoric. Culturally-based explanations follow several discourses.[59] A tradition of public band violence, the socialization of violence replete with rituals, mythologies and traditions which valorize respective histories of resistance and an inherent distrust of the modern state are among the reasons offered to explain the protracted use of violence in Ireland.

Interpretations of political violence based on either culture or religion are flawed for a number of reasons. First, and foremost, we simply have no empirical evidence to support these views. For example, we cannot attribute fluctuations in the levels of violence to any measure of religiosity such as church attendance. Second, if religion underpins conflict then those areas most affected by the use of violence should also have higher markers of religious affiliation. There are no statistical data to support this position and, moreover, my own research renders quite opposite conclusions. In several affected areas in Belfast, I found that community members (and this was particularly the case in republican areas) reflected secular attitudes. Last, and perhaps most compelling, if religion lies at the core of conflict and theocratic doctrines facilitate violence, the converse should also be true; secularism and ecumenism would bring about peace. There is little evidence to support this supposition.

Cultural explanations also fail on empirical testing. If we accept culturalist explanations of violence then participation in political violence by militant agents is, in many ways, predetermined. Results from both formal and informal interviews contradict this theory. My findings suggest that paramilitants had, in fact, carefully weighed the decision to engage militarily and that engagement was a rational response to identity-related fears activated by movement on the constitutional question or as a result of actions by the state or outgroup members, a finding consistent with that of other researchers.[60]

Rational Discourses

Several collective rational choice theories attempt to explain the how and the whys of participation in collective violence. From this perspective, grievances are a constant. Therefore, as in other forms of collective action, the decision to participate in political protest does not stem from deprivation or grievance, but rather from whether the benefits of participation outweigh its costs.[61] The shift from peaceful protest to political violence depends, in large part, on what Tilly describes as the group's *repertoire of collection action*; quite simply what is the alternative available to the group[62] and 'the appropriateness and efficiency of the means the group actually uses and the alternative means which are theoretically available'.[63]

Notwithstanding economic interpretations,[64] when applied to Northern Ireland, the rational choice approach to analysis of participation in political violence has merit. Far from an emotive reaction to grievance, the use of violence becomes, to invoke von Clausewitz's dictum, 'simply a continuation of politics by other means'. Surveying patterns of violence by loyalist and republican paramilitants illustrates that they are, in fact, the ultimate rational pragmatists. As the security force apparatus grew in number and sophistication in early 1977, the IRA responded by changing to a cell structure.[65] Shifts in republican paramilitary target and tactics from the indiscriminate use of force in the mid-1970s to a refined and targeted campaign clearly reflected the organization's cost/benefit analysis. When no-warning car bombs in Belfast city centre alienated community support, republicans shifted gear and stepped up their campaign in England, selecting targets such as the London Underground designed to create the maximum disruption and publicity. Clearly eager to appeal to an international, mainly American-based audience, the republicans have proved to be masters at generating publicity and changing direction when it proved profitable. The republican shift from indiscriminate to targeted campaigns was accompanied by what has been referred to as 'war talk'. A demarcation was drawn, albeit blurred at times, between noncombatants and 'legitimate targets'. As Darby observes, the effect has been to introduce a 'principle of limited liability'.[66] These self-imposed boundaries between Protestants and Catholics, and between nationalist paramilitants and the British Army, have moderated intercommunal relations, limited confrontation and controlled levels of violence.

On first examination, loyalist paramilitarism seems to escape the realms of rational analysis. Loyalists have consistently been viewed as more sectarian than their nationalist counterparts. Most victims of loyalist paramilitaries are civilian with no apparent paramilitary or political ties. Members of Sinn Féin, nationalist paramilitants and, more recently, SDLP

POLITICAL VIOLENCE IN ETHNICALLY DIVIDED SOCIETIES   45

members comprise approximately 15 per cent of loyalist paramilitant targets. The majority of loyalist killings, 77 per cent, were sectarian in nature.[67] These factors give weight to nationalists' claims that for loyalist paramilitants 'any taig will do'. Loyalist paramilitants are, however, 'the political and paramilitary expressions of their respective ethnic communities, rather than the by-products of cultural pathologies'.[68] The seemingly sectarian nature of loyalist paramilitant violence reflects the wider loyalist community perception that they are fighting an 'enemy within'. From this precept, loyalist violence is, in fact, 'rational', and stems from a sense of rival nationalities. Among many loyalists, being a Catholic remains a political act. Loyalist paramilitants, when referring to the republican community, often failed to distinguish between community members and republican paramilitants. Among the loyalist community as a whole the perception is that Catholics living in strongly republican enclaves give succor to republican paramilitants and are, therefore, culpable for their acts. Blankets of legitimacy and justification are then laid which, in the name of security, allow even the most arbitrary of killings to be justified.

Much like their republican counterparts, loyalist paramilitants shift and adapt to circumstance. When, in the late 1980s, loyalists concluded that the British simply could not and would not cope with the IRA, loyalists changed tactics deciding to 'take two Catholics for every one Prod' (e.g. Greysteel after the Shankill).[69] Similarly, the cessation of violence by the IRA forced the Combined Loyalist Military Command (CLMC) to instate a cease-fire as they could not realistically continue to act unilaterally while at the same time claiming to be reactive to republican violence and protectors of the Protestant community. A cost/benefit analysis can also explain why despite renewed IRA activity in February 1996, the CLMC cease-fire held. Political components of loyalist paramilitaries have assessed and concluded that (to date) the benefits are greater remaining within rather than outside of the political process.

To summarize, the levels of republican violence are most affected by organized and unorganized state repression, while loyalist violence is most affected by republican violence and activated when loyalists feel threatened. The decision to engage in acts of violence is calculated, and not the by-product of socio-economic factors or cultural or religious divisions. Using qualitative data collected from a series of ethnographic studies undertaken in loyalist and republican communities in Northern Ireland, I conclude that political violence is justified by a perceived collective victimization within both communal groups and underpinned by the absence of political legitimacy which prevents the state from having a monopoly on the use of force.

'Water and Fish': Communal Support for Paramilitary Violence

When the underpinning of communal support for the use of political violence are examined, questions of legitimacy and challenges to state legitimacy resurface.[70] In contradistinction to theories which posit the community as a passive force that does not shape the dynamics of political violence, I argue that the community is integral to analysis of political violence in Northern Ireland. Political violence, as Burton has convincingly argued, must be understood within the social and historical context from which it stems.[71] As we examine civil society in Northern Ireland, three characteristics emerge: a strong sense of community; ethnic separatism; and a tradition of loyalism and republicanism in both its cultural and political forms. These factors are interdependent as each affects and is, in turn, affected by the other. Core to paramilitarism in Northern Ireland is communalism. With basic security needs left unfulfilled and fear of identity loss prevalent in both republican and loyalist communities, strong intra-communal infrastructures have evolved which protect and promote communal cohesion. Communal cohesion is fostered, in part, by ethnic separatism, an ability to identify one's group in opposition to the outgroup. Taken together, these factors not only form and explain the 'social basis' of paramilitary violence[72] but reinforce and serve to reproduce the exclusionary ethos of republicanism and loyalism.

The structural conditions which, according to Burton, the IRA has successfully used to 'activate...a politics of civil rights through national liberation',[73] are complemented by two basic functions: defense and social control. A dependency exists between structure and function. The 'fear factor', evident in both communities, strengthens communalism as well as ethnic separatism and creates a space for republicanism and loyalism in both its political and paramilitary forms. Strong communal cohesion demands social order and control. To insure social order and control, republican and loyalist paramilitants have constructed alternative legalities to that of the state. Intra-communal support for the use of political violence can be categorized as *active* and *passive* support, with some gradations of grey within each grouping. Active support denotes a willingness to engage with paramilitants by providing safe houses, storing munitions or providing financial contributions. Passive support may include electoral support for political parties associated with paramilitary organizations (Sinn Fein, IRSP, UDP, PUP) or espousing sympathy for (engaging in verbal defense of) paramilitants and their objectives.

Communal reactions to paramilitants in both republican and loyalist communities were often contradictory, temporal and, in many cases, dependent on political movements. Support was, with small pockets of exceptions,[74] conditional while criticisms often drifted into justifications. As paramilitaries reflect the ethos of their respective communities, it was unsurprising to find that paramilitant attitudes towards the use of violence were mirrored in the wider loyalist and republican communities where security-related concerns are prevalent. Heightened or decreased security concerns produced concomitant shifts in support given paramilitants, which, in turn, influenced paramilitant activities.

Within loyalist communities, perceptions of abandonment, betrayal and vulnerability surfaced and resurfaced during both formal and informal interviews. 'If we didn't have these paramilitaries', one loyalist respondent argued, 'who would we have to defend [us]'.[75] During the last phase of field work, perceptions among loyalist respondents that they had been left to 'go it alone', were particularly strong. This, in turn, created a space for loyalist paramilitants.

Within republican areas, security related concerns also framed discourses on the use of political violence. While respondents who were members of Sinn Féin were more likely to concentrate on threats from security forces, community members' security concerns were directed towards loyalist paramilitaries. While most respondents living in republican areas did not actively support paramilitants, few challenged the commitment of PIRA members, as one community member observed, 'I do believe republicans have convictions cause they know what can happen to them know what I mean? I believe that they know what can happen to them and what they're gettin' themselves into and fair play to them if their heart is in it'.[76]

Within both communities, respondents who supported paramilitary goals and tactics, either actively or passively, struggled with the question of legitimacy. Respondents' interpretations of political violence reflect ideological and moral struggles framed within a discourse of legitimacy. There are no absolutes. Violence is conditional and for most respondents a painful last resort. In accepting or condoning political violence, members of both republican and loyalist communities contextualized its use, making the event or killing not an individual entity but part of a larger whole. As a former priest living in West Belfast explained, 'I think people do rationalize violence and fit it into their perception of the world'.[77] Rationalizing violence often entailed categorizing the victim. The victim was connected or an unintended, casualty of war. Acts of violence were justified in terms of defense or:

> [In] another sense it's justification because of retaliation, in other words 'well they did that to us so we can do that to them'. Or 'our ones', there's a sense of 'well why don't our ones go out and do these things?' Justification because of retaliation is a strong one.[78]

48 TERRORISM AND POLITICAL VIOLENCE

One of the most vivid accounts of this practice was provided by a long time resident of a West Belfast republican community. This respondent recalled the events that followed the killings of two soldiers in Casement Park. In March 1988 (in what is commonly referred to as the Casement Park case) two British Army corporals (Wood and Howes) drove into the funeral procession of Caoimhín Mac Brádaigh in West Belfast. They were dragged from their vehicle, beaten by the crowd, taken to Casement Park and later by Black Taxi to a waste ground on Penny Lane where they were executed by the PIRA.[79] The respondent observed that in the immediate wake of killings, there was an unusual quiet in the streets, people passed without eye contact as if, in her opinion, 'we were all guilty'. When information came to light that the two individuals killed were corporals in the British Army, attitudes among community members changed. The killings were justified, even provoked. The victims were no longer two 'young lads', but British agents and, therefore, legitimate targets.[80]

Alternative Justice: Inner Policing and Intimidation

The second function of paramilitary groups in Northern Ireland is to maintain social order and control within their respective communities. Counterinsurgency theorists argue that national liberation or guerrilla movements achieve social order and control by intimidation and coercion. In divesting political violence from the social, historical or political base from which it stems, arguments are reduced to states of black and white. Paramilitants are either zealots or profiteers. Subjugation of the community is necessary to maintain a defensive and, in some cases, financial base. As I will argue, when applied to Northern Ireland, this reductionist argument fails.

Paramilitant involvement in policing was, as John Darby notes, '...greatly facilitated by the fact that alternative forms of policing were not acceptable'.[81] In a July 1992 Human Rights Watch/Helsinki report on the abuse of children by security forces and paramilitaries, the issue of policing in nationalist areas was addressed. The report found that the RUC was unwilling to undertake a normal policing role in certain nationalist (mostly republican areas) as, 'they believe that there is a good chance [when responding to complaints of crime] that they are being set up for an attack, which has happened in the past...'. Additionally the report noted that many within the Catholic community are unwilling to contact the RUC when incidents occur, 'because they don't trust them, seeing them as representatives only of the Unionist Community'.[82] While particularly strong in republican enclaves, the rejection of state security forces is increasing in loyalist communities. My research findings suggest that

Protestant attitudes towards the security forces underwent a transition following the signing of the Anglo-Irish Agreement (AIA) in 1985. Not only did this period mark a rise in attacks against the security forces by the loyalist community but, concurrently, an increase in reports of security force harassment in Protestant districts.[83]

I found that paramilitary involvement in social control is tolerated, even demanded, but communal support is conditional. When addressing the question of paramilitary policing, Sinn Fein has distanced itself from role-player but has argued that republican involvement in policing is necessitated, targeted and indeed the better of two options.[84] Perceptions within the republican community that the RUC is biased and sectarian lend this assessment some merit. Paramilitants, through inner-policing, have constructed an alternative legality to the state. While adopting a law and order role contributes to the paramilitaries' legitimacy (especially true within republican areas), the task is a 'double edged sword'.[85] For both loyalist and republican paramilitaries to maintain credibility they must meet communal demands to control hooding, drugs and petty crime. Administering 'rough justice', however, risks alienating or reducing the paramilitant's support base.

A small number of loyalist respondents characterized the relationship between paramilitaries and the community as solely antagonistic. During the course of my study, I interviewed two respondents – one living with a republican, the other within a loyalist community – who had been directly affected by paramilitant inner-policing and 'punishment attacks'. Not surprisingly, these respondents were the most critical of paramilitary activity. Within republican areas, incidents of intimidation were related but criticisms were muted. I did not attribute this tendency to the respondent's fear of openly criticizing paramilitants as opinions expressed during formal interviews were often replicated in non-formal settings. Rather, I think that these findings illustrate the complexity of the relationship between paramilitant and community. For most respondents, the subject of intimidation and control by paramilitaries in Northern Ireland often led to discourses of grey. Complexities and contradictions emerge when republican and loyalist respondents were asked to explain the role and legitimacy of paramilitants within their respective communities. My findings support Burton's argument that generalizations which posit paramilitants' relationship with their community as one forged through 'naked force' are too simplistic.[86] Instead, as Burton observed in republican Anro, there is a 'see-saw' relationship between paramilitary and community.[87]

50   TERRORISM AND POLITICAL VIOLENCE

Conclusion

States exist, among other reasons, to adjudicate between citizens and administer justice. The legitimacy of the state is measured, in part, by its ability to meet citizens' basic needs. Political legitimacy may be challenged and justice disputed if the state fails in this role, or if the state machinery has been effectively coopted by one or more dominant identity groups. Northern Ireland is a case in point. Challenges to the legitimacy of the state have created a space for paramilitarism in Northern Ireland. Where state authority is challenged, paramilitants have, and in many way successfully, created alternative legalities and labour markets to that of the state.

Paramilitants serve two basic functions: defence and social control. A co-dependency between the community and paramilitary groups exist. Paramilitants require strong communal cohesion for security. In turn, community members demand protection. To maintain social order and control, republican and loyalist paramilitants have adopted a policing role. While this role provides legitimacy to paramilitary groups, administering justice within communities can also create tension between paramilitants and their support base. Interpretations of political violence which characterize the community as passive are flawed. As my findings reveal, the role of the community is integral to analysis of political violence, as the interconnectedness between paramilitary and community in Northern Ireland directly affects paramilitary tactics and strategies.

NOTES

An earlier version of this paper was prepared for presentation at the Annual Meeting of the American Political Science Association, San Francisco, 29 August – 1 September 1996. I should like to note that in preparation of this paper, I am indebted to the seminal work of a number of researchers, particularly that of political scientists, Professors Brendan O'Leary and John McGarry, and sociologists Frank Burton and Robert White. I have noted their contributions where appropriate.

1. David Held, *Political Theory and the Modern State* (Stanford: Stanford UP 1989) p.146.
2. Anne Norton, *Reflections on Political Identity* (Baltimore: The Johns Hopkins University Press 1988) p.146.
3. Violence may also put on the mask of the law.
4. Interviews were conducted in Belfast, Northern Ireland with paramilitants, as well as community members during four separate time intervals (1985, 1990, 1994 and 1995). Some paramilitant respondents were, at the time, militarily engaged while others had moved from the military to political party activism (as active and, at times, visible members of Sinn Fein, IRSP, UDA [in 1985], UDP [in 1994, 1995], and PUP). With few exceptions I will provide only a summary of these findings.
5. On 30 Jan. 1996, Gino Gallagher was killed on the Falls Road in West Belfast. Initially the IRSP, INLA's political wing, denied reports that this was due to an internal feud. The organization later stated that Gallagher was killed by breakaway members of its group. Gallagher's death led to a series of reprisal beatings, murders and attempted murders of

POLITICAL VIOLENCE IN ETHNICALLY DIVIDED SOCIETIES 51

INLA members that continued throughout 1996.

6. Often referred to by community members as 'the boys', 'the Provies' or 'the Rah' ('RA).

7. The split, ostensibly, was the demise of the Officials eventually reforming into Official Sinn Féin (Sinn Féin: the Workers Party in Northern Ireland) and, in 1982, the Workers Party. In 1992, the Workers Party split with most of its southern membership forming a new party, Democratic Left. Flackes and Elliot, *Northern Ireland: A Political Directory 1968–1993* (Belfast: Blackstaff Press 1994) pp.356–7. While political offshoots of the Officials continue to reject paramilitarism, recent post-cease-fire activities suggest that at least some remnants of the Officials are active and have maintained armaments.

8. See the critique by Ronnie Munck, 'Rethinking Irish Nationalism', *Canadian Review of Studies in Nationalism* (1987) pp.31–48. Also see Anthony McIntyre's, 'Modern Irish republicanism: the product of British state strategies', *Irish Political Studies* 10 (1995) pp.97–122. McIntyre argues that republican strategies, including the use of violence, have actually been far more reactive than analysts have noted. He argues that republican tactics and ideology since the early 1970s have been adapted 'to survive in the face of British state strategies', p.102.

9. This has been referred to as the 'armolite and ballot box' phase, a phrase adapted from Danny Morrison's 1981 Ard Feis speech.

10. See Iris Bheag uimh. a. 8. (March 1987) pp.19–20.

11. See Iris Bheag uimh. a 9. (April 1989), pp.20–25.

12. This departure from traditional republican strategy and analysis is outlined in Sinn Fein's, *Towards a Lasting Peace* (Belfast: Sinn Fein 1992).

13. See Mitchel McLaughlin, 'Protestantism, Unionism and Loyalism', *The Starry Plough* 1/ 2 (Nov. 1991) pp.13–16.

14. UDA leadership claimed that this was not the result of decreasing support but a deliberate policy to downsize in order to better maintain the group.

15. The UDA is said to presently be split between those involved and those against UDA involvement in the drug trade.

16. Spence now serves in the leadership of the PUP.

17. The UVF drew its name from Carson's Ulster Volunteer Force (UVF) established in 1912 to fight against Home Rule. According to David Boulton, recruitment and training of the UVF:

> was done essentially by the Orange Order as the lodge room was no place for conscientious objectors or political opponents. Likewise, drilling was carried on in Orange Halls, but when the weather and landowners permitted, drilling was done openly. The UVF were given suite offices in the Belfast Town Hall where the provincial government sat. Belfast businessmen underwrote the UVF to the tune of one million.

The organization grew to some 10,000 men. It successfully infiltrated both industrial and rural sectors of Northern Ireland. By the early 1920s, the UVF became the Ulster Special Constabulary with the authorization of Lloyd George. See David Boulton, *The U.V.F. 1966–1973: an anatomy of loyalist rebellion* (Dublin: Torc Books 1973) pp.16–17, 21.

18. In a special Forum election held in Northern Ireland on 30 May 1996, the PUP polled 26,082 votes or 3.47 per cent of the electorate, and the UDP polled 16,715 votes or 2.22 per cent of the electorate.

19. Ted R. Gurr, *Why Men Rebel* (Princeton: Princeton University Press 1970).

20. Denis O'Hearn, 'Catholic Grievances, Catholic Nationalism: A Comment', *British Journal of Sociology* 34/3 (1983) pp.438–45.

21. J. Stacy Adams, *Equity Theory: Toward a General Theory of Social Interactions* (New York: Academic Press 1976).

22. Elaine Walster, G. William Walster and Ellen Berscheid, *Equity: theory and research* (Boston: Allyn and Bacon 1978) pp.50–56.

23. See Coopers & Lybrand, *Northern Ireland Economy: Review and Prospects* (Belfast: Coopers & Lybrand 1994) pp.22, 33.

24. In the republican study area (and its three adjacent wards) the male unemployment rate for 1993 was 47 per cent. Long term unemployment (12 months or more) as a percentage of all unemployed was set at 58 per cent for this area (Belfast Action Team 1994, 77). In the

52   TERRORISM AND POLITICAL VIOLENCE

loyalist study area, a 1991 Census revealed an overall unemployment rate for the greater ward of approximately 21 per cent. The unemployment rate among males aged 16+ was 50 per cent, and long term unemployment for all unemployed was 50.5 per cent.

25. See Robert White, 'Political Violence by the Nonaggrieved: Explaining the Political Participation of those with no Apparent Grievances', *International Social Movement Research* 4 (1992) p.84. White found that IRA supporters in the Republic were drawn from both working, farming and middle class social backgrounds. A comparable study conducted by White in Northern Ireland yielded similar results – activists were drawn from a mixed social background. White used ethnographic study to interpret results from time series regression analysis and concluded that 'political violence was not a function of economic deprivation'. See White, 'From Peaceful Protest to Guerrilla War: Micromobilization of the Provisional Irish Republican Army', *American Journal of Sociology* 94 (1989) p.1297. An early study by Boyle, Hadden and Chesney examined the socio-economic grouping and social class of Diplock Defendants. The findings confirmed that most, *but not all*, defendants were drawn from working class homes. See K. Boyle, R. Chesney and T. Hadden, 'Who are the Terrorists?', *Fortnight* 126 (1976) pp.6–8. Christopher Hewitt's 'Catholic Grievances, Catholic Nationalism in Northern Ireland 1968–1971: A Reinterpretation', *British Journal of Sociology* 32 (Sept. 1981) pp.362–80 was a seminal piece for the nationalist argument.

26. In choosing unemployment as an indicator of deprivation levels within the Catholic community Robert White argues that 'Discrimination in employment is probably the key form of economic deprivation in the North of Ireland and in Derry in particular' (note 25b) p.1284. His findings are consistent with Peroff and Hewitt, 'who show that the unemployment rate but not the level of 'new Homes completed' was related to the frequency and severity of rioting in the North between 1968 and 1973'. Kathleen Peroff and Christopher Hewitt, 'Rioting in Northern Ireland: The Effects of Different Policies', *Journal of Conflict Resolution* 24 (1980) pp.593–612.

27. Brendan O'Leary and John McGarry, *Explaining Northern Ireland: Broken Images* (Oxford: Blackwell Publishers 1995) p.289–90. O'Leary and McGarry concede that a more sophisticated analysis of the data is necessary but are quite right to note that their results are in concert with other more detailed studies (p.486).

28. Respondents often cited more than one contributing factor when explaining the causes of political violence in Northern Ireland or their own personal involvement in a paramilitary organization. However, in most cases there were reasons that were core to the individuals decision to engage, and those that were secondary or contributing factors.

29. A partner of a paramilitant described their marriage as his second; 'his first', she recalled, 'was to politics of this place' (Interview, 1994).

30. As I shall explore in subsequent sections, communal support of paramilitants was not unconditional.

31. Term used to describe petty criminals.

32. One respondent did relate vague memories of his family having been 'burnt out from Lenadoon' (now an all-Catholic housing estate in West Belfast).

33. Interview with Loyalist, male, UDA, 1985.

34. Interview with Loyalist, male, UVF, 1994.

35. Robert White, 'On Measuring Political Violence: Northern Ireland, 1969 to 1980', *American Sociological Review* 58 (1993) p.582. Similar conclusions can be found in O'Leary and McGarry (note 27) p.291.

36. For example, Labour Force Survey data for February 1997 indicate that the unemployment rate for Belfast was 7.7 per cent. The rate of unemployment in Glasgow during the same time period was 7.9 per cent, and in Dublin the rate was 17.17 per cent! Boyle and Hadden compared Northern Ireland with other less economically prosperous regions of the UK and Republic of Ireland. Their data set reveals similar patterns of economic deprivation. Disparities are noted, however, when the figures are broken down between Protestants and Catholics within Northern Ireland. See Kevin Boyle and Tom Hadden, *Northern Ireland: The Choice* (London: Penguin Books 1994) pp.52–3.

37. It should be noted that survey data also suggest that a greater consensus on this issue exists for Protestants than for Catholics.

38. For a summary of survey data see Boyle and Hadden (note 36) pp.90–91.
39. Interview with Loyalist, male, Taughmonagh estate, 1994.
40. Edward Azar, *The Management of Protracted Social Conflicts* (Dartmouth: Dartmouth Publishing 1990) p.13.
41. Azar (note 40) p.16.
42. A.M. Gallagher, 'Freedom to Change', *Community Relations* (July 1992) p.3.
43. Azar (note 40) p.17.
44. Peter Stringer and Gillian Robinson (eds), *Social Attitudes in Northern Ireland: The Third Report* (Belfast: Blackstaff Press 1994) p.37.
45. Paul Compton, *Demographic Review: Northern Ireland 1995* (Belfast: Northern Ireland Economic Development Office 1995) p.144.
46. Stringer and Robinson (note 44).
47. See John Darby, Seamus Dunn and Kenneth Mullan (eds), *Education and community in Northern Ireland: schools apart? schools together?* (Coleraine: Centre for the Study of Conflict, University of Ulster 1989). Also, Robert Coles, *The political life of children* (Boston: Houghton Mifflin 1986); Dominic Murray, *Worlds Apart: Segregated Schools in Northern Ireland* (Belfast: Appletree 1985) and Ken Heskin, *Northern Ireland: A Psychological Analysis* (Dublin: Gill and Macmillan 1980).
48. William Hazleton, 'Constitutional Uncertainty and Political Deadlock: Overcoming Unionist Intransigence in Northern Ireland', *Conflict Quarterly* (Summer 1993) p.27.
49. See Donald Horowitz, *Ethnic Groups in Conflict* (Berkeley: University of California Press 1985).
50. W.D. Flackes and Sydney Elliott (note 7) pp.359–412.
51. Paul Mitchell, 'Party competition in an ethnic dual party system', *Ethnic and Racial Studies* (Oct. 1995) p.776.
52. Mitchell (note 51).
53. John Darby, *Intimidation and Conflict in Northern Ireland* (Dublin: Gill and Macmillan 1986) p.169.
54. Rosemary Harris, *Prejudice and Tolerance in Ulster: A study of neighbors and 'strangers' in a border community* (Manchester: Manchester University Press 1972) p.xi.
55. John Whyte, *Interpreting Northern Ireland* (Oxford: OUP 1991) p.50.
56. The Catholic Church's 'just war' theory is detailed in Fionnuala O'Connor's, *In Search of State* (Belfast: Appletree 1993) pp.295–6. Definition and examination of Protestant Covenant Theology can be found in Marianne Elliot's, *Watchman in Sion: the Protestant idea of liberty* (Belfast: Field Day Pamphlet No 8 1985).
57. See Stringer and Robinson (note 44) and Richard Breen, Paula Devine and Gillian Robinson (eds), *Social Attitudes in Northern Ireland, Fourth Report: 1994–95* (Belfast: Appletree 1995).
58. See Table 5.1 in O'Leary and McGarry (note 27) p.174.
59. An in-depth discussion of this approach can be found in O'Leary and McGarry (note 27) Ch.6.
60. See Jeffrey Sluka, *Hearts and Minds, Water and Fish: Support for the IRA and INLA in a Northern Irish Ghetto* (Greenwich: JAI Press 1989); Frank Burton, *The Politics of Legitimacy: Struggles in a Belfast Community* (London: Routledge & Kegan Paul 1978); and White (notes 26 and 35).
61. Bert Klandermans, 'Social-Psychological Expansions of Resource Mobilization Theory', *American Sociological Review* 49 (1984) pp.583–600; Edward N. Muller and Karl-Dieter Opp, 'Rational Action and Rebellious Collective Action', *America Political Science Review* 89 (1986) pp.471–87.
62. The unit of analysis here is the organization, not the individual.
63. Charles Tilly, *From Mobilization to Revolution* (Reading, MA: Addison-Wesley 1978) pp.151–66.
64. For a critique of this approach see O'Leary and McGarry (note 27) pp.292–6.
65. Flackes and Elliot (note 7) p.277.
66. Darby (note 53) p.5.
67. Victims were killed because they were (or were assumed to be) Catholic. Sectarian killings

54   TERRORISM AND POLITICAL VIOLENCE

of Protestants by nationalist militant agents comprise eight per cent of the total during the same time period. Percentages represent deaths related to conflict between July 1969 and March 1996. Tabulated from Malcolm Sutton, *An Index of Deaths from the Conflict in Ireland: 1969–1993* (Belfast: Beyond the Pale Publications 1994) pp.196–203; *Fortnight Magazine's* 'Chronology of Troubles', Jan. 1994–March 1996; and statistics obtained through RUC information services (for 1995 only). For an informative debate on this matter, see Robert White and Steve Bruce's article on sectarianism victim and selection, *TPV* 9/1 (Spring 1997) pp.20–71 and *TPV* 9/2 (Summer 1997) pp.120–31.

68. O'Leary and McGarry (note 27) p.263.
69. A significant rise in loyalist paramilitary killings occurred between 1991 and 1993.
70. See Burton, Sluka, White (note 60) and Darby (note 53).
71. Burton (note 60) p.2.
72. Burton (note 60) p.1.
73. Burton (note 60) p.128.
74. Within republican and loyalist communities I found that paramilitants had a small but core group of support that remained consistent and was impervious to external factors or concerns.
75. Interview with Loyalist, male respondent, 1995.
76. Interview with Republican, female respondent, 1994.
77. Interview, 1995.
78. Interview with Catholic respondent, male, 1994.
79. Amnesty International, *United Kingdom, Northern Ireland: fair trial concerns in the Casement Park trials* (London: AI Index: EUR 45/07/93).
80. Interview with Catholic respondent, female, 1990.
81. Darby (note 53) p.162.
82. Human Rights Watch (Helsinki), *Children in Northern Ireland: Abused by Security Forces and Paramilitaries* (New York: Human Rights Watch 1992) p.36.
83. The Helsinki Watch report referred to security harassment in Protestant areas. Helsinki Watch (note 82) pp.31–2.
84. In an interview with Human Rights Watch (Helsinki), Sinn Fein councillor Joe Austin states:

> The policing role is not played by Sinn Fein, but by the Republican movement – the IRA. The community should police itself – the IRA shouldn't do it. But the dilemma is that if the movement does nothing, people will resort to self-help and take matters in their own hand. Helsinki Watch (note 82) p.39.

Austin maintains that shootings were a last option and only used when an individual 'habitually create[s] problems, and commit[s] violent crimes like armed robbery, rape and muggings', p.41.

85. Burton (note 60) p.109.
86. Burton (note 60) p.106.
87. Burton (note 60) p.85.

[29]

Animal Rights and Violent Protest

RACHEL MONAGHAN

The arguments for the better treatment of animals underwent a dramatic change in the 1970s with the publication of Peter Singer's *Animal Liberation* and the work of Tom Regan. These new works challenged the previous moral orthodoxy which had suffused the animal welfare/protection movement and espoused the view, in the case of Regan, that animals had rights or, according to Singer, that they should be granted 'equal consideration'. The 1970s also saw the emergence of new groups, such as the Animal Liberation Front (ALF), who were not only willing forcibly to free animals from laboratories, but also to employ violence in the fight against animal abuse. This article seeks to show that the appearance and development of such groups is related to the growth of the demand for animal rights/liberation at a philosophical level.

The purpose of this article is to map the growth of the demand for animal rights/liberation at a philosophical level against the evolution of violent animal rights protest. This will involve a brief outline of Singer's and Regan's work,[1] before concentrating on those groups willing to use violence, for example, the ALF and Animal Rights Militia (ARM). These groups will be analysed in terms of their ideologies, tactics employed and targeting. The discussion will also draw on recent developments in violent animal rights protest with the appearance of the Justice Department, a group willing to injure and maim humans in the pursuit of their cause.

The debate concerning the moral status of animals dates back to at least the sixth century BC.[2] Much of the traditional western view on animals, and man's relationship with them, is based upon Judaeo-Christian morality in which there is a hierarchy of life in which man, made in the image of God, reigns supreme over all the creatures on earth. To quote the book of Genesis (Gen.1:27-28),

> So God created man in his own image, in the image of God he created him; male and female he created them. And God blessed them, and God said to them, 'Be fruitful and multiply, and fill the earth and subdue it; and have dominion over the fish of the sea and over the birds of the air and over every living thing that moves upon the earth'.[3]

A version of this article was presented at the Alternative Futures and Popular Protest Conference, Manchester Metropolitan University, 24–26 March 1997. I should like to thank Professor Christie Davies and Dr Ken Robertson for their valuable comments on earlier drafts of this article. They are in no way responsible for the views presented here.

Terrorism and Political Violence, Vol.9, No.4 (Winter 1997), pp.106–116
PUBLISHED BY FRANK CASS, LONDON

This belief in the lack of moral status of animals gave way to a new position of moral orthodoxy in the nineteenth century, whereby animals were accorded a moral status but one inferior to that of humans. Humans, while having an obligation to avoid inflicting unnecessary suffering on animals, were entitled to use them for their own benefit, for example, for food, clothing and to experiment upon. Organisations were established to protect and promote the welfare of animals and, as Garner notes, by the early part of the twentieth century the framework of modern welfare legislation in Britain was in place.[4] Over the past twenty years the animal protection movement has experienced a revival, not only in terms of membership of established groups such as the League Against Cruel Sports (LACS), but also in the proliferation of new groups including Animal Aid and the Compassion in World Farming.[5] The movement has also witnessed an ideological change in its character, and it is possible to trace a move away from a discourse centred on compassion towards animals to the notion that animals have rights.

Singer's *Animal Liberation* is the work most often cited as the inspiration or catalyst for this change. Singer writes from within the utilitarian tradition of moral philosophy whose central theme is that pleasure is good and pain is bad. A moral act for Singer as for Bentham is one which takes account of the desire of all sentient creatures not to experience increases in pain or suffering. The proposition that all creatures that can suffer pain have an equal interest in avoiding it, is the essence of Singer's morality. For Singer, the supreme principle is that of equality. Hence, all sentient beings are entitled to equal consideration of their interests. A being possesses interests if it is capable of suffering and enjoyment (features of sentiency); this capacity is the fundamental prerequisite for having interests at all. Equal interests must be equally respected, without regard to the species of the beings whose interests they are.[6] For example, whether the beings under consideration are members of royalty or are laboratory rats – both are due equal consideration. Singer is not advocating animal rights but an end to prejudice and a right to equal consideration. Hence, his work is entitled *Animal Liberation*: 'A liberation movement ... is a demand for an end to prejudice and discrimination based on an arbitrary characteristic like race or sex' or species.[7]

The work of Regan differs from that of Singer in that Regan believes that animals have intrinsic rights. Regan asserts that certain animals at least, especially mammals, have consciousness. Mammalian animals have beliefs and desires upon which they act. This claim is supported by appeals to common sense, ordinary language, evolutionary theory and observable behaviour.[8] A number of implications arise from this notion, namely that animals have perception, memory, intention and a sense of future and interests. Utilitarianism is rejected given that it views individuals as 'mere receptacles' for value whereas Regan is advocating the inherent value of all creatures. All individuals have a value that is logically independent of the value of their experiences and of their value to others. Regan argues,

> We are each of us experiencing subjects of a life, a conscious creature having an individual welfare that has importance to us whatever our usefulness to others. We want and prefer things, believe and feel things, recall and expect things. And all these dimensions of our life, including our pleasure and pain, our enjoyment and suffering, our satisfaction and frustration, our continued existence or our untimely death – all make a difference to the quality of our life as lived, as experienced, by us as individuals.[9]

Thus, animals can be seen as subjects who experience life and therefore have an inherent value of their own. Following on from this is the respect principle or 'equality of individuals view', which entails that we must treat those individuals that have inherent value in ways that respect their inherent value. Although animals, like children, are 'moral patients', that is to say individuals unable to control their own behaviour in ways that would make them morally accountable, this does not mean that they have less inherent value than do 'moral agents' (those who can recognise right from wrong and are able to act accordingly). All creatures/individuals can be victims of injustice, but only moral agents can commit injustices, for only they can violate rights.[10] Furthermore, the existence of a 'respect principle' implies the co-existence of a harm principle. This tells us that, as moral agents, we must not harm other moral agents or patients because to harm them is to treat them in ways which fail to respect their inherent value. Regan argues that it is from these principles that basic rights are generated and it follows that creatures who have inherent value have basic rights.[11]

Not only has the emergence of a 'rights' vocabulary led to a revival in the animal protection movement but it has also had an effect on campaigning styles.[12] Newer groups tend to promote local activism by engaging their members in rallies, market stalls and non-violent direct action such as the picketing of establishments selling animal products. In contrast, the older welfare groups have relied upon more traditional styles of campaigning, for example, consultation with government officials and advertisements in national newspapers. As Garner notes,

> the growth of mass activism is clearly linked to the belief, derived from an animal rights perspective, that since so much more is wrong with our treatment of animals than was previously thought, only permanent and sustained activism will help put things right. Likewise,

it is no accident that the use of – sometimes violent – direct action has corresponded with the development of a rights position.[13]

The Animal Liberation Front's origins can be traced back to 1972 with the formation of a new group calling itself the Band of Mercy.[14] Two members of the Hunt Saboteurs Association, Ronnie Lee and Cliff Goodman, founded this group because they 'began to feel that action should also be taken to save animals in laboratories and factory farms' and not just on behalf of animals hunted for recreation.[15] The group embarked upon a campaign of property damage including arson and the destruction of equipment at various laboratories throughout England and Wales. This campaign was shortlived as both Lee and Goodman were apprehended by the police in the process of breaking into an animal breeding centre in Bicester. They were convicted at Oxford Crown Court and sentenced to three years imprisonment.[16] Released early from gaol, Lee formed the ALF in 1976 with initially thirty members.[17] According to the *Animal Liberation Frontline Information Service*, the purpose of the ALF is as follows,

> the Animal Liberation Front carries out direct action against animal abuse in the form of rescuing animals and causing financial loss to animal exploiters, usually through the damage and destruction of property. The ALF's short term aim is to save as many animals as possible and directly disrupt the practice of animal abuse. Their long term aim is to end all animal suffering by forcing animal abuse companies out of business. It is a nonviolent campaign, activists taking all precautions not to harm any animal (human or otherwise). Because ALF actions are against the law, activists work anonymously, either in small groups or individually, and do not have any centralized organization or coordination.[18]

The ideology of the ALF is one which embraces the notion of animal rights and the sin of 'speciesism'.[19] Simply put, speciesism is the exploitation of one species by another, most usually the exploitation of non-humans by humans. As already noted, within animal rights theory, animals have 'rights' parallel and equal to those of humans, but such 'rights' cannot be defended by animals themselves. Therefore, humans must recognise their clear moral duty and must take on the responsibility of advocating and ensuring animal rights. As Henshaw notes,

> the implications of the new philosophy were rather more urgent than traditional and rather cosy notions of welfare. These were groups that were going to get things done, groups for activists who wanted more out of membership than demonstrations of de-infestation techniques and the annual charity social.[20]

The group believes its campaign to be one characterised by an absence of violence, as violence in their view can only be perpetrated against sentient beings. Sentient beings have a right to be free of suffering, whereas an inanimate object such as a meat truck has no such interest and is not concerned if it is destroyed. It is the infliction of violence or pain on a sentient being which has the right to be free from suffering that is inherently wrong. By contrast they argue that the destruction of property is not inherently wrong and may even be the right thing to do.[21] For example, the smashing up of laboratory equipment at an establishment where animals are used for experiments and their subsequent 'liberation' not only results in the freedom of those animals from further experiments, but also in a financial loss for their exploiters. As Lee notes, 'if you damage a laboratory, they have to increase their security and that's less money spent on animal research'.[22]

As already noted, the ALF's short term aim is to rescue animals from 'animal abuse' and to disrupt its practice, while their long term aim is to end all animal suffering by forcing 'animal abuse' companies and individuals out of business. In the year following its formation the ALF employed a variety of tactics and targeted a range of establishments connected with 'animal abuse'. Butcher's shops, furriers, animal breeders, fast food restaurants and race courses were all targeted. Methods employed included arson, the supergluing of locks, the releasing of animals, the pouring of paint stripper on vehicles and the breaking and etching of windows.[23] It has been estimated that in its first year of operation the ALF caused more than £250,000 worth of damage.[24] This pattern of targeting and tactics continued up until the early 1980s where one could detect a shift in targeting and tactics away from impersonal attacks on property to personal threats to and attacks on individuals.[25] It should also be noted that at this stage some activists broke away from the ALF and formed so-called Animal Liberation Leagues. These Leagues tended to target large animal laboratories and were more concerned with the gathering of information through the use of video cameras and publicity as opposed to damaging property.[26]

The period between 1982 and 1988 was one characterised by a resort to letter bombs, product contamination threats and car bombs. It was also the period marked by the emergence of a new group willing to use violence against people in the pursuit of animal rights and an end to animal suffering. In 1982, letter bombs were sent to the leaders of the four main political parties.[27] A previously unheard of group, the Animal Rights Militia (ARM) claimed responsibility for these attacks. The ARM holds similar views to that of the ALF but it differs with respect to attitudes on the use of violence directed at people. The ARM was later to claim responsibility for six minor bomb attacks on scientists' homes in 1985 and four car bombs in January of the following year. These attacks were preceded by warnings but a further car bomb in April 1986 marked a change in policy to one of 'no more warnings'.[28] As Paton notes, the ARM 'reappeared later with a reported threat to break the hands of scientists who work with animals, "so they won't be able to torture anymore"', further reinforcing their commitment to violence against people.[29] Some writers such as Henshaw and Geldard question whether the ARM is actually a new distinct group; they suggest instead that members of the ALF have invented names for supposedly new groups that then take notional responsibility for acts too violent to accord with the ALF's public stance of non-violence to sentient beings.[30]

The product contamination threats of the 1980s also marked a shift in tactics and targeting, in that the general public at large were now being targeted. The most notable hoax in 1984 concerned the alleged adulteration of Mars Bars with rat poison. Suspect bars were planted in shops around the country. Each potentially contaminated bar was marked with an 'x' and contained a note which read:

> this confection has been adulterated. We have no desire in [sic] endangering life, but those who persist in buying cruelty based products must accept full responsibility for their actions.[31]

It is estimated that Mars lost £6 million as a result of this hoax.[32] Subsequent contamination threats have included spiked baby oil, mercury in turkeys and bleach added to shampoo.[33]

The early 1980s were also characterised by the utilisation of bombs of varying design and refinement. Bombs are very effective and not just because they cause economic losses; this is especially true of the planting of incendiary devices. These devices are sophisticated and yet small enough to fit into a cigarette packet. For example, in the summer of 1987 they resulted in £9 million worth of damage to three separate fur departments in Debenhams' stores.[34] Bombs also cause psychological fear in the intended victim. The employment of letter bombs has even led to the introduction of specially designed machines to check the contents of incoming mail. High explosives were not used until 1989 in an attack on Bristol University. The use of bombs in their various forms has progressed from the targeting of property to the targeting of individuals.

The ARM has claimed responsibility for a number of actions during the 1980s, but it has not mounted a steady campaign, unlike the ALF which claims an estimated fifteen to twenty actions every night.[35] The 1990s have witnessed an escalation in the levels and quantities of violence. In 1994, the ARM claimed responsibility for a number of incendiary devices planted in a variety of shops including Fads DIY (owned by Boots), Boots, the Cancer Research Fund Shop and Halfords (again, owned by Boots). Furthermore, the group was involved in an alleged product contamination incident whereby Boots' own brand toothpaste was contaminated with mercury.[36] Another new animal rights group has also emerged which, like the ARM, is willing to harm humans in the pursuit of an end to animal suffering. In October 1993, a package later found to be addressed to an individual connected with fieldsports exploded at a sorting office in Watford. More devices followed and were claimed by a previously unheard of group calling itself the Justice Department. In a statement from the group after its campaign of letter and parcel bombs, they stated:

> We've sat back for years and watched AR activists ask nicely for all the abuse to stop – the more daring risk their lives and liberty but still the unacceptable number of tortured animals keep rising....We won't be asking anyone to stop messing with animals and make no more excuses for our violent intervention – they've had it too good for too long. NO MORE TORTURE, NO MORE LIES ... [37]

In the last three months of 1993, the group claimed responsibility for 31 attacks; these were predominantly poster tube and video cassette bombs but also included a number of timed incendiary devices.[38] Their targets ranged from individuals connected with fieldsports to companies involved in animal experimentation and to furriers.[39] The following year the group claimed some one hundred attacks. Again the methods utilised varied. Although there was a reduction in the number of letter bombs, two serious car bombs were exploded; these devices were planted under vehicles belonging to individuals linked with animal testing.[40]

As already noted the ALF began as a group of some thirty individuals. No official membership lists are available and in the strict sense of the word one does not join the ALF. The ALF guidelines say: 'Any group of people who are vegetarians or vegans and who carry out actions according to ALF guidelines have the right to regard themselves as part of the ALF.'[41] Today the group claims 2,500 activists with an estimated hard core of 'dedicated activists' of around one hundred who are prepared to use explosives and incendiary devices.[42] In addition, Henshaw suggests that around 2,000 individuals contribute money or other resources to the ALF through its supporters group (ALFSG).[43] The ALFSG provides financial aid to help pay the legal costs of activists as well as books and educational material for those in prison. Contributors receive a regular bulletin informing them of ALF actions, animal liberation prisoners and articles on issues concerning animals. There is debate within the animal protection movement as to the nature of the support base for the ALF. Some such as Richard Course of the LACS attributes the use of violence and the growth of the group to anarchists:

> There is a hard core who have turned their back...[on the parliamentary process] ... and they are anarchists. They see the animal rights issue growing and regard it as fertile, attractive ground.[44]

This view is not supported by Henshaw, who argues that the support base is broad, ranging from anarchists to fascists to Conservative-voting pensioners to teenagers.[45] One can also see evidence of this in the recent demonstrations against live animal exports where housewives and pensioners were to be found alongside punks on the picket lines.

Within the animal protection movement there has been much debate regarding the effectiveness of the direct action groups especially those which utilise violence, whether it be against property or targeted at individuals. There have been around three hundred prosecutions, most of them successful, and activists have served time in prison. Most received six or seven years for property damage connected with the ALF.[46] According to recent postings on the Internet, there are currently ten animal liberation prisoners serving out their sentences ranging from three years to eleven years in the case of Keith Mann. A further four are being held on remand.[47]

The classic ALF tactic of breaking into laboratories together with the undercover work of activists disguised as employees have also provided a large amount of material that can be used in anti-vivisection campaigns. The 'liberation' of animals from laboratories removes them from further possible pain and suffering, although the ones taken represent only a tiny proportion of the number of animals involved. ALF activities have severe financial cost for those targeted. The Mars hoax and the arson at three branches of Debenhams together account for some £15 million worth of damage. Garner suggests that the positive results of direct action have been limited but they have not had much of a negative impact either. Such actions have not prevented a rise in membership numbers or donations to the animal protection movement in general. Furthermore the planting of incendiary devices in department stores' fur sections does not appear to have hindered the activities of those anti-fur groups working within the confines of the law.[48] However, not everyone within the movement takes such a view. Animal Aid are very hostile to ALF activities and are quoted in the wake of the Bristol car bomb as saying that they are 'sick of this tiny bunch of half-witted pseudo-terrorists undermining all the vital work being done by ourselves and many others'.[49]

In conclusion, from the arguments outlined in this article one can suggest that the emergence and evolution of groups willing to use violence against property and individuals is related to the growth of the demand for animal rights/liberation at a philosophical level. The relationship between holding a philosophical conviction that animals have rights and a practical defence of these rights has profound implications. As Henshaw correctly asserts,

> Of course, a belief in animal rights didn't necessarily make you a bomb thrower, but it lined you up behind the rationale for bomb throwing. It meant you at least could understand the idea of threatening human life on behalf of the animals.[50]

As already noted a belief in animal rights contends that animals have 'rights' parallel and equal to those of humans, and that such 'rights' cannot be defended by animals themselves. Humans, as moral agents, have a duty to advocate and ensure these rights. For the majority of activists in the animal rights movement this does not involve violence or the breaking of laws. Some activists, though, argue that the law may be broken since it is ephemeral; government legislation is not constant and what may be illegal now may be legal in years to come. By contrast, what is morally right and wrong is constant and the breaking of unjust laws cannot be morally wrong. Activists involved with the ALF, ARM and Justice Department take this kind of argument one step further with the utilisation of violence in their demand for an end to animal suffering. Their activities gain media attention and, given the increase in the number of activists involved, encourage recruitment and support. Traditional lobbying had not produced the desired results and so the ALF was formed with the long term aim of forcing 'animal abuse' companies and individuals out of business by a campaign of property damage. This was followed by the emergence of groups willing to use violence against people, such as the ARM and, most recently, the Justice Department. The tactics used by these groups have continually escalated. For example, the tactic of breaking and entering laboratories and destroying equipment has been replaced by the sending of poster tube bombs containing hypodermic needles and the planting of car bombs. These groups contend that they need to exist and fight because animals are being abused and that they will cease to exist when and only when there is no more animal abuse. Although individuals have been injured by the actions of these groups, no deaths have occurred but, as Garner notes, 'it seems only a matter of time before someone is killed in the name of animal liberation'.[51]

NOTES

1. Peter Singer, *Animal Liberation*, 2nd ed. (London: Thorsons 1993); Tom Regan, *The Case For Animal Rights* (London: Routledge 1988).
2. For a more detailed discussion see Helena Silverstein, *Unleashing Rights: Law, Meaning and the Animal Rights Movement* (Ann Arbor: University of Michigan Press 1996) and Robert

ANIMAL RIGHTS AND VIOLENT PROTEST   115

Garner, *Animals, Politics and Morality* (Manchester: MUP 1993).

3. *The Holy Bible*, Revised Standard Version (New York: Collins 1973) p.1.
4. Garner, *Animals, Politics and Morality* (note 2).
5. The LACS saw its membership levels rise from 6,000 in 1950 to 15,000 in 1989 to 35,000 in 1994. Figures quoted from Robert Garner, 'The Road to Shoreham: Ideological and Political Aspects in the Evolution of the British Animal Rights Movement', unpublished paper from *Alternative Futures and Popular Protest Conference*, Manchester Metropolitan University, March 1995. For a more detailed account of this revival see Garner's paper. Recent figures put membership/supporters of the LACS at 40,000 in 1997. See Rachel Wollett, 'The anti-hunting lobby', *The Independent*, 10 July 1997, p.3.
6. Singer (note 1); John Benson, 'Duty and the Beast', *Philosophy* 53/206 (Oct. 1978); David Lamb, 'Animal Rights and Liberation Movements', *Environmental Ethics* 4 (Fall 1982); and Keith Tester, *Animals and Society* (London: Routledge 1992).
7. Singer (note 1) p.iv.
8. Silverstein (note 2).
9. Tom Regan, 'The Case for Animal Rights', in Tom Regan and Peter Singer (eds), *Animal Rights and Human Obligations*, 2nd ed. (New Jersey: Prentice Hall 1989) pp.111–12.
10. Regan argues that 'in claiming that we have a prima facie duty to assist those animals whose rights are violated, therefore, we are not claiming that we have a duty to assist the sheep against the attack of the wolf, since the wolf neither can nor does violate anyone's rights', quoted in Dale Jamieson, 'Rights, Justice and Duties to Provide Assistance: A Critique of Regan's Theory of Rights', *Ethics* (Jan. 1990) p.351.
11. Regan, *The Case For Animal Rights* (note 1); Silverstein (note 2) and Tester (note 6).
12. Garner, 'The Road to Shoreham' (note 5) pp.8–12.
13. Garner, 'The Road to Shoreham' (note 5) p.12.
14. The only booklength study of the ALF is David Henshaw's *Animal Warfare* published by Fontana in 1989. See also Richard Ryder, *Animal Revolution* (Oxford: Blackwells 1989) and Garner, *Animals, Politics and Morality* (note 2).
15. Quote taken from Ryder (note 14) p.273.
16. For more details see Ryder (note 14) and Garner, *Animals, Politics and Morality* (note 2).
17. See Henshaw (note 14) for more details.
18. Taken from the *Animal Liberation Frontline Information Service* posting on the ALF found at http://envirolink.org/ALF/orgs/alforg.html.
19. 'Speciesism' was first coined by Richard Ryder and refers to the exploitation of one species by another. For a more detailed discussion see Ryder (note 14).
20. Henshaw (note 14) p.38.
21. Taken from Freeman Wicklund, *Animal Rights in Britain* (http://envirolink.org/arrs/ar_uk.html, 1995).
22. Lee quoted from David T. Hardy, *America's New Extremists: What You Need to Know About the Animal Rights Movement* (Washington, DC: Washington Legal Foundation 1990) p.17.
23. See William Paton, *Man and Mouse*, 2nd ed. (Oxford: OUP 1993); Maureen Duffy, *Men and Beasts* (London: Paladin 1984) and Henshaw (note 14) for more details.
24. Hardy (note 22).
25. Garner, *Animal, Politics and Morality* (note 2) and Paton (note 23).
26. Garner, *Animal, Politics and Morality* (note 2).
27. Only the bomb addressed to Mrs Thatcher exploded, injuring an office clerk at No. 10. See Paton (note 23) for more details.
28. See Ryder (note 14) and Henshaw (note 14).
29. Paton (note 23) p.232.
30. Henshaw (note 14) reports that Lee has called for the invention of new names and quotes Tim Daley, a 'leading' ALF activist as saying: 'I can support petrol bombings, bombs under cars, and probably shootings at a later stage. It's a war,' p.91. See also Ian Geldard, 'New Militancy Grips Animal Rights Groups', *Terror Update* 7 (March 1989) p.8.
31. Henshaw (note 14) p.64.
32. Garner, *Animal, Politics and Morality* (note 2).
33. See Paton (note 23) and Henshaw (note 14) for more details.

34. Ryder (note 14).
35. Figures quoted by Robin Webb, ALF Press Officer taken from Wicklund (note 21).
36. Information taken from the Internet, http://envirolink.org/ALF/ezines/ug1_1html and covers the period from February to early October 1994.
37. Taken from the Justice Department's press release located at http://envirolink.org/ALF/orgs/jd1.html and in _Liberator_ (Winter 1994/Spring 1995).
38. A poster tube bomb is made using a poster tube packed with explosives and usually contains hypodermic needles. A video cassette bomb is as it sounds – a video cassette box filled with explosives.
39. http://envirolink.org/ALF/orgs/jd1.html.
40. http://envirolink.org/ALF/orgs/jd1.html.
41. Taken from the ALF Guidelines found at http://envirolink.org/ALF/orgs/alforg.html.
42. Writing in 1993, Garner, _Animal, Politics and Morality_ (note 2) puts the figure of dedicated activists at fifty. In contrast, Michael Durham, 'Animal Passions', _The Observer_, 12 Nov. 1995, p.19, estimates a hundred such individuals.
43. Henshaw (note 14) says the ALFSG has an annual income of at least £50,000 a year.
44. Quoted in G. Davidson Smith 'Political Violence in Animal Liberation', _Contemporary Review_ 247 (July 1985) p.28.
45. Henshaw (note 14).
46. Durham (note 42).
47. Information taken from http://envirolink.org/ALF/people/prlist.html.
48. Garner, _Animals, Politics and Morality_ (note 2).
49. Taken from Garner, _Animals, Politics and Morality_ (note 2) p.221.
50. Henshaw (note 14) p.157.
51. Robert Garner, 'The Animal Lobby', _Political Quarterly_ 62/2 (1991) p.288.

Name Index